The Changing Scope of Technoethics in Contemporary Society

Rocci Luppicini
University of Ottawa, Canada

A volume in the Advances in Information Security,
Privacy, and Ethics (AISPE) Book Series

Published in the United States of America by
IGI Global
Information Science Reference (an imprint of IGI Global)
701 E. Chocolate Avenue
Hershey PA, USA 17033
Tel: 717-533-8845
Fax: 717-533-8661
E-mail: cust@igi-global.com
Web site: http://www.igi-global.com

Library of Congress Cataloging-in-Publication Data

Names: Luppicini, Rocci, editor.
Title: The changing scope of technoethics in contemporary society / Rocci
  Luppicini, editor.
Description: Hershey, PA : Information Science Reference, [2018] | Includes
  bibliographical references.
Identifiers: LCCN 2017035443| ISBN 9781522550945 (h/c) | ISBN 9781522550952
  (eISBN)
Subjects: LCSH: Technology--Moral and ethical aspects. | Technology--Social
  aspects. | Technology and state.
Classification: LCC BJ59 .C45 2018 | DDC 174/.96--dc23 LC record available at https://lccn.loc.gov/2017035443

This book is published in the IGI Global book series Advances in Information Security, Privacy, and Ethics (AISPE) (ISSN: 1948-9730; eISSN: 1948-9749)

British Cataloguing in Publication Data
A Cataloguing in Publication record for this book is available from the British Library.

For electronic access to this publication, please contact: eresources@igi-global.com.

Advances in Information Security, Privacy, and Ethics (AISPE) Book Series

Manish Gupta
State University of New York, USA

ISSN:1948-9730
EISSN:1948-9749

MISSION

As digital technologies become more pervasive in everyday life and the Internet is utilized in ever increasing ways by both private and public entities, concern over digital threats becomes more prevalent.

The **Advances in Information Security, Privacy, & Ethics (AISPE) Book Series** provides cutting-edge research on the protection and misuse of information and technology across various industries and settings. Comprised of scholarly research on topics such as identity management, cryptography, system security, authentication, and data protection, this book series is ideal for reference by IT professionals, academicians, and upper-level students.

COVERAGE

- Tracking Cookies
- Cookies
- Privacy Issues of Social Networking
- Computer ethics
- Cyberethics
- Security Information Management
- Telecommunications Regulations
- Technoethics
- Electronic Mail Security
- Security Classifications

IGI Global is currently accepting manuscripts for publication within this series. To submit a proposal for a volume in this series, please contact our Acquisition Editors at Acquisitions@igi-global.com or visit: http://www.igi-global.com/publish/.

Titles in this Series

For a list of additional titles in this series, please visit: www.igi-global.com/book-series

Critical Research on Scalability and Security Issues in Virtual Cloud Environments
Shadi Aljawarneh (Jordan University of Science and Technology, Jordan) and Manisha Malhotra (Chandigarh University, India)
Information Science Reference • copyright 2018 • 341pp • H/C (ISBN: 9781522530299) • US $225.00 (our price)

The Morality of Weapons Design and Development Emerging Research and Opportunities
John Forge (University of Sydney, Australia)
Information Science Reference • copyright 2018 • 216pp • H/C (ISBN: 9781522539841) • US $175.00 (our price)

Advanced Cloud Computing Security Techniques and Applications
Ihssan Alkadi (Independent Researcher, USA)
Information Science Reference • copyright 2018 • 350pp • H/C (ISBN: 9781522525066) • US $225.00 (our price)

Algorithmic Strategies for Solving Complex Problems in Cryptography
Kannan Balasubramanian (Mepco Schlenk Engineering College, India) and M. Rajakani (Mepco Schlenk Engineering College, India)
Information Science Reference • copyright 2018 • 302pp • H/C (ISBN: 9781522529156) • US $245.00 (our price)

Information Technology Risk Management and Compliance in Modern Organizations
Manish Gupta (State University of New York, Buffalo, USA) Raj Sharman (State University of New York, Buffalo, USA) John Walp (M&T Bank Corporation, USA) and Pavankumar Mulgund (State University of New York, Buffalo, USA)
Business Science Reference • copyright 2018 • 360pp • H/C (ISBN: 9781522526049) • US $225.00 (our price)

Detecting and Mitigating Robotic Cyber Security Risks
Raghavendra Kumar (LNCT Group of College, India) Prasant Kumar Pattnaik (KIIT University, India) and Priyanka Pandey (LNCT Group of College, India)
Information Science Reference • copyright 2017 • 384pp • H/C (ISBN: 9781522521549) • US $210.00 (our price)

Advanced Image-Based Spam Detection and Filtering Techniques
Sunita Vikrant Dhavale (Defense Institute of Advanced Technology (DIAT), Pune, India)
Information Science Reference • copyright 2017 • 213pp • H/C (ISBN: 9781683180135) • US $175.00 (our price)

701 East Chocolate Avenue, Hershey, PA 17033, USA
Tel: 717-533-8845 x100 • Fax: 717-533-8661
E-Mail: cust@igi-global.com • www.igi-global.com

Table of Contents

Section 3
Emerging Trends and Future Directions

Detailed Table of Contents

Section 1
Ethical Perspectives on Advancing Human-Technological Relations

Chapter 1
Ben van Lier, Centric Gouda, The Netherlands & Steinbeis University Berlin, Germany

Technology is responsible for major systemic changes within the global financial sector. This sector has already developed into a comprehensive network of mutually connected people and computers. Algorithms play a crucial role within this network. An algorithm is in essence merely a set of instructions developed by one or more people with the intention of having these instructions performed by a machine such as a computer in order to realize an ideal result. As part of a development in which we as human beings have ever higher expectations of algorithms and these algorithms become more autonomous in their actions, we cannot avoid including possibilities in these algorithms that enable ethical or moral considerations. To develop this ethical or moral consideration, we need a kind of ethical framework that can be used for constructing these algorithms. With the development of such a framework we can start to think about what we as human beings consider to be a moral action executed by algorithms that support actions and decisions of interconnected and self-organizing machines. This chapter explores an ethical framework for interconnected and self-organizing moral machines.

Chapter 2
Jose-Luis Perez-Trivino, Pompeu Fabra University, Spain

Doping, or in more morally neutral terms, enhancement, has always been present in sport practice and not only at the present time, which is marked by professionalism and competitiveness. The latest development in doping seems linked to biotechnological advances, and one of the techniques that will apparently be particularly important in the near future is neuroscience, notably through pharmacological enhancers and transcranial stimulators. These devices promise to improve not only physiological aspects in sport performance, but also mental and emotional ones. On the other hand, they can seriously affect sport ethics insofar as they can be economically accessible to professional and amateur athletes. This chapter explores these issues.

This chapter examines the dialectical role of science in its promotion of public policy and the manner in which scientific autonomy has been challenged to further political ends. Various episodes in the ever-expanding technological reach of the marriage of science and politics are historically recounted to demonstrate the threat to scientific self-rule and to individual scientists who have been relegated to instrumentally functional roles. It is argued that the emergent class status of scientists has been subverted by the triumvirate of technology, industry, and religion. Moreover, science has met its greatest challenge from those entities which understand how the use of technology and scientific discovery translate into regulatory measures.

This chapter advocates a re-introduction of the notion of cyborg in order to acquire a new perspective on studies concerning the development of human cognition in highly technological environments. In particular, it shows how the notion of cyborg properly engages cognitive issues that have a powerful resonance especially as far as social cognition is concerned, and may consequently provide a new tool for tackling the emergent safety issues concerning sociality mediated by the internet, and the moral panic occasionally surrounding it. The conclusion suggests how the notion of cyborg accounts for a better understanding and recognition of the victims of cyberbullying.

This chapter addresses concerns that the development and proliferation of human enhancement technologies (HET) will be dehumanizing and a threat to our autonomy and sovereignty as individuals. The chapter argues contrarily that HET constitutes nothing less than one of the most effective foreseeable means of increasing the autonomy and sovereignty of individual members of society. Furthermore, it elaborates the position that the use of HET exemplifies—and indeed even intensifies—our most human capacity and faculty, namely the desire for increased self-determination, which is referred to as the will toward self-determination. Based upon this position, the chapter argues that the use of HET bears fundamental ontological continuity with the human condition in general and with the historically ubiquitous will toward self-determination in particular. HET will not be a dehumanizing force, but will rather serve to increase the very capacity that characterizes us as human more accurately than anything else.

Although most unmanned systems that militaries use today are still unarmed and predominantly used for surveillance, it is especially the proliferation of armed military robots that raises some serious ethical questions. One of the most pressing concerns the moral responsibility in case a military robot uses violence in a way that would normally qualify as a war crime. In this chapter, the authors critically assess the chain of responsibility with respect to the deployment of both semi-autonomous and (learning) autonomous lethal military robots. They start by looking at military commanders because they are the ones with whom responsibility normally lies. The authors argue that this is typically still the case when lethal robots kill wrongly – even if these robots act autonomously. Nonetheless, they next look into the possible moral responsibility of the actors at the beginning and the end of the causal chain: those who design and manufacture armed military robots, and those who, far from the battlefield, remotely control them.

Weapons research seeks to design new or improved weapons and their ancillary structures. This chapter argues that weapons research is both morally wrong and morally unjustified. This "case against weapons research" requires lengthy discussion and the argument given here is a summary of that discussion. The central claim is that the "standard justification" for all forms of weapons acquisition and deployment, which appeals to defense and deterrence, does not stand up for weapons research because the harms caused by the latter projects into the future in unknowable ways. Weapons research produces practical knowledge in the form of designs for the means to harm, and its practitioners cannot know how this knowledge will be used in the future.

Chapter 8

Technology has always allowed agents of war to separate themselves from the harm that they or their armed forces inflict with spears, bows and arrows, trebuchets, cannons, firearms, and other modern weaponry, all serving as examples of technologies that have increased the distance between belligerents and supposedly made warfare less sickening than the close-quarters combat of the past. This chapter calls into question the claims of some proponents of a ban moratorium on lethal autonomous weapons systems regarding a responsibility gap and contends that most implications associated with the introduction of autonomous technologies can be resolved by recognizing that autonomy does not mean the elimination of a human influence on the battlefield and advocates for a black-box-type recorder to ensure compliance with just war theory and the laws of war.

Chapter 9

Elena Grebenshchikova, Institute of Scientific Information for Social Sciences of the Russian Academy of Sciences, Russia

One of the key trends in the development of technoscience is associated with the NBIC-convergence projects, which create not only unprecedented means for transformation of society and human but also raise the risks that require integrated approaches to ethical assessment and examination. Today, the foundations of the "NBIC-tetrahedron" have ethical projections in the form of nanoethics, bioethics, ICT-ethics, and neuroethics. However, their ability to discuss and resolve complex problems is limited. Technoethics can be considered a relevant way of combining different approaches to the ethical issues of converging technologies and science to discuss and solve not only actual situations but prospects as well.

Chapter 10

Nils-Frederic Wagner, University of Duisburg-Essen, Germany
Jeffrey Robinson, Royal Ottawa Health Care Group, Canada
Christine Wiebking, Ulm University, Germany

Using cognitive enhancement technology is becoming increasingly popular. In another paper, the authors argued that using pharmacological cognitive enhancers is detrimental to society, through promoting competitiveness over cooperation, by usurping personal and social identifies and thus changing our narrative and moral character. In this chapter, the authors seek to expand that argument by looking at an emerging technology that is rapidly gaining popularity, that of transcranial stimulation (TS). Here the authors explore TS via two major methods, transcranial magnetic stimulation (TMS) and transcranial electrical stimulation (TES). In this, the authors seek to demonstrate that artificial cognitive enhancement is detrimental to society. Furthermore, that the argument can be applied beyond the moral dubiousness of using pharmacological cognitive enhancement, but applied to new, emergent technologies as well. In other words, artificial cognitive enhancement regardless of the technology/medium is detrimental to society.

Chapter 11

Brett Lunceford, Independent Researcher, USA

For many, cosmetic surgery holds the promise that one can reshape his or her body to remove perceived defects and thus have a more perfect body. However, the decision to undergo elective cosmetic surgery is not made in a vacuum, and it is easy to overlook the full range of ethical considerations surrounding cosmetic surgery. Many medical ethicists subscribe to an ethical code that centers mainly on the relationship between the doctor and patient, with a focus on respect for autonomy, nonmaleficence, beneficence, and justice. This chapter builds on this framework by extending the scope of actors to include not only the surgeon and the patient but also the media and the overall society. To illustrate this framework, the author uses the example of actress Heidi Montag, who underwent 10 different plastic surgery procedures in one day. The chapter concludes with a discussion of potential correctives for ethical failures in each of these areas.

Today, technology is being integrated in all social environments, at home, school, or work, shaping a new world in which there is a closer interaction between human and machine than ever before. While every new technology brings along the expected "blessings," there is also the thick end of the stick, namely the potential undesired effects it might cause. Explorative research in smart and enhancing technologies reveals that the current trend is for them to transcend to persuasive technologies, capable of shaping human behavior. In this context, this chapter aims at identifying the social and ethical implications of such technologies, being elaborated after reviewing literature from various research domains. It addresses the implications of today's smart and enhancing technologies on several levels: health repercussions, the social and behavioral changes they generate, and concerns of privacy and security. Also, the chapter emphasizes the need for scientists and researchers to engage not only with the technical considerations, but also with the societal implications mentioned above.

This chapter employs the framework of contextual integrity related to privacy developed by Nissenbaum as a tool to understand consumer response to implementation of residential smart metering technology. To identify and understand specific changes in information practices brought about by the introduction of smart meters, energy consumers were interviewed, read a description of planned smart grid/meter implementation, and were asked to reflect on changes in the key actors involved, information attributes, and principles of transmission. Areas where new practices emerge with the introduction of residential smart meters were then highlighted as potential problems (privacy violations). Issues identified in this study included concern about unauthorized use and sharing of personal data, data leaks or spoofing via hacking, the blurring distinction between the home and public space, and inferences made from new data types aggregated with other personal data that could be used to unjustly discriminate against individuals or groups.

Section 3
Emerging Trends and Future Directions

The internet, the landmark invention of our lifetime, has brought us great benefit, but along with it, risk and antisocial behavior, including online bullying, hate speech, extremist content, and other ills. Prevention lies in promoting digital citizenship—safe, responsible, and appropriate use of technology and services—and a newer concept, digital civility—online interactions rooted in empathy, respect, and kindness. And, while no one entity can combat these issues alone, internet companies can play their part, as exemplified by the robust tools and resources offered by Microsoft and others. A collective focus, however, is needed to help raise awareness and change behavior, and the responsibility must be shared among the technology industry and government policy makers as well as everyone who uses the internet, including parents and caregivers, educators, and young people. This chapter explores these ideas.

Chapter 15

Rick Searle, IEET, USA

From the time of its emergence onto the public scene, the internet has been understood in light of both its dystopian potential for total surveillance and control and its utopian possibilities to enable enhanced forms of freedom. The reality has proven far more complicated with the internet having both helped to weaken institutions and strengthened new forms of authoritarian populism. This chapter argues that these two potentials are deeply interconnected and that the long-term sustainability of democracy requires that we understand and address the connections between our fears and hopes regarding the internet's future.

Chapter 16

Alejandra Emilia Iannone, Sparkle Theatricals, USA

Over the last two decades, an impactful phenomenon called virality (i.e., when content circulates via internet among an increasingly broad audience at an exponentially rapid rate) has developed. Not all information achieves virality, so the phenomenon invites reflection. Yet, the academic literature on viral artwork is quite sparse. This chapter helps fill a gap in the literature by demonstrating the academic significance of viral art through comparative analysis of three cases where web-based artworks went viral: Ten Hours of Princess Leia walking in NYC, New Beginnings, and McKayla Is Not Impressed. The author argues that viral art merits rigorous study because doing so could, first, augment existing research on other topics; second, fortify philosophy of art investigations; and third, establish aesthetic principles to guide audience engagement with viral artwork.

Chapter 17

Baha Abu-Shaqra, University of Ottawa, Canada
Rocci Luppicini, Universisty of Ottawa, Canada

Ethical hacking is an important information security risk management strategy within higher education applied against the growing threat of hacking attacks. Confusion regarding the meaning and ethics of ethical hacking within broader society and which resonates within organizations undermines information security. Confusion within organizations increases unpredictably (equivocality) in the information environment, which raises risk level. Taking a qualitative exploratory case study approach, this chapter pairs technoethical inquiry theory with Karl Weick's sensemaking model to explore the meanings, ethics, uses and practices, and value of ethical hacking in a Canadian university and applies technoethical inquiry decision-making grid (TEI-DMG) as an ethical decision-making model. Findings point to the need to expand the communicative and sociocultural considerations involved in decision making about ethical hacking organizational practices, and to security awareness training to leverage sensemaking opportunities and reduce equivocality in the information environment.

Online and media cultures have a dominant influence on modern society. This type of culture is characterized by specific forms of expression and ethical and aesthetic features mediated by technology. Virtual communication is one reflection of the phenomena of culture reflected through technology. The chapter identifies the typology of virtual communication using a systems approach as an example of online and media culture. This is based on the analysis of the development of social networks and forms of communication and shows the trends in the dynamics of virtual communication. The new environment, with its distinctive characteristics, indicators, forms, and images, creates new opportunities and new risks for humans and their cultures.

Preface

OVERVIEW

Where Did We Come From and Where Are We Going (Or Want To)?

As human beings, we are vulnerable to confusing the unprecedented with the improbable. In our everyday experience, if something has never happened before, we are generally safe in assuming it is not going to happen in the future, but the exceptions can kill you and climate change is one of those exceptions.
– Al Gore

This heartfelt statement from Al Gore illustrates the very real vulnerability of humans amidst the clashing forces of human innovation, society, and the environment. It is safe to say that the advancement of technologies in the twentieth century has changed life and transformed our world in weird and wonderful ways. Many of these transformations are obvious like new building materials and energy sources to create and power our cities. Other technologies, as Al Gore recognizes, are not so obvious and easy to ignore and even disbelieve in the face of preexisting beliefs. Many of these not so obvious transformations are that way because they are directed inward at the human condition and challenge the very nature of human existence and what it means to be human and interact with others in society. Advances in genetic research, reproductive technologies, and human enhancement technologies provide us with new powers that we quickly integrate into our lives and forget about. Other not so obvious transformations are at the level of complex systems and beyond our individual grasp. The advancements in computer networking, wireless devices, and big data provide opportunities for new forms of communication, community building, and economic growth. At the same time, they also provide a perfect stage for information overload, security and privacy risks, crime and human exploitation. This sets the stage for the present volume which deals with new ethical issues and and dilemmas accompanying the challenging co-evolution of technology and human society.

The term, *technoethics* was first coined in the 1960s by philosopher, Mario Bunge (Bunge, 1977), becoming entrenched with academia over the last decade as an interdisciplinary field of research. A number of seminal publications can be cited as key drivers in the formalization of Technoethics as an interdisciplinary research field, namely *The Handbook of Research on Technoethics: Volume I and II* (Luppicini & Adel, 2009), the *Evolving Knowledge Society: Ethical Issues in Technological Design, Research, Development, and Innovation* (Luppicini, 2010a), and the *International Journal of Technoethics. The Handbook of Research on Technoethics: Volume I and II* pulled together over 100 experts from around the world working on a diversity of areas where technoethical inquiry was being pursued. Following this, the first reader in Technoethics, *Technoethics and the Evolving Knowledge Society: Ethical Issues in Technological Design, Research, Development, and Innovation* (Luppicini, 2010a) was published for use at the undergraduate and graduate level in a variety of courses that focus on technology and ethics in society. In the same year, the *International Journal of Technoethics* (Rocci Luppicini – Founding Editor-in-Chief) was established as a peer-reviewed journal to provide an ongoing forum for scholarly exchange. The mission of the journal was as follows:

The mission of the International Journal of Technoethics (IJT) is to evolve technological relationships of humans with a focus on ethical implications for human life, social norms and values, education, work, politics, law, and ecological impact. This journal provides cutting edge analysis of technological innovations, research, developments policies, theories, and methodologies related to ethical aspects of technology in society. IJT publishes empirical research, theoretical studies, innovative methodologies, practical applications, case studies, and book reviews. IJT encourages submissions from philosophers, researchers, social theorists, ethicists, historians, practitioners, and technologists from all areas of human activity affected by advancing technology. (Luppicini, 2010b, p. i)

In 2018, the field of Technoethics has never been stronger as public interest and concern continue to focus on controversial new emerging technologies, technologies that we have that are being used in new ways, and future technologies that have yet to be developed but which could transform life and society in profound and unpredictable ways. Current research in technoethics continues to focus on all areas of human life, society, and the environment where technological development is having a profound impact. For instance, what it means to be human amidst a myriad of human enhancement technologies that allow us to augment human bodies and minds in substantive ways (e.g., plastic surgery, prosthetic limbs, exoskeletons, performance and mind enhancing drugs, biosensors, neural implants, wearable computers, etc.). Although there is continual fear in the world concerning disruptive force new emerging technologies on human life, individuals like, Chapter 5 author, Francesco Albert Bosco Cortese author see the opposite as more probable, "It is through the development of human enhancement technologies in general and the development of increasingly precise and extensive neuromodulation technologies for the controlled induction and modulation of an agent's own neural activity in particular that we can gain more control than we've ever had before over the determining conditions of the material systems constituting our minds and bodies."

Another area of technoethical inquiry examines the moral dilemmas revolving around the boundaries of the social world itself as we struggle to navigate the juxtaposition of humans and advancements in autonomous robotics which, for some, warrant social rights and responsibilities. This type of ethical inquiry brings the debate concerning human enhancement to a new level of importance. Can humans teach machines and algorithms to learn some form of ethics and morality? How can we ensure moral responsibility in the context of military research and autonomous weapons systems. Beyond the realm of human enhancement and moral agency in autonomous weapons in autonomous systems, there are also everyday technological applications revolving around the Internet and social networking technologies that invoke public concern (digital democracy, media ethics, cybercrime and online plagiarism). What are the ethical problems and dilemmas that individuals face in cyberspace? What are the privacy concerns with posting personal information online and how much is too much? What are the trends in cyberbullying activity and other areas of ethical misconduct that occur using the Internet? These questions and others that place human ethics and values at the centre of technological inquiry are taken up in this volume within research domain of technoethics.

OBJECTIVES AND ORGANIZATION

This edited book continues to expand the growing body of work on the existing intellectual platform within the field of technoethics. The topics covered in this volume expand on scholarship covered in the International Journal of Technoethics and supporting publications. It provides up to date coverage of cutting edge work from a variety of areas where technoethical inquiry is currently being applied.

The book contains 18 chapters divided into three sections to highlight a logical flow of writing organized into key thematic areas of technoethical inquiry. Section 1, "Ethical Perspectives on Advancing Human-Technological Relations" contains five chapters: Chapter 1, "An Ethical Framework for Interconnected and Self-Organizing Moral Machines" (Ben van Lier); Chapter 2, "Enhancing the Brain and the Ethics of Sport" (José Luis Pérez Triviño); Chapter 3, "The Political Use and Abuse of Science (Gabriel R. Ricci); Chapter 4, "Cyber-Bullies as Cyborg-Bullies" (Tommaso Bertolotti, Selene Arfini, and Lorenzo Magnani); and Chapter 5, "The Techoethical Ethos of Technic Self-Determination: Technological Determinism as the Ontic Fundament of Freewill" (Francesco Albert Bosco Cortese). Section 2, "Current Applications of Emerging Technologies and Their Ethical Implications," contains eight chapters: Chapter 6, "Lethal Military Robots: Who is Responsible When Things Go Wrong" (Lambèr Royakkers); Chapter 7, "The Case Against Weapons Research" (John Forge); Chapter 8, "Humans, Autonomous Systems, and Killing in War" (Jai Galliot); Chapter 9, "Ethical Dimensions of NBIC-Convergence" (Elena Grebenshchikova); Chapter 10, "The Societal Hazards of Neuroenhancement Technologies" (Wagner); Chapter 11, "Surgeon, Media, Society, Patient: Four Factors in Determining the Ethics of Cosmetic Surgery" (Brett Lunceford); Chapter 12, "Socio-Ethical Impact of the Emerging Smart Technologies" (Octavian M. Machidon); and Chapter 13, "Energy Consumers' Perspectives on Smart Meter Data: Privacy and Unjust Algorithmic Discrimination" (Winter). Section 3, "Emerging Trends and Future Directions" contains five chapters: Chapter 14, "Encouraging Digital Civility: What Companies and Others Can Do" (Jacqueline F. Beauchere); Chapter 15, "Algorithms vs. Hive Minds: Preserving Democracy's Future in the Age of AI" (Rick Searle); Chapter 16, "Viral Art Matters: Using Web-Based Artwork to Fortify Academic Efforts" (Alejandra Emilia Iannone); Chapter 17, "A Technoethical Study of Ethical Hacking Communication and Management Within a Canadian University" (Baha Abu-Shaqra and Rocci Luppicini); and Chapter 18, "Communication in the E-Culture and Media: New Trends and Features" (Liudmila Vladimirovna Baeva).

More detailed descriptions of the chapters are as follows:

- Chapter 1, "An Ethical Framework for Interconnected and Self-Organizing Moral Machines," by Ben van Lier explores an ethical framework to deal with interconnected and self-organizing moral machines in life and society. In particular, the chapter focuses on the driving force of algorithms created by humans for machines and how moral actions can be programmed into these machines. The chapter raises importance questions concerning how humans, if at all, could teach machines and algorithms that act increasingly autonomously to learn some form of ethics and morality. Drawing on social systems theory of Luhman (and other scholars), the author posits an innovate ethical model for framing for guiding the creation of algorithms that support the actions and decisions of interconnected self-organizing machines in a world of human actors, intentionality, and information complexity.

- Chapter 2, "Enhancing the Brain and the Ethics of Sport," by José Luis Pérez Triviño explores the brave new world of sport and sport ethics amidst the latest development in sport doping linked to biotechnological advances, pharmacological enhancers and transcranial stimulators. What is striking in this chapter is how it demonstrates the extreme disruptive power of technology to influence well entrenched societal traditions and practices. This chapter provides the reader with an overview of the evolution of doping including more recent developments in cognitive and emotional doping. The chapter highlights the need for more attention to the importance of ethical and neuroscientific aspects of sport within contemporary society.

- Chapter 3, "The Political Use and Abuse of Science," by Gabriel R. Ricci provides an excellent birds eye view look at the political influence on science by exploring the role of science on public policy and how scientific autonomy has been, at times, subverted to political agendas. The chapter highlights the important role of political influence on the real world advancement of science and technology where scientists often find themselves in the back seat of their own discoveries and innovations. This chapter does an excellent job at showcasing how an underrepresented area of Technoethical Inquiry (political perspective) exerts an ongoing pressure on value systems (religious, scientific, political) on scientists and technological innovations that result. The chapter focus on the past US Bush administration will resonate with current readership on the recent history of the war on science and the complexities that can block ethical scientific and technological progress.

- Chapter 4, "Cyber-Bullies as Cyborg-Bullies," by Tommaso Bertolotti, Selene Arfini, and Lorenzo Magnani provides another useful step back to reconceptualize how cyber bullying is viewed. The chapter presents a compelling case to look at cyber-bullies as cyborg-bullies in order to appreciate the important nuances of the bullying in the technological age. The chapter highlight how the term 'cyborg' had, and continues to have, an important theoretical value and strong explanatory and predictive power in dealing with current cyber-bullying situations. As stressed by the chapter authors, "The definition of cyborg-bullying, by paying attention to the medium of the violence as the cognitive shaper of the violent acts, not only improves the comprehension of the different possibilities that a violent SNS user could exploit, but also provides a better understanding of what kind of damage is actually caused by violent acts online."

- Chapter 5, "The Techoethical Ethos of Technic Self-Determination: Technological Determinism as the Ontic Fundament of Freewill," by Francesco Albert Bosco Cortese provides a much needed optimistic spin on the human enhancement debate as the author discusses it as a means of increasing the autonomy of individual members of society in alignment with the changing human condition and the natural desire for increased self-determination. To this end, the chapter posits the need for an ontology of self-determination that acknowledges the human capacity for self-modification and self-modulation of material systems and processes that influence the body and mind to effect change. The author sees human enhancement technologies driven by advances in neurotechnologies as a key means of leveraging human self-determination.

- Chapter 6, "Lethal Military Robots: Who Is Responsible When Things Go Wrong," by Lambèr Royakkers explores the moral responsibility of lethal military robots by critically examining the chain of responsibility in relation to the deployment of semi-autonomous and autonomous lethal military robots in contexts that lead to violence and the human loss of life. Following a critical overview of the current situation and highlights the need to create ethical responsibility practices that minimize risk and delineate clear lines of responsibility that can be observed by all.

- Chapter 7, "The Case Against Weapons Research," by John Forge builds the previous chapter by making a case against weapons research. The chapter argues that current justifications for keeping and deploying weapons in the spirit of defence and deterrence do not outweigh their potential harms when factoring in the unforeseen ways in which these weapons could be used in the future. This, the author believes, provides a solid deterrence against continued weapons research. As stated in the chapter," Weapons research produces practical knowledge in the form of designs for the means to harm, and its practitioners cannot know how this knowledge will be used in the future."

- Chapter 8, "Humans, Autonomous Systems, and Killing in War," by Jai Galliot provides an interesting angle on the alleged responsibility gap that exists in the context of autonomous weapons systems use. Given the complexity of autonomous systems, problem of moral distancing, human actions, and responsibility, the chapter calls for solutions that take human, technical and regulatory aspects of autonomous weapons systems use into consideration. One way suggested in the chapter is to use black box-type recorders on the battlefield to ensure more appropriate autonomous weapons systems use in accordance with just war theory and the laws of war, "A kind of 'black box recorder' that tracks human input into autonomous systems throughout the system lifecycle might be the best way forward in this scenario and ensure technical actors are held responsible to the same standards as their military equivalents and do not slip the cracks left open by distance." This chapter adds a fresh perspective and practical insights into autonomous weapons systems work.

- Chapter 9, "Ethical Dimensions of NBIC-Convergence," by Elena Grebenshchikova provides a sobering look at the ethical dimensions of the complex world of NBIC-convergence. The chapter provides a useful review of new trends in technoethics (nanoethics, bioethics, ICT-ethics, and neuroethics) in response to the synergetic merging of nanotechnology, biotechnology, information technology and cognitive sciences in recent years. The chapter places moral dimensions of technoscience under a single theoretical framework of technoethics to highlight the need for an integrated approach to deal with NBIC-convergence as an example of an inter- and multi-disciplinary innovation that combines knowledge and specialists from various fields and disciplines to solve complex socio-technical system problems. The chapter emphasizes, "The problems that arise at the intersection of different knowledge fields require complex optics to measure their social impact and ethical issues. Formation of different ethical approaches to various areas of technology (nanoethics, neuroethics, ICT ethics) reflects their specificity, but is limited. The complex problem requires stereoscopy view, which offers technoethics, which is an effective guide in understanding the complexity of the various ethical NBIC implications."

- Chapter 10, "The Societal Hazards of Neuroenhancement Technologies," by Wagner takes an in-depth look at the world of cognitive neuroenhancement drugs (aka drugs) to improve cognitive cognitive function and performance. The chapter provides a focused review of psychostimulants and how these drugs work in terms of brain functioning, psychological experiences, and long-term effect. The chapter also reviews at transcranial stimulation, a non-pharmacological approach, cognitive enhancement. A number of insightful ethical considerations and concerns are aidentified that warrant future attention and continued research. The chapter raises concludes by raising the following important question to ponder, "Do we really want to live in, and promote, a society where people aspire to enhance their cognitive capacities to answer and thereby reinforce the increasing societal demands of competition?"

- Chapter 11, "Surgeon, Media, Society, Patient: Four Factors in Determining the Ethics of Cosmetic Surgery," by Brett Lunceford looks at the ethical considerations surrounding cosmetic surgery. The chapter discusses ethical codes grounded in doctor-patient relationships that emphasize respect for autonomy, nonmaleficence, beneficence, and justice. In line with a technoethical lens, the chapter extends ethical codes grounded in doctor-patient relationships to include media and societial for a a more complete understanding the key factors involved in establishing an ethics of cosmetic surgery. Drawing on the famous case of Heidi Montag, the chapter also illustrates the dark side of plastic surgery and its ethical failures.

- Chapter 12, "Socio-Ethical Impact of the Emerging Smart Technologies," by Octavian M. Machidon explores the social and ethical implications of emerging smart technologies. The chapter takes a multi-level approach to the topic addressing health repercussions, possible social and behavioral changes, as well as privacy and security concerns. The chapter reviews key areas of smart technology impact on society while drawing attention to very serious risk posed to humans, "Being 'smart,' and thus offering context-aware feedback, and a multitude of functions meant to ease the owner's life, these devices raise concerns due to the risk of over-relying on technology at the expense of using the natural cognitive functions as before." The chapter extends existing work in technoethics and makes useful suggestions for future research.

- Chapter 13, "Energy Consumers' Perspectives on Smart Meter Data: Privacy and Unjust Algorithmic Discrimination," by Jenifer Winter builds on the previous chapter through a focused empirical research study on consumer response to implementation of residential smart metering technology. The chapter attests to the growing concern over smart technologies which the public is increasing willing to voice. He first hand reports indicate that smart technologies are not free from ethical challenges. The chapter makes useful recommendations for moving forward in line with the public it serves.

- Chaper 14, "Encouraging Digital Civility: What Companies and Others Can Do," by Jacqueline F. Beauchere explores the important role that companies play in the promotion of digital citizenship. As the Chief Online Safety Officer, Microsoft Corporation, the author, provides a useful roadmap for companies and other to follow to leverage the safe, responsible, and appropriate use of technology and services. The chapter reviews some of the steps that Microsoft is taking to promote digital civility. In line with a technoethical systems approach, the chapter addresses the need for multiple perspectives understanding and support from stakeholder groups including the technology industry, policy makers, the broader Internet community, educators, parents, and youth. This chapter takes a forward looking gaze at how the internet can be used to foster greater civility.

- Chapter 15, "Algorithms vs. Hive Minds: Preserving Democracy's Future in the Age of AI," by Rick Searle expands on the discussion on the Internet and its potential role in shaping democracy. The author effectively weaves a path between two opposing visions of the Internet, one with a dystopian potential for surveillance and control versus its utopian possibilities for enhancing freedom and social democracy. Rather than taking a particular side, the author takes an alternative position that views the internet as complex and entrenched in both dystopian and utopian ideals entrenched in human society which need to be understood to better navigate the fears and hopes of the Internet's future, In the end the author predicts, "There is no final utopia out there that awaits us so long as we follow the Internet's inherent logic, but this is not a pessimistic thought. For neither does there await us in the future some everlasting dystopia, so long as we remain human."

- Chapter 16, "Viral Art Matters: Using Web-Based Artwork to Fortify Academic Efforts," by Alejandra Emilia Iannone digs into a much neglected area of media ethics, art appreciation, human values. Why is it that we are drawn to some YouTube videos? What makes something go viral and what underlies this phenomenon? This chapter draws our attention to the need to reflect more and invest more academic efforts in unravelling the powerful influence of viral art. The author writes a compelling chapter that demonstrates just how art matters and challenges scholars to continue exploring this area to advance ethics, art appreciation, and human understanding.
- Chapter 17, "A Technoethical Study of Ethical Hacking Communication and Management Within a Canadian University," by Baha Abu-Shaqra and Rocci Luppicini explores ethical hacking as an important new information security risk management strategy within higher education used to combat hacking attacks. This chapter presents the findings from a case study that paired technoethical inquiry theory with Karl Weick's sensemaking model to explore the meanings, ethics, uses and practices, and value of ethical hacking in a Canadian university. Valuable findings revolved around a lack in current communicative and sociocultural considerations involved in decision making about ethical hacking organizational practices. The chapter suggests that security awareness training is required to address growing hacking threats.
- Chapter 18, "Communication in the E-Culture and Media: New Trends and Features," by Liudmila Vladimirovna Baeva discusses the changing landscape of communication in e-culture and media. Based on a social network analysis, the chapter sketches out a typology of virtual communication using a systems approach to illustrate contemporary e-culture. The chapter ends this volume by reflecting on a serious technoethical concern for future researchers to deal with, "There are more possibilities and conditions to violate common morals and ethics of behavior online and that means there are more temptations to do so. Human beings continue to be "condemned to freedom" online, with its new levels and forms. It is much more difficult to keep on behaving morally under the ethical pluralism than under an environment of strict control."

CONCLUSION

Taken together, the above chapters nicely illustrate the diversity of areas of research opening up to technoethical inquiry from lethal military drones, to human enhancement technologies to internet related challenges to human privacy and security. At the same time, many of the current chapters leave unanswered questions for future researchers to take up. It is expected that scholarly work will continue to flourish within the expanding landscape of technoethical research for years to come.

REFERENCES

Abbott, T. K. (1898). *Kant's Critique Of Practical Reason And Other Works On The Theory Of Ethics*. London: Longmans, Green.

Britannica Online Encyclopedia. (2012). *Cybercrime*. Retrieved, October 15, 2012, from: www.britannica.com/EBchecked/topic/130595/cybercrime

Gore, A. (n.d.). *BrainyQuote.com*. Retrieved August 31, 2017, from BrainyQuote.com Web site: https://www.brainyquote.com/quotes/quotes/a/algore457743.html

Luppicini, R. (2008). Introducing technoethics. In R. Luppicini & R. Adell (Eds.), *Handbook of research on technoethics* (pp. 1–18). Hershey, PA: Idea Group Publishing. doi:10.4018/978-1-60566-022-6.ch001

Luppicini, R. (2009). Technoethical inquiry: From technological systems to society. Global Media Journal – Canadian Edition, 2(1), 5-21.

Luppicini, R. (Ed.). (2012a). *Handbook of Research on Technoself: Identity in a Technological Society* (Vols. 1-2). Hershey, PA: Idea Group Publishing.

Luppicini, R. (Ed.). (2012b). *Ethical Impact of Technological Advancements and Applications in Society*. Hershey, PA: Idea Group Publishing. doi:10.4018/978-1-4666-1773-5

Luppicini, R. (2010a). *Technoethics and the evolving knowledge society*. Hershey, PA: Idea Group Publishing. doi:10.4018/978-1-60566-952-6

Luppicini, R., & Adell, R. (Eds.). (2009). *Handbook of Research on Technoethics* (Vols. 1-2). Hershey, PA: Idea Group Publishing. doi:10.4018/978-1-60566-022-6

Luppicini, R. (2010b). The technological r/evolution. *International Journal of Technoethics, 1*(1), i–ii.

Section 1
Ethical Perspectives on Advancing Human–Technological Relations

Chapter 1
An Ethical Framework for Interconnected and Self-Organizing Moral Machines

Ben van Lier
Centric Gouda, The Netherlands & Steinbeis University Berlin, Germany

ABSTRACT

Technology is responsible for major systemic changes within the global financial sector. This sector has already developed into a comprehensive network of mutually connected people and computers. Algorithms play a crucial role within this network. An algorithm is in essence merely a set of instructions developed by one or more people with the intention of having these instructions performed by a machine such as a computer in order to realize an ideal result. As part of a development in which we as human beings have ever higher expectations of algorithms and these algorithms become more autonomous in their actions, we cannot avoid including possibilities in these algorithms that enable ethical or moral considerations. To develop this ethical or moral consideration, we need a kind of ethical framework that can be used for constructing these algorithms. With the development of such a framework we can start to think about what we as human beings consider to be a moral action executed by algorithms that support actions and decisions of interconnected and self-organizing machines. This chapter explores an ethical framework for interconnected and self-organizing moral machines.

INTRODUCTION

The theme of this essay is the major systemic changes confronted by the global financial sector in general and particularly in the trade in financial products. Within this essay I will focus specifically on the dominant role played by technology and technological applications within the context of these changes. Algorithms play an essential and valuable role within the financial sector. Take, for example, the visualization of all sorts of information and being able to exchange and share this information between the parties involved, irrespective of their time and location. Algorithms have become increasingly autonomous during the past decade, their artificial intelligence has increased and this artificial intelligence has allowed

DOI: 10.4018/978-1-5225-5094-5.ch001

them to act more independently and make complicated decisions at speeds that exceed human powers of observation. Whether we like it or not, these algorithms currently dominate the financial markets and the large majority of the global financial transactions are performed without any human interference. The development of systems that are ever more interconnected with networks in which algorithms act autonomously and influence the global trade in financial products raises new questions concerning, for example, the need for an '*ethical framework*'. This framework could enable us to further consider if and how these machines and their algorithms could be taught a form of morality as part of their development. In the second part of this essay, I will deal specifically with the question of whether and how concepts such as ethics and morality could be related to technology and whether and how machines and algorithms that act increasingly autonomously could be taught a form or ethics and morality.

Enframing

Many foundations of the current financial and social crisis lie in the unstoppable rise of technology and the use of technological applications during the past decade and mankind's inability to give sufficient meaning to these developments. The rise of the personal computer, the Internet and the mobile phone has been unstoppable during the past twenty years, as noticed by van Lier (2015). We can now conclude that a mobile phone is available for each average world citizen. Of all the mobile phones sold worldwide, more than 40% are smartphones with a memory capacity that exceeds that of a desktop computer from eight years ago. On the basis of the resulting networking, new technological applications were invented, which became a social and economic force. I am referring to developments also known as social media such as Facebook, Twitter, Instagram, LinkedIn and Whatsapp. Who would have thought twenty years ago that the largest companies in the world would be IT companies such as Google, Apple, Microsoft or Samsung. And that a small company such as Whatsapp with approximately 100 employees is able to show the global telecommunications giants that their existing business model based on modern elements such as calling and texting has come to the end of its life cycle. These telecommunications giants are now also forced to sit and watch how their crucial role, which arose in the middle of the previous century, is replaced with data bundles and devices that communicate with each other in networks of the postmodern society. Whether we like it or not, all of these changes have an unprecedented influence on our daily life and work and our experience of reality. The end of this technological revolution is not yet in sight and in the years to come we will be confronted with more technological developments and applications arising therefrom. We are on the brink of a new phase in technological evolution and, in addition to people, more and more objects are interconnected in these networks and enabled to exchange and share information mutually and with people. As van Lier (2015) states, apparently ordinary and traditional objects such as cars, televisions, passport, books, sports shoes and medical implants will be or have already been interconnected in these networks. We also want to use and wear more portable information elements such as Google glasses, smart watches, OMsignal t-shirts or Nike shoes so that we are able to share information about ourselves with others. And as if this is not yet enough, we are also confronted with new developments resulting from the convergence of nano-, bio- and cognitive technology with IT. This convergence has been possible because our understanding of nanoscience and nanotechnology and how to manipulate matter with this technology is growing. According to Bainbridge and Rocco (2005), these new combinations of technology will enable:

Human intellectual and social performance [to] be greatly enhanced by nano-enabled portable infor-mation systems and communication devices, by biotechnology treatments for disorders of the mind or memory, and by increased understanding of how the human brain and senses actually function. (Rocco, 2005, p.4).

The aforementioned technological developments and the applications that result from them will be or have already been incorporated to a greater or lesser extent in everyday products such as coatings, glass, food and medicine. However, over the coming decades there is an entirely new technological development on the horizon: quantum computing. Although many scientists are convinced that it will take decades before it is possible to build the first practical quantum computer, new possibilities and applications are presenting themselves at breakneck speed in this area as well. Dowling (2013) argues for example that an exponential acceleration of search algorithms using quantum informatics could be useful for all manner of functions not directed at cryptography. He mentions by way of an example of such usefulness, among other things, the digital possibilities for stock trading that uses very high-quality software on supercomputers that operate at the speed of light. He therefore states:

In such a cutthroat business, if your quasi-quantum computer trading machine is a few milliseconds faster than the classical computer trading machine of your competitor, you stand to make millions. A quantum quadratic speed-up on a 100-milliseconds stock trade would be 10-millisecond stock trade that would leave your competitors to eat the dust of your electron cloud competitor. (Dowling, 2013, p.192).

It is not without reason that the philosopher Heidegger (1927) asked the question towards the middle of the previous century of how we as human beings through 'Dasein' (presence) in our world relate to the phenomenon of technology. He states that we owe it to ourselves as human beings to continuously search for the essence of technology in our world and the manner in which this technology influences us as human beings as well as our 'presence' in our daily life and actions. According to Heidegger, the search for the essence of technology also constitutes a form of revealing (Heidegger, 1977, p.12), in the sense of exposing or showing how our 'presence' in our relationship with technology has changed. Investigating and revealing the essence of technology and in particular the manner in which it relates to us as human beings will hopefully enable us to come to terms with a new form of shared reality and to redefine our 'presence' in this new reality. The development of this new reality of human beings and technology is formed, according to Heidegger, by technology 'enframing' our reality. We seem to take it for granted that technology surrounds us ever more in different manifestations in our contemporary society, and we are don´t even notice. However, Heidegger states that the question concerning the essence of technology always comes too late, as it does not arise until mankind experiences that the essence of technology has already enframed its daily existence and has already influenced our actions and our daily experience of reality. The fact that the question concerning the essence of technology always comes too late does not release us as human beings from responsibility towards ourselves concerning the manner in which we redefine our 'presence' in the new reality, as Heidegger argues. Such a development of enframing and revealing de facto also exists for the global financial sector and in particular for High Frequency Trading as we are now able to conclude throughout the world.

Forty years after Heidegger, Smith (1991) added to Heidegger's argument that mankind first has to let go of its traditional way of thinking about technology before it is able to consider its relationship with new and developing technology in its surroundings. Smith states that modern man first needs to learn to accept that he is no longer the most important entity in this universe; an entity that is able to control and manage everything around it and can continue to consider technology merely a neutral instrument that supports him as a human being. Technology and technological applications oblige us, according to Smith, to learn to think more and in a fundamentally different way about ourselves as human beings and our relationship with the technology that has been developed and that surrounds us. The development of technology and the use of new technological applications thus very naturally creates a new reality in which we will have to learn to hold our own as human beings, whether we like it or not. In the new reality of the global financial sector, we will have to acknowledge that technology and technological applications are drastically changing the global financial system and that new networks of interconnected machines have been created, such as computers that have a high level of autonomy. These are machines that have become incredibly complex as a result of their interconnection and interaction and slowly but surely take over more responsibilities from human beings.

The increase in autonomy and complexity of technology results, according to Braidotti (2013), is a shift in "*the location of moral intentionality from autonomous transcendental consciousness to the technological artifacts themselves*" (Braidotti, 2013, p.42). She states that this drastic change should be reason for a fundamental reconsideration of our relationship with technology. Contrary to the common anthropocentric notion that technology or manifestations thereof such as algorithms, robots, computers etc. are subordinate to human beings, she states that we will have to develop towards a post anthropocentric notion in which technology and the mutual connection between mankind and machine are central and whereby decisions within this interconnected system are no longer made, or can be managed and controlled, solely by human beings. Braidotti disputes this new mutual connection: "*The relationship between the human and the technological other has shifted in the contemporary context, to reach unprecedented degrees of intimacy and intrusion*" (Braidotti, 2013, p.89). Slowly but surely, we will have to acknowledge that mankind and technology are simultaneously and equally present in postmodern society and this simultaneous 'presence' of mankind and technology has a major impact on our experience of reality in this world. The transformation to a post anthropocentric perspective of the relationship between human beings and technology demands new frameworks, however, and new and shared points of reference will have to be developed for this purpose. New frameworks that can provide new points of reference for the new reality between the post human and the surrounding complexity of people, machines and technology connected in networks. From the above, it can be concluded that technology and technological applications have created a new reality for mankind. Technology and technological applications have changed the global financial sector too. Within this evolutionary change, the agency between man and technology has also shifted in favor of technology. Within this new, developing complex and globally connected ecosystem of communication and interaction, humans and machines in the financial sector need new and shared points of reference that could help develop new frameworks for this new reality.

High Frequency Trading

As I have argued previously, the global financial sector has already developed into a comprehensive network of mutually connected people and computers that are constantly evaluating and approving millions of transactions, as argued by Wallach (Wallach, 2009, p.3). Wallach states that the complexity of this whole of mutually connected hardware, communication networks, software, algorithms and people who exchange and share information in these global networks and make decisions based on this information and perform further activities, demands specific, ethical subroutines within these networks. Ethical subroutines are necessary for further development towards autonomous and interconnected machines, according to Wallach, because: *"the greater the freedom of a machine, the more it will need moral standards"* (Wallach, 2009, p.23). Although machines in financial markets cannot cause direct physical injury to a person - as can be done by an autonomous car robot or combat robot for example - decisions made in ever increasing freedom by autonomous machines in financial networks can have far-reaching social and financial consequences that will have a major impact on the wellbeing of large groups of people. However, the development and the role of machines within financial markets is, according to Farmer and Skouras (2012), an *"inherently dynamic process that can only be properly understood from an ecological and evolutionary perspective"* (Farmer and Skouras, 2012). They consider that the technical domination of the current financial markets results from subsequent changes that took place during the history of these markets. But these changes do not result exclusively from technological progress and innovation; also from specific design problems in the structure of these markets, changing legislation and regulations, habits and conventions and, more generally, from the trading patterns of people in these markets. Farmer and Skouras are of the opinion that more research into the behind the specific combination of digital trading strategies that are used by computers in these markets is needed in order to be able to properly understand these developments in the financial markets. Such research will enable us to learn to understand how these strategies interact with each other and how these interactions cause the strategy to change over time and at the same time alter our perception of the financial markets as a result of these changes.

According to Hendershott (2011), research into the fundamental changes in the financial sector that in recent years, among other things, have led to the creation and rapid development of High Frequency Trading, starts with the DOT system that was taken into use at the New York Stock Exchange in 1976. This system made it possible to electronically request transactions of up to 100 shares. Once they arrive on the trading floor, the stock exchange dealers process these digital requests in their traditional stock exchange activities of purchase and sale. The number of electronic trade activities and the number of trade activities performed by human beings was still almost the same towards the end of the previous century. However, the number of trade activities performed by human beings on the trading floor started to drop substantially as of 2002. The number of trade transactions performed by human beings dropped even further after 2006 to ultimately less than 20% of the activities on the New York Stock Exchange. Hendershott is of the opinion that this transformation mainly due to the possibility of automatically executing digital transactions, which was introduced in 2006. From then on, the size of transactions was no longer limited, but now they can involve as many as 1 million shares per automatic transaction. The execution time of these transactions is reduced to less than one second. It is observed in a report from Finance Watch (2012) that the combination of the introduction of the real time quotation system to the stock exchange, as well as the rapidly increasing IT possibilities, have led to a rapid development and application of algorithms within the financial sector. Current estimates of the volume of transactions in the financial markets initiated and executed by algorithms vary. Based on their research, Ahlstedt and Villyson (2012) conclude that 73% of the trade in the US equity market consists of activities initiated by High Frequency Trading, while these activities are applied by only 2% of the 20,000 trading companies worldwide. The reduction in the volume of transactions executed by human beings thus keeps pace with the development of a high level of fragmentation of the financial markets, argues Brogaard (2011). This means that only a fraction of the shares are still traded by the NYSE or the NASDAQ. The overwhelming majority of the share transactions is performed on new stock exchanges, such as BATS or in digital communication networks such as Island ECN and other alternative trading systems. According to Brogaard, this fragmentation of the financial market also leads to differences in the information position, because current information that is used during transactions on the digital stock exchanges differs from the information that is recorded in the computer systems of the stock exchange and is later (re)used to obtain an 'up-to-date' picture of the trading situation by human traders. This means that the speed with which these markets can dispose of information for the purpose of financial transactions has become very valuable. Technological communication networks, necessary connections, information that is exchanged and shared and people and machines that use this information jointly form a connected whole that operates at speeds and volumes that have become incomprehensible to us as human beings. Johnson et al. (2013) determine on the basis of millisecond analyses that the most powerful socio-technical network worldwide, the financial sector, has developed in its current form into a *"new all-machine phase, characterized by large numbers of sub-second extreme events"* (Johnson et al., 2013). A new multi-billion dollar technological arms race is taking place in this new phase to further increase the speed of computer processing and the communication between computers at speeds that are several factors higher than humans beings are even able to observe, let alone respond to. The only limit that cannot be broken yet in this connection is the limit of the speed of light, as formulated by Einstein in the previous century. By way of an example of this arms race, Johnson et al. (2013) refers to the new transatlantic connection created between American and British traders just to be able to realize a 5 millisecond speed gain. Or a new iX-eCute chip that was developed specifically for this sector and that prepares orders in 740 nano seconds. However, a form of dark trading has developed in this new market structure in order to be able to operate within these networks and in order to prevent other traders from being able to observe buying or selling orders prematurely. The report from Baseline Capital (Walsh, 2012), Australia, describes Dark Trading as executing orders without providing transparency in advance to the market concerning that specific order.

According to Hendershott (2011), the composite whole of people and machines in the financial sector arises from two simultaneous technological developments that have transformed this sector worldwide in a relatively short period of time. On the one hand, there is an increasing number of traders who wish to use technology and technological applications to place their orders and, on the other hand, the stock exchanges on which these transactions take place are being reorganized in such a way that they have basically become nothing more than electronic limit order books. The speed and quality of access to electronic markets subsequently encourages further use of algorithms to be able to make automatic decisions quickly, to be able to place and execute orders and to be able to monitor the orders after they have been placed. Algorithms that operate in the global financial sector as autonomous software 'agents' are defined by Luca et al. (2011) as:

Self-contained entities that could sense their environment and somehow combine this sensor reading with their internal state via learning or reasoning mechanisms to take actions that are appropriate in that environment in the pursuit of the agent's aims or goals without the need of external control. (Luca et al, 2011).

In the current financial markets, these autonomous algorithms can exist in the form of software or robot traders which are constantly busy, in a non-physical form, probing the various flows of information that are present within the global digital financial markets. These non-physical traders can combine and analyze the available information on the basis of their internal capabilities and act independently by buying, selling or withdrawing financial orders within the digital market from the outcome of these analyses. The arrival of these autonomous software 'agents' in the current financial markets means that these markets have become a worldwide, shared playing field for people and financial trading systems controlled by algorithms in which transactions amounting to billions of dollars are performed each day. Luca et al. consider that, despite these factual developments, only a little scientific research into the combination of transactions performed by human beings and machines is carried out. In short, the global financial sector can be seen as a socio-technical ecosystem consisting of autonomous systems. Within this new global ecosystem, systems will be increasingly autonomous and self-organizing, relying on the mutual exchange and sharing of information within these ecosystems for their decisions. The evolutionary development within the global financial sector of autonomous systems that are making decisions by themselves creates a need for new knowledge and more holistic perspectives based on connections, interactions and communications between humans and machines within this new entity.

Flash Crash

The implications of the creation of this global '*interconnected ultra large scale*' and '*complex socio-technical*' system for the financial sector cannot be foreseen at this time, argue Cliff et al. (2010). Presently, the risks inherent in a mutually connected global system in the field of technology, finance and economy are almost impossible to comprehend. Analysis and quantification of the possible financial risks run by an individual financial organization are also almost impossible. The whole that arises from the compound systems, the trade strategies applied by them, the variety of digital trading places, the automated trading systems of the various investment banks and hedge funds have turned the global financial sector into a system-of-systems. The enormous size and complexity of this socio-technical system-of-systems means that new types of problems or risks can arise anywhere, at any time. These new risks and problems cannot be foreseen or prevented using the knowledge that is available at this time until these problems and risks actually manifest themselves. When these unpredictable risks of problems become reality it will no longer be possible to intervene and relatively minor incidents can lead to major and uncontrollable crises that can develop at a speed that makes it almost impossible for human beings to respond adequately to them. Cliff et al. (2010) therefore consider that it has become necessary to study the increasing interaction between human traders and their digital counterpart in further detail, in order to better understand the ensuing whole. One of those major problems took place on Thursday, May 06, 2010 and has become known as the Flash Crash. This problem can be classified as an entirely unexpected and dramatic error in one of the relevant software systems. In hindsight, this flash crash can also be considered and possibly understood to be a normal anomaly in an ultra-large-scale complex socio-technical system-of-systems. The events that took place during this Flash Crash were reason for Adler (2012) to question whether High Frequency Trading does not raise the existential question as to why we still actually have stock exchanges. After all, the current financial trade has become an end in itself. Performing High Frequency Trading demands the availability of the fastest possible computer systems and connections and these have therefore become essential in the global trade in financial products.

Within the context of ever more increasing and ever faster data communication, the Dow Jones Industrial Average lost dropped 1000 points of its value in almost 20 minutes on Thursday, May 06, 2010. This rapid price drop and the subsequent return to the former level that occurred just as rapidly gave this event the name 'Flash Crash', argues Ramirez (2011). The SEC (2010) published an investigation report five months after this event in which responsibility for this Flash Crash was attributed fully to a single large sell order concerning futures, according to Lewis (2014). This order was placed mistakenly with an electronic stock exchange in Chicago by a small High Frequency Trading firm in Kansas City. According to Kirilenko (2011), this sell order was executed by an algorithm programmed specifically to submit special sell orders to the June 2010 E-mini exchange with the aim of realizing "*an execution rate set of 9% of the trading volume calculated over the previous minute*". Lewis (2014), however, is of the opinion that the conclusion drawn by the SEC can only have come about by accident. He states that the supervisors of this stock exchange do not have the knowledge or access to the information required to draw such far-reaching conclusions. Lewis bases his opinion on the fact that the speed of such transactions takes place at the microsecond level while the registrations that are maintained by the stock exchange are processed by the second.

Major disruptions to the trading traffic were again caused in 2012 and 2013, which resulted, among other things, in market maker Knight Capital losing 400 million dollars in 45 minutes in 2012. This almost caused the company's bankruptcy. This time, the rapid and significant losses were caused by an error in the software produced by the company, the consequence of which were not sufficiently tested when it was taken into use. Browning of the Wall Street Journal is of the opinion that all these disruptions can be summarized by a single word: complexity. He states that complexity is shaped by the ever larger number of places where trade is performed, including at least 13 stock exchanges in the US, at least 40 dark pools and an innumerable number of trade activities performed by internal traders employed at banks and institutional investors. These 'agents' create an increasing number of mutual transactions and new and as yet unknown characteristics which we have never experienced before arise from this ever increasing quantity. However, the new and unknown characteristics can no longer be reduced to the responsibility of only a single agent, because the whole of the financial sector is more than the sum of its individual parts. The global financial sector can therefore be characterized as a huge software ecosystem. Within this new software system, new and as yet unknown risks and properties may emerge which cannot merely be explained by the sum of the individual components.

Algorithms and Ethics

According to Steiner (2013), an algorithm is in essence merely a set of instructions developed by one or more people intending them to be performed by a machine such as a computer, a software robot or a physical robot in order to realize an ideal result. Information is fed into the algorithm, after which it is checked and approved on the basis of the combination of rules. However, by definition, algorithms are not a stable unit. For example, genetic algorithms, which are also used in the financial sector. As described by Holland (1992), genetic algorithms for instance can develop independently in an evolutionary manner and autonomously learn to solve new problems during this development in a manner that even their developers find difficult to understand. In our modern society, algorithms have developed into a crucial element that enables us to control the ever increasing flow of information, according to Gillepsie (2014). These algorithms also determine how information is perceived and used by end users, whether these are humans, machines or combinations of the two. These elements were not the most important reasons for Gillepsie to further consider algorithms. He argues for more research into the: "*multi-dimensional entanglement between algorithms put into practice and the social tactics of the users who take them up*" (Gillepsie, 2014). According to Gillepsie, we should thus search for a mutual connection between algorithms and their creators and/or users and the considerations applied by them in the development and/or the use of these algorithms. He states that we as human beings should stop considering algorithms as merely a form of computer code, but we should rather consider these algorithms to be the current socially-constructed new knowledge logics that are used and controlled by organizations. According to Gillepsie, research in this area should mainly focus on the complex operation of these new knowledge logics. This research is important because algorithms are increasingly able to act, make decisions and process information without human intervention on a scale that is difficult to conceive for us as human beings.

Kraemer et al. (2011) are of the opinion that algorithms are essentially value-specific if it is impossible to make a purely rational decision between two or more options and ethical considerations play an implicit or explicit role in this decision. They consider that developers are morally responsible for the software they create if the developers of these algorithms are unable to prevent the algorithm from making such ethical choices in its selection of information. Kraemer et al. (2011) define such a value judgment as: "*any proposition expressing a view on how things ought to be or not to be, or what is good or bad, or desirable or undesirable*" (Kramer et al., 2011, p.252). They are of the opinion that, if such implicit value judgments are or have been included in algorithms, these value judgments should be transparent and easily identifiable by the users. Allen, Wallach and Smit (2006) also call attention for such value judgments that have been included in algorithms, intentionally or otherwise. System developers and software developers should at least be aware of whose values are involved and who contributed those values during the development of the algorithms. However, they also draw attention to the fact that the modular design and the development of mutually connected technological systems means that it is no longer possible for a single person or a group of people to oversee the entire interaction or response that arises from the complexity of the new algorithms that are used. As part of a development in which we as human beings have ever higher expectations of algorithms and these algorithms become ever more autonomous in their actions, we cannot avoid including possibilities in these algorithms that enable ethical or further considerations. Crnkovic (2012) is of the opinion that such a form of artificial morality should be considered a skill on the part of machines to perform activities that we as human beings would have performed in the same way. In his opinion, the argument that such systems do not have a capacity that allows for a conscious form of intentionality is incorrect because defining what such a conscious capacity actually is or involves generally problematic. Even for people, intentionality is described on the basis of observed behavior, because we do not have direct access to how the human brain operates. Crnkovic states that we should see 'intelligent agents' such as algorithms more as parts or components of a larger socio-technical environment. From this perspective, responsibility is also a distributed and mutually connected whole, because within the overall socio-technical environment only part of the responsibility can be attributed to an intelligent agent such as a software robot or physical robot. When considered from the perspective of a global financial network, Moor (2006) is of the opinion that all transactions related to cash or value should also be characterized as ethically important.

Van der Poel and Royakkers (2011) argue that ethics are a systematic reflection on morality. They consider that morality in turn consists of opinions, decisions and actions that are expressed by an individual or a group of people concerning what they consider to be right or wrong. Standards are formed by the rules that prescribe necessary, desirable or prohibited action within a specific context. Or as Abney suggests: "*Morality always involves an "ought (not)" – it is about the way the world ought (or ought not) to be, as opposed to the way it actually is*" (Abney, 2014, p. 36). For Floridi it is essential that the ethical discourse is not limited to individual agents because this will hinder: "*the development of a satisfactory investigation of distributed morality, a macroscopic and growing phenomenon of global moral actions and collective responsibilities resulting from the invisible hand of systematic interactions among several agents at a local level*" (Floridi, 2013, p. 137). In view of these descriptions, it can be quoted from Anderson and Anderson (2007) that "*the ultimate goal of machine ethics is to create a machine that itself follows an ideal ethical principle or set of principles*" (Anderson and Anderson, 2007, p.15) This objective brings us according to Gunkel (2012) to a new boundary where we as human beings are confronted with new and fundamental challenges to our moral philosophy. The fact that we as human beings develop and use ever more intelligent and autonomous machines means that the machines will each time present us with new questions concerning the fundamental human assumptions at the basis of the question as to who or what shapes being a moral subject or, in the present case, a moral object. According to Gunkel, we can and should distinguish in both cases between moral 'agents' and moral 'patients'. Moral agents can then be described in a general sense as a class of agents and patients that can qualify in principle as a source for moral actions. Moral actions in this sense are a result of the complex communications and interactions among these interconnected agents such as described in the financial sector. As Floridi states: "*What we are discovering is that we need an augmented ethics for a theory of augmented moral agency*" (Floridi, 2013, p. 160). Within the context of this introduction, Menkveld (2014) and Menkveld and Zoican (2014) state that this could be for example algorithms that: "*implement a long term-position change at the lowest possible cost*". This is contrasted by the moral 'patients', in other words, a class that is formed by 'agents' that can qualify in principle as receivers of these moral actions. According to King (1995), it can be determined from the perspective of intentionalism that the intention with which an action is performed by an agent is decisive for the moral value of this action. In order to be able to evaluate the actions that have been performed on the basis of their moral value, we should, according to King, search for the reason why the specific action was performed and not limit ourselves to evaluating the action itself. For Scharre, autonomy of a machine or combinations of machines in its most simple form: "*is the ability of a machine to perform a task without human input. Thus an autonomous system is a machine, whether hardware or software, that once activated performs some task or function of its own* (Scharre, 2015, p. 8). Tonkens (2009) states that in addition to the intentionality of the action performed by the agent, the agent's degree of autonomy when performing the action is also important. He is of the opinion that autonomy can be distinguished into a negative and a positive form of autonomy. Negative autonomy arises when the agent is restricted in his actions by an outside influence which determines what the agent should do. Positive autonomy exists if the agent is the only party that determines what rules are performed by him when performing his activities. The terms 'moral agent' and 'moral patient' and the terms 'intentionality' and 'autonomy' can be used as the basis for the development of an ethical framework that can be used to develop moral machines and the ensuing new interactions between human beings and machines. We can also start to think about what we as human beings consider to be moral action by machines within the financial sector on the basis of such a framework. The next step in developing this framework is to define 'actors' within this framework who perform activities within the digital system of the global financial sector and that are focused on performing High Frequency Trading, for example. According to German sociologist Niklas Luhmann, the concept 'system' in its abstraction refers "*to something that is in reality a system and thereby incurs the responsibility of testing its statement against reality*" (Luhmann, 1995, p.12). On the basis of this general description, human beings, organizations and the technology used by them in the global financial sector can be considered separate systems, as referred to by Luhmann. New systems that come into being in this larger whole, such as High Frequency Traders, are different from the systems that already exist within this sector when considered from the traditional system perspective because they focus on technology in their actions and use the activities that arise from this technology to trump the traditional possibilities of human actions within the financial sector. These new combinations of human beings and technology are referred to by Hissam, Klein and Moreno (2013) as socio-technical systems. They describe such socio-technical systems as: "*systems in which human and computational elements interact as peers. The behavior of the systems arises from the properties of both types of elements and the nature of their collective reaction to changes in their environment, the mission they support, and the availability of resources they use*" (Hissam et al., 2013). This description allows us to also determine that, contrary to more traditional organizations, High Frequency Traders, as a socio-technical system, satisfy the post- anthropocentric assumption of equality between human beings and technology and jointly use the new ensuing possibilities to create the new possibilities previously mentioned.

Systems are required to satisfy two essential criteria within the system concept developed by Luhmann, namely self-reference and autopoiesis. First and foremost, systems must have the capacity to establish relationships within the system itself (for example human-technology) and be able to distinguish these internal relationships from the relationships established by the system with its environment. Luhmann refers to this power to distinguish as 'self-reference' (Luhmann, 1995, p.13). The relationship between the system and its environment is not just an incidental and accidental relationship that merely serves as adaptation to impulses that arise from the environment, but is also a structural relationship without which the system could not continue to exist, according to Luhmann. The system distinguishes itself from other systems in its environment by the relationships established by the socio-technical system with its environment. The second criterion of the system concept formulated by Luhmann is the principle of autopoiesis. The term autopoiesis was originally formulated by Chilean biologists Maturana and Varela and was composed by them from the terms 'auto' which means 'self' and 'poiesis' which means 'create'. Luhmann uses the term to indicate that the communication elements used by the system are created by the system itself. These communication elements are, in turn, involved in the continued existence of the system itself and the relationships between the system and its environment. The activities that are performed by a system in its environment are therefore always related to the raison d'être of the system and the relationships that already exist within the system. Together, they form the basis for the intentionality with which the system performs it activities. In figure 1 the moral agent is represented diagrammatically.

The socio-technical system involved in High Frequency Trading intends to establish a communication connection with the other systems in its environment by means of the elements created by and of itself in the form of algorithms. The system's intention with these relationships is to collect as much data as possible as quickly as possible and to perform digital financial transactions on the basis of this information as effectively and as efficiently as possible within a certain period of time. Luhmann states that the connection between two socio-technical systems that is created by means of communication in the form of algorithms is not the same as sending and receiving messages between a sender and receiver as formulated by Shannon (1948). The metaphor of sending and receiving messages focuses only on the manifestation of sending and/or receiving the message, according to Luhmann (1995). This manifestation is defined by him as the 'utterance'. To him, said 'utterance' is merely a suggestion of a selection of information. Communication connections between socio-technical systems can therefore be considered not just a selection process of information in which only two elements are involved, namely the sender and the receiver, but, according to Luhmann, they should be considered to be a three-part selection process. According to him, the synthesis that arises from the unity of the three elements of 'selection of information', the 'utterance of information' and the possible 'understanding' of the selected information that is included in the communication connection should be assumed for the communication connection between two or more systems. Communication can be considered successful if the receiving socio-technical system is able to attribute a correct meaning as van Lier (2013) states to the synthesis

Figure 1. Moral Agent

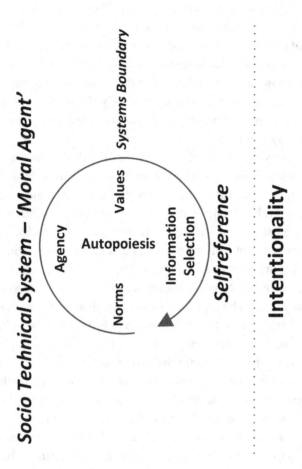

that arises from the trinity of information, utterance and understanding, without further intervention. The information can be incorporated within the system's complexity and used for further action, operation or creation with the aid of the meaning assigned by the receiving system. It will be clear that the synthesis arising from the trinity of information, utterance and understanding can also form a possible basis for including moral considerations. The element of communication is represented in figure 2

When the communication element - consisting of the synthesis of the selection of information, utterance and understanding - arrives at the receiving system, in the present case a 'moral patient', the receiving system will be able to allow or refuse this communication element access within its system boundaries. The system performs selections in both situations in order to determine whether the communication element can be accepted and incorporated in the complexity of the receiving system itself or whether it should be rejected. In figure 3 the moral patient is represented diagrammatically

Access to the receiving systems and incorporation in the complexity within this system is described by Luhmann with the term 'interpenetration'. According to van Lier (2010, 2013, 2013) Luhmann uses this term to indicate the special manner in which systems in the sending system's environment of the contribute to the design of the receiving system. Luhmann does not apply the term interpenetration until the system makes its own complexity available for construction by another system.

Figure 2. Communication Element

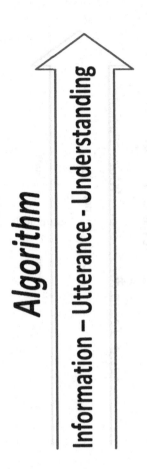

The response that will be expressed by the receiving 'moral patient' (a new synthesis of information, utterance and understanding) to the communication element that it has received and given meaning to, can be considered from a cybernetic perspective as equivalent to a feedback loop as formulated by Wiener. Feedback is, according to Wiener (1948): *"to return the information into the system, which the system can use for correcting its own action"* (Shannon, 1948, p.3). The feedback loop can create a cycle of machine learning in which moral elements are simultaneously included. When represented diagrammatically in figure 4, we then arrive at the full diagram on the basis of which further research can be carried out into the further expansion of an ethical framework for the possible development, management and maintenance of moral machines and algorithms within the global financial sector.

To summarize this part, we can conclude that software and algorithms are becoming increasingly autonomous and capable of making decisions by themselves. Decisions made by autonomous machines, software and algorithms within the global financial market could be seen as being ethically important. According to Van de Voort et al. (2015), a decision can be considered a moral decision when a person could have made a similar decision in the same situation. Ethical decisions made by autonomous humans or machines always have an intention which is decisive for the moral value of this action. The action performed by autonomous systems within the global financial ecosystem is usually a result of communication elements based on information and algorithms which could be accepted by other systems. By

Figure 3. Moral Patient

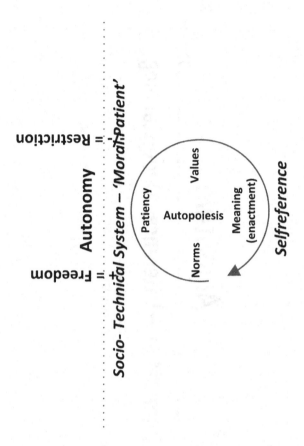

accepting these communication elements, they will interpenetrate the receiving system and the system's own complexity. Within this complexity, the accepting system will assign meaning to this communication element. The assigned meaning can be reused by the accepting system in a communication feedback loop that can help teach the sending machine to correct its own actions. This conclusion is in line with recent developments described by Deng (2015), who states:

With this kind of 'machine learning', a robot can extract useful knowledge even from ambiguous inputs. The approach would in theory help the robot to get better ethical decision making as it encounters more situations. But many fear that the advantages will come at a price. The principles that emerge are not written into the computer code. (Deng, 2015, p.25).

Figure 4. Feedback Loop

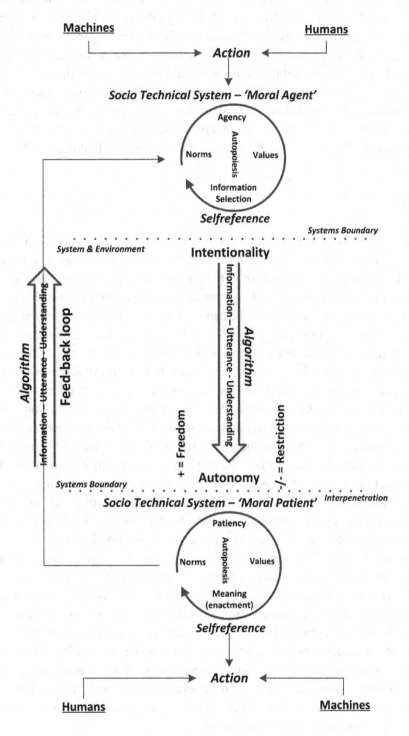

The increasing ability to learn causes the autonomy and intelligence of the machines connected within networks to increase further on the basis of the algorithms used. We therefore cannot avoid, as suggested by Coeckelbergh (2014), associating the notion of moral standing with *"interpretations of encounters and interactions between humans and machines"* (Coeckelbergh, 2014, p.67), especially where these connections also see machines make more and more decisions that have moral elements or consequences. According to Hammond (2005), an essential part of this development is for us to involve all active entities of this decision-making process in our scientific thought and actions. He states that this *"is perhaps one of the most fundamental ethical principles emerging out of a systems-oriented world view – the "reverence for the living" to which Bertalanffy appeals"* (Hammond, 2005 p. 25).

CONCLUSION

According to Weaver (1948), complexity emerges from problems which involve dealing simultaneously with a sizable number of factors which are interrelated into an organic whole. The increasing pressure of technological developments means that we as human beings, organizations and a society are turning into a complex and interconnected whole. The same applies to the financial sector in which as Floridi states: *"moral actions are the result of complex interactions among the distributed systems integrated on a scale vastly larger that the single human being"* (Floridi, 2013, p. 160). The end of the technological revolution is nowhere in sight and new technological possibilities for the coming decades are already presenting themselves. We have clung on to an anthropocentric world image in which technology and technological applications are subordinate to mankind as the central entity for too long. We are now realizing too late that we as human beings are undergoing a transformation from a modern society into a postmodern society based on technology and mutual connection. The consequences of this transformation have uncontrollable consequences for the global financial sector. We are therefore forced to think about how this transformation is changing us as human beings, organizations and society and how we can shape a development towards a new 'presence' within a postmodern society which can be characterized as a globally connected ecosystem of communicating and interacting humans and machines. Within this new socio-technical ecosystem, there will be an urgent need for new knowledge, perspectives and ethical frameworks to give shape and substance to this 'presence' in a postmodern society.

An ecosystem is as Tansley describes: *"the whole system, including not only the organism-complex, but also the whole complex of physical factors forming what we call the environment of the biome –the habitat factors in the widest sense"*. (Tansely, 1935, p. 299). The global financial sector can also be regarded as such a whole, an ecosystem which is formed by humans, organizations and machines connected together with software and algorithms. Within this new ecosystem, systems will not only be more autonomous and self-organizing, but will also rely on exchanging and sharing information in order to make their decisions. The trend towards more autonomous systems that can make decisions by themselves, and thus influence people's lives, can be considered ethically important decisions. This kind of decision making by autonomous but connected machines creates an urgent need for a more holistic perspective based on connections, interactions and communication.

The software and algorithms used for such decisions thus form the new knowledge logics for mankind, organizations and society. Algorithms are becoming more intelligent, operating more independently and taking more and more decisions. Algorithms are certainly not free of values and it is therefore advisable to focus more on the value-specific choices that have been and will be included in these algorithms.

From this perspective, it is clear that there is a need for a new ethical framework that devotes attention to the development of algorithms such as those used in the global financial sector. More attention to the development of such an ethical framework for algorithms can support the development, management and maintenance of moral physical and software-based robots that assist us as human beings in performing tasks or achieving a specific objective. The framework could be useful for making these autonomous systems more self-organizing and learning. This idea is not new and already appears in the works of Ashby after the Second World War. According to Ashby (1962),

The system would be self-organizing if a change were automatically made to the feedback, changing it from positive into negative, then the whole would have changed from a bad organization to a good" (1962, p.267). Ashby states that: "the appearance of being self-organizing can be given only by a machine when this machine is coupled to another machine. (1962, p.269).

Heylighen et al. also notice that self-organization *"can be seen as the more efficient, synergetic use of interaction"* (Heylighen et al., 2004, p.7). According to Heylighen et al., these complex ecosystems are inherently difficult to model, control or predict. In their opinion: *"all dynamic systems tend to self-organize, i.e. evolve to a relatively stable configuration of states"* (Heylighen et al., 2004, p.6). For them, the most important characteristic of self-organization is that: *"connectionist networks inherently support learning by means of the continuous adaptation of the link strengths to the ways in the ways they are used"* (Heylighen et al., 2004, p.9). Heylighen et al. are convinced that this kind of learning can create new possibilities *"through the emergence of structures that are more than the sum of the parts"* (Heylighen et al., 2004, p.110). Maybe we can use these insights from complexity science to develop connected self-organizing and moral acting machines within the global financial ecosystem.

REFERENCES

Abney, K. (2014). Robotics, ethical theory, and metaethics: A guide for the perplexed. In Robot Ethics. The ethical and social implications of robotics. MIT Press.

Adler J. (2012, August 3). Raging Bulls: How Wallstreet got addicted to light-speed trading. *Wired*.

Ahlstedt, J., & Villyson, J. (2012). High Frequency Trading. *Research Paper,* 1-8.

Allen, C., Wallach, W., & Smit, I. (2006). Why machines ethics. *IEEE Intelligent Systems, 21*(4), 12–17. doi:10.1109/MIS.2006.83

Anderson, M., & Anderson, S. L. (2007). Machine Ethics: Creating an Ethical Intelligent Agent. *AI Magazine, 28*(4), 15–26.

Ashby, W. R. (1962) Principles of the self-organizing system. In *Principles of self-organization: Transactions of the University of Illinois Symposium*. London: Pergamon Press.

Bainbridge, W., & Rocco, M. (Eds.). (2005). Managing Nano-, Bio-, Info- Cogno Innovations: Converging Technologies in Society. National Science Foundation.

Braidotti, R. (2013). *The posthuman*. Cambridge, UK: Polity Press.

Brogaard, J.A. (2011). High Frequency Trading, information, and profits. Government of Science. *The future of computer trading in Financial markets – Foresight Driver Review – DR 10.*

Cliff, D., Brown, D., & Treleaven, Ph. (2010a). Technology trends in the financial markets: A 2020 vision. In UK Governments Foresight Project, The Future of Computer Trading in Financial Markets. Government Office for Science London.

Cliff, D., & Northrop, L. (2010b). The global financial markets: an Ultra-Large-Scale Systems Perspective. In *The future of Computer Trading in Financial Markets Driver review - DR 4* (p. 47). Government Office for Science London.

Coeckelbergh, M. (2014). The moral standing of machines: Towards a relational and non-cartesian moral hermeneutics. *Philosophy & Technology, 27*(1), 61–77. doi:10.100713347-013-0133-8

Crnkovic, G. D., & Curuklu, B. (2012). Robots: Ethical by design. *Ethics and Information Technology, 14*(1), 61–71. doi:10.100710676-011-9278-2

Deng, B. (2015, July). The robot's dilemma. Working out how to build ethical robots is one of the horniest challenges in artificial intelligence. *Nature, 523*, 25–26.

Dowling, J. P. (2013). *Schrodinger's killer app. Race to build the world's first quantum computer.* Boca Raton, FL: Taylor & Francis. doi:10.1201/b13866

Farmer, J. D., & Skouras, Sp. (2010). *An ecological perspective on the future of computer trading.* Government Office for Science London.

Finance Watch. (2012). Investing not Betting. Making Financial markets serve society. *Finance Watch.*

Floridi. (2013). *The ethics of information.* Oxford, UK: Oxford University Press.

Gillepsie. (2014). *The relevance of algorithms.* Retrieved from http://www.tarletongillespie.org/essays/Gillespie%20-%20The%20Relevance%20of%20Algorithms.pdf

Gunkel, D. J. (2012). The machine question. Critical perspectives on AI, robots, and ethics. Cambridge, MA: The MIT Press.

Hammond, D. (2005). Philosophical and Ethical Foundations for systems thinking. *TripleC (Cognition, Communication, Co-operation), 3*(2), 20-27.

Heidegger, M. (1927). *Being and time (Dutch edition).* Nijmegen: SUN.

Heidegger, M. (1977). *The question concerning technology and other essays.* New York: Harper & Row Publishers Inc.

Hendershott, T., & Moulton, P. C. (2011). Automation, speed, and stock market quality: The NYSE's hybrid. *Journal of Financial Markets, 14*(4), 568–604. doi:10.1016/j.finmar.2011.02.003

Hendershott & Riordan, R. (2009). *Algorithmic Trading and Information.* Econ papers No. 09-08. Working Papers NET Institute.

Heylighen, F., Heath, M., & Van Overwalle, F. (2004). The emergence of distributed cognition: a conceptual framework. *Proceedings of Collective Intentionality IV*.

Hissam, S., Klein, M., & Moreno, G. A. (2013). *Socio-Adaptive systems challenge problem Workshop report*. Carnegie Mellon Software Engineering Institute Chicago. CMU/SEI-2013-SR-010.

Holland, J. H. (1992). Genetic Algorithms. *Scientific American*, *267*(July), 66–72. doi:10.1038cientifi camerican0792-66

Johnson, N., Zao, G., Hunsader, E., Qi, H., Johnosn, N., Meng, J., & Tivnan, B. (2013). Abrupt rise of new machine ecology beyond human response time. *Scientific Reports*, *3*(1), 2627. doi:10.1038rep02627 PMID:24022120

King, P. (1995). Abelard's Intentionalist Ethics. *The Modern Schoolman*, *72*(2), 213–231. doi:10.5840choolman1995722/316

Kirilenko, A., Kyle, A.S., Samadi, M., & Tuzun, T. (2011). *The Flash Crash: The impact of High Frequency Trading on an Electronic Market*. DOI: 10.2139/ssrn.1686004

Kraemer, F., van Overveld, K., & Peterson, M. (2011). Is there an ethics of algorithms. *Ethics and Information Technology*, *13*(3), 251–260. doi:10.100710676-010-9233-7

Lewis, M. (2014). Flash boys. Cracking the money code. New York, Penguin Group.

Lier, B. (2015). Advanced Manufacturing and Complexity Science Ultra-Large-Scale Systems, Emergence and Self-Organisation. ICSTCC 2015.

Lier, B., & Hardjono, T. W. (2010). Luhmann meets the Matrix. Exchanging and sharing information in network-centric environments. *Journal of Systemics, Cybernetics and Informatics*, *3*, 68–72.

Lier van B. (2013). Can machines communicate? The Internet of Things and Interoperability of Information. *Engineering Management Research*, *2*(1), 55–66.

Lier van B. (2013). Luhmann meets Weick: Information Interoperability and Situational Awareness. *Emergence*, *15*(1), 71–95.

Luhmann, N. (1995). *Social systems*. Stanford, CA: Stanford University Press.

Menkveld, A. J. (2014). High-Frequency Traders and Market Structure. *Financial Review*, *49*(2), 333–344. doi:10.1111/fire.12038

Menkveld, A. J., & Zoican, M. A. (2014). Need for Speed? Exchange Latency and Market Quality. *Journal of Financial Economics*, *14*, 71–100.

Moor, J. H. (2006, July). The nature, Importance and Difficulty of Machine Ethics. *IEEE Intelligent Systems*, *21*, 18–21. doi:10.1109/MIS.2006.80

Poel, I., & Royakkers, L. (2011). Ethics, technology and engineering. Chichester, UK: John Wiley and Sons Ltd.

Ramirez. (2011). *High Frequency Trading*. Retrieved from http://www.google.nl/url?sa=t&rct=j&q=&esrc=s&source=web&cd=2&ved=0CCkQFjAB&url=http%3A%2F%2Fre.vu%2Fdoc-download%2Fluzorlandoramirez%2F129619%2Fwork_example-luz.orlando.ramirez-highfrequencytrading.149252.1340385848.pdf&ei=4O8uVIm8CYSjPKO3gdgE&usg=AFQjCNF8239BS1WMAB865KebjUqmDDklig&bvm=bv.76802529,d.ZWU

Report of the Staffs of the CFTC and SEC to the Joint Advisory Committee on Emerging Regulatory Issues. (2010). *Findings regarding the market events of May 6, 2010*. Author.

Scharre, P. D. (2015). The opportunity and challenge of autonomous systems. In Autonomous systems. Issues for Defence Policymakers. NATO Headquarters Supreme Allied Command. Allied Command Transformation.

Shannon, C. E. (1948). A mathematical theory of communication. *The Bell System Technical Journal, 27*(3), 379–423. doi:10.1002/j.1538-7305.1948.tb01338.x

Smith, G. B. (1991). Heidegger, Technology and Postmodernity. *The Social Science Journal, 28*(3), 369c–389. doi:10.1016/0362-3319(91)90019-Z

Steiner Chr. (2013). *Automate this: How algorithms took over our markets, our jobs, and the world*. New York: Penguin Group.

Szostek. (2011). Studies of Interactions between human traders and Algorithmic trading systems. Government Office for Science London.

Tansley, A. G. (1935, July). The use and abuse of vegetational concepts and terms. *Ecology, 16*(3), 284–307. doi:10.2307/1930070

Tonkens, R. (2009). A challenge for Machine Ethics. *Minds and Machines, 19*(3), 421–438. doi:10.100711023-009-9159-1

Van de Voort, M., Pieters, W., & Consoli, L. (2015, March). Refining the ethics of computer-made decisions: A classification of moral mediation by ubiquitous machines. *Ethics and Information Technology, 17*(1), 41–56. doi:10.100710676-015-9360-2

van Lier, B. (2015). The enigma of context within network-centric environments. *Cyber-Physical Systems, 1*(1), 46–64. doi:10.1080/23335777.2015.1036776

Wallach, W., & Allen, C. (2009). *Moral machines. Teaching robots right from wrong*. New York: Oxford University Press. doi:10.1093/acprof:oso/9780195374049.001.0001

Walsh, D. (2012). *Changing Technology in Capital Markets: A Buy side evaluation of HFT and Dark Trading*. Commissioned research for the Financial Services Council.

Weaver, W. (1948). Science and Complexity. *American Scientist, 36*, 536–544. PMID:18882675

Wiener, N. (1948). *Cybernetics or control and communication in the animal and the machine*. New York: John Wiley & Sons.

ADDITIONAL READING

Anderson, M., & Anderson, S. L. (2010). Robot be good. *Scientific American, 303*(October), 72–77. doi:10.1038cientificamerican1010-72 PMID:20923132

Davis, J. (2016). Program good Ethics into Artficificial Intelligence. *Nature*. doi:10.1038/538291a

Loukides, M. (2017) On computational Ethics. Is it possible to imagine an AI that can compute Ethics. O'Reilly Media https://www.oreilly.com/ideas/on-computational-ethics

Pritchard, M. S. (2012). Moral Machines. *Science and Engineering Ethics, 18*(2), 411–417. doi:10.100711948-012-9363-x

Tamburrini, G. (2009) Robot Ethics: A view from the philosophy of science pp. 11-22 in: Ethics and Robotics (eBook) eds. Rafael Capurro; Michael Nagenborg Heidelberg, IOS Press.

Chapter 2
Enhancing the Brain and the Ethics of Sport

Jose-Luis Perez-Trivino
Pompeu Fabra University, Spain

ABSTRACT

Doping, or in more morally neutral terms, enhancement, has always been present in sport practice and not only at the present time, which is marked by professionalism and competitiveness. The latest development in doping seems linked to biotechnological advances, and one of the techniques that will apparently be particularly important in the near future is neuroscience, notably through pharmacological enhancers and transcranial stimulators. These devices promise to improve not only physiological aspects in sport performance, but also mental and emotional ones. On the other hand, they can seriously affect sport ethics insofar as they can be economically accessible to professional and amateur athletes. This chapter explores these issues.

INTRODUCTION

Technology has penetrated in most aspects of our lives (economy, education, society) (Luppicini, 2012; Luppicini, 2009) and sport is one these areas (Miah, 2011). In this context we need to think reflectively about the consequences of technology on the traditional practice and ethics of sport, given the fact that each technical innovation can imply an ethical dilemma. In this sense sport authorities should question themselves how to adapt these new advances to the conventional moral principles or if it is convinient to adapt our moral comprehension of sport. In this sense the increase of technology in sport is a challenging topic for technoethics.

Classical historic studies dealing with sports have identified two so-called golden eras, ancient Greece and Victorian England, where athletes practiced sport without spoiling its playful nature. At these times, sport took place as an end in itself (Young, 1984 p.7). It was clear for participants that what was important was taking part in the activity and having fun while at the same time testing of their physical abilities. The aim, therefore, was not to win, but to reach the highest level of development of these physical skills, physical excellence. Victory would be merely the result of excellence.

DOI: 10.4018/978-1-5225-5094-5.ch002

However, recent historical studies cast doubt on the existence of these golden ages, demonstrating in fact, that wherever the sport has existed, its protagonists have always tried to make use of all possible means available to gain a competitive advantage over other contestants. The idea of a pure sport, practiced by itself as a means of achieving physical excellence is therefore nothing more than fiction.

This is especially true today, where professionalized sport prevails. In this kind of sport, the primary purpose is victory, not only for the economic benefits, but for cultural reasons: the social glorification of the winner and consequently the loser's oblivion. The excessive desire for victory that governs sport in our time has driven participants to extreme rationalization. Athletes follow specific diets and perfectly controlled workouts; they take all sorts of nutritional supplements and use sports equipment designed exclusively for them, all in order to achieve that slight advantage that puts their performance above the rest. Thus, our sports world is more than ever linked to interests and elements that go beyond the pure sport practiced by Greek and British amateur athletes.

It is therefore not surprising that given these peculiarities, many athletes choose to artificially improve their sport performance. The consumption of substances with the aim of improving performance is one of the strategic tools used to achieve that result. Doping has always been present in sport due to athletes' desire to gain a competitive advantage or simply facilitate their quest to be physically superior to the rest. The following four phases in the history of doping can be noted (López-Frías, 2014):

1. Natural doping
2. Single or first generation chemical doping
3. Systematic and second generation chemical doping
4. Biotechnological doping

The aim in this article is to provide a short overview of one of the pharmacological and transcraneal enhancements in the brain that could have become notoriously relevant in the practice of sport: neuroscience, particularly transcranial stimulators and pharmacological cognitive enhancers. But before going into this area, it seems appropriate to offer a brief summary of how neuroscience enhancements are involved in a vision of sport performance in terms of a combination of physiological and brain elements (which include cognitive and emotional or mood components).

A SHORT CHRONICLE OF DOPING

Natural Doping

The quest for all possible means of improving physical performance is a constitutive element of competition in sport, and this psychological attitude was even present in ancient societies. This search for a "competitive advantage" was carried out mainly through training and diet, but also by consuming naturally-found products which increase an individual's physical performance by affecting an athlete's organs (Vesali, 2002, p. 42).

Cases of this type of doping have already been found in ancient Greece. At that time empirical knowledge was held regarding the use of anabolic and androgenic testicles through the study of the effects of neutering pets. For example, Greek athletes thought something related to physical performance must reside in the testes, and in a way, their view was not entirely misguided, considering what is known about the actual role of testosterone in the body. Intake lamb testicles became common practice among them in order to gain that vital force that castrated animals seemed to lack due to their lack of testicles.

During this time, athletes were also aware that diet was key to their physical performance, so they designed diets based on certain types of herbs, mushrooms, hallucinogenic plants, cheese, and flour-based products, and specific diets of wheat and meat. Mushrooms and pain-relieving plants allowed physical symptoms of fatigue and overwork to be overcome in order to allow a high level of competition to be maintained. Many of the uses of these substances are documented in mythological texts from ancient civilizations, such as those which document Greek Dionysian rituals.

Chemical Doping

With the development of civilization and modern science, especially medicine, began the stage of 'chemical doping.' It is feasible to distinguish two generations within this stage. The first is characterized by the simplicity of doping treatments, which were carried out through pure chemicals products such as cocaine, heroin, caffeine, and alcohol. As they had immediate short-term effects on performance, they had to be taken in key moments of the competition, for example, at the start of a competition.

As in the classical period, there were athletes who designed their diets following the advice of some medical experts with certain scientific knowledge. Science offered to athletes pure chemical substances whose effects on the body were beneficial to sport practice. At this time it was common to use coca leaves and other alkaloids, whose main effect was to eliminate feelings of fatigue and tiredness. For example, in the 19th century, cyclists ingested a chemical called 'speedball,' mixing heroin and cocaine, which had an effect identical to that of natural hallucinogens from handmade products extracted from nature by the Greeks. It was precisely in 19th century, in the era of amateurism, when the term "doping" appeared. According to Verroker (2005), it is likely this term comes from the term "dop used in South Africa in the 1700s to refer to a stimulant alcoholic beverage. Others point out that it may come from the Dutch term 'doop,' which later came to designate in English a substance with sedative and hallucinogenic effects. At the end of the 19th century, the term was used to refer to beverages with narcotic effects and at the turn of the 20th century, it began to be used in reference to enhancement on physical performance, although initially it referred to the enhancement of race horses.

The first documented case of chemical doping in a sport competition is that of Thomas Hicks in the St. Louis Olympics of 1904 (Vesali, 2002, p. 6). Having just crossed the finish line and winning the marathon, he fell to the ground, having taken doses of alcohol and strychnine throughout the race.[1]

Chemical Doping: Second Generation

In the second stage of chemical doping, chemical products and chemical enhancement treatments were of a more complex nature, with longstanding and dangerous effects. They were not used individually, but rather in a systematic way, controlled by doctors and specialists. Amphetamines, anabolic steroids and blood doping were the prevalent enhancement treatments throughout the second half of the 20th century.

Anabolics were used for the first time by Soviet weight lifters in the 1950s. The doctor of the US track team, John Bosley Ziegler, applied them to their athletes after observing the excellent results of the Soviet team. Given the great rivalry between the capitalist and communist countries, the respective national sports associations developed what came to be known as 'Doping State,' whose most extreme cases occurred in the German Democratic Republic. But the truth is that the use of doping during this decade was not exclusive to Eastern countries.[2]

From the 1960s, knowledge about the disastrous health effects of anabolic substances ingested in massive quantities was generalized. Thus, in 1960 the first victim of doping fell during the Rome Olympics Rome: the Danish cyclist Knut Jensen died from the effects of Ronicol, an amphetamine. In 1967 the effects of doping was seen by millions of spectators during the Tour de France: the British cyclist Tom Simpson[3] died during the race, the cause of death being the excessive use of amphetamines and brandy.[4]

At the end of the Cold War, it was discovered that several Eastern European countries had carried out systematic doping in order to show the world the superiority of the communist regime. But health effects of that systematic doping were devastating: suicide, sex changes, injuries and disease. However, this systematic and scientifically controlled doping did not disappear. Rather, it began to be adopted by associations or economically powerful individuals who had the economic resources to access to the best scientific and medical treatments.

Biotechnologycal Doping

The recent decades have seen more profound changes to the relationship between human beings and technology: the development of genetics, robotics, cybernetics, nanotechnology, and biomedicine are making it possible to posit that in the future human beings will be able to genetically modify and clone themselves; they will be able to create hybrid beings or interact with computers or other components from within the human body itself. A transhuman world, in which human beings are not limited by constraints imposed by nature, in which they can experience whatever physical change with the goal of increasing their physical or mental capacity, is for some the Fukuyama case, the most dangerous idea that lies in wait for humanity (Fukuymana). But not everybody agree with that pessimistic forecast (Savulescu, 2007).

Scientific and biotechnological developments will have an inevitable impact on the sport through genetic engineering (Miah, 2004; Pérez-Triviño, 2011) and enhancements provided by body implants and prosthetics that can lead to the creation of cyborgsportsperson (Pérez-Triviño, 2013). But the enhancing athletic technique to wich I devote my attention here is neuroscience. But to better understand the effects of these stimulators it seem necessary a previous presentation of the different types of sports performance enhancements. Indeed, historically the focus of doping has been only physiological performances. But in sport practice there are combination of factors besides physiological one, cognitives and emotionals (mood). Insofar these factors can be boosting intervening in the brain, neuroscience will be relevant in the near future as a mean to enhance sport performance. Before going to examine cognitive enhancers and transcranial stimulators, let me explaining briefly physical, cognitive and mood enhancing.

Cognitive Enhancements: Cognitive Doping

Physical enhancement has been understood as any type of development that enhances a physical function of a human body (Holme & McNamee, 2011, 291). Sport performance is, by definition, an expression of physiological abilities, and the constitutive aim of sport is the improvement of physical performance in its different expressions such as speed, endurance or flexibility. The tools for improving physical performance– in different areas such as training techniques, equipment or nutrition – have been evolving and continue to do so.

The connection between physiology and sport performance means that substances and methods of physical improvement that enhance traits tied to movement or endurance have been the focus of anti-doping efforts. The majority of prohibited substances influence physical performance directly, such as anabolic androgenic steroids (AAS), hormones, beta-2 agonists, anti-estrogens, stimulants, narcotics, cannabinoids, glucocorticosteroids, alcohol, and beta blockers. Most effort has been focused on the now infamous erythropoietin (EPO) (which enhances endurance by creating red blood cells to deliver oxygen to working muscles) and AAS (assisting strength and recovery by increasing protein synthesis in muscle cells).

As the understanding of enhancing sporting performances has evolved, there is growing interest in non-physical factors, and in particular cognitive enhancements[5]. In fact, the recognition that cognitive abilities are involved in sport performance arose almost simultaneously with the knowledge of the importance of the physiological elements, but its radical development has taken place in recent decades (Sánchez & Lejeune, 1999). In the short span of sport history the interest in how psychology can enhance sporting performance has grown remarkably (LeUnes, 2011). This has been captured by Hoberman's (1992) observation that from the outset of natural science:

..early sport physiologists discovered that scientific study of athletic performance must operate at this frontier where physiology and psychology overlap. (p. 157).

Fort that reason, a variety of stimulants also appear on the Prohibited List of World Anti-Doping Association which have a direct effect on physical performance, and also leave a trace in the peripheral nervous system. As Foddy (2011) explains:

The purpose of this story is to show how many neural processes are involved in the execution of physical actions. Even in producing basic physical motion like a kick, a player needs to engage a large and complex web of neural mechanisms. Some of these mechanisms, like decision making and judgment are confined to the central nervous system and the brain. Others, like stage fright and elevated heart rate, are primarily involved with the peripheral nervous system. (p. 315).

"Neurophysical enhancements" can positively affect sport performance. These mechanisms can be treated pharmacologically to produce neural improvements. For example, amphetamines activate some adrenergic receptors in the organs of the body, including the brain, which act to increase heart rate, eliminate fats, supply glycogen, and dilate blood vessels. These improvements can have an impact on the abilities and skills that any athlete can develop.

There have been two ways through which cognitive improvements are relevant for sport performance. The first is that there are sporting competitions which demand both a physiological test and one of cognitive character; chess provides a standard case. In some sport events success depends on strategising the event, such that the physical ability also relies on superiority on psychological factors. The second is that it is impossible to sever the link between body and the brain; between physical performance and brain activity. Thus, in all sport performance the brain plays a role. As Foddy (2011, p. 313) points out

All such variations (physical actions) in performance are mediated, at least in part, by the actor's brain, spinal cord and peripheral system. Neurological systems play a role in determining how far we throw

a javelin, how deeply we breathe while swimming... how long we can withstand the pain of endurance cycling. (see also Foddy, 2008).

Cognition can be understood as the process an organism uses to organize information, a process that includes the following abilities: i) acquisition (perception); ii) selection (attention); iii) representation (understanding) and iv) retention (memory), and usage of abilities to guide behaviour (reasoning and coordination of motor outputs) (Sandberg, 2011, p. 71). Thus, cognitive improvement can be defined as all increase of the capacities involved in the process of cognition by any system, internal or external, of information processing. However, although there is a symbiosis between physiological and cognitive factors, I will treat them separately insofar they have been analysed historically as separated.

The concern over how cognition influences sport performance has been present since the birth of modern sport. In this regard, Hoberman (1992) examined the birth of sport psychology during the first decades of 20th century, arguing that:

The idea of manipulating the mind to enhance human performances -a popular preoccupation of our own era- seldom appears during this period. (p. 157)

The progressive importance of cognitive processes in sport performance has doubtlessly had a substantial impact on this area. Some authors point this out, although perhaps in a somewhat exaggerated fashion. For example, Sanchez and Lejeune (1999) cite two famous quotes suggesting that "the difference between winning and losing is 99% psychological" and that "90% of the sport is mental and the other half is in the head". Such characterisations of the influence of cognition on sport outcomes underpin the commonly accepted notion that sports performance can be improved by methods focusing on mentation, such as guided imagery and cognitive restructuring. Training using imagination is "the symbolic repetition of a physical activity in absence of any big muscular movement" (p. 22). The athlete imagines metadynamically, consciously and repeatedly, a sport action without carrying out the practical execution, to facilitate the motor skills improving the sport execution, control attention and concentration and accelerate recovery from injuries (28). Cognitive restructuring refers to "the group of techniques that aim to directly change athletes' thoughts to better face the demands of competition" (p. 26). With this, athletes can improve their self-confidence, motor abilities and control over attention and concentration.

Emotional Enhancements: Emotional Doping

The part of human mental reality that has seen recent remarkable development relates to the understanding of emotions. The expansion of understanding of the role of emotion in mental health has spurred studies in this area of psychology. Mental health (e.g. depression, fear, and shyness) represents an ongoing challenge for sport, and can noticeably affect physical performance. An athlete might have great physical potential, talent, or technical aptitude, but can fail at the time of competition due to anxiety or depression. Athletes can suffer "emotional blocks", arising from performance pressure exerted by coaches, family, or fans, or the loneliness of being an elite athlete, expressed as fear or lack of confidence that prevents normal sport performance. Equally, an elite athlete who has a fear of flying is unable to travel to important international matches. More famously, the steep decline in the tennis player Rafa Nadal's performance was attributed to depression following his parents' divorce. Anxiety and depression can be so severe that there are famous cases of athletes who have committed suicide, such as Gary Speed and Robert Enke.

Hoberman (186) points out that from the beginning of the 20th century psychologists have been trying to help athletes suffering from anxiety, depression, fear or other emotional disorders to reach peak performance. With this goal in mind, multiple techniques or psychological methods were developed to improve the emotional state of athletes to prevent it from affecting normal physiological functioning. Like pharmaceutical substances, the therapeutic approaches to psychology were adapted to achieve performance outcomes among those in the normal range of the curve. This is what is known as "the medicalisation of normality" (Berghmans, ter Meulen & Vos, 153). Sandel (2007) offers a deeper account of this phenomenon.

Emotional or mood doping in sport therefore occurs when psychological therapies are used to make athletes experience states of optimism, confidence, plenitude or aggression to enhance sport performance. Problems for the anti-doping policy emerge when substances mediate the emotional state of athletes rather than psychological therapies.

Generally speaking mood enhancement is defined negatively as the treatment directed at the lack of good mood, or in the case of depression the inability to find pleasure in aspects of everyday life. However, these products are being prescribed for individuals without such illnesses. In these cases, mood enhancers have the effect of making people feel "better than well". Individuals usually recognize that such substances make them feel energetic, more alert and better suited to face reality (Liao-Roache, 246). In the initial approach, improving negative mood into a state of positive mood is desirable and thus the goal of any technology or chemical is to improve negative mood in a safe and effective form is positive (Berghmans et al,161). Psychological therapy has been a longstanding treatment for mood, although progress in neuroscience is increasing the understanding of how the patterns of brain chemicals lie at the root of some of these emotional disorders. Psychological treatment has been replaced in some instances with pharmacological substances that affect states of emotion or mood (e.g. sadness, depression, fear, shyness, etc.), such as fluoxetine (e.g. Prozac). Fluoxetine is used to treat a range of psychological disturbances from depression to obsessive-compulsive disorder to premenstrual dysphoric disorder to alcoholism, migraines and Tourette's syndrome (Berghmans et al, 154).

The main problem arises when these substances are applied with the aim of enhancing performance among individuals with no mood disturbance. This phenomenon leads to a blurring of lines between psychiatric and psychopharmacological issues and the medicalisation of emotional and social problems (Sandel, 2007).

Sport must consider the implications that arise from the increasing use of substances that enhance mood states. Indeed athletes could use such substances as a tool that allows them to compete in a better psychological state than their rivals in order to achieve a competitive advantage. For example, dextroamphetamine might be used to reduce impulsivity, which is particularly relevant in sports where inhibiting action is crucial, such as baseball or cricket.

Neuroscience and Sport

As we have seen before, cognitive enhancement in sport is moving from traditional psychological approaches towards neuroscience (Davis, 2013). The early 21st century has seen significant developments in this area, opening up the possibility to examine brain processes in depth. Neuroscience roughly consists of the study of the cerebral mechanisms at the base of the essential cognitive functions of the individual: the capacity to remember, to argue, to decide, etc. Such functions are observed through powerful instruments such as functional magnetic resonance imaging [fMRI], positron emission tomography [PET scans], and magnetoencephalography [MEG] (which monitors the electrodynamic flow of the neurons). Advances in measurement of the brain have seen the ideas advanced by psychology regarding the connection between brain and the movement functions measured and explained by neuroscience. In some ways the neuroscience revolution can be compared to Galileo's impact on the field of the physics or Darwin's on biology; this puts sport as a potentially significant contributor and recipient of significant advances in knowledge that were unthinkable in the 20th century (Tamorri, 10).

Neuroscience can inform sport by introducing the possibility to identify which structures (circuits) in the brain are associated with specific movements, with strategising sport events, or with intuition in game situations. Tamorri (2004) is so confident in this line of research that he believes that it will be possible to discover the mechanisms that turn an athlete into a champion:

A champion is a mix of muscle and biomechanical reaction, possible and developed through a fragile, fine and complex process of gathering information, decoding and programming in the brain, in his biology, in its neurotransmitters and finally, in its cognitive processes, in its organic background but also, in its emotional and cultural elements. (p. 11).

Progress in understanding and boosting the brain's role in physiological performance has seen pharmaceutical laboratories identify substances that improve cognitive skills and abilities. These cognitive enhancers were initially designed for the treatment of neurodegenerative illnesses that primarily affected people as they age. However, such medicines have recently found a market in healthy people and are used to increase the duration of a wakeful state, maintain high levels of attention and concentration even under conditions of mental stress and improve memory (Eronia, 2012, p. 7; Porsdam-Sahakian,). These replicate the effect of other stimulants that have appeared on the Prohibited List of WADA (e.g. amphetamines, cocaine and caffeine), although they make use of different mechanisms.

Among these medicines modafinil (Provigil) and methylphenidate (Ritalin) stand out for their effects on memory and concentration abilities. Modafinil, probably the most interesting cognitive enhancer, particularly enhances wakefulness, but it also improves reaction time, pattern recognition, working memory and spatial planning ability (Foddy, 2011, 316). The first individuals who tested these substances were pilots and soldiers since they allowed the individuals improve the potential for concentration and avoid the effects of fatigue (Housden et al, 118). Methylphenidate was originally used for the treatment of attention deficit disorder and hyperactivity. However, it is widely used because of the perception that it also can provide similar effects in people without these conditions. Its use has spread to university staff, university students and high school students who that have discovered that the stimulant improves concentration (Housden et alii, 17). The influence of such cognitive enhancers on physical performance emerges in terms of increases in information transmission speed and ability to focus on specific tasks. Improvements in information transmission and focus can have a significant impact in sports such as javelin, archery and golf (Foddy, 2011, p. 316).

Cognitive enhancers appear to be prohibited for their potential effect on sporting performance and also for their health implications. Some studies have shown that these substances can have unwanted side effects on health, such as dependency (Foddy, 2011, 318; Dubljević-Ryan 2015, 26). Thus, it is unsurprising that these substances would be added to the Prohibited List. However, unlike other stimulants, the effect of cognitive enhancers is less about enhancing a person and instead about enabling a different kind of functioning within normal neural limits, and the safety data indicates the risks to athletes' health is approximately the same as some permitted prescription substances (Foddy, 2011, 318). This raises the question if the prohibition of cognitive enhancers is justified.

But there are other neurotechniques capable of enhancing the brain functions. As Merkel et al point out, beyond pharmacological substances there are three more main types of physiological interventions in the brain: genetic, electro-magnetic and surgical. The latter may be differentiated further into four subclasses: a) the implantation or neuroprostheses, including brain computer interfaces (bionics), b) the intracranial grafting or implantation of cells (neural non neural, or embryonic stem cells) for tissue repair or cell-containing devices for the local delivery of bioactive compounds, c) intracranial gene transfer techniques to enhance or dampen protein expression for cure. But here we will focus on techniques for electrical stimulation of defined brain areas.

Brain Stimulation Techniques

Although at the beginning of experiments of brain stimulation techniques there was a limited hope in its use in sport (Goodall, 2012, p. 7), recent advances in neuroscience suggest that the skills and abilities underpinning sport performance can be enhanced using technologies that change the activity of the brain. These factors may include motor learning, enhanced muscular strength or reduced fatigue, or even changes to mental state or concentration.

Davis suggests that

Modulating the activity of the brain during training or during sport will lead to benefits comparable to those of using drugs. The devices needed to generate these effects are already available, and are currently in use in laboratories or clinics to produce short or long-term changes in performance. (649).

There are other advantages to these devices so the risks of using brain stimulators are relatively low, when used within established safety parameters. Only the case of multi-session stimulation could alter the risk. Nonetheless, currently there is not sufficient knowledge to determine appropriate doses of stimulation in a given situation, specially when it is used outside the laboratory or the clinic. More research will be needed to guarantee safety and efficacy. And finally, there is no security regarding how brain stimulation could affect mood or mental state.

Two main brain stimulation techniques are available:

1. Transcranial magnetic stimulation (TMS) is a method to cause depolarization or hyperpolarization of the neurons of the brain. TMS uses electromagnetic induction to induce weak electric currents using a rapidly changing magnetic field; this can cause activity in specific or general parts of the brain, allowing for study of brain functioning and interconnections. The immediate effect of this is to generate action potentials in those cells, followed by a refractory period as the cell recovers. These effects outlast the stimulation phase by several dozen minutes of minutes, with the possibility of longer-term reorganisation of brain activity if the stimulation is applied at regular intervals. (Davis, 2013, p. 649-650)

2. Transcranial current stimulation (tCS) comes in two common variants:

    a. **Transcranial direct current stimulation (tDCS):** A form of neurostimulation which uses constant, low current delivered directly to the brain area of interest via small electrodes. The magnitude and polarity of the electric field at the brain surface near the electrodes determines its effect: cells in the vicinity of the anode will tend to increase in excitability, through a process thought to involve a modulation of the resting membrane potential of the cells. Although it was originally developed to help patients with brain injuries such as stroke, tests on healthy adults have demonstrated that tDCS can increase cognitive performance on a variety of tasks, depending on the area of the brain being stimulated (Kanai et al.).

Other recent experiments have studied the effects of 20 min of tDCS with the anode over the left temporal cortex (T3) on trained cyclists during an incremental cycling test. The result was the significantly improved peak power, as well as reduced heart rate and perception of effort at submaximal workloads. Hight performance were partially attributed to the effects of tDCS on perception (reduced fatigue and improved threat detection) (Okano et al. 2013). On the other hand, Angius et al. (2016) reported reduced perception of effort and increased endurance in cyclist after anodal stimulation.

Borduchi et al. (2016) observed a positive effect of tDCS in cognitive performance of different athletes, including a significant improvement in alternated, sustained, and divided attention and in memory scores[6]. According their study: "tDCS interventions can increase cognitive performance and diminish depression scores in professional athletes, which in our point of view may contribute to performance gains, greater well-being, and faster recovery" (Borduchi et al., 7).

b. **Transcranial Alternating Current (tACS):** Uses a similar principle, except that the current alternates at a specific frequency.

As Davis points out, there are some relevant differences between two these techniques. TMS is a more focal technique, with a relatively small area of the brain being affected by the stimulation, whereas the electric field induced by tCS is spread across the whole brain surface; tCS has a number of advantages over TMS.

TCS technology is cheaper and more portable. Indeed, wireless tCS stimulators are now commercially available, and websites exist that give instructions for home-made tCS stimulators. For that reason Davis argues that neurodoping will become a key technology for the future of sport and sports medicine, although given the current state of development, the use of brain stimulation must be carefully considered.

Davis foresees two domains where neurodoping may potentially change performance in sport. The first benefit takes place immediately following stimulation, a time at which participants have demonstrated enhanced motor skills including: improved time-to-fatigue, response time, and tremor suppression. After this time, approximately 20 to 60 minutes, the effects begin to decline. In any case, the enhanced motor skills could be very useful for these initial minutes in sports like shooting a pistol or jumping out of the gates on a ski slalom.

The second use of neurodoping is related to skill acquisition:

Skills learned in the context of anodal tDCS are acquired more rapidly, and reproduced more accurately, than those learned without. Sports performance at the highest levels require good technique and good timing. These are skills learned during training, so enhancing the efficiency of learning during the training phase will be of greater benefit at competition time. I suggest that an athlete could use these techniques to make training more efficient and thereby gain an advantage. (Davis, 2013, p. 652)

It is not difficult to foresee that an area of development will be the application of neurodoping is sport training and performance. Coaches will be in a better position to understand how and when to incorporate brain stimulation into training. It is likely that as more brain stimulation is used there will be a reduced dose of stimulation delivered to the athlete.

In any case given that each sport determines its own functioning and values, the tolerance of brain stimulation could be diverse according to each competition. For example, performance in a sport such as pistol-shooting would be greatly improved by tremor reduction so governing bodies will have to decide whether shooters should be prevented from using tACS during or immediately before competing to reduce tremor, just as beta-blockers are banned in many sports. Conversely, a tennis player's performance in a match is heavily influenced by the probability of regularly getting the first serve in, which is a skill learned in training and therefore potentially susceptible to neurodoping. Neurodoping is one of many potential forms of enhancement that may affect sport performance, and the development of technology should be mirrored by a development in how such enhancements are viewed and dealt with.

But there still doubts about the efficacy of tDCS in the real world of sport performance. As Dylan et al. (2017) points out some questions remain:

1. THE comparison between results in laboratory conditions and results in field events
2. the comparison between results in athletes and healthy non-athletes
3. Improvements in strenght vs endurance.

Meanwhile sport authorities are determining whether or not tDCS fits in the regulatory framework at sport elite level, other problem is the extension of usage of tDCS in ordinary people. The dangers of uncontrolled use (DYI practices) should cause authorities to take precautionary measures (Wexler, 2016).

Some Normative Remarks About Brain Enhancement and Sport

The cases of brain enhancers who have been examined highlight some of the problems that sport authorities will have to deal with in the future given that enhancements will produce athletes with better potential cognitive and emotional abilities, leading to the conclusion that modified athletes would have the upper hand when compared to "normal" athletes. What should be done? Should these advantages be considered something similar to doping and then be banned them from participating in competitions, as is now the case? Or rather should they be able to compete head-to-head with normal athletes? Or should specific competitions be created for them only?

As we have pointed out before, the first critical observation are purely technical: these techniques has not been tested under real competitive sport conditions or for specificactions. In addition, as Davis points out, the tests have not been carried out on athletes but rather on normal people, that is, non-athletes. As a result, Davis is sceptical about applying them to elite sports.

Much like problems raised to doping, the reasons informing objections against technological intervention in the sportpeople brain can be categorized into: 1) the unnecessary of efforts in sport; 2) health problems; 3) the authenticity problem; 4) the quesion of artificiality; 5) the problem of dehumanization of sport;

A first objection would be that with neuroenhancement the athlete would not need to strive to make an effort or a sacrifice to obtain results. The acquisition of physical power, or other relevant skills for the sport would make the physical sacrifice of the sportsman irrelevant to obtaining the sport victory. But the impact of neurodoping in sport practice will likely not affect equality to such an extent. Neurodoping, at least in its current state, does not offer such miraculous effects that the athlete will obtain stratospheric results. The athlete still needs to train and make sacrifices to ensure top performance. In the end, neurodoping simply offers a small difference in the results; if an athlete were to rely on the miraculous effects of a pill or an electromagnetic session and stop training, it is highly unlikely that he would be in the elite of his field.

A second objection stems from dangers of potential generalized use, as well uncontrolled use by fans who are also athletes. The effects of doping in the gyms and athletic facilities of sport aficionados are well known, making it highly likely that the use of cognitive enhancers and cranial stimulators may also become widespread. Clearly this could bring about pressing public health concerns resulting from irreversible harm to the brain that could be caused by improper use.

A more general objection to cognitive and emotional enhancement is that any attempt to intervene in the brain can raise hotly debated issues such as authenticity and practical relevance when it comes time to judge the actions of an individual. There are others, such as McNamee and Loland, who believe that the imposition of paternalistic measures is in fact justified in that they keep sport from becoming the field for experiments in which athletes are used as human guinea pigs.

The first objection is that a possible side effect of this kind of enhancements is the creation of inauthentic personalities. The second objection argues that enhancers would change our mind in such a way that it will be difficult for us to attribute moral accountability. There are two possible answers to both criticisms. Firstly, it is unclear why the enhanced self is evaluated as inauthentic, especially if the enhancement is ongoing rather than momentary. The sport person who has inferior memory skills could negate these traits as the inauthentic by-product of a biological weakness. The authentic person is the one who fights against their imposed weak nature.

Regarding the second objection, Kahane (2011) offers an interesting defence of enhancers as authentically coherent insofar as one tries to conform to one's own desires, preferences or values. For these points of view, these techniques represent no more than advances over traditionally used techniques in education.

Such discussion warns of the possible consequences of enhancement for sporting purposes. Under the current anti-doping policy, athletes have the capacity to make informed choices about the use of enhancers in terms of their short- and long-term impacts: the possible enhancement (or not) of sport performance relative to a potentially reduced (or higher) level of welfare in future life.

Other reason to forbid this kind of mood enhancement in sport would be that this mechanism to increase sport performance is not natural, but artificial. But this argument relies on the vague distinction between natural and artificial. On one hand, artificiality is already well installed in sport with new forms of training, nutrition, equipment, etc. Currently, many athletes recover from their injuries very quickly in comparison to the past, where complicated, painful and long rehabilitation processes were needed. These long suffering recovery processes belong to the past: recovery times are remarkably shorter due to new medical technologies. What about new and sophisticated nutritional complements in form of pills? For good or bad, sport has changed so much that little has to do with sport practiced in antiquity or even in the times of Coubertain. To be consistent, the prohibition of these substances on the basis of being artificial will drag other forms of enhancing technics.

The fifth objection againts brain enhancements in sport is the concern about the dehumanization of sport. As Sandel (2003) pointed out againts genetic doping, it brain enhancements reduces the scope of an element that has been considered part and parcel of fair competition. They may lead to a situation in which we are incapable of identifying the original 'I' whose performance we want to improve" (Schneider, 2000). That is to say, brain enhancement can be considered a the loss of meaning in the sports spectacle.

The problem here is with the characterization of "humanity" (Culbertson, 2007; Savulescu, 2007; Schneider, 2009). On some occasions, human beings as moral agents have been identified by belonging to the human species; on others, by their ability to feel. But perhaps currently the most widespread conception of "humanity" resides in the possession of superior cognitive abilities such as rationality, autonomy, consciousness, and self-consciousness. If this conception is adopted, it does not in any way seem that technologically modified athletes (at least to a certain point) lose their humanity: they reflect and feel, they are self-conscious, and they can establish future life plans.

One variant of this criticism comes from Michael Sandel, who expresses the fear that human beings are playing God and are going against Nature (Sandel, 2003). Leaving aside the religious interpretation, in which the concern is that humans literally usurp the role of a superior being, we will center our analysis on the secular interpretation: the main concern that humans may not recognize their own limitations. To put it another way, they express "hubris," an exaggerated self-pride in their abilities as natural beings.

But the answer to this fear is that

The history of humanity has always consisted of modifying the world for good reasons. The natural state of man would be 'disagreeable, brutal and short' to use Hobbes' words if it were not for the many improvements obtained by modifying the world. Vaccines, antibiotics and practically all medicine entail powerful interventions. The objection that we would be playing God is only valid as a precaution against ill-informed actions, to which humans are undoubtedly predisposed (Savulescu, 2007).

On the other hand, experts in favor of the use of new technologies in sport question the arbitrary and binary methods that are at times used to define what constitutes a human being (Butryn, 2003). Along these lines, they highlight that all individuals (and consequently all athletes, too) exercise freedom to question the limits imposed by nature. Bostrom says something similar in relation to the challenge of becoming cyborgs "to challenge the projected limited of modern sport, including those dealing with humans, machines and technology, and to explore new ways of being 'cyborg' though the interaction with technologies at our disposal" (Bostrom, 2003). The continual efforts carried out by sport bureaucracy have also been denounced, as they forcibly impose a rigid separation between "natural" and "technological" competitors

Another strategy to demonstrate the inefficiency of excluding technologically modified athletes stems from highlighting the contradiction that this involves when compared to the current situation in which athletes have undergone therapeutic treatments that were unimaginable a number of years ago and without which they would not achieved their actual level success. In this way, for example, Messi – the now famous footballer – took growth hormones as an adolescent and Tiger Woods had eye surgery to overcome problems with short-sightedness. It is clear that these are cases of therapeutic treatments, but perhaps it will have to be considered that 1. There are already enhancement treatments (like vaccines); 2. As long as it is possible in the future that these initially-therapeutic treatments allow the patient to improve on his previous abilities, or to broaden the spectrum of the human average, we will be on slippery ground. This boundary between therapeutic and enhancement treatments may become fuzzy. No one criterion exists to denote what is considered a "disease", and, consequently, no limiting criterion is known for "therapies", either. For example, Borse offers a biological-determinist conception of disease, while Daniels advocates a social- constructivist focus. Depending on which criteria are adopted, (therapeutic) treatments can be more or less widespread. In other words, the scope of therapy could increase and, in this way, diffuse what an enhancement treatment would be (Miah, 2004).

Finally, what remains to be made known is the position taken by the World Anti-Doping Agency. Whether these substances should be included on the agency's famous list of prohibited substances is not a simple issue. Certainly, as we have just seen, the effects of these techniques on athlete performance are as of yet unknown; thus it would be risky to venture an opinion on that matter. But given their characteristics, these stimulation techniques still may receive identical treatment to hyperbaric or cryogenic chambers, whose effects are similar to those included on the WADA list although these treatments are not included in it. In any case, cognitive enhancers and transcranial techniques would avoid the objections to technological unfair play given that their affordability would increase athletes' equal access opportunities.

From my point of view, cognitive enhancement techniques open up an interesting field in terms of sport performance, an arena which demands close examination. In the first place, the lack of conclusive evidence regarding their efficacy under actual competitive conditions leads us to recommend not taking hasty decisions regarding their use.

CONCLUSION

Enhancement methods have actually been present in sport practice from its origin. However, from the first natural forms used to carry out this enhancement to the present time there have been many varied treatments and substances experimented by athletes. In the near future, it seems that the more prevalent enhancements will be biotechnological due to the fact that these appear to promise better and safer sport performance enhancement.

On the other hand, such treatments and substances will not necessarily have the athletes' physiology (muscles mainly) at their core of action. So far scientific knowledge has offered certainties about the connection between the brain (cognitive and emotional factors) and the rest of the human body in sport performance; this will be also at the core of the experiments aimed at enhancing sport performance. For that reason, it is easy to understand the increasing importance of the neuroscience for sport.

In the other section of the chapter I have tried to show the novelty that cognitive pharmacological enhancers and transcranial stimulators could suppose. Particularly, it is essential to highlight that these stimulators which act on brain neurons can directly improve sport performance by increasing reaction times or by reducing fatigue; they can better athletes' capacity to learn sport skills. These traits would make it possible to describe these enhancement treatments as other products that belong on the list of substances prohibited by the World Anti-Doping Association (WADA). But their peculiarity does not stop here. The use of these stimulators could be extended to both professional or amateur athletes, since they are commercially accessible.

To conclude, it has been highlighted some of the normative problems spawned by the use of these techniques in sport, analyzing five relevant fears that arise with the brain enhancemen in sportspeople: 1) the unnecessary of efforts in sport; 2) health problems; 3) the authenticity problem; 4) the quesion of artificiality; 5) the problem of dehumanization of sport.

I pointed out that given the lack of conclusive evidence for their eficacy in actual competitive situations, it would not be prudent to adopt definitive decisions with regard to them. It it reasonable to defend that, as occurs with any other brain interventions, they must be governed by meticulous respect for the principle of precaution in order to maintain the absence of undesirable harm to the primary organ of the human being. Lastly, we attempted to balance the arguments in favour of the advantages provided by easy access with those that warn against the possible risks to public health generated by inappropriate usage of the same.

ACKNOWLEDGMENT

This research was supported by DER2016-80471-C2-1-R (AEI/FEDER, UE).

REFERENCES

Borducchi, D., Gomes, J. S., Akiba, H., Cordeiro, Q., Borducchi, J. M., Valentin, L., ... Dias, Á. M. (2016). Transcranial direct current stimulation effects on athletes' cognitive performance: An exploratory proof of concept trial. *Frontiers in Psychiatry*, *7*, 183. doi:10.3389/fpsyt.2016.00183 PMID:27965597

Bostrom, N. (2003). Human Genetic Enhancements: A transhumanist Perspective. *The Journal of Value Inquiry*, *37*(4), 493–506. doi:10.1023/B:INQU.0000019037.67783.d5 PMID:17340768

Culbertson, L. (2007). "Human-ness", "dehumanisation" and performance enhancement. *Sport. Ethics and Philosophy*, *1*(2), 195–217. doi:10.1080/17511320701439877

Davis, N. J. (2013). Neurodoping: Brain Stimulation as a Performance-Enhancing Measure. *Sports Medicine (Auckland, N.Z.)*, *43*(8), 649–653. doi:10.100740279-013-0027-z PMID:23504390

Dubljević, V., & Ryan, C. J. (2015). Cognitive enhancement with methylphenidate and modafinil: Conceptual advances and societal implications. *Neuroscience and Neuroeconomics*, *4*.

Dubljević, V. (2015). Principles of Justice as the Basis for Public Policy on Psychopharmacological Cognitive Enhancement. *Law, Innovation and Technology*, *4*, 1.

Edwards, Cortes, Wortman-Jutt, Putrino, Bikson, Thickbroom, & Pascual-Leone. (2017). Transcranial Direct Current Stimulation and Sports Performance. *Frontiers in Human Neuroscience*. 10.3389/fnhum.2017.00243

Eronia, O. (2012). Doping mentale e concetto di salute: A possibile regolamentazione legislative? *Archivio penale*, *3*.

Foddy, B. (2008). Risks and asterisks: neurological enhancements in baseball. In *Your Brain on Cubs: Inside the Heads of Players and Fans*. Washington, DC: Dana Press.

Foddy, B. (2011). Enhancing Skill. In Enhancing Human Capacities. Oxford, UK: Blackwell. doi:10.1002/9781444393552.ch23

Fukuyama, F. (2002). *Our Posthuman Future: Consequences of the Biotechnology Revolution*. London: Profile Books.

Goodall, S., Howatson, G., Romer, L., & Ross, E. (2012). Transcranial magnetic stimulation in sport science: A commentary. *European Journal of Sport Science*. doi:10.1080/17461391.2012.704079 PMID:24444227

Harris, J. (2012). Chemical cognitive enhancement: is it unfair, unjust, discriminatory, or cheating for healthy adults to use smart drugs?—-2. In J. Illes & B. Sahakian (Eds.), *Oxford Handbook of Neuroethics*. Oxford, UK: Oxford University.

Hoberman, J. (1992). *Mortal Engines. The Science of Performance and the Dehumanization of Sport*. New York: The Free Press.

Holme, S., & McNamee, M. (2011). Physical Enhancement: What Baseline, Whose Judgment? In Enhancing Human Capacities. Oxford, UK: Blackwell.

Housden, C. R., Morein-Zamir, S., & Sahakian, B. J. (2011). Cognitive Enhancing Drugs: Neuroscience and Society. In Enhancing Human Capacities. Oxford, UK: Blackwell.

Kahane, G. (2011). Reasson to Feel, Reasons to Take Pills. In R. Ter Muelen, J. Savulescu, & G. Kahane (Eds.), *Enhancing human capacities*. Malden, MA: Blackwel.

Kanai, R., Chaieb, L., Antal, A., Walsh, V., & Paulus, W. (2008). Frequency-dependent electrical stimulation of the visual cortex. *Current Biology*, *18*(23), 1839–1843. doi:10.1016/j.cub.2008.10.027 PMID:19026538

LeUnes, A. (2011). *Sport Psychology*. London: Icon Books.

Loland, S. (2009). The ethics of performance-enhancing technology in sport. *Journal of the Philosophy of Sport*, *36*(2), 152–161. doi:10.1080/00948705.2009.9714754

López-Frías, J. (2014). *Mejora humana y dopaje en la actual filosofía del deporte* (Unpublished doctoral dissertation). Facultad de Filosofía, Universidad de Valencia.

Luppicini, R. (2009). Technoethical Inquiry: From Technological Systems to Society. *Global Media Journal*, *2*(1), 5–21.

Luppicini, R. (2012). *Ethical Impact of Technological Advancements and Applications in Society*. Hershey, PA: IGI Global. doi:10.4018/978-1-4666-1773-5

Merkel, R., Boer, G., Fegert, J., Galert, T., Hartmann, D., Nuttin, B., & Rosahl, S. (2007). *Intervening in the brain. Changing psyche and society*. Berlin: Springer.

Miah, A. (2004). Genetically Modified Athletes. London: E&FN Spon (Routledge).

Miah, A. (2011). Physical Enhancement: The State of Art. In Enhancing Human Capacities. Oxford, UK: Blackwell.

Okano, A., Fontes, E., Montenegro, R., Farinatti, P., Cyrino, E., Li, L., ... Noakes, T. D. (2013). Brain stimulation modulates the autonomic nervous system, rating of perceived exertion and performance during maximal exercise. *British Journal of Sports Medicine*, *49*(18), 1213–1218. doi:10.1136/bjsports-2012-091658 PMID:23446641

Pérez-Triviño, J.L. (2011). Gene Doping and the Ethics of Sport: Between Enhancement and Posthumanism. *International Journal of Sports Science*, *1*(1).

Pérez-Triviño, J.L. (2013). Cyborgsportpersons: Between Disability and Enhancement. *Physical Culture and Sport Studies and Research*, *57*(1). doi:10.2478/pcssr-2013-0003

Pérez-Triviño, J.L. (2015). Equality of Access to Enhancement Technology in a Posthumanist Society. *Dilemata*, *19*.

Porsdam,, M. S., & Sahakian, B. J. (2015). The increasing lifestyle use of modafinil by healthy people: Safety and ethical issues. *Current Opinion in Behavioral Sciences*, 4.

Ron, B., Meulen, R., Malizia, A., & Vos, R. (2011). Scientific, ethical, and social issues in mood enhancement. In Enhancing Human Capacities. Oxford, UK: Blackwell.

Sánchez, X., & Lejeune, M. (1999). Práctica Mental y deporte. ¿Qué sabemos después de casi un siglo de investigación? *Revista de Psicología del Deporte*, *8*(1).

Sandberg, A. (2011). Cognition Enhancement: Upgrading the Brain. In Enhancing Human Capacities. Oxford, UK: Blackwell.

Sandel, M. (2007). *The case against Perfection*. Cambridge, MA: Harvard University Press.

Savulescu, J. (2007). Gene therapy, transgenesis and chimeras: is the radical genetic alteration of human beings a threat to our humanity? In J. Savulescu (Ed.), *Quest of Ethical Wisdom: How the Practical Ethics of East and West Contribute to Wisdom*. Oxford, UK: Oxford Uehiro Centre for Practical Ethics.

Simon, R. (1993). *Fair Play. Sports, values and society*. Boulder, CO: Westview Press.

Tamorri, S. (2004). *Neurociencias y deporte. Psicología deportiva y procesos mentales del atleta*. Barcelona: Ed. Paidotribo.

Verroker, M. (2005). Drug use and abuse in sport. In D. R. Mottram (Ed.), *Drugs in Sport*. London: Routledge.

Vesali, C. E. (2002). History of Drugs in Sport. *International Sports Studies*, *24*(1).

Wall, Croarkin, McClintock, Murphy, Bandel, & Sim, & Sampson. (2013). Neurocognitive effects of repetitive transcranial magnetic stimulation in adolescents with major depressive disorder. *Frontiers in Psychiatry*, *4*(1).

Wexler, A. (2016). The practices of do-it-yourself brain stimulation: Implications for ethical considerations and regulatory proposals. *Journal of Medical Ethics*, *42*(4), 211–215. doi:10.1136/medethics-2015-102704 PMID:26324456

Young, D. C. (1984). *The Olympic Myth of Greek Amateur Athletics*. Chicago: Ares Publishers.

ENDNOTES

1.   The participants in these 1904 Olympic were only amateurs, who did not receive any award, payment or reward for winning. Thus, as I mentioned previously, natural doping and chemical doping were in fadt present at times which some experts had conceived of as the golden (or pure) age of sport.

2.   Recently, the discovery of documents has demonstrated that West German athletes players would have taken some type of amphetamines in the 1954 Football World Cup final. At the time it was quite surprising that West Germany team defeated the favorites, the Hungarian team.

3.   Simpson had been appointed in 1965 as a "Sports Personality" by the BBC.

4.   That same year, the IOC set up the Medical Commission against Doping whose aim was protecting athletes' health, sport, medical ethics, and equality among athletes. As a result, in 1968 the first victim of the drug testing took place in Mexico Olympics. Out of 667 tests performed, only one athlete tested positive: Hans-Gunnar Liljwewall a pentathlete who was stripped of his bronze medal for consuming excessive alcohol.

5.   The concern about the use of this type of substance that improves cognitive and emotional capacities is increasing. Currently it is estimated that between 5 and 35% of American students have taken them with the aim of improving their academic performance (Dubljevic 2015, 30). The Presidential Commission for the Study of Bioethics has included cognitive drugs among its four main priorities. Ethical considerations of neuroscience research and the application of neuroscience research findings for the Presidential Commission for the Study of Bioethical Issues (2014). *J Law Biosci*:1-6.

6.   The conclusions they achieved were that tDCS sessions could have competitive advantages for professional athletes and recommend the deepening of the discussion on its ethical use in sports, which is ultimately tied to the wider debate around the risks and opportunities that neuromodulation brings to the table.

Chapter 3
The Political Use and Abuse of Science

Gabriel R. Ricci
Elizabethtown College, USA

ABSTRACT

This chapter examines the dialectical role of science in its promotion of public policy and the manner in which scientific autonomy has been challenged to further political ends. Various episodes in the ever-expanding technological reach of the marriage of science and politics are historically recounted to demonstrate the threat to scientific self-rule and to individual scientists who have been relegated to instrumentally functional roles. It is argued that the emergent class status of scientists has been subverted by the triumvirate of technology, industry, and religion. Moreover, science has met its greatest challenge from those entities which understand how the use of technology and scientific discovery translate into regulatory measures.

INTRODUCTION

When scientific investigation and experiment was first formalized within associations like the Royal Society, the Acadèmie des Sciences and the American Philosophical Society in the United States, government had little to do with their ongoing operation.[1] Over time governments have routinely insinuated themselves into the workings of the scientific community. Between the two world wars, for example, totalitarian ideologies guided the practical outcomes of science. In the case of Aryan racial policy and the Nazification of the university system, some speculative aspects of science were sidelined because they were too closely associated with Jewish scientists. It is estimated that the physics community was gutted by 15% to 25% and pure research was suppressed in favor of the practical and technical applications of knowledge, all in service to the needs and goals of the mythical *Volk*. According to Alan Beyerchen, the remaining scientific community ranged from those who gave into a "prudential acquiescence", a phrase he borrowed from Joseph Haberer, or sheer opportunism in service of the Nazi agenda.[2] Similarly, while Marxism may have found some innovations in psychoanalysis too bourgeois, Marxism in general embraced the application of technology and science for the benefit of humanity.[3] However, by the 1930s science in

DOI: 10.4018/978-1-5225-5094-5.ch003

the Soviet Union had been absorbed by the five-year-planning mentality and centralized control through a Commissariat. As with Nazism, science was directed by production and industrial goals that eclipsed basic research in favor of the construction of a socialist and industrialized state. Centralized control had effectively aligned professional ambitions to the aims of party organs.[4] Scientists were pressured to avoid speculative reason and to pursue applicative and productive processes. Communication outside the Soviet Union became suspect and the inability to accurately forecast future research according to the demands of five-year planning undermined the vitality of scientific investigation. If these demands were not coercive enough, the Soviet scientific community would also suffer from both the short-lived Cultural Revolution and the Great Purge; in the first instance, unqualified party members supervised seasoned scientists, and in the latter, many scientists were sent to the gulag. A special challenge was presented by reconciling dialectical materialism with science; ideologues triumphed and dictated which methods best served the proletarian. Infamously, a public debate on the direction of research in genetics resulted in its abolition from textbooks.[5] Independent scientific associations would have to wait until *glasnost* under Gorbachev.

In the United States, it was only after the war in a public report to President Truman that the director of the Office of Scientific Research and Development, Vannevar Bush, promoted a prominent role for science. [6] Bush's report, *Science: The Endless Frontier* (July 25, 1945), which addressed the question first raised by Franklin Delano Roosevelt: What can be done, consistent with military security, and with the prior approval of the military authorities, to make known to the world as soon as possible the contributions which have been made during our war effort to scientific knowledge?, argued that the fruits of science were not only synonymous with the goals of government, but consistent with the historical narrative of the United States. Bush's statement was reinforced by repeated references to Frederick Jackson Turner's frontier thesis.[7] In this storyline, Jonathan Moreno credits the American pragmatist C.S. Peirce, who proposed that the meaning of ideas be calculated in their practical effects, for elevating the status of technical achievement alongside theoretical innovations. (Moreno, p.44) Additionally, Peirce's concept of the community of inquiry promised that progressive scientific inquiry would ultimately produce a more precise view of the real world. The spirit of open dialogue within the scientific community can also take some credit for advancing innovation, which would outpace the Soviet Union where lack of open communication among researchers stifled competition and progress.

Vannevar Bush could not have predicted, but following the war, scientific and technological advances remained infused with deliberations of war and military ambitions, lending credence to Randolph Bourne's assessment that the modern state is essentially militaristic.[8] The shift from private institutional funding to government subsidy for research fueled the marriage between science and politics. Bush's appeal for an institutional role for science in service of national welfare was garnered in his position as director for the Office of Scientific Research in which he oversaw wartime research and development, including supervision of The Manhattan Project (Haberer, 1969, p.185). Bush's early appeal for an active role for the scientific community in the welfare of the state persisted with the establishment of the President's Science Advisory Committee (PSAC) in 1951. Twenty years after the Second World War, action by the PSAC confirmed the alliance between science and government policy. Following the revelations of Rachel Carson, the PSAC would establish a precursor to the Environmental Protection Agency, the Environmental Pollution Panel (EPP). This panel would release a spirited statement, *Restoring the Quality of Our Environment* (The White House, November 5, 1965), which boldly promoted the need for environmental leadership at the level of the federal government in order to protect the very heritage of the United States.[9] The EPP also expressed the clear obligation that the government had in underwriting a favorable cultural setting which would produce scientists and engineers whose expertise would guarantee a healthy environment (Nash, 1990, pp. 195-201)

Government, Science, and War

The use of the scientific community to produce a weapon of mass destruction during the Second World War forged a lasting relationship between government and science by which the two are not easily separated. This relationship has been marked by internecine strife with very public arguments. There is a prehistory of this tension that is well known to us through the iconic cases in which political authority has determined that certain scientific ideas must be suppressed in order to safeguard worldviews which supported institutional doctrine. Galileo, who exacerbated his problems with the Church by demonstrating that he was as exegetically equipped as the next favorite Jesuit, is perhaps the most notorious incident. Giordano Bruno, though more a speculative thinker than a scientist, was burned at the stake for his controversial multiple worlds view. Similarly, Francis Bacon, who primarily articulated a framework for the sociology of knowledge, became vulnerable to political vagaries.

The cases of Galileo and Bruno were driven by the desire to protect a hegemonic worldview. In our time, it has been the Oppenheimer case which was fueled by Cold War hysteria that has had such obvious global ramifications. The parallel case of Andrei Sakharov was also a warning to scientists that public political and moral dissent could upend a career; by 1968 Sakharov's political activity undermined any further military research and he fell back on fundamental science. Though Sakharov would win the Nobel Peace Prize in 1975, he suffered internal exile and was perpetually hounded by the state. The fact that their respective governments accused both Oppenheimer and Sakharov of being arrogant and stepping beyond their jurisdiction is at the core of the perennial tension between science and government according to the insights of David Guston and Kenneth Keniston.[10] In the United States the history of this tension can be traced to the Allison Commission of 1884 which addressed jurisdictional concerns, scientific priorities and the responsibilities of existing scientific offices, like the US Geological Survey. Commissions in the 1960s and 1985 provided congressional forums for analyzing government's ongoing relationship to scientific research.[11] That the tension persists to this day may seem to result from clashes between scientific elite and democratically elected politicians, but Guston and Keniston trace the problem to the fundamental disparity between how the scientific community is organized and how the democratic polity turns on popular will. (Guston and Keniston, p. 25) Scientific method does not bypass experimentation, dialogue and peer-review in order to vote on scientific consensus. Guston and Keniston suggest that this chronic friction may be relieved if scientists increase outreach activities. (Guston and Keniston, pp. 31-33) However, as we have learned from public challenges to the authority of science since the end of the twentieth century, scientists must be prepared for challenges of scientific uncertainty from competitive voices equally invested in discretionary government funding and regulatory restrictions.

Oppenheimer did not help when he ventured a position on foreign policy after the war. He had already reported that policy concerns for scientists had become controversial at the time of the first successful testing of an atomic device, after which opinions from scientists became either irrelevant or suspect by policy makers.[12] After the war, Oppenheimer maintained the reciprocity of science and policy in his various advisory roles, but being outspoken about policy matters only undermined his status. The loyalty of a scientist at that time was very fragile and any echoes of leftist sympathies could undercut a career.[13] Oppenheimer had been hounded by investigations during the Manhattan Project because of his circle of left-leaning friends and associates but after the war he became vulnerable because he mixed science and political policy. His skepticism about the Hydrogen Bomb and the need to guard against an arms race was not only construed as a breach of loyalty, but a kind of trespassing.[14] After succumbing to pressure to leave the chairmanship of the General Advisory Committee (serving the Atomic Energy Commission) Oppenheimer produced a policy statement, "Atomic Weapons and American Policy," which was published in *Foreign Affairs* (Oppenheimer, 1953, pp. 523-535). Later republished in the *Bulletin of the Atomic Scientists*, IX (July,1953): 203-205, Oppenheimer made an argument for transparency on various fronts: 1) He recommended that knowledge of the nature and the likely effects of atomic weapons should be made public; 2) he argued that the state of knowledge of the so-called enemy should be revealed and 3) he thought that our allies, who do not share our land expanse, should be made aware of methods of interception and the expected damages from the deployment and use of tactical nuclear weapons which, in 1954, when they were first deployed in Europe, only had a range of thirty miles (Oppenheimer, 1953).[15] In this argument, Oppenheimer was reiterating the "open world" policy that Niels Bohr advocated in 1944.[16] In 1953, open communications with the Soviets must have appeared naïve, though it was on the table immediately following the cessation of the Second World War and when Oppenheimer publicly expressed his concern over war with Russia and an arms race to numerous political figures at a conference in Washington, D.C. in October 1945. (Bird and Sherwin, 330)

In 1965 Peter Watkins produced the drama-documentary, *The War Game*, which dramatically presented a scenario that was implicit in Oppenheimer's last recommendation. The film imagines how nuclear war would play out in Britain following a US pre-emptive nuclear strike. The film was declared too controversial and horrific to show on BBC, but was later aired in 1985, after which it received an Academy Award for Best Documentary.[17] If Peter Watkins's docudrama met such criticism twenty years following the war after which Europe had settled into détente, Oppenheimer's advice in 1953 must have been even more troublesome. Oppenheimer had naively gone over the line and the ultimate revocation of his security clearance was a statement that science, if it were to remain vital, should restrict itself to practical and technological aspects of science and leave speculation about the future to policy makers. In 1953, the geopolitical scope of Oppenheimer's policy recommendations disclosed the global reach of the marriage of science and politics. In hindsight Oppenheimer's frankness showed that scientists must be especially careful when they weigh in politically. Politicians, on the other hand, operate with a different standard when they liberally digress on scientific matters with little or no knowledge of the subject. This double standard has become engrained in the political landscape and has become even more exaggerated thanks to a contemporary cultural milieu in which the findings of science are regularly challenged by mere opinion and religious conviction.

When Albert Einstein first brought the reality of an atomic weapon to the attention of Franklin Delano Roosevelt, he could not have anticipated how its creation and use would later lock the world in an uneasy détente guaranteed by mutual fear and which produced spontaneous proxy wars across the globe.[18] However, it is clear from Einstein's recommendations to Roosevelt that he imagined a critical role for scientists in government policy. Einstein advised that the government have ongoing contact with the physicists engaged in producing chain reactions and that an individual be assigned the job of communicating to the administration in order to apprise the various government offices of any further advances and how the United States might procure a ready supply of ore, which, he noted, was abundant in Czechoslovakia and Africa. Einstein clearly indicated that he had information that Germany was anxious to pursue such a weapon and that the resources in recently conquered Czechoslovakia made this a plausible threat. Einstein also appealed to Roosevelt for financial assistance and cooperation from industrial labs that were properly resourced.[19] Einstein's dutiful appeal received immediate attention and along with The Manhattan Project Einstein must take some credit for forging an alliance between science and government. Though he may have compromised his pacifism when he assumed this interventionist role, Einstein was aware of the catastrophic destructive potential of an atomic weapon which he imagined capable of being delivered by ship and totally destroying a port city and its surrounding territory. This was a technological innovation that threatened the globe.

The Scientific Estate

If it is the case that war is an extension of policy/politics by other means, then the military success won by technological innovation in the Second World War is proof that scientific power can transform into real political power. Since the pursuit of science during the war corresponded to the ends of political power, then there could be no question that Bacon's methodological innovations were ultimately and convincingly realized. Furthermore, the new alliance between science and military power endowed the scientific community with a new status. As redeemers of civilization the scientific community was elevated to an institution that commanded respect and gratitude for preserving our future. Consequently, support was in order and the government was in a position and motivated to continue to offer subvention. In a manner of speaking this meant that the conventional separation between church and state, according to Don K. Price, had been breached, since the government's enthusiasm for endowing science amounted to the promotion of a new kind of messianism (Price, 1965, p.12). Price was not just indulging in metaphor, the title of his book, *The Scientific Estate*, is an allusion to the hierarchically ordered medieval society which was upset by the French Revolution and in which today science has achieved an emergent class status. The way in which the estates were reconfigured in the eighteenth century meant that this new scientific estate had the potential to threaten traditional values as well as the prevailing economic and constitutional system. Price, who was the founding Dean of the Kennedy School of Government at Harvard University and political advisor to three presidential administrations, was echoing the famous admonition of Eisenhower who in his final address to the nation warned of an emergent military-industrial complex. Eisenhower's warning was presaged in the work of Randolph Bourne, the social critic and pacifist, who described the natural symbiosis between the state and militarism. Bourne's personal experience during the First World War also made him keenly aware that a state's ambition for democratic principles abroad can go hand in hand with their suppression at home, as with the Sedition Act of 1918. Stuart W. Leslie points out that the wedding of industry and the military was disbanded after the Armistice when industry turned to new commercial interests[20] but this would not be the case following The Second World War. Bourne, in fact, argued that the state manifests itself in aggression and militarism and thus devotes most of its energy to war and defense, "developing the powers and techniques which make for destruction."[21] Naturally, the consequence of this militaristic organization is a "crippling of the productive and life-enhancing processes of national life." [22] Whichever way it is expressed and organized, the alliance incorporating the state, research initiatives and the military industrial complex has achieved cultural supremacy in the United States with its ever-expanding defense budget. In this vein, David Dickson, in *The New Politics of Science*, expressed alarm that by the 1980s the military-industrial alliance had become a coterie of university administrators, defense contractors and scientists, who while still dependent on public funding, were no longer subject to democratic control and public-decision making.[23] Dickson's analysis of the mutual evolution of science and politics confirmed Price's suspicions in 1965.

Eisenhower's military and political trajectory privileged him to the need for such development but it also made him aware of the industry's newly acquired influence. In order to preserve both security and liberty, Eisenhower promoted a vigilance that would prevent the emergence of scientific and technological elite who were vulnerable to the power of money which might usurp democratic processes.[24] What was at stake, according to Price's analysis, was the encroachment of the private economic order into the public sector, a tangled bureaucracy with multiple layers of technocratic management and potential disruption to a constitutionally sanctioned system of checks and balances (1965, p. 186). While Price had always supported a vital role for science in government affairs, some reviewers took the opportunity to warn against the hegemony of science. Arthur Selwyn Miller provided a timely message to the legal profession (1966, pp. 622-629). Miller cautioned that Price's message that science, while it professed to provide regular panacea, could not ameliorate all of society's woes. Miller argued that no matter how informed we become through science, no matter how many problems are resolved by science, science alone cannot provide principles for political and legal action (p.625). Miller was especially alarmed with Price's suggestion that, while science would not result in a heartless, managed dystopia, it might very well erode humanity's sense of purpose (p. 625). In a world that is predominantly focused on technological innovation, lawyers, whose work relies on the repository of precedent and established laws, would find themselves sidelined in a political process driven by forward-looking technologies. Miller urged lawyers to do what scientists do: address problems that have a global scope (p. 628). Thus, he counseled the legal profession to find a voice to address pressing problems like population growth, atmospheric and environmental blight and war, all of which threaten the welfare of humanity. The technocrats will otherwise threaten a coup d'état. Miller urged lawyers to mobilize in order to preserve the humanistic elements in rationalism; they need to learn how to do what technologists and scientists are doing (p. 628). To clarify the intellectual reach of the lawyer Miller invoked the celebrated jurist Oliver Wendell Holmes who claimed that there is no discipline remote from the law. In fact, to become proficient in any discipline should compel us to know all the subjects at its fringes (p. 628). Holmes's message is advice for those who must work in a competitive intellectual environment in which a technique or fashionable discipline can rise to the standing of an insulated and esoteric political estate complete with a militant priesthood. [25]

At the time, Miller and others may have overstated the priestly status of the emergent scientific estate, since technicians do not actually set the political agenda, they only contribute specialized knowledge. Oppenheimer sadly discovered that scientists were mere functionaries in service to the government machine; their ambitions are not the same as politicians for the simple reason that scientists only further the goals of policy makers. This instrumental function of science has been thoroughly appropriated in the network of skilled scientists assembled by the state in what John Kenneth Galbraith called a techno-structure or the institutional manner in which the technical ends of science become yet another way to achieve political goals. Within this structure science loses the independent status it may have achieved within academia and scientific associations, and becomes subservient to political machinations (Galbraith, 1967, p. 294) Jean-Jacques Salomon (1973) inferred the idea of a technonature from Galbraith's economic conception of technostructure to further identify the manipulation of natural resources on the part of scientific managers; thus, emphasizing their role as means to the ends of the state (p. 174). The term is also an incarnation of Bacon's insights about the power of knowledge through which nature is framed by commodification. Constrained in this way, humanity, as Martin Heidegger would echo in his critique of technology, is closed off to more primordial aesthetic, spiritual, and psychological interconnections which sustain culture.

The Limits of Reason

The hard lesson that Oppenheimer learned when he became enmeshed in this newly forming institutional structure was that science was restricted to informing policy, its function was not to form policy. Galileo's predicament anticipated this dynamic when he instructed his detractors on the separate jurisdictions of defining how the heavens go and how one might get to heaven. The Church was adamant that they governed both spheres. The authoritative absorption of the technical prowess of science in both cases corrupt the ends that devolve from the momentum science produces on its own and allows authorities to determine ends that serve the arbitrary needs of transitory power structures.

If the strategies which informed the nuclear arms race have taught us a lesson, it is that technical solutions cannot substitute for political ones. In the final analysis, what the use of reason and technology has done is to give the irrational (the prospect of mutual destruction) the appearance of being reasonable. [26] Science is far off its enlightenment course of freeing humans from the constraints and vicissitudes of nature if in its wake it has left us facing residual pollutions and ecological insecurities, not to mention the threatening instabilities of an emerging geopolitical landscape that was percolating when international politics was technologically dominated by regulating the tensions between the two super powers.

The Enlightenment has not gone without its critics. Hegel was the first to point out how the appeal of rationality produced a disenchantment of nature and a purging of the spiritual. Critical theorists, Theodor Adorno and Max Horkheimer, followed suit in their *Dialectic of Enlightenment* (1947), which viewed the Holocaust as the culmination of this technological domination of man and nature, all ironically in the name of making history or human interaction less irrational. Before scientific research was misdirected by politics, it had already been infiltrated by a competitive and Faustian spirit that overshadowed idealistic goals. [27] The prospects for any technology assessment that might oversee the state's role as both the producer and consumer of knowledge must first deal with the appeal of Bacon's identity of knowledge and power and its modern corollary: substituting technical solutions for political ones. This dialectic agitated the scientific community during the war years, challenged the loyalties of individual scientists after the war and has produced a political and cultural atmosphere that freely challenges and even debunks scientific theory in the name of sacred market forces, hallowed economic growth and sacrosanct religious fundamentalism. The history of the Reagan and the George W. Bush Administrations bear witness to this evolution.

The War on Science

In many respects, the administration of George W. Bush was a recapitulation of Ronald Reagan's, particularly in the way that industry and religion united to produce an ambiguous brand of science. Presidents have had science advisory teams since the administration of Truman, but the collusion between industry and religion is a phenomenon that could not have been imagined with the first stirrings of the anti-scientific attitude and distrust of the intellectual elite in the early days of William Buckley's *New Republic*. The *New Republic* broadcast these views, but it was Buckley's *God and Man at Yale* that first began to question the cooperation between government and science that had prospered during the war. Buckley took aim at the social scientist of his day, but his criticism was intended for all scientists; he considered them to be much too critical of religion (Mooney, 2005). Buckley, perhaps unwittingly, set the stage for the more strident critique of science and scientists that would mark the Nixon administration and that would be resuscitated in the special merger between industry and religion in the Reagan administration and later in the second Bush administration.

Richard Nixon did not devise the clever strategies that subvert conventional science but he was publicly angered when the community of scientists voiced their opposition to the Vietnam War. Scientists had had Nixon's ear for not only did he establish a full-bodied regulatory agency in the EPA, he also passed environmentally friendly legislation in the Endangered Species Act and strengthened the Clean Air Act. Nixon could not abide any criticism, and he soured on science and scientists. It was in 1972 that the EPA would ban DDT after the heroic efforts of Rachel Carson to reveal the devastating effects of its commercial use. This was the moment when industry took note of the way in which scientific discovery could be transformed into regulatory measures that would affect their bottom line. The subsequent smear campaign against Rachel Carson was not only driven by sexism; it also challenged the validity of her science. Carson was painted as an alarmist who subscribed to the cult of environmentalism, but industry was really agitated by the role that science began to take in informing laws designed to protect health and welfare and to prevent environmental degradation. Industry's attack against Rachel Carson ushered in the accusation of *scientific uncertainty* that would be bolstered and fortified during the Reagan administration.

Since Carson the cry of *scientific uncertainty* has been brandished against policy informed by science. After the historic controversy following Alfred Wegener's theory of continental drifts, Naomi Oreskes cites the case of Rachel Carson and the impact of *Silent Spring* as instrumental in clarifying how the weight of scientific opinion may guide policy choices. Policy has never waited for the elusive standard of abstract truth or ultimate proof; informed public policy has always been directed by the "consensus of relevant scientific experts."[28] Critics of environmentalism, like Bjørn Lomborg, have exploited the declarations of environmentalists precisely on this point; labelling environmental claims as myth. Oreskes acknowledges the various commitments that may sway even a scientist's conclusions, and in the case of Rachel Carson it was her combined sympathies for the world around us and her science that informed her opinion. For Lomborg and others, Carson's respect for nature is not scientifically intelligible since it is not quantifiable. Carson's holistic vision embraced living things, Oreskes argues, that even though they can't be quantified, they still count. (Oreskes, 376) Carson only raised the ethical question of eliminating entire bird species in the pursuit of better living through chemistry.

There are still conservative, industry-friendly politicians who beat the drum against Rachel Carson. At the time of the centenary of her birth in 2007, Carson was denied recognition for her accomplishments, thanks to the efforts of Senator Tom Coburn of Oklahoma. He joined other detractors from the far right, including proponents of Ayn Rand's Objectivism, to impugn her scientific reputation and to accuse Carson of genocide for all the lives lost to malaria thanks to her revelations which lead to banning the use of DDT in the United States. This charge, of course, ignores the fact that even mosquitoes eventually become immune to DDT applications, while it continues to do its destructive work across the food chain. Coburn's Republican colleague James Imhofe, chairman of the Senate Environment and Public Works Committee, is perhaps the most vocal opponent of global warming. As Oreskes and Conway (2010) point out in *Merchants of Doubt*, the libelous campaign against Carson reached a fever pitch when some conservative think tanks compared Carson to a mass murderer that surpassed Adolf Hitler. [29] It is ironic that the state that has suffered one of the most catastrophic, anthropogenic ecological disasters in the twentieth century, the Dust Bowl, is home to such environmental skeptics.

The public display made by Newt Gingrich and his cohorts in 1994 to revive a conservative Republican agenda was accompanied by a systematic attack on the mainstream scientific community. Under

Gingrich's grandiose intellectual leadership an autonomous scientific program took shape, a position that first emerged under the auspices of Ronald Reagan who as governor of California encouraged a unique form of creationism, one that was informed by an ambiguous scientific approach. The result was scientific creationism or creationist science in which idiosyncratic interpretations of the scripture were aligned with conventional science, like Darwinism. In another incarnation, creationism also tried to demonstrate the invalidity of evolution on scientific grounds. The political ambition in both cases was to introduce creationism alongside evolution in the curriculum. Reagan would take this new science to the Whitehouse; and, in addition, he would introduce industry-friendly personnel into the EPA and the Department of Interior, two government offices dedicated to the protection and prudent use of the nation's natural resources.

Dorothy Nelkin places creationism in a larger wave of social activism which began in the 1970s. Representing a range of political positions and beliefs, social activism introduced challenges to the independence and objective authority of science. Nelkin writes that this general movement was fueled by rights discourse, whether it was in defense of animal rights or fetal tissue, and demanded a role in policy formation.[30] In some cases activists succeeded but creationism suffered a major setback with the Supreme Court decision Edwards v. Aguillard, 107 S.Ct 2573 (1987) which found that it violated the establishment clause. Dissenting opinions by Antonin Scalia and William Rehnquist recognized that it was protecting academic freedom. Soon after the expression intelligent design was substituted for creationism and the textbook *Of Pandas and Peoples* explored the alternative theory in scientific terms.

Under the leadership of Anne Gorsuch, the EPA would gain notoriety for drawing up a so-called "hit list" of scientists who were deemed unfriendly to industry (Mooney, 2005, p. 40). Reagan's scientific team was questionable for all the foolish statements he made in public about acid rain at the time. They were all justified under the mantle of scientific uncertainty, just as scientific assertions about global warming face today. Still the Reagan use and abuse of science was not yet systemic; this would be left to the intellectual bravado of Gingrich and his fellow-travelers. Reagan, however, must be credited with the most concerted effort to turn a fantasy into a science with his Star Wars program (SDI). What we do see that would become even more troubling in the years ahead was the pressure placed upon science administrators to place an ideological spin on scientific information. For example, in an effort to redirect and get control over the abortion debate, Dinesh D'Souza, a Reagan advisor, hatched a plot to use the public face of the Surgeon General, who so successfully alerted the public to the dangers of smoking (Mooney, 2005. P. 46). C. Everett Koop was pressured by D'Souza to produce a study suggesting that there were dangerous health consequences to abortion. Koop resisted and made it clear that there was no scientific data to support these conclusions. This was "science" getting the cart before the horse; an attitude that persisted into the second Bush administration where censorship and the debunking of science and scientists would be raised to a political art.

The practice of debunking science was cultivated and widely put into practice in the anti-regulatory campaign of the Gingrich Republican revolution. The Reagan administration revealed the problems associated with manipulating science advisors; Gingrich's crew would avoid this problem by pretending to be scientists themselves. Gingrich was a self-proclaimed futurologist, having been deeply moved by Alvin Toffler's work, and he liked to think that he had a grasp of the technological and scientific trends that would evolve over time. Before his political downfall, he publicly proclaimed that his sensitivity to technological and scientific discoveries gave him insights into social and cultural developments over centuries. He did not just envision a Republican revolution; he made pronouncements on cutting edge science like nanotechnology after claiming to have studied at the country's most renowned science institutions. Informing public policy with the right sort of science had already been institutionalized in organizations like the Heritage Foundation and the George C. Marshall Institute, but Gingrich's intellectual audacity made him a one-man science and policy foundation.

The groundwork for Gingrich's scientific agenda had previously been established by Big Tobacco which had cultivated the technique known as "manufacturing uncertainty." This method is sanctioned by science itself which promotes a perennial skepticism in order to further the ends of inquiry at the heart of science. Big Tobacco had shown that instilling doubt was the most efficient way of producing controversy and challenging an accepted body of fact, as in the case of the risks of being exposed to second hand smoke. As far back as 1969 Brown & Williamson expressed their strategy: "Doubt is our product, since it is the best means of competing with the 'body of fact' that exists in the mind of the general public. It is also the means of establishing controversy" (Mooney, 2005, p. 67) The Advancement of Sound Science Coalition (TASSC), founded in 1993, would take up this banner. The group was heavily financed by Philip Morris. The group's mandate was to restrain politicians they deemed to abuse science. In the industry–friendly environment created by Gingrich et al. the banner of "sound science" led the way to regulatory reform. If regulatory reform could not be scuttled, the overbearing criteria for scientific review and the strict rules for risk assessment would at least slow down the process and wear down the opposition. At the time David Vladeck, a Georgetown University law professor, described the political climate as "paralysis by analysis" (Mooney, 2005, p.70). The strategy of adopting the call for "sound science" was cunning since it gave the appearance of taking the higher intellectual road and because it gave the appearance of an analytical and logical position; one that could only be accused of erring on the side of caution.

Industry did not have to rely on sympathetic legislators; there were eager enough consultants in Washington, D.C. to do their bidding. The long and illustrious career of James Tozzi is emblematic of the growing anti-regulatory ethos that challenged the validity of governmental science. Tozzi was a jazz musician manqué who had begun his career in the regulatory offices of the Corps of Engineers and progressively worked his way up to the Office of Management and Budget where he was able to make a close study of regulatory mechanisms and procedures. From the moment he left the Reagan administration, Tozzi actively worked on behalf of industrial entities whose bottom line could be affected by government science. The culmination of his career was shepherding the little-known Data Quality Act in 2002. The brief two sentence amendment to a budgetary measure provided industry with information about any study that might affect the bottom line. Under the guise of regulatory efficiency Tozzi provided industry with an inside track to challenging the validity of government science. [31]

The most notorious use and abuse of the facts in the second Bush administration must be the manipulation of evidence of WMDs in Iraq. This propaganda campaign has had disastrous consequences. The strategies employed in this campaign of misinformation were the same used against the scientific opposition to the Bush administration's manipulation of advisory and regulatory bodies mandated to guide national and international policy. Censorship and accusations of disloyalty became the primary tools employed against the opposition, just as they were utilized in the Oppenheimer case. Before her resignation in 2003, Christie Whitman had been accused of disloyalty for seeking "the facts." Anthony Zinni, a former commander-in-chief of Central Command, when he broke ranks with the Bush administration, was accused of treason. Being a wartime president meant creating a sensitive political atmosphere intolerant of dissent. This was the same environment the administration created for the scientific advisory community from its very beginning when it became obvious that George W. Bush was having difficulty appointing a lead scientific advisory team. It was well into the first year of the administration when John Marburger received the call to be the President's lead science advisor.

When the Union of Concerned Scientists (UCS) produced a public statement on scientific integrity in the Bush administration in 2004, even Marburger, who had been in lockstep to Bush's control of scientific information, took note of the seriousness of this outcry. The federal government followed up that same year with legislation that forbade inquiry into a scientist's political background when they were being considered for advisory positions. The use of so-called litmus tests had been one of the administrations primary tactics in screening for loyal scientists; the other major strategy against the scientific community were well placed gate keepers intent on overriding any obstacles to the political goals articulated by the administration.

The Revolving Door

When he first came into office George W. Bush made quite a spectacle of the faith-based initiatives that were to substitute for meaningful domestic policy. This display made it quite clear that religion was going to be a major component of his administration. The fate of science would be reflected in the desultory way he appointed scientific advisors. While religion, in the form of creationism, did trump evolution, dictate stem-cell research and inform birth control policy, it would not always be religion that blocked, censored and obfuscated the facts. Industry-friendly advocates were well-schooled at this sort of sabotage. Before Jim Hansen accused the administration of censorship in 2006, the federal government had already established strictures that required scientists to receive permission to publish their scientific work and the two most regulation-conscious agencies in the government, the EPA and the Department of Interior, were led by enforcement officers like Jeffrey Holmstead (EPA) and Stephen Griles (Department of Interior) both of whom were adept at manipulating the data to satisfy ideological and commercial goals.[32] Hansen's accusation that the Bush White House was deliberately interfering with scientists' communication with the public did not disclose the systemic institutional interference that had been going on for some time. Hansen's case has come to the fore because of his admonitions about global warming, but the story of the chronic manipulation and censorship of the facts is told in the meddling and obstruction of ideological bureaucrats like Holmstead and Griles, both of whom cut their teeth with legal firms that represented big industrial polluters. This experience put them in the ideal position to control scientific data. Holmstead repeatedly ignored the suggestions of his science advisors when they counseled him on the amount of retooling required in order for polluting industries to install state of the art, environmentally friendly technology. The figures were so skewed as to place extensive repairs and retooling beyond the mandated threshold. The Clear Skies Initiative, which Holmstead was invested in, would be guided not by science but by the market place. This policy was a subversion of the Clean Air Act whose standards Holmstead and others deemed to be a financial burden to industry. Having clean air would be determined by what was considered to be an optimal level of pollution across the board, and all the big polluters would participate in a system of trading pollution rights in order to maintain that level of optimal pollution. The policy, of course, ignored the fact that a really big polluter could buy up all available pollution rights and turn a region into an environmental nightmare.

Similarly, Stephen Griles served in the Department of Interior as an industry advocate. Previous to government service he represented the mining industry and for all intents and purposes he did the same while serving as a deputy secretary at the Department of Interior. In this capacity Griles oversaw an Environmental Impact Study (EIS) for strip mining. Typically, an EIS would require a committee to investigate more environmentally benign ways of extracting coal from a mountain, other than removing their tops, deforesting the area and producing toxic run off. Under Griles's direction technical teams were told to remove language from their reports that might indicate a severe or negative environmental impact. Griles's real focus became expediting the permit process. [33]

Though John Marburger would call for a full investigation into the UCS's criticism of the Bush administration's politicization of science, he would ultimately dismiss their claims as grossly wrong on all counts (Mooney, 2005, p. 232). In a pathetic attempt to defend Bush, Marburger strained to make it seem that George W. Bush agreed with the consensus view on global warming, when it was obvious to everyone that the administration would not admit to the role of human activity. Howard Gardner, one of Marburger's most outspoken critics, did not hold back when he referred to Marburger as a prostitute on Diane Rehm's radio show (Mooney, 2005, p. 230).[34]

The Bush administration had multiple problems with facts. Whether it be in the form of concealing information, like the names of those attending Dick Cheney's notorious energy task force meeting in the early days of the administration, censoring important data from advisory committees or simply fabricating information, the Bush administration produced a separate reality that was sustained by friendly think tanks and monotonous talking points devoid of critical insight. The scientific community had to suffer the abuse of the Bush administration but so too did high ranking military officers, like Tony Zinni and Antonio Taguba, both of whom elected to reveal the facts. Taguba had the unenviable job of investigating what turned out to be the routine violation of the Geneva Convention and military protocol at Abu Ghraib. In all these cases, the Bush Administration waged a war on the truth, when it pretended to fight wars on more traditional fronts. The war on truth was a campaign against the facts. The Bush Administration confused having two sides to a story with having two sides to the facts, but its intellectual and psychological problems run deeper. The manner in which the Bush administration consistently held up and inflexibly defended questionable evidence; routinely manufactured apocalyptic scenarios on the basis of slim evidence; maintained false beliefs in spite of countervailing evidence; and denied evidence that undermines preconceived ideas suggests a psychological profile that Richard Hofstadter eloquently outlined in his essay *The Paranoid Style in American Politics*, published in Harper's Magazine in 1964, and which later served as the title essay of a larger work the same year. Hofstadter wrote at a time in which a paranoid mentality dominated the American political landscape, but he also took pains to historically review the various forms this syndrome has assumed, whether it be anti-Masonic, anti-Jesuit or in its anti-Semitic form. Whatever its incarnation, one can expect the same political pathology: the denial of compromise and mediation, a militant leader who sees things in terms of absolute good and absolute evil, and the demand that the evil enemy be totally eradicated. Partial success is construed as a sign of weakness and tantamount to defeat. Whatever form the enemy comes in, the paranoid personality perceives it as having special powers to influence the mind: it may be foreign, religious demagogues, it can be the press, it could be elite Eastern intellectuals or even wayward scientists alarmed about global climate change. These powers, according to Hofstadter, are projections of the self and so the paranoid personality adopts the manners of its enemy in the way that the KKK modeled itself on Catholicism, down to the vestments, the rituals and the hierarchy (Hofstadter, 1964). As the Bush administration faced off its scientific opposition it tried to outdo them in what Hofstadter called the "apparatus of scholarship" and in uncovering the facts (Hofstadter, p. 32). The result was a war on the truth, a war on science and a betrayal of the American trust.

These strategies now inform the current Trump Administration, whose surrogates have even made a case for alternative facts. There is much that is threatened by this attitude. The recent makeover of the EPA webpage epitomizes this mindset. Under the leadership of an ardent opponent of the EPA, Scott Pruitt, the new face of the EPA, has introduced a so-called Back-to-Basics Agenda. Like his boss, Pruitt is skeptical of global warming and he wants the EPA webpage to correspond to the current president's attitudes, one of which came in the public announcement that global warming was a hoax promulgated by the Chinese. On June 1, 2017, Donald Trump withdrew the United States from the Paris Climate Accord and has stonewalled answering questions on his belief or disbelief in climate change. The Back-to-Basics Agenda rests on the three pillars of protecting the environment, sensible regulations that allow economic growth and engaging with state and local partners. The fact that Donald Trump opposes the Clean Power Plan, which was previously promoted by the EPA and designed to counter anthropogenic climate change, makes it obvious that business and the economy will override science and environmental protection in the new EPA. [35] The effects of regulatory rollbacks are heralded in Devon Energy's recent decision not to introduce promised state-of-the-art equipment to reduce hazardous emissions in their Wyoming plant.[36] Devon is a known polluter and has admitted violating the law in the past, but its new resistance to checking hazardous emissions is being cheered by the industry. Four years before assuming his post at the EPA, Pruitt, then Attorney General of Oklahoma, forecasted his oil-industry ties when he essentially forwarded an appeal from Devon Energy to the EPA which challenged government restrictions on methane emissions from drilling operations.

The Religious Turn

The Bush Administration's campaign to justify war in the Middle East involved a new triumvirate, combining technology, the military and religion. This new iteration of the military-industrial complex revived the Crusades, deployed just war theory and resuscitated Manicheism. This was a complex that had God on its side, a full-bodied Christian Spirit cut with the punitive features of an Old Testament God.

Invoking God has a long pedigree as a call to battle. The motto Gott mit uns, for example, had an entrenched cultural presence in Germany before it was inscribed on the belt buckle of German soldiers in the First World War. The phrase first graced the Prussian Order of the Crown from its inception in 1861 and it later appeared on the imperial standard from 1870 to 1918 and on silver and gold coins from this period. The slogan was intended as a nationalistic cry to smite the enemy and by the end of the nineteenth century it played a role in politically infusing the state with a romantic religious ideology. To some extent this took the form of making Lutheranism the state religion. This revitalized Christian spirit followed in the wake of Bismarck's challenge to the growing independence of the various Churches, particularly the Catholic Church and what was perceived as the growing threat of Judaism. In *Infected Christianity: A Study of Modern Racism,* Alan T. Davies interprets Bismarck's Kulturkampf as a subterfuge for a romantic nationalism that had been percolating since the rise of the organic conception of the state and the emergence of Volkstudien earlier in the nineteenth century. The Jews who had found some political relief in the Weimar moment, with its parliamentary procedures and liberal constitution, would lose their political foothold as the German nation became identified with the mystical body of Christ, thus equating German history with sacred history. In this moment of "unity of altar, throne and Volk," according to Davies, Gott mit uns became both a Protestant and imperial slogan. [37]

In the Crusades initiated by Pope Urban II we have the most notorious nexus between religious authority and the justification for war and violence. Whether it took the form of recapturing territory in the Holy Land, fortifying borders in the Eastern Roman Empire or subjugating idiosyncratic expressions of Christian theology within Europe, the High Middle Ages saw the papacy mount a campaign of military conquest and vigilant vindication of Christian doctrine. This particular unity of religious fervor and militaristic mobilization was resurrected during the Bush Administration's campaign to suppress the contrived national security threat posed by Sadam Hussein's potential use of WMDs.

Bush, who personally declared the war on terror a "crusade", routinely received intelligence updates from the then Secretary of Defense Rumsfeld; memoranda with cover sheets that combined biblical quotations with inspirational images. First disclosed by GQ in May of 2009, it was suspected that Rumsfeld was fueling Bush's commitment with a dose of homegrown fundamentalist zeal. The neo-conservative think tanks had already been mobilized to preach that Bush's justification for war had solid religious roots. Rumsfeld's rousing memo campaign only fortified this religious justification for war. Among the illuminated intelligence updates there is one dated April 8, 2003, showing American tanks passing under one of the Swords of Qādisīyah or Victory Arches in Baghdad with the biblical lines, "Open the gates that the righteous nation may enter, the nation that keeps faith," Isaiah, 26.2. No doubt we can easily imagine that the primary faith of the conquered territory would be inclined to counter with a personalized religious riposte for the gathering western infidels. After all, these victory arches are named after a key battle in the Muslim expansion into Persia in 683CE. Ironically, the religious fundamentalism that fed the invasion of Iraq and instilled religious hostility placed an ancient indigenous Christian community at risk.

During the Iraq War, there were some in the military that did not conceal their belief that the conflict was a holy war sanctioned by their God. After the war Chris Kyle, the acclaimed sniper, gained notoriety for establishing an international business dedicated to honing military assault skills and for poignantly perishing at the hands of a fellow soldier with PTSD. While in service in Iraq, he and his companions decorated their helmets with their personal version of the Totenkopf. Kyle would adapt this international symbol of death for the logo of Craft International by placing a Templar's cross, which is suggestive of sniper crosshairs, at the right eye. With a crusader's cross tattooed on his left bicep, Chris Kyle went into battle shrouded in Christian symbolism.

William G. Boykin, because of his high rank and high-profile status in the military, created a dustup when he couched his political and military views in religious terms. Boykin stirred controversy when he pitted his Judeo-Christian God against a lesser Islamic God who personified Satan, when he challenged the Somali warlord and dissident, Osman Atto. Even George W. Bush would distance himself from his Under Secretary of Defense for Intelligence. Boykin was found to have overstepped his boundaries by his military superiors in some of his public proclamations, but even after his retirement from the military in 2007 he continued to battle what he viewed as the threat of Shariah law to the American way of life.

When George W. Bush conjured up a reincarnated axis of evil, political commentary characterized his dualistic mindset as Manichean and/or Zoroastrian.[38] However it was theologically parsed, this cosmic drama evoked Carl Schmitt's analysis of the true function of the state. Ever vigilant about delineating friends from enemies, Schmitt's core conception of the state meant that political unity required purging alien and potentially schismatic forces. Schmitt was responding to the unstable political situation in 1930s Germany, but these dualisms are so culturally and religiously entrenched that they can be spontaneously retrieved to suit rhetoric of fear and anarchy. When Bush described the war on terror as a crusade, he also announced that even if the threat of terror was eliminated, his personal spiritual reality would demand a long line of perpetual dualisms, at least until an ultimate messianic moment eliminates the cosmic polarity. Bush audaciously created a messianic role for himself so he was not a Manichean. A truly Manichean interpretation of these dueling forces does not entail the elimination of the other, since in Manicheism the structure of reality originates in the strife and tension produced by these antagonistic forces.

Given the theatrical scope of the violence perpetrated by religious zealots of all stripes, following Mark Juergensmeyer's prevailing analysis, it is more the case that these acts of violence are not intended to accomplish tactical objectives as much as they are perpetrated for their symbolic significance.[39] This only intensifies the pious quality of events that are already grounded in spiritual ideology, since as performance acts and spectacles they are logical extensions of liturgical rituals which are designed to spiritually and ideologically transform victims and perpetrators alike. As a drama steeped in patriotism, national pride and liturgy, when Rumsfeld made good on his threat of "shock and awe" the night sky over Baghdad lit up in March 2003 like a fireworks display and provided TV viewers with the same feelings that one can reverently enjoy on the 4th of July. After such an image, it is no wonder that there followed a rush to commercially employ the trademark "shock and awe" and that fireworks companies would be the first to seek advantage on the very day of the Baghdad bombing. Likewise, the attacks on the World Trade Centers on September 11, 2001, were charged with symbolism intended to demonstrate that the United States, despite the imposing structures which housed global commercial networks, was indeed vulnerable. The fact that the US had its own technology turned on itself lent the spectacle that much more ideological advantage. While this irony was not lost on the American public, perhaps the new nexus of technology, industry and religion was overlooked. This incestuous trinity meant that venerating any facet of the union probably made the worship of the god almighty dollar inevitable.

REFERENCES

Barke, R. (1986). Science Technology and Public Policy. Washington, DC: Congressional Quarterly Press.

Bernal, J. D. (1939). *The Social Function of Science*. London: Routledge and Kegan Paul.

Bird, K., & Sherwin, M. J. (2005). *American Prometheus The Triumph and Tragedy of J. Robert Oppenheimer*. New York: Alfred A Knopf.

Davies, A. T. (1988). *Infected Christianity*. Montreal: McGill-Queen's University Press.

Dickson, D. (1988). *The New Politics of Science*. Chicago: The University of Chicago Press.

Einstein, A. (n.d.). *Correspondence with Franklin Delano Roosevelt from August 2, 1939*. Retrieved from http://hypertextbook.com/eworld/einstein.shtml#first

Eisenhower, D. (n.d.). *D. Farewell address to the nation on January 17, 1961*. Retrieved from http://www.ourdocuments.gov/doc.php?flash=true&doc=90

Galbraith, J. K. (1967). The New Industrial State. Boston: Houghton Mifflin.

Goethe, J. W. v. (1988). *Faust, Part I* (German-English ed.). New York: Bantam Classics.

Guston, D. H. & Keniston, Kenneth. Editors. (1994). The Fragile Contract, University Science and the Government, Cambridge, MA: The MIT Press.

Haberer, J. (1969). *Politics and the Community of Science*. New York: Van Nostrand Reinhold.

Hofstadter, R. (1964). *The Paranoid Style in American Politics and Other Essays*. Cambridge, MA: Harvard University Press.

Jacob, M. C. (Ed.). (2000). *The Politics of Western Science*. Amherst, MA: Humanity Books.

Juergensmeyer, M. (2000). *Terror in the Mind of God: The Global Rise of Religious Violence*. Oakland, CA: University of California Press.

Miller, A. S., & Price, D. K. (1966). Review of The Scientific Estate. *Duke Law Journal*, 2(Spring), 622–629. doi:10.2307/1371547

Mooney, C. (2005). *The Republican War on Science*. New York: Basic Books.

Moreno, J. D. (2011). *The Body Politic, The Battle Over Science in America*. New York: Bellevue Literary Press.

Nash, R. F. (Eds.). (1990). American Environmentalism, Readings in Conservation History. New York: McGraw Hill.

Oppenheimer, R. (1953, July). Atomic Weapons and American Policy. *Foreign Affairs, 31*, 523–535.

Oppenheimer, R. (1955). *The Open Mind*. New York: Simon and Schuster.

Oreskes, N. (2004, June). Science and Public Policy: What's proof got to do with it? *Environmental Science & Policy, 7*(5), 369–383. doi:10.1016/j.envsci.2004.06.002

Oreskes, N., & Conway, E. M. (2010). The Merchants of Doubt. New York: Bloomsbury Press.

Pitzer, K. S. (n.d.). *Letter dated April 2, 1952*. Retrieved January 16, 2015 from http://vault.fbi.gov/rosenberg-case/robert-j.-oppenheimer

Price, D. (1965). *The Scientific Estate*. Cambridge, MA: The Bellknap Press of Harvard University.

Resek, C. (Ed.). (1964). *War and the Intellectuals*. Indianapolis, IN: Hackett Publishing Co.

Salomon, J.-J. (1973). *Science and Politics* (N. Lindsay, Trans.). Cambridge, MA: MIT Press.

Shulman, S. (2008). *Undermining Science, Suppression and Distortion in the Bush Administration*. Oakland, CA: University of California Press.

The White House. (1965). *Restoring the Quality of our Environment, Report of the Environmental Pollution Panel*. President's Science Advisory Committee.

Watkins, P. (n.d.). Filmography and an account of the controversy over the film *The War Game*. Retrieved January 10, 2015 from http://pwatkins.mnsi.net/warGame.htm

ENDNOTES

[1]   An early history of the Royal Society by Bishop Spratt in 1667, for example, indicated that neither religion nor politics were to be the subject of the Society's endeavors. Nature alone should be the subject of reflection, Joseph Haberer, *Politics and the Community of Science*, (New York: Van Nostrand Reinhold 1969):1. It was only in the early seventeenth century that scientists were publicly and professionally identified; by the mid-twentieth century scientists, like Robert Oppenheimer, had not only achieved celebrity status, they had an active role in government policy. This is not say that scientists were not aware of the ways in which science could contribute to the social order. Following Condorcet's enthusiasm for a relationship between science and political power, Antoine François, comte de Fourcroy (1755-1809) publicly promoted, in 1795, a role for science in the defense of the Republic. See *Rapport sur les arts qui ont servi à la defense de la Republique* cited in Jean-Jacques Salomon, translated by Nöel Lindsay. *Science and Politics*, (Cambridge: MIT Press, 1973): 16. Members of the early Royal Society also expressed enthusiasm for the potential for science-driven industry to ameliorate the extremes of excessive wealth and debilitating poverty and to produce wealth and what James R. Jacob refers to as a moral economy in "The Political Economy of Science in Seventeenth-Century England," *The Politics of Western Science*, edited by Margaret C. Jacob, (Amherst: Humanity Books, 2000): 45.

[2]   See Alan Beyerchen's "What we know about Nazism and Science" in *The Politics of Western Science*, edited by Margaret C. Jacob, 129-155. This article is a summary of Beyerchen's major work *Scientists Under Hitler, Politics and the Physics Community in the Third Reich* (New Haven: Yale University Press, 1977) which primarily treats of the Third Reich's effects on the community of physicists and the rise of "Aryan Physics" and "German Science" purged of so-called undesirables.

[3]   The progressive scientist J.D. Bernal presented an argument for government support of research and development in his book *The Social Function of Science* (London: Routledge and Kegan Paul, 1939). Bernal began working for the war effort in 1939 when he joined the Ministry of Home Security. His book describes the Marxist State as most congenial to the alliance of science and human welfare, 22.

[4]   See Paul R. Josephson's "Soviet Scientists in the State," in The Politics of Western Science, edited by Margaret C. Jacob, (Amherst: Humanity Books,2000): 104-128.

[5]   Led by the agronomist Trofim Lysenko, the movement purged information about genetics from textbooks until 1965. Josephson, 116.

[6]   There were US presidents who advocated for science as A. Hunter Dupree relates in "Science Policy in the United States: The Legacy of John Quincy Adams," *Minerva*, XXVIII (Autumn 1990), pp 259-71. John Quincy Adams promoted a national observatory and what would become the Smithsonian, and Theodore Roosevelt promoted science education, went on scientific expeditions and was a strong voice for conservationism

[7]   Jonathan D. Moreno, *The Body Politic, The Battle Over Science in America*, (New York: Bellevue Literary Press, 2011): 51-52.

[8]   See Stuart Leslie's discussion in "Science in Cold War America," in *The Politics of Western Science*, (Amherst: Humanity Books, 2000): 211-214. How political culture was informed by militaristic discourse was manifest in how the appropriation of Nazi rocket technology enabled American space science.

[9]   Anticipating a heated contemporary debate, Appendix Y4, Atmospheric Carbon Dioxide (p.121) clearly spells out how consumption of fossil fuels and increased carbon dioxide emissions will progressively raise the temperature near the surface of the earth.

[10]   See David H. Guston's and Kenneth Keniston's introduction "The Social Contract for Science," in *The Fragile Contract* (Cambridge, MA, The MIT Press, 1994): 24-26.

[11]   Richard Barke, *Science Technology and Public Policy*, (Washington, D.C.:Congressional Quarterly Press, 1986): 24.

[12]   Haberer, 196. Haberer refers to Oppenheimer's *The Open Mind* (New York, Simon and Schuster, 1955): 39 in which Oppenheimer weighed the value of participating in policy making to the organization of efficient team work.

[13]   Kenneth Sanborn Pitzer notified the FBI in 1952 that he had changed his position on Oppenheimer's loyalty which he pledged in 1947. In the public hearing for Oppenheimer Pitzer testified about policy differences with Oppenheimer but the FBI records indicate that he had information that changed his mind about Oppenheimer's loyalty. See the letter dated April 2, 1952, that can be found on the Web at http://vault.fbi.gov/rosenberg-case/robert-j.-oppenheimer

[14]   What Julius and Ethel Rosenberg would be executed for in 1953, Oppenheimer advocated in his famous policy statement in *Foreign Affairs* that same year; that is, the sharing of scientific information with America's allies. Oppenheimer was also suspected of being a courier and secreting documents out of Los Alamos for the Soviets at the time.

[15]   In 1955, when I first encountered Honest John missiles, the first thermonuclear weapons to be deployed on European soil, in nearby woods, I am sure that few people, if any, were aware of their potential threat. This was a time in which live bombs were still being unearthed in Europe, displaced populations were still unsettled and everyone was on a war footing since Soviet tanks were only thirty kilometers away.

[16]   Kai Bird and Martin J. Sherwin, *American Prometheus The Triumph and Tragedy of J. Robert Oppenheimer*, (New York: Alfred A Knopf, 2005): 274, 286, 288-289.

[17]   Peter Watkins's filmography and an account of the controversy over *The War Game* can be found at the following site: http://pwatkins.mnsi.net/warGame.htm

[18]   Einstein's letter dated August 2, 1939 apprised Roosevelt of the work of Szilard and Fermi and how the Germans might also be similarly involved in exploiting the power in uranium, which was abundant in Czechoslovakia.

[19]   Einstein's correspondence with Roosevelt is readily available on the Web and can be found at http://hypertextbook.com/eworld/einstein.shtml#first

[20]   Leslie's "Science in Cold War America," in *The Politics of Western Science*, edited by Margaret C. Jacob, (Amherst: Humanity Books, 2000): 200.

[21]   Randolph S. Bourne, "The State," in *War and the Intellectuals*, edited by Carl Resek, (Indianapolis: Hackett Publishing Co., 1964): 80-81.

[22]   Bourne, 81.

[23]   David Dickson, *The New Politics of Science*, (Chicago: The University of Chicago Press,1988):5.

[24]   Eisenhower delivered his farewell address to the nation on January 17, 1961, from the President's Office at 8:30 PM. The warning of the military industrial complex is the turn of phrase that is most memorable but threat of "the disastrous rise of misplaced power exists and will persist" is rarely quoted. Don K. Price's book is testimony to the gravity of Eisenhower's warning.

[25]   From a speech by Holmes titled *The Profession of the Law* delivered at Harvard University on February 17, 1886.

[26]   Salomon, 241. While Enlightenment science promised the progressive amelioration of society, Salomon argues that there has been an anarchic escalation of the instrumental function of science that can no longer be reined in by the power of knowledge itself. He compares this anarchic advance of technique and knowledge to the laissez-faire sensibility of capitalism in which we can expect corresponding injustices to prevail.

[27]   Goethe's Faust provides a literary warning. Before his encounter with Mephisto, Faust despairs that his father's scientific apparatus was unable to penetrate Nature's secrets; what she is unwilling to reveal on her own one cannot pry loose with "thumbscrews, wheel or lever." In his moment of despair he bears the effrontery of a grinning skull and turns his attention to a potion whose essence is derived from slumber-bearing flowers [Schlummersäfte], lines 675-695 in Johann Wolfgang von Goethe, *Faust, Part I*, (New York: Bantam Classics, 1988).

[28]   Naomi Oreskes, "Science and public policy: what's proof got to do with it?" Environmental Science & Policy 7 (2004) 369-383. Alfred Wegener first postulated his continental drift theory in 1912 on the basis of data from various sciences and the optics of the "jigsaw-puzzle" fit of the continents, but it was not until the mid-1980s that satellite interferometry resolved the issue once and for all.

[29]   Naomi Oreskes and Eric M. Conway, *The Merchants of Doubt*, (New York: Bloomsbury Press, 2010): 217.

[30]   Dorothy Nelkin, "The Public Face of Science: What Can We Learn from Disputes?," in *The Fragile Contract*, David Guston and Kenneth Keniston, editors, (Cambridge, MA, The Mit Press, 1994): 106-112).

[31]   In a repeat of the Rachel Carson controversy, Tozzi worked with the Kansas Corn Growers Association and a group called the Atrazine Network to challenge a study by the EPA which called into question the use of the herbicide, atrazine, which was suspected of causing harm to the endocrine systems of frogs. See Mooney pp. 108-109. David Dickson, The New Politics of Science, (Chicago: The University of Chicago Press,1988).

[32]   Hansen minced no words when he compared the Bush administration's behavior to Nazi Germany and the Soviet Union. As reported by Juliet Eilperin in The Washington Post on Saturday, February 11, 2006, Hansen also accused the National Oceanic and Atmospheric Administration for suppressing the voices of scientists studying Global Warming.

[33]   Shulman, Seth, *Undermining Science, Suppression and Distortion in the Bush Administration*, (University of California Press, 2006), p. 77. In a memo to the White House on Environmental Quality, Griles spelled out that a EIS draft should "focus on centralizing and streamlining coal-mining permitting" instead of thinking about the consequences of mountain removal.

[34]   On March 4, 2004, Howard Gardner was a guest following an interview with Marburger.

[35]   For all the inconsistent, inflammatory and uninformed things Donald Trump has said about climate change see the history that Jeremy Schulman, *Mother Jones*' senior news editor, provides in his extensive timeline, http://www.newsweek.com/timeline-every-ridiculous-thing-trump-has-said-about-climate-change-576238.

[36]   See "How Rollbacks at Scott Pruitt's E.P.A. Are a Boon to Oil and Gas," by Hiroko Tabuchi and Eric Lipton, The New York Times, May 20, 2017, https://www.nytimes.com/2017/05/20/business/energy-environment/devon-energy.html?hp&action=click&pgtype=Homepage&clickSource=story-heading&module=first-column-region&region=top-news&WT.nav=top-news&_r=0

[37]   Alan T. Davies, *Infected Christianity*, (Montreal: McGill-Queen's University Press, 1988): 42.

[38]   David Frum, George W. Bush's speechwriter, after a close study of Roosevelt's speech to Congress on December 8, 1941, was able to revive the threat of the axis powers and enshrine it in a universal struggle against what Bush would pronounce as the axis of evil. In both cases, there was a clear justification for war and the presumption that the enemy was evil personified. Bush was only returning the insult that opposing religious forces had already leveled against the West and the United States in particular, the enemy was Satan incarnate.

[39]   See Mark Juergensmeyer, *Terror in the Mind of God: The Global Rise of Religious Violence* (Oakland: University of California Press, 2000) particularly Part III, The Logic of Religious Experience, for an analysis of religious violence as performance and as an extension of ritual which is inherently designed to transform personal experience.

Chapter 4
Cyber–Bullies as Cyborg–Bullies

Tommaso Bertolotti
University of Pavia, Italy

Selene Arfini
University of Chieti and Pescara, Italy

Lorenzo Magnani
University of Pavia, Italy

ABSTRACT

This chapter advocates a re-introduction of the notion of cyborg in order to acquire a new perspective on studies concerning the development of human cognition in highly technological environments. In particular, it shows how the notion of cyborg properly engages cognitive issues that have a powerful resonance especially as far as social cognition is concerned, and may consequently provide a new tool for tackling the emergent safety issues concerning sociality mediated by the internet, and the moral panic occasionally surrounding it. The conclusion suggests how the notion of cyborg accounts for a better understanding and recognition of the victims of cyberbullying.

INTRODUCTION

There is no *ethics* in *cybernetics*. The missing *h* is a spy of the different etymology, but there is more to that. The Oxford American dictionary defines cybernetics as the "science of communications and automatic control systems in both machines and living things," and indeed its etymology is strictly bound to the notion of control. The root is that of the Greek verb *gubernan*. Does it sound familiar? It does, because it is the same origin from which *govern* developed, as the mastery of steering, of control. As such, the cybernetics was associated since the late 40s with the fast-developing computer science, especially as far as the evolution of control was concerned.

After being around for more than 70 years, the *cyber–* prefix sounds vintage, in a way. More precisely, it resonates with a vision of the future that belongs to the past. In the Western world, cybercafés remind us of a time where personal computers were less than widespread, let alone tablets and smartphones. The notion of cyberwar evokes vividly immersive, yet abstract, virtual realities in which opposing factions

DOI: 10.4018/978-1-5225-5094-5.ch004

fight each other, in something like Tron or Matrix. Popular culture, especially science-fiction, nearly appropriated the notion of cyborg, a cybernetic organism where the machine components can control the biological ones or vice versa: famous cyborgs range from the Terminators to Darth Vader, from Robocop to the Bicentennial Man.

What is less known to lay culture is that the notion of cyborg had an important theoretical value laden with a strong explanatory and predictive power, as proven for instance by Clark's and Haraway's perspectives. The aim of this paper is to show how the fertility of that notion, together with its ethical depths, still matter to current societal issues about how the Internet and computer mediated communications are affecting our lives.

While the bulk of our argumentation will focus on the behavior known as cyber-bullying, we will conclude by broadening our analysis to see how the theory of cyborg-bullies can shed light on topics such as international terrorism or foreign meddling in national elections.

A QUICK AND CRITICAL HISTORY OF THE CYBORG

The concept of cyborg was not coined in science-fiction, but by two scientists at the Rockland State Hospital, Orangeburg, N.Y.:

For the exogenously extended organizational complex functioning as an integrated homeostatic system unconsciously, we propose the term "Cyborg." The Cyborg deliberately incorporates exogenous components extending the self-regulatory control function of the organism in order to adapt it to new environments. (Clynes & Kline, 1960, p. 27)

Cyborgs (obtained by endowing men with transparent implants) were advocated for allowing man's adaptation to new environments – think of outer space – that either could not be adapted, or would require a major genetic (hence hereditary) adaptation, spontaneous or induced. It is important to note that since the beginning the notion of cyborg was connoted by what, today, could be seen as an *ecological-cognitive* necessity (Magnani, 2009). The cyborg's eco-cognitive nature derives from the stress on adaptation and on the cognitive functions: the artifactual additions have always been considered as something that ought to be transparent to one's cognition and often capable of expanding one's cognitive capabilities (Pino, 2010).

We will now briefly review two insightful positions in cyborg-related studies, which will be crucial for the rest of our argument: Donna Haraway's feminist theory (1991) and Andy Clark's cognitive-oriented approach (Clark, 2003).

Haraway's Uncomfortable Cyborg

Waite and Bourke (2013), exploring the cyborg-like features of Facebook, recently showed the untarnished fertility of Haraway's *Cyborg Manifesto*. While we will later return on its recent use, it is worth sparing a few words on the Haraway's contentions. As presented by Haraway herself, the theory is deeply embedded in Feminist arguments. Nevertheless, some of her takes may be discussed and accepted regardless of one's sharing the ideology they are meant to support. Haraway inserted in her definition of cyborg a trait that was seminal (or concerning an elite) at the time of her writing, but that is fully developed now: the strict dependence of our "cyborg an" nature on social cognition.

A cyborg is a cybernetic organism, a hybrid of machine and organism, a creature of social reality as well as a creature of fiction. Social reality is lived social relations, our most important political construction, a world-changing fiction. (Haraway, 1991, p. 149)

Haraway's further insight about the relationship between cyborgs and boundaries is perhaps the one that is most useful to the actual discourse. Her pivotal claim is that high-tech culture, epitomized by the actualization of the cyborg, openly challenges the dualisms that have been determining the practical and intellectual lives of human beings for millennia: "some of those troubling dualisms are self/other, mind/ body, culture/nature, male/female, civilized/primitive, reality/appearance, whole/part, agent/resource, maker/ made, active/passive, right/wrong, truth/illusion, total/partial, God/man" (p. 177). With this respect, it is extremely interesting to consider how the actual "being cyborgs" impacts our perception of the World, the way we make sense of our perceptual judgments and how we direct attention: it is the issue explored by Verbeek as *augmented intentionality* (2008), essential to phenomenology and cognitive science. As noticed by Waite and Bourke (2013), this denotation of the cyborg is most fitting to investigate actual phenomena such as the use of social networking websites (SNS), considering to what extent they habitually collapse dualisms and dichotomies such as the *real/virtual* one, which was left relatively unharmed in previous modalities of virtual pro-sociality (i.e. forums, chat rooms) which would foster a juxtaposition of different social worlds rather than a homogenous blend.

Andy Clark's Brilliant Intuitions and the Explosion of the Cyborg Concept

One of the largest debates in cyborg-related studies has been on where to set the line dividing what is a cyborg and what is not (yet) a cyborg. Inclusive and exclusive positions would argue about the use of extensions to one's physical and cognitive capabilities (esthetic or prosthetic) and the possibility (or lack thereof) to detach the extension. The most remarkable and successful attempt to go beyond this debate (and its dangerous scholasticism) was carried out by philosopher and cognitive scientist Andy Clark. His fundamental goal was to perform a gestalt shift and discard the iconic view (highly influenced by decades of sci-fi interweaving with philosophy and cognitive science) of the cyborg as an esthetically intriguing mixture of man and machine, and rather focus on the fact that:

[what] is special about human brains, and what best explains the distinctive features of human intelligence, is precisely their ability to enter into deep and complex relationships with non-biological constructs, props, and aids. This ability, however, does not depend on physical wire-and-implant mergers, so much as on our openness to information-processing mergers. Such mergers may be consummated without the intrusion of silicon and wire into flesh and blood, as anyone who has felt himself thinking via the act of writing already knows. (Clark, 2003, p. 5)

Clark's contention, explained by the oxymoronic expression depicting human beings as "natural-born cyborgs," is coherent with his studies concerning the extended mind and the distribution of cognition (Clark, 2008), and cannot be overlooked firstly because of the *naturalization* of the cyborg he performed. From his view, we can sensibly contend that, if we look for a cyborg, a student massively relying on her iPhone should be a satisfactory instance. From the perspective of distributed cognition, we can admit that there is indeed no qualitative shift from using pen and paper to spell out a complicate choice, to relying on one's smartphone to evaluate the best course of action.[1]

Nevertheless, our epistemologically critical view on Clark's theory is that albeit being coherent from a cognitive perspective, his convincing expansion of the concept of cyborg eventually *exploded* it, defusing the explanatory power concerning a cyborg that is not made of human plus *any* kind of cognitive enhancement, but rather depending on a peculiar kind of highly technological endowments.[2] In the next two sections we will first define this kind of cyborg (whose main characteristics are being *diffused* and being hybridized with forms of *artificial cognition*), and then show some of its possible applications in reframing a common safety concern such as cyber-bullying.

INTRODUCING THE DIFFUSED-AC CYBORG (DACC)

The Internet, and those devices that rely on it to the point of being meaningless offline, empower us to become this peculiar kind of cyborg.

Thanks to the Internet, our "selves" today largely consist of an externally stored quantity of data, information, images, and texts that concern us as individuals (sometimes produced by ourselves, sometimes not), and the result is a "cyborg" of both flesh and electronic data that relate to us. The "implant places" of this kind of cyborg consists in a series of devices we use actively and passively (from smartphones and computers to GPS receivers and highway cameras), which contribute to create a mutual interaction between our offline and online presence, making the two less and less separable. To have a better picture of this mechanisms, we could say that most alterations (of any kind, physical, geographical, emotional) of our offline variables provoke a modification in our online presence, which first of all cause in their turn a series of modifications of the original physical variables,[3] and secondarily (but not of least importance) they interfere with other online presences causing modification in the physical variables of other people.

The "traditional" idea of cyborg focused on the connection between a human being and high-tech artifacts. Andy Clark suggested that the *high* in high-tech is not qualitatively crucial in defining a cyborg. Our take is that two elements, relating to contemporary available technologies, do indeed matter in the individuation of at least a peculiar kind of cyborg concept whose explanatory power could much benefit the current debate. These are:

1. Technologies that diffuse and de-localize the activity of the subject, yet without transporting her in a cognitively separate world;
2. Technologies that let the user rely on more or less complex forms of artificial cognition.

This can be summed up by the notion of a *Diffused and Artificially-Cognizing Cyborg* (hence *DACC*). Let us analyze it in greater detail, starting with its *diffused* nature.

Since the early 2000's the virtualization of the Internet usage, first understood as the creation of a decoupled universe, witnessed an inverted trend. Popular websites and services such as MSN, Myspace and later Facebook and Twitter dramatically impacted our cyborgean nature in a way that would not affect our virtualization but rather the organism-side of the cyborg. Indeed, the text-and-image-based interfaces of websites such as Facebook, Twitter, Amazon, Wikipedia (or even the infamous Ask.fm) are scarcely impressing, and require far less ability than most video-games, no matter how intuitive the latter can be.[4] Yet, the former subtly play an incredible role in turning users into diffused cyborgs – not only at the cognitive level, but also at the perceptual and emotional one. As Waite and Bourke (2013) contend, referring to social networking sites:

In one instance, Facebook is a website clearly identifiable as virtual online space, but simultaneously, it is thoroughly embedded in, and informed by the material lives of the individuals without whom it would not exist in its current, recognizable form. [. . .] More than a 'space' or a 'destination', Facebook can be conceived of as a virtual network of interacting 'digital bodies' (p. 4).

Waite and Bourke, referring to a research they conducted in an Australian rural community, stressed the cyborgean nature of social networking itself: phones and computers are the gateways to a world that is not self-standing (as a Second Life, or World of Warcraft would be), but augments the material reality that people live in every day. Anticipating some conclusive remarks of this paper, it must be acknowledged how the subtlety displayed by social networking websites, and other kinds of pro-social technologies, in determining our existence as cyborgs begs for a cognitive and philosophical analysis. If being cyborgs meant for instance carrying around powerful implanted weaponry, then the effects would be apparent to anyone: conversely, we are mostly unaware of the effects of our diffused social colorization apart from brief moments of wonder after some peculiar coincidences, or – we will see it in the next section – when the outcomes become violent. As already suggested by Bertolotti and Magnani (2013), evolutionarily-oriented cognitive studies cannot be spared from having their say about the matter inasmuch as pro-social technology are effective by reproducing and simulating our social-cognitive affordances (for instance our inclination towards gossip), making the cyborgization of our selves utterly transparent.

Another reason justifying the cognitive interest in the diffused cyborg is still spelled out by Waite and Bourke (2013), in their contention that Facebook itself, as most SNS, can be conceptualized as a massive, loosely bordered, cyborg – blending human and cybernetic parts. In this sense, it may be valuable to add that the dualism-collapsing might of the cyborg does not only concern the human/machine dichotomy, but the self/other one as well. The diffused cyborg that prosocial technology is turning us into does not only absolve us from the physical boundaries – still replicating and augmenting a kind of sociality that is based upon the functioning of the "real world" one – but blends us in a real super-cyborg (just similar to the sociobiological notion of super-organism) not only as we epistemologically partake of an objectified shared knowledge base more real than any *collective unconscious* (real inasmuch it is hard stored on data servers), but also because by functions such as tagging and commenting one's possession over texts and images becomes in some cases undistinguishable from the possession of other users.[5]

Such widening of the field of our analysis, and of the agent it concerns, requires the introduction of the second element defining the DACC cyborg, namely the reliance on forms of *Artificial Cognition*. The Artificial Cognition capabilities displayed by the technologies we connect through (and with) can be extremely modest,[6] still they represent the possibility to react smartly to modifications in one's environment. Such cognitive capabilities to "make sense" of a given environment in order to pursue a certain scope may be perceived by users as *randomness*: this is especially true if we consider all of the cases in which an artificial system *suggests* something to the user, for instance, Amazon's recommendations or Facebook's *People you might know*.

The historical division between organic and inorganic – to rely once again on dualisms – would correspond to the division between constructor and constructed (in the lexicon of cognitive niche theory): decision-making processes (connected with cognition) could be only ascribed to biological organisms.

As shown macroscopically by the actual debate about the development of autonomous killer drones (Krishnan, 2009), the computational revolution introduced *constructed constructors*, artificially cognizing, non-biologic systems able to make autonomous assessments and forecasts, and initiate courses of actions (from simple safety recognition devices to elaborate financial applications capable of determining the fate of entire nations). The presence of such artifactual cognizers becomes further complicate once, as cyborgs, we start becoming hybridized with them, turning into beings that embed a biologic brain and several artificial forms of auxiliary cognition on which our primary cognition (often unawarely) relies. The awareness of being hybrid not only with artifactual extensions, but also with artifactual cognitive extensions interestingly relates with the cognitive literature concerning an agent's will: according to Benjamin Libet, the results of his famous experiment suggested that initiating a voluntary act was an unconscious cerebral process put in motion before the person consciously knew that she wanted to act: an involuntary neural impulse would be the process, not free will, as was widely held (Libet, Gleason, Wright, & Pearl, 1983). From this perspective, an individual feeling of conscious free will is just a superficial, after-the-fact explanation of other internal processes and does not reflect the actual mechanism that generates action. It is then extremely thought provoking to read the hybridization of humans (whose will is already cognitively compound) with external artificial cognizers in the light of Daniel Dennett's review of Libet's experiment:

Once you distribute the work done by the homunculus (on this case, decision making, clock-watching, and decision-simultaneity judging) in both space and time in the brain, you have to distribute the moral agency around as well. You are not out of the loop; you are the loop. (Dennett, 2003)

In agreement with Clark's takes, once could contend that the *loop* has not changed qualitatively, but just became wider so to accommodate the new artificial cognitive wirings that instead of being in the person's nervous system, or in the interplay between a person and some cognitive delegations around her (epistemic mediators such as paper and pencil), are diffusely allocated partially in her device and partially in some servers around the globe.

Consider the SNS user: we showed how it could be convincingly framed as a *diffused* cyborg, but that was not the end to it. In order to function, the super-cyborg relies on a series of standalone algorithms handling searches (and their priorities), reports, suggestions, and order of the news. Facebook, for instance, actively impacts the "real lives" of its cyborg users (who in turn are users because of the impact that Facebook has in their real lives), but they are not necessarily aware of how, in their being cyborgs, their lives are partially determined by the artificial cognitive processes implanted in the network they holistically partake of, for instance deciding which updates are more "important" and showing them first. One picture seen on Facebook can trigger an unthinkable chain reaction in a user's life, but it was the system (hybridized with the user) that picked what picture would be more relevant for the user to see first.

Such reflections can be easily extended to most contemporary technologies mediating pro-sociality through the Internet. Whereas the diffusion of remote communication systems (mail, telephone, text messages, emails. . .)[7] turned human beings into diffused cyborgs (it's not impossible, in agreement with Clark's idea, to imagine a Renaissance man as cyborg made up of body, paper, and ink as he would engage in correspondence with his fellows over Europe), contemporary technologies add the artificial cognition element, determining users as *Diffused and Artificially-Cognizing Cyborgs*. This is not only true as far as social cognition is concerned, but also the reliance on geo-localization and guiding devices (assessing road conditions and making forecasts about traffic and weather), or eCommerce: basically, just as SNS make human beings into social DACCs, advanced eCommerce platforms such as Amazon turn consumers into DACC consumers, because of the integration between the buyer's desires, her possibilities and their processing operated by the website. The same can be said of most contemporary and foreseen "augmented" experiences, as they will rely on a diffusion of the self through the internet in order to achieve a maximized experience in her real life, but this can happen only if massively supported by transparent artificial decision makers assisting the user, ranging from contemporary artificial cognition to a full blown artificial intelligence.

CYBER-BULLIES AS CYBORG-BULLIES

The aim of this section is to show the utility of the reintroduction of the (DACC) cyborg notion in the current debate, by applying it to the widespread issue in Internet-related safety known as cyber-bullying. Cyber-bullying – that is bullying carried out through means related to the Internet, that is via Instant Messages, Social Networks and so on – has received ever-growing attention by the media, and by political and intellectual actors.[8]

The standard, and not fruitless, approach usually involves a techno-ethical reflection, dealing with processes of e-empowerment, digital literacy and pedagogical issues, together with a psychological and social enquiry connecting the dimension of real-life bullying with its online counterpart (Rigby & Smith, 2011; Sontag, Clemans, Graber, & Lyndon, 2011; Kowalski, Limber, & Agatston, 2012). The latter research shows interesting but relatively unpractical correlations between online and offline bullying, leaving vast percentages in which the two phenomena do not overlap that are still to be efficaciously explained in order to find a long-term solution to the threat. A viable idea would be, indeed, to reframe cyber-bullying as cyborg-bullying, of course understanding the cyborg in its DACC conceptions described so far. A number of reasons seem to favor this perspective shift:

1. The rupture of moral proximity brought about by computer screens and anonymous avatars is often advocated as one of the causes of the lack of empathy which results in particular verbal violence, threats and so on that would not be carried out so openly in real life. Our claim is that this presumed moral gap is a biased artifact of the analysis, informed by the honest (but untrue) answers of the subjects: what is perceived as a distance between the virtual world and real life is actually caused by the loss of references of the biological organisms (with the evolutionary inherited endowments concerning sub moralities and the enforcement of coalitions (Bingham, 1999; Magnani, 2011)), and the acquisition of the new references (social, too) pertaining to the DACC cyborg. Empirical research carried out to study "the transferability of basic interpersonal affect, or affinity/disaffinity, from nonverbal to verbal communication accompanying the alternative communication channels of [Face to Face] versus [Computer Mediated Communication]." Walther, Loh, & Granka (2005, p. 56) seem to confirm that moral proximity is indeed not impaired by the lack of physical presence:

Although concerns about the lack of cues in CMC may persist with regard to determining participants identity, or the reduction of message equivocality, as functions of bandwidth and interface design, affinity issues may be different and readily translatable from one cue system to another. (p. 58)

2. Considering what we exposed so far, we could indeed see how this configuration equals setting a ring, a fight arena between human beings that became DACCs, as they obtained an ubiquitous access to their social cognition (and its enhancement by bits of artificial cognition) and, in return, paid the price of forsaking (at least as long as they act-as-DACCs) the real lives subdivision that separate them but also protect them, and the groups they belong to, from each other (Bertolotti & Magnani, 2013; Debatin, Lovejoy, Horn, & Hughes, 2009).

3. Many instances of cyber-bullying and cyber-violence seem affected by an element of randomness and self-righteousness, where on the one hand it becomes hard to tell the aggressor from the victim, and on the other hand the perpetrated violence embeds instances of extreme moral reactions following a perception of relevance that is different from that of the "real life." The perceived randomness depends on the artificial cognitive processes embedded in the DACC, presenting certain information instead of others to users. Furthermore, as the boundaries between DACC and groups of DACCs do not reflect those between real-life humans (because of their diffused nature, as seen in the previous section), a user might find that a remote event justifies her moral and violent intervention against another DACC, who is not "remote" in the cyberspace they connect within. Such a view does not justify, but explains why teenagers engage in violent mobbing aggressions against "peers" they never met on websites such as *Ask.fm*, or why so many Twitter users thought they had to pursue the public shaming and threatening of Alicia Ann Lynch, a 22-year-old from Michigan, who tweeted and Instagrammed a photo of herself at work dressed as a Boston Marathon bombing victim for Halloween 2013.

4. The different perception of relevance is also due to the fact that whereas real-life human beings cope with a diversity of truth regimes, where truth is generally perceived as less reliable as it gets further from its source, DACCs can rely on a copy-and-paste truth regime, which does not let distance (both chronological and physical) defuse the truth-value, and hence the pragmatic relevance, of the information they stumble upon (Bertolotti, 2011).

Considering all this, it might be indeed interesting to consider instances of Internet-related violence such as cyber-bullying (but the paradigm can easily accommodate other examples) as clashes between cyborgs. This is particularly interesting as far as the incidents – albeit they induce serious real-life consequences – sometimes involve no real-life relationship between the victim and the aggressor who, in their real-life existences, have no connection whatsoever.

Conferences, workshops and studies focusing on (real or perceived) emergencies relating to Internet safety, such as cyber-bullying, have been ever increasing in the recent past, also as the media coverage becomes more and more intensive. Most analyses (and the solutions they inform) tend to concentrate on the aging distinction between an online and an offline world. This dualism more or less explicitly serves the purpose of reiterating pedagogical and moral axiologies tacitly connecting *online* and *offline* with *safe* and *unsafe*, fundamentally reverberating the dualism between good and evil.

The increasing corporate effort to make the Internet a *safer* place (Beaucherc, 2013, 2017) can only be integrated with the awareness that we are not users separate from it, but rather our cognitive endowments were prone to seamlessly connected with the possibilities offered by the new technologies, especially (so far) in as much as social cognition is concerned.

Such a seamless connection between humans and technology has been studied since long as defining the dualism-collapsing notion of cyborg, but the issues at stake might benefit from the explanatory power of a particular concept: the *Diffused and Artificially-Cognizing Cyborg* (DACC). This concept describes, and fosters the reflection on how contemporary human beings, thanks to a number of devices mediating their Internet use, experience the cyborgization not as a virtualization but as an augmentation of their real-lives, actualized by the *diffusion* of their selves beneath the geographical and chronological constraints, but still connecting with similarly diffused humans, and whose interactions are sensibly determined by a transparent layer of artificial cognitive processing.

If Internet-related unpleasant issues can be interestingly reframed as clashes between cyborgs, the protean essence of the cognitive links bonding humans and the Internet are so unapparent that the lack of awareness concerning one's cyborg nature can be seen as the cause of many of the direst consequences of Internet use. Therefore, future efforts to establish digital literacy should first of all aim at teaching users to be aware of, and to explore, their very *being cyborg*.[9]

A BROADER VIEW

Being cyborg-bullies does not only affect teenagers as they replicate online, *as cyborgs*, certain behaviors that are generally not approved of in real life. Anyone can be a cyborg-bully as far as we develop behaviors that are massively influenced by our way of relying on the Internet for communication and decision-making activities. Ultimately, cyborg-bullying is about acquiring a leverage that could hardly be achieved in the offline world. And, as the "cybernetics" we set off from included the notion of automated control, a specificity of cyborg-bullying is its potential to replicate automatically, its self-enforcing nature. Let us star with some mild examples to understand harsher ones.

I get some bad food at a restaurant, or the service is not as nice as I would like it to be. I can either speak up to the waiter or the owner, or I can post a bad review. Reviews, idealistically, should equally guide peers to good spots and steer them away from bad ones. Realistically, the level of goodness or badness that prompts us into writing a review is not symmetric. In other words, reviews are a double-edged weapon for businesses because while food, service, accommodation and so on and so forth have to be really outstanding to prompt us into writing a positive review, it takes a much lesser amount of badness for us to grab a keyboard and blast away (always trying to read as civilized as possible). The review is supposed to make fellow customers or travelers avoid the same situation we found ourselves into, but as a matter of fact we are essentially trying to get back at the business. We are offloading our resentment and anger on the Internet knowing that, as other people will supposedly see it, the power of our negative remark will be far greater than if we spoke to the manager or dropped them an email. There is also no corrective goal in the review, since we are extremely unlikely to check after a few weeks if our comment made a difference in how the business is handled.

Something similar goes on when we vent on social networks tagging the customer service of this and that business who did us wrong. We know the public dimension makes it is more efficacious than if we privately addressed the issues, but at the same time we are indeed engaging in some cyborg-bully like behavior, namely taking advantage of the medium affordances to the extent that they lay in our favor. After all, this is akin to what is shown by Rigby and Smith (2011), as they suggest that online bullying can take the form of revenge bullying against real life bullies: in everyday consumer dynamics, we feel "bullied" by the businesses we buy from, who stand on the higher ground, and we bully them back in an attempt to revert the power dynamics.

Cyber warfare, CITA, sometimes fathomed as the aseptic work of military-hackers able to shut down vital infrastructures in enemy countries stealthily and without unneeded bloodshed, has recently proved to take the much uglier face of cyber bullying. Instead of shutting down utilities, state sponsored hackers infiltrate emails and personal accounts to harvest details to be used for crushing the reputation of the adversaries. What happened during the 2016 US electoral campaign is indeed much more similar to a large-scale brawl between geeky teenagers than to War 2.0.

Last but not least, the recent wave of terror caused (or sponsored) by the so-called Islamic State revealed the ability to co-opt many of the tactics used by teenage bullies, namely leveraging the public appearance and media resonance of one's deed in order to add, literally, insult to injury.

These cases we just described do differ, of course, and a lot, in magnitude, scopes, and effects. Posting an angry review won't make anyone a terrorist, not even close. Perhaps it will even do good and avoid someone a nasty sickness. What we wanted to point out, though, is how notwithstanding their differences these examples all partake of the bullying mechanism, namely the cyborg-bullying mechanism. When engaging in violent behaviors online, our psychological and computer-based networks influence, not to say control, each other. New opportunities of leveraging reach and effect trigger new ways of acting because we think as cyborg, namely as diffused-artificially cognizant cyborgs. Terrorism has always been about resonance, but since the quasi-complete diffusion of social networking websites, terrorists have developed an esthetic compulsion to think and stage their deeds so to obtain, graphically and verbally, the highest and scariest reach, to the point of being dubbed "pornographic." Again, we are not on the same level, but the dynamic is the same as that of a bunch of teens ganging up against a peer making sure they have a "good angle" to film the beating, which will be later shared on the appropriate social media.

All of these different phenomena can be comprehended in the definition of *cyborg-bullying* for the valuable extension of the concept with respect to the milder and stricter version of *cyberbullying*. Indeed, the definition of cyborg-bullying, by paying attention to the medium of the violence as the cognitive shaper of the violent acts, not only improves the comprehension of the different possibilities that a violent SNS user could exploit, but also provides a better understanding of what kind of damage is actually caused by violent acts online. In the next and final section, we will then discuss how the performance of cyborg-bullying acts specifically affects other users' online vulnerability.

CONCLUDING REMARKS: CYBORG-BULLIES AND CYBER-VICTIMS

Online vulnerability has been so far used as an umbrella concept to include different ways individuals can experience loss of psychological, reputational, or physical wellbeing as a result of engaging in online activities (Davidson and Martellozzo, 2013). It is the reciprocal concept to the traditional notion of cyberbullying, since the latter describes different ways in which internet users exploit "ICTs to support intentional, recurrent and mean-spirited actions with the aim of harming others" (Akbulut et al., 2010, p. 47); perform behaviors designed to "embarrass, threaten, hurt, or exclude" (Bhat, 2008, p. 58); begin "repeated, unwanted, hurtful, harassing, and/or threatening interaction through electronic communication media" (Rafferty & Vander Ven, 2014, p. 364). All of these traditional definitions aim at describing the activities of cyberbullying as the acts that primarily cause online vulnerability in the same way in which traditional bullying actions cause harassment and humiliation in the offline world. The good of these definitions is the focus on the violence of the actions performed, and the connection to the online vulnerability pays attention to the damage these kinds of activities involve and cause. Their downside is represented by the looser reference to the particular means of the offence, namely online tools and SNS in particular, which, as we argued before, completely transform the possibilities of action of the perpetrators. However, as cyberbullying can be reframed as cyborg-bullying by extending our view on the cognitive possibilities that SNS give to the Internet users, by the same measure we can also reconsider the way target users can be affected by online vulnerability.

Thus, the point here is to consider what an actual cyborg-bully can do online to the targeted user and what the latter can do to repel the attack. As we already mentioned, the use of SNS does not represent the utilization of a mere tool for communication in the hands of the users, but it consists in obtaining a ubiquitous access to their social cognition and its enhancement through the engagement with artificial cognition. Users of SNS, by becoming cyborg, achieve ways to generate and frame their social boundaries and connections through the use and modification of online platforms according to their preferences and style. As highlighted by Buglass *et al.* (2017), this means engaging in practices of self-presentation, self-exposure, and self-promotion: these activities could lead to positive achievements, namely the healthy exploitation of the richness of the networks, as well as negative outcomes, such as the risk of increasing the individuals' online vulnerability. The cyborg-bully plays a dramatic role in shifting the balance between these two extreme outcomes for the targeted users. Experiences such as the humiliating diffusion of personal data or repeated online harassments can foment distress in the targeted users, such as the fear of having some personal data shared online or the fear of missing out –the famous FOMO, (Buglass *et al.*, 2017)– which can seriously compromise a healthy approach to the use of SNS for the targeted users. Cyborg-bullies, by increasing the online vulnerability of other user, jeopardize the latter's possibilities to actually become self-sufficient and confident DACC. They thwart her very *being cyborg*. This is showed by the fact that more than often the only possibility perceived by the victims of online bullying to escape their attackers is to leave the platforms where they were harassed. Leaving the platform means to reject the possibility to benefit from a cognitive and social enhancement that can be achieved by the advanced engagement with SNS.

When referring to cyborg-bullying we should therefore continue to use the term cyber-victims for their targets. This specification both reckons a sensible adjustment of the concept of cyberbullying and an increased value for the damage suffered by the victims. The cyber-victims have no chance to develop into functional DAACs and the loss they feel should be considered more than just online vulnerability, which is defined in terms of psychological, reputational, or physical damage, but also as eco-cognitive disadvantage and limitation. Moreover, these terminological clarifications suggest the need for interventions that do not just aim at improving the safety of the online environments, but invite the creation of programs to educate users to the self-aware engagement with SNS and provide them equal possibilities to actually become functional and confident Diffused and Artificial-Cognizing Cyborgs.

REFERENCES

Akbulut, Y., Sahin, Y. L., & Eristi, B. (2010). Development of a scale to investigate cybervictimization among online social utility members. *Contemporary Educational Technology*, *1*, 46–59.

Beauchere, J. (2013). Online 'safety' as a state of being. *Microsoft on the Issues*. Retrieved from http://bit.ly/1eiOJCE

Beauchere, J. (2017). *Encouraging Digital Civility: What Companies and Others Can Do*. Academic Press.

Bertolotti, T. (2011). Facebook has it: The irresistible violence of social cognition in the age of social networking. *International Journal of Technoethics*, 2(4), 71–83. doi:10.4018/jte.2011100105

Bertolotti, T., & Magnani, L. (2013). A philosophical and evolutionary approach to cyber-bullying: Social networks and the disruption of submoralities. *Ethics and Information Technology*, 15(4), 285–299. doi:10.100710676-013-9324-3

Betts, L. R. (2016). *Cyberbullying: Approaches*. Springeralden, MA: Consequences, and Interventions. doi:10.1057/978-1-137-50009-0

Bhat, C. S. (2008). Cyber bullying: Overview and strategies for school counsellors, guidance of officers, and all school personnel. *Australian Journal of Guidance & Counselling*, 18(01), 53–66. doi:10.1375/ajgc.18.1.53

Bingham, P. M. (1999). Human uniqueness: A general theory. *The Quarterly Review of Biology*, 74(2), 133–169. doi:10.1086/393069

Buglass, S. L., Binder, J. F., Betts, L. R., & Underwood, D. M. (2017). Motivators of online vulnerability: The impact of social network site use and FOMO. *Computers in Human Behavior*, 66, 248–255. doi:10.1016/j.chb.2016.09.055

Clark, A. (2003). *Natural-Born Cyborgs. Minds, Technologies, and the Future of Human Intelligence*. Oxford, UK: Oxford University Press.

Clark, A. (2008). *Supersizing the mind. embodiment, action, and cognitive extension*. Oxford, UK: Oxford University Press. doi:10.1093/acprof:oso/9780195333213.001.0001

Clynes, M., & Kline, N. (1960, September). Cyborgs and space. *Astronautics*, 26–27, 74–76.

Davidson, J., & Martellozzo, E. (2013). Exploring young people's use of social networking sites and digital media in the internet safety context: A comparison of the UK and Bahrain. *Information Communication and Society*, 16(9), 1456–1476. doi:10.1080/1369118X.2012.701655

Debatin, B., Lovejoy, J. P., Horn, A. K., & Hughes, B. N. (2009). Facebook and online privacy: Attitudes, behaviors, and unintended consequences. *Journal of Computer-Mediated Communication*, 15(1), 83–108. doi:10.1111/j.1083-6101.2009.01494.x

Dennett, D. (2003). *Freedom Evolves*. New York: Viking.

Dredge, R., Gleeson, J., & de la Piedad Garcia, X. (2014). Presentation on Facebook and risk of cyberbullying victimization. *Computers in Human Behavior*, 40, 16–22. doi:10.1016/j.chb.2014.07.035

Faiola, A., & Matei, S. A. (2005). Cultural cognitive style and web design: Beyond a behavioral inquiry into computer-mediated communication. *Journal of Computer-Mediated Communication*, 11(1), 375–394. doi:10.1111/j.1083-6101.2006.tb00318.x

Haraway, D. (1991). A cyborg manifesto: Science, technology, and socialist feminism in the late twentieth century. In D. Haraway (Ed.), *Simians, Cyborgs and Women: The Reinvention of Nature* (pp. 149–182). New York, NY: Routledge.

Kowalski, R. M., Limber, S. P., & Agatston, P. W. (2012). Cyberbullying: Bullying in the Digital Age (2nd ed.). Malden, MA: Academic Press.

Krishnan, A. (2009). *Killer robots: Legality and ethicality of autonomous weapons*. Burlington, VT: Ashgate.

Libet, B., Gleason, C. A., Wright, E. W., & Pearl, D. K. (1983). Time of conscious intention to act in relation to onset of cerebral activity (readinesspotential): The unconscious initiation of a freely voluntary act. *Brain*, *106*, 623–642. doi:10.1093/brain/106.3.623 PMID:6640273

Magnani, L. (2007). *Morality in a Technological World. Knowledge as Duty*. Cambridge, UK: Cambridge University Press. doi:10.1017/CBO9780511498657

Magnani, L. (2009). *Abductive Cognition: The Epistemological and Eco-Cognitive Dimensions of Hypothetical Reasoning*. Berlin: Springer. doi:10.1007/978-3-642-03631-6

Magnani, L. (2011). *Understanding Violence. Morality, Religion, and Violence Intertwined: a Philosophical Stance*. Berlin: Springer.

Pino, B. (2010). Re-assessing ecology of tool transparency in epistemic practices. *Mind & Society*, *9*(1), 85–110. doi:10.100711299-010-0071-4

Rafferty, R., & Vander Ven, T. (2014). "I hate everything about you": A qualitative examination of cyberbullying and on-line aggression in a college sample. *Deviant Behavior*, *35*(5), 364–377. doi:10.1080/01639625.2013.849171

Rigby, K., & Smith, P. K. (2011). Is school bullying really on the rise? *Social Psychology of Education*, *14*(4), 441–455. doi:10.100711218-011-9158-y

Rizza, C., & Pereira, A. G. (Eds.). (2013). *Social networks and Cyber-bullying among teenagers: EU Scientific and Policy report*. Publications Office of the European Union.

Sontag, L. M., Clemans, K. H., Graber, J. A., & Lyndon, S. T. (2011). Traditional and cyber aggressors and victims: A comparison of psychosocial characteristics. *Journal of Youth and Adolescence*, *40*(4), 392–404. doi:10.100710964-010-9575-9 PMID:20680425

Verbeek, P.-P. (2008). Cyborg intentionality: Rethinking the phenomenology of human–technology relations. *Phenomenology and the Cognitive Sciences*, *7*(3), 387–395. doi:10.100711097-008-9099-x

Waite, C., & Bourke, L. (2013). Using the cyborg to re-think young people's uses of Facebook. *Journal of Sociology*. DOI: 10.1177/1440783313505007

Walther, J. B., Loh, T., & Granka, L. (2005). Let me count the ways: The interchange of verbal and non-verbal cues in computer-mediated and face-to-face affinity. *Journal of Language and Social Psychology*, *24*(1), 36–65. doi:10.1177/0261927X04273036

ENDNOTES

1. Magnani (2007) carried out a thorough reflection about the increasing hybridization of human beings, considering its philosophical and cognitive implications. One of the cores of the analysis, resonating in this paper, concerned the lack of knowledge possessed by users facing with ever more intelligent devices – a lack of awareness coupled with a similar lack of the necessary technical skills that would allow humans to responsibly navigate the technological present.

2. Paradoxically, Clark himself anticipated certain scenarios that materialized a decade later, such as the "Datagate" scandal concerning the NSA, or the ethically arguable conditions of Amazon workers, whose efficacy is measured by tracking devices they have to wear and which monitor their movements. The paradox rests in the fact that the concept of cyborg was not used to achieve a better understanding of these situations, while it could have been of great use, as claimed by this paper.

3. Consider this example. You develop an interest in apiculture (offline), and browse for some manuals on the Internet (online). Being intercepted by some e-seller, your new interest modifies your online profile, and makes the e-seller's algorithms recommend you a book on mead brewing. You would have never thought of that but you buy it and become a passionate mead brewer (offline).

4. Faiola & Matei (2005) proposed cognitive correlations between culture and ease of use of determinate web design: these studies further corroborate contentions about the distribution of cognitive tasks between users and the Internet.

5. This uncertainty is legally reverberated by the Terms and Conditions users must subscribe to, usually conceding to the SNS the non-exclusive, unlimited license for what is posted online: albeit legally meaningful, this just enforces the notion of a super-cyborg (specifically a network-cyborg) transcending the individual (yet cyborgized) selves into a greater entity.

6. That is why we prefer this expression to the more demanding Artificial Intelligence.

7. It can be argued that also the reception of emails and text messages depend on services establishing the priority of their recovery, but they do not rank the relevance. The SPAM filters, conversely, can be considered as a kind of pro-social mediator inasmuch as they perform kinds of guessing and establish a course of action affecting the users real-life.

8. Also a EU report, deriving from a number of studies and a workshop reuniting experts from different disciplines, was released on the matter (Rizza & Pereira, 2013).

9. This paper was originally presented at the 36th Annual Conference of the Cognitive Science Society, held in Quebec City (Quebec, Canada) from the 23rd to the 26th of July 2014.

Chapter 5
The Techoethical Ethos of Technic Self–Determination:
Technological Determinism as the Ontic Fundament of Freewill

Francesco Albert Bosco Cortese
Institute for Ethics and Emerging Technologies, USA

ABSTRACT

This chapter addresses concerns that the development and proliferation of human enhancement technologies (HET) will be dehumanizing and a threat to our autonomy and sovereignty as individuals. The chapter argues contrarily that HET constitutes nothing less than one of the most effective foreseeable means of increasing the autonomy and sovereignty of individual members of society. Furthermore, it elaborates the position that the use of HET exemplifies—and indeed even intensifies—our most human capacity and faculty, namely the desire for increased self-determination, which is referred to as the will toward self-determination. Based upon this position, the chapter argues that the use of HET bears fundamental ontological continuity with the human condition in general and with the historically ubiquitous will toward self-determination in particular. HET will not be a dehumanizing force, but will rather serve to increase the very capacity that characterizes us as human more accurately than anything else.

INTRODUCTION

The present article first articulates an ontology of self-determination based upon self-modification and self-modulation (i.e. deliberate modification or modulation of the material processes and systems constituting our bodies and brains), characterizing self-determination as a modality (i.e. that there can be degrees of self-determination, or that it isn't an absolute, all-or-none category) that encompasses any act of manipulating the material systems and processes underlying the body and mind so as to effect certain changes to the emergent operation, function or capacities of the body or to the modes of experience, thought and perception available to the mind.

DOI: 10.4018/978-1-5225-5094-5.ch005

Secondly, it illustrates (1) how HET constitutes a distinct modality of self-determination, which we refer to as technic[1] self-determination, that is encompassed by the broader ontology of self-determination previously articulated, (2) how technic self-determination nevertheless bears ontological continuity with existing and historical (predominantly non-technological) means and modalities of self-determination as practiced by contemporary and historical humans, as well as (3) why technic self-determination (and the use of HET in general and neurotechnology in particular that underlie it) constitute humanity's most effective and most extensive means of self-determination, and thus of *increasing* their available capacity for self-determination.

Thirdly, the article turns to the topic of human nature and human dignity, arguing that it is humanity's will toward self-determination that best distinguishes humans as such, and accordingly that the will toward self-determination constitutes the best available candidate for a universal human condition.

Fourthly, the article analyzes the extent with which limited availability of HET across different geographic, sociopolitical and economic classes could cause a net decrease in society's capacity for self-determination by giving those who can afford HET an increased capacity for technological self-determination at the expense of those who cannot.

The article concludes by arguing (1) that technic self-determination (and the use of HET that underlies it) will not be dehumanizing because HET will simply serve to increase our *existing* degree of and capacity for self-determination and (2) that HET bears ontological continuity with the existing tools and techniques for affecting the substratum of self, and as such with human nature itself. Quite to the contrary of critics concerned with the potential for dehumanization and a violation of human dignity, technic self-determination and HET will maintain, continue and extend rather than rend asunder that which makes us most human.

Technoethics is an interdisciplinary field focusing on the moral and ethical aspects and repercussions of technology upon society (Luppicini and Adell, 2008; Luppicini, 2010). While the field encompasses all technology and is in no way limited to emerging technologies in general and HET in particular, such technologies are of particular importance to the field due to their heightened capacity to increase the physical and mental capacities of individuals, and due to the stark and intense ethical issues that HET are enshrouded by. The field has never been so poignant and prescient, and the need for its continued development so pressing, when one considers the ever-increasing rapidity with which advances in science, technology and medicine are occurring, and due to the increasing ever-increasing gravity of the ethical issues surrounding such advances. Today more than ever before technology serves as a prosthetic Prometheus, holding the potential to turn man into titan, and the ethicacy of this potential begs our attention. This chapter presents an ontology of self-determination that connects the timeless human drive toward self-determination to technology in general and emerging technologies in particular, arguing that particular sets of emerging technologies (with particular emphasis on HET) will increase humanity's capacity for self-determination to as-yet unseen heights, and subsequently connects this thesis with the modalities of self-determination in general and technological (or more specifically technic) modalities of self-determination in particular that humanity has used to effect self-determination throughout its history. The present article's relevance to technoethics lies in the extent with which a technologically-mediated increase in humanity's capacity for self-determination, both as individuals and as a society, is ethical and desirable. Summarily, the article argues in favor of the ethicacy of an increased capacity for self-determination via the use and proliferation of HET in general and neurotechnology in particular, positing that rather than constituting a disruption of the human condition this new form of technic self-determination constitutes an ontological continuation of the human condition. The article's fourth topic – namely, the extent with which the availability of such HET in general and neurotechnology in particular might be limited to certain geographic, sociopolitical and/or economic classes, and what this might mean for the ultimate ethicacy and desirability of its development – is of particular relevance to the field of technoethics because one of its central issues as it pertains to HET in particular is the possibility that such emerging technologies (which pose the unquestionable potential to increase the capacity of its users to determine the controlling circumstances of society and the world) might be of limited availability to large portions of humanity, to the net-detriment of society as a whole.

BACKGROUND

Determinism and Self-Determination

The 'free will problem' is almost as almost old as philosophy itself. The posed problem is a fatal inconsistency between freewill and causal determinism that necessitates at least one to be illegitimate or inexistent. Causal determinism can be defined as the thesis that every event is the necessary result of prior events combined with the laws of nature. If everything in the universe has been predetermined, then it would appear that free will is an illegitimate notion. On the other hand, if freewill exists, then determinism must be false (because free will couldn't exist with true determinism). This notion is known as 'the dilemma of determinism'. The dilemma refers to the fact that either free will or determinism *must* be false.

There are several positions one can take in this philosophical debate. Incompatibilists accept the premises of the dilemma and argue that one must be false; most incompatibilists side with determinism, arguing that free will must not exist (Inwagen, 1975). Compatibilists argue that freewill and determinism are not incompatible, arguing that the dilemma of determinism is a false dilemma to begin with, and that causal determinism does not illegitimate the notion of free will.

Some compatibilists wrongly turn to determinism's antithesis, indeterminism, to solve the dilemma, positing that indeterminism, by invalidating determinism, should allow free will to legitimately exist. But we would agree with many others in arguing that this is no better than determinism. "Indeterminism does not confer freedom on us: I would feel that my freedom was impaired if I thought that a quantum mechanical trigger in my brain might cause me to leap into the garden and eat a slug" (Smart and Haldane, 2003). Joshua Greene puts this position thusly:

There are three standard responses to the problem of free will. The first, known as 'hard determinism', accepts the incompatibility of free will and determinism ('incompatibilism'), and asserts determinism, thus rejecting free will. The second response is libertarianism (again, no relation to the political philosophy), which accepts incompatibilism, but denies that determinism is true. This may seem like a promising approach. After all, has not modern physics shown us that the universe is indeterministic? The problem here is that the sort of indeterminism afforded by modern physics is not the sort the libertarian needs or desires. If it turns out that your ordering soup is completely determined by the laws of physics, the state of the universe 10,000 years ago, and the outcomes of myriad subatomic coin flips, your appetizer is no more freely chosen than before. Indeed, it is randomly chosen, which is no help to the libertarian. (Greene 2004).

Our position implicit within the thesis of this chapter falls within compatibilism. Indeed, we contend that freewill is not only compatible with determinism – but that determinism is actually a *necessary precondition* for free will (which we will use synonymously in this chapter with autonomy and self-determination). The dilemma of determinism is a false dilemma. During the millennia in which it was engendered and established within the western philosophical tradition, the ability for humans to determine the parameters and conditions of the material systems and processes of their bodies and brains was severely limited. It made more sense for most of human civilization – indeed, perhaps until as little as two hundred years ago – to see free will and determinism as incompatible, when we didn't have such things as routine surgery, prosthesis, implants and other instances of significantly modifying the human body while it was still alive – i.e. of partially *determining* the material systems and processes underlying our bodies. Indeed, for the most part of the dilemma's history we didn't even have a rudimentary understanding of how our bodily systems operated. Today we not only have such an understanding (or at least one vastly better than was available for the majority of the past few thousand years), but also medicine (a means of modifying the body's systems that necessitates a good understanding of the body's underlying operational mechanisms), routine surgery, transplants, implants, and other intuitively-apprehensible examples of modifying the body's underlying systems and processes to as to effect targeted changes to their structure or operation – in other words of determining the determining condition of the material systems and processes underlying our bodies and brains. Indeed, today we even have a diverse set of psychopharmacological agents able to enact specific changes to our own *phenomenal[2] experience* (i.e. thought, perception). Today we have tools for making targeted (i.e. predictable) changes to not only our own bodies, but our brains and *minds* as well.

If such means of partial determination (and thus of partial *self*-determination) were available during the millennia in which the seeming incompatibility between free will and causal determinism became entrenched within the western philosophical tradition, then it is likely that the dilemma of determinism wouldn't have posed such an unquestionable affront to the ontic legitimacy of our autonomy and agency.

Neurotechnology in general, and neuromodulation in particular, poses the potential to vastly increase the precision and extent of our existing capacity for self-determination, and constitutes the apex of the other means of technic self-determination mentioned above (e.g. medicine). It is these and other means of enacting changes to the physical processes and systems of our bodies and minds that render obvious the fumbled foundation underlying the dilemma of determinism.

Human Enhancement Technology and Neurotechnology

Human Enhancement Technology (HET) is typically defined as any technological attempt to overcome or obviate the biological limitations of the human body and brain or extend the capacities and faculties of the human body and brain beyond their normative range of capacities and faculties. HET encompasses a broad range of technological domains (i.e. types of technology), but the term is often used synonymously with NBIC (Nano-Bio-Info-Cogno) technologies because these four technological domains encompass the large majority of contemporary and conceptualized HET (Roco, 2004; Bainbridge & Roco, 2006; Bainbridge, 2013). However, NBIC technologies have a wide range of applications beyond their use on the human body, and so in the strictest sense should not be synonymized with HET.

While the notion of technic self-determination articulated in this chapter encompasses the use of HET on the body, some emphasis will be placed upon neurotechnology (Banks, 1998; Farah et al., 2004) because it constitutes one of the most extensive and exemplary means of technic self-determination as outlined in the present article.

Neurotechnology[3] encompasses any technology used to directly modify or modulate the structure or activity of the brain (Lynch, 2004; Eaton, and Illes, 2007; Isa et al., 2009; Giordano, 2012). Some definitions also encompass technologies that give us better insight into the operation of the brain, such as neuroimaging technologies, but within the context of the chapter it will refer exclusively to technologies for the modification and modulation of neural activity and structure.

A more precise definition of neurotechnology is given by Geelen:

Technical and computational tools that measure and analyze chemical and electrical signals in the nervous system, be it the brain or nerves in the limbs. These may be used to identify the properties of nervous activity, understand how the brain works, diagnose pathological conditions, or control external devices (neuroprostheses, 'brain machine interfaces'); and

Technical tools to interact with the nervous system to change its activity, for example to restore sensory input such as with cochlea implants to restore hearing or deep brain stimulation to stop tremor and treat other pathological conditions (Geelen, 2012).

Neurotechnology thus encompasses any technological means of stimulating the brain, modulating the brain, interfacing technology with the brain (e.g. brain-computer interfacing) and/or replacing any portion of the brain with a functional prosthetic. This broad definition includes such fields as brain stimulation, deep-brain-stimulation and transcranial magnetic stimulation (Breit, Schulz, and Benabid, 2004; Perlmutter, and Mink, 2006; Kringelbach and Aziz, 2009), neuromodulation (Serruya, Hatsopoulos, Paninski, Fellows and Donoghue, 2002; Gazzaley, Cooney, McEvoy, Knight, and D'esposito, 2005; Fetz 2007), neuroengineering (Sanguineti, Giugliano, Grattoarola and Morasso 2001), and neuroprosthesis (Loeb, McHardy, Kelliher, and Brummer, 1982; Heetderks, 1988; Bankman, and Janselewitz, 1995; Stieglitz, Schuettler, and Meyer, 2000; Isaacs, Weber, and Schwartz, 2000; Hetke and Anderson 2002; Ju et al., 2002; Shain et al., 2003; Chapin, 2004; Schwartz, 2004; Gasson, Hutt, Goodhew, Kyberd, and Warwick, 2005; Stieglitz, Schuetter, and Kock, 2005; Jackson, Moritz, Mavoori, Lucas, and Fetz,. 2006; Chan, Aslam, Wiler, and Casey, 2009; Berger, and Glanzman, 2009; Berger et al., 2011).

The scope of the present article will give comparatively greater emphasis to the subdomain of neurotechnology known as neuromodulation. However, it is important to note that other subdomains of neurotechnology can also constitute an instance and means of technic self-determination. For instance, the sub-domain of neuroprosthesis (and indeed even non-biomimetic brain computer interfaces) could be used to augment one's own neural activity via the replacement of existing portions of the brain with systems possessing alternate functional modalities than the portion(s) being replaced (as in neuroprosthesis) or by the addition of systems possessing alternate functional modalities than the human brain normally possesses (as in both neuroprosthetic and brain computer interfacing). However, the role of neurotechnology as a means of technic self-determination – i.e. as a means of inducing and modulating one's own neural activity (Fetz, 2007) – is given comparatively greater emphasis because it serves to illustrate the ontology of self-determination articulated in the present article better than other instances of neurotechnology-mediated technic self-determination, and because it constitutes one of the most extensive and arguably the most effective means of technic self-determination.

Neuromodulation has been achieved pharmacologically, magnetically, electrically and ontogenetically[4]. Continuing advances in the field of nanoelectronics, brain computer interfacing and neurobiology will only work to increase the precision, control and reliability of our available means of neuromodulation. This trend will culminate in the controllable, differential induction and modulation of neural activity at the scale of single neurons, integrated so as to modulate the coordinated activity of whole populations of neurons. It is conceivable that user-interfaces operatively-connected to a means of neuromodulation will allow users to modulate their own neuronal activity, thereby allowing them to modulate their emergent functional capacities and faculties, as well as their experiential or phenomenal modalities (i.e. thought and perception). The dynamic neural correlates of a given experience could conceivably be recorded by extensive, neuron-level brain scanning technology so as to record the pattern of neural induction of a given experience. A database of such recordings could be kept such that, through the use of neuro-modulatory user-interfaces as described above, a given agent could induce previously-recorded patterns of neural activity correlating with a given phenomenal (i.e. subjectively-perceivable) experience, the specificity of which is a function of the resolution of available brain-scanning technology. Though due to the unique wiring (i.e. synaptic profile, or organizational structure on the scale of neurons) possessed by each brain, the ability to transfer such patterns of neural induction to a different mind than the one it was initially recorded in will be limited to the degree of similarity between the two brains on the scale of induction (i.e. so if the modulation of single neurons was incurred, the scale of induction would be the scale of single neurons). This is advantageous for the thesis and conclusions of the present article, because this biases the use of such patterns pf neural induction by agents upon others, for the purposes of modulating another agent's brain rather than one's own. In other words, these consideration bias the use of specific patterns of neural induction (actuated by a sufficiently-precise means of neuromodulation) toward being used by agents upon themselves as a means of technic self-determination, rather than upon other minds as a means of determining other minds.

We have been modulating our own minds by varying degrees, both intentionally and non-intentionally, for all of human history. Certain historical technological and techniques, like meditation and psycho-pharmacological drugs, have allowed us to do so more precisely and more extensively. And through continuing developments in neurotechnology in general and neuromodulation in particular, tomorrow may yield yet another tangible increase in the scope and scale of our capacity to manipulate the activity of our own brains and minds. This, we argue, could constitute the most extensive means of not only technic self-determination but of self-determination in general yet seen by human history, and one that will serve to explicate why self-determination has never been incompatible with self-determination.

Neurotechnology and the "Dilemma of Determinism"

Decades of development in neurotechnology and its underlying technological and methodological base present new possibilities and capabilities that pose new questions and challenges to the "dilemma of determinism" and the freewill-determinism debate in general. However, the field of neuroethics (Illes, Kirschen, and Gabrieli, 2003; Farah, 2005; Levy, 2007) has given a much greater emphasis to the extent with which the newfound ability to modify and modulate our own or others' neural activity could endanger human self-determination and the freedom and autonomy of the individual. A prominent example of this position is the possibility that neurotechnology could be used to violate the autonomy of others by giving agents (or agency, e.g. government, military, industry) the capacity to manipulate – i.e. modify or modulate –the neural activity of others.

Meanwhile field of neurolaw (Taylor, 1995; Annas, 2007; Wolf, 2008; Schleim 2012; Spranger, 2012) has given emphasis to the legal implications of neurotechnology, such as the implications of neuroimaging and its potential to be used as a lie-detector with sufficient accuracy and reliability to justify its use during court testimony, or of advances in our understanding of neural activity and the ethical ramifications posed by the possibility of discovering neural correlates for criminal tendencies. The field has given comparatively less emphasis to the legal ramifications of the capacity to modulate one's own neural activity through a sufficiently-precise means of neuromodulation.

Similarly, the emerging field of neurosecurity has also addressed neurotechnology in the context of autonomy, freewill and self-determination, particularly in the context of the extent with which means of neuromodulation could be used to facilitate mind-control by government, military and industry (Fins, 2007; De Jong, Olds, and Giordano, 2001; Denning, Matsuoka, and Kohono, 2009; Benanti, 2010; Costa, Stevens, and Hansen, 2011; Xuyang and Yuzhuo, 2011; Takagi, 2012; Geelen, 2012). The comparatively greater emphasis given to the ethical, legal and philosophical concerns of neurotechnology's use as a means of controlling the other or infringing upon the privacy of the other in the fields of neuroethics, neurolaw and neurosecurity have helped to emphasize the dangers of neurotechnology in the public eye and popular mind rather than the potential benefits. But as we will argue, the use of neuromodulation upon one's own self has the potential to constitute one of the most extensive and effective means of self-determination available to us, and as such, the field of neurotechnology holds at least as much potential to increase people's capacity for self-determination as it has potential to decrease people's capacity for self-determination

THE WILL TOWARD SELF-DETERMINATION

In this section we articulate an ontology of self-determination, of which technic self-determination is a subset, which identifies self-modification and self-modulation as the ontological fundament of self-determination and the heart of the ontology of self-determination articulated in the present article.

Self-Determination Necessitates Determinism

Self-determination as self-modification and self-modulation is not in contradiction with determinism. Indeed, determinism is actually *necessary* to the particular ontology of self-determination articulated in the present chapter. If there were a high degree of indeterminacy in the processes and material systems constituting our minds and bodies, then there would be no reliable method of making specific changes to such material processes and systems in order to achieve specific modifications to the operation or capacities of those material processes and systems – i.e. no way of implementing a series of changes to the operation or constitution of the mind or body whose outcome can be confidently estimated or predicted. This applies to our actions in the external world as well: if there were no way of translating an objectified goal into a series of actions able to achieve that goal, as would be the case in any sufficiently-indeterministic process, then our capacity to shape the world – i.e. physical environments, laws, social customs and infrastructure – according to our own desires, values and ideals would be severely curtailed.

We argue contrarily to incompatibilists that the fact that humans lack conscious control over the circumstances of our own births, i.e. of the parameters defining our genetics or our environments, does *not* evidence the illegitimacy of self-determination. It is true we did not decide ourselves, consciously and volitionally, to come into existence. But if a material system is made through the deterministic actions of other, external material processes and systems *so as to be* self-determining (by whatever degree) thereafter, then this, we contend, is enough to legitimately characterize it as a system of partial self-determination. Indeed, we hold that any legitimate ontological schema of self-determination *must* concede that no self-determining system can be *absolutely* self-determining (i.e. to the point of having determined its own birth or initial creation), as such would constitute a temporal tautology. There is no such thing as absolute self-determination; there are only degrees of self-determination.

Humans come into existence through no choice of their own, and increasing degrees of autonomy are demonstrated to and bestowed upon us as we are reared and educated with the general aim of making us as autonomous and independent – i.e. as self-determining – as we can be.

Once one accepts that 'true' self-determination does not necessitate that one determines all the determining conditions of themselves to the point of and even preceding birth, then one if forced to recognize that self-determination is a modality rather than an absolute or all-or-nothing category. This effectively obviates the largest barrier to seeing partial determinations of the material and procedural conditions underlying our bodies and minds as veritable acts of self-determination.

Self-Modification and Modulation as the Ontological Fundament of Self-Determination

There is a distinction to be made between self-modulation and self-modification. Self-modification corresponds to the act of adding to, removing or rearranging the constitutive material processes and systems of our minds and bodies. Thus the addition of artificial neural networks to the existing biological brain, or changing the wiring of our connectomes (i.e. the pattern of synaptic connection in our brain, which to a large extent define who we are and distinguish us from one another as persons with distinct skills, knowledge, behavioral-inclinations and memories), the deletion of an existing neural sub-system (e.g. network, cluster, emergent neural circuit) and the addition of cochlear implants that expand the range of frequencies one can hear, would all constitute variations of self-modification.

By contrast, self-modulation corresponds with (varying degrees of) conscious control over the procedural steps constituting the activity of the material systems and processes constituting one's body and brain, or of the various parameters defining the material systems constituting their body and brain (e.g. stimulating a specific series of neurons at specific time intervals so as to externally-induce a specific pattern of synaptic firing – in other words external control over the neural activist constituting and determining one's own phenomenal, i.e. subjective, experience).

Self-modification involves actually changing the capabilities (or more precisely the "system states") of the material systems constituting one's mind and/or body, whereas self-modulation involves controlling or consciously manipulating (i.e. modulating) the *existing* abilities or "system states" of the material systems constituting one's mind and/or body. "Playing" a memory by inducing a specific sequence of action potentials in specific neurons (i.e. controlling the sequence of synaptic connections made during a chunk of neural activity) would be an instance of self-modulation, whereas changing the neural connections encoding or determining the parameters of a given memory so as to remove or alter the memory, on the other hand, would be an instance of self-modification. Adding new genes to one's genome would be an instance of self-modification, while consciously modulating the expression of existing genes so as to alter one's resultant phenotype would be an instance of self-modulation. Directly controlling the levels of various hormones in one's circulatory system would be an instance of self-modulation, while removing the presence of a given hormone completely would be an instance of self-modification.

ESSENCE AS DISSENT[5]

In this section we will outline a taxonomy for the various modalities of self-determination encompassed by the ontological schema of self-determination articulated above, and analyze it against the background of humanity's existing and historical modalities and means of self-determination, ultimately demonstrating ontological continuity between technic self-determination via HET and neurotechnology, on the one hand, and the largely-non-technological means and modalities of self-determination practiced by society today and in the past, on the other. By demonstrating such continuity, we elaborate the position that HET in general and neurotechnologies in particular are a vital and necessary step on the path to *staying* human, rather than a potential source of dehumanization, and that they both exemplify and have the potential to *increase* and *intensify* the very feature that designates us better than any other as human: namely our will toward self-determination.

To Have a Bod Is to Mod

Humans have modified themselves by varying degrees since the inception of recorded culture. While we argue that humans' inclination toward and desire for increased self-determination is the feature that most distinguishes us as humans (and that underlies the desire to change our selves, our communities, our societies and our world for the better – a desire ubiquitous throughout time and geography), it does not necessarily constitute an ontological break from the animals we are evolutionarily derived from. It distinguishes us from animals as a matter of not category but degree – that is, we are the only animal to have made a *deliberate* effort to increase our own degree of self-determination, and it is that metaconditional consideration that marks us starker than anything else as human, and not the act or fact of being, like most other animals, partially self-determining. Every living system is to some extent self-modifying, insofar as they attempt to change or utilize their environments in specific ways impacting their own existence. Self-determination could arguably even be traced all the way down to the ever-present survival instinct itself. If an organism performs a series of actions with the aim of living instead of dying, then they are making actions meant to directly affect the defining conditions of their existence –in this case whether they exist or not.

But that a series of actions, perceptions of thoughts leads to a change in the wiring of our brains, thus constituting an instance of self-modification, does not necessitate that it also constitute an instance of self-modification. The categorical differentiator here is that for it to constitute an instance of self-determination, an instance of self-modification must be conscious – i.e. must be made with the *intent* of modifying oneself (which is synonymous with modifying the way one acts in the future). Thus whereas passive perception would not constitute an instance of self-determination (ignoring the extent with which we modulate, or consciously direct, our perception, for instance by choosing where we look or our point of focus), a series of thoughts in which one evaluates past decisions, reflecting upon what one wants to have accomplished in X years, and decides that they want to consciously make an effort to be more X (focused, patient, knowledgeable, etc.), *would* be an instance of self-modification that also constitutes self-determination.

Methodological Self-Determination: Autogenic Thoughts Steer Morphogenic Knots

One of the ways in which humans – and organisms in general – change the wiring of their brains is in response to thought and perception. Due to the fact that the activity of neurons is impacted by their past *history* of activity (e.g. the more frequently neurons that make synaptic connection with one another, the more likely they will be to make synaptic connection with one another in future, which is the source of the idiom "neurons that fire together wire together"), any neural activity involving the synaptic or ephaptic connection between neurons has the potential to affect future neural activity. For this reason, perception and thought constitute a modality of self-determination in and of themselves, insofar as they can facilitate changes to the material systems and processes underlying our brains, thereby facilitating the modification of our emergent intellectual and experiential capacities and faculties constituted thereby.

Perception

One likely criticism we anticipate is the notion that unlike thought, which is internal to the self, perception would fail to constitute a modality or means of self-determination because it is initiated from systems and processes external to the self. But this fails to take account of (1) the ways in which our sensory organs process, filter and otherwise-modify our raw sensory data, (2) internal sensory modalities like proprioception that sense conditions internal to the body, (3) the ways in which we can actively modulate our perception through the modulation of bodily-activity (e.g. by deciding where to turn our heads, or where to focus our eyes within a given point of view, or walking to a different physical environment, or closing one's eyes), (4) the ways in which we can actively modulate our perception through the changes made to one's immediate environment (e.g. putting on a film or song to induce a specific sequence of perception) and (5) the ways in which we can internally invoke sensory modalities normally focused on the outward environment (e.g. sight and sound) by internally inducing sensory impressions, as used in dreaming and in what we colloquially refer to as acts of "imagination".

Our non-technological (i.e. methodological) ability to control or self-modulate (1) and (2) are rather limited. But our ability to methodologically affect our categories (3) – (5), which can be affected or "modulated" by thought, is by contrast rather extensive. We can be driven by a series of thoughts to change one's environment (through physically moving to another location or by, say, putting on some form of media in one's proximal physical environment). It is this capacity for thought to affect and modulate these externally-initiated perceptual events that distinguishes perception as a means of self-determination.

Moreover, the line between thought and perception is indistinct and, we would argue, more a pragmatic tool than a real ontological truth as-such. When we think on a conscious level, we employ sensory impressions to convey or "embody" the informational substrata of our thoughts – whether by way of visualizing a process being articulated through time or the relative organization of components and/or sequences of events, or via the explicit use of words (i.e. "thinking in sentences").

Thus to characterize thought as a modality of self-determination without also categorizing perception as being encompassed by that modality of self-determination would be to implicitly reify the claim that thought and perception are distinct processes without interplay or intertwine.

Thought

Thought itself has a determining impact on other thoughts. The history of activity in a given neural network, cluster or emergent neural circuit will impact its present and future activity. For this reason act of thought can constitute a modality of self-determination because it can be used as a means of changing the determining conditions of our minds (which have a much larger determining impact on our available experiential modalities and our available capacities and faculties than do the determining conditions of our non-cognitive bodily systems.

The predominant theory of memory in neurology is the neural activation theory – that when we imagine or recall performing a certain action, perceiving a certain perception or thinking a certain thought, the same neurons and neural connections activated during the doing are the same neurons and neural connections being activated during the recalling, perceiving or thinking. When we think about walking up stairs, the same motor neurons that would be activated during a walk up the stairs are activated; the same neurons fire, just at a lower magnitude. An analogous mechanism is thought to underlie mirror neurons as well; when I perceive another agent picking up an object, the same neurons that would be activated if *I* were picking up the object are activated.

This demonstrates that it is possible to deliberatively and methodologically change the organization of our own brains via deliberative activities made through our brains. Deliberative acts of learning and memorizing are a very good intuitive example of this. We repeat a given line of thought (or facts, or association between two or more facts) over until it seems to "come on its own". The increased ease we feel in recalling a given line of thought, conclusion or notion is the phenomenal correlate of an increased synaptic weighting between the neurons repeatedly activated concomitantly during the "learning" or "repeated recall" session.

Other instances that are less obviously deliberative acts of repeating certain neural activities are also encompassed by this modality of self-determination. When we read in order to acquire knowledge or new information, we implicitly understand that by reading a given book and thinking about it, we will encode that information into the neural activities (or structures) constituting our minds. The fact that we do not consciously correlate the act of newly acquired knowledge with newly acquired changes to one's neural activities or connections – i.e. that we associate it with the phenomenal result (the ability to recall something one couldn't before) rather than with the physical result underlying that phenomenal result – does not obviate the fact that we are still nonetheless *deliberatively* changing our own neural activity through the deliberative activation of our own neural activity.

We will refer to the modality of self-determination that encompasses the ways in which thought and perception can be utilized to effect changes to the determining conditions of our minds (i.e. our phenomenal experience) as *methodological* self-determination, both to contrast it with technic self-determination (thereby distinguishing it therefrom) and to emphasize its non-physical nature (i.e. the fact that we effect changes and subsequently feel such effected changes phenomenally, rather than as say a quantitative increase in synaptic connections between certain neurons – even though that is what it physically correlates with).

Reciprocal Self-Determination: Essence, Embodiment, Environment

Humanity's most effective and predominantly-utilized means of self-modification thus-far, besides methodological self-determination, has been *reciprocal causation* – i.e., changes made to one's external environment that result in subsequent changes to the material systems and processes constituting one's body and mind. When such reciprocal causation is done in a way that is deliberately meant to (i.e. expected to) directly affect the physical parameters determining one's material and/or phenomenal existence, it constitutes what we will call *reciprocal self-determination.*

An illustrative instance of reciprocal self-determination would be the act of turning on the fireplace in order to manipulate or affect the physical parameters of one's body (e.g. body temperature) and of one's phenomenal experience (e.g. initiating a series of actions leading to the perception of warmth). We refer to this process as reciprocal causation to denote the *recursive* fashion in which the actions of an agent are directed outward in such a way as to feedback with the agent that initiated the actions, via causal connection between the material systems constituting the agent and those constituting their environment.

A more intuitively-apprehensible example would be dimming the lights in manipulate one's mood or phenomenal experience. In such a case one would be changing environmental conditions known to directly affect his or her phenomenal experience. An even more precise instance of reciprocal self-determination is the deliberate act of perceiving some form of media – e.g. a song or movie – in order to induce a specific series of perceptions and emotions, i.e. a specific phenomenal experience (either because we remember such media doing so in the past or because we have been told that it would by someone who *has* viewed it). Note here that just as there can be differential degrees of self-determination in general (i.e. it is a broader modality rather than an absolute, all-or-nothing category), there can be differential degrees of self-determination in different instances of a particular modality of self-determination. In this case, certain instances of reciprocal self-determination (e.g. putting on media) effect more precise changes to one's perceptual experience than another instance of reciprocal self-determination (e.g. dimming the lights to manipulate one's mood).

Prosthetic Essence: The Co-Constitution of Man and Techné

Moreover, the constitution of one's environment has a large impact on what an agent is able to do. For instance, the possible actions available to a human living in a contemporary city are very different than the possible actions available to a human living in a prehistoric environment, and those discrepancies derive more than anything else from the differences in the conditions of their external environments, because genetically speaking we remain largely equivalent to prehistoric human.

Thus modifications to one's environment that *do not* result in subsequent changes to the material systems and processes of the initiating-agent can also be argued to constitute a means and modality of self-determination. An articulated series of modifications to the environment (i.e. physical objects and resources) that result in the addition of new capacities and abilities, e.g. the construction of a new tool or device, can also be legitimately characterized as an act of self-determination in that it affects (i.e. partly determines) the available capacities of the agent as a result of the actions of that very agent.

The developmental progression of humans from birth onward involves interaction and interplay between both nature and nurture, determined by both our genetic as well as epigenetic constitution. The environment (e.g. historical period, geographic location) we are born into will have a large determining impact on the range and extents of our capacities and faculties. Born today, we have the capacity to cross an ocean in a matter of hours; born a few hundred years ago, and one would have the capacity to cross an ocean in a matter of months. The technologies and techniques we develop extend our capacities and faculties – they open up new positive freedoms (i.e. freedom *to* do something, as opposed to freedom *from* some external force or circumstance) for us.

Moreover, technology is increasingly becoming our *predominant* means of effecting change. "Technology is man's foremost mediator of change; it is by and large through the use of technology that we expand the parameters of the possible" (Cortese, 2013a). Most every technology can be characterized as a new configuration or arrangement of existing technologies. This can also be true for technologies that aren't obviously an emergent system comprised of distinct subsystems; a new paradigm of technology is built upon the preceding paradigm of technology, which then becomes the technological and methodological infrastructure or fundament underlying the new technological paradigm. This seemingly-anecdotal fact – that technologies are build out of other existing technologies – leads to the non-anecdotal conclusion that the potential for technological development is continuously growing, because the underlying base of technologies that can be used and combined to create any given new technology is continuously growing. Thus our capacity to effect change in the world has been increasingly biased towards the use of technology rather than methodology, because the capacity for technology to foster new faculties and capacities has been increasing, while our methodological infrastructure increases at a comparatively slower rate. The fact that technology now constitutes our predominant means of affectation reifies the argument that technologies, insofar as they partly determine our faculties and capabilities, can legitimately be considered to co-constitute 'the human'. And that both technology and methodology constitute a means of determining the conditions of the self means that technic self-determination shares continuity-of-impetus and continuity-of-fundament with methodological self-determination. To think that the most essential characteristic of each modality is the way in which they effect change, rather than the fact that they can both be used to affect change in general, would be "miss the end for the means and the mark for a lark. The point is that we are trying to consciously improve the state of self, society and world; technology has simply superseded methodology as the most optimal means of accomplishing that, and now constitutes our best means of effecting our affectation" (Cortese 2013b). As we will demonstrate in a later section, this continuity-of-impetus between technic self-determination and methodological self-determination also helps to illegitimate the claim that the proliferation and use of HET will be dehumanizing and/or an affront to out 'human dignity'.

Thus, another way in which changes made to one's environment can be seen to constitute an act of self-determination is through a view of personhood that encompasses one's environment (in addition to the material systems constituting one's mind and body as such) as belonging to or co-constituting one's self.

Of relevance to this view of selfhood is the 'extended cognition thesis' (Clark, 1998a, 1998b, 1999, 2008). The extended cognition thesis posits "an active externalism, based on the active role of the environment in driving cognitive processes" (Chalmers, and Clark 1998), contending that any tools actively used by a mind, and which play an integral role in the activities of that mind, should be recognized as partly constituting that mind; in other words that the the mind and its tools are co-constitutive. Views of personhood characterizing the mind as a single, distinct and definitive system causally insulated from the tools it uses and the environment it acts within fail to account for the ways in which our tools play an active part in our cognitive processes.

Within the bounds of the extended cognition view of personhood, changes made by an agent to their environment that afford them new capabilities or experiential (e.g. mental, perceptual) modalities, insofar as such an environment partly constitutes that agent and impacts the range and extents of his capacities and faculties, would qualify as an instance of self-modification or self-modulation, and thus as an instance of self-determination. This is distinct but highly similar to the above case, wherein an agent's environment is considered co-constitutive because an agent's environment impacts his or her available capacities and faculties. The extended cognition thesis posits a level of co-constitution even more integral than was articulated in the preceding context, because in the extended cognition thesis, tools play an active and integral role in *existing* cognitive processes (rather than merely fostering new positive freedoms in the creation of new capacities and faculties or the extension of existing capacities or faculties).

A third distinct-but-convergent view on the co-constitutive relationship between humans and their technologies, tools and techniques concerns itself with the ways in which certain technologies are extensions of the mind, the senses, or another human body-part or faculty (Brey, 2000; Lawson, 2010). These views would characterize the mass communications network facilitated by the telephone, the television and now the internet as extensions of the senses and vehicles as extensions of our capacity to move or travel. The most well-known figure to have espoused this view is Marshal McLuhan (1964, 1966, 1967, 1968, 1988, 2000), who is commonly credited with contending that media are an extension of the senses and the mind:

During the mechanical ages we had extended our bodies in space. Today, after more than a century of electric technology, we have extended our central nervous system itself in a global embrace, abolishing both space and time as far as our planet is concerned. Rapidly, we approach the final phase of the extensions of man - the technological simulation of consciousness, when the creative process of knowing will be collectively and corporately extended to the whole of human society, much as we have already extended our senses and our nerves by the various media. (McLuhan, 1966, p. 19).

Indeed, McLuhan even went so far as to contend (much in the spirit of the extended cognition thesis) that media are extensions not only of the senses (which many consider to be passive faculties) but also extensions of the mind itself. "It is a persistent theme of this book that all technologies are extensions of our physical and nervous system to increase power and speed" (Ibid., p. 91). He distinguishes technologies by the domain or faculty they extend. Mechanical technologies constitute extension of the body:

What makes a mechanism is the separation and extension of separate parts of our body as hand, arm, foot, in pen, hammer, wheel. And the mechanization of a task is done by segmentation of each part of an action in a series of uniform, repeatable, and movable parts. (Ibid, p. 218).

Communications technologies constitute extensions of the senses; the telephone and radio correspond to sound, visual media like television, writing and print are extensions of sight. And a subset of electronic communications technologies characterized most aptly by the computer constitutes an extension of our mental faculties and capacities: "[Man is] an organism that now wears its brain outside its skull and its nerves outside its hide" (Ibid, p. 64). McLuhan also argues that such technologies constitute our most effective and also our most predominant means of extending human capacities and faculties. "Again, unless there were such increases of power and speed, new extensions of ourselves would not occur or would be discarded." (Ibid p. 91).

Within the context of this view, the deliberative use of technologies to extend the human body and/or mind would constitute a means of self-determination insofar as such technologies are viable extensions (i.e. parts) of the human body and mind.

These three views of the symbiotic and co-constitutive relationship between humans and their technologies, tools and techniques, while distinct from one another, each reify the argument that our environments, and especially our epigenetic environments (of which are technological environment is a subset), form part of the overall determining conditions of our selves. Thus all three views allow for the characterization of technology as means of self-determination.

It is worth noting here, somewhat anecdotally, that these three views of the co-constitutive relationship humans have with their techné would effectively characterize all technologies that are encompassed by the respective conditions of each view (e.g. for the first view, technologies that add new capacities or expand existing capacities and faculties; for the second view, technologies that play an integral role in our cognitive processes; for the third view, technologies that extend our bodies, senses and minds) as human enhancement technologies, here defining HET as any technology integrated with the human mind or body for the purposes of changing the capacities and faculties of the human mind or body. While this chapter will limit its use of the term 'HET' to its normative meaning (for purposes of clarity and consistency), we also acknowledge that within the context of the above views on human-technology co-constitution, the distinction between HET and normal technology is ambiguous at best, and possibly illegitimate to begin with at worst. Furthermore, this ambiguity works to reify the argument, outlined in a later section, that the use and proliferation of HET are not dehumanizing and a threat to human dignity any more than the use of automobiles or antibiotics are. If technology as general category can be considered as an extension of or integral addition to existing human capacities or faculties, then we have been immersed in HET since the very inception of culture.

This modality of self-determination (which encompasses all three of the above views on human-technology-co-constitution) is distinct from reciprocal self-determination as outlined in the preceding section. As such, we will refer to it as *prosthetic self-determination*, in which the (normative, i.e. physically-external) tools, techniques and technologies used by an agent is seen to co-constitute the agent (insofar as our capacities and faculties are among our distinguishing or 'defining' characteristic, and insofar as the techniques and technologies we have available to us is a large factor determining the type and extents of our capacities and faculties). Within the context of this modality of self-determination, changes made to or through technology are accordingly characterized as self-directed changes (i.e. instances of self-determination) made to the agent's constitutive sub-systems. We refer to this modality of self-determination as *prosthetic* self-determination because the view of personhood that underlies it characterizes technology as having an ontologically symbiotic or co-constitutive relationship to humans, and as such would characterize all technology of that sort as fundamentally prosthetic, despite the fact that they are at times extensions of our existing functional capacities, faculties and modalities, rather than the restoration of a lost or diminished functional capacity, faculty or modality.

The ancient Greek notion of *techné*[6] (Rawlins 1950; Dunne 1993; Meagher 1988) is of some relevance to this discussion. Rather than unambiguously distinguishing between technique and technology, the ancient Greeks used the notion of techné (most often translated as "craftsmanship", "craft" or "art"), which encompasses both technology *and* technique (Wadia 2010). Techné meant in the simplest sense a 'way of doing', and thus encompassed everything from art to technology. Both the tool and the way in which it was operated were equally considered techné to the ancient Greeks.

The notion that technique and thought – works of the mind – are equally viable and vital components of the human condition is met with much less resistance than the notion that technology is so, perhaps merely because technique and methodology cannot be physically separated from the mind (except when it is embodied in technology), and could not continue existing if humanity went extinct tomorrow – in contrast to technology, which could do both. The Greek notion of techné reifies the above positions pertaining to the co-constitutive relationship humans have with their technology because it demonstrates that a clean and clear ontological distinction between technology and technique, tool and thought, or device and mind is neither necessary nor more appropriate than avoiding such a distinction.

Indeed, one could make the case that the distinction between technology and technique *is* in fact illegitimate, in that technology and technique are themselves co-constitutive in relation to each other. Every technology either employs or implicitly embodies technique (e.g. if it performs a technique previously performed by humans, as in the case of a computer; if there is a technique to its use, in the case of any manually-operated technology, as in the case of a crossbow; if there is a technique underlying its manufacture or construction, as in the case of most every technology). Similarly, many techniques either (a) involve the use of tools or technologies (as in the case of any technique for sewing, which requires a needle, or contemporary techniques of weather forecasting, which require meteorological instrumentation) or (b) couldn't have been formulated without the use of technologies (e.g. information or data involved in the use of the technique may have required scientific instruments to initially obtain and verify them). Thus many (if not all) technologies either use or embody techniques, and many techniques either employ technologies or require underlying technologies for their initial formulation. Writing can be categorized as technique – but without the technological infrastructure of something to write with and something to write on, one would be hard-pressed to employ it. We build upon this interplay between technology and technique recursively, using available techniques in our newest technologies and available technologies in our newest techniques.

Technic Self-Determination

Reciprocal self-determination and methodological self-determination constitute, by and large, rather indirect ways of making changes to the material systems and processes constituting our minds and bodies. In these modalities of self-determination, we must rely on the probabilistic tendency for certain actions or processes to change the material systems and processes comprising our bodies and brains; for instance the strengthening of synaptic connections between neurons activated concomitantly during a given physical routine, thought or memory. Technic self-determination, by contrast, would allow us to *directly* affect our underlying bodily and mental parameters, without having to invoke the methodological repetition of a routine in order to effect such changes.

Nevertheless, reciprocal self-determination and methodological self-determination have been for most of human history our most effective means and medium of self-determination. For instance, when we repeat actions or procedures we gradually gain the capacity to perform them with less and less conscious effort. This is due to several neurological mechanisms that strengthen the synaptic weighting between neurons making synaptic connection with each other frequently during same activity, thought-association or memory; neurons that 'fire together' during a given activity, thought-association or memory are more likely to do so when the same activity, thought-association or memory occurs in future, while neurons that 'fire together' less frequently will be accordingly less likely to 'fire together' in future.

In order to improve our fidelity in a given skill, we typically practice performing the skill repeatedly so as to facilitate the sequence of strong synaptic-connections that correspond with proficiency in a given skill (i.e. physical or mental operation). Likewise, to increase the probability of remembering something (or put another way, to increase the strength of a given memory), we typically repeat the information in some perceptual form (e.g. as words) until it can be recalled with less conscious effort, and/or associate it with a higher number of existing concepts or memories (i.e. increasing the number of strengthened synaptic connections rather than the strength of existing connections per-se).

But if we had a means of directly modifying the synaptic weighing between neurons, or the connections between existing neurons and neutral networks, then we could facilitate changes to our behavioral-inclinations, memories, skillsets, etc. – essentially any modality encompassed by the material systems and processes of our bodies and brains – much more quickly and readily – e.g. without having to make the neurons fire together a number of times manually in order to modify the weighting or their synaptic connection(s) – and with vastly-greater precision.

The same applies for modifications involving the addition of neurons (neurogenesis) or the addition of synaptic connections to existing neurons (synaptogenesis), which we will refer to as additive modifications, as opposed to subtractive modifications (i.e. the removal or a certain neural structure) and reorganizational modifications (i.e. the rearrangement of neural structures). Currently, methodological self-determination allows us to practice routines that strengthen the weighting of synaptic connections between the neurons in use during that routine, thereby allowing for the self-directed modification of the relative weightings of our own synaptic connections. Certain varieties of neuromodification farther out on the developmental horizon could facilitate the addition and integration of new neurons and the addition of new synaptic connections to existing neurons directly, bypassing the need for the repetition of certain practices that is incurred by methodological self-determination. Genetic engineering applied to the brain could utilize the brains endogenous mechanisms for neurogenesis and synaptogenesis. This would include the use of growth factors correlating with synaptogenesis, in-vivo gene modification to selectively up-regulate neuron growth-factors promoting synaptogenesis in certain neurons and not others, and the direct transplantation (or targeted migration) of pluripotent cells (such as induced pluripotent stem cells, or iPSCs) cells to the central-nervous-system. Farther out on the developmental horizon, continuing progress in nanobiotechnology (Lowe, 2000; Niemeyer, 2000; Niemeyer, 2004; Müller, and Dufrene, 2008; Cheon, and Lee, 2008; Burns, Ow, and Wiesner, 2006), nanomedicine (Freitas, 1999, 2002, 2003, 2005; Freitas, and Hayukkala, 2005; Cavalcanti and Freitas, 2005; Kostarelos, 2006) and nanoneurotechnology (Giordano, Akhouri, and McBride, 2009) could allow for the addition and integration of non-biological (i.e. nanotechnological or computationally-emulated) neurons functionally equivalent to biological neurons and interacting with them in their own language (i.e. via electrical and chemical synaptic connections and ephaptic connection). Both shorter-future and farther-future embodiments of neurotechnology constitute a means of directly facilitating additive neuromodification without the need for the methodological repetition involved in methodological self-determination. Furthermore, they can also allow us to make additive neuromodifications that are simply not possible via methodological self-determination (i.e., in this case, by exercising more or changing one's diet), as well as at a rate disallowed by the body's endogenous neurogenic and synaptogenic mechanisms.

It is important to note that the term 'technic self-determination' denotes both the use of HET applied to the body and neurotechnology applied to the brain. We can taxonomically distinguish between the two by referring to the self-directed use of neurotechnology as *neurotechnic self-determination*, and referring to the integration of HET on the body as *somatotechnic self-determination*, recognizing both as subsets encompassed by the larger category of *technic self-determination*. However, for the most part we will refer to both subsets as technic self-determination, recognizing that the emphasis is on neurotechnologies (simply because the conditions and parameters of the material systems and processes underlying our brains have a much larger determining impact on our overall capacities and faculties than the conditions and parameters of those underlying the rest of our bodies, and thus because neurotechnology has a greater capacity for self-determination than HET applied to the body) and that 'HET' as employed in the present chapter encompasses both neurotechnology and 'somatic technology'.

HET constitutes but a vastly-better means to the same end humanity has had in mind since the very start. HET is not a break from normality or from humanity. Humans have been partially self-determining since our first dawn in Sumer and on. HET in general and neurotechnology in particular are but the modern-most tools we have on-hand for doing what we've always done – that is, considering who, what, how and why we want to be, and overcoming ourselves in a fit of becoming toward the projected objective of what it might be better to be(come) instead.

Thus the use of HET does not constitute a disconnect from our most human ways of seeing and being; on the contrary, HET bears fundamental continuity with the other modalities of self-determination that humans have practiced for millennia, in that both constitute a means of using our own thoughts and actions so as to partly determine the determining conditions of our *possible* thoughts and actions (i.e. capacities and faculties).

It is only when we as humans *halt* our upward-mission and forward-march to increase our own degree of self-determination through increasingly precise and extensive tools for shaping self, society and landscape that we lose any part or parcel of our humanity. HET, if used to increase the control we have over the determining conditions of our *own* selves, rather than over each other, can only serve to make us more human by increasing and intensifying the very aspect that makes us human more than anything else – our incessant essence to make our own, to defy and retry, to continually better-determine ourselves – ultimately, to be by becoming instead.

Homo-Autopoietic

The will toward self-determination has been at the heart of the human since the very inception of culture. Indeed, we argue that the will-toward self-determination is either embodied by, exemplified by or implicit in many contemporary and historical cultural practices and beliefs.

Democracy exemplifies our will toward self-determination on the societal level. We seek to determine the laws we live under ourselves, rather than have an arbitrary monarch or despot do the deciding. Moreover, we want to reserve the right to continually change our minds, to reserve the ability to redecide in future. This exemplifies the progressive nature of the will *toward* self-determination, and our desire for successively-*increasing* degrees of self-determination.

The enlightenment tradition, characterized by the use of rationality and the scientific method to determine things rather than tradition, and the decline of religious political and scientific authority – exemplifies our will toward increased self-determination on an epistemological level. Indeed, one could argue that the scientific method itself also exemplifies our will toward increased self-determination on the level of epistemology, for much the same reasons that the enlightenment tradition does – an eschewing of tradition, and the exclusive reliance on *self-directed* study and investigation.

The notion of human rights, of inalienable liberties possessed by all humans, exemplifies our want for and belief in our autonomy on the level of the individual. Indeed, all notion of human rights imply our individual autonomy and freedom as a core value and desire.

The notion of morality and ethics not only exemplifies our want to self-determination, but constitutes one of the ends to which we actually apply methodological self-determination. On a very intuitive level, morality and ethics perhaps more than any other methodological pursuit is clearly an act of self-modification, and an exemplification of the will toward self-determination.

Education, and even more generally the raising of a child into adulthood, exemplifies both our will toward self-determination as well as the modal nature of self-determination. Children are born and gradually are guided and taught to become increasingly independent, autonomous, self-determining – in other words of gradually taking their own becoming in-hand. This is exemplified in obvious ways, like being taught how to live in society so as to survive (i.e. food and shelter), and in less obvious ways, like urging children to be who they want to be, to get the kind of employment they want, to live life more than anything else for the pursuit of their own happiness.

The contemporary value of individualism and relativism, and the pressure to accept people's beliefs without judgment or discrimination, exemplifies the will toward self-determination on the level of our minds – freedom from the external determination of our thoughts and beliefs.

Indeed, these and a great many other things exemplify, embody and imply the ubiquitously-human will toward self-determination, as value, as desire and as actuality.

For we human beings, naturality is unnatural... we who have crafted clothes, codes, cities, symbols, and culture. Since the very inception of human civilization, we have very thoroughly ceased to be natural, and to such an extent that unnaturality has become our first nature. (Cortese, 2013c)

Indeed, this highlights an all-too-common misperception of the underlying impetus and overarching end of transhumanism (a philosophical position that espouses the feasibility and desirability of the ethical use of human enhancement technologies) and technoprogressivism. This misnomer is that transhumanism is about eschewing our humanity. This isn't exactly a surprising misconception given the monikers transhumanism and posthumanism, but it is one that is nonetheless troubling, for it is not contrary to the thesis we have articulated here, but antithetical to it as well. Transhumanism, i.e. the position that it is both feasible and desirable to use technology to improve the human condition, constitutes nothing less than our best means of *maintaining* the human condition, which we have argued here is characterized by our desire to choose our own determining conditions ourselves. We will not be posthuman; on the contrary, we will be more human than we ever have been before.

The emphasis on technology in H+ and Tech[no]Prog[ressive] communities does not come from disdain for our humanity (i.e. the silly "contempt-of-the-flesh" trope) or sheer technophilia. Rather it is because (1) we seek to better determine the determining conditions of world and of self (which are to some extent symbiontic and interconstitutive), [to] leave more up to choice and less down to chance, and (2) because technology is simply Man's foremost mediator of change, of effecting our affectation, and thus the best means of shaping the state of self and world for the better, whatever your definition of better happens to be. (Cortese, 2013b).

Thus the will-toward self-determination is exemplified by a wide array of contemporary and historically deep-rooted practices, beliefs, values and ideals.

In *Posthumanity: Thinking Philosophically About The Future*, Brian Cooney presents an ontology of life, i.e. of living organisms, rooted in autopoiesis – Greek for "self-creating", based upon homeostasis and self-maintenance. "The organism remains this organism (what philosophers call numerical identity) by *making itself*, at each point in its duration, an *instance* of the same *kind* of system. For this reason, we call it a *self-instantiating system*." (Cooney, 2004, p. 79). Interaction with the environment in a reciprocal and recursive feedback process is integral to this autopoietic process. Cooney extends this autopoietic ontology of life across scales, from DNA to unicellular organisms to multicellular organisms, culminating in the characterization of the human self and brain as an autopoietic process bearing ontological continuity with life itself, at all scales and times, down the evolutionary tree and all the way back to self-replicating RNA. Cooney's ontological scheme for life and mind as a self-creating and self-maintaining process reify the argument, presented here, that technic self-determination is ontologically-continuous with the human condition today and in the far past, and exemplified by or implicit in many contemporary and historical values, practices and beliefs. Indeed, Cooney extends it all the way across life itself.

OUR HUMANITY IS A FUCTION OF OUR CAPACITY FOR SELF-DETERMINATION

A common criticism against the desirability of HET is that it is dehumanizing – i.e. that the use of HET will mark the departure of the very qualities that make us human. In this section we will argue that the ontology of self-determination as self-modification and self-modulation articulated above (in which HET in general and neurotechnologies in particular are shown to play an integral role in maintaining and expanding our liberty and autonomy by constituting our most comprehensive and extensive means of self-determination) can serve to illustrate how the dehumanization criticism is based upon a naïve and outdated conception of human nature as static and predetermined. This line of reasoning can be utilized to not only illegitimate this criticism, but to invert it as well – to make it eat its own words in a sense.

The predominant view through the history of the western philosophical and religious tradition has been one that is static. We argue that this derives from the fact that metaphysical dualism – i.e. the notion of an immaterial soul causally-insulated from the physical universe – was the by-far-predominant paradigm in which the notion of a universal human condition, i.e. human nature, have been constructed and considered. The aspects of being (1) causally insulated from the physical universe and (2) eternal bias the conception of human nature possible within the context of metaphysical dualism to staticity. This, in turn, has biased most historical notions of human nature towards staticity as well.

The increasing predominance of scientific materialism (also known as metaphysical naturalism – i.e. the position contrary to metaphysical-dualism) has undermined the belief in a causally-insulated, non-physical human soul. The philosophical underpinnings of static conceptions of human nature have yet to feel the reverberations of the soul's fall.

A static or preordained human nature also fails to account for developments in evolutionary biology and evolutionary psychology, which demonstrate that the material systems and processes capable of determining the capacities and faculties of humans (e.g. genotype, developmental environment) are *not* static but are instead under a constant state of flux. Static conceptions of human nature were formulated at a time when most everyone thought that humans were distinct from or ontologically-discontinuous with the rest of the animal kingdom; this is likely to have reinforced the bias towards characterizing human nature as static and eternal. We now know that, rather than each organism being created by a deity separately, we along with the rest of the ecosphere constitute an evolutionary continuum, and that on the contrary we bear ontological continuity with the rest of the animal kingdom because of it.

Thirdly, static conceptions of human nature also fail to account for the epigenetic domain of human constitution and activity – i.e. the ways in which our tools, techniques and technologies – our techné – constitute a portion of humans' 'determining conditions' just as much as the genetic domain of human constitution and activity does, as described in the section 'Prosthetic Essence: The Co-Constitution of

Man & Techné.' The notion that culture and our available cultural and technic environment are constantly changing. This notion is even accepted by those who remain dubious that our genetic constitution changes over multi-generational time as well. The conjunction of the premises that (1) man and his technic environment are co-constitutive and that (2) man's technic environment changes serves to further undermine static conceptions of human nature.

Furthermore, we contend that it is precisely due to their staticity that certain views of human nature incline one to see any changes made to human nature as indignifying – i.e. because change is the antithesis of staticity. The conception of human nature articulated here, as the will toward self-determination (which is characterized both by our own partial self-determination as well as our desire to increase our degree of self-determination), put self-directed change at the heart of the human. If change, self-determination and "the Becoming underlying life's self-overcoming" (Cortese, 2014) is what distinguishes the human as such, then changes made to one's self, so long as they are mediated upon the self by and for the self, could be anything but indignifying.

Lastly, the characterization of human nature as the will toward self-determination is able to achieve the universality sought-after in most, if not all, conceptions of human nature *through* its lack of a constant 'nature' (e.g. constitution or range of capacities and faculties), or in other words through its seeming lack of 'universality' as-such. If each of us are free to choose ourselves, to make our own natures (or, put another way, to associate our first and foremost natures with that very condition of making our own natures – the human metacondition), to *differ*, then we are united through our difference. If each of us are free to determine to as great an extend we can or wish the determining conditions of our being, if each is free to forfeit static being for ecstatic becoming, then each of us is the same at radical-root.

Conceptions of human nature that are not so restrictive – i.e. that do not make it easy to characterize a given person or organism as inhuman – is desirable because static, restrictive ontologies of human nature engender large-scale acts of cruelty unto enslavement and genocide. A wrongly-perceived 'lack of humanity' is what led white westerners to enslaving the African people, and what could very well engender the discrimination or outright enslavement or genocide of future non-biological intelligences (including significantly-self-modified humans).

The will toward self-determination is exclusively capable of encompassing a range of possible secondary-natures by making its first-most 'constitutive composition' a metaposition on conditioning the human condition itself.

ADDRESSING ANTICIPATED CRITIQUES: LIMITED TECHNOLOGICAL SELF-DETERMINATION AS NET-DISENFRANCHISEMENT?

One possible criticism of the argument, outlined above (i.e. that it is both desirable and ethical to develop HET because they constitute our best means of self-determination), is that if HET is only available to a wealthy elite then it could increase *their* degree of self-determination *at the expense of* everyone else, whose autonomy and sovereignty are severely threatened by the increased capabilities (e.g. intelligence) of such wealthy HET-recipients. According to this critique, even if HET do constitute our best potential means of self-determination, their development and proliferation could have a net-detrimental effect to society's cumulative autonomy and degree of self-determination by only increasing the degree-of-self-determination possessed by select members of society.

In this section we argue that, while limited initial availability of HET is a legitimate concern that should be mitigated as effectively as possible, this criticism fails to justify avoiding the development of HET. The potential decrease in net-autonomy that the above criticism is concerned with is outweighed by the vast increase in autonomy possible through the development of HET. We also argue that other considerations surrounding the use of HET – some militaristic and political, some commercial – force the conclusion that the most effective means of determining how HET is developed, proliferated (i.e. made available) and used (which would encompass any attempt to maximize the initial availability of HET) is through the deliberative development of HET, rather than relinquishment. In particular, we argue that militaristic, political and economic considerations of HET create a situation in which avoiding the development of HET completely (for fear that it will foster a net-decrease in autonomy as outlines in the above criticism) impels its development elsewhere (where we have less oversight over its development and proliferation), thereby creating the exact situation the criticism is concerned with – namely HET (and the increase in capabilities and faculties it affords) being made available to a select few and not others.

It is true that HET pose the potential to cause drastic disparity between the existential modalities (e.g. modalities of experience, functional capabilities, embodiment, environment, lifestyle) available to different members of society. The vast rich-poor divide could severely limit the availability of HET, especially during the early years if their availability. Indeed, disparity of wealth is a particularly pressing concern in regards to HET because if HET the resource in question in this case has non-negligible potential to bestow significant advantages (such as intelligence amplification and augmentation) upon HET-recipients that could maximize their ability to retain their current wealth. Because most emerging technologies cost so much during the initial years of their availability, they are almost invariably a luxury item for a number of years before improvements in design and manufacturing (funded by the revenues generated by the technologies' sales during its initial high-cost period) allow the cost to be driven down into the price-range of the average consumer (Rothblatt, 2011). This was as true for washing machines and VCRs as it was for cell-phones. But never before have such emerging technologies posed the potential to actually facilitate the volitional control of the determining conditions of our very selves. Never before have we been presented with a potential situation wherein the amount of assets one has could determine fundamental conditions and parameters of their very existence and experience, and make financial disparity correlative with existential and experiential impoverishment to such an extensive and fundamental degree. And never before have emerging technologies held such potential to foster such dramatic increases in the ability of emerging-technology-recipients to increase their own wealth or to deliberately deter the widespread proliferation of a given emerging technology.

But while HET do pose the potential to increase the magnitude of difference among members of society, they also have the potential to mitigate the disenfranchising consequences of *existing* differences amongst members of society. The likely health, longevity and intelligence of a given person is impacted both by upbringing (i.e. interaction with an external environment) as well as genetics. As a result some people are born into circumstances (e.g. parents, environment) and/or genotypes conferring an arbitrarily higher probability of high intelligence or good health than others. The proliferation of HET would allow us to minimize such arbitrary disparities by minimizing the degree of arbitrariness in the phenotypic-biases or developmental-biases conferred by the genes or the developmental environment one is born into. If our children happen to be born with less genetic bias towards high intellect or happiness – or any other such near-ubiquitously-desired human trait or characteristic – then it is through the use of HET that we can remediate that and undo such undue biases and arbitrary instances of genetic or developmental impoverishment.

This is *not* to say that differences amongst the capabilities and predispositions of the members of society is in any way an absolute evil. On the contrary, difference and diversity are things to be celebrated – indeed, things that are *vital* to the will toward self-determination that marks us as human more than anything else. We would go so far as to contend that it is solely *through* our difference that humans find true equality and union; i.e. that we are each the same solely in our ceaseless will and thrust to better-determine for ourselves the determining conditions of our selves.

There may, however, be a heretofore-unseen advantage in the sheer severity or magnitude of some of the dangerous, disenfranchising and marginalizing potentials of emerging (e.g. NBIC) technologies in general and HET in particular. The severity of such dangers, as well as the likelihood of their being manifest, have a significant impact on the demand to participate in the determination of regulations pertaining to the safe and ethical development and proliferation of HET in ways that reinforce our values and, more importantly, our liberties. By and large, the more severe a given technology's dangerous potentials, the more pressing the demand to ensure that it is developed, proliferated and used safely and ethically, in ways that maximize their beneficial potentials and minimize their dangerous ones. The unethical use of HET in general and neurotechnologies in particular by institutions and organizations such as government and industry, or by individuals upon one another, constitutes perhaps the greatest danger to our near-future liberty, autonomy and safety. For this reason it is likely that societies will have a readily-apprehensible interest in deliberately participating in the regulatory processes and laws impacting the development, proliferation and use of HET, with the aim of maximizing their liberating and beneficial potentials while minimizing their disenfranchising, marginalizing an dangerous potentials.

It is both important and relevant to note that, somewhat counter-intuitively, the most effective means of minimizing the negative potentials of HET is through a deliberative effort to develop them safely and ethically – in other words to actually go out and develop them, with as much participation from the public and relevant experts and scientists as possible. The only alternative is to avoid their development completely on the basis that their destructive potentials are simply *too* severe to warrant being made possible by their development. This position is known as *technological relinquishment* (Joy, 2000; Kass 2001; Kaczynski 2008). But the problem with this solution-paradigm is that relinquishing the development of a given technology in one nation does not necessitate, or even make likely, the relinquishment of that technology or technological domain in all other nations with the economy or infrastructure necessary to support such development (Cortese, 2013c). The only way that legislatively-instigated technological relinquishment will see success is if the ban on a given area of technological development is unanimously extended by all developed nations (i.e. all nations with the necessary resources and infrastructure to develop such areas of technology) across the globe. Different nations have different laws, policies and stances on political issues, and this all but ensures, at least in cases where there is a clear use and market for the technology in question, that technological relinquishment in one country will simply lead to the technology in question being developed elsewhere.

Another flaw with the technological relinquishment solution-paradigm derives from the fact that many of the technological domains (e.g. nanotechnology, biotechnology, neurotechnology, information technology) that underlie the more extensive forms of HET also have many other applications, including commercial and military applications. The point of technological relinquishment is not to legally prohibit certain uses of a given technology, but to relinquish development of a given technological domain so that we don't have the capacity to actually produce the kinds of technologies that are encompassed by that technological domain. Thus the opposition to relinquishing development in any of the NBIC technology-domains will consist of not only those in favor of HET, but also everyone interested in the vast number of other commercial applications of biotechnology, nanotechnology, neurotechnology and information technology. The significant militaristic potential of NBIC technology-domains also significantly decreases governments' incentive to relinquish their development, as to do so with the knowledge that a non-allied foreign military is developing them, or even that they could develop them, would effectively be to forfeit their defensive and offensive footing and put them at a significant militaristic disadvantage.

Thus the outright relinquishment of a given technological domain is likely to increase the probability that it is developed elsewhere (perhaps in a less democratic nation with less transparency and less public oversight into the development of emerging technologies), in a context where we will have far less power to shape the ultimate embodiments of such technologies into ones that exemplify our liberties, values and desires, and far less power to steer the development of such technologies into beneficial arenas and out of deleterious and disenfranchising ones. Indeed, this is particularly true for say molecular nanotechnology or bioweapons, wherein the potentially-dangerous effects can be global in scale.

The technological relinquishment position is contrasted by *differential technological development* (Bostrom, 2002), wherein resources or funds are preferentially allocated to the development of certain technologies and not others, or to the implementation of the beneficial uses and potentials of a given technological domain (e.g. nanotechnology, biotechnology, information technology) and not to the dangerous or disenfranchising uses of such technological domains.

Similarly, the best way to ensure that the development of HET is regulated in a way that allows the public to participate in the determination of its ultimate embodiments – i.e. to ensure that society-at-large has a chance of steering HET and neurotechnology toward their beneficial potentialities an away from their dangerous and disenfranchising ones – is by actually developing it. The only way that any sort of regulations or regulatory bodies for the safe, ethical and self-empowering development of HET are going to form is if we they are actually developed. This is a safer state of affairs than avoiding their development because in that case such technologies would be developed, here or elsewhere, in the absence of any regulations or laws pertaining to their safe development and use.

Thus, avoiding the development of HET for the fear that limitations on its initial availability will cause a net-decrease in autonomy will only work to create a worse version of that very situation, wherein HET is develoeped in another nation, thereby increasing their degree of self-determination *at the expense* of those nations who relinquished HET development and/or use.

CONCLUSION

It is through the development of human enhancement technologies in general and the development of increasingly precise and extensive neuromodulation technologies for the controlled induction and modulation of an agent's own neural activity in particular that we can gain more control than we've ever had before over the determining conditions of the material systems constituting our minds and bodies. The precision of our available means of self-modification and self-modulation correspond with our capacity for self-determination (i.e. with their effectiveness). It is for this reason that neuromodulation *ipso facto* constitutes our most promising (i.e. most precise and extensive) means of self-determination – because it is the technological and methodological domain that encompasses the induction and modulation of neural activity, and because it is the induction and modulation of an agent's own nervous system that constitutes our most extensive and precise means of self-determination. The proliferation of HET in general and neurotechnology in particular, will serve to increase humanity's existing but comparatively-limited capacity for self-determination, or in other words our capacity to change the material systems determining the parameters (e.g. distinguishing characteristics) of our selves, which encompasses both our functional capabilities and our experiential modalities. This capacity is today exemplified for the most part by the ways in which we modify ourselves through methodological, prosthetic and reciprocal self-determination, as outlined above. Each and every one of these means of self-determination constitute a means of facilitating changes to our experiential and functional capacities, faculties and modalities that manifest themselves as changes to the wiring, i.e. the organization, of our brains, and as such legitimately constitute, respectively, viable means of self-determination. And it is because we as humans are defined more by our will toward self-determination than by anything else that the development and proliferation of HET will be anything but dehumanizing.

REFERENCES

Annas, G. J. (2007). Imagining a New Era of Neuroimaging, Neuroethics, and Neurolaw. *American Journal of Law & Medicine*, *33*(2-3), 163–170. doi:10.1177/009885880703300201 PMID:17910155

Bainbridge, W. S. (Ed.). (2013). *Converging technologies for improving human performance: Nanotechnology, biotechnology, information technology and cognitive science*. Springer Science & Business Media.

Bainbridge, W. S., & Roco, M. C. (2006). *Managing Nano-Bio-Info-Cogno Innovations*. Springer. doi:10.1007/1-4020-4107-1

Bankman, I. N., & Janselewitz, S. J. (1995, September). Neural waveform detector for prosthesis control. In *Engineering in Medicine and Biology Society, 1995., IEEE 17th Annual Conference* (Vol. 2, pp. 963-964). IEEE. 10.1109/IEMBS.1995.579382

Banks, D. (1998). Neurotechnology. *Engineering Science and Education Journal*, *7*(3), 135–144. doi:10.1049/esej:19980306

Benanti, P. (2010). From Neuroskepticism to Neuroethics: Role of Morality in Neuroscience That Becomes Neurotechnology. *AJOB Neuroscience*, *1*(2), 39–40. doi:10.1080/21507741003699264

Berger, T. W., & Glanzman, D. L. (Eds.). (2005). *Toward replacement parts for the brain: implantable biomimetic electronics as neural prostheses*. MIT Press.

Berger, T. W., Hampson, R. E., Song, D., Goonawardena, A., Marmarelis, V. Z., & Deadwyler, S. A. (2011). A cortical neural prosthesis for restoring and enhancing memory. *Journal of Neural Engineering*, *8*(4), 046017. doi:10.1088/1741-2560/8/4/046017 PMID:21677369

Bostrom, N. (2002). Existential risks: Analyzing Human Extinction Scenarios and Related Hazards. *Journal of Evolution and Technology / WTA*, 9.

Boyden, E. S., Zhang, F., Bamberg, E., Nagel, G., & Deisseroth, K. (2005). Millisecond-timescale, genetically targeted optical control of neural activity. *Nature Neuroscience*, *8*(9), 1263–1268. doi:10.1038/nn1525 PMID:16116447

Breit, S., Schulz, J. B., & Benabid, A. L. (2004). Deep brain stimulation. *Cell and Tissue Research*, *318*(1), 275–288. doi:10.100700441-004-0936-0 PMID:15322914

Brey, P. (2000). Technology as extension of human faculties. *Metaphysics, Epistemology, and Technology. Research in Philosophy and Technology, 19.*

Burns, A., Ow, H., & Wiesner, U. (2006). Fluorescent core–shell silica nanoparticles: Towards "Lab on a Particle" architectures for nanobiotechnology. *Chemical Society Reviews, 35*(11), 1028–1042. doi:10.1039/B600562B PMID:17057833

Cavalcanti, A., & Freitas, R. A. Jr. (2005). Nanorobotics control design: A collective behavior approach for medicine. *NanoBioscience. IEEE Transactions on, 4*(2), 133–140. PMID:16117021

Chalmers, D., & Clark, A. (1998). The extended mind. *Analysis, 58*(1), 7–19. doi:10.1093/analys/58.1.7

Chan, H. Y., Aslam, D. M., Wiler, J. A., & Casey, B. (2009). A novel diamond microprobe for neurochemical and-electrical recording in neural prosthesis. *Microelectromechanical Systems. Journalism, 18*(3), 511–521.

Chapin, J. K. (2004). Using multi-neuron population recordings for neural prosthetics. *Nature Neuroscience, 7*(5), 452–455. doi:10.1038/nn1234 PMID:15114357

Cheon, J., & Lee, J. H. (2008). Synergistically integrated nanoparticles as multimodal probes for nanobiotechnology. *Accounts of Chemical Research, 41*(12), 1630–1640. doi:10.1021/ar800045c PMID:18698851

Clark, A. (1998a). *Being there: Putting brain, body, and world together again.* MIT Press.

Clark, A. (1998b). Embodiment and the Philosophy of Mind. *Royal Institute of Philosophy, 43*(Supplement 43), 35–51. doi:10.1017/S135824610000429X

Clark, A. (1999). An embodied cognitive science? *Trends in Cognitive Sciences, 3*(9), 345–351. doi:10.1016/S1364-6613(99)01361-3 PMID:10461197

Clark, A. (2008). *Supersizing the Mind: Embodiment, Action, and Cognitive Extension: Embodiment, Action, and Cognitive Extension.* Oxford University Press. doi:10.1093/acprof:oso/9780195333213.001.0001

Cooney, B. (2004). *Posthumanity: thinking philosophically about the future.* Rowman & Littlefield.

Cortese, F. (2013a). *Transhumanism, Technology & Science: To Say It's Impossible Is To Mock History Itself.* Institute for Ethics & Emerging Technologies. Retrieved November 17, 2015, from http://ieet.org/index.php/IEET/more/cortese20130612

Cortese, F. (2013b). The Hubris of Neoluddism. *H+ Magazine.* Retrieved November 17, 2015, from http://hplusmagazine.com/2013/06/07/the-hubris-of-neo-luddism/

Cortese, F. (2013c). Three Spectres of Immortality: A Talk From the Radical Life Extension Conference in Washington D.C. *H+ Magazine.* Retrieved November 17, 2015, from http://hplusmagazine.com/2013/10/16/three-spectres-of-immortality-a-talk-from-the-radical-life-extension-conference-in-washington-d-c/

Cortese, F. (2014). Heidegger On The Existential Utility Of Death. In C. Tandy (Ed.), Death And Anti-Death, Volume 12: One Hundred Years After Charles S. Peirce (1839-1914) (pp. 131-136). Ann Arbor, MI: Ria University Press.

De Jong, K., Olds, J., & Giordano, J. (2011). *National Neuroscience: Ethics, Legal and Social Issues Conference* (No. 202069). George Mason University.

Denning, T., Matsuoka, Y., & Kohno, T. (2009). Neurosecurity: Security and privacy for neural devices. *Neurosurgical Focus*, *27*(1), E7. doi:10.3171/2009.4.FOCUS0985 PMID:19569895

Dunne, J. (1993). *Back to the Rough Ground: "Phronesis" and "Techne"*. Modern Philosophy and in Aristotle.

Eaton, M. L., & Illes, J. (2007). Commercializing cognitive neurotechnology—the ethical terrain. *Nature Biotechnology*, *25*(4), 393–397. doi:10.1038/nbt0407-393 PMID:17420741

Farah, M. J. (2005). Neuroethics: The practical and the philosophical. *Trends in Cognitive Sciences*, *9*(1), 34–40. doi:10.1016/j.tics.2004.12.001 PMID:15639439

Farah, M. J. (2005). Neuroethics: The practical and the philosophical. *Trends in Cognitive Sciences*, *9*(1), 34–40. doi:10.1016/j.tics.2004.12.001 PMID:15639439

Farah, M. J., Illes, J., Cook-Deegan, R., Gardner, H., Kandel, E., King, P., ... Wolpe, P. R. (2004). Neurocognitive enhancement: What can we do and what should we do? *Nature Reviews. Neuroscience*, *5*(5), 421–425. doi:10.1038/nrn1390 PMID:15100724

Fetz, E. E. (2007). Volitional control of neural activity: Implications for brain–computer interfaces. *The Journal of Physiology*, *579*(3), 571–579. doi:10.1113/jphysiol.2006.127142 PMID:17234689

Fins, J. J. (2007). Mind wars: Brain research and national defense. *Journal of the American Medical Association*, *297*(12), 1382–1383. doi:10.1001/jama.297.12.1382

Freitas, R. A. (1999). *Basic capabilities*. Georgetown, TX: Landes Bioscience.

Freitas, R. A. (2002). The future of nanofabrication and molecular scale devices in nanomedicine. *Studies in Health Technology and Informatics*, 45–60. PMID:12026137

Freitas, R. A. Jr. (2005). Nanotechnology, nanomedicine and nanosurgery. *International Journal of Surgery*, *3*(4), 243–246. doi:10.1016/j.ijsu.2005.10.007 PMID:17462292

Freitas, R. A., & Havukkala, I. (2005). Current status of nanomedicine and medical nanorobotics. *Journal of Computational and Theoretical Nanoscience*, *2*(1), 1–25.

Freitas, R. A., & Nanomedicine, V. I. (2003). *Biocompatibility*. Georgetown, TX: Landes Bioscience.

Gasson, M., Hutt, B., Goodhew, I., Kyberd, P., & Warwick, K. (2005). Invasive neural prosthesis for neural signal detection and nerve stimulation. *International Journal of Adaptive Control and Signal Processing*, *19*(5), 365–375.

Gazzaley, A., Cooney, J. W., McEvoy, K., Knight, R. T., & D'esposito, M. (2005). Top-down enhancement and suppression of the magnitude and speed of neural activity. *Journal of Cognitive Neuroscience*, *17*(3), 507–517. doi:10.1162/0898929053279522 PMID:15814009

Geelen, J. (2012). *The Emerging Neurotechnologies: Recent Developments and Policy Implications*. Policy Horizons Canada.

Giordano, J. (Ed.). (2012). *Neurotechnology: Premises, potential, and problems.* CRC Press. doi:10.1201/b11861

Giordano, J., Akhouri, R., & McBride, D. K. (2009). Implantable Nano-Neurotechnological Devices: Consideration of Ethical, Legal, and Social Issues and Implications. *Journal of Long-Term Effects of Medical Implants, 19*(1), 83–93. doi:10.1615/JLongTermEffMedImplants.v19.i1.80 PMID:20402632

Greene, J. (2004). Article. *Philosophical Transactions of the Royal Society of London. Series B, Biological Sciences, 359*, 1776.

Han, X., Qian, X., Bernstein, J. G., Zhou, H. H., Franzesi, G. T., Stern, P., ... Boyden, E. S. (2009). Millisecond-timescale optical control of neural dynamics in the nonhuman primate brain. *Neuron, 62*(2), 191–198. doi:10.1016/j.neuron.2009.03.011 PMID:19409264

Heetderks, W. J. (1988). RF powering of millimeter-and submillimeter-sized neural prosthetic implants. *Biomedical Engineering. IEEE Transactions on, 35*(5), 323–327. PMID:3397079

Hetke, J. F., & Anderson, D. J. (2002). Silicon microelectrodes for extracellular recording. Handbook of Neuroprosthetic Methods, 163-91.

Illes, J., Kirschen, M. P., & Gabrieli, J. D. (2003). From neuroimaging to neuroethics. *Nature Neuroscience, 6*(3), 205–205. doi:10.1038/nn0303-205 PMID:12601375

Isa, T., Fetz, E. E., & Müller, K. R. (2009). Recent advances in brain–machine interfaces. *Neural Networks, 22*(9), 1201–1202. doi:10.1016/j.neunet.2009.10.003 PMID:19840893

Isaacs, R. E., Weber, D. J., & Schwartz, A. B. (2000). Work toward real-time control of a cortical neural prothesis. *Rehabilitation Engineering. IEEE Transactions on, 8*(2), 196–198. PMID:10896185

Jackson, A., Moritz, C. T., Mavoori, J., Lucas, T. H., & Fetz, E. E. (2006). The Neurochip BCI: Towards a neural prosthesis for upper limb function. *Neural Systems and Rehabilitation Engineering. IEEE Transactions on, 14*(2), 187–190.

Joy, B. (2000). Why the future doesn't need us. *Nanoethics–The Ethical and Social Implications of Nanotechnology*, 17-39.

Kaczynski, T. J. (2008). *Industrial Society and Its Future.* Wingspan Press.

Kass, L. (2001). Preventing a brave new world. *Technology and Values: Essential Readings*, 311-322.

Kostarelos, K. (2006). The emergence of nanomedicine: A field in the making. *Nanomedicine (London), 1*(1), 9–12. doi:10.2217/17435889.1.1.1 PMID:17716200

Kringelbach, M. L., & Aziz, T. Z. (2009). Deep brain stimulation. *Journal of the American Medical Association, 301*(16), 1705–1707. doi:10.1001/jama.2009.551 PMID:19383961

Lawson, C. (2010). Technology and the extension of human capabilities. *Journal for the Theory of Social Behaviour, 40*(2), 207–223. doi:10.1111/j.1468-5914.2009.00428.x

Levy, N. (2007). *Neuroethics: Challenges for the 21st century.* Cambridge University Press. doi:10.1017/CBO9780511811890

Loeb, G. E., McHardy, J., Kelliher, E. M., & Brummer, S. B. (1982). Neural prosthesis. *Biocompatibility in Clinical Practice, 2*, 123-149.

Lowe, C. R. (2000). Nanobiotechnology: The fabrication and applications of chemical and biological nanostructures. *Current Opinion in Structural Biology, 10*(4), 428–434. doi:10.1016/S0959-440X(00)00110-X PMID:10981630

Luppicini, R. (2010). *Technoethics and the Evolving Knowledge Society: Ethical Issues in Technological Design, Research, Development, and Innovation.* Hershey, PA: IGI Global; doi:10.4018/978-1-60566-952-6

Luppicini, R., & Adell, R. (2009). *Handbook of Research on Technoethics* (Vols. 1–2). Hershey, PA: IGI Global; doi:10.4018/978-1-60566-022-6

Lynch, Z. (2004). Neurotechnology and society (2010–2060). *Annals of the New York Academy of Sciences, 1013*(1), 229–233. doi:10.1196/annals.1305.016 PMID:15194618

McLuhan, M. (1964). *The Gutenberg galaxy: The making of typographic man.* Toronto: University of Toronto Press.

McLuhan, M. (1966). *Understanding media: The extensions of man.* Toronto: University of Toronto Press.

McLuhan, M., & Fiore, Q. (1967). *The medium is the massage.* New York: Random House.

McLuhan, M., Fiore, Q., & Agel, J. (1968). *War and peace in the global village* (Vol. 127). New York: Bantam books.

McLuhan, M., & McLuhan, E. (1988). *Laws of media: The new science* (Vol. 1). Toronto: University of Toronto Press.

Meagher, R. (1988). Techne. *Perspecta, 24*, 159–164. doi:10.2307/1567132

Müller, D. J., & Dufrene, Y. F. (2008). Atomic force microscopy as a multifunctional molecular toolbox in nanobiotechnology. *Nature Nanotechnology, 3*(5), 261–269. doi:10.1038/nnano.2008.100 PMID:18654521

Niemeyer, C. M. (2004). *Nanobiotechnology.* Nanobiotechnology. Encyclopedia of Molecular Cell Biology and Molecular Medicine. doi:10.1002/3527602453

Perlmutter, J. S., & Mink, J. W. (2006). Deep brain stimulation. *Annual Review of Neuroscience, 29*(1), 229–257. doi:10.1146/annurev.neuro.29.051605.112824 PMID:16776585

Rawlins, F. I. G. (1950). Episteme and Techne. *Philosophy and Phenomenological Research, 10*(3), 389–397. doi:10.2307/2103272

Roco, M. C. (2004). Science and technology integration for increased human potential and societal outcomes. *Annals of the New York Academy of Sciences, 1013*(1), 1–16. doi:10.1196/annals.1305.001 PMID:15194603

Rothblatt, M. (2011). Won't mindclones only be for the rich and famous? *Institute for Ethics & Emerging Technologies.* Retrieved November 17, 2015, from http://ieet.org/index.php/IEET/more/rothblatt20110321

Sanguineti, V., Giugliano, M., Grattoarola, M., & Morasso, P. (2001). 14 Neuro-Engineering: From neural interfaces to biological computers. *Communications Through Virtual Technologies: Identity, Community, and Technology in the Communication Age, 1*, 233.

Schleim, S. (2012). Brains in context in the neurolaw debate: The examples of free will and "dangerous" brains. *International Journal of Law and Psychiatry, 35*(2), 104–111. doi:10.1016/j.ijlp.2012.01.001 PMID:22289293

Schwartz, A. B. (2004). Cortical neural prosthetics. *Annual Review of Neuroscience, 27*(1), 487–507. doi:10.1146/annurev.neuro.27.070203.144233 PMID:15217341

Serruya, M. D., Hatsopoulos, N. G., Paninski, L., Fellows, M. R., & Donoghue, J. P. (2002). Brain-machine interface: Instant neural control of a movement signal. *Nature, 416*(6877), 141–142. doi:10.1038/416141a PMID:11894084

Shain, W., Spataro, L., Dilgen, J., Haverstick, K., Retterer, S., Isaacson, M., & Turner, J. N. (2003). Controlling cellular reactive responses around neural prosthetic devices using peripheral and local intervention strategies. *Neural Systems and Rehabilitation Engineering. IEEE Transactions on, 11*(2), 186–188. PMID:12899270

Smart, J. J. C., & Haldane, J. J. (2003). *Atheism and theism.* Blackwell Publishing. doi:10.1002/9780470756225

Spranger, T. M. (Ed.). (2012). *International neurolaw: A comparative analysis.* Springer. doi:10.1007/978-3-642-21541-4

Stieglitz, T., Schuetter, M., & Koch, K. P. (2005). Implantable biomedical microsystems for neural prostheses. *Engineering in Medicine and Biology Magazine, IEEE, 24*(5), 58–65. doi:10.1109/MEMB.2005.1511501 PMID:16248118

Stieglitz, T., Schuettler, M., & Meyer, J. U. (2000). Micromachined, polyimide-based devices for flexible neural interfaces. *Biomedical Microdevices, 2*(4), 283–294. doi:10.1023/A:1009955222114

Takagi, M. (2012). Safety and Neuroethical Consideration of Deep Brain Stimulation as Psychiatric or Dementia Treatment. *Asian Bioethics Review, 4*(1), 48–64.

Taylor, J. S. (1995). Neurolaw: Towards a new medical jurisprudence. *Brain Injury: [BI], 9*(7), 745–751. doi:10.3109/02699059509008230 PMID:8680401

Van Inwagen, P. (1975). The incompatibility of free will and determinism. *Philosophical Studies, 27*(3), 185–199. doi:10.1007/BF01624156

Wadia, P. (2010). The Notion of 'Techne' in Plato. *Philosophical Studies, 31*, 148–158.

Wolf, S. M. (2008). Neurolaw: The big question. *The American Journal of Bioethics, 8*(1), 21–22. doi:10.1080/15265160701828485 PMID:18236328

Xuyang, W., & Yuzhuo, Z. (2011). Law philosophy analysis: Application of medical instruments for direct reading and influence of the activities of cranial nerve. In *Computer Science & Education (ICCSE), 2011 6th International Conference on* (pp. 293-296). IEEE.

ENDNOTES

[1]   The word 'technic' is here used in the sense of encompassing both technology and technique. It derives from the ancient Greek notion of 'techne', which was a category that made no distinction between technology and technique, or technology and methodology.

[2]   We will use the term 'phenomenal' in the sense of 'pertaining to subjective experience'. This includes everything from perception to thinking to memory and imagination and subconscious (but not autonomic) functions – i.e. all possible mental phenomena.

[3]   For a review of the technical aspects of neurotechnology, see Banks, 1998. For a review of the ethics of neurotechnology, see Farah et al, 2004.

[4]   Optogenetic induction of neural activity involves via the application of light to neurons genetically engineered so as to generate an action potential in the presence of a certain frequency of light through the incorporation of photosensitive proteins that change their conformational shape in response to certain frequencies of electromagnetic radiation. See Boyden, 1995, and Han et al., 2009 for empirical examples of optogenetic neural induction.

[5]   Dissent. From Latin *dissentire* (*dis:* "differently"; *sentire:* "to feel, think").

[6]   For a historical review of the notion of techné in ancient Greece, see Meagher, 1988.

Section 2

Current Applications of Emerging Technologies and Their Ethical Implications

Chapter 6
Lethal Military Robots:
Who Is Responsible When Things Go Wrong?

Lambèr Royakkers
Eindhoven University of Technology, The Netherlands

Peter Olsthoorn
Netherlands Defence Academy, The Netherlands

ABSTRACT

Although most unmanned systems that militaries use today are still unarmed and predominantly used for surveillance, it is especially the proliferation of armed military robots that raises some serious ethical questions. One of the most pressing concerns the moral responsibility in case a military robot uses violence in a way that would normally qualify as a war crime. In this chapter, the authors critically assess the chain of responsibility with respect to the deployment of both semi-autonomous and (learning) autonomous lethal military robots. They start by looking at military commanders because they are the ones with whom responsibility normally lies. The authors argue that this is typically still the case when lethal robots kill wrongly – even if these robots act autonomously. Nonetheless, they next look into the possible moral responsibility of the actors at the beginning and the end of the causal chain: those who design and manufacture armed military robots, and those who, far from the battlefield, remotely control them.

INTRODUCTION

Although the use of unmanned systems is still in its infancy in most armed forces, some militaries, especially those of the US and Israel, have developed and deployed highly advanced drones. Even though the majority of these unmanned systems used in operations today are unarmed and mainly used for reconnaissance and mine clearing, the increase of the number of armed military robots, especially airborne ones, is undeniable. Certainly, on the face of it, unmanned systems have some strong benefits that could reduce the number of 'unfortunate incidents' on the battlefield. To start with, the main causes of misconduct on

DOI: 10.4018/978-1-5225-5094-5.ch006

the battlefield: frustration, boredom, and anger are diminished.[1] What's more, these unmanned systems have no instinct of self-preservation, and are able to hold their fire in critical situations. On the other hand, the use of robots raises some serious ethical questions. For instance, under what circumstances, and to what extent, do we allow robots to act autonomously? What precautions should (and can) we take to prevent robots from running amok? Would the use of military robots not be counterproductive to winning the hearts and minds of occupied populations, or result in more desperate terrorist-tactics given an increasing asymmetry in warfare? (See for an overview Lin, Bekey, and Abney, 2008; Lichocki, Kahn & Billard. 2011; Olsthoorn & Royakkers 2011; Schwarz 2017). A particularly pressing question is what to do when things go wrong: who, if anyone, can be held morally accountable *in reason* for an act of violence that a) involves a military robot; and b) would normally be described as a war crime?

The answer to that latter question depends on the answer to a prior one: when is there reasonable ground to hold an agent morally responsible for a certain outcome in the first place? Following Fischer & Ravizza (1998) on moral responsibility, we will assume here that agents can only in reason be held responsible if they are *moral* agents, that is, persons (or organizations) who have *control* over their behavior and the resulting consequences. This means that agents can be held responsible for a certain decision only insofar as they have been able to make it *in freedom* and *knowingly*. The first term means that it is not reasonable to hold agents responsible for actions or their consequences if they were not coerced or under duress. The second term, 'knowingly,' has an important normative aspect in that it relates to what people should know, or can with reason be expected to know, with respect to the relevant facts surrounding their decision or action.[2]

According to some authors (Asaro, 2007; Sparrow, 2007; Sharkey, 2008), the use of armed military robots makes the attribution of responsibility problematic, as it is not sufficiently clear who can be held responsible for civilian casualties and other collateral damage that result from the use of military robots, whether by mechanical error or failing judgment. Is it the designer/programmer, the field commander, the robot manufacturer, the robot controller/supervisor, or the nation that commissioned the robot? The answer to that question depends on a number of factors. For instance, was the cause a programming error, a malfunctioning, an accident, or intentional misuse? Or did the procedure include a 'man-in-the-loop,' that is, an element of human control, or was the military robot a fully autonomous or even learning machine?

As to that last question, this paper distinguishes between semi-autonomous robots, autonomous (but non-learning) robots, and learning robots. To start with the latter, learning robots are able to develop new behavioral patterns without human intervention; these robots are able to go beyond the parameters they left the factory with, as the robot itself can change them in its interaction with the operating environment (Matthias, 2004). An example is a system that was developed for the automatic diagnosis of lung cancer, and which is able to learn to identify cancer cells on the basis of microscope images of specimens of needle biopsies obtained from the bodies of the persons to be diagnosed (Matthias, 2004). More learning systems are in development, and most of them will pose no moral problems. But this would be different in the case of lethal military learning robots: seeing that it will often be impossible to predict the future behavior of these robots, it is hard to see how one could have sufficient *control* over their actions, which in its turn makes it difficult to determine who can be held responsible with reason.

Autonomous robots are robots that are based on conclusions derived from gathered information and preprogrammed constraints, and are capable of independently selecting and engaging targets (Crootof 2015). This in contrast to semi-autonomous robots where a human must take some affirmative action before a specific target is elected or engaged, that is, they require a 'man-in-the-loop.' This means that the decision to open fire, or more in general, the taking of any action that could threaten human life, is to be considered and approved by a human agent. According to Sparrow (2007) and Singer (2009), this precondition is essential to avoid the problems with respect to the attribution of responsibility; it is not without reason that the "International Law of Armed Conflict dictates that unmanned systems cannot fire their weapons without a human operator in the loop" (Isenberg, 2007).

Yet, while it is certainly true that currently human agents are kept 'in-the-loop,' it is not certain, or even likely, that this will remain so. The logic that brought unmanned systems more or less leads naturally to the wish to take the human agent out of the system altogether (Sparrow, 2011, 121; see also Sullins, 2010), and it seems almost a given that the future will bring more autonomous, and possibly learning, robots. Illustrative for this direction is that The United States is investing heavily in autonomous robots, and the U.S. Department of Defence has described increasing autonomous capabilities as a high priority. One of the ultimate goals is to take the man out-of-the-loop (US Department of Defense 2013), which raises the essential moral question: should we relinquish the decision to kill a human to a non-human machine? (Johnson & Axinn, 2013). That a lethal decision should be made only by a human and not a machine was one of the main reasons that in 2009 four leading scientists (Noel Sharkey, Peter Asaro, Robert Sparrow and Jürgen Altmann) established the International Committee for Robot Arms Control, ICRAC. The committee wants to restrict the use of armed robots for military purposes as much as possible (Altmann et al., 2013). In 2010 in Berlin, the committee organised the expert workshop Limiting Armed Tele-Operated and Autonomous Systems and invited scientists, politicians and military delegates. Following the workshop, a statement was made – signed by a large majority of those present – which emphasised that a ban ought to be imposed on autonomous armed military robots because a human must always take life-and-death decisions. Part of the statement read,

It is unacceptable for machines to control, determine, or decide upon the application of force or violence in conflict or war. In all cases where such a decision must be made, at least one human being must be held personally responsible and legally accountable for the decision and its foreseeable consequences.[3]

In 2015, the Future of Life Institute gained considerable publicity in 2015 when it distributed an open letter signed by more than twenty thousand artificial intelligence and robotics researchers (and others), which called for a "ban on offensive autonomous weapons beyond meaningful human control"[4]. "Meaningful human control" has been identified as key for the responsible design of autonomous systems operating in circumstances where human life is at stake. By preserving meaningful human control human safety can be better protected and "responsibility gaps" can be avoided. However, we still lack a satisfactory definition of what meaningful human control precisely means in relation to killer robots (Ekelhof, forthcoming, see also Crootof, 2016). Sparrow (2007) was one of the first authors to discuss this question, and he claims that since no one can reasonably be held responsible for autonomous robots' behavior, robots should not be allowed to make life-and-death decisions. In Sparrow's reasoning, considerations of responsibility occupy centre stage. Mukerji (2016) agrees with Sparrow's conclusion that robots should not be allowed to make life-and-death decisions, but on a different argument. He argues that only subjects who are capable of responsibility should make morally significant choices. Since autonomous robots seem to lack that capability, it follows that they should not be entrusted to make life-and-death decisions and act on them. However, some researchers dispute these arguments and that the problem of determining responsibility for autonomous military robots can be solved by addressing it within the context of the military chain of commands (e.g., Schulzke, 2013, and Champagne and

Tonkens, 2015), or by developing responsibility practices that clearly establish lines of accountability (Noorman & Johnson, 2014, and Noorman, 2014).

The above raises plenty of issues to critically assess the attribution of responsibility with respect to the deployment of both semi-autonomous and (learning) autonomous lethal military robots. In this article, we will argue that, in contrast to what some other authors hold, that we can reasonably assign responsibility for the development and deployment of these robots to their developers and commanders. A neglected problem, however, regards the assignment of responsibility at the end of the causal chain: the human operators who remotely control armed military robots from behind a computer screen. The depersonalization of war, the dehumanization of the enemy, and the moralization of technology strengthened by the speed of decision-making, can disengage the human operator morally and emotionally. We will show that to make deliberate, and thus responsible, decisions it is essential that operators have control over their decisions, and a vivid awareness of what is at stake. We will start by looking at the role of those with whom responsibility normally lies, the commanders. After that, we will turn to those at the beginning and the end of the causal chain, respectively the manufacturers and designers, and the human operators. We end by drawing some conclusions.

ULTIMATELY RESPONSIBLE: THE COMMANDING OFFICER

Discrimination and proportionality are the two-main *jus in bello* principles of the Just War Tradition. The first forbids the intentional killing of 'the innocent,' and the underlying idea is that civilians should not be made to suffer in war; overall, this is a rights-based principle. The principle of proportionality is a consequentialist one: enemy combatants should not be subjected to unnecessary suffering and superfluous injury, and a mission is permitted only if the expected military gain outweighs the expected number of unintended (the intended killing of civilians being prohibited anyway) civilian casualties. These principles have materialized in international humanitarian law and, for instance, in international treaties banning, regulating, or limiting the possession and use of certain weaponry.

Sparrow has pointed out that these principles assume that "we can identify the persons responsible for the actions that these principles are intended to govern" (Sparrow, 2007; see also Fieser & Dowden, 2007). Although some authors (Sparrow, 2007; Asaro, 2007; Sharkey, 2008) hold that the use of military robots makes this attribution of responsibility complex, it seems evident that the ultimate responsibility for, for instance, a war crime that crucially involved a military robot lies in the hands of the operators, the commanding officers who ordered the deployment of that robot, the military organization on whose behalf they did so, and the state of which that military is an instrument of. So, at the heart of it, the use of unmanned systems is, as far as responsibility concerns at least, not *very* different from using an aircraft to drop a bomb from a high altitude.

Still, this straightforward approach only works as long as there is 'a human in the loop' – from a legal and ethical perspective that human element seems a precondition for the attribution of responsibility (cf. Singer, 2009). Some have therefore argued that the attribution of responsibility in the case of autonomous military robots is so problematic that for that reason alone their use should be forbidden (Asaro, 2007; Sparrow, 2007). One of the most outspoken advocates of this position on the use of autonomous military robots is Noel Sharkey. In his view, the problem is that armed autonomous robots simply cannot be held accountable for their actions, as "[t]here is no way to punish a robot" (2010, 380). According to Sharkey this "leaves the question about who is responsible somewhere along the long causal chain that includes: the manufacturer for the description they gave, the programmer, the designer, the Department of Defense, the generals or admirals in charge of the operation and the operator" (2010, 380-1). If it proves impossible to establish where the responsibility lies, the use of unmanned robots should be, according to Sharkey, illegal. Other experts in the field hold similar views: a majority of the participants of an Expert Workshop on "Arms Control for Robots – Limiting Armed Tele-Operated and Autonomous Systems" organized by the International Committee for Robot Arms Control (ICRAC) in 2010, for example, found it 'unacceptable for machines to control, determine, or decide upon the application of force or violence in conflict or war. In all cases in which such a decision must be made, at least one human being must be held personally responsible and legally accountable for the decision and its foreseeable consequences' (Altmann et al., 2013).[5] The general drift of these comments is that responsibility evaporates without a human in the loop.

But on second though it seems clear that, also without a human agent directly controlling the robot, it is still a human agent that has decided on whether or not to deploy this robot: 'even if a system is fully autonomous, it does not mean that no humans are involved. Someone has to plan the operation, define the parameters, prescribe the rules of engagement, and deploy the system' (Quintana, 2008). Krishnan therefore thinks that

The legal problems with regard to accountability might be smaller than some critics of military robots believe. (...) If the robot does not operate within the boundaries of its specified parameters, it is the manufacturer's fault. If the robot is used in circumstances that make its use illegal, then it is the commander's fault. (2009, 105).

The basis of this argument is the Doctrine of Command Responsibility, and although this doctrine, 'that goes back to the dawn of time' (Garraway 2009, 704), is interpreted differently by different authors (Garraway, 2009), it will usually cover the deployment of armed military robots. So, if such a robot is used in circumstances that make its use illegal, then it is the commander's fault. The question then arises: what degree of knowledge must a commander have about the workings of a military robot in order to be reasonably responsible? Commanders are expected to take "all necessary and reasonable measures in their power" to prevent war crimes (Heckaerst & Doswald-Beck, 2006), and that requires according to Dunlap (forthcoming) a reasonable understanding of the foreseeable consequences of the deployment of armed military robots, and that we cannot hold the commanding officer responsible if an armed military robot would perform unforeseeable consequences. The latter is in line with the argument of Sparrow (2007), that it is unfair to assign responsibility to the commanding officer of learning autonomous robots, since "[t]he use of autonomous weapons (…) involves a risk that military personnel will be held responsible for the actions of machines whose decisions they did not control". This problem, however, can be overcome by using a more explicit social contract or "blank check". According to Champagne and Tonkens (2015), Sparrow overlooks the possibility of a sufficient high-ranking commanding officer accepting responsibility for the robot's performance, and thus being responsible for any violation of the rules for the ethical conduct of warfare. So,

The moral blame and accompanying punishment could be placed squarely on a human agent (or agents) who, through her own volition, has traded a part of her freedoms for the prestige of occupying a high-ranking position in a given social hierarchy (...). If no one in willing to accept this responsibility, then they should not deploy autonomous killer robots in the first place. (Champagne & Tonkens, 2015, 136; see also Schulzke 2013).

That the future will hold more autonomous systems seems almost a given, and although renouncing certain types of autonomous robots might be a good idea for many reasons, a lack of clarity as to who is responsible for their use is probably not among them (see also Kershnar, 2013). Whether one would want to have that responsibility is a different question altogether.

RESPONSIBILITY OF DESIGNERS

Although in general commanders can be held responsible for the decisions they make, in particular cases the matter is not that clear cut; in some specific cases it might be unjust to hold a commanding officer responsible for the actions of military robots. For instance, it is dubious whether we can hold a commanding officer responsible if, for example, civilian casualties (or casualties among own military personnel) are the result of a malfunctioning military robot, or of a programming error. There have already been instances of such malfunctioning: in October 2007 in South Africa a malfunctioning robotic gun fired five hundred high explosive rounds, killing nine soldiers and seriously injuring fourteen (Shachtman, 2007), while in April 2008 a SWORDS, an armed unmanned ground vehicle, produced unintended movements (Magnuson, 2008). Although partly a result of their flying low and slow, the relatively high loss rate of military robots in military operations is perhaps also an indication of their unreliability. For example, some years ago the US Air Force reported that it had lost 50 percent of its then 90 Predators (Jordan, 2007). Although it is clear that both military personnel and local civilians should be protected from malfunctioning military robots, the question is whether designers can be reasonably held responsible for casualties caused by a malfunctioning system. This is a difficult question for more than one reason. Especially with regard to learning autonomous robots, since according to Sparrow (2007) the designers then lose their responsibility for how the robot will act in the future: "[t]he connection between programmers/designers and the results of the system, which would ground the attribution of responsibility, is broken by the autonomy of the system" (Sparrow 207, p. 70). Sparrow treats the autonomy of military robots as a 'black box', leaving its working opaque, and then drawing out implications as if the autonomy of military robots are the same as human autonomy (Noorman & Johnson, 2014). This is, however, misleading since although autonomous military robots "would be able to go beyond their programming by learning new information and developing novel solutions to problems, the range of possible actions open to them would still constrained by their initial programming" (Schulzke, 2013, 213), and do not exhibit random behavior. These robots are designed to perform particular tasks and the extent to which their actions can vary is constrained by the designers. These constrains for military robots should be based on International Humanitarian Law (including the principle of discrimination, the principle of proportionality, and the principle of superfluous injury or unnecessary suffering) and the rules of engagement.

The possibility that a military robot may engage the wrong targets – because it cannot adequately distinguish citizens from soldiers – could be an acknowledged limitation of the system. If the designers have made this clear to those who have purchased or deployed a system, then, Sparrow (2007) argues, they can no longer be held responsible should this occur; in that case the responsibility should be assumed by the nation or commanding officer who (willfully and knowingly) decided to send the robot into the battlefield despite its known limitations. Conversely, one could argue that designers have an (at least moral) obligation to make products that are 'safe' and satisfy the legal and ethical conditions, and that it poses an unacceptable risk to soldiers and civilians alike to introduce a robot with such 'an acknowledged limitation' onto the battlefield. Although it might seem somewhat inconsistent to require armed military robots to be safe, as their main purpose is to destroy, in reality there is of course ample reason to be extra cautious with systems that are designed to be lethal. As it stands, there is, regarding the responsibility of designers of military robots (and militaries that deploy them), no lack of relevant legal and ethical concepts we can turn to, with *liability* seeming to be the most appropriate one (see also Lucas, 2011). The advantage of responsibility as liability *in this case*, that is, of malfunctioning robots, is that it does not require the government to foresee the consequences of new technology but rather – under certain conditions – makes the ones developing the technologies legally liable for these consequences. This places the responsibility where it can be met best: in the hands of the ones developing the technology. They have the best knowledge of new innovations and their possible effects and they are in the best position to avert certain disadvantages. Moreover, a scheme of liability would stimulate them to take their (active) moral responsibility seriously (Van de Poel & Royakkers, 2011).

Regrettably, in an international environment liability issues are not always that straightforward; for starters, the conditions that have to be met for someone to be liable depend on national laws that differ from country to country. Generally speaking, however, in the Western world the main condition for liability is negligence. Negligence implies that a manufacturer failed to do something that was morally or legally required, and thus can be held responsible for certain harms produced by his product – in legal terminology this is called *reasonable care*. Reasonable care is based on the sometimes implicit moral responsibilities of programmers and designers – it is not something made explicit in law. In military practice, however, designers are rarely held responsible for accidents caused by poor design (Thompson, 2007). It is therefore important that there will be a regulatory framework that entails 'reasonable care' to be met by designers of armed military robots. A good candidate to offer some guidelines for a formal approach of reasonable care would be the *precautionary principle*.[6] This principle was initially proposed to deal with environmental problems, yet it has far wider applications. It is especially suited for situations in which it is not possible to calculate the risks because we have insufficient scientific knowledge. In general, the precautionary principle states that precautionary measures must be taken if there are indications that there are certain hazards despite the fact that the precise nature and extent of these hazards cannot be scientifically established (Raffensperger & Tickner, 1999). Applying the precautionary principle to armed military robots would imply that the potential hazards of military robots should first be properly assessed before they could be introduced into the armed forces on a large scale, and that these robots, for example, should design with some emergency stop mechanism in case of malfunctioning such as happened in South Africa with a SWORDS (see above). The present practice to test if a system is properly functioning is done through simulations and experiments in laboratories or in small-scale field tests. Although such simulations, experiments, and tests are very important with respect to technological innovations, they do not always provide complete and reliable knowledge of the functioning of technological products and the potential hazards and risks involved. For example, laboratory and field tests are not always representative of the dynamic and complex circumstances in which military robots have to function. Evidently, it is difficult to capture the fog of war in a test setting.

Nevertheless, it seems that regulation on risk assessment can provide us with a regulatory framework for the design of military robots by formulating a set of boundary conditions for the design, production, and use of military robot technologies, such as that a military robot follows the rules of engagement and the safety protocols. If such a regulatory framework meets certain criteria, it could be considered an adequate way of dealing with the ethical issues the design of a technology raises with regard to safety and responsibility. Such a regulation for risk management should be laid down in specific norms, such as the ISO 10218 requirements for industrial robots. This norm 'specifies requirements and guidelines for the inherent safe design, protective measures, and information for use of industrial robots. It describes basic hazards associated with robots, and provides requirements to eliminate or adequately reduce the risks associated with these hazards' (ISO 2011). Although this ISO norm was developed for industrial robots, it can be used outside that context: "Examples of non-industrial robot applications include, but are not limited to: undersea, military and space robots" (ISO 2011).

Until now, however, such a regulatory framework specifically for military robots has been lacking (see also Lin et al., 2008, and Lucas, 2011). The potential use of military robots in saving 'friendly' human lives possibly explains why most of today's governments refrain from regulation with respect to the design of military robots, and especially from regulation that could lead to a ban on certain designs of military robots. On the other hand, if no-one is legally responsible for the malfunction of a military robot, there is hardly any incentive to learn from mistakes or do better in future.

Driven by this faith in the rationalisation of warfare by constraining autonomous armed robots so that they meet certain criteria, Arkin (2009) investigates the introduction of an adequate artificial ethical conscience into the armed robots by programming international humanitarian law and the rules of engagement into the robot. An advantage of these robots is that they "have the potential capability of independently and objectively monitoring ethical behaviour in the battlefield by all parties and reporting infractions that might be observed. This presence alone might possibly lead to a reduction in human ethical infractions" (Arkin, 2007). The idea of the development of autonomous machines with an additional ethical dimension is quite a new emerging field of machine ethics. These robots, with the help of formal logic, are "able to calculate the best action in ethical dilemmas using ethical principles" (Anderson & Anderson, 2007). It is thus assumed that it is sufficient to represent ethical theory in terms of a logical theory and to deduce the consequences of that theory. Beavers (2012) sees machine ethics as a threat to *ethical nihilism,*

The doctrine that states that morality needs no internal sanctions, that ethics can get by without moral 'weight,' that is, without some type of psychological force that restrains the satisfaction of our desire and that makes us care about our moral condition in the first place. (Beavers, 2012, 343).

According to Johnson and Axinn (2013), robots with an artificial ethical conscience can only mimic moral actions with no human emotions and no feelings about the seriousness of killing a human. Therefore, they conclude that autonomous robots cannot be moral.

This view that ethics can be made computable also misunderstands the unique – non-reducible – nature of ethics. Arkin (2009) agrees that some ethical theories, such as virtue ethics, do not lend themselves well by definition to a model based on a strict ethical code. But he claims that the solution is simply to eliminate ethical approaches that refuse such reduction. However, the hallmark of ethics is its non-reducibility (Royakkers & Topolski, 2014). While many ethical situations may be reducible, it is the ability to act ethically in situations that call for a judgement that is distinctly human. A consequence of this approach is that ethical principles themselves will be modified to suit the needs of a technological imperative:

Technology perpetually threatens to co-opt ethics. Efficient means tend to become ends in themselves by means of the 'technological imperative' in which it becomes perceived as morally permissible to use a tool merely because we have it. (Kaagman & Kaufman, 2009).

Another problem concerning the attempt to program the rules of the law of war and engagement into robots is that these rules are subject to interpretation and they do not provide a ready answer in any given situation. Moreover, the application of these rules is context dependent and requires the ability to understand complex social situations (Asaro, 2009). This ability is necessary in order to make ethical decisions, and as long as robots lack this ability, they will certainly not be able to take better ethical decisions than humans (Sullins, 2010).

In conclusion, although risks are inherent to the use of military robots, there is a moral obligation to limit these risks to an acceptable level by procedures of risk assessment. To ensure the allocation of responsibility for malfunction or program errors of military robots, it should be specified what this acceptable level is. Still, the possibility of an accident remains, and Krishnan suggests that in such cases all the military robots of the type that was involved in the accident should be abandoned: "If the weapon is not withdrawn from service, it can only be interpreted as a failure of politics and maybe as a war crime or crime against humanity committed by the political leadership of a state" (2009, 105).

RESPONSIBILITY OF HUMAN OPERATORS

What is often underplayed in the literature on responsibility and military robots is the role of the human operators; an omission that is all the more regrettable since it is, in fact, especially there where a number of complexities lie. In this section, we will work out the position of the human operator, often working far away from the actual battlefield. Today's UAVs connect human operators with the war zone; they are the eyes – and sometimes hands – of the tele-soldier. Partly autonomous military robots such as the Predator or the Reaper, which are able to navigate independently to their objective but require a human operator to open fire, send GPS-coordinates and camera images back to an operator who then, based on the information projected on his computer screen, decides whether or not to engage a target.

The point is that the things they see on screen can emotionally and psychologically affect these human operators, influencing their decision-making. Although fighting from behind a computer is not as emotionally potent as being on the battlefield, killing from a distance remains stressful; various studies have reported physical and emotional fatigue and increased tensions in the private lives of military personnel operating the Predators in Iraq and Afghanistan (Donnelly, 2005; Kaplan, 2006; Lee, 2012). For example, a drone pilot may witness war crimes which he is unable to prevent, or he may even see how his own actions kill civilians; unfortunately no longer a hypothetical case.

The ensuing 'residual stress' of human operators has led to proposals to diminish these tensions. In particular, the visual interface can play an important role in reducing stress; interfaces that only show abstract and indirect images of the battlefield will probably cause less stress than the more advanced real images (Singer, 2009). From a technical perspective this proposal is a feasible one, since it will not be hard to digitally recode the war scene in such a way that it induces less psychological discomfort with the war operator. This cure may have some unwanted side-effects though. Showing abstract images would in fact dehumanize the enemy, and as a result could desensitize military personnel operating unmanned systems.

Today's operators already find it at times difficult to distinguish between playing a video war game and operating an actual drone (Singer, 2009). From a technological perspective it is only a minor step to let operators think they are playing a computer game, and destroying enemy 'avatars,' while they are actually killing real people at the other side of the globe. In that case, it would be no longer the real war that would numb the soldier, but the digital recoding of it. From a moral point of view this would mean that a soldier is likely to become even further physically and emotionally detached from his actions than is already the case at present (cf. Royakkers & Van Est, 2010). Thus, where increased detachment may reduce or even eliminate human operator stress, it could at the same time limit reflection; human operators only focused on the outcome – the targeting of the blips on a screen – might not be fully aware of the consequences of their decisions.

This last observation brings us to the important role dehumanization can play. Social psychologists point out that dehumanization, that is, seeing people for something less than human, can open the door to more serious forms of unethical conduct (see for instance Bandura, 1999, 200; Mastroianni, 2011; Moller & Deci, 2010, 43-4; see also Slim, 2007, 218). It is rather hard to imagine how to have respect for the local population, a vital element of the hearts and minds approach, from, for instance, a control room in Nevada (where the pilots of Predators and Reapers mostly work from). The most effective remedy for preventing unethical conduct is 'humanization,' a not so clearly defined concept that, however, includes the affirmation of common humanity, instead of distancing oneself 'from others or divesting them from human qualities' (Bandura, 1999, 202-3). Hugo Slim explains in *Killing Civilians* that, to be effective, civilian immunity "requires that armed people find a fundamental *identification* with those called civilians and not an excessive *distinction* from them" (2007, 34). As shown by the famous Milgram experiments on obedience, it is easier to be cruel when the other does not have a face (Milgram, 1974). At a time that unmanned aerial vehicles take out insurgents from afar, and a human operator thinks that his job is "like a video game. It can get a little bloodthirsty. But it's fucking cool" (Singer, 2009, 332), that 'face' is hardly ever there. With such a distance – physical, but also psychological – between a soldier and the horrors of war, it has to be feared that this can limit, or even eliminate, proper reflection of the human operators on their decisions to open fire (see for a different view Lee, 2012; Vincente, 2013).[7]

Unclear responsibility plays a role here: the social-psychologist Albert Bandura counts the displacement and diffusion of responsibility among the "many social and psychological manoeuvres by which moral self-sanctions can be disengaged from inhumane conduct" (1999, 194), which leaves the answer to the question of responsibility of the human operator far from straightforward.

Sullins (2010) believes that in the foreseeable future such inhumane conduct could be a thing of the past, as life-and-death decisions might then be mediated by a computer-aided diagnosis of the war situation, and that military robots may even have ethical constraints built into their design – a so-called 'ethical governor' that suppresses unethical lethal behavior. For example, Arkin (2007) has done research (sponsored by the US Army) to create a mathematical decision mechanism consisting of prohibitions and obligations derived directly from the laws of war. The idea is that future military robots might give a warning if orders, according to their ethical governor, are illegal or unethical. For example, a military robot might advise a human operator not to fire because from an evaluation of the camera images the robot informs the operator that he or she is about to attack non-combatants, that is, the software of the military robot diagnosing a war situation provides a human operator with ethical advice.

Achterhuis (1998) has called this development, in which for instance an ethical governor helps to shape moral decision-making, the 'moralization of technology.' Instead of only moralizing the *human operator* ('do not shoot non-combatants'), it is the *material environment* that should be moralized, Achterhuis claims. In our case, the military robot should then see to it that no rules of engagement are violated (cf. Verbeek, 2005). Achterhuis' plea for a moralization of technology has received severe criticism, with the main criticism being that human freedom is diminished when human actions are explicitly and deliberately steered with the help of technology (cf. Verbeek, 2009). A consequence may be that humans would simply show a type of behavior that was desired by the designers of the technology instead of explicitly choosing to act this way, diminishing the freedom of, and control over, their actions. According to Cummings (2006), this would also be the case with ethical governors, since they may form a 'moral buffer' between human operators and their actions, allowing human operators to tell themselves that it was the military robot that took the decision.

The moralization of military robots could blur the line between semi-autonomous and autonomous systems, as the decision of a human operator is not the result of human deliberation, but is mainly determined or even enforced by a military robot. Another possible effect is that human operators may come to over-rely on military robots (Cummings, 2006). This is bound to happen more often in future, due to an ongoing shift from controlling to monitoring.

In brief, the moralizing of a military robot may deprive the human operator from *controlling* the situation; his future role may be restricted to *monitoring*. For our case, this would imply that we could no longer hold a human operator in reason responsible for his decisions, since it would not really be the operator taking the decisions but a military robot. This could have consequences for the question of responsibility in another way too: Detert et al. (2008) have argued that people who believe that they have little personal control in certain situations – such as those who monitor – are more likely to go along with rules, decisions, and situations even if they are unethical or have harmful effects. However, Leveringshaus (2016) argues that this "lack of moral awareness" does not relieve the human operator of taking "adequate steps to attain the morally relevant facts that enabled him to assess the risks arising from automation", and that he can still be judged negligent for deploying and relying on a technology that put innocent lives at risks.

CONCLUSION

Niccolò Machiavelli held that in war nothing ever really changes, and hence thought that the invention of the firearm amounted to nothing more than just a new variety of the age-old catapult. It is tempting to think likewise about the progress of unmanned systems, that is, as a development that does not really raise issues different from those raised a long time ago by artillery, and more recently by highflying bombers. And in part, there is something to be said for this view. But the fact is that Machiavelli was, of course, wrong; the invention of the firearm proved as crucial for warfare as the spread of the stirrup some thousand years before. Possibly, the use of unmanned systems will prove to be equally significant, especially since the development of these systems has only just begun. That will raise a host of ethical issues that are truly new, and this article addressed one of them.

We have seen that most military robots currently find their applications in surveillance, reconnaissance, and the location and destruction of mines and IEDs. These robots are unarmed, harm no one, and save lives. But not all military robots are unarmed; different types of armed military robots are currently used on the battlefield. This development may cause an important ethical problem in the assignment of responsibility in the long causal chain involved in the design and deployment of armed military robots, stretching from the manufacturer, programmer, and designer, to the departments of defense, commanding commander, and human operator. According to Sparrow (2007) a necessary condition for fighting a just war, under the principle of *jus in bello*, is that there is someone that can reasonably be held responsible for an atrocity, such as killing non-combatants, in the course of war; this condition also applies when a military robot is employed. Especially with respect to armed learning military robots there are serious legal and ethical questions regarding responsibility due to the problematic attribution of responsibility: since no-one can have sufficient *control* over the actions of these robots, and no one can foresee the consequences of these actions.

The issue of responsibility is the main reason why many lawyers and ethicists argue that a human agent should remain in-the-loop, so that traditional accountability can be ensured, and that this would therefore avoid the problem of the allocation of responsibility. Yet, in section 2 we have argued that even in the case of learning autonomous robots the assignment of responsibility is still very well possible: it normally lies with the commanding officer. However, in the subsequent two sections we have shown that the existence of responsibility gaps cannot always be avoided. Müller (2016) states that possibility of this existence should not morally preclude the use of autonomous weapons, since in civil life we only expect 'due care' from those involved. He states that if technology produces rare cases of killings where no person is responsible, this does not by itself compel a ban of autonomous robots, but that we have to regulate autonomous robots is such a way that they reduce the frequency of responsibility gaps. Therefore, we should be focused on developing responsibility practices that work to minimize risk and that clearly establish lines of responsibility. This means, that we have to negotiate about how to best assign responsibility and what that entails. Noorman and Johnson conclude that "[d]elegation of responsibility to human and non-human components is a sociotechnical design choice, not an inevitable outcome of technological development. Robots for which no human actor can be held responsible are poorly designed sociotechnical systems (Noorman & Johnson 2014, 61; see also Noorman 2014). This will be a significant challenge, since this implies that this shared responsibility is distributed broadly and which can lead to 'the problem of many hands' (see Van de Poel et al. 2015), meaning that it can be very difficult to determine what share of responsibility each person has in this sociotechnical system when something goes wrong.

For example, developing responsibility practices is necessary for a lethal mishap due to a malfunctioning of a military robot. The application of the legal concept of 'product liability' is inadequate to deal with this problem since it misses a clear regulatory framework for the design of military robots about safety and risk assessment, and more specifically, what degrees of reliability should autonomous robots meet in terms of proportionality and discrimination in their decision to attack. Therefore, governments should have a moral obligation to determine the appropriate tolerance level for autonomous robots, and to licence them for use only after a thorough testing and inspection process (Simpson and Müller 2016).

As far as semi-autonomous robots are concerned, we have discussed the largely neglected problem of the responsibility of those at the other end of the causal chain, the human operators. After all, they are the ones who decide to use lethal force, and at first sight it might seem that the attribution of responsibility is clear-cut in their case. We have seen, however, that the criteria for attributing responsibility might not always be met. The depersonalization of war, the dehumanizing the enemy, and the moralization of technology, emotionally and morally disengages the human operator. The aim of this disengagement is to reduce the psychological stress among human operators being simultaneously 'present' in and absent from the battlefield. Unfortunately, this can also limit, or even eliminate, proper reflection on their decisions; human operators have partly lost control over their decisions. Hence, if we want to hold human operators in reason responsible for their decisions, it is essential that they have control over their decisions, and a clear awareness of what is at stake.

It is, in all, important to strike a proper balance between emotional and moral attachment and detachment. This requires a lot from the computer systems that human operators use to make their life-and-death decisions. On the one hand, such systems should communicate the moral reality of the consequences of the decisions of human operators, and on the other hand such systems should reduce the strong emotions human operators feel to reduce the number of war crimes (Sparrow 2009). To develop such systems is a real challenge, but necessary to solve the problem of the attribution of responsibility, and a precondition for fighting justly in the robotic era.

REFERENCES

Achterhuis, H. (1998). *De erfenis van de utopie*. Amsterdam: Ambo.

Alley, R. (2013). *The drone debate. Sudden bullet or slow boomerang?* New Zealand: Victoria University of Wellington.

Altmann, J., Asaro, P., Sharkey, N., & Sparrow, R. (2013). Armed military robots. *Ethics and Information Technology*, *15*(2), 73–76. doi:10.100710676-013-9318-1

Anderson, M., & Anderson, S. L. (2007). Machine ethics: Creating an ethical intelligent agent. *AI Magazine*, *28*(4), 15–26.

Arkin, R. C. (2007). *Governing lethal behavior: Embedding ethics in a hybrid deliberative/reactive robot architecture* (Technical report GIT-GVU-07-11). Atlanta, GA: Georgia Institute of Technology.

Arkin, R. C. (2009). Ethical robots in warfare. *IEEE Technology and Society Magazine*, *28*(1), 30–33. doi:10.1109/MTS.2009.931858

Asaro, P. (2007). Robots and responsibility from a legal perspective. In *Proceedings of the 8th IEEE 2007 International Conference on Robotics and Automation*. IEEE.

Asaro, P. M. (2008). How just could a robot war be? In A. Briggle, K. Waelbers, & Ph. Brey (Eds.), *Current issues in computing and philosophy* (pp. 50–64). Amsterdam: IOS Press.

Asaro, P. M. (2009). Modeling the moral user. *IEEE Technology and Society, 28*(1), 20–24. doi:10.1109/MTS.2009.931863

Bandura, A. (1999). Moral disengagement in the perpetration of inhumanities. *Personality and Social Psychology Review, 3*(3), 193–209. doi:10.120715327957pspr0303_3 PMID:15661671

Beavers, A. F. (2012). Moral machines and the threat of ethical nihilism. In P. Lin, K. Abney, & G. A. Bekey (Eds.), *Robot ethics. The ethical and social implications of robotics* (pp. 333–344). Cambridge, MA: The MIT Press.

Champagne, M., & Tonkens, R. (2015). Bridging the responsibility gap in automated warfare. *Philosophy & Technology, 28*(1), 125–137. doi:10.100713347-013-0138-3

Coeckelbergh, M. (2013). Drones, information technology, and distance: Mapping the moral epistemology of remote fighting. *Ethics and Information Technology, 15*(2), 87–98. doi:10.100710676-013-9313-6

Crootof, R. (2015). War, responsibility, and killer robots. *North Carolina Journal of International Law and Commercial Regulation, 40*(4), 909–932.

Crootof, R. (2016). A meaningful floor for 'meaningful human control'. *Temple International and Comparative Law Journal, 30*, 53–62.

Cummings, M. L. (2006). Automation and accountability in decision support system interface design. *Journal of Technology Studies, 32*(1), 23–31. doi:10.21061/jots.v32i1.a.4

Detert, J. R., Treviño, L. K., & Sweitzer, V. L. (2008). Moral disengagement in ethical decision making: A study of antecedents and outcomes. *The Journal of Applied Psychology, 93*(2), 374–391. doi:10.1037/0021-9010.93.2.374 PMID:18361639

Donnelly, S. B. (2005, December 4). Long-distance warriors. *Time Magazine.*

Dunlap, Ch. J. Jr. (n.d.). Accountability and autonomous weapons: Much ado about nothing. *Temple International and Comparative Law Journal.* (forthcoming)

Ekelhof, M. A. C. (n.d.). Complications of a common language: Why it is so hard to talk about autonomous weapons. *Journal of Conflict and Security Law.* (forthcoming)

Fielding, M. (2006). Robotics in future land warfare. *Australian Army Journal, 3*(2), 99–108.

Fieser, J., & Dowden, B. (2007). Just war theory. *The Internet Encyclopedia of Philosophy.* Retrieved June 26, 2017, from http//www.iep.utm.edu/j/justwar.htm

Fischer, J. M., & Ravizza, M. (1998). *Responsibility and control: A theory of moral responsibility.* Cambridge, UK: Cambridge University Press. doi:10.1017/CBO9780511814594

Garraway, C. (2009). The doctrine of command responsibility. In J. Doria, H.-P. Gasser, & M. C. Bassiouni (Eds.), *The legal regime of the international criminal court* (pp. 703–725). Leiden: Nijhoff. doi:10.1163/ej.9789004163089.i-1122.194

Hellström, T. (2013). On the moral responsibility of military robots. *Ethics and Information Technology, 15*(2), 99–107. doi:10.100710676-012-9301-2

Henckaerts, J.-M., & Doswald-Beck, L. (2009). Customary international humanitarian law: Vol. I. *Rules.* Cambridge, UK: ICRC and Cambridge University Press.

Human Right Council. (2013). *Report of the special rapporteur on extrajudicial,summary or arbitrary executions, Christof Heyns (A/HRC/23/47).* United Nations.

International Organization for Standardization. (2011). *Robots for industrial environments - Safety requirements.* Retrieved June 26, 2017, from http://www.iso.org/iso/iso_catalogue/catalogue_tc/catalogue_detail.htm?csnumber=36322

Isenberg, D. (2007). Robots replace trigger fingers in Iraq. *Asia Times Online.* Retrieved June 26, 2017, from http://www.atimes.com/atimes/Middle_East/IH29Ak01.html

Johnson, A. M., & Axinn, S. (2013). The morality of autonomous robots. *Journal of Military Ethics, 12*(2), 129–141. doi:10.1080/15027570.2013.818399

Jordan, B. (2007). Half of predators fielded have been lost. *Air Force Times.* Retrieved June 26, 2017, from http://www.airforcetimes.com/news/2007/02/AFpredatorlosses070223

Kaag, J., & Kaufman, W. (2009). Military frameworks: Technological know-how and the legitimization of warfare. *Cambridge Review of International Affairs, 22*(4), 585–606. doi:10.1080/09557570903325496

Kaplan, R. D. (2006, September). Hunting the Taliban in Las Vegas. *Atlantic Monthly,* 81–84.

Kershnar, S. (2013). No moral problem. In B. J. Strawser (Ed.), *Killing by remote control: The ethics of an unmanned military.* Oxford, UK: Oxford University Press. doi:10.1093/acprof:oso/9780199926121.003.0011

Krishnan, A. (2009). *Killer robots. Legality and ethicality of autonomous weapons.* Farnham, MA: Ashgate Publishing Limited.

Lee, P. (2012). Remoteness, risk and aircrew Ethos. *Air Power Review, 15*(1), 1–19.

Leveringhaus, A. (2016). Drones, automated targeting and moral responsibility. In E. D. Nucci & F. Santoni de Sio (Eds.), *Drones and responsibility. Legal, philosophical and socio-technical perspectives on remotely controlled weapons* (pp. 169–181). London: Routledge.

Lichocki, P., Kahn, P. Jr, & Billard, A. (2011). The Ethical Landscape of Robotics. *IEEE Robotics & Automation Magazine, 18*(1), 39–50. doi:10.1109/MRA.2011.940275

Lin, P., Bekey, G., & Abney, K. (2008). *Autonomous military robotics: Risk, ethics, and design.* San Luis Obispo: California Polytechnic State University. doi:10.21236/ADA534697

Lucas, G. (2011). *Industrial challenges of military robotics.* Paper presented at the conference The Ethics of Emerging Military Technologies of International Society for Military Ethics (ISME), San Diego, CA. Retrieved from http://isme.tamu.edu/ISME11/isme11.html

Magnuson, S. (2008, May). Armed robots sidelined in Iraq. *National Defense Magazine.*

Mastroianni, G. R. (2011). The person–situation debate: Implications for military leadership and civilian–military relations. *Journal of Military Ethics, 10*(1), 2–16. doi:10.1080/15027570.2011.561636

Matthias, A. (2004). The responsibility gap: Ascribing responsibility for the actions of learning automata. *Ethics and Information Technology*, *6*(3), 175–183. doi:10.100710676-004-3422-1

Milgram, S. (1974). *Obedience to authority: An experimental view*. London: Tavistock.

Moller, A. C., & Deci, E. L. (2010). Interpersonal control, dehumanization, and violence: A self-determination theory perspective. *Group Processes & Intergroup Relations*, *13*(1), 41–53. doi:10.1177/1368430209350318

Mukerji, N. (2016). Autonomous killer drones. In E. D. Nucci & F. Santoni de Sio (Eds.), *Drones and responsibility. Legal, philosophical and socio-technical perspectives on remotely controlled weapons* (pp. 197–214). London: Routledge.

Müller, V. C. (2016). Autonomous killer robots are probably good news. In E. D. Nucci & F. Santoni de Sio (Eds.), *Drones and responsibility. Legal, philosophical and socio-technical perspectives on remotely controlled weapons* (pp. 67–81). London: Routledge.

National Research Council. (2005). *Autonomous vehicles in support of naval operations*. Washington, DC: The National Academies Press.

Noorman, M. (2014). Responsibility practices and unmanned military technologies. *Science and Engineering Ethics*, *20*(3), 809–826. doi:10.100711948-013-9484-x PMID:24142234

Noorman, M., & Johnson, D. G. (2014). Negotiating autonomy and responsibility in military robots. *Ethics and Information Technology*, *16*(1), 51–62. doi:10.100710676-013-9335-0

Olsthoorn, P., & Royakkers, L. M. M. (2011). *Risks and robots – Some ethical issues*. Paper presented at the conference The Ethics of Emerging Military Technologies of International Society for Military Ethics (ISME), San Diego, CA. Retrieved from http://isme.tamu.edu/ISME11/isme11.html

Orend, B. (2006). *The morality of war*. Orchard Park, NY: Broadview Press.

Raffensperger, C., & Tickner, J. (Eds.). (1999). *Protecting public health and the environment: Implementing the precautionary principle*. Washington, DC: Island Press.

Royakkers, L. M. M., & Topolski, A. R. (2014). Military robotics & relationality: criteria for ethical decision-making. In J. van den Hoven, N. Doorn, T. Swierstra, B.-J. Koops, & H. Romijn (Eds.), *Responsible innovation 1. Innovative solutions for global issues* (pp. 351–367). Dordrecht: Springer. doi:10.1007/978-94-017-8956-1_20

Royakkers, L. M. M., & Van Est, Q. (2010). The cubicle warrior: The marionette of digitalized warfare. *Ethics and Information Technology*, *12*(3), 289–296. doi:10.100710676-010-9240-8

Schulzke, M. (2013). Autonomous weapons and distributed responsibility. *Philosophy & Technology*, *26*(2), 203–219. doi:10.100713347-012-0089-0

Schwarz, E. (2017). *Death machines: The ethics of violent technologies*. Manchester, UK: Manchester University Press.

Shachtman, N. (2007, October 18). *Robot cannon kills 9, wounds 14*. Wired.com.

Sharkey, N. (2008). Cassandra or false prophet of doom: AI robots and war. *IEEE Intelligent Systems, 23*(4), 14–17. doi:10.1109/MIS.2008.60

Sharkey, N. (2010). Saying 'no!' to lethal autonomous targeting. *Journal of Military Ethics, 9*(4), 369–383. doi:10.1080/15027570.2010.537903

Simpson, T. W., & Müller, V. C. (2016). Just war and robots' killings. *The Philosophical Quarterly, 66*(263), 302–322. doi:10.1093/pq/pqv075

Singer, P. W. (2009). *Wired for war: The robotics revolution and conflict in the twenty-first century.* New York: Penguin Books.

Slim, H. (2007). *Killing civilians: Method, madness and morality in war.* Hurst Company.

Sparrow, R. (2007). Killer robots. *Journal of Applied Philosophy, 24*(1), 62–77. doi:10.1111/j.1468-5930.2007.00346.x

Sparrow, R. (2009). Building a better warbot: Ethical issues in the design of unmanned systems for military applications. *Science and Engineering Ethics, 15*(2), 169–187. doi:10.100711948-008-9107-0 PMID:19048395

Sparrow, R. (2011). Robotic weapons and the future of war. In P. Tripodi & J. Wolfendale (Eds.), *New wars and new soldiers: Military ethics in the contemporary world* (pp. 117–133). Farnham, UK: Ashgate.

Sullins, J. (2010). RoboWarfare: Can robots be more ethical than humans on the battlefield? *Ethics and Information Technology, 12*(3), 263–275. doi:10.100710676-010-9241-7

Thompson, M. (2007). V-22 Osprey: A flying shame. *Time.* Retrieved June 26, 2017, from http://www.time.com/time/politics/article/0,8599,1665835,00.html

US Department of Defense. (2013). *Unmanned systems integrated roadmap 2013-2038.* Washington, DC: Government Printing Office.

Van de Poel, I. R., & Royakkers, L. M. M. (2011). *Ethics, engineering and technology.* Oxford, UK: Blackwell.

Van de Poel, I. R., Royakkers, L. M. M., & Zwart, S. D. (2015). *Moral responsibility and the problem of many hands.* New York: Routledge.

Verbeek, P. P. (2005). *What things do: Philosophical reflections on technology, agency, and design.* University Park, PA: Pennsylvania State University Press.

Verbeek, P. P. (2009). Moralizing technology: On the morality of technological artifacts and their design. In D. M. Kaplan (Ed.), *Readings in the philosophy of technology* (pp. 226–242). Plymouth: Rowman & Littlefield Publishers.

Vicente, J. P. (2013). The American way of remote air warfare. *Journal of Military Studies, 4*(1). doi:10.1515/jms-2016-0185

Welsh, A. (2008). *What is Honor? A Question of Moral Imperatives.* New Haven, CT: Yale University Press.

ENDNOTES

[1] As the authors of a report on autonomous military robots, written for the US Navy, put it: unmanned systems are 'unaffected by the emotions, adrenaline, and stress that cause soldiers to overreact or deliberately overstep the Rules of Engagement and commit atrocities, that is to say, war crimes' (Lin, Bekey, and Abney 2008, 1).

[2] There are more criteria to hold someone reasonably responsible, such as a *causal relationship* between the behavior and the consequences, but in this paper we focus on *control*.

[3] For the statement see www.icrac.co.uk/Expert%20Workshop%20Statement.pdf.

[4] https://futureoflife.org/open-letter-autonomous-weapons/ (retrieved July 3, 2017).

[5] A footnote made clear to what kind of decisions this principle should apply to 'The decision to kill or use lethal force against a human being; The decision to use injurious or incapacitating force against a human being; The decision to initiate combat or violent engagement between military units; The decision to initiate war or warfare between states or against non-state actors.' The statement can be found at http://icrac.net/statements/ (retrieved July 4, 2017).

[6] This principle originates from the Rio Declaration, the closing statement of the first conference of the United Nations on sustainable development, which was held in Rio de Janeiro in 1992.

[7] According to Coeckelbergh (2013), the practice of using drones is illustrative of the claim that new technological practices that aim to bridge physical distance create more moral distance and make it difficult for people to exercise moral responsibility.

Chapter 7
The Case Against Weapons Research

John Forge
University of Sydney, Australia

ABSTRACT

Weapons research seeks to design new or improved weapons and their ancillary structures. This chapter argues that weapons research is both morally wrong and morally unjustified. This "case against weapons research" requires lengthy discussion and the argument given here is a summary of that discussion. The central claim is that the "standard justification" for all forms of weapons acquisition and deployment, which appeals to defense and deterrence, does not stand up for weapons research because the harms caused by the latter projects into the future in unknowable ways. Weapons research produces practical knowledge in the form of designs for the means to harm, and its practitioners cannot know how this knowledge will be used in the future.

INTRODUCTION

One of the most morally challenging, and most enduring, forms of technology is *military* technology, technology that is associated with the organised violence that has been in the stock-in-trade of armed forces since ancient times. Military technology covers a broad area, including some forms that are similar if not identical to civilian technologies, so-called dual use technologies (Forge 2010). However, there are other forms that are unmistakably military and these include all of those that enable weapons to be produced. My concern here is with the endeavour that leads to such technologies, what I call *weapons research*. The aim of weapons research is thus to produce the technology, or more directly the design, for a new or improved weapon, or for the ancillary structures, such as platforms, necessary for using a weapon (Forge 2012: 13-14). This topic has been almost entirely neglected by moral philosophers and others.[1] I suspect that this may be because it is thought to be subsumable under discussion about the morality of war, and that moral judgements about weapons research follow from moral judgements about war. I believe that this is wrong and that weapons research is a topic for discussion in its own right. Having said this, I do of course acknowledge that certain particular classes of weapons research, namely

DOI: 10.4018/978-1-5225-5094-5.ch007

those directed towards weapons of mass destruction, especially nuclear weapons, have been discussed at length, and judgements have been made about the morality of such research. My own interest in the topic stemmed from my work on the responsibility for the use of the atomic bombs on Japan, but it has since expanded to cover weapons research as a whole.[2]

My topic also clearly falls with the relatively new, or newly named, field of technoethics, as it is certainly a judgement in regard to the 'impact of ethics on technological advance'. Indeed, if we look back to one of the seminal works on technoethics by Mario Bunge, we find a clear statement to the effect that not all technology is good and he explicitly mentions military technology. Bunge writes: "Just think of thanatology or the technology of killing: the design of tactics and strategies of aggression, of weaponry" (Bunge 1977: 100). Moreover, Bunge makes it clear that those who design technologies must accept moral responsibility for the impacts of their work. I agree completely and entirely with these sentiments. I also note that Bunge, and following him Luppicini (see Luppicini 2008: 1-2), stress that technoethics is a highly inter-disciplinary field. This accords with my own experience in regard to the morality of weapons research.

The purpose of this paper is to set out an argument that aims to establish that weapons research is both morally wrong and not morally justified.[3] I have made this 'case against weapons research' on several occasions (Forge 2004, 2007a), but most fully in *Designed to Kill: The Case against Weapons Research* (Forge 2012) and *The Morality of Weapons Design and Development: Emerging Research and Opportunities* (Forge 2017b). This paper is a sketch of the argument and makes no claim to be anything more that an outline – it takes a whole book (or two) to fully present the case. One way to mount such a case is to begin by affirming some form of pacifism, and then maintain that if war is wrong, so is weapons research. But this is not a good option, even granted that we could come up with a coherent version of pacifism. If weapons research provided the means for robust defence, then this might keep the peace by deterring war. In general, it is hard to see why weapons *research* is wrong if fighting is wrong. A better option is to address what I believe to be assumption behind the assimilation of weapons research to questions about the morality of war, namely that war and all that is needed for fighting wars is justified by appeal to defence and deterrence. The only justified war, or just war, is war which resists aggression. Hence weapons research is justified for the purposes of defence, and, even better because it prevents war, for deterrence. I refer to this as the *standard justification* for war and for all forms of defence spending, weapons procurement, etc. (Forge 2017b: Chapter 1) However, I believe that while the standard justification can apply to certain wars, it does not serve to justify weapons research. The case against weapons research can be seen in this sense to be a argument against the standard justification. It is now even more important to reveal the standard justification for what it is, as something based both on confusions and conflations and something that serves as a smokescreen to hide the special interests that profit from weapons development (Forge 2017b *passim*). The new US President plans to sharply increase spending on 'defence' while cutting social security programmes and is urging others to do the same. This is completely and utterly the wrong thing to do.

As a final comment by way of introduction, I claim that weapons research is not something relatively new, something that came about when scientific theory was applied to weapons design. The best-known instance of the latter, indeed of any episode of weapons research, is the Manhattan Project. It is clear that the very idea of the atomic bomb, let alone its detailed design, could not have been thought up without the experimental discoveries in, and theories about, nuclear physics that became available in the 1930s. Science had been applied to weapons design a century earlier, but hardly at all before that. However, systematic research has informed weapons research since at least the fourth century BCE. I have in mind here the designs of torsion catapults developed by Greek engineers in Sicily, Athens, Rhodes and elsewhere in the ancient world that were codified in manuals and expressed by mathematical equations. The work is both interesting and remarkable (Marsden 1969, Rihill 2007). Given a broad definition of "research", this work qualifies, and I see no reason why we are not at liberty to adopt it and hence to see weapons research as having a long history.[4] I note that torsion catapults were the first 'heavy' projectile weapons: projectile weapons, and I include free fall bombs and well as ballistic and guided ordnance, artillery, etc., are the truly dangerous and harmful ones. I will therefore proceed as follows: I will identify a number of key propositions or premises, and discuss them as much as I can in the space available, and this will serve as a summary of my case against weapons research. The first three premises are concerned with the (*prima facie*) wrongfulness of weapons research, and the remainder with the justification, or lack thereof, of the activity.

The Case Against Weapons Research

1. It is morally wrong to harm moral subjects, members of our species and other sentient creatures, without justification.

This is a moral principle, and it is surely not contentious: *any* system of morality that denied 1 would not be acceptable. However, not every moral system will use 1 explicitly as a starting point. For example, standard act consequentialism maintains that moral agents should maximise 'the good', and there are different views on what is good. My own preference is for a moral system that makes 1 explicit at the outset, and for this reason I have adopted Common Morality, the moral system developed by Bernard Gert (Gert 2004, 2005). The core of Common Morality is a set of ten rules, eight of which prohibit specific harms – for instance, the first two rules are "Do not kill" and "Do not cause pain".[5] These rules are not absolutely binding: it is permissible to break or 'violate' them if there is adequate justification. In essence, an adequate justification establishes that one anticipates that 'comparable' harm will be prevented by the act in question, and moreover that any moral agent could accept that the violation of the moral rule in question be publicly allowed.[6] 1 therefore amounts to a one sentence description of Common Morality. Returning for a moment to consequentialism, the demand to maximise 'the good' must be understood to incorporate its converse, namely minimisation of what is bad and, clearly, harm is bad. Right action for the consequentialist cannot entail, for instance, making some happy while harming many more. So while the question of the justification of acts that harm is separate from judgements about moral wrongdoing on non-consequentialist systems such as Common Morality, it is part and parcel of consequentialist judgements of right and wrong action. I have argued elsewhere that in the situations I am concerned with, namely making judgements about weapons research, act and especially rule consequentialists will address the same sorts of issues when making judgements about the rightness and wrongness of such activities as I do when appealing to Common Morality to consider whether these activities are justified.[7]

Now consider

2. It is morally wrong to provide the means to harm moral subjects, members of our species and other sentient creatures, without justification. 2 is more contentious. Suppose person P designs household items like knives and scissors and these are used, on occasion, to harm. Setting aside for the moment whether it is correct to say that a designer 'provides' the artefact she designs, it seems that we should not class P's actions as wrong because of such deviant or unintended use. P expected the

artefacts she designs to be used for mundane household tasks, not for harming innocents. I agree with this response, so I would not assert 2 without qualification. My qualification is that what is provided *is intended to be* the means to harm, to be a weapon.[8] What ever else can be said about 2, for instance how it might figure in discussions of dual use items, I believe it applies to weapons research.

In that case one must accept:

3.   The primary purpose of a weapon is to harm and (hence) weapons are the means to harm. The notion that artefacts can only be used in ways that their creators intend when they design and make them is not generally accepted – Don Ihde calls it the "Designer Fallacy" and gives many examples of things that have had quite different, sometimes entirely unanticipated, uses from what their designers had in mind (Ihde 2009). I agree with much of what Ihde and others have to say on this subject, but I think there has been some confusion about, or lack of reflection on, what counts as a use and for this reason I prefer to talk about *purposes*. What I understand the primary purpose of an artefact is what it is intended to do. It may seem that this is what Ihde and others deny, that artefacts cannot have anything like a 'primary' purpose. It will help explain what I have in mind by using one of his favourite examples, the typewriter. Ihde tells us that this was originally designed to enable unsighted persons to write, but of course it has come to be used by sighted people as well. On my account, however, the *primary* purpose of a typewriter is to produce symbols, such as letters, on paper. That is what the typewriter mechanism was designed to achieve. That it then enables unsighted persons to write is what I call a *derivative* purpose, something for which the primary purpose of the artefact is necessary but not conversely (Forge 2012: 142-47). Typically, derivative purposes tend to be contextual, a function of the context, situation or occasion of the use of the artefact. A good example of this is deterrence. That one country feels it needs to deter another is something that occurs at some time and in some place - it is what we might call an historical state of affairs – but circumstances can change and the need for deterrence may pass. So for a weapon to be used for the ends of deterrence certain (contingent) matters of fact need to obtain. However, weapons can only be used for deterrence, or for defence or making threats or to coerce, if they can be used to harm. But the converse is not true, which is why all of these other purposes weapons can be used for are derivative.

Going back to the previous example, I would say that the primary purpose of the household scissors is to enable all manner of domestic cuttings up, and that its use as a weapon is derivative. Following on from this, my view is that designers are committed to the primary purpose of the artefacts they create, in the sense that they have responsibility for those instances in which the primary purpose is realised, but not necessarily so for derivative purposes, as these depend in addition on further considerations and the designer may not be able to anticipate these. I claim that the primary purpose of a weapon is to harm: this is what weapons do and when they are designed, they are designed in such a way as to be an efficient means to carry out this function. For example, when a projectile weapon is designed, then its designer (and her team of experts) works out how to send the projectile as accurately as possible to its target, given the constraints specified by the brief she has been given. What she is doing could not be anything but undertaking research into the means to harm – we have seen that weapons can be used for defence and deterrence *presupposes* that they are the means to harm. Indeed, in order defend, weapons must be capable of harming.

The standard justification for weapons research states that defence justifies all forms of weapons procurement, including weapons research. That defence is a derivative purpose of a weapon, combined with one other aspect of weapons research that I shall come to in a moment, is crucial for the case against weapons research. However, it is necessary first to address a response to the effect that even if it is accepted that weapons are the means to harm in the sense that this is what they really 'are', nevertheless some of these are defensive weapons, weapons that can only be used for defence. For that class of weapons, it would be necessary to qualify the primary purpose to something like "means to harm, but only in defence". I deny that there are any weapons which are defensive in the *requisite* sense and it is important to be quite clear on what this is. Suppose w is a weapon that is very well-suited to defend an asset; perhaps that is the only purpose w could fulfil. But this is *not* a defensive weapon in the requisite sense, for what one is looking for is a class of weapons that cannot be use to aid *any* type of aggression. Those who embark on aggressive wars need to defend their assets, both at home and in the field, and hence need weapons that are suitable for this purpose.[9] The requisite sense is therefore of what one may call an *inherently* defensive weapon, one that cannot aid an aggressive war in any way. I claim that there can be no such weapon, except in science fiction. For example, suppose that there was a weapons system that was totally effective, in that it defended a country from any form of attack, but it was only activated when the borders of the country were crossed by attackers. A state which has such a weapon would be able to attack others without fear of retaliation, and in this sense it would really be the ultimate offensive weapon.[10] It is only if every single state in the world had such a weapon that there could be no aggression. But this is science fiction for three reasons: there can (surely) be no such weapon; if there were such a weapons, not everyone would be able to build it, and if everyone could build it, there would be so much international upheaval as states tried to frustrate others' programmes that they would never be built.

Premises 2 and 3 imply that we should judge weapons research to be morally wrong and to hold to that judgement unless and until there is adequate justification. My aim in formulating the premises was (of course) to arrive at this conclusion. As I have said already, it is only really possible here explain briefly what they amount to and for an adequate discussion and defence of them, I can only offer the reader further references. Recall that the case against weapons research divides into two parts: first it is necessary to show that we can make a preliminary judgement to the effect that the activity is morally wrong, but in the second place it is necessary to show that that judgement can be maintained in the face of attempted justifications. I now need to outline this second part of the case, and to this end I put forward four more propositions. A quick comment before I proceed: when I claim that there is no justification for weapons research, I mean that there is no adequate or acceptable justification, that there is nothing that would persuade a reasonable person to revoke the judgement that weapons research is morally wrong. Of course, all manner of *attempted* justifications are possible, and those with vested interests in weapons research will no doubt be inclined to accept one of them. I claim, however, that a unbiased person will not.

The other aspect of weapons research which I mentioned above concerns the nature of its product, namely

4.   Weapons research produces knowledge, in the form of designs for weapons, and as such is to be sharply distinguished from weapons manufacture. Weapons research has this feature, the produciton of knowledge, in common with all other forms of research, including basic or 'pure' research. There

are different kinds of design, depending on how finely specified the instructions are for making the artefact in question. For example, what is known as an engineering specification is a set of instructions which gives precise and minute details for all the relevant parameters needed to realise the artefact. There has been a qualitative change in the relationship between design and production, with the advent of computer-driven three-dimensional printers which can be programmed to print artefacts directly - it is no surprise (to me at any rate) that some of the first examples have involved the 'printing' of plastic guns. At the other end of the scale, one might include under the heading much less detailed specifications, that require (much) more work before they can be realised. For example, Szilard had the idea of a chain reaction in a fissile substance being used in a bomb of terrible power, before much of the background physics had been done. This is perhaps not so much a design itself and as idea for a design, one that became progressively articulated up until 1945, when it was realised. There is even a sense in which an artefact itself can represent its own design. An artefact that has been bought, stolen or captured could be reverse engineered by experts to work out how it was made, and subsequent copies produced. To summarise we can say this: a design is whatever information allows the 'production unit' to produce the artefact in question (Forge 2012: 17-24). What counts as a design is therefore contingent on there being a production unit available with the requisite skills and materials.

It follows from 4 that

5. Unlike the artefacts that they enable, designs do not decay, wear out and so become useless. Because they are items of knowledge, designs are, if not immortal, potentially very long-lived. Nowadays, storage and transmission of all forms of data is extremely easy and hence designs can be readily copied and shared. Hence it is much less likely than it once was that designs will get lost. What this means is that the relationship of designer to design, and hence to the artefacts that the design realises, will not be such that the designer can exert a great deal of control or influence – unless she never releases her design and tells no one about it. This would be true even if the designer has a patent – which will not normally be the case - because patent rights lapse, because of theft, and for other reasons. Indeed, the norm will be that she works for others, often a state-owned enterprise, which holds the rights to the design. The most celebrated case of the designers losing control of their work is once again the atomic bomb. Once they had enrolled in the Manhattan Project, Szilard and his colleagues were eventually only able to offer advice on how their invention might be used, but they had no actual say in the matter.[11]

Some of the Manhattan scientists agreed with the atomic bombing of Japan, and so the fact that a designer may have no control over the products of her work does not mean that she will always disagree with how it is used. And it would be most surprising if that were true for most instances of run of the mill civilian design and R&D. However, weapons research is unique in that it produces the means to harm, so if someone engages in weapons research and the products of her work are used to harm people that she thinks should not be harmed, then she has contributed to something that she believes to be wrong, indeed believes to be morally wrong. This of course was why many of the Manhattan scientists were troubled after Hiroshima and Nagasaki: they did not believe atomic bombs should have dropped on civilians. Not everyone is moved by moral concerns; some dismiss such things as irrelevant in the 'real world' or are simply too selfish and egotistical to care. I have nothing to say here, and little to say elsewhere, about why one should be moral.[12] But I am assuming that to say that (one believes that) something is morally wrong is a very good reason not to do it, and to find out that one has done something that is morally wrong may place a burden on one's conscience, as it did for Szilard, Oppenheimer, Franck, Rotblat and many others who worked on the atomic bomb project. However, there are examples of weapons researchers who have designed weapons in situations where they could anticipate and completely endorse the ways in which their weapons would be used, and it seems that they were quite justified in these expectations and beliefs (unlike the Manhattan Project scientists who endorsed the atomic bombing of Japan). For instance, the improvements to the designs of the T-34 tank and the Yakolev fighter in the World War Two (WW2) helped the Red Army defeat the Wehrmacht. This was a just war on the part of the Soviet Union and their weapons researchers helped them win it.

Weapons research intended to produce new systems, and not (marginal) improvements of existing systems, takes a lot of time. For instance, while very minor improvements were made to the T-34 in between the German attack on the Soviet Union in midsummer 1941 and the Battle of Stalingrad – such as a new hatch and rails for 'tank riders' - it took another two years to upgrade to an 85mm gun. In contrast, the Kalashnikov assault rifle was not ready until 1947, hence its name, even though work on it began in 1941. The AK-47 is the most widely produced and widely used weapon of all time, but it was never used for the purpose envisaged by its creator, namely to help repel the Germans in WW2 (Forge 2007b). Indeed there are parallels here with the atomic bomb. Szilard, Fermi and others were concerned about a German atomic bomb, and their efforts to interest the US government in it were motivated by what they saw as the need to get the means to deter any use of such a weapon by the Germans. So just as they did not expect to see the atomic bomb used against Japanese cities, Kalashnikov did not expect to see 'his gun' used by child soldiers in Africa. This leads to

6. Weapons designers cannot foresee (all) the uses to which the products of their work will be put. I believe that 6 is well-supported by many other examples of weapons research.[13] Moreover, the fact that new weapons research often builds on work done in the past should also be acknowledged. I have mentioned improvements to existing systems, and this obviously presupposes that those systems already exist. But there are also weapons which are truly innovations but which are 'based on' existing systems. A thermonuclear warhead combines both nuclear fusion and nuclear fission, the latter being the physical principle by which atomic bombs function. Without the Manhattan Project, and comparable work done in the Soviet Union, Britain, France and elsewhere, there could be no thermonuclear systems. I understand 6 to cover both the direct effects of weapons research, the uses to which the weapons in question are put, and the *indirect* effects, the uses to which new weapons are put whose design is based on the work in question.

Weapons designers are by no means alone in not knowing all the particular ways in which their work will used, as I have acknowledged. But weapons design stands out from *all* other forms of design and technology – it is unique – in that it provides the means to harm in the sense explained. *No* other form of endeavour does this. It follows from 6 that weapons designers cannot know about all the particular ways in which the products of their work will be used: they cannot know about all the actual harms that are caused by the weapons, their primary function, nor whether these are for defence or aggression, and they cannot know if the weapons will used for deterrence, coercion, threatening, or any other derivative purposes. A weapons researcher therefore cannot satisfy the following demand:

7. In order to provide justification for a morally wrong action, it must be possible at least in principle for an agent who commits such an action to know about all the harms that the action typically gives rise to. Is this a reasonable demand?

The idea behind 7 is that if an agent does something that is morally wrong in the sense understood here, then the only possible justification is that at least comparable harms are prevented - or if a great deal of 'positive' benefit ensues (not a view I subscribe to).[14] The harms must therefore be knowable for the agent to decide to go ahead and act. 7 should not be understood to demand that an agent must know all the harmful consequences of *any* action that she undertakes before she is permitted to act, because it is possible even for the most mundane and simple act to give rise to dreadful unforeseeable consequences in which many people are harmed. If we were to require that any such act is morally wrong and condemn the agent, then this would not only be unfair, it would lead to a kind of paralysis. 7 should not be understood this way because, in the first place it applies only to actions which are already judged to be morally wrong, and where the issue now is with justification. Even with this qualification, it may seem to demand too much. Suppose the agent believes that by causing a little harm, she will save a lot of future harm and therefore performs a given act. But she is wrong, and it turns out that more harm is done than prevented. It is possible that she did all she could to estimate the consequences of her act, but through not fault of her own, things did not turn out as expected. Again it seems unfair to condemn her. But 7 includes the qualification "…all the harms that the action typically gives rise to."

The harms which weapons research typically gives rise to are the harms that weapons cause, the killing, the destruction and so forth. No weapons researcher should be surprised when her work is used in these ways, because it is what weapons primarily do. That something which is designed to kill and destroy is used for this end is, on the contrary, to be expected. What cannot be anticipated are the particular occasions in which weapons are used: who is killed, what is destroyed, when and why these acts are carried out. So what should be expected is that weapons will be used to kill and destroy, what cannot be foreseen are the *particular* occasions on which they are used. So what cannot be foreseen is whether the particular uses to which a weapon is put, and here I include those in which it is used to deter and coerce, on the whole prevent more harm that would have otherwise occurred. But it is this demand that I claim *must* be satisfied before weapons research can be justified. 7 does not, I think, apply to many kinds of action; in fact it may only apply to weapons research. But for the reasons I have given, I believe it does so apply, and if I am correct, then we have:

8. Weapons research is not only morally wrong, it is not morally justifiable.

CONCLUSION

What happens in wars is morally wrong: people are killed and otherwise harmed, their property destroyed and their livelihood taken away. It is therefore necessary to justify war if one is to be remain a moral agent. The same is true of weapons research. Weapons research gives rise to harms because it seeks to design the means to harm, and this is the first step in the process that leads to killing and destruction on the battlefield. It is not enough by way of justification to give what I have called the standard justification and say that the research is done in the interest of defence, as it is not enough when justifying war to say that it is done in self defence. And as is the case for war, it is necessary to show that the harms caused by the weapons in question (and those that comprise the next generations of systems) are balanced by harms prevented, avoided and reduced. But this is not possible. Weapons research is therefore morally wrong and cannot be justified.

REFERENCES

Arigo, J. (2000). The Ethics of Weapons Research: A Framework for Discourse between Insiders and Outsiders. *Journal of Power and Ethics*, *1*, 303–327.

Bunge, M. (1977). Towards a Technoethics. *The Monist*, *60*(1), 96–107. doi:10.5840/monist197760134

Forge, J. (2004). The Morality of Weapons Research. *Science and Engineering Ethics*, *10*(3), 531–542. doi:10.100711948-004-0010-z PMID:15362709

Forge, J. (2007a). What are the Moral Limits of Weapons Research? *Philosophy in the Contemporary World*, *14*(1), 79–88. doi:10.5840/pcw200714120

Forge J. (2007b). No Consolation for Kalashnikov. *Philosophy Now*, 6-8.

Forge, J. (2008). *The Responsible Scientist: A Philosophical Analysis*. Pittsburgh, PA: Pittsburgh University Press.

Forge, J. (2009). Proportionality, Just War Theory and Weapons Innovation. *Science and Engineering Ethics*, *15*(1), 25–38. doi:10.100711948-008-9088-z PMID:18802788

Forge, J. (2010). A Note on the Definition of Dual-Use. *Science and Engineering Ethics*, *16*(1), 111–117. doi:10.100711948-009-9159-9 PMID:19685170

Forge, J. (2011). *The Morality of Weapons Research*. Wiley-Blackwell International Encyclopaedia of Ethics.

Forge, J. (2012). *Designed to Kill: The Case Against Weapons Research*. Dordrecht: Springer.

Forge, J. (2017a). *Science, Ethics and Weapons Research in Encyclopedia of Information Science and Technology* (4th ed.). Hershey, PA: IGI Global.

Forge, J. (2017b). *The Morality of Weapons Design and Development: Emerging Research and Opportunities*. Hershey, PA: IGI global.

Gert, B. (2004). *Common Morality*. Oxford, UK: Oxford University Press. doi:10.1093/0195173716.001.0001

Gert, B. (2005). *Morality: Its Nature and Justification* (Revised Edition). Oxford, UK: Oxford University Press. doi:10.1093/0195176898.001.0001

Ihde, D. (2009). The Designer Fallacy and Technological Imagination. In P. Vermass & ... (Eds.), *Philosophy and Design* (pp. 51–60). Berlin: Springer.

Leveringhaus, A. (2016). *Ethics and Autonomous Weapons*. London: Palgrave. doi:10.1057/978-1-137-52361-7

Luppicini, R. (2008). The Emerging Field of Technoethics. In R. Luppicini & R. Adell (Eds.), *Handbook of Research on Technoethics*. Academic Press. Retrieved from www.igi-global.com/emerging-field-technoethics

Marsden, E. (1969). *Greek and Roman Artillery: Historical Development*. Oxford, UK: Oxford University Press.

Resnick, D. (2013). Is Weapons Research Immoral? *Metascience, 23*(1), 105–107. doi:10.100711016-013-9834-y

Rhodes, R. (1986). *The Making of the Atomic Bomb. Harmonsworth, UK*. Penguin.

Rihill, T. (2007). *The Catapult*. Yardley, PA: Westholme.

Sinnott-Armstrong, W. (2002). Gert Contra Consequentialism. In W. Sinnott-Armstrong & R. Audi (Eds.), Rationality, Rules and Ideals. Lanham, MD: Roman and Littlefield.

ENDNOTES

[1]   When I was asked to write on the "Weapons Research and Development" for the Wiley-Blackwell International Encyclopaedia of Ethics I was hard pressed to find references to anything others that my own work, see Forge 2011. In this paper many of the references will be to my own work. However, others are beginning to take more interest in the 'ethics of weapons research', see for instance, Leveringhaus 2016.

[2]   For a general account of the bomb and the decision to bomb Japan, see Rhodes 1986. For my account of the responsibility for that decision, see Forge 2008 Chapter 2.

[3]   This way of expressing the moral judgement implies that some actions that are morally wrong may nevertheless be permissible under certain special conditions. Most modern systems of morality allow for this.

[4]   One might also claim that composite bows and bronze swords were the products of weapons research, but that would be an inference based on the weapons themselves, not on any independent evidence about their genesis.

[5]   Common Morality has been construed as negative rule consequentialism, though not by Gert himself, see Sinnot-Armstrong 2002. It appears to be a system of defeasible duties, but Gert himself did not like this description either!

[6]   I need to refer the reader to Gert for more on this. Gert 2004 is a short introduction to his system, and well worth reading.

[7]   For instance in Forge 2014 Chapter 3 I look in more detail than I do in Forge 2012 at the way in which a consequentialist moral system can be used to support the case against weapons research. I should add that I do not think that it is *necessary* to show that this is possible.

8   To anticipate a possible objection, I do not claim, and am not committed to the view, that the wrongfulness of an action is always a function of what the agent intends, nor do I think that agents are responsible for all and only their intended actions – Forge 2008 is a sustained defence of wide view of responsibility in which agents are responsible for (much) more than their intended actions. Premise 2 refers to the special situation in which agents are designers, the providers of certain means. Intention is important here, once we have identified what the means are for – this qualification is critically important.

9   The Wehrmacht, notorious for being highly aggressive, was skilled at conducting defensive missions and operations. It is well-known that after Operation Citadel failed in 1943, the Wehrmacht was continuously on the defensive in the East, though it is less well known that it was engaged in defence along most of the front for much of August 1941. Germany was able to hold out until May 1945 because of its defensive ability.

10   The Soviets, for instance, interpreted the US SDI, 'Star Wars', as a highly aggressive move, whereas President Reagan famously wanted an ultimate defensive weapon (Forge 2012: 98-103)).

11   For my views on the Manhattan Project, including the responsibility for dropping the bombs, and for further references, see Forge 2008 Chapters 2 and 3, and Forge 2012 Chapter 5.

12   Philosophers have struggled with this question for many centuries and I do not think that anyone has come up with a good answer. For my own view here, see Forge 2012: 111-13.

13   I note that the T-34 tank and later generations of Soviet tanks were used to impose Soviet hegemony on Eastern Europe after the end of WW2, something that is clearly not in accordance with Just War Theory.

14   7 also accords with Gert's two stage method for evaluating attempted justifications of moral wrongdoing, see Gert 2005, Chapter 6, although as I have indicated, the proposition has been formulated with weapons research in mind.

Chapter 8
Humans, Autonomous Systems, and Killing in War

Jai Galliott
The University of New South Wales, Australia

ABSTRACT

Technology has always allowed agents of war to separate themselves from the harm that they or their armed forces inflict with spears, bows and arrows, trebuchets, cannons, firearms, and other modern weaponry, all serving as examples of technologies that have increased the distance between belligerents and supposedly made warfare less sickening than the close-quarters combat of the past. This chapter calls into question the claims of some proponents of a ban moratorium on lethal autonomous weapons systems regarding a responsibility gap and contends that most implications associated with the introduction of autonomous technologies can be resolved by recognizing that autonomy does not mean the elimination of a human influence on the battlefield and advocates for a black-box-type recorder to ensure compliance with just war theory and the laws of war.

INTRODUCTION

Despite strong opposition from various quarters, it remains an open question as to whether increasing levels of autonomy and distancing in weapon systems will have any significant effect on states' or individuals' ability to meet ethical and legal obligations. As neither the law of armed conflict nor just war theory refers specifically to levels of autonomy systems or indeed the impact of technologically facilitated spatial-moral distancing, the obligations which states currently bear in relation to the use of those systems with a degree of autonomy are those which apply to use of any weapon system that is not, by its nature, illegal or immoral. There are, of course, weapon systems in use today that arguably conform to the commonly accepted definitions of 'autonomous', such as the defensive and offensive close-in-weapon systems commonly installed on naval warships for detecting and destroying missiles and aircraft, as well as similar systems which are all capable of identifying targets of interest and firing without needing human input at the point of action execution. Not only are such weapon systems in use today, there are no serious claims that the use of such systems in armed conflict is intrinsically illegal

DOI: 10.4018/978-1-5225-5094-5.ch008

or immoral. This chapter focuses on the trail of humanity tied to the development of distancing weapons and argues that more advanced systems, capable of complex behaviour in less predictable environments, while perhaps morally problematic in that they facilitate moral distancing and disengagement, would not reach the threshold beyond which our existing normative instruments and frameworks cannot adequately account for their use. The fundamental tendency obscuring the capacity of the relevant instruments to deal with the challenge of what are, in fact, little more than semi-autonomous weapons, is that through which stakeholders attribute blame to technology, rather than the people deciding how to use the technology. Such arguments are often labelled 'too reductive', but such claims are argued to be, at best, counterproductive, and, at worst, nonsensical. The actual task, it is argued and partly addressed here, is to identify the places in which compliance with the existing frameworks will be challenged as levels of autonomy on the battlefield increase. The main responsibility in this regard, it is suggested, is to focus on those areas throughout the lethal autonomous weapon systems product life cycle in which direct human-interaction takes places and to record said interaction.

THE ROLE OF THE INDIVIDUAL IN MODERN CONFLICT

While many of the campaigns to halt the development of lethal 'autonomous' weapons systems choose to focus on high-level decision makers, as they are central to the initial decision to develop said systems and engage them in warfare, it is, in fact, the individual who defends his state and society by operating, designing or engineering increasingly autonomous weapon systems that must be most unconditional in exercising moral restraint and adhering to just war theory. Michael Ignatieff (1998) writes that more than any other warmaking agential group, it is the soldiers who actually conduct war that have the most influence on its outcomes and the ability to introduce the moral component that regulates warfare and justifies it as a step toward a better state of peace. In his words, 'the decisive restraint on inhuman practice on the battlefield lies within the warrior himself – in his conception of what is honourable or dishonourable for a man to do with weapons' (Ignatieff 1998, p. 118). Ironically, soldiers are the primary agents of both physical violence and compassion and moral arbitration in war. As Darren Bowyer (1998) remarks, they deliver 'death and destruction one moment...[and deal] out succour to the wounded (of both sides) and assistance to the unwittingly involved civilian population, the next' (p. 276). Of course, the intended definition of 'soldier' and 'warrior' is today changing. We more commonly refer to airmen and women when referring to low-level semi-autonomous systems and, increasingly, contractors, engineers and designed others involved in the technological practice enabling more highly autonomous systems and who are, more or less directly, also involved in the wielding of lethal power. The specific concern examined here is whether, with each shift in the definition of the word 'soldier' or indeed 'warfighter', and in allowing individuals to fight and participate in/facilitate killing via a technologically mediated proxy and increasingly indirect algorithmic means, we may, through a process of psycho-moral disengagement and emotional desensitisation lower their ability or willingness to exercise restraint and compassion in warfare and adhere to the moral laws of war and/or, with the more autonomous systems, render completely useless the principles of discrimination and proportionality, and others enshrined within just war theory. It will be argued that the development of autonomy in weapon systems in some ways tracks unethical decision-making and/or lowers barriers to killing, and that it is the human involvement in warfare that we can never eliminate and which results in these undesirable consequences at the lower end of the spectrum of autonomy that paradoxically means that we will never be at risk of endangering or ruling out the moral conduct of highly autonomous warfare involving artificial intelligence.

Most human beings are born with what can only be described as a primitive survival instinct that, without unchecked counter force, would lead to a degree of violence and savagery. But in most societies, people are raised and socialised in such a way that typically leads them to hold an aversion to harming other human beings, which might be why some choose to participate in warfare via wielding ones and zeroes rather than guns and bullets. In a military context and as applied to lower-end autonomous systems, this socialised reluctance to kill is evidenced by recounts and statistics from earlier wars. David Grossman (1995), a self-proclaimed 'killogist' or military psychologist, writes of two World War veterans. The first confirms that many WWI infantrymen never fired their weapons and relied instead on artillery, while the second says that platoon sergeants in WWII had to move up and down the firing line kicking men to get them to fire and that they felt they were doing good if they could 'get two or three men out of a squad to fire' (Grossman 1995, p. xiv). While some have criticised his methodology, S. L. A. Marshall gave further supporting evidence in arguing from personal experience and studies conducted on firing ratios, which revealed that 'on average not more than 15 per cent of the men had actually fired at the enemy' (Marshall 2000, p. 54). He attributed this startling inhibition to kill to an 'ingrained fear of aggression' that was based on society's teaching that killing is fundamentally wrong (Marshall 2000, p. 71). For Marshall, success in combat and the welfare of the state and its people demanded that action be taken to correct or overcome this problem. For those with an aversion to highly autonomous weapon systems, the problem is reversed, as will be later discussed.

In the years following publication of the first edition of Marshall's book – that is, in those following WWII – there is evidence that Marshall's calls for corrective action were answered. The claims of very low firing rates had been replaced by very high and morally concerning firing rates. By the time of the Korean War, the American firing rate was said to be up to fifty-five percent and, in Vietnam, it was reported to be up to ninety or ninety-five percent (Meagher 2006). Some expressed doubts about these firing rates too, with some finding troops with unspent ammunition in the rear of troop formations, but they were generally satisfied that among those who actually sighted the enemy, there appeared to have been extraordinarily high and consistent firing rates (Grossman 1995). From a strictly military or operational perspective, this is a remarkable success story. In order to overcome the hesitancy to fire and kill that most people develop over time, Russel Glenn says that staff sergeants and platoon commanders watched their troops to ensure that they were actually engaging with the adversary and that in Vietnam, they listened for the steady roar of machine gun fire which indicated to them that their soldiers were unhesitatingly firing their weapons (Marshall 2000). However, this corrective action seems unlikely to account for such a radical shift in the firing ratios. The real cause for the difference in the firing rates, it could be argued, has much more to do with technology employed in later conflicts and changes in military training which, together, allowed and continues to allow, individuals to achieve a physical, emotional and/ or moral distance from their enemies, thus enabling them to kill somewhat easier. It is these distances that need to be explored in more detail, as even the most advanced autonomous unmanned systems that can be conceived of today or the near future will only further these distances and the disengagement and the accompanying desensitization. They may further them to a point that gives rise to unique problems affecting their operators' ability to wage discriminate and proportional warfare, but the problems, even in the face of artificial intelligence, are uniquely human problems and well within the domain of just war theory and theories similarly seeking to govern human behaviour.

The link between physical and emotional distance, ease of aggression and waging warfare is in no way a new discovery and thus it is puzzling why critics of autonomous weapon platforms ignore the relationship that this link has with the modern programmer come warfighter. As Grossman (1995) writes, it has long been understood that there is a positive relationship between the empathetic and the spatial proximity of the victim and the resultant difficulty and personal trauma caused by the kill, or the morally problematic ease of killing, more generally. This relationship has been a cause for concern among anthropologists, philosophers, psychologists, theologians and, of course, soldiers themselves, who often struggle to understand their own actions. Jesse Glenn Gray (1959), an American philosophy professor whose career was interrupted by a period of service as a WWII counter-intelligence officer, wrote that unless one is caught in some sort of overwhelming murderous ecstasy where rage takes over, killing and destroying is much easier when done at a little remove and that with every foot of distance, there is a corresponding decrease in the accurate portrayal of reality. He argues that there is a point at which one's representation of the world begins to flag and another at which it fails altogether (Gray 1959). Glenn put forward this argument over fifty years ago and the valid concern is that autonomous weapons systems seem to increase the relevant distances to the flagging point that he referenced, where the moral inhibitions of those operating, overseeing or designing/engineering autonomous systems are almost totally overcome but, the corollary of this is that, the advancement of digital warfare with high levels of artificially intelligent autonomous systems cannot surpass point that has already been reached. That is, the worry is not that we have reached another morally significant point in the history of weapons development, but that we are looking at a new enactment of an old trend. This is to say that to truly understand the relationship between soldiers, technical actors, autonomy and their ethicality for today's purposes, we have to think about autonomous systems in the wider context of weapons that increase physical distance to the target and lower resistance to killing, as well how this maps onto increasing levels of artificial intelligence.

AUTONOMOUS SYSTEMS: KILLING AT KEYBOARD RANGE

In order to fully understand the issues associated with autonomy, one must place lethal autonomous weapon systems on a spectrum with other forms of autonomous weaponry. At one end we have close range, then middle range and long range at other end. Close range, for our sake, involves any easily attributable kill at 'point-blank' range, whether with one's bare hands, an edged weapon or even a projectile weapon. According to Grossman (1995), the key factor in close range killing is the undeniable responsibility one holds for the act. John Keegan and Richard Holmes (1986) cite the story of an Israeli paratrooper during the capture of Jerusalem in 1967: 'we looked up at each other for half a second and I knew that it was up to me, personally, to kill him' (p. 266). When a soldier kills at this range, more than any other, it's an intensely vivid and personal matter (Grossman 1995, p. 115). One can see the raw emotions on their enemy's face, hear their cries and smell the gunpowder. The Israeli paratrooper mentioned above goes on to say that having shot his enemy at close range, he could see the hate on his enemy's face and that 'there was so much blood...[he] vomited, until the rest of the boys came up' (Keegan and Holmes 1986, p. 266). Combat at close proximity is an interpersonal affair, so much so that it is incredibly difficult to deny the enemy's humanity. For this reason, Grossman says, the resistance to close-range killing is 'tremendous' (Grossman 1995, p. 118). At midrange – where you can still see and engage the enemy with handgrenades, sniper rifles and so on, but usually without being able to gauge the extent of the wounds inflicted – the experience of killing changes. At this range in the spectrum, the soldier can begin to deny responsibility for the fatal shot or blow if there are others present and participating in the act of killing. One is still located on the battlefield and can hear the gunfire and feel the stress, but the distance between adversaries makes the act of killing both physically and psychologically easier, and thus more morally troubling (Grossman 1995, p. 113).

At long range, at which one must use some sort of mechanical, electrical or digital assistance to view or interact with others and potential victims, there is evidence to suggest that killing is made even easier. Among those who we have historically considered least reluctant to kill are pilots, artillery numbers and missile silo attendees. Gwynne Dyer (2010, p. 57) writes that while being observed by their fellows puts pressure on them to kill (as was the case with the gunners in Vietnam), it has much more to do with the distance between them and their targets and how it acts as an emotional and moral buffer. She aptly notes that on the whole, 'gunners fire at grid references they cannot see; submarine crews fire torpedoes at 'ships' (and not, somehow, at the people in the ships); and pilots launch their missiles at 'targets'' (Dywer 2010). Grossman (1995) also reports that in his extensive career researching and reading on the subject of killing in combat, he is not aware of a single instance in which an individual operating at such long range has refused to kill. We also have numerous examples of long distance killing made easy. Dyer (2010) reminds us that in the early nineteen forties, for instance, the British Royal Airforce 'firebombed' Hamburg. Using early bomber aircraft, munitions blew in windows and doors over four square miles and resulted in a firestorm which left seventy thousand people dead, mostly women, children and the elderly (Grossman 1995). A further eighty thousand died in the firebombing of Dresden, two hundred and twenty-five thousand in Tokyo and many millions more in bombing conflicts since (Grossman 1995). If the bomber crews had to kill each of these people with a flamethrower or, as Whetham (2012) writes, slit each of their throats with a knife, the majority would be unable to do it. The awfulness of killing people at such close proximity and the emotional trauma inherent to each act, and to the collective acts, would have been of such magnitude that they simply would not have happened.

Figure 1. Distance, Technology and Resistance to Killing

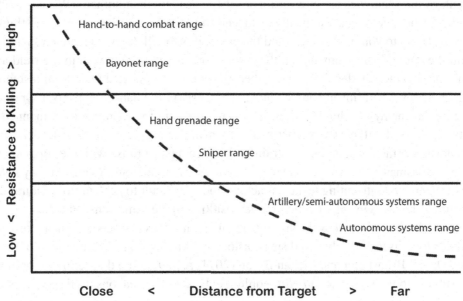

As indicated on the chart above, killing conducted with the most basic semi-autonomous systems belongs at the beginning end of the long-range killing spectrum, followed by higher level autonomous systems, which when roughly grouped together, might even be worthy of its own designation: killing at keyboard range. The contention here is that there is no other tactical weapon on the battlefield today that facilitates killing with such physical and psychological ease and that it becomes a rather clinical and dispassionate matter, easing any of their operators' existing moral qualms. Noel Sharkey (2010) offers support this argument in drawing attention to reports collected by Singer. Amongst a variety of other disturbing statements, he cites one twenty-one year old soldier who talks about his acts of killing with casual indifference: 'the truth is, it wasn't all I thought it was cracked up to be. I mean, I thought killing somebody would be this life-changing experience. And then I did it, and I was like, 'All right, whatever' (Singer 2009, p. 391). Later, he says that 'killing people is like squashing an ant. I mean, you kill somebody and it's like 'all right, let's go get some pizza' (Singer 2009, p. 392). In this clinical killing environment, in which it seems reasonable to propose that some human targets are divested of their humanity, respect for the laws of war wanes. Many 'war porn' videos show raw footage of Predator strikes with people being reduced to little more than 'hot spots' or 'blips' on the screen, with operators often failing to take the necessary precautions to ensure noncombatants are protected. And, of course, it is not difficult to imagine how someone coding an artificially intelligence autonomous weapon might come to minimise the impact of their effort in reducing decisions regarding people to keystrokes. Again, it seems that obscuring 'targets' in this way and increasing the distance to the maximum possible, makes it easier for to kill in an indiscriminate and disproportionate fashion.

While the distances involved show the powerful role of distance and autonomous systems in over-coming moral-emotional qualms and the socialised inhibition to killing, there are a range of other mechanisms that further this and make it even easier for systems operators, designers, programmers and the like to contribute to deployment of lethal force without regard for the consequences of their individual actions or *jus in bello* norms. The first additional mechanism that Grossman (1995, p. 161) explicitly notes – and the one that is most relevant to America's use of autonomous platforms, but will only mention briefly here – is cultural difference, which perpetuates racial and ethnic differences and allows warfighters to further dehumanise the enemy. Military forces have long been trying to get their troops to think of the enemy/ies as 'inferior forms of life...as less than human' (Watson 1978, p. 250). Put simply, the further one is technologically distanced from the enemy, the easier it is to think that they are distinctly different to you in some way and the easier it is to kill them. Unmanned systems separate soldiers from the cultural environment that they would operate in if they were in the field and, in that sense, permit them to racially demonise and 'other' the enemy. Connected to cultural distance is moral distance, which involves legitimising oneself and one's cause (Grossman 1995, p. 164). Once it has been determined that the enemy is culturally inferior, it is not difficult for operators of unmanned platforms to incorrectly suppose that their counterparts are either misguided or share their leaders' moral guilt and think that this warrants waging unconstrained violence against those with the supposedly morally inferior cause (Grossman 1995, 164-7). In the case of highly autonomous systems, it may involve a less overt process, whereby contributing technical actors find it difficult to account for cultural differences in code, whether it be in a sensing or action mode, resulting in the same consequences.

However, not all are convinced by the argument that autonomous systems present a moral problem in making it easier to indiscriminately and disproportionately kill, even at the higher end of the spectrum of autonomy. Daniel Brunstetter and Megan Braun (2011, p. 339) argue that semi-autonomous robotic systems are subject to the same *jus in bello* requirements as other weapons used in war, but that their technological advantages coupled with the removal of risk to soldiers means that they should, at the least in theory, make satisfying the principles of discrimination and proportionality an easier task and perhaps make operators more reluctant to kill in situations where doubt exists as to the legitimacy of the potential victim of aggression. They say that the in the case of surveillance, at the very least, the distance or what they call 'separation factor', arguably offers an increased level of control over lethal targeting decisions and ought to actually reduce the emotional toll and unnecessary killing (Brunstetter and Braun 2011, p. 339). They regard a drone operator's ability to confer with a superior officer as being a critical factor encouraging ethical decision making in war. In some instances, this may be the case, and may even apply in the case of highly autonomous systems if the relevant coding and engineering is sufficiently detailed and comprehensive to account for all relevant morally relevant inputs and outputs, but in others, it might be that having a mission commander or a test overseeing the operator's/programmer's actions only places additional pressure on them to perpetrate lethal acts, just as the sergeants walking the trenches of WWI aimed to encourage reluctant soldiers to kill. Yet Christian Enemark (2013) also questions some of the assumptions relied on here. He says that there is reason to suppose that being physically absent from the battlefield is *more* conducive to discrimination (Enemark 2013). In his view, the removal of risk allows decisions to be made in a more deliberate manner and also removes anger and emotion that he thinks might otherwise lead to morally unsanctioned killings. That is, if a drone operator working from a desk in Nevada encounters the enemy, adherence to *jus in bello* protocol should improve as the operator is at little or no personal risk. It could be suggested, however, that if an operator or technical contributors is so emotionally removed, they are in fact likely to develop the sort disengagement referred to above or an even more morally concerning callousness. In case of highly autonomous system with little input other than through code, the concern that it such a callousness might pervade said code and perhaps even go unnoticed by virtue of being concealed within the system and being evident only from its highly complex actions, having even more severe and long-lasting consequences.

It is also becoming increasingly difficult to distinguish whether one is playing a video game or operating a real system with weapons that will also have very real consequences for those at which they are directed. As Nolen Gertz (2011) notes, while it should be rather clear that video games try to approximate the reality of combat insomuch as it is possible for such a medium to do so – with attempts at this reaching new levels with the designers of video games such as 'Medal of Honor' turning to former members of the military and its special forces for technical guidance – what is probably less well-known is that the military and its weapons designers often also try to approximate the reality of war gaming. Semi-autonomous system designers are now trying to model the controllers of these platforms to those of video game consoles or, in some cases, actually using the very same controllers, wired especially for use with these systems. Singer (2009) cites a project manager who was responsible for designing an unmanned ground vehicle and said that they modeled the controller after the PlayStation because that's what these 18-, 19-year-old Marines have been playing with pretty much all of their lives. The argument is not just that these systems create a militaristic mentality; that would be too reductive. What is being said is that recruits that are already familiar with the technology have a premediated and probably distorted idea of war. The related moral concern, of course, is that people often do things in video games that they would not do in normal life and that this may somehow carry over to the use of semi-autonomous systems. That is, they may be unable to separate the reality from virtual reality, making them prone to launching the indiscriminate and disproportionate attacks that are characteristic of most violent video games, further supporting the argument that the increasing employment of unmanned systems tracks unethical conduct in war.

It is therefore reasonable to claim that killing is made most easy and morally problematic at keyboard range, but not so fundamentally problematic that it prevents the relevant normative instruments from standing up to the challenge. What needs to be recognised, and follows on particularly well from the point immediately above about the design of semi-autonomous systems, is that the disengagement and depersonalisation of war can go so far that it is not just the operators that begin to lose sight of the fact that they are actually involved in real wars. An individual who designs or programs a system to operate like or benefit from gaming systems is disconnected from the harsh realities of the battlefield and what is required for individuals and states to meet their obligations on these battlefields and, more importantly, is less clearly demarcated conflict zones. Therefore, the problems at maximum range are certainly therefore going to extend to the programmers, designers and engineers of more highly autonomous systems, such that the issue at this furthest end of the spectrum is less a matter of the technology, or how the technology designed to take advantage of certain premeditations or distortions, but more so the ignorance of the people involved in designing and developing the technology. After all, in the case of highly autonomous systems where humans are increasingly removed from the direct operating loop and reduced to providing oversight, it is the programmer, engineer and logician who has become the warfighter and these individuals need to be urgently reminded of their level of culpability for errors has been altered with technological progress, and is now on par with that of a regular warfighter in regular warzone, such that they might be liable for a single misstroke, intentional or otherwise, that could result in unjustifiable lethal action.

EMOTION, SELF-LIMITATION AND KEYBOARD WARRIORS

In the previous section, it was argued that autonomous systems and the physical and emotional distances that they create magnify the challenges that warfighters face in applying and adhering to *jus in bello* norms, but that these challenges are not insurmountable, even at 'keyboard range'. With this argument made, I now turn to highlighting an important difference between semi-autonomous and more highly autonomous systems and the importance that this difference has for recognition of the human actor's role in highly autonomous warfare. In what follows, there is less focus on the mindset-altering effect or psychological impact that these systems have on the warfighting role of unmanned systems operators and more on the impact of psychological and emotional stresses as important mechanisms of self-limitation to immoral conduct that may be less evident at keyboard range.

Some suggest that killing via proxy does not have a significant adverse psychological or emotional effect on the distance warfighter as the operator of a semi-autonomous system and this of great consequence for the future of autonomous warfare where there are individuals making what may be lethal decisions at the ultimate distance: programmers coding systems and other technical persons providing input to design, guidance, logic and operation. Lambèr Royakkers (2010), for instance, says that 'creating moral disengagement reduces or even eliminates the stress of cubicle warriors' (p. 291). Grossman (1995) also writes that in his years of reading and research on the subject of killing, he has never come across a single instance of psychiatric or psychological trauma associated with such long-range killing. Sharkey (2010, p. 372) gives further anecdotal evidence supporting these claims in citing the commander of 432nd Wing at Creech Air Force Base, who said that 'on only four or five occasions had sensor operators gone to see the chaplain or their supervisors and that this was a very small proportion of the total number of remote operators'. The reasoning here seems to follow from an idea examined in a study conducted by

Michael Osofsky, Albert Bandura and Philip Zimbardo (2005), which hypothesised that the selective disengagement that similarly distancing systems or processes facilitate, allow them to perform their role and go about killing people and conducting themselves in an injurious fashion while maintaining their emotional wellbeing. However, Sparrow (2009) expresses the concern that while distancing unmanned systems operators from the risk of death and allowing them to become disengaged might be thought to reduce stress, killing by the push of a button can still be a stressful job and might actually expose operators to new, somewhat different or unexpected stressors. In this section, the argument is that something is missing from previous evaluations of what autonomy can reasonably achieve and that it is particularly important to understand these psychological stressors because they will also influence moral decision-making keyboard warriors just as much as the typical semi-autonomous system operator and guide public opinion as to whether autonomous warfare really is an improvement over earlier forms, which links to a point made in the first section of this chapter. That is to say that the harmful stress Sparrow speaks of in relation to semi-autonomous systems operators, which might lead to the self-limitation of lethal action or the immoral use of lethal force that is quickly identified by others, might be completely absent as per Royakkers' and Grossman's suggestions and that in the highly autonomous context, may be a negative in the sense that the programmers and designers of autonomous systems already lack context with which to guide their actions.

Before delving deeper into the psychological issues that affect semi-autonomous sytems operators and those involved in the design of highly autonomous systems, we must comment more generally on the burden of killing as it affects conventional warfighters in regular close and midrange warfare. As has already been mentioned, the resistance to killing at these distances can often be so extreme that it overcomes one's own innate self-preservation mechanism and the coercive force exerted by sergeants and platoon commanders in an attempt to encourage killing. Furthermore, it can override the expectations of one's peers and the more general obligation, that of defending the state and its otherwise vulnerable population. As such, the ordinary warfighter is put in a situation such that they cannot avoid some sort of psychological trauma because of conflicting feelings, stresses and moral obligations that are reinforced by society and a range of regulations and procedures that govern wartime conduct. It has been claimed that if the conventional soldier can overcome the socialised resistance to harm and kill individuals in close or midrange combat, he will forever be burdened by guilt. As an example, William Manchester (1979), novelist and United States Marine veteran of WWII, describes his feelings after killing a sniper in a fishing shack who was, one by one, picking off the Marines in his company: 'I shot him with a 45 and I felt remorse and shame. I can remember whispering foolishly, 'I'm sorry' and then just throwing up... I threw up all over myself. It was a betrayal of what I'd been taught since a child' (pp. 3-6). If for some reason the soldier does not kill, he has also failed to fulfil his duty to his comrades. John Early, a former mercenary and Vietnam veteran, explains that 'you're depending on him [the man next to you] for the most important thing you have, your life, and if he lets you down you're either maimed or killed. If you make a mistake, the same thing happens to him, so the bond of trust goes extremely close' (Dywer 2010, p. 34). Furthermore, the reluctant soldier is subject to the shame that comes with failing his profession, fellow citizens and state. In Grossman's (1995) words, the soldier is 'damned if he does, and damned if he doesn't' (p. 87).

For conventional soldiers, it becomes a matter of balancing the obligation to kill that is generated by the society that one serves and the comrades that one serves alongside, with the toll of guilt that inevitably follows killing in war. From their comments above, Royakkers and others seem to imply that due to the moral and emotional buffers introduced by semi-autonomous systems, this balancing act is made significantly easier for the soldiers-turned-autonomous systems operators. If we follow Grossman's line of thought, we may even conclude that this balancing act is totally insignificant or not even a factor for these distance warriors. To make a comparison to combat at close or mid-range, it might be said that the psychological stress profile of a semi-autonomous operator is much more similar to that of a higher commander, who may have some operational function, but is much more strategically focused. Unlike the average soldier, but quite like an unmanned systems operator, high level military decision makers generally do not face the same sort of risk that burdens those troops that are physically present at the frontline (Evans & Ryan 2000). Most of the time, they can go to sleep at night knowing that they are very unlikely to be bombed or mortared during their sleep; they do not have to worry that field communication lines might be cut or that resupply might not happen; and they generally are not faced with the task of retrieving the dog tags of those who have been killed in action beside them, or writing personal letters home to their loved ones (Evans & Ryan 2000). Now this would be problematic at the higher level of autonomous operation because, as abovementioned, those programming and otherwise technically design autonomous systems already lack much of the context from which semi-autonomous systems benefit in terms of guiding their actions and this may therefore lead to more immoral conduct, especially if certain proponents in the lethal autonomous weapons systems debate continue to divert attention away from the enabling role of human beings in autonomous warfare.

Of course, if it were to turn out that the more relevant similarity to higher commanders and semi-autonomous systems operators were that they both face a range of other psychological stresses that, while qualitatively different, seem to equal or surmount those faced by conventional combatants and combatant commanders, the concerns might be different. For instance, higher commanders may not have to worry about being killed by the enemy, but they too have to be concerned about the enemy's movements and how they impact operations. They may not be worried about impediments to their own progress or dangers to their own life, but they are likely to be worried about ensuring that their troops have sufficient resources to conduct their campaign, their commanders' ability to conduct operations and the views of the public and the media (Evans & Ryan 2000). Likewise, it might be argued that semi-autonomous systems operators face their own unique problems. While some remote operators may be spared from the raw first-hand experience of seeing people die on the battlefield, in many ways, they may actually see more of war and its deadly outcomes than any typical soldier engaged in close or midrange warfare. There are two key reasons for this, one more convincing than the other. Firstly, while it has been argued that most of today's semi-autonomous systems reduce targets to a 'blip' on the screen, many say that some systems have such high-resolution optics that operators can see the impact of their actions with greater clarity than most conventional air force pilots (Kaurin 2013). Again, there is doubt about this because of the physical limitations with which optical technologies must operate, but technological developments may make this more of a concern as time passes. However, semi-autonomous systems do improve loiter capability over conventional manned systems, meaning that an operator may observe a target for twelve or more hours before taking lethal action (Singer 2009). Thus, even if the raw footage is not particularly clear and the operator is somewhat disengaged, this extended surveillance period in which many disturbing events may unfold, has potential to be psychologically damaging, if not at the time of operation, at a later stage when the operator has had time to come to a realization concerning what has happened and what role they have played. Yet for those distanced to the point of being involved at the design level, there are no real blips on the screen and no actual footage pertinent in advance, so the concerns may persist.

Another associated stress rarely mentioned in the academic literature is that related to limited participation in these events. Like a higher commander who has to exert influence on the ground via troops that he is not directly in control of, with only that information conveyed by field-based combatant commanders, a semi-autonomous system operator has to contend with having limited capacity to intervene or influence events that are unfolding in the combat zone. Sparrow (2009) recognizes that this general concern is more significant than it perhaps seems because despite the 'hype' surrounding them, many semi-autonomous systems are limited in the information they can relay, the force they can actually exert and the range of actions that they make possible. It is not always the limitations of the systems themselves, but often the capacity of these systems to be utilized within particular environmental surroundings that limits adherence to just war theory and creates the psychological problem. In his first-hand account of piloting drones, Martin (with Sasser, 2010) details the anguish he experienced resulting from being unable to shape or rectify some injustices he witnessed on the battlefield. He describes how he had carefully planned to kill a group of enemy combatants and recounts the feelings he experienced when two children walked into the attack path post-missile release: 'there was nothing I could do to save them... we could only stare in abject horror as the silent missile bore down upon them' (Martin & Sasser, p. 21). The feeling of helplessness and shame that Martin tells of is compounded when it is the enemy waging the violence and one's own comrades that stand to be injured or killed. In much the same way as a missile release gone badly, a semi-autonomous system may limit the distance warrior's moral agency in the sense of limiting their capacity to act in reference to right and wrong. In a combat scenario, this means they cannot aid fellow warfighters in the way that they could if they were physically present on the battlefield. Benjamin cites a young sensor operator who said, having witnessed the death of troops from afar, that 'it was a traumatic experience. It shocked me' (Benjamin 2012, p. 97). This experience of sitting in a peaceful country in relative safety and taking indirect action, while seeing fellow military personnel die, is one that is unique to semi-autonomous systems operators and one that operators need time to process and understand. More unique, though, is having direct input into the killing process via programming and engineering without having any physical presence to the later use these systems and code, and being completely absent any concerns of time. While the impact of this is unknown, the fear is that this might result in a disregard for ethical outcomes.

All of the aspects of combat stress and trauma discussed here have the potential to profoundly impact not only the wellbeing of the warfighter, whether it be the semi-autonomous systems operator or the technical contributor to the design and engineering of more autonomous systems, but also the individual's contribution to the war effort and the aggregate contribution of arrangements of individuals that we call squadrons and military units. If we better realise how humans are involved in autonomous warfare, and seek to understand the range of responses of autonomous systems operators, we can begin to understand how mediating warfighting technologies and technical design processes influence ethical conduct in warfare and then seek to make the necessary changes. We do not yet have the psychological profiles that are necessary to select the most psychologically well-suited candidates for either semi-autonomous systems service or the building of more autonomous systems and, even then, there is no guarantee that this will lead to more discriminate and proportional warfare. We also have a situation whereby political and military leaders may utilize autonomy to alter the public mindset regarding engagement in war and lower barriers to killing. For these reasons, many have suggested that we focus on technical solutions to what is a technologically mediated but largely human problem and I briefly detail some of these misguided solutions before putting forward what I believe is the only solution that can genuinely ensure that autonomous warfare is regulated (rather than banned).

TECHNICAL OR HUMAN SOLUTION?

Unfortunately, when it comes to trends in adherence to legal and ethical norms, the human record in adhering to the dictates of *jus in bello* principles is questionable, at best. In fact, Ronald Arkin dedicates an entire chapter in his book *Governing Lethal Behavior in Autonomous Robots* (2009) to human failings on the battlefield. He cites the US Surgeon General's report into battlefield ethics and the mental health of soldiers deployed in Operation Iraqi Freedom, which details some concerning findings. Among them were claims that: approximately ten percent of soldiers reported mistreating noncombatants; less than fifty percent agreed that noncombatants should be treated with dignity and respect; roughly fifteen percent agreed that all noncombatants should be treated as insurgents; and close to thirty percent reported facing ethical situations in which they did not know how to respond (Office of the Surgeon General 2006). Arkin (2009) suggests that with the increasing use of technology like semi-autonomous drones, the figures noted in these reports will become even more concerning and that atrocities in war will also become increasingly worse. His primary conclusion is that we cannot expect human warfighters, because of their fallible nature, to adhere to wartime standards when confronted by the horrors of the battlefield and that we ought to develop technology that extends beyond the limits of human warfighters (Arkin 2009).

In other words, his solution is not to take the moderate step of tailoring the weapons control interface to encourage ethical decision making in war, but rather to eliminate the importance of the human and human-machine interface altogether and look at how one might actually provide unmanned systems with the capacity to make ethical decisions and carryout different kinds of actions, some of them lethal. He is deeply convinced of the possibility of ethical programming that would not only meet the normative requirements of international humanitarian law and just war theory, but would ultimately surpass their requirements, writing that: 'I am convinced that they [unmanned systems] can perform more ethically than human soldiers are capable of' (Arkin 2009, p. 36). Arkin (2009) proposes that we equip unmanned systems with an 'ethical governor', which is based on Watt's mechanical governor for the steam engine. This governor acts as a transformer or suppressor of automatically generated lethal action, so in much the same way that the mechanical governor would shut down a steam engine running too hot, the ethical governor shuts down the autonomous machine when it is about to do something unethical, such as firing too closely to civilians. But this is just one component. The second is the 'ethical behavioral control' unit, which monitors all of the systems behaviours and ensures that they evolve from within set constraints (Arkin 2009). The third is the 'ethical adaptor'. It allows the system to learn, adapt and overcome by updating the system's set of constraints (Arkin 2009). It is presumably intended to act in place of human guilt or remorse in the case of unethical conduct managing to pass the previous two components. The final component is the responsibility advisor, which ensures that in the event of a lethal action occurring, responsibility can be clearly allocated between human and machine, in the case of joint interaction (Arkin 2009).

Arkin believes that with these sub-systems working effectively together, autonomous machines would possess the capability to operate morally, ensuring that any force is delivered proportionally and with maximum discrimination between combatant and noncombatant targets. However, he does not seem to recognise that there is a difference between a machines that act in accordance with the dictates of morality and what Wendell Wallach and Colin Allen call a 'moral machine' (Wallach and Allen 2009). That is, he fails to recognise that there is a distinct difference between following rules or laws and actually being moral, in the full and proper sense of the word. While the technical acts of discriminating between targets and determining proportionality may be a necessary condition for moral conduct in war, they are not, alone, sufficient. For instance, Andreas Matthias (2011) has said that Arkin seems to view discrimination as a mere matter of technical classification between friend and foe and between legitimate and illegitimate targets of potentially lethal military action. He reduces discrimination down to a cognitive level operation that the machine mimics. It identifies all those targets within its specified radius of operation and sorts them into various categories, combatants and noncombatants, children, wounded persons and so on. While this is an important capacity for any moral agent in war, Arkin's system does not actually establish these categories, it presupposes them. 'Individual X standing beside weapon Y is Z' (an instance of discrimination), is a straightforward classification result and there is no sort of moral deliberation involved. To ask whether it is morally right for the machine to kill Individual X standing next to Weapon Y, on the other hand, involves genuine moral evaluation. For this very reason, if no other, it seems that Arkin is incorrect in saying that his proposed system can outperform human warfighters. His system can only be as good as the individuals who design it.

Part of the problem is that Arkin takes the laws of armed conflict, rules of engagement and just war theory to be mutually compatible and translatable into a set of rules that are also compatible with his control architecture and programming language. When the principles of just war theory are viewed in this way, it is easy to mistakenly think that what is left is a technical matter of ensuring that the machinery is capable of correctly and reliably carrying them out. In reality, while many military and political leaders also portray these sources of restraint as if they were a clear and steadfast set of rules amenable to automation, each is actually a set of highly context-dependent guidelines. The law of armed conflict is, in Asaro's (2009, p. 21) words, a 'menagerie of international laws, agreements and treaties' that are open to considerable interpretation. Rules of engagement, which are devised to instruct warfighters how to act in specific situations, can also be rather vague as they are an attempt to combine legal, political and strategic concerns on one small card and leave much up to the individual soldier. Likewise, just war theory is often presented as though it is an entirely coherent theory, when in most formulations it is necessarily, and by its very nature, a set of principles that, while setting certain values and rules of thumb, require a great deal of moral deliberation to be put to effective use. Take the *jus in bello* proportionality principle, for instance. There are a host of difficulties in operationalising this principle and in carrying out the necessary calculations in the field. As Lucas (2011) says, we do not have anything like a 'formal proportionality algorithm' and it requires weighing and comparing incommensurable goods under conditions of extreme epistemic uncertainty. How many men, women and children, for example, is it permissible to kill for a given military objective? Questions like these require a kind of moral evaluation of which Arkin's system is incapable. He might advance the more limited claim that his autonomous drones might outperform humans in classificatory tasks, but he wants to make the stronger claim that his proposed system will perform more ethically than humans.

Even if we put aside the fact that he glosses over the difference between representing morality and acting morally, both Lucas (2011) and Sparrow (2011) highlight that there is an additional conceptual problem associated with saying that an autonomous system might perform better than a human warfighter. As has already been said, one ought to be willing to concede that Arkin's proposed system might function better in classificatory tasks and thus might perform better under certain limited wartime conditions. We might discover through an empirical study, for example, that the failure rate of human warfighters confronting some specific sort of decision making scenario is ten percent or, alternatively, that they comply with the necessary legal and moral restraints ninety percent of the time. In this instance, it means that the human warfighters are fallible. Suppose that we can reliably track compliance with the relevant rules and principles. Arkin simply demands that his system perform as well or better than this ninety percent benchmark set by the human warfighter. When we send a human warfighter into battle, we expect one hundred percent compliance with the laws of war and just war theory, even though we know all to well that for those reasons stated earlier, soldiers are often statistically unlikely to meet these standards. But when human warfighters fail to do so, they are held accountable and punished. The problem with Arkin's argument is that he is effectively lowering the moral benchmark for conduct in war, which may result in further breaches of the law of armed conflict and the proportionality and discrimination principles. If we know in advance that in a particular scenario, Arkin's system will perform with less than one hundred percent compliance with the relevant laws and moral principles, it would be unethical to have it operate.

The solution may be to go beyond the sort of robotic architecture that Arkin proposes and develop systems that truly have full autonomy or what others call 'strong artificial intelligence'. That is, it might be morally preferable to develop a system that would, unlike Arkin's system that calls on a human to make certain decisions when it cannot, can create and complete its own tasks without the need for any human input, with the exception of the decision to build such a system (the human is so far removed from the loop that the level of direct influence on this sort of system is totally negligible). Such a system would display capacities that imitate or truly replicate the moral capacities of sentient human warfighters and would therefore be able to engage in the sort of moral deliberation that the laws of war and just war theory demand. There is considerable disagreement in the disciplines of artificial intelligence and philosophy as to when we can reasonably expect machines to become as capable as human warfighters on the battlefield or whether this 'strong artificial intelligence' or above human intelligence is at all possible. In 1965, Gordon Moore, Chairman Emeritus of Intel Corporation, described 'Moore's law', which predicted the doubling of transistors on silicon chips with each new generation leading to rapid acceleration in the power of computer, and it has held true to date (Moore 1965). With this in mind, futurist Ray Kurzweil (2005) has prophesised that we will reach the 'technological singularity' – the point at which machine intelligence will surpass human intelligence – by 2045. Some are more reserved and say that while computers may exceed human intelligence in a few rather narrow domains, they will be never be as universally intelligent as is necessary for moral conduct in war. At the other end of the scale, there are those who hold no hope. Joseph Weizenbaum (1977) has famously stated that 'no other organism, and certainly no computer, can be made to confront human problems in human terms' (p. 233). The philosopher John Searle (1980) has also argued that a computer may be able to solve a complex problem, such as those in war, but without having any actual understanding of it.

Despite the fact that Weizenbaum and Searle seem to dismiss the idea of fully autonomous systems as the stuff of science fiction, it is wise to briefly consider whether they could even be a solution to immoral conduct both in resorting to war and conducting war these technological possibilities since a great deal of money is being invested toward the goal of creating them and it seems impossible to rule out their invention at this early stage. To be sure, the potential problems are many. One of the immediate concerns that surfaces about waging warfare with artificial moral agents is that they may eventually turn on human beings. Again, this might sound fantastical or highly unrealistic, but if we want to endow our unmanned systems with full moral agency (this cannot be assumed), this will involve giving them the capacity to contemplate both moral and immoral actions and it is a matter of conjecture as to what sorts of decisions autonomous military systems would make. A robot warfighter may not be motivated by sexual desire, power or dominance as human warfighters are, and may not have the same natural killer instinct, but they too may come to develop what some might claim are needs and aspirations that they will need to compete for with other agents for (Sullins 2010). There is no guarantee that these systems will not evolve into the functional equivalent of today's unethical warfighters. What is more worrying is that these systems and the moral decisions they make may become so complex that humans are incapable of understanding them. Imagine that these systems eventually become so powerful that we come to cede power to one super system and entrust it to make *jus ad bellum* decisions in lieu of human political and military leaders, a possibility taken seriously by many technological optimists given that the latter often deceive the public. The variables it would take into consideration might be so many that no human could understand whether a particular war was just or unjust. Strawser (2011) argues that with machines filling the decision-making niche that humans once did, it could eventually get to a point where there is no point to humans making personal choices at all, a situation whereby they are better off surrendering their moral agency altogether. Both war and human life could be made meaningless. Of course, while this is logically conceivable, it does not mean it is worthy of any closer examinination. What we do need to consider is whether might be some sort of more moderate technological solution, for those above do not overcome the emotional and mind-set altering effect that is linked to unethical conduct in unmanned warfare. That is, the solution to this technologically induced human problem is not necessarily to introduce more advanced autonomous technology, but work on adapting human-focusing rules and regulations to better deal existing and future technology to yield the best results.

TOWARD AN AI BLACK BOX

What has been shown in this chapter is that we need to focus on the trail of humanity tied to the development of distancing weapons and on the fact that more advanced autonomous systems, capable of complex behaviour in less than predictable environments, while perhaps morally problematic in that they facilitate moral distancing and disengagement, will not reach the threshold beyond which our existing normative instruments and frameworks cannot adequately account for their use. The fundamental tendency obscuring the capacity of the relevant instruments to deal with the challenge of what are, in fact, little more than semi-autonomous weapons, is that through which stakeholder's attribute blame to technology, rather than the people deciding how to use the technology. What is needed, I want to suggest in closing, is a compromise between a human, technical and regulatory solution. No solution will be easy. Complexity will inevitably stem from the need to decode inputs and review autonomous weapon systems that can exchange information with other autonomous systems, such as in a swarming scenario. The number of possible interactions between individual systems would increase exponentially with the number of systems that can exchange information, greatly complicating the task of understanding the likely behaviour of the system as a whole, giving rise to the need for systems and processes that are effective in determining whether a proposed weapon system, or a proposed/past use of a weapon system, would be/was consistent under applicable ethical and legal constraints. A kind of 'black box recorder' that tracks human input into autonomous systems throughout the system lifecycle might be the best way forward in this scenario and ensure technical actors are held responsible to the same standards as their military equivalents and do not slip the cracks left open by distance. This, in itself, might be sufficient to limit the proliferation of autonomous weapon systems in the developed world.

ACKNOWLEDGMENT

The author has received funding from the Department of Defense, but the views expressed here are his alone. This paper is adapted with the publisher's authority from: Galliott, J 2016, 'War 2.0: Drones, Distance and Death', *International Journal of Technoethics*, vol. 7, no. 2.

REFERENCES

Arkin, R. (2009). *Governing lethal behavior in autonomous robots*. Boca Raton, FL: CRC Press. doi:10.1201/9781420085952

Asaro, P. M. (2009). Modeling the moral user. *IEEE Technology and Society*, *28*(1), 20–24. doi:10.1109/MTS.2009.931863

Benjamin, M. (2012). *Drone warfare: Killing by remote control*. New York: OR Books.

Brunstetter, D., & Braun, M. (2011). The implications of drones on the just war tradition. *Ethics & International Affairs*, *25*(3), 337–358. doi:10.1017/S0892679411000281

Chappelle, W., McDonald, K., & McMillan, K. (2011). *Important and critical psychological attributes of USAF MQ-1 predator and MQ-9 reaper pilots according to subject matter experts*. School of Aerospace Medicine. doi:10.21236/ADA545552

Dyer, G. (2010). *War: The new edition*. New York: Random House.

Fitzsimonds, J. R., & Mahnken, T. G. (2007). Military officer attitudes toward UAV adoption: Exploring institutional expediments to innovation. *Joint Forces Quarterly*, *46*(3), 96–103.

Galliott, J. C. (n.d.). *Military robots: Mapping the moral landscape*. Farnham: Ashgate. (forthcoming)

Gertz, N. (2011). *Technology and suffering in war*. Paper presented at Technology and Security, University of North Texas.

Gray, G. J. (1959). *The warriors: Reflections on men in battle*. New York: Harper & Row.

Grossman, D. (1995). *On killing: The psychological cost of learning to kill in war and society*. Boston: Little, Brown and Company.

Kaurin, P. (2013). Courage behind a screen. In B. J. Strawser (Ed.), *Killing by remote control: The Ethics of an unmanned military*. New York: Oxford University Press.

Keegan, J., & Holmes, R. (1986). *Soldiers: A history of men in battle*. New York: Viking.

Kurzweil, R. (2005). *The singularity is near: When humans transcend biology*. New York: Viking Penguin.

Lucas, G. Jr. (2011). Industrial challenges of military robotics. *Journal of Military Ethics*, *10*(4), 274–295. doi:10.1080/15027570.2011.639164

Manchester, W. (1979). *Goodbye darkness: A memoir of the pacific war*. New York: Dell Publishing Company.

Marshall, S. L. A. (2000). *Men against fire: The problem of battle command.* Norman, OK: University of Oklahoma Press.

Martin, M. J., & Sasser, C. W. (2010). *Predator: The remote-control air war over Iraq and Afghanistan: A pilot's story.* Minneapolis, MN: Zenith Press.

Matthias, A. (2011). *Is the concept of an ethical governor philosophically sound?* Paper presented at the Tilting Perspectives: Technologies on the Stand: Legal and Ethical Questions in Neuroscience and Robotics, The Netherlands.

Meadors, T. (2011). *Virtual jus in bello: Teaching just war with video games.* Paper presented at the The Ethics of Emerging Military Technologies, University of San Diego.

Meagher, R. E. (2006). *Herakles gone mad: Rethinking heroism in an age of endless war.* Northampton, UK: Olive Branch Press.

Moore, G. E. (1965). Cramming more components onto integrated circuits. *Electronics (Basel), 38*(8), 114–117.

Office of the Surgeon General. (2006). Mental health advisory team (MHAT) IV Operation Iraqi Freedom 05-07, Final Report. Washington, DC: United States Department of the Army.

Osofsky, M. J., Bandura, A., & Zimbardo, P. G. (2005). The role of moral disengagement in the execution process. *Law and Human Behavior, 29*(4), 371–393. doi:10.100710979-005-4930-1 PMID:16133946

Royakkers, L., & van Est, R. (2010). The cubicle warrior: The marionette of digitalized warfare. *Ethics and Information Technology, 12*(3), 289–296. doi:10.100710676-010-9240-8

Searle, J. (1980). Minds, brains, and programs. *Behavioral and Brain Sciences, 3*(3), 417–457. doi:10.1017/S0140525X00005756

Sharkey, N. (2010). Saying 'no!' to lethal autonomous targeting. *Journal of Military Ethics, 9*(4), 369–383. doi:10.1080/15027570.2010.537903

Singer, P. W. (2009). *Wired for war: The robotics revolution and conflict in the 21st century.* New York: The Penguin Press.

Singer, P. W. (2010). The future of war. In G. Dabringer (Ed.), *Ethical and legal aspects of unmanned systems: Interviews* (pp. 71–84). Vienna: Institute for Religion and Peace.

Sparrow, R. (2009). Building a better warbot: Ethical issues in the design of unmanned systems for military applications. *Science and Engineering Ethics, 15*(2), 169–187. doi:10.100711948-008-9107-0 PMID:19048395

Sparrow, R. (2011). Robotic weapons and the future of war. In J. Wolfendale & P. Tripodi (Eds.), *New wars and new soldiers* (pp. 117–133). Burlington: Ashgate.

Strawser, B. J. (2011). *Two bad arguments for the justification of autonomous weapons.* Paper presented at Technology and Security, University of North Texas.

Sullins, J. P. (2010). RoboWarfare: Can robots be more ethical than humans on the battlefield? *Ethics and Information Technology, 12*(3), 263–275. doi:10.100710676-010-9241-7

Wallach, W., & Allen, C. (2009). *Moral machines: Teaching robots right from wrong.* Oxford, UK: Oxford University Press. doi:10.1093/acprof:oso/9780195374049.001.0001

Watson, P. (1978). *War on the mind: The military uses and abuses of psychology.* New York: Basic Books.

Weizenbaum, J. (1977). *Computer power and human reason: From judgement to calculation.* New York: W. H. Freeman & Company.

Whetham, D. (2012). Remote killing and drive-by wars. In D. W. Lovell & I. Primoratz (Eds.), *Protecting civilians during violent conflict: Theoretical and practical issues for the 21st century* (pp. 199–214). Aldershot, UK: Ashgate.

Chapter 9
Ethical Dimensions of NBIC–Convergence

Elena Grebenshchikova
Institute of Scientific Information for Social Sciences of the Russian Academy of Sciences, Russia

ABSTRACT

One of the key trends in the development of technoscience is associated with the NBIC-convergence projects, which create not only unprecedented means for transformation of society and human but also raise the risks that require integrated approaches to ethical assessment and examination. Today, the foundations of the "NBIC-tetrahedron" have ethical projections in the form of nanoethics, bioethics, ICT-ethics, and neuroethics. However, their ability to discuss and resolve complex problems is limited. Technoethics can be considered a relevant way of combining different approaches to the ethical issues of converging technologies and science to discuss and solve not only actual situations but prospects as well.

INTRODUCTION

One of the key trends in the development of techno-science associated with a NBIC-convergence project, which was proposed by M. Roco and W. Bainbridge – organizers "Converging Technologies: Improving Human Performance" workshop in 2002, where a new stage in the science and technology development was designated as the New Renaissance (Roco & Bainbridge, 2002). NBIC-initiative identified two focus-attractors: the first placed the emphasis on the synergetic merging of nanotechnology, biotechnology, information technology and cognitive sciences at the nanometric scale, promising a stream of different technological innovations; the second focused on the change of the human, expansion of its performance. The latter caused a wave of enthusiasm among the adherents of the trans-humanist movement who saw it as a real tool for a transition towards a post-human future. Both vectors – economic-technological innovation and improvement of man – promised the global transformation of human and society in totality, opening up new horizons for the evolution of humanity as a consciously directed transformative process. However, the question of the nature of this evolution is fundamentally open. The complexity of the answer to this question is connected with the fact that initially NBIC-initiative has been instrumental and technocratic in nature, as indicated by many critics.

DOI: 10.4018/978-1-5225-5094-5.ch009

The cumulative effect of technology convergence can create not only unprecedented transformation of society and human, but also the risks that require integrated approaches to ethical evaluation and social expertise. One of the relevant approaches is technoethics, proposed by M. Bunge in 1977.

As Bunge (1977) wrote

The technologist must be held not only technically but also morally responsible for whatever he designs or executes: not only should his artifacts be optimally efficient but, far from being harmful, they should be beneficial, and not only in the short run but also in the long term.

In formalizing technoethics as a contemporary field of research, R. Luppicini acknowledges

Bunge brought to the forefront the core idea that technology should be moderated by moral and social controls and that the pursuit of such technology related issues requires special consideration and expertise, what eventually would become the field of technoethics. (Luppicini, 2008).

After some time, new dimensions of responsibility and responsibility for the future in particular, became the basis for creation of ethics of a technological civilization by G. Jonas (1984). The discussion of many modern technologies has a clear prognostic vector, where expectations and fears, hopes and risks intersect. The unprecedented pace of innovation requires not only operational, but also balanced approaches, taking into account the existing experience of solving complex problems. In this context, technoethics, bringing together different moral projection in the development of technoscience in a single theoretical framework, has a great potential (Figure 1 Conceptual map of technoethics, Handbook of technoethics, 8).

This potential is of interest in the context of discussions about the "ethical myopia" described by S. Alpert (2008) through the example of neuroethics and nanoethics, which he sees as "trajectories of bioethical inquiry". From this point of view, technoethics can be seen as a way of preventing "ethical myopia" in the evaluation of NBIC-convergence, bringing together the potential of neuroethics, nano-ethics, ICT-ethics and bioethics.

- **Bioethics:** Formation of bioethics in the middle of the 20th century can be seen as a kind of response to the development of new biomedical technologies (Jonsen, 1998; Hester, 2001; Callahan, 2012). The ethical issues that have arisen as a result of the development of reproduction, intensive care, transplant et al. technologies demonstrated that the matrix of traditional medical ethics are not able to answer the pressing questions. New theoretical approaches, ethical procedures and decision-making mechanisms emerged. Promises and prospects of medical innovations actualized predictor vectors in bioethics and expanded responsibility for the future, in terms of Jonas (Jonas, 1984). Formation of NBIC projects were an important step in the development of bioethical issues, in particular the human enhancement matters. In terms of G. Khushf, NBIC projects became a starting point, which marked the emergence of a new stage in the enhancement debate in bioethics (Khushf, 2005). The first phase of technological reshaping, associated with cosmetic surgery, "smart drugs", mood enhancers, sports doping, and growth hormones. Khushf focuses on five shared attributes of the first stage of the enhancement debate: 1) The enhancements are medical and require a physician to legally prescribe the treatment; 2) The enhancements are discrete; 3) The enhancements usually serve a narrow, specific purpose; 4) The enhancements have harms that can be studied and quantified in the same way, and by the same tools we use to study benefits and harms in other areas of medicine; 5) While the enhancements do have clear, documented effects (although many are not well-studied), they are, in the end, relatively modest effects.

Almost revolutionary prospects of NBIC convergence promise radical changes that include advanced human / machine interfaces, significant extension of the human life span, genetic engineering, and the complete transformation of formal educational systems. So, the researcher highlights the following features of "second stage enhancements": 1) The enhancements provide radically new capacities; 2) The enhancements are multi-functional, and alter how we approach disability. 3) The lines between diverse enhancements blur, and they involve the convergence of multiple kinds of technology. 4) The enhancements develop at an accelerating rate. 5) The enhancements will provide significant advantages to those who obtain them. In competitive contexts of education, business, and the military, the pressure to use these enhancements will grow, and the problems raised by this will become prominent and pervasive in the everyday life of all people.

Whether we agree or disagree with the Khushf`s statement that «we stand on the horizon of a brave new world», it is difficult to criticize his stance that «we lack the social and intellectual tools to conceptualize appropriately and to address responsibly this new world» (Khushf, 2005). Of course, many of the technological possibilities are desirable and can positively improve the quality of life. However, there is fear of the negative consequences that are not always predictable. They all require thoughtful consideration and understanding of their impact on human life and society. For example, close association of the body with technology, which could trigger a negative change in attitudes towards the body. Firstly, the body and its functions will become intertwined with technology. ... Secondly, the body will progressively become a part of technological systems and networks. ... Both developments will contribute to a more technologically inspired image of the body as something very similar to a machine. The body will increasingly be regarded as a whole, made up of many different components that might be fixed, enhanced or replaced if necessary. Development, functions, and appearance of the body will seem less and less established by nature and less frequently accepted without change, and more frequently controlled by technology. Instead of being in charge of our own health we might increasingly trust technology to take over this responsibility. In the process however, the body will be treated almost like the inanimate material of a machine. Hence, the body might become increasingly de-hallowed and de-mystified. (Gordijn, 2006).

Bioethical issues of converged technologies also affect the wider social context. Convergence of biomedical and nanotechnologies is enabling the enhancement of genetization trend. The term "genetization" was proposed by researcher Abby Lippman in a paper ''Prenatal Genetic Testing and Screening: Constructing Needs and Reinforcing Inequities'' (Lippman, 1991). Genetization focuses on how biomolecular technology affects a man`s attitude towards health, including his attitudes to social structures of the health system. Not stressing specifically interpretation of medicalization, biomedicalization and genetization, it is important to emphasize that the development of modern biomedicine increasingly captures a person's life (cf. «..biology is becoming technology. ... Technology is becoming biology»). Accordingly, the complex emerging challenges require a more relevant ethical approach that may be offered by technoethics. In this formulation of the problem it is important to pay attention to the role of bioethics, which already has considerable experience in the discussion and decision-making processes, it already formed mechanisms and gained opportunities for regulation.

- **Neuroethics:** The term"neuroethics" was introduced by Anneliese Pontius in the paper "Neuro-ethics of 'walking' in the newborn"in the journal "Perceptual and Motor Skills" (Pontius,1973). Several factors determined the development of neuroethics. First was an exponential growth in neuroscience over the last few decades. New research centers were formed, and the grant organizations provided opportunities for researches. Second, these sciences promised us not only understanding of our mind, but unprecedented capability of controlling it. Third, they promised to create new links between mind and brain, the private and subjective world of experience, feeling and thought with the public and objective world of hard physical data (Zeman, 2003).

As an emerging field Neuroethics, includes two main branches; the ethics of neuroscience and the neuroscience of ethics (Roskies, 2002). The ethics of neuroscience refers to the branch of neuroethics that aims to develop an ethical framework for regulating the conduct of neuroscientific researches and the application of neuroscientific knowledge to human beings; the neuroscience of ethics refers to the effect of neuroscientific knowledge upon our understanding of ethics itself.

Neuroethics covers a wide range of ethical issues. Among the highlighted issues is the problem field, which is associated with the use of invasive and non-invasive neurotechnology for non-cure tasks. Nowadays EEG (electroencephalography), fMRI (functional magnetic resonance imaging), TMS (transcranial magnetic stimulation), and DBS (deep brain stimulation) are mostly used in research and medical purposes, but all of these neurotechnologies may be used for human enhancement or more specifically for neuroenhancement. A good example of the transition from therapy to enhancement is methylphenidate (Ritalin) and beta blockers, which healthy people used to boost concentration or reduce exam anxiety. The use of such practices can gradually form an instrumental approach to mental health and become the basis for a more active intrusion of technology in biology. As such, the ability to improve memory may lead to a "social order" for those who have such memory. But is it good, if one remembers many events of the past, especially a negative experience?

Active neurotechnology development for the treatment of patients has raised a number of ethical issues that bring together neuroethics and bioethics. As bibliography analysis show, «... what have been called "traditions"of neuroethics both mirror traditional bioethical discussions (such as debates about the safety of technological and pharmaceutical advances and ethical implications of new scientific and technological discoveries) and directly engage neuroscientific investigations of (protomoral and moral) cognition, emotions and behaviors, and philosophical, ethical and legal reflections upon what such findings may mean for human beliefs and conduct - from the individual to the political levels» (Buniak et al., 2014). Indeed, the ethical problems of Ritalin have been the subject of bioethical discussions, and also have constituted an ethical issue of neuroethics (Wagner, Robinson & Wiebking, 2015).

Many neuroethical problems are discussed as promising and possible in a future. As some researchers argue vision for the new technologies future play a fundamental role in building technoscientific projects (Morrison, 2012). In itself, the claim that science and technology was initially oriented to the future is not new. The development of hormonal drugs in the 1930s, the "war on cancer" in 1970, the project "Human Genome" or nano and neuro-technological developments of our time are based on the hopes and expectations of desired results. Specificity of modern ethical approach is based on developmentof preventive strategies and includes all stakeholders in the discussion of the benefits and risks. Consideration of trends at an advanced stage creates the conditions for a more efficient preparation of new regulatory and legislative norms.

- **Nanoethics:** Nanoethics is a response to rapidly growing scientific and technological development of nanoscience and technologies. Nanoethics deal with ethical, social, and policy issues associated with developments and applications in technology on nanoscale. Nanotechnologies is a multidisciplinary area of scholarship which connects physicists, chemists, biologists, and engineers. So, ethical issues of nanotechnologies usually touches up on different sectorsissues (medical, environment), rather than specific characteristics of nanoscience and technology. Academics and other researchers «who pursue nanoethics tend to come from backgrounds in engineering, hard sciences, Science and Technology Studies, and/or the social sciences (political science, sociology, anthropology, economics), while those who pursue neuroethics tend to come more from the humanities, the neurosciences, and medicine» (Alpert, 2008).

One of the most prominent areas of nanotechnology application is nanomedicine. According to the European Technology Platform (ETP) definition "Nanomedicine exploits the improved and often novel physical, chemical and biological properties of materials at the nanometre scale. Nanomedicine has the potential to enable early detection and prevention, and to essentially improve diagnosis, treatment and follow-up of diseases."Three subareas are accented by the ETP: nanodiagnostics, nanopharmaceutics and regenerative medicine (Malsch & Hvidtfelt-Nielsen, 2010). Another point of view separates nanomedicine and medical applications of nanotechnology.

Nanomedicine is based on molecular knowledge of the human body and it involves molecular tools for the diagnosis and treatment of disease. Medical nanotechnologies are more general: these concern public health monitoring, the integration of medical practices into daily patterns of work and leisure, the redefinition of the physiological body as a body of data, and the reorganization of the therapeutic context with its medical experts, insurance companies, state interests, and healthcare institutions. (see ETP Nanomedicine, web resource).

Some authors came to the conclusion that nanobioethics can be considered a sub area of nanoethics dealing with biomedical, biotechnological or agrifood applications of nanotechnology (Malsch & Hvidtfelt-Nielsen, 2010). It can also be considered a sub area of bioethics where nanotechnology plays a role. Sometimes it is interpreted broader, including ethical, legal and societal aspects as well as philosophical ethics.

Another attempt to revise nanoethics is the approach of Tsjalling Swierstra and Arie Rip. They argue that «there might not be a specific nano-ethics, but there definitely is an ethics of new & emerging science and technology (NEST) with characteristic tropes and patterns of moral argumentation» (Swierstra, 2007). The prefix NEST stands for New and Emerging Science and Technology (similar to the title of the EU funding program NEST in the 6th Framework Program). The questions of the independent status of nanoethics researchers decide addressing bioethics. «This is different from the case of bio-ethics, where aspects and issues derived from living creatures are a shared starting point. Nanotechnology has no such common referent other than that phenomena and manipulations occur at the nanoscale. It is an umbrella term covering a host of heterogeneous technologies, from electronics to materials and on to medical use of nanoparticles » (Swierstra, 2007).

An additional conceptualization based on nanoethics argues the need for a new decision ethics (Berube, 2012). David M. Berube considers nanotechnology as a platform technology that will allow for making of better alloys, polymers, etc. as well as making products with better characteristics. Emerging technologies distinguishes two determinations: (1) prominent technologies and (2) technologies that are the product of emergence. He offers ten principles for the conceptualization of a new ethics of decision-making. But the important thing is the author's attempt to uncover nanoethics as part of a wider ethical reflection of technoscience.

- **ICT-Ethics:** ICT-ethics aims to analyze and evaluate ethical issues arising from information and communication technology (ICT). It brings together ICT professionals, across the variety of IT roles and experts in ethics and moral philosophy in addressing complexity of issues and dilemmas in this field. Despite the relative novelty of ICT-ethics, there are already articles and monographs, seminars and specialized magazines, research groups and projects. For example, the endeavor to implement an integrated approach to ethical, social and legal ICT issues presented in the ETICA project. It identified a number of technologies: affective computing, ambient intelligence, artificial intelligence, bioelectronics, cloud computing, future internet, human-machine symbiosis, neuro-electronics, quantum computing, robotics, virtual / augmented reality (e.g., ETICA Project). As ethical analysis showed there are numerous ethical issues and some of them are repetitive: privacy, data protection, intellectual property, and security. Moreover, there are issues that require more attention from different specialists for further development. Furthermore, there were numerous ethical issues that are less obvious and currently not regulated. These include: autonomy, freedom, agency, possibility of persuasion or coercion, responsibility, liability, the possibility of machine ethics, access, digital divides, power issues, consequences of technology for our view of humans, conceptual issues (e.g. notions of emotions, intelligence), link between and integration of ethics into law, culturally different perceptions of ethics (Stahl, 2009).

Convergence of ICT with nanotechnology and biotechnology opens up opportunities in health care. Possible applications of medical innovation through ICT can be divided into three areas: preventive medicine, disease treatment and disability alleviation. For example, convergence enables small diagnostic and monitoring devices for early warning of the disease. If they are implanted in the body, the control will be carried out for the man himself quietly. Moreover, they can be integrated into a larger network of significant computational power. A comprehensive assessment of the body can be accessed online and with a sufficient number of indicators for rapid preventive responses to change. In fact, the selected preventive strategies will determine life styles. However, these developments can also limit individual and group privacy and liberty.

The use of ICT in the treatment of diseases opens up opportunities for the cure and the possibilities of interaction with the patient. For example, ICT advances have led to the development of telemedicine, which erases the distance and borders between doctors and patients. However, further development of telemedicine should be accompanied by the development of means of communication channels protection to ensure the privacy of the patient. Another dimension of the complexity of medical devices for self-care requires high technical competence of the patient. In all cases, the doctor must be sure that the patient is using the device properly and correctly interprets the results. Indeed, a lot of work is required from a physician for some groups of patients in order to achieve an acceptable level of patients' training. One can also argue that the further development of ICT in medicine will fundamentally change the practice of the organization and conduct of clinical trials, and thus require new mechanisms of protection for individual dignity and autonomy of volunteers and patients.

Another direction, which is welcomed by patients and new technology advocacy group, is disability alleviation. Already there is some progress in establishing the interface between the brain and electronic devices, which is important in helping disabled people. These devices can also be used by healthy people for enhancements. ICT achievements are also important, not only for patients, but also for services providing the care. Social services of modern societies is experiencing considerable burden. Social services will welcome such devices, even if that will be able to only partially solve the problem. However, this raises the question of financial security (initially, many innovations are quite expensive), free choice and movement of the boundaries between therapy and enhancement.

Even this cursory look at the specifics of the problems shows that incorporating technological systems is ambivalent: on one hand the convergence of ICT and other technologies are aimed at benefiting the patient, and on the other they call a new relationship in medicine, which will be mediated by technological systems. This requires an integrated approach ICT ethics, nanoethics and bioethics. In this vision, the experience of "new types of ethics" can be useful for developing new approaches to confidence, autonomy and privacy and responsibility. The latter, as some authors argue, «are more current now than ever before due to the ongoing health care paradigm shift in the western highly industrialized countries where responsibility of one" s personal care is becoming more and more one "s personal matter» (Collste, 2006).

Ethical Dimensions of NBIC-Convergence and Technoethics

According to many experts, the further integration of different areas of science and technology will determine the prospects of solving complex problems in different areas of society that will inevitably raise questions about the forms and mechanisms of social and ethical evaluation of innovation (National Research Council, 2014). The relevance of "borderline ethics", as in the case of telemedicine and e-health, where it is important to take into account ICT-ethics and bioethics, is inevitably going to increase (Rippen & Risk, 2000). Yet, further it is more, especially if we take into account the development of socio-technical systems. In a sense, the convergence of science and technologies initiates "the convergence of ethics", which shouldn't be taken literally. However, it is important to emphasize the process of mutual strengthening of their resources for a shared vision of ethical issues as well as resolving the contradictory dynamics of modernity.

Convergence is a principle of inter- and multi-disciplinary projects that combine knowledge and specialists from life, health and computational sciences, physical, mathematical, engineering disciplines to problem solving. Transitional effect of disciplinary boundaries and comprehensive synthetic framework lead to innovation in basic science discovery and could be translated into new products. The problems that arise at the intersection of different knowledge fields require complex optics to measure their social impact and ethical issues. Formation of different ethical approaches to various areas of technology (nanoethics, neuroethics, ICT ethics) reflects their specificity, but is limited. The complex problem requires stereoscopy view, which offers technoethics, which is an effective guide in understanding the complexity of the various ethical NBIC implications. In addition, there are many technologies that are currently regarded as promising. An integrated approach within the overall theoretical frame can become the most claimed tool for reducing uncertainty and preventing the negative effects of the early stages.

Some authors who understand convergence as a way of an integrated response to large civilizational challenges, have come to the conclusion that it is necessary to include a social component in the NBIC-tetrahedron (Bainbridge, 2007; Budanov, 2015; Tonn, 2006), where the role of technoehics is obvious and necessary. This role is not limited to discussing possible solutions, but involves posing questions that it is necessary to think about in advance. In particular, what might be the consequences of intervention in the various structures at the molecular and atomic levels, of micro-devices implantation in the human body, etc. In this context, technoscience becomes more reflexive because it is included in the understanding of possible effects of socio-technical development of "risk society". However, there are conditions for active development of social technology, where the ethical component is important also to discuss and solve today's and future challenging problems.

REFERENCES

Alpert, S. (2008). Neuroethics and nanoethics: Do we risk ethical myopia? *Neuroethics*, *1*(1), 55–68. doi:10.100712152-007-9001-5

Bainbridge, W. (2007). Governing Nanotechnology: Social, Ethical and Human Issues. In Springer Handbook of Nanotechnology (pp. 1823-1840). Springer Berlin Heidelberg.

Berube, D. M. (2012). Decision ethics and emergent technologies: The case of nanotechnology. *European Journal of Law and Technology*, *1*(3), 1–8. Retrieved from http://ejlt.org/article/view/78

Budanov, V. G. (2015) Conceptual model of socio-anthropological projections of converging NBICS-technologies In Socio-anthropological resources transdisciplinary research in the context of innovative civilization: Collected papers of international scientific webinar. Kursk.

Bunge, M. (1977). Towards a technoethics. *Monist*, *60*(1), 96–107. doi: 013410.5840/monist19776

Buniak, L., Darragh, M., & Giordano, J. (2014). A four-part working bibliography of neuroethics: part 1: overview and reviews – defining and describing the field and its practices. *Philosophy, Ethics, and Humanities in Medicine; PEHM*, *9*(9), 1–14. doi:10.1186/ 1747-5341-9-9 PMID:24885037

Callahan, D. (2012). *The roots of bioethics: Health, progress, technology, death*. Oxford University Press. doi:10.1093/acprof:oso/9780199931378.001.0001

Collste, G., Duquenoy, P., George, C., Hedström, K., Kimppa, K., & Mordini, E. (2006). ICT in medicine and health care: Assessing social, ethical and legal issues. Social Informatics: An Information Society for all? In *Remembrance of Rob Kling. Proceedings of the Seventh International Conference on Human Choice and Computers* (pp. 297-308). Retrieved August 1, 2017, from https://eprints.mdx.ac.uk/2040/1/ Duquenoy-ICT_in_Medicine_and_Health_Care_social_ ethical_issues_preprint.pdf

ETICA Project. (2011). Retrieved August 1, 2017, from http://www.etica-project.eu/

ETICA Report Summary. (2011). Retrieved August 1, 2017, from http://cordis.europa.eu/result/ rcn/56066_en.html

Gordijn, B. (2006). Converging NBIC technologies for improving human performance: A critical assessment of the novelty and the prospects of the project. *The Journal of Law, Medicine & Ethics, 4*(34), 726–732. doi:10.1111/j.1748-720X.2006.00092.x PMID:17199814

Hester, D. M. (2001). *Community as healing: pragmatist ethics in medical encounters*. Rowman & Littlefield.

Jonas, H. (1984). The Imperative of Responsibility. In *Search of Ethics for the Technological Age*. University of Chicago Press.

Jonsen, A. R. (1998). *The Birth of Bioethics*. Oxford University Press.

Khushf, G. (2005). The use of emergent technologies for enhancing human performance: Are we prepared to address the ethical and policy issues? *Public Policy and Practice, 4*(2), 1-17. Retrieved August 1, 2017, from http://www.ipspr.sc.edu/ejournal/ej511/ George%20Khushf%20Revised%20Human%20 Enhancements1.htm

Lippman, A. (1991). Prenatal genetic testing and screening: Constructing needs and reinforcing inequities. *American Journal of Law & Medicine, 1-2*(17), 15–50. PMID:1877608

Luppicini, R. (2008). The emerging field of technoethics. In R. Luppicini & R. Adell (Eds.), *Handbook of Research on Technoethics* (pp. 1–19). Hershey, PA: Idea Group Publishing. doi:10.4018/978-1-60566-022-6.ch001

Malsch, I., & Hvidtfelt-Nielsen, K. (2010). *Nanobioethics: ObservatoryNano 2nd Annual Report on Ethical and Societal Aspects of Nanotechnology*. ObservatoryNano.

Morrison, M., & Cornips, L. (2012). Exploring the role of dedicated online biotechnology news providers in the innovation economy. *Science, Technology & Human Values, 3*(37), 262–285. doi:10.1177/0162243911420581

National Research Council. (2014). *Convergence: facilitating transdisciplinary integration of life sciences, physical sciences, engineering, and beyond*. National Academies Press; doi:10.17226/18722

Pontius, A. A. (1973). Neuro-ethics of 'walking' in the newborn. *Perceptual and Motor Skills, 37*(1), 235–245. doi:10.2466/pms.1973.37.1.235 PMID:4728008

Rippen, H., & Risk, A. (2000). e-Health code of ethics (May 24). *Journal of Medical Internet Research, 2*(2), e9. doi:10.2196/jmir.2.2.e9 PMID:11720928

Roco, M. C., & Bainbridge, W. S. (Eds.). (2002). Converging technologies for improving human performance: nanotechnology, biotechnology, information technology and cognitive science. NSF-DOC Report, June 2002, Arlington, VA.

Roskies, A. (2002). Neuroethics for the new millenium. *Neuron, 35*(1), 21–23. doi:10.1016/S0896-6273(02)00763-8 PMID:12123605

Stahl, B. C., & Rogerson, S. (2009). Landscapes of ethical issues of emerging ict applications in europe. In *Proceedings of the Eighth International Conference of Computer Ethics: Philosophical Enquiry* (pp. 719 – 738). Nomiki bibliothiki.

Swierstra, T., & Rip, A. (2007). Nano-ethics as NEST-ethics: Patterns of moral argumentation about new and emerging science and technology. *NanoEthics*, *1*(1), 3–20. doi:10.100711569-007-0005-8

Tonn, B. (2006). Co-volution of Social Science and Emerging Technologies. *Managing nano-bio-info-cogno innovations*, 309-335.

Wagner, N.-F., Robinson, J., & Wiebking, C. (2015). The ethics of neuroenhancement: Smart drugs, competition and society. *International Journal of Technoethics*, *6*(1), 1–20. doi:10.4018/ijt.2015010101

Zeman, A. (2003). *Consciousness: A user's guide*. London: Yale University Press.

Chapter 10
The Societal Hazards of Neuroenhancement Technologies

Nils-Frederic Wagner
University of Duisburg-Essen, Germany

Jeffrey Robinson
Royal Ottawa Health Care Group, Canada

Christine Wiebking
Ulm University, Germany

ABSTRACT

Using cognitive enhancement technology is becoming increasingly popular. In another paper, the authors argued that using pharmacological cognitive enhancers is detrimental to society, through promoting competitiveness over cooperation, by usurping personal and social identifies and thus changing our narrative and moral character. In this chapter, the authors seek to expand that argument by looking at an emerging technology that is rapidly gaining popularity, that of transcranial stimulation (TS). Here the authors explore TS via two major methods, transcranial magnetic stimulation (TMS) and transcranial electrical stimulation (TES). In this, the authors seek to demonstrate that artificial cognitive enhancement is detrimental to society. Furthermore, that the argument can be applied beyond the moral dubiousness of using pharmacological cognitive enhancement, but applied to new, emergent technologies as well. In other words, artificial cognitive enhancement regardless of the technology/medium is detrimental to society.

DOI: 10.4018/978-1-5225-5094-5.ch010

INTRODUCTION: THE SOCIETAL HAZARDS OF NEUROENHANCEMENT TECHNOLOGIES

Background: What Is Cognitive Neuroenhancement?

By and large, cognitive neuroenhancement drugs (colloquially also referred to as 'smart drugs') is a label given to prescription drugs such as Ritalin that are taken with the intent of improving cognitive performance. Smart drugs improve cognitive function such as alertness, attention, concentration, and memory; and psychological function such as mood and sleep, with the intent to indirectly enhance cognitive performance. By taking these drugs, users hope for amplification and/or extension of core cognitive capacities in order to perform better at the task at hand.

"Ultimately, our drug use is a reflection of our society" so the authors of a recent *Nature* commentary tell us, "and should never be considered without the broader context of why healthy people choose to use the drugs in the first place" (Sahakian & Morein-Zamir, 2007). According to a recent study, one in seven healthy college students in Switzerland uses neuroenhancement drugs to enhance their cognitive capacities aiming at improving their academic performance (Maier et al., 2013). In fact recent meta-analysis indicate that improved academic and sports performance was the greatest reasons given to using non-prescribed medication (Bennett & Holloway, 2017). In a recent survey conducted in Canada, 15% of medical students admitted non-medical and/or off-label use of one or more pharmaceutical stimulants (Kudlow et al., 2013). Many other studies confirmed the widespread use of these drugs in the academic environment; not only students but also faculty members reported use of such substances (Maher, 2008). There is evidence to suggest that European students, at least, perceive non-prescribed use of stimulants by peers is higher than their own personal usage and that this perception along with perceived higher peer approval for its use was associated with higher level of personal use (Helmer et al., 2016).

In what follows, the authors will approach the ethics of neuroenhancement from the perspective of the emerging field of *technoethics*—a term that has been coined by Mario Bunge (1977) in the late 1970s. Ever since, this fascinating and growing interdisciplinary research area aims at exploring ethical aspects of technology and its impact on society. Technoethics has been defined as dealing "with human processes and practices connected to technology which are becoming embedded within social, political, and moral spheres of life. It also examines social policies and interventions occurring in response to issues generated by technology development and use. This includes critical debates on the responsible use of technology for advancing human interests in society. To this end, it attempts to provide conceptual grounding to clarify the role of technology in relation to those affected by it and to help guide ethical problem-solving and decision making in areas of activity that rely on technology" (Luppicini, 2008). One of the key areas of technoethics is 'biotech ethics'; a subfield that is concerned with, "the use of biotechnologies [that] spread rapidly to medical research, health care, and industrial applications" (Luppicini, 2009). This key area of technoethics involves analyzing pressing ethical issues that arise from the application of neuroscientific research leading to growing possibilities of artificially enhancing human cognition. We have seen an unprecedented growth in medical technologies such as magnetic resonance imaging (MRI) and associated research investigating the function and anatomy of the human brain. Following something akin to Moore's law, this will only continuously increase in the future. Therefore, the examination of technoethics and more specifically, biotech ethics are becoming increasingly important and relevant to society.

In order to set the stage, some disclaimers regarding our take on cognitive enhancement are important: the authors are not concerned here with non-prescription substances such as caffeine that can be regarded as 'soft enhancers', but with a narrow understanding of artificial, and, for that matter, 'unconventional' cognitive enhancement by means of using technology that is designed to directly alter the functioning of particular neurological systems When reflecting on moral issues of neuroenhancement, it has been argued that there may not be a difference in kind between caffeine and prescription smart drugs (Meyers, 2014); but this does not undermine the assumption that there might be a morally significant difference in degree. This is, in part, due to the fact that the efficacy of caffeine on more complex and cognitively demanding tasks is controversial (Dresler et al., 2013). Presumably, no amount of caffeine is going to make a decisive difference in performing cognitive tasks, whereas the use of psychostimulants or transcranial stimulation (TS) could potentially tip the balance and enable the user to perform at a pace that would not have been achievable without artificial enhancement of this sort. In other words, caffeine is not going to elevate the peak of one's cognitive capacities, whereas pharmaceutical and neural stimulation technologies have the potential to raise the level of the peak performance. This difference in degree, then, might well be a morally significant factor.

The authors are also not concerned with a wider notion of enhancement including external technological and institutional structures that support and improve cognition such as education and training, which the authors take to be too wide of a notion of enhancement. Using the term enhancement regarding these kinds of external technological and institutional structures bears the risk of committing a fallacy of ambiguity. Here, the idea of enhancement is fundamentally different, involving long lasting educational traditions that serve not only the goal of immediate cognitive enhancement, but also aim to shape and educate people holistically. Compared to the immediate and potentially damaging effects of psychostimulants and TS on the neural level, which might be described as deliberately induced invasive interventions, the features of external technological structures might be considered as non-invasive and intrinsic effects on the function and structure of the brain. However, this is not to ignore that the ethics of cognitive enhancement should also be considered more broadly (as for example done by Bostrom & Sandberg, 2009). Nevertheless, it seems that these issues need to be distinguished from cognitive enhancement by means of pharmacological drug interventions because these are different in kind from external and educational enhancement practices. In response to increased neural activity through repetition and practice, education and training approaches lead to strengthened synapses (on the cellular level) and neural networks (on the global level) involved in learning and memory, amongst others (e.g., Bernardinelli, Nikonenko, & Muller, 2014). Benefiting from neural plasticity changes requires a much longer time frame, but in turn leads to more stable and long lasting enhancing neural effects. Education and training subsumes the degree of scholarly effort compared to pharmacological and TS enhancement. Conceding that education does have a neurological impact on the brain through repetition and practice; however, this occurs over a much longer time frame compared to the almost immediate effect of stimulants on the brain. Interestingly, the use of transcranial stimulation technologies may be a stepping stone in this direction through, as research has shown that cognitive training while undergoing rTNS can improve deep level cognitive processing (Snowball et al., 2013).

So, what are the authors concerned with? The so called off-label use of smart drugs has to be distinguished from therapeutic interventions as its aim is not to cure and restore natural abilities but to enhance the given; in other words, to become able to perform better than well. The debate over where to draw the line between therapy and enhancement is controversial but need not be solved here, since the article will focus on cases that are clearly on the non-therapeutic side. In these instances, neuroenhancement technologies are used by people that do indicate a clinical need that would justify the use of these technologies. On the contrary, the authors are discussing cases in which drugs or TS are used in the academic environment involving people that, arguably, already perform cognitively above average. Nonetheless, a few remarks on the difference between therapy and enhancement might be helpful in wrestling with ethical issues that arise when the line between these dimensions gets blurry. Treatment does not override natural capacities but permits them to flourish. The purpose that guides medical treatment is thus to restore and preserve the natural human functions that constitute health. Needless to say that the question of what counts as normal human functioning is not merely an empirical question, and there is reasonable disagreement on the matter. This disagreement, however, does not undermine the assumption that medical treatment aims at promoting health and cure disease. Enhancement, on the contrary, aims at elevating cognitive capacities beyond the individual physiological and psychological limitations.

The following reflections explicitly focus on present-day actual methods of off-label use of psychostimulants and their known effects and side-effects, rather than speculating on possible future scenarios and hypotheticals. As cognitive neuroscience has advanced, the list of prospective internal, biological enhancements has steadily expanded (Farah et al., 2004). Hereafter, the authors will give an overview over how these drugs work, both physiologically in terms of brain functioning and psychologically in terms of subjective experience. Furthermore, the authors will discuss known side effects and health risks. In doing so, it will become clear that, for one, the effects of present-day available drugs are by far not as straightforward as it is often assumed; and they come at a high cost—possibly resulting in long-term effects on brain plasticity and personality (Urban & Gao, 2014). Whether or not this is a principled limitation of these drugs is subject for further empirical research. In an update to the original article the authors will expand our argument by reviewing several emerging TS technologies that are demonstrating potential for cognitive enhancement.

Michael Sandel writes: "When science moves faster than moral understanding, as it does today, men and woman struggle to articulate their unease" (Sandel, 2012, p. 93). For this reason, a solid understanding of the neuroscientific underpinnings of artificial cognitive enhancement is indispensable when evaluating their moral status; that is, both from the viewpoint of the individual user, and, maybe even more so—for reasons that will become clear later—from the perspective of a society that promotes or permits the use of these technologies.

General Neuropharmacological Mechanisms of Methylphenidate (Ritalin)

Methylphenidate (MPH) is a psychostimulant drug and a derivative of amphetamine. It is known under trade names such as Ritalin or Concerta and became the drug of first choice mainly prescribed for the treatment of attention-deficit/hyperactivity disorder ADHD (Greenhill et al., 2002; Morton & Stockton, 2000), but it may also be involved in the treatment of Alzheimer's disease (AD), Parkinson's disease (PD) or major depressive disorder (MDD) (Auriel, Hausdorff, & Giladi, 2009). MPH acts on the dopaminergic system of the brain. Its primary mechanism of action is the interaction with the presynaptic dopamine transporter (see Figure 1B). Stimulants such as MPH and cocaine (Volkow et al., 1999; Volkow et al., 2012) bind to the transporter and decrease the possibility of dopamine reuptake back into the presynaptic cell after dopamine release. Hence, the concentration of dopamine molecules in the synaptic cleft increases, leading to an increase of the postsynaptic dopamine receptor firing rate, which in turn significantly effects neuronal transmission and plasticity. When MPH is orally taken the molecular concentration peaks around one or two hours (Patrick et al., 1987); however it can be abused by crushing and taken intranasally or even intravenously, causing a feeling of euphoria similar to the 'high' experienced by cocaine (e.g., Morton & Stockton, 2000; Shaw et al., 2008). In addition, MPH (and the structurally similar amphetamine) promotes the release of presynaptic dopamine (Calipari & Jones, 2014). In contrast to MPH, amphetamine also disrupts vesicular storage of dopamine, which might explain lower neurotoxicity features of MPH (Berman et al., 2008). MPH-induced effects of structural and synaptic plasticity are highly complex processes (Markowitz et al., 2006) and dependent on many factors such as regional localisation of the neuron, drug dosage, duration of MPH-usage (Kim et al., 2009; Russo et al., 2010) as well as ethnic background (Shumay et al., 2011) and genetic factors (Faraone et al., 2014) amongst others (see Figure 1D). Assuming an inverted U-shaped dose/response curve of MPH effects, low as well as high drug levels may lead to impaired cognitive and executive performance, whilst moderate drug levels may improve these functions (Arnsten & Li, 2005; Urban & Gao, 2014). Due to its influence on the dopamine system, MPH-induced changes occur broadly along the projections of dopaminergic neurons terminating in the striatum, nucleus accumbens and frontal brain areas (Figure 1A,C). However, effects of MPH are multifaceted and emerging research is beginning to shed more light on the associated neurobiological and behavioral mechanisms.

Enhancing Effects of Methylphenidate (Ritalin) on Brain and Behavior?

A one-to-one mapping between circumscribed drug effects of MPH on a) a single neurotransmitter system, b) specific effects on brain activity or plasticity and c) selective effects on certain cognitive functions would represent an oversimplified assumption. On the level of neurotransmitters, for example, MPH is predominantly associated with the dopaminergic system. However, dopamine can interact with different subtypes of dopamine receptors resulting in very different neuronal effects, which again depend on the regional localization of the dopaminergic neurons (Robbins & Arnsten, 2009). Many other confounding factors need to be considered when planning and/or interpreting neuroimaging/behavioral studies investigating the effects of MPH including age, gender, dosage, clinical diagnoses and baseline levels of neurotransmitters, pharmacological history and other individual psychophysiological differences (Figure 1D).

Regarding the abuse of MPH by individuals without a diagnosis of ADHD, the current literature contains inherent limitations and heterogeneity, specifically in terms of the tested cognitive abilities (e.g., working memory, attention, reward, wakefulness, etc.). With no standard battery of tests applicable, which might also lack sensitivity if adapted from clinical trials, it is difficult to compare effect sizes for different drugs across studies (Husain & Mehta, 2011). However, a systematic review investigating the non-medical use of prescription stimulant medication such as MPH, amongst others, in non-clinical/healthy (neurotypical) participants suggest moderate effects on measures for cognitive or motivational factors (Repantis et al., 2010). This review provided no consistent evidence for neuroenhancement effects—specifically the enhancement of attention—of MPH, but described a positive effect on spatial working memory. As this review finding seems not sufficient to justify the high (and still increasing) number of non-medical MPH users, the authors speculate about other, rather subjective enhancing effects. Supporting this assumption, another study showed that placebo effects for MPH significantly influenced subjective mood (feeling high and stimulated) in college students (Looby & Earleywine, 2011). Besides mood enhancing placebo effects, MPH-induced emotional changes and their possible positive effect on neural activity and cognition have not been investigated yet. Tentative links between MPH-induced behavioral/neural changes and affective disorders are subject to debate. Repantis and colleagues concluded that "the lack of positive objective effects of MPH found in this review should be propagated so as to discourage people who consider using it to achieve an enhancement of cognitive capacities" (Repantis et al., 2010).

A straightforward conclusion about MPH-induced enhancing effects on neural activity and plasticity changes in healthy participants cannot be drawn yet. Instead, recent articles provide scientific support that pharmacological enhancement is accompanied by rather negative and long-term neural costs. In the article "Performance enhancement at the cost of potential brain plasticity: neural ramifications of nootropic drugs in the healthy developing brain" (Urban & Gao, 2014), the authors review and highlight the risks and concerns of pharmacological interventions (MPH, modafinil and ampakines) particularly in the healthy juvenile and adolescent brain. Pointing out the impossibility to predict the effect of a certain MPH dose on an individual (due to the inverted U-shaped dose-response curve of MPH in combination with individual fluctuations of dopamine levels), the authors point out that early life treatment with MPH may alter circadian rhythms, induce anxiety that persists into adulthood and impair object-recognition memory (see Urban & Gao, 2014 for details). Alternating dopamine levels during the particularly long maturation of the human prefrontal cortex might disrupt these processes and have powerful and lasting behavioral effects. The most replicated finding of alterations in the brain structure of children with ADHD include significantly smaller volumes of the dorsolateral prefrontal cortex, caudate, pallidum and abnormalities in frontal cortex areas (Frodl & Skokauskas, 2012; e.g., Makris et al., 2007; Seidman et al., 2005). These findings might be causally related to the underlying disorder, but might also be modulated by stimulant treatment. Whilst low dose MPH treatment in neurotypical adolescents might improve attention and decrease hyperactive behaviour, behavioral inflexibility and impaired working memory might indicate some of the downside consequences (Urban & Gao, 2012). Behavioral flexibility is critically involved in interpersonal skills and also in substance abuse. Although some studies reported that early clinical ADHD treatment with stimulant medication had no long-term effects on substance abuse in adulthood (Volkow, 2012; Volkow and Swanson, 2008) or was associated with a reduction in subsequent substance abuse (Wilens et al., 2003), other prospective studies identify it as a risk factor for substance abuse (Lambert & Hartsough, 1998). Recent animal studies point out that early adolescent exposure to stimulants had consequences that persist into adulthood with gender-specific MPH effects (Shanks et al., 2015). Compensatory changes occurred on the cellular level due to MPH self-administration, which resulted in increasing susceptibility to abuse other dopamine releasing compounds such as amphetamines, independent of the pattern of administration (intermittent, which is typically seen in healthy MPH users, or continuous) (Calipari & Jones, 2014). As MPH exhibits properties of both dopamine blockers and releasers and affects glutamatergic signaling as well, it can increase the probability to develop obsessive-compulsive or addictive behaviour, similar to which is seen in cocaine addicts (Kalivas & Volkow, 2011; Urban & Gao, 2014).

Understanding the neural long-term effects of pharmacological enhancement on the developing brain is key to reduce undesirable or maladaptive long-term effects such as rigid attention and behavioral inflexibility. Amongst others, the influence of age in individual responses to MPH seems to be of particular interest (Andersen, 2005). Turner and colleagues examined healthy elderly adult male volunteers receiving MPH (Turner et al., 2003). Whilst MPH had significant cardiovascular and subjective effects, no effects were seen in behavioral tests to objectify working memory, response inhibition and sustained attention. The results suggest clear age-dependent effects of MPH, with elderly subjects showing a lack of cognitive enhancing effects (Turner et al., 2003). Other studies in animals used multimodal magnetic resonance imaging (MRI) such as pharmacological MRI or diffusion tensor imaging (DTI) to assess long-term effects of MPH treatment (van der Marel et al., 2014). They observed MPH effects on the volume and myelination in the striatum of healthy rats. Interestingly, these effects were opposite in adolescent and adult rats, highlighting again the importance of further research in age factors when exposed to MPH, but do not suffer from ADHD.

Studying neural effects of MPH in humans using MRI are usually carried out and interpreted within the context of ADHD, which further hampers a simple one-to-one transfer of effects to casual users without ADHD. In a recent neuroimaging study, Mueller and colleagues investigated the effects of MPH on intrinsic functional connectivity using resting state fMRI (Mueller et al., 2014). They performed a double-blind, randomized, placebo-controlled study in 54 healthy male participants. Having in mind the various confounding factors such as gender or administration schedule (see also Figure 1D), the results demonstrate that MPH does not selectively affect brain regions involved in sustained attention or other executive functions. MPH induced more complex changes within networks of the resting brain, including cortico-cortical and cortico-subcortical connectivity of many other cognitive and sensory-motor networks. Interestingly, the authors linked MPH-induced changes of intrinsic connectivity, which include brain stem and midbrain regions, to typical side effects of MPH on the body. As MPH frequently causes gastrointestinal upset or nausea and nervousness, amongst others (Husain & Mehta, 2011; Yildiz et al., 2011), connectivity changes in brain areas involved in somatic regulation processes might be connected to these physical symptoms, which again underlines the multifaceted and still not well understood effects of MPH on the human physiology. In addition to resting state changes caused by MPH, blood oxygen level dependent (BOLD) functional MRI is increasingly used to study the differential effects of MPH on human brain function. For the interpretation of task-evoked neural activity changes (and resting state changes) in responses to a broad range of cognitive tasks in combination with MPH administration, several physiological parameters such as the regional cerebral blood flow need to be considered. Marquand and colleagues used arterial spin labeling MRI to measure these changes in healthy participants after administration of MPH, atomoxine and placebo (Marquand et al., 2012). MPH-induced effects showed a specific pattern of changes in regional cerebral blood flow. The authors were thus able to discriminate the neural effects of each drug and provided information about differential brain activity patterns. It should be noted that MPH increased the cerebral blood flow significantly in the caudate, substantia nigra and the thalamus, whilst the cerebellum showed relatively decreased blood flow compared to atomoxetine (Marquand et al., 2012). Thus, measures derived from BOLD-MRI might be significantly influenced by these vasoactive effects of MPH. Therefore, it will be important to consider the vasoactive effects of MPH in future studies investigating neural activity (during certain tasks or at rest) to disentangle its relationship to drug-induced neural activity changes.

Taken together, various confounding variables need to be addressed carefully and thoroughly in the field of MPH research, specifically with respect to increasing numbers of neurotypical individuals without an ADHD diagnosis abusing those stimulating drugs (ranging from parents taking Ritalin from their children to boost their energy level, students trying to improve their grades, professors trying to enhance their productivity, military personnel trying to increase vigilance, etc.; Farah et al., 2004; Husain & Mehta, 2011; Repantis et al., 2010). Currently, though, the scientific literature less confirms enhancing effects of MPH, but rather causes underlying concerns about negative long-term consequences of neurotypical individuals using/abusing MPH.

Interestingly, non-pharmacological enhancement strategies have been shown to be more efficacious compared to pharmacological interventions, such as physical exercise or meditation (see Dresler et al., 2013 for a detailed review): positive effects of non-pharmacological interventions such as meditation were reported on the behavioral level showing increased attentional capacities and cognitive flexibility (Moore & Malinowski, 2009; Zeidan et al., 2010), but also on the level of brain activity and plasticity. Interestingly, non-pharmacological techniques showed reduced neural activity in people who meditate compared to non-meditators, suggesting improved neural efficiency possibly via improved attention and impulse control (Kozasa et al., 2012). Corresponding to the described pharmacological effects of MPH on dopaminergic synapses, a PET study showed increased dopamine release during meditation (Kjaer et al., 2002). Moreover, non-pharmacological enhancement had positive effects on brain plasticity, such as increased volumes of grey matter in the hippocampus and orbitofrontal regions (Hölzel et al., 2011; Luders et al., 2009).

Abbreviations: ADHD (attention-deficit/hyperactivity disorder), AD (Alzheimer's disease), BOLD (blood oxygen level dependent), COMT (Catechol-O-methyltransferase), DA (dopamine), IQ (intelligence quotient), MDD (major depressive disorder), MPH (methylphenidate), PD (Parkinson's disease), VTA (ventral tegmental area)

Transcranial Stimulation

While the discussion of cognitive enhancement has tended to focus on pharmacological approaches of altering the functioning of the brain which require introducing foreign chemicals (medications) to the body and brain, other technologies are also being explored. Research into new non-evasive technologies that do not require physical contact with the brain itself to modulate neuronal activity is gaining in popularity. In general, TS uses electromagnetism projected through the scalp, skull and into the brain to produce neural changes. Simply put, since neuronal activity involves tiny electrical impulses, applying an electromagnetic force can modulate these impulses by increasing or decreasing neural excitability. There are two principle methods of neuromodulation via TS; TMS (using magnetic fields) and TES (using electrodes to apply electrical current through the brain). In the following section, we all too briefly introduce these technologies along with some evidence of their potential as a cognitive enhancer. For an excellent and more technical summary, the interested reader is directed to the article "Non-Invasive Human Brain Stimulation on Cognitive Neuroscience: A primer" by (Parkin, Ekhtiari, & Walsh, 2015).

Transcranial Magnetic Stimulation

TMS is based on Faraday's law of electromagnetic induction, where basically a magnetic field can interact with an electric circuit (and vice versa). In this case an electric current is run through a coil of wire creating an electromagnet (the stimulator and wand), which in turn produces a focussed electromagnetic field. When the wand is placed near the brain, the electromagnetic field then passes through the scalp/skull and interacts with the electrically charged molecules between and within neurons, creating or inhibiting action potentials, essentially controlling neuronal firing through depolarization. TMS uses brief high intensity magnetic fields to depolarize neurons in a specific region of the brain, increasing or decreasing cortical activity in a given region. The frequency of the magnetic fields can increase or decrease the activity; around 1 Hz generally decreases cortical activity (inhibition) and pulses around 5 to 20 Hz generally increases cortical activity (excitation). Repetitive TMS (rTMS), that is, using multiple bursts at specific frequencies, can modulate cortical activity beyond the stimulation period (Machado, et al., 2013; Rossi, et al., 2009).

Figure 1. A) Brain regions typically affected by the use of methylphenidate (MPH) such as frontal (colored in blue and copper) and subcortical brain areas (caudate in green, putamen in yellow, nucleus accumbens in red, hippocampus in magenta/cyan). Brain areas are taken from the Harvard-Oxford Structural Atlas; numbers indicate coordinates in standard stereotaxic MNI space (x, z). B) Cellular effects of MPH on the dopaminergic synapse. One of the main consequences of MPH is the blockade of dopamine (DA) reuptake back into the presynaptic neuron. C) Dopaminergic pathway in the human brain. Dopaminergic cell bodies are located in the ventral tegmental area (VTA) and the substantia nigra. Dopaminergic neurons project to the nucleus accumbens, frontal cortex and striatum, respectively. D) Some confounding factors that need to be considered when interpreting and/or planning research studies on MPH effects. Please note that illustrations show simplified representations, e.g. about processes at the dopaminergic synapse and pathways. MPH-induced effects of structural and synaptic plasticity are highly complex processes (Markowitz et al., 2006) and dependent on many factors such as regional localization of the neuron, drug dosage and time period of MPH-usage (Kim et al., 2009; Russo et al., 2010). Future research needs to further clarify the exact mechanism of MPH-induced functional and structural changes.

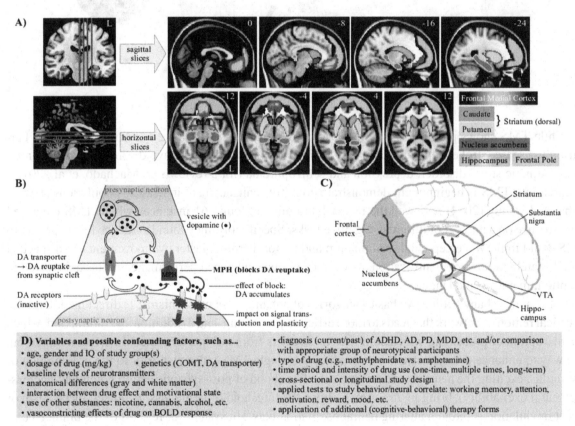

Figure 2. A visual example of a typical TMS set-up and basic functions

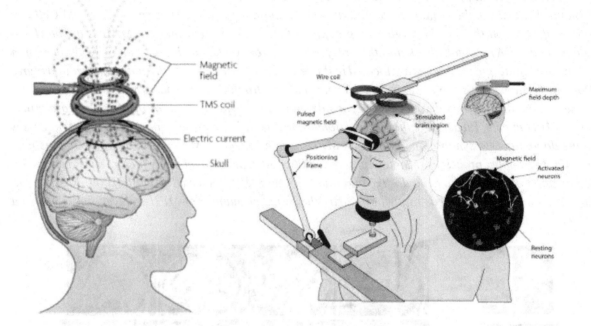

While TMS shows promise as a therapeutic tool for various psychiatric conditions, including Parkinson's disease, stroke, generalized anxiety disorder, obsessive-compulsive disorder, panic disorder, post-traumatic stress disorder, depression and schizophrenia (for a review see: Machado, et al., 2013); research into TMS is beginning to demonstrate cognitive enhancement in healthy populations as well. Luber & Lisanby (2014) reviewed the recent literature and found 61 instances where TMS enhanced performance on a number of different cognitive tasks. Specifically, they found evidence that exposure to TMS could improve perceptual discrimination and motor learning, faster eye movements, and speeded visual search and object identification, as well as produce enhanced performance on tasks involved in attention, memory, and language.

Luber and Lisbany outline two basic categories of enhancement mechanisms; 1) direct modulation of a cortical region or network that leads to more efficient processing, and 2) addition-by-subtraction, which is a disruption of processing which competes or distracts from task performance. In direct modulation, one way to enhance performance is by introducing a single TMS pulse just prior to the presentation of a stimulus, exciting the neurons, and boosting the likelihood of post-synaptic action potentials (increasing neural excitability), bringing the stimuli above the threshold of awareness. A related mechanism of direct modulation is through altering neural oscillation between systems or regions of the brain. Neural oscillation between neural systems has been correlated with cortical integration, memory, attention and perception; and TMS can disrupt and/or drive these oscillations. For example, using TMS Thut et al., (2011) found that they could mimic or artificially induce naturally occurring neural oscillation typically activated by a cognitive task (neural entrainment). In addition-by-subtraction, (Luber & Lisanby, 2014), suggests that TMS can enhance task performance through temporarily disrupting the neural processing that is competing with or distracts from the task performance (somewhat akin to using white noise to block out distracting sounds). For example, (Sauseng et al., 2009) were able to modulate working memory by delivering ipsilateral or contralateral rTMS stimulation to the posterior parietal cortex, where (essentially) the information of the given task was being processed. Additionally, Estocinova et al., (2016) were able to demonstrate that TMS applied over the lateral occipital cortex of healthy participants facilitated distractor suppression in a visual discrimination task, thus enhancing attentional focus on target stimuli.

Using fMRI along with TMS, Wang et al., (2014) were able to demonstrate enhanced associative memory, when targeting the hippocampus over several stimulation/exposure sessions. Interestingly, not only did repeated stimulation improve associative memory but the changes were evident 24 hours after stimulation, suggesting enhanced long-term plasticity via long-term potentiation (increase neural connectivity). They suggested that their results are analogous to other research using invasive (neurosurgical) techniques to directly stimulate areas of the hippocampus (Suthana et al., 2012). While human studies exploring the biological factors involved with TMS are relatively rare, animal models may shed some light on some of these factors. For example, (Shang et al., 2016) were able to demonstrate that rTMS can facilitate spatial learning in rats. In a spatial cognition task (the Morris water maze), they found that rats who received rTMS performed significantly better on the task compared to the sham group. Upon biological analysis they found that the rTMS group had significantly higher expressions of brain-derived neurotrophic factor (BDNF), presynaptic protein synaptophysin (SYP), and postsynaptic protein NR2B compared to the sham group. This suggested that rTMS increased the expression of BDNF, SYP and postsynaptic protein NR2B, which in turn increased the synaptic plasticity of the animals, and thus facilitated learning.

While the duration of the enhancement caused by TMS is still being explored, it appears that there may be some evidence for longer term effects. Depending of the protocol used, the effects can vary from seconds to hours or longer. Single pulse TMS or brief trains tend only to last for a few seconds (Hamidi, Johnson, Feredoes, & Postle, 2011), whereas Galea et al., (2010) found significant improvement on a serial reaction task after 8 hours of theta burst rTMS. However, as this technology develops, efficacy of this technology will only increase. In fact, there is some evidence that the beneficial effects of TMS can last up to 1 year in depressed patients (Dunner et al., 2014).

Like any other technology, it can be safely assumed that over time the efficacy of TMS technology will continue to develop. Spatial resolution might be increase via improved apparatus technology; while more precise stimulation protocols may yield longer lasting more and more precise neurocognitive enhancements.

Transcranial Electric Stimulation

Transcranial electric stimulation (TES) can be considered an umbrella term, with three distinct methods that fall under it, that is, Transcranial Direct Current Stimulation (tDCS), Transcranial Alternating Current Stimulation (tACS) and Transcranial Random Noise Stimulation (tRNS).

Transcranial Direct Current Stimulation

tDCS is a non-evasive method to modulate cortical activity, through the application of weak electrical currents via two electrodes placed on the scalp. Depending on the polarity of the electrical current (anodal versus cathodal), it can increase or decrease the likelihood of producing an action potential via up or down regulation of the of the neuron's membrane resting potential (Andrea Antal & Herrmann, 2016;

Inukai et al., 2016). In general, anodal stimulation (positively charged) can increase the excitability of neurons compared to cathodal stimulation (negatively charged) which reduces the excitability, though neural alignment plays a role (Zhao et al., 2017).

Transcranial Alternating Current Stimulation

tACS is quite similar to tDCS, but unlike tDCS, where each electrode is either considered an anode or cathode, in tACS each electrode constantly fluctuates as an anode or cathode via alternating current (AC). Specifically, in the first half of the AC cycle, one electrode is serving as the cathode and the other the anode, but during the second half of the cycle, they switch polarity and become reversed (Woods et al., 2016). On average the overall membrane potential does not change because of this rapid fluctuation, but it appears that this fluctuation affects cortical systems by inducing neural oscillation, leading to entrainment (Andrea Antal & Herrmann, 2016).

Transcranial Random Noise Stimulation

tRNS is probably the most recent to appear on the scene. It could be considered a variant of tACS, but it is differentiated by randomly varying the intensity and frequency of the oscillation (typically from 0.1Hz to 640Hz; (Woods et al., 2016)). One theories of the mechanism of rTNS is stochastic resonance. This operates by "improving" the signal-to-noise ratio. Briefly, as (Andrea Antal & Herrmann, 2016) explains, stochastic resonance refers to the phenomenon that a signal that is too weak to exceed a threshold is amplified by adding noise. For example, if a neural oscillation in a particular system is subthreshold where a weak stimulus induced signal would not be enough to bring it above threshold and induce and action potential, introducing "noise" via tRNS can augment the oscillation, whereby the weak signal could then bring it above threshold.

Figure 3. TMS compared to tDCS stimulators. tACS and tRNS use a very similar set-up to tDCS. Used with permission from https://thebrainstimulator.net, (2017).

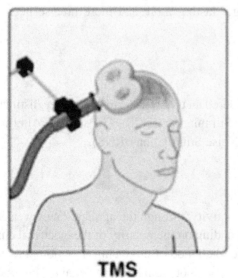
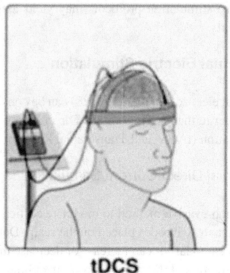

TMS **tDCS**

The Cognitive Enhancement Effects of Transcranial Electric Stimulation

Multiple studies have shown that TES can improve performance on a variety of tasks including, but not limited to; mathematical cognition, reading, memory, mood, learning, sleep, perception, decision making, pain, motor skills, creativity, anxiety, dyslexia, motivation, moral reasoning (Parkin et al., 2015). Of course, as with TMS, the region of interest/stimulation plays an extremely significant role. Much of research using TES as a means of cognitive enhancement has focused on the prefrontal and parietal cortices, which are considered to house the central executive network. This network plays a significant role in attention, sense of self, working memory, goal seeking/oriented behaviours, and planning (Fox et al., 2005; Mulquiney, Hoy, Daskalakis, & Fitzgerald, 2011; Robinson, Wagner, & Northoff, 2015; Sridharan, Levitin, & Menon, 2008; van der Meer, Costafreda, Aleman, & David, 2010; Vanhaudenhuyse et al., 2011). In this, the dorsolateral prefrontal cortex (DLPFC) has received much attention in the research, a recent meta-analysis of the effects of tDCS on working memory, concluded that that there is some support for dose-dependent improvements in working memory when tDCS is applied to the DLPFC. Specifically, when anodal tDCS was applied to the DLPFC in healthy populations they found a trend towards improving working memory and significantly improving reaction time even after stimulation (off-line) (Hill, Fitzgerald, & Hoy, 2016). Other meta-analyses have also shown this trend (Dedoncker, Brunoni, Baeken, & Vanderhasselt, 2016), while others have not (Horvath, Forte, & Carter, 2015), though differences in methodologies and stimulation protocols might account for some of the discrepancies. Similar studies but using rTNS delivered to the DLPFC have also shown cognitive enhancement. For example, (Snowball et al., 2013) found that rTNS, delivered bilaterally to the DLPFC, combined with cognitive training could enhance cognitive performance, even up to 6 months after stimulation. They had participants undergo cognitive training for five consecutive days, where half the participants received tRNS to the DLPFC and the other half received sham stimulation. Two arithmetic tasks served as behavioural measures; a shallow (drill-learning/rote recall) and a deeper (calculation) processing task, along with physiological measures (using a near-infrared spectroscopy to measure changes in several variants of hemoglobin concentrations). While both groups were initially equal on the measures, after the five days of cognitive training and stimulation, the group that received the rTNS demonstrated significantly faster calculation and memory-recall relative to sham group (along with significant differences in the physiological measurements). In a six month follow-up session, they found that there was no difference in performance of the shallow learning task but the experimental group still outperformed the control group in the deeper calculation based task. They concluded that tRNS along with cognitive training can improve learning for complex (deep-level) cognitive tasks, not only initially but over the long term. In another example, but using tACS, by applying theta band tACS to the left DLPFC (Sela, Kilim, & Lavidor, 2012) were able to significantly reduce participant's ability to process and adapt responses based on feedback on a risk taking task. They used a modified Balloon Analog Risk Task, which serves as a measurement of risk taking behaviour. In this task participants chose to pump a virtual balloon to accumulate more points or bank the points that they had already earned. Each pump risk increases the risk of explosion and the loss of all points accumulated thus far. The decision to stop and bank the points or to continue pumping and risk an explosion, thus losing all their points, combined with the number of explosions, was used as a measurement of risk taking behaviour. They randomly assigned participants into one of three stimulations groups, receiving theta band stimulation to the left or right DLPFC or sham stimulation. They found that the group that received tACS to the left DLPFC demonstrated riskier decision making style compared to the other groups. While in this study, learning was disrupted, but other studies have shown that tACS can enhance working memory. For example, working memory was improved by applying theta band (4-7 Hz) tACS to the parietal cortex, but interestingly, not when applied to the frontal region (Jausovec & Jausovec, 2014; Jausovec, Jausovec, & Pahor, 2014). Additionally, (Lustenberger, Boyle, Foulser, Mellin, & Fröhlich, 2015) were able to demonstrate enhanced creativity, as measured by the Torrance Test of Creative Thinking, by applying Alpha band (7-14Hz) tACS to the frontal cortex of healthy participants.

Regarding long-term effects of TS, there are two principle avenues to measure, the physiological and the behavioural. Depending on the stimulation protocol (ex. frequency, duration, repetitiveness, etc...) the physiological after effects are relatively transient. The absolute duration of after effects of TMS as measured by EEG, demonstrated that neural activity was back to baseline after an average of 37 mins, with the greatest being 70 minutes (Rossi, Hallett, Rossini, & Pascual-Leone, 2009). The reported after effects of TES varied, with some research reporting physiological effects lasting up to 90 minutes after tDCS stimulation (Nitsche et al., 2003), and up to 70 minutes following tACS (Kasten, Dowsett, & Herrmann, 2016).

It appears that many of the detectable long-term effects in behavioural measures are most likely caused by facilitated synaptic plasticity via LTP or LTD effects during stimulation. For example, as discussed above, cognitive enhancing effects were found up to 6 months after stimulation (Snowball et al., 2013). They concluded that, depending on the learning regime (shallow versus deep) during training, rTNS can facilitate long-term learning. Additionally, TMS has been shown to improve working memory up to 18 hours after stimulation in sleep deprived participants (Luber et al., 2008, 2013). Long-term benefits in clinical populations are also reported. In a clinical study using tDCS to treat depression, the authors found significant improvement in clinical depression ratings one month after treatment. In the double-blind study, they randomly assigned 40 individuals diagnosed with major depression disorder into three TES treatment groups (tDCS applied to the DLPFC, the occipital cortex or a sham group). The groups received 10 sessions of 20 minutes of stimulation over a two week period. One month after the termination of the stimulation protocol, the group that received stimulation to the DLPFC reported the greatest improvement in depression scores with approximately 40% reduction in depression scores (as measured by the Hamilton Depression Rating Scale), compared to the occipital cortex (a 21% reduction) and the sham group (a 10% reduction)(Boggio et al., 2008).

There is not a great deal of research into the long-term effects of tES, though in order to mitigate any potential risks certain safety protocols have been introduced and continually developed. This lack of well-established safety guidelines, combined with some of the data of some of the lasting effects of TES can raise some concern (Parkin et al., 2015). In a well-reasoned article, (Davis, 2014) identifies four gaps in the knowledge regarding TS: (1) the direct effects of stimulation are fully understood; (2) the side-effects of stimulation are not known; (3) there is a lack of clear dosing guidelines, and (4) there is a lack of translational studies from adults to children. However, this is changing. In a recent large collaboration of some of the most prevalent researchers in the field, upon reviewing the research literature, it was concluded that TES appears safe. They found that in over 18,000 sessions of tDCS, tACS, or tRNS, in both healthy and clinical populations, no serious adverse events were reported. Moderate adverse events were rare, with skin burns from tDCS due to improper electrode application and some correlational evidence of induced mania or hypomania in patients diagnosed with depression (11 cases). Mild adverse events included, headache, fatigue, itching/pricking/burning sensation at the electrode site in tDCS. They also found that these mild adverse events were found in both placebo/sham groups and stimulated groups (A. Antal et al., 2017). These conclusions are also similar to other reviews and meta-analyses (Andrea Antal & Herrmann, 2016; Luber & Lisanby, 2014; Woods et al., 2016), granted the studies selected are not mutually exclusive. In regards to TMS and rTMS, similar guidelines have been developed through the collaboration of many researchers. The most serious side-effect reported from TMS is seizures, which are extremely rare (less than 1% in a health population); with transient headaches and short-term minor hearing loss as the most frequently reported (Rossi et al., 2009).

Research into the mechanisms and effects of TS is still in its infancy but interest in this technology as a cognitive enhancement tool is growing. As future research continues to develop and hone experimental methods, it will only serve to help bring this type of technology out of the lab and into the real world. While the authors acknowledge that we are still a ways from wide spread usage of TS as a cognitive enhancer, compared to MPH, there are the same ethical considerations to be made.

Ethical Considerations

After having shed some light on the neurobiological, safety and behavioral consequences of psycho-stimulant drug use and TS, the authors will now turn to ask related moral questions that arise when considering the increasing use of these technologies as cognitive enhancers. The authors will elaborate on some considerations as to why these practices can be seen as morally reprehensible. The reasons adhered to might seem obscure to some, for they inevitably, as science advances, arise from questions that were largely lost from view. These are

questions about the moral status of nature, and about the proper stance of human beings toward the given world. Since these questions verge on theology, modern philosophers and political theorists tend to shrink from them. But our new powers of biotechnology make them unavoidable. (Sandel, 2012, p. 94)

Our attempt is to reflect on the attitudes and dispositions that prompt the personal and societal drive for neuroenhancement from a secular point of view.

While cognitive neuroenhancement via pharmacological means (e.g. MPH) will likely remain much more popular than using TS technologies for quite a while, continued development and refinement of TS technologies may start to move it into an increasingly viable means of CE. Furthermore, as TS technologies become more advanced, more cost-effective and thus more attainable, additional consideration of the legitimacy and even general acceptance these technologies must be taken into account in the field of technoethics in the future.

The ethics of neuroenhancement must take into account different settings in which this occurs. There seems to be a morally significant difference between using these technologies in competitive settings like entrance exams to universities, or when used by surgeons and nurses who work long shifts. Whilst the former might be seen as an egocentric arms race for limited resources, the latter serves rather an altruistic goal of being better able to help others in need. It is for these differences in purpose, that there are no straightforward general answers to the ethics of neuroenhancement and any fruitful debate must address each situation in turn (Sahakian & Morein-Zamir, 2007). The authors concede with this point, and thus largely focus on situations that involve the use of these drugs in settings that can broadly be construed as competitive (i.e., situations that are characterized by individuals competing directly or indirectly for limited resources).

That being said, a moral predicament arises when non-medically indicated neuroenhancement is used to elevate cognitive abilities in order to gain an edge over competitors in situations where, one way or another, the setting in which cognitive enhancement technologies are used can be described as a competition for limited resources. This is clearly the case when students aim at lifting themselves above the norm, or as the case may be, from the top five to, say, the top one percentile in order to score higher on entrance exams or regular exams leading to better grades which then, in turn, lead to a higher likelihood of getting a more prestigious job after school. This, of course, involves some unfair advantage over unenhanced competitors. Take another example: in competitive chess (where on the highest level people make a living out of it), the usage of drugs that enable longer periods of concentration might provide a decisive edge over unenhanced players and result in winning an unfairly higher share of prize money.

Philosophers have taken issue with several versions of the fairness argument, since it seems not to be an inherent moral problem that comes with enhancement technologies, but rather a derivative result of its uneven distribution. For example, it has been claimed that "the socio-economic unfairness argument is largely irrelevant to practices like sports, science, or scholarship, since people working in these fields would probably not have significantly different access to enhancements (Meyers, 2014)." The authors concede with this claim, however, we posit that this does not necessarily render the fairness problem as an insignificant issue. Even given the possibility that enhancers would be equally available for all, if some refuse to take enhancers themselves for health or moral reasons (or both), the disadvantage remains. Fair distribution and availability does not necessarily entail the willingness of all to use these technologies, and thus a measure of unfairness remains. In the case of professional sports where neuroenhancement might play a role, such as in chess, there is another reason for why these practices are morally reprehensible even if the fairness objection is answered. The reason is this: players that are winning because of artificial and invasive cognitive enhancement corrupt the idea of sportive competition as a societal activity that honors the cultivation and display of natural giftedness in combination with practice and training.

When considering neuroenhancement in a wider sense, it becomes apparent that the underlying idea is to provide a shortcut for success. For example, rather than cultivating appropriate healthy habits (schedule times for learning/sports/free time, sufficient amounts of sleep, healthy nutrition), and thereby achieving the ability to be able to take an exam well-rested and fresh, students might use Ritalin for compressed learning right before/at an exam; or use TS to reduce the negative impact that sleep deprivation can cause, thus, they gain a decisive time advantage. "Though there is much to be said for this argument," Michael Sandel writes,

I do not think the main problem with enhancement and genetic engineering is that they undermine effort and erode human agency. The deeper danger is that they represent a kind of hyperagency—a Promethean aspiration to remake nature, including human nature, to serve our purposes and satisfy our desires. The problem is not the drift to mechanism but the drive to mastery. And what the drive to mastery misses and may even destroy is an appreciation of the gifted character of human powers and achievements. (Sandel, 2007).

Acknowledging the giftedness of life is to recognize that our talents and powers are not wholly our own doing, nor even fully ours, despite the efforts we expend to develop and to exercise them. Recognizing that not everything in the world is open to any use we may desire or devise leads to an ethics of constraint. An appreciation of the giftedness of life constrains the human desire for enhancing beyond the natural and conduces to a certain humility. The problem with ignoring this humility and surrendering to using every possible means of enhancing our cognitive capacities beyond what we have naturally been equipped with is that it endorses the superiority of molding our nature over beholding and accepting the given. The world is not just at our disposal. Why is this so? To give a theological answer would be the easy way out. Molding our nature at whim would be to confuse our role as humans with the role of God. However, a secular answer can be given as well: if due to technological advances the wish of some to change their natural capacities comes true, it will become difficult to view our capabilities at least to some degree as gifts for which we are indebted, rather than as achievements for which we are responsible. Hereafter, the authors will flesh out in more detail how this would transform our moral landscape and societal value orientations to the worse.

Winning isn't everything; it's the only thing! Competition over Cooperation

In further elaborating on why neuroenhancement is morally objectionable, it seems important to ask for the reasons as to why people seek to artificially enhance their cognitive capacities in the first place. By reasons the authors do not mean here the concrete purpose to enhance one's capacities, say, for a particular exam, but more generally the reasons for why people consider these methods to achieve their goals more easily—or achieve goals they would otherwise maybe not have been able to achieve at all.

As a matter of fact, in most of the eastern and western world (certainly in liberal societies), we live in meritocratic societies. That is to say, greater effort leads to higher achievements—at least in principle. The more we put into our formal education, say, the better we score on tests, the higher the likelihood of getting a well-paid job, and thereby climbing up the societal ladder. It seems natural and legitimate that we try everything to improve our chances to get our share of limited resources. However, if this is a prevalent feature of how we cope with meritocracies, then this comes with a pivotal amount of social pressure resulting from the inevitable competition. Resources are limited and so, for example, if you are on the job market, every job in your field that is taken by someone else is one less opportunity for you.

Now, the question the authors want to submit to reflection is whether the use of artificial neuroenhancement technologies increases the social pressure for people that refuse use them. This, then, leads to the underlying question of whether we should care more about competitiveness or cooperation as a form of solidarity being a bearing component of what Karl Popper called "open societies" (Popper, 1947). What is, or rather should be a more salient feature of a liberal society, competition or cooperation? In addressing this question, the authors are not asserting that 'competition versus cooperation' is the only available option for any society; neither are the authors suggesting that cooperation is the default position. Although, arguments based on evidence from neuroendocrinology and evolutionary neurobiology have been made indicating that bonding and cooperative behavior are vital for human survival, and as such form the basis of morality (Suhler & Churchland, 2011).

In what follows, the authors will outline why they believe that the deepest moral objection to enhancement lies less in the concrete goal that it seeks (elevating cognitive capacities), than more in the human disposition it expresses and promotes. Widespread use of neuroenhancement, so the authors claim, contributes to changing the expectations society has for cognitive performances and thereby putting pressure on those who refuse to comply, as a consequence of which three core values of liberal societies are subtly transformed: humility, responsibility and solidarity. The moral thread of artificially enhancing our cognitive capacities, then, comes from the pursuit of misguided ends, since it reflects and endorses a hyper-competitive society that values the output highest—even if this is achieved by wilfully acting against solidarity, cooperation and humility as qualities of character that have been building blocks of liberal societies. Important in this regard is to emphasize again that the neuroenhancement drugs in question are not a source of recreation but become a bid for compliance—a way of answering a competitive society's demand to improve our performance in order to be able to keep up with, and ultimately outsmart, competitors in an arms race for limited resources. This demand for hyper-performance then animates the impulse to rail against the given. Here is where the deepest source of the moral trouble with enhancement lies.

Take two examples. "Winning isn't everything; it's the only thing!"—is a well-known quotation in sports, attributed to the UCLA football coach Henry Russell Sanders. While the shift in the purpose of sports from recreation and health to winning competitions is legitimate and to some extent the nature of professional sports, it is widely accepted that this does not justify any means to achieve this end. This is not only for the reason that it is unfair to outperform opponents by using doping in sports, but also because sports resembles an important part of society and thus reflects and influences to some degree the underlying values in society—the way we want to structure and organize our daily lives with each other. Imagine we would allow the usage of neuroenhancement in sports where applicable, why should it then be illegitimate, one might ask, if a chess player was allowed to use smart drugs to perform above his natural skill level, for a student not to be permitted for using these drugs to score better at her exams? The way we manage the usage of drugs in one sphere of our daily life does naturally influence the way we see it in other domains.

This leads us to a second more salient example. Academia as a microcosm of society is a highly competitive endeavor, resembled in the wrestle for positions, tenure, promotion, journal space and the "publish or perish" mentality, grants, funding, fellowships, awards, honors and prizes; in short, the competition for academic survival, for fame and fortune. Like in sports, the academic output serves not only a purpose in itself, the acquisition and dissemination of knowledge, but also a purpose to maintain one's position, to compete for grants, or whatever it may be. This resulted in the widespread use of smart drugs in academia (Sahakian & Morein-Zamir, 2007). Granted that it might increase the scholarly output as well, it also subtly transforms the expectations scholars have of one another. For example, expecting collaborators being able to work longer hours, be more prolific and enable themselves to walk the extra mile. Natural human limitations as to how long one can concentrate, for example, become less acceptable when fewer people refuse to take widely available smart drugs, thus giving in to social pressure. That is, the given is less accepted when it becomes more a matter of choice than of chance. In fact, in sports this already starts happening when unenhanced players are accused by their teammates of "playing naked"—it is not too difficult to foresee this happening in academia as well. If, say, winning the competition for grants becomes the ultimate goal and almost any means is justifiable, then this transforms not only the values inherent in academia itself, but in the long run also affects society at large. In a society in which winning is everything, there is hardly any room for humility and solidarity. In like manner, if smart drugs become commonly accepted in academia, unenhanced scholars will find themselves "playing naked." This is at odds with the admittedly humanistic conviction that human nature is not a mere object at our disposal, open to any use we may desire, but a gift for which we should be thankful. Here it becomes pivotal to bear in mind the earlier mentioned difference between treatment in order to restore natural abilities and enhancement aimed at elevating our performance beyond the given.

Another problem that comes with neuroenhancement is our capacity to act freely, for ourselves, by our own efforts, and to consider ourselves praiseworthy and responsible for our achievements. It is, for example, one thing to memorize chemical formulas for an exam in medical school as the result of disciplined studying, and another thing to having been able to memorize them with the help of neuroenhancement drugs or even TS to augment memory performance. Of course, this is not an all-or-nothing matter; but as the role of enhancement increases, our admiration for the achievement fades. One might even say that the moral unease in these cases comes with a diminished agency of the person whose achievement is enhanced. The more students rely on artificial neuroenhancement, the less the objectified performance represents a measure of personal achievement. Accordingly, neuroenhancement might pose a threat by eroding human agency, undermining human freedom and transforming moral responsibility. Why is this so? Consider again the widespread use of cognitive enhancement drugs leading to what the authors earlier referred to as the problem of hyperagency. If molding our nature by means of neuroenhancers becomes acceptable, responsibility expands to disconcerting proportions. That is, a student being too tired or occupied to study all day and night and thus reducing the likelihood to score an A in the exam is hold to be responsible for poor time management. Additionally, the student becomes responsible of not having taken artificial measures enabling to study all night.

In other settings the problem of responsibility explosion becomes even more evident. Take a surgeon that has to perform a long and exhausting operation and makes a mistake that, maybe, could have been avoided by taking cognitive enhancement drugs. It is easy to see how this might change expectations of human abilities that were perfectly acceptable before the invention of these drugs. This might lead to transforming attributes of both personal and social identity.

How Cognitive Neuroenhancers Might Transform Personal and Social Identity

In this section, the authors will sketch some issues as to how the widespread acceptance of cognitive enhancement drugs bears the risk of changing, for one, how we see ourselves in a group of relevant others (here personal identity is at stake), and also, how others see us within a group of relevant others (here social identity is at stake).

How does one perceive their personal identity in a group of relevant others? Let's assume for the moment that one is in a group of newly admitted medical students at the University of Nebraska's College of Medicine. Soon the individual finds out that their fellow students don't shy away from taking Ritalin in order to increase their academic performance. However, for both moral and health reasons, the individual has been able to convince themselves to take these drugs and shortly thereafter find themselves becoming an outcast—this not only because their academic performances are lower than the performances of their peers, but also because they are not taking part in using cognitive neuroenhancers, and thus implicitly refuse to subscribe to the group's ethos. This is an expression of their personal values conflicting with the values that are governing the group which might lead to peer-group pressure.

Let's take the perspective of the group and evaluate my social identity. How do others see an individual within the group? It seems, that there is a great societal risk that comes both from the expectation to achieve excellence in order to be socially accepted in such a group, as well as from the social pressure to subscribe to values that others share. That is, not only will the individual see themselves as an outcast, but also will others see them as an outcast. It doesn't take much to imagine how this might look like a little further down the road.

Let's say an individual and their peer's graduate medical school with comparable results, with those peers who regularly consume neuroenhancers score slight better. Now not only will it become difficult for the individual to compete for jobs with them now, but also, if the individual continues to refuse taking these drugs, they might be no longer able to compete with their colleagues once they get a job. If a significant amount of, say, surgeons are able to work longer hours, perform operations with greater ability of concentration due to artificially enhancing their cognitive capacities, they might soon find themselves coming under pressure for failing to offer an explanation of their underperformance. As social acceptance of other enhancements increases, and if these are available at a reasonable price," Bostrom and Sandberg tell us, "it is possible that social support for people who refuse to take advantage of enhancements will diminish" (Bostrom & Sandberg, 2009, p. 329).

Narrative and Moral Character

To take what has been said in an even wider notion, the authors will now turn to some reflections on how a society that endorses the use of cognitive neuroenhancers might change their moral values and become less governed by solidarity and more by competition.

As Alsdair MacIntyre (1981) has famously argued, our lives are structured in the form of narratives. Both how we see ourselves and how we are seen by others is, in large part, the degree to which our lives fit into a coherent whole.[1] Narratives are, to some extent, teleological in that they are guided by some vision of the future—some variety of ends and goals. However, narratives also provide an outlook of an uncertain future. The unpredictable and teleological natures of narratives coexist, so that we never know what will happen next in our lives, but nonetheless our lives have a shape which guides us towards our future. We make sense of our lives only through the stories of which we find ourselves a part, and so we can only understand a society through the stock of stories that it tells. As Noam Chomsky would attest, this stock of stories becomes more and more a story of competition; thereby a change in viewing others as competitors rather than as collaborators becomes inevitable. It, then, becomes natural and even praiseworthy to strive for competition at any cost. But what happens to those, arguable in fact to most of us, who are not hyper-competitive in nature? Hypothesizing an individual having difficulties to make sense of their life in light of hyper-competitive societal demands, this person is "complaining that the narrative of their life has become unintelligible to them, that it lacks any point, any movement towards a climax or a telos" (MacIntyre, 1989, p. 103). The unity of a personal narrative requires a unity of character, an understanding of how a person could at various points be a character in different narratives. "The narrative of any one life is part of an interlocking set of narratives" (MacIntyre, 1981, p. 218); and the unity of an individual life is the unity of a narrative embodied in that life. It is the notion of a quest towards particular goals, in which obstructions are encountered and dealt with, and in so dealing, the goals of the quest come to be fully understood. Thus, the virtues are to be understood as those dispositions which enable us to achieve the goods internal to practices and to engage in the overall quest for the good. The good life, then, is "the life spent in seeking for the good life for man, and the virtues necessary for the seeking are those which will enable us to understand what more and what else the good life for man is" (MacIntyre, 1981, p. 218). When the good life is seen as a way in which our moral character fits the society in which we live in, then the ascription of moral character, arguably, stands as it were at the top of the self-constitution ethical pyramid. It matters whether my character, as MacIntyre argued, is that of the 'Aesthete', the 'Therapist', or the 'Bureaucratic Manager' (MacIntyre, 1981). The latter character appears even more disenchanted and locked into Max Weber's "iron cage" in a post-2008 global recession world that puts more and more importance on winning competitions for limited resources. Here, the authors would suggest the character of the 'Libertarian Wall Street Trader', which is characterized by hyper-competitiveness, egoism pure and simple, with the addition that our contemporary dominant characters simply chalk up their costs and trillions of dollar debts to future generations. Crucial in MacIntyre's understanding of persons as characters in enacted narratives are the inevitable consequences of moral behavior.

[P]ossessing only the resources of psychological continuity, we have to be able to respond to the imputa-tion of strict identity. I am forever whatever I have been at any time for others—and I may at any time be called upon to answer for it—no matter how changed I may be now. There is no way of founding my identity—or lack of it—on the psychological continuity or discontinuity of the self. (MacIntyre, 1981, p. 251).

The way in which we see ourselves fitting into the demands of society is important and inevitably shapes the way in which others see themselves fitting in. Thus, personal and social identity extended into moral character in the unity of one's moral life has implications for the freedom and well-being of all other human beings and, down the road, for society as a whole. The feeling of being intimately linked to a set of shared values is something we seek for its own sake, not as a means to some further end. When seeing society first and foremost as an organized competition, by contrast, our shared values become primarily pragmatic and strategic; enabling us to better compete with others for limited resources, its primary value becomes instrumental. The unrestricted quest for competitiveness might then change social values towards more selfishness and reduced cooperation.

CONCLUDING REMARKS

It is tempting to think of enhancing our cognitive capacities to gain a competitive edge as a legitimate way of expressing the ideal of freedom allowing us to get more than our fair share in a meritocracy. However, the social costs of this are likely to outweigh the benefits. We should bear in mind that by changing our nature to fit society—rather than trying to create a society that fits our nature—we may inadvertently subjugate ourselves to the brute ideal of 'survival of the most competitive' at any sacrifice. Rather than encouraging a hyper-competitive society, we would do well to aspire and promote a more humanitarian society allowing for and accepting the limitations of innate human cognition. This involves the recogni-tion and appreciation of the fact that our talents and limitations are not subject to our absolute control or entirely our own doing. In this sense, none of us can be exclusively responsible for their success or failure. This is an important insight but no general disproof of meritocratic societies. To the contrary,

It saves a meritocratic society from sliding into the smug assumption that the rich are rich because they are more deserving than the poor. Without this, the successful would become more likely than they are now to view themselves as self-made and self-sufficient, and hence wholly responsible for their success. Those at the bottom of society would be viewed not as disadvantaged, and thus worthy of measure of compensation, but simply as unfit, and thus worthy of eugenic repair. (Sandel, 2012, p. 103).

Such a society, more and more driven by choice, and less and less by chance, would become harsh, less forgiving and undermine the solidarity that we have with the less gifted due to recognizing the measure of contingency when pondering our own capabilities.

The vision of ungluing our cognitive limitations from the given has something appealing to it as it resembles our quest for freedom and might even be deeply rooted in the human urge to strive for perfection. However, it is also intelligible to view the wish of enhancing ourselves beyond the given differently. "It can be seen," Michael Sandel says,

As the ultimate expression of our resolve to see ourselves astride the world, the masters of our nature. But that vision of freedom is flawed. It threatens to banish our appreciation of life as a gift, and to leave us with nothing to affirm or behold outside our own will. (Sandel, 2007, p. 99f.).

A crucial question when reflecting on the ethics of neuroenhancement is this: do we really want to live in, and promote, a society where people aspire to enhance their cognitive capacities to answer and thereby reinforce the increasing societal demands of competition—thus becoming what Nietzsche called the "Übermensch"? Taking artificial enhancement drugs raises the worry of, as it were, 'pharmacologization' of the entire life course, or as Healy (2008) puts it short and to the point: "Birth, Ritalin, Prozac, Viagra, Death." The authors propose that instead, we would do better to adhere to a certain degree of humility considering our place in nature and to accept our natural limitations. By doing so, we would refrain from abandoning solidarity and view our joint human quest as cooperative rather than competitive.[2]

REFERENCES

Andersen, S. (2005). Stimulants and the developing brain. *Trends in Pharmacological Sciences*, 26(5), 237–243. doi:10.1016/j.tips.2005.03.009 PMID:15860370

Antal, A., Alekseichuk, I., Bikson, M., Brockmöller, J., Brunoni, A. R., Chen, R., ... Paulus, W. (2017). Low intensity transcranial electric stimulation: Safety, ethical, legal regulatory and application guidelines. *Clinical Neurophysiology*, 34(0), 4022–4026. PMID:28709880

Antal, A., Alekseichuk, I., Bikson, M., Brockmöller, J., Brunoni, A. R., Chen, R., ... Paulus, W. (2017). Low intensity transcranial electric stimulation: Safety, ethical, legal regulatory and application guidelines. *Clinical Neurophysiology*, 34(0), 4022–4026. doi:10.1016/j.clinph.2017.06.001 PMID:28709880

Antal, A., & Herrmann, C. S. (2016). Transcranial Alternating Current and Random Noise Stimulation: Possible Mechanisms. *Neural Plasticity*. PMID:27242932

Antal, A., & Herrmann, C. S. (2016). Transcranial Alternating Current and Random Noise Stimulation: Possible Mechanisms. *Neural Plasticity*, 2016, 1–12. doi:10.1155/2016/3616807 PMID:27242932

Arnsten, A., & Li, B. (2005). Neurobiology of executive functions: Catecholamine influences on prefrontal cortical functions. *Biological Psychiatry*, 57(11), 1377–1384. doi:10.1016/j.biopsych.2004.08.019 PMID:15950011

Arun, P., & Sahni, S. (2014). Methylphenidate and suicidal ideation: Report of two cases. *Indian Journal of Psychiatry*, 56(1), 79–81. doi:10.4103/0019-5545.124721 PMID:24574564

Auriel, E., Hausdorff, J., & Giladi, N. (2009). Methylphenidate for the treatment of Parkinson disease and other neurological disorders. *Clinical Neuropharmacology*, 2(32), 75–81. doi:10.1097/WNF.0b013e318170576c PMID:18978488

Bennett, T., & Holloway, K. (2017). Motives for illicit prescription drug use among university students: A systematic review and meta-analysis. *The International Journal on Drug Policy*, 44, 12–22. doi:10.1016/j.drugpo.2017.02.012 PMID:28343063

Bennett, T., & Holloway, K. (2017). Motives for illicit prescription drug use among university students: A systematic review and meta-analysis. *The International Journal on Drug Policy*, 44, 12–22. doi:10.1016/j.drugpo.2017.02.012 PMID:28343063

Berman, S., O'Neill, J., Fears, S., Bartzokis, G., & London, E. (2008). Abuse of amphetamines and structural abnormalities in the brain. *Annals of the New York Academy of Sciences*, 1141(1), 195–220. doi:10.1196/annals.1441.031 PMID:18991959

Bernardinelli, Y., Nikonenko, I., & Muller, D. (2014). Structural plasticity: Mechanisms and contribution to developmental psychiatric disorders. *Frontiers in Neuroanatomy*, 8. PMID:25404897

Bilder, R., Volavka, J., Lachman, H., & Grace, A. (2004). The catechol-O-methyltransferase polymorphism: Relations to the tonic-phasic dopamine hypothesis and neuropsychiatric phenotypes. *Neuropsychopharmacology*, 29(11), 1943–1961. doi:10.1038j.npp.1300542 PMID:15305167

Boggio, P. S., Rigonatti, S. P., Ribeiro, R. B., Myczkowski, M. L., Nitsche, M. A., Pascual-leone, A., & Fregni, F. (2008). A randomized, double-blind clinical trial on the efficacy of cortical direct current stimulation for the treatment of major depression. *The International Journal of Neuropsychopharmacology*, 11(2), 249–254. doi:10.1017/S1461145707007833 PMID:17559710

Boggio, P. S., Rigonatti, S. P., Ribeiro, R. B., Myczkowski, M. L., Nitsche, M. A., Pascual-leone, A., & Fregni, F. (2008). A randomized, double-blind clinical trial on the efficacy of cortical direct current stimulation for the treatment of major depression. *The International Journal of Neuropsychopharmacology*, 11(2), 249–254. doi:10.1017/S1461145707007833 PMID:17559710

Bostrom, N., & Sandberg, A. (2009). Cognitive Enhancement: Methods, Ethics, Regulatory Challenges. *Science and Engineering Ethics*, 15(3), 311–341. doi:10.100711948-009-9142-5 PMID:19543814

Bunge, M. (1977). Towards a Technoethics. *The Monist*, 60(1), 96–107. doi:10.5840/monist197760134

Calipari, E., & Jones, S. (2014). Sensitized nucleus accumbens dopamine terminal responses to methylphenidate and dopamine transporter releasers after intermittent-access self-administration. *Neuropharmacology*, 82, 1–10. doi:10.1016/j.neuropharm.2014.02.021 PMID:24632529

Clatworthy, P., Lewis, S., Brichard, L., Hong, Y., Izquierdo, D., Clark, L., ... Robbins, T. (2009). Dopamine release in dissociable striatal subregions predicts the different effects of oral methylphenidate on reversal learning and spatial working memory. *The Journal of Neuroscience*, 29(15), 4690–4696. doi:10.1523/JNEUROSCI.3266-08.2009 PMID:19369539

Coghill, D., Seth, S., Pedroso, S., Usala, T., Currie, J., & Gagliano, A. (2014). Effects of methylphenidate on cognitive functions in children and adolescents with attention-deficit/hyperactivity disorder: Evidence from a systematic review and a meta-analysis. *Biological Psychiatry*, 76. PMID:24231201

Davis, N. J. (2014). Transcranial stimulation of the developing brain: A plea for extreme caution. *Frontiers in Human Neuroscience*, 8(August), 8–11. PMID:25140146

Davis, N. J. (2014). Transcranial stimulation of the developing brain: A plea for extreme caution. *Frontiers in Human Neuroscience*, 8(August), 8–11. doi:10.3389/fnhum.2014.00600 PMID:25140146

Dedoncker, J., Brunoni, A. R., Baeken, C., & Vanderhasselt, M.-A. (2016). The effect of the interval-between-sessions on prefrontal transcranial direct current stimulation (tDCS) on cognitive outcomes: A systematic review and meta-analysis. *Journal of Neural Transmission (Vienna, Austria)*, 123(10), 1159–1172. doi:10.100700702-016-1558-x PMID:27145765

Dedoncker, J., Brunoni, A. R., Baeken, C., & Vanderhasselt, M.-A. (2016). The effect of the interval-between-sessions on prefrontal transcranial direct current stimulation (tDCS) on cognitive outcomes: A systematic review and meta-analysis. *Journal of Neural Transmission (Vienna, Austria)*, 123(10), 1159–1172. doi:10.100700702-016-1558-x PMID:27145765

Dresler, M., Sandberg, A., Ohla, K., Bublitz, C., Trenado, C., Mroczko-Wąsowicz, A., ... Repantis, D. (2013). Non-pharmacological cognitive enhancement. *Neuropharmacology*, 64, 529–543. doi:10.1016/j.neuropharm.2012.07.002 PMID:22828638

Farah, M., Illes, J., Cook-Deegan, R., Gardner, H., Kandel, E., King, P., ... Wolpe, P. (2004). Neuro-cognitive enhancement: What can we do and what should we do. *Nature Reviews. Neuroscience*, 5(5), 421–425. doi:10.1038/nrn1390 PMID:15100724

Faraone, S., Spencer, T., Madras, B., Zhang-James, Y., & Biederman, J. (2014). Functional effects of dopamine transporter gene genotypes on in vivo dopamine transporter functioning: A meta-analysis. *Molecular Psychiatry*, 19(8), 880–889. doi:10.1038/mp.2013.126 PMID:24061496

Fettahoglu, E., Satilmis, A., Gokcen, C., & Ozatalay, E. (2009). Oral megadose methylphenidate ingestion for suicide attempt. *Pediatrics International*, 51(6), 844–845. doi:10.1111/j.1442-200X.2009.02929.x PMID:20158630

Fox, M. D., Snyder, A. Z., Vincent, J. L., Corbetta, M., Van Essen, D. C., & Raichle, M. E. (2005). The human brain is intrinsically organized into dynamic, anticorrelated functional networks. *Proceedings of the National Academy of Sciences of the United States of America*, 102(27), 9673–9678. doi:10.1073/pnas.0504136102 PMID:15976020

Fox, M. D., Snyder, A. Z., Vincent, J. L., Corbetta, M., Van Essen, D. C., & Raichle, M. E. (2005). The human brain is intrinsically organized into dynamic, anticorrelated functional networks. *Proceedings of the National Academy of Sciences of the United States of America*, 102(27), 9673–9678. doi:10.1073/pnas.0504136102 PMID:15976020

Frodl, T. (2010). Comorbidity of ADHD and Substance Use Disorder (SUD): A neuroimaging perspective. *Journal of Attention Disorders*, 14(2), 109–120. doi:10.1177/1087054710365054 PMID:20495160

Frodl, T., & Skokauskas, N. (2012). Meta-analysis of structural MRI studies in children and adults with attention deficit hyperactivity disorder indicates treatment effects. *Acta Psychiatrica Scandinavica, 125*(2), 114–126. doi:10.1111/j.1600-0447.2011.01786.x PMID:22118249

Greenhill, L., Pliszka, S., & Dulcan, M. (2002). Practice Parameter for the Use of Stimulant Medications in the Treatment of Children, Adolescents, and Adults. *Journal of the American Academy of Child and Adolescent Psychiatry, 41*(2), 26S–49S. doi:10.1097/00004583-200202001-00003 PMID:11833633

Hamidi, M., Johson, J. S., Feredoes, E., & Postle, B. R. (2011). Does high-frequency repetitive transcranial magnetic stimulation produce residual and/or cumulative effects within an experimental session? *Brain Topography, 23*(4), 355–367. doi:10.100710548-010-0153-y PMID:20623171

Hamidi, M., Johson, J. S., Feredoes, E., & Postle, B. R. (2011). Does high-frequency repetitive transcranial magnetic stimulation produce residual and/or cumulative effects within an experimental session? *Brain Topography, 23*(4), 355–367. doi:10.100710548-010-0153-y PMID:20623171

Healy, D. (2008). Birth, Ritalin, Prozac, Viagra, Death. In T. C. Bennett & I. Karpin (Eds.), *Brave New World of Health* (pp. 112–128). Sydney: The Federation Press.

Helmchen, H., & Sartorius, N. (Eds.). (2010). *Ethics in Psychiatry European Contributions.* Springer. doi:10.1007/978-90-481-8721-8

Helmer, S. M., Pischke, C. R., Van Hal, G., Vriesacker, B., Dempsey, R. C., Akvardar, Y., ... Zeeb, H. (2016). Personal and perceived peer use and attitudes towards the use of nonmedical prescription stimulants to improve academic performance among university students in seven European countries. *Drug and Alcohol Dependence, 168*, 128–134. doi:10.1016/j.drugalcdep.2016.08.639 PMID:27639131

Hesapcioglu, S., Goker, Z., Bilginer, C., & Kandil, S. (2012). Methylphenidate Induced Psychotic Symptoms: Two Cases Report. *Journal of Medical Cases.*

Hill, A. T., Fitzgerald, P. B., & Hoy, K. E. (2016). Effects of Anodal Transcranial Direct Current Stimulation on Working Memory: A Systematic Review and Meta-Analysis of Findings from Healthy and Neuropsychiatric Populations. *Brain Stimulation, 9*(2), 197–208. doi:10.1016/j.brs.2015.10.006 PMID:26597929

Hill, A. T., Fitzgerald, P. B., & Hoy, K. E. (2016). Effects of Anodal Transcranial Direct Current Stimulation on Working Memory: A Systematic Review and Meta-Analysis of Findings from Healthy and Neuropsychiatric Populations. *Brain Stimulation, 9*(2), 197–208. doi:10.1016/j.brs.2015.10.006 PMID:26597929

Hölzel, B., Carmody, J., Vangel, M., Congleton, C., Yerramsetti, S., Gard, T., & Lazar, S. (2011). Mindfulness practice leads to increases in regional brain gray matter density. *Psychiatry Research, 191*(1), 36–43. doi:10.1016/j.pscychresns.2010.08.006 PMID:21071182

Horvath, J. C., Forte, J. D., & Carter, O. (2015). Quantitative review finds no evidence of cognitive effects in healthy populations from single-session transcranial direct current stimulation (tDCS). *Brain Stimulation, 8*(3), 535–550. doi:10.1016/j.brs.2015.01.400 PMID:25701175

Horvath, J. C., Forte, J. D., & Carter, O. (2015). Quantitative review finds no evidence of cognitive effects in healthy populations from single-session transcranial direct current stimulation (tDCS). *Brain Stimulation, 8*(3), 535–550. doi:10.1016/j.brs.2015.01.400 PMID:25701175

Husain, M., & Mehta, M. (2011). Cognitive enhancement by drugs in health and disease. *Trends in Cognitive Sciences, 15*(1), 28–36. doi:10.1016/j.tics.2010.11.002 PMID:21146447

Inukai, Y., Saito, K., Sasaki, R., Tsuiki, S., Miyaguchi, S., Kojima, S., ... Onishi, H. (2016). Comparison of Three Non-Invasive Transcranial Electrical Stimulation Methods for Increasing Cortical Excitability. *Frontiers in Human Neuroscience, 10*(December), 1–7. PMID:28082887

Inukai, Y., Saito, K., Sasaki, R., Tsuiki, S., Miyaguchi, S., Kojima, S., ... Onishi, H. (2016). Comparison of Three Non-Invasive Transcranial Electrical Stimulation Methods for Increasing Cortical Excitability. *Frontiers in Human Neuroscience, 10*(December), 1–7. doi:10.3389/fnhum.2016.00668 PMID:28082887

Jausovec, N., & Jausovec, K. (2014). Increasing working memory capacity with theta transcranial alternating current stimulation (tACS). *Biological Psychology, 96*(1), 42–47. doi:10.1016/j.biopsycho.2013.11.006 PMID:24291565

Jausovec, N., & Jausovec, K. (2014). Increasing working memory capacity with theta transcranial alternating current stimulation (tACS). *Biological Psychology, 96*(1), 42–47. doi:10.1016/j.biopsycho.2013.11.006 PMID:24291565

Jausovec, N., Jausovec, K., & Pahor, A. (2014). The influence of theta transcranial alternating current stimulation (tACS) on working memory storage and processing functions. *Acta Psychologica, 146*(1), 1–6. doi:10.1016/j.actpsy.2013.11.011 PMID:24361739

Jausovec, N., Jausovec, K., & Pahor, A. (2014). The influence of theta transcranial alternating current stimulation (tACS) on working memory storage and processing functions. *Acta Psychologica, 146*(1), 1–6. doi:10.1016/j.actpsy.2013.11.011 PMID:24361739

Kalivas, P., & Volkow, N. (2011). New medications for drug addiction hiding in glutamatergic neuroplasticity. *Molecular Psychiatry, 16*(10), 974–986. doi:10.1038/mp.2011.46 PMID:21519339

Kasparbauer, A., Rujescu, D., Riedel, M., Pogarell, O., Costa, A., Meindl, T., ... Ettinger, U. (2014). Methylphenidate Effects on Brain Activity as a Function of SLC6A3 Genotype and Striatal Dopamine Transporter Availability. *Neuropsychopharmacology*. PMID:25220215

Kasten, F. H., Dowsett, J., & Herrmann, C. S. (2016). Sustained aftereffect of α-tACS lasts up to 70 minutes after stimulation. *Frontiers in Human Neuroscience, 10*, 245. doi:10.3389/fnhum.2016.00245 PMID:27252642

Kasten, F. H., Dowsett, J., & Herrmann, C. S. (2016). Sustained aftereffect of α-tACS lasts up to 70 minutes after stimulation. *Frontiers in Human Neuroscience, 10*(May), 245. doi:10.3389/fnhum.2016.00245 PMID:27252642

Kim, Y., Teylan, M., Baron, M., Sands, A., Nairn, A., & Greengard, P. (2009). Methylphenidate-induced dendritic spine formation and FosB expression in nucleus accumbens. *Proceedings of the National Academy of Sciences of the United States of America*, *106*(8), 2915–2920. doi:10.1073/pnas.0813179106 PMID:19202072

Kjaer, T., Bertelsen, C., Piccini, P., Brooks, D., Alving, J., & Lou, H. (2002). Increased dopamine tone during meditation-induced change of consciousness. *Brain Research. Cognitive Brain Research*, *13*(2), 255–259. doi:10.1016/S0926-6410(01)00106-9 PMID:11958969

Kozasa, E., Sato, J., Lacerda, S., Barreiros, M., Radvany, J., Russell, T., ... Amaro, E. Jr. (2012). Meditation training increases brain efficiency in an attention task. *NeuroImage*, *59*(1), 745–749. doi:10.1016/j.neuroimage.2011.06.088 PMID:21763432

Kudlow, P., Treurnicht Naylor, K., Xie, B., & McIntyre, R. (2013). Cognitive enhancement in Canadian medical students. *Journal of Psychoactive Drugs*, *45*(4), 360–365. doi:10.1080/02791072.2013.825033 PMID:24377176

Lambert, N., & Hartsough, C. (1998). Prospective Study of Tobacco Smoking and Substance Dependencies Among Samples of ADHD and Non-ADHD Participants. *Journal of Learning Disabilities*, *31*(6), 533–544. doi:10.1177/002221949803100603 PMID:9813951

Looby, A., & Earleywine, M. (2011). Expectation to receive methylphenidate enhances subjective arousal but not cognitive performance. *Experimental and Clinical Psychopharmacology*, *19*(6), 433–444. doi:10.1037/a0025252 PMID:21875224

Luber, B., & Lisanby, S. H. (2014). Enhancement of human cognitive performance using transcranial magnetic stimulation (TMS). *NeuroImage*, *85*, 961–970. doi:10.1016/j.neuroimage.2013.06.007 PMID:23770409

Luber, B., & Lisanby, S. H. (2014). Enhancement of human cognitive performance using transcranial magnetic stimulation (TMS). *NeuroImage*, *85*, 961–970. doi:10.1016/j.neuroimage.2013.06.007 PMID:23770409

Luber, B., Stanford, A., Bulow, P., Nguyen, T., Rakitin, B., Habeck, C., ... Lisanby, S. (2008). Remediation of sleep-deprivation-induced working memory impairment with fMRI-guided transcranial magnetic stimulation. *Cerebral Cortex*, *18*(9), 2077–2085. doi:10.1093/cercor/bhm231 PMID:18203694

Luber, B., Stanford, A., Bulow, P., Nguyen, T., Rakitin, B., Habeck, C., ... Lisanby, S. (2008). Remediation of sleep-deprivation-induced working memory impairment with fMRI-guided transcranial magnetic stimulation. *Cerebral Cortex*, *18*(9), 2077–2085. doi:10.1093/cercor/bhm231 PMID:18203694

Luber, B., Steffener, J., Tucker, A., Habeck, C., Peterchev, A. V., Deng, Z.-D., ... Lisanby, S. H. (2013). Extended remediation of sleep deprived-induced working memory deficits using fMRI-guided transcranial magnetic stimulation. *Sleep*, *36*(6), 857–871. doi:10.5665leep.2712 PMID:23729929

Luber, B., Steffener, J., Tucker, A., Habeck, C., Peterchev, A. V., Deng, Z.-D., ... Lisanby, S. H. (2013). Extended remediation of sleep deprived-induced working memory deficits using fMRI-guided transcranial magnetic stimulation. *Sleep*, *36*(6), 857–871. doi:10.5665leep.2712 PMID:23729929

Luders, E., Toga, A., Lepore, N., & Gaser, C. (2009). The underlying anatomical correlates of long-term meditation: Larger hippocampal and frontal volumes of gray matter. *NeuroImage*, *45*(3), 672–678. doi:10.1016/j.neuroimage.2008.12.061 PMID:19280691

Luppicini, R. (2008). Introducing technoethics. In R. Luppicini & R. Adell (Eds.), *Handbook of research on technoethics* (pp. 1–18). Hershey, PA: Idea Group Publishing. doi:10.4018/978-1-60566-022-6.ch001

Luppicini, R. (2009). The emerging field of technoethics. In R. Luppicini & R. Adell (Eds.), *Handbook of research on technoethics* (pp. 1–19). Hershey, PA: Idea Group Publishing. doi:10.4018/978-1-60566-022-6.ch001

Lustenberger, C., Boyle, M. R., Foulser, A. A., Mellin, J. M., & Fröhlich, F. (2015). Role of Frontal Alpha Oscillations in Creativity HHS Public Access. *Cortex*, *67*, 74–82. doi:10.1016/j.cortex.2015.03.012 PMID:25913062

Lustenberger, C., Boyle, M. R., Foulser, A. A., Mellin, J. M., & Fröhlich, F. (2015). Role of Frontal Alpha Oscillations in Creativity HHS Public Access. *Cortex*, *67*, 74–82. doi:10.1016/j.cortex.2015.03.012 PMID:25913062

MacIntyre, A. (1981). *After Virtue*. Notre Dame, IN: University of Notre Dame Press.

MacIntyre, A. (1989). The Virtues, the Unity of a Human Life and the Concept of a Tradition. In S. Hauerwas & L. Gregory Jones (Eds.), *Why Narrative?* (pp. 89–110). Grand Rapids, MI: W.B. Eerdmans.

Maher, B. (2008). Poll results: Look who's doping. *Nature*, *452*(7188), 674–675. doi:10.1038/452674a PMID:18401370

Maier, L., Liechti, M., Herzig, F., & Schaub, M. (2013). To Dope or Not to Dope: Neuroenhancement with Prescription Drugs and Drugs of Abuse among Swiss University Students. *PLoS One*, *8*(11), e77967. doi:10.1371/journal.pone.0077967 PMID:24236008

Makris, N., Biederman, J., Valera, E., Bush, G., Kaiser, J., Kennedy, D. N., ... Seidman, L. (2007). Cortical thinning of the attention and executive function networks in adults with attention-deficit/hyperactivity disorder. *Cereb cortex*, *17*(6), 1364–1375. doi:10.1093/cercor/bhl047 PMID:16920883

Markowitz, J., Devane, C., Pestreich, L., Patrick, K., & Muniz, R. (2006). A Comprehensive In Vitro Screening of d-, l-, and dl- threo-Methylphenidate: An Exploratory Study. *Journal of Child and Adolescent Psychopharmacology*, *16*(6), 687–698. doi:10.1089/cap.2006.16.687 PMID:17201613

Marquand, A., O'Daly, O., De Simoni, S., Alsop, D., Maguire, R., Williams, S., ... Mehta, M. (2012). Dissociable effects of methylphenidate, atomoxetine and placebo on regional cerebral blood flow in healthy volunteers at rest: A multi-class pattern recognition approach. *NeuroImage*, *60*(2), 1015–1024. doi:10.1016/j.neuroimage.2012.01.058 PMID:22266414

McCarthy, H., Skokauskas, N., & Frodl, T. (2014). Identifying a consistent pattern of neural function in attention deficit hyperactivity disorder: A meta-analysis. *Psychological Medicine*, *44*(04), 869880. doi:10.1017/S0033291713001037 PMID:23663382

Meyers, C. (2014). Neuroenhancement in Reflective Equilibrium: A Qualified Kantian Defense of Enhancing in Scholarship and Science. *Neuroethics*, *7*(3), 287–298. doi:10.100712152-014-9212-5

Moore, A., & Malinowski, P. (2009). Meditation, mindfulness and cognitive flexibility. *Consciousness and Cognition, 18*(1), 176–186. doi:10.1016/j.concog.2008.12.008 PMID:19181542

Morton, W., & Stockton, G. (2000). Methylphenidate Abuse and Psychiatric Side Effects. *The Journal of Clinical Psychiatry, 2,* 159–164. PMID:15014637

Mueller, S., Costa, A., Keeser, D., Pogarell, O., Berman, A., Coates, U., ... Meindl, T. (2014). The effects of methylphenidate on whole brain intrinsic functional connectivity. *Human Brain Mapping, 35*(11), 5379–5388. doi:10.1002/hbm.22557 PMID:24862742

Mulquiney, P. G., Hoy, K. E., Daskalakis, Z. J., & Fitzgerald, P. B. (2011). Improving working memory: Exploring the effect of transcranial random noise stimulation and transcranial direct current stimulation on the dorsolateral prefrontal cortex. *Clinical Neurophysiology, 122*(12), 2384–2389. doi:10.1016/j. clinph.2011.05.009 PMID:21665534

Mulquiney, P. G., Hoy, K. E., Daskalakis, Z. J., & Fitzgerald, P. B. (2011). Improving working memory: Exploring the effect of transcranial random noise stimulation and transcranial direct current stimulation on the dorsolateral prefrontal cortex. *Clinical Neurophysiology, 122*(12), 2384–2389. doi:10.1016/j. clinph.2011.05.009 PMID:21665534

Nakao, T., Radua, J., Rubia, K., & Mataix-Cols, D. (2011). Gray Matter Volume Abnormalities in ADHD: Voxel-Based Meta-Analysis Exploring the Effects of Age and Stimulant Medication. *The American Journal of Psychiatry, 168*(11), 1154–1164. doi:10.1176/appi.ajp.2011.11020281 PMID:21865529

Nitsche, M. A., Fricke, K., Henschke, U., Schlitterlau, A., Liebetanz, D., Lang, N., ... Paulus, W. (2003). Pharmacological modulation of cortical excitability shifts induced by transcranial direct current stimulation in humans. *The Journal of Physiology, 553*(1), 293–301. doi:10.1113/jphysiol.2003.049916 PMID:12949224

Nitsche, M. A., Fricke, K., Henschke, U., Schlitterlau, A., Liebetanz, D., Lang, N., ... Paulus, W. (2003). Pharmacological modulation of cortical excitability shifts induced by transcranial direct current stimulation in humans. *The Journal of Physiology, 553*(1), 293–301. doi:10.1113/jphysiol.2003.049916 PMID:12949224

Parkin, B. L., Ekhtiari, H., & Walsh, V. F. (2015). Non-invasive Human Brain Stimulation in Cognitive Neuroscience: A Primer. *Neuron, 87*(5), 932–945. doi:10.1016/j.neuron.2015.07.032 PMID:26335641

Parkin, B. L., Ekhtiari, H., & Walsh, V. F. (2015). Non-invasive Human Brain Stimulation in Cognitive Neuroscience: A Primer. *Neuron, 87*(5), 932–945. doi:10.1016/j.neuron.2015.07.032 PMID:26335641

Patrick, K., Mueller, R., & Gualtieri, C. (1987). *Psychopharmacology: The Third Generation of Progress* (H. Y. Meltzer, Ed.; 3rd ed.). New York: Raven press.

Popper, K. (1947). *The Open Society and its Enemies* (Vol. 1). London: Routledge.

Repantis, D., Schlattmann, P., Laisney, O., & Heuser, I. (2010). Modafinil and methylphenidate for neuroenhancement in healthy individuals: A systematic review. *Pharmacological Research, 62*(3), 187–206. doi:10.1016/j.phrs.2010.04.002 PMID:20416377

Robbins, T., & Arnsten, A. (2009). The Neuropsychopharmacology of Fronto-Executive Function: Monoaminergic Modulation. *Annual Review of Neuroscience, 32*(1), 267–287. doi:10.1146/annurev.neuro.051508.135535 PMID:19555290

Robinson, J. J. D., Wagner, N.-F., & Northoff, G. (2015). Is the Sense of Agency in Schizophrenia Influenced by Resting-State Variation in Self-Referential Regions of the Brain? *Schizophrenia Bulletin, 42*(2), 270–276. doi:10.1093chbulbv102 PMID:26221048

Robinson, J. J. D., Wagner, N.-F., & Northoff, G. (2015). Is the Sense of Agency in Schizophrenia Influenced by Resting-State Variation in Self-Referential Regions of the Brain? *Schizophrenia Bulletin.* doi:10.1093chbulbv102 PMID:26221048

Rossi, S., Hallett, M., Rossini, P. M., & Pascual-Leone, A. (2009). Safety, ethical considerations, and application guidelines for the use of transcranial magnetic stimulation in clinical practice and research. *Clinical Neurophysiology, 120*(12), 2008–2039. doi:10.1016/j.clinph.2009.08.016 PMID:19833552

Rossi, S., Hallett, M., Rossini, P. M., & Pascual-Leone, A. (2009). Safety, ethical considerations, and application guidelines for the use of transcranial magnetic stimulation in clinical practice and research. *Clinical Neurophysiology, 120*(12), 2008–2039. doi:10.1016/j.clinph.2009.08.016 PMID:19833552

Rubia, K., Alegria, A., Cubillo, A., Smith, A., Brammer, M., & Radua, J. (2013). Effects of Stimulants on Brain Function in Attention-Deficit/Hyperactivity Disorder: A Systematic Review and Meta-Analysis. *Biological Psychiatry, 76*(8), 616–628. doi:10.1016/j.biopsych.2013.10.016 PMID:24314347

Russo, S., Dietz, D., Dumitriu, D., Morrison, J., Malenka, R., & Nestler, E. (2010). The addicted synapse: Mechanisms of synaptic and structural plasticity in nucleus accumbens. *Trends in Neurosciences, 33*(6), 267–276. doi:10.1016/j.tins.2010.02.002 PMID:20207024

Sahakian, B., & Morein-Zamir, S. (2007). Professor's little helper. *Nature, 450*(7173), 1157–1159. doi:10.1038/4501157a PMID:18097378

Sandel, M. (2007). *The Case against Perfection: Ethics in the Age of Genetic Engineering.* Belknap Press of Harvard University Press.

Sandel, M. (2012). The Case against Perfection. In S. Holland (Ed.), *Arguing About Bioethics* (pp. 93–105). New York: Routledge.

Sattler, S., Sauer, C., Mehlkop, G., & Graeff, P. (2013). The rationale for consuming cognitive enhancement drugs in university students and teachers. *PLoS One, 8*(7), e68821. doi:10.1371/journal.pone.0068821 PMID:23874778

Sauseng, P., Klimesch, W., Heise, K. F., Gruber, W. R., Holz, E., Karim, A. A., ... Hummel, F. C. (2009). Brain Oscillatory Substrates of Visual Short-Term Memory Capacity. *Current Biology, 19*(21), 1846–1852. doi:10.1016/j.cub.2009.08.062 PMID:19913428

Sauseng, P., Klimesch, W., Heise, K. F., Gruber, W. R., Holz, E., Karim, A. A., ... Hummel, F. C. (2009). Brain Oscillatory Substrates of Visual Short-Term Memory Capacity. *Current Biology, 19*(21), 1846–1852. doi:10.1016/j.cub.2009.08.062 PMID:19913428

Schechtman, M. (2014). *Staying Alive—Personal Identity, Practical Concerns, and the Unity of a Life*. New York: Oxford University Press. doi:10.1093/acprof:oso/9780199684878.001.0001

Schweren, L., Hartman, C., Zwiers, M., Heslenfeld, D., van der Meer, D., Franke, B., ... Hoekstra, P. (2014). Combined stimulant and antipsychotic treatment in adolescents with attention-deficit/hyperactivity disorder: A cross-sectional observational structural MRI study. *European Child & Adolescent Psychiatry*. PMID:25395383

Seidman, L., Valera, E., & Makris, N. (2005). Structural brain imaging of attention-deficit/hyperactivity disorder. *Biological Psychiatry*, *57*(11), 1263–1272. doi:10.1016/j.biopsych.2004.11.019 PMID:15949998

Sela, T., Kilim, A., & Lavidor, M. (2012). Transcranial alternating current stimulation increases risk-taking behavior in the Balloon Analog Risk Task. *Frontiers in Neuroscience*, *6*, 1–11. doi:10.3389/fnins.2012.00022 PMID:22347844

Sela, T., Kilim, A., & Lavidor, M. (2012). Transcranial alternating current stimulation increases risk-taking behavior in the Balloon Analog Risk Task. *Frontiers in Neuroscience*, *6*(FEB), 1–11. doi:10.3389/fnins.2012.00022 PMID:22347844

Shang, Y., Wang, X., Shang, X., Zhang, H., Liu, Z., Yin, T., & Zhang, T. (2016). Repetitive transcranial magnetic stimulation effectively facilitates spatial cognition and synaptic plasticity associated with increasing the levels of BDNF and synaptic proteins in Wistar rats. *Neurobiology of Learning and Memory*, *134*, 369–378. doi:10.1016/j.nlm.2016.08.016 PMID:27555233

Shang, Y., Wang, X., Shang, X., Zhang, H., Liu, Z., Yin, T., & Zhang, T. (2016). Repetitive transcranial magnetic stimulation effectively facilitates spatial cognition and synaptic plasticity associated with increasing the levels of BDNF and synaptic proteins in Wistar rats. *Neurobiology of Learning and Memory*, *134*, 369–378. doi:10.1016/j.nlm.2016.08.016 PMID:27555233

Shanks, R., Ross, J., Doyle, H., Helton, A., Picou, B., Schulz, J., ... Lloyd, S. (2015). Adolescent exposure to cocaine, amphetamine, and methylphenidate cross-sensitizes adults to methamphetamine with drug- and sex-specific effects. *Behavioural Brain Research*, *281*, 116–124. doi:10.1016/j.bbr.2014.12.002 PMID:25496784

Shaw, S., Shah, L., Jolly, A., & Wylie, J. (2008). Identifying heterogeneity among injection drug users: A cluster analysis approach. *American Journal of Public Health*, *98*(8), 1430–1437. doi:10.2105/AJPH.2007.120741 PMID:18556614

Shumay, E., Chen, J., Fowler, J., & Volkow, N. (2011). Genotype and Ancestry Modulate Brain's DAT Availability in Healthy Humans. *PLoS One*, *6*. PMID:21826203

Snowball, A., Tachtsidis, I., Popescu, T., Thompson, J., Delazer, M., Zamarian, L., ... Cohen Kadosh, R. (2013). Long-term enhancement of brain function and cognition using cognitive training and brain stimulation. *Current Biology*, *23*(11), 987–992. doi:10.1016/j.cub.2013.04.045 PMID:23684971

Snowball, A., Tachtsidis, I., Popescu, T., Thompson, J., Delazer, M., Zamarian, L., ... Cohen Kadosh, R. (2013). Long-term enhancement of brain function and cognition using cognitive training and brain stimulation. *Current Biology*, *23*(11), 987–992. doi:10.1016/j.cub.2013.04.045 PMID:23684971

Spencer, T., Brown, A., Seidman, L., Valera, M., Makris, N., Lomedico, A., ... Biederman, J. (2013). Effect of Psychostimulants on Brain Structure and Function in ADHD: A Qualitative Literature Review of MRI-Based Neuroimaging Studies. *The Journal of Clinical Psychiatry, 74*(09), 902–917. doi:10.4088/JCP.12r08287 PMID:24107764

Sridharan, D., Levitin, D. J., & Menon, V. (2008). A critical role for the right fronto-insular cortex in switching between central-executive and default-mode networks. *Proceedings of the National Academy of Sciences of the United States of America, 105*(34), 12569–12574. doi:10.1073/pnas.0800005105 PMID:18723676

Sridharan, D., Levitin, D. J., & Menon, V. (2008). A critical role for the right fronto-insular cortex in switching between central-executive and default-mode networks. *Proceedings of the National Academy of Sciences of the United States of America, 105*(34), 12569–12574. doi:10.1073/pnas.0800005105 PMID:18723676

Suhler, C. L., & Churchland, P. S. (2011). The Neurobiological Basis of Morality. In J. Illes & B. J. Sahakian (Eds.), *The Oxford Handbook of Neuroethics* (pp. 33–58). Oxford, UK: Oxford University Press.

Suthana, N., Haneef, Z., Stern, J., Mukamel, R., Behnke, E., Knowlton, B., & Fried, I. (2012). Memory Enhancement and Deep-Brain Stimulation of the Entorhinal Area. *The New England Journal of Medicine, 366*(6), 502–510. doi:10.1056/NEJMoa1107212 PMID:22316444

Suthana, N., Haneef, Z., Stern, J., Mukamel, R., Behnke, E., Knowlton, B., & Fried, I. (2012). Memory Enhancement and Deep-Brain Stimulation of the Entorhinal Area. *The New England Journal of Medicine, 366*(6), 502–510. doi:10.1056/NEJMoa1107212 PMID:22316444

Tobaiqy, M., Stewart, D., Helms, P., Williams, J., Crum, J., Steer, C., & McLay, J. (2011). Parental reporting of adverse drug reactions associated with attention-deficit hyperactivity disorder (ADHD) medications in children attending specialist paediatric clinics in the UK. *Drug Safety, 34*(3), 211–219. doi:10.2165/11586050-000000000-00000 PMID:21332245

Turner, D., Robbins, T., Clark, L., Aron, A., Dowson, J., & Sahakian, B. (2003). Relative lack of cognitive effects of methylphenidate in elderly male volunteers. *Psychopharmacology, 168*(4), 455–464. doi:10.100700213-003-1457-3 PMID:12734634

Urban, K., & Gao, W. (2012). Evolution of the Study of Methylphenidate and Its Actions on the Adult Versus Juvenile Brain. *Journal of Attention Disorders*. PMID:22923783

Urban, K., & Gao, W. (2014). Performance enhancement at the cost of potential brain plasticity: Neural ramifications of nootropic drugs in the healthy developing brain. *Frontiers in Systems Neuroscience, 8*, 38. doi:10.3389/fnsys.2014.00038 PMID:24860437

Van der Marel, K., Klomp, A., Meerhoff, G., Schipper, P., Lucassen, P., Homberg, J., ... Reneman, L. (2014). Long-term oral methylphenidate treatment in adolescent and adult rats: Differential effects on brain morphology and function. *Neuropsychopharmacology, 39*(2), 263–273. doi:10.1038/npp.2013.169 PMID:23851400

Van der Meer, L., Costafreda, S., Aleman, A., & David, A. S. (2010). Self-reflection and the brain: A theoretical review and meta-analysis of neuroimaging studies with implications for schizophrenia. *Neuroscience and Biobehavioral Reviews, 34*(6), 935–946. doi:10.1016/j.neubiorev.2009.12.004 PMID:20015455

Van der Meer, L., Costafreda, S., Aleman, A., & David, A. S. (2010). Self-reflection and the brain: A theoretical review and meta-analysis of neuroimaging studies with implications for schizophrenia. *Neuroscience and Biobehavioral Reviews, 34*(6), 935–946. doi:10.1016/j.neubiorev.2009.12.004 PMID:20015455

Vanhaudenhuyse, A., Demertzi, A., Schabus, M., Noirhomme, Q., Bredart, S., Boly, M., ... Laureys, S. (2011). Two distinct neuronal networks mediate the awareness of environment and of self. *Journal of Cognitive Neuroscience, 23*(3), 570–578. doi:10.1162/jocn.2010.21488 PMID:20515407

Vanhaudenhuyse, A., Demertzi, A., Schabus, M., Noirhomme, Q., Bredart, S., Boly, M., ... Laureys, S. (2011). Two distinct neuronal networks mediate the awareness of environment and of self. *Journal of Cognitive Neuroscience, 23*(3), 570–578. doi:10.1162/jocn.2010.21488 PMID:20515407

Volkow, N. (2012). Long-term safety of stimulant use for ADHD: Findings from nonhuman primates. *Neuropsychopharmacology, 37*(12), 2551–2552. doi:10.1038/npp.2012.127 PMID:23070200

Volkow, N., & Swanson, J. (2008). Does Childhood Treatment of ADHD With Stimulant Medication Affect Substance Abuse in Adulthood? *The American Journal of Psychiatry, 165*(5), 553–555. doi:10.1176/appi.ajp.2008.08020237 PMID:18450933

Volkow, N., Wang, G., Fowler, J., Fischman, M., Foltin, R., Abumrad, N., ... Pappas, N. (1999). Methylphenidate and cocaine have a similar in vivo potency to block dopamine transporters in the human brain. *Life Sciences, 65*(1), 7–12. doi:10.1016/S0024-3205(99)00225-8 PMID:10403500

Volkow, N., Wang, G.-J., Fowler, J., & Tomasi, D. (2012). Addiction Circuitry in the Human Brain. *Annual Review of Pharmacology and Toxicology, 10*(1), 321–336. doi:10.1146/annurev-pharmtox-010611-134625 PMID:21961707

Wilens, T., Faraone, S., Biederman, J., & Gunawardene, S. (2003). Does Stimulant Therapy of Attention-Deficit/Hyperactivity Disorder Beget Later Substance Abuse? A Meta-analytic Review of the Literature. *Pediatrics, 111*. PMID:12509574

Woods, A. J., Antal, A., Bikson, M., Boggio, P. S., Brunoni, A. R., Celnik, P., ... Nitsche, M. A. (2016). A technical guide to tDCS, and related non-invasive brain stimulation tools. *Clinical Neurophysiology, 127*(2), 1031–1048. doi:10.1016/j.clinph.2015.11.012 PMID:26652115

Woods, A. J., Antal, A., Bikson, M., Boggio, P. S., Brunoni, A. R., Celnik, P., ... Nitsche, M. A. (2016). A technical guide to tDCS, and related non-invasive brain stimulation tools. *Clinical Neurophysiology, 127*(2), 1031–1048. doi:10.1016/j.clinph.2015.11.012 PMID:26652115

Yildiz, O., Sismanlar, S., Memik, N., Karakaya, I., & Agaoglu, B. (2011). Atomoxetine and methylphenidate treatment in children with ADHD: The efficacy, tolerability and effects on executive functions. *Child Psychiatry and Human Development, 42*(3), 257–269. doi:10.100710578-010-0212-3 PMID:21165694

Zeidan, F., Johnson, S., Diamond, B., David, Z., & Goolkasian, P. (2010). Mindfulness meditation improves cognition: Evidence of brief mental training. *Consciousness and Cognition*, *19*(2), 597–605. doi:10.1016/j.concog.2010.03.014 PMID:20363650

Zhao, H., Qiao, L., Fan, D., Zhang, S., Turel, O., Li, Y., ... He, Q. (2017). Modulation of Brain Activity with Noninvasive Transcranial Direct Current Stimulation (tDCS): Clinical Applications and Safety Concerns. *Frontiers in Psychology*, 8. PMID:28539894

KEY TERMS AND DEFINITIONS

Cognitive Neuroenhancement: Using technology to artificially increase cognitive functions such as attention, memory, executive function, etc. beyond a healthy individual's natural/normal functioning baseline.

Ethics of Restraint: The normative idea that there is often ethical virtue in beholding natural conditions rather than trying to mold them according to what often turns out to be instances of hubris.

Methylphenidate: A derivative of the psychostimulant amphetamine. Often used as a first line treatment for attention deficit hyperactive disorder (ADHD). It primarily acts as a norepinephrine-dopamine reuptake inhibitor. Currently traded under the brand names Ritalin, Concerta, and Biphentin, amongst others.

Neuroethics: A sub-field of ethics that is concerned with the ethical aspects of neuroscience and neurotechnology that can be used to alter the functioning of the brain.

Personal Identity: The philosophical inquiry as to what conditions are necessary and sufficient for a person to persist through time.

Social Identity: A person's sense of who they are based on their group membership(s), or lack thereof.

Transcranial Stimulation: Using various non-evasive technologies to stimulate the brain and alter its functioning, without physical contact with the brain. These technologies include transcranial magnetic stimulation (TMS) which uses strong magnetic field(s) to alter neuronal activity, and transcranial electrical stimulation (TES) which passes a small electrical field through the brain from an anode to a cathode applied to the scalp.

ENDNOTES

[1]   In contemporary analytically minded philosophy of mind and action, the notion of narrativity plays a fundamental role in the constitution of personhood and personal identity. In this tradition, Marya Schechtman is a leading proponent of a narrative view on personal identity. In her latest book *Staying Alive*, Schechtman develops the 'Person Life View' which holds that persons are defined in terms of the characteristic lives they lead, and seen as unified loci of practical interaction (Schechtman, 2014).

[2]   We are grateful to Niall W. Duncan and Rocci Luppicini for valuable feedback on earlier versions of this paper.

Chapter 11
Surgeon, Media, Society, Patient:
Four Factors in Determining the Ethics of Cosmetic Surgery

Brett Lunceford
Independent Researcher, USA

ABSTRACT

For many, cosmetic surgery holds the promise that one can reshape his or her body to remove perceived defects and thus have a more perfect body. However, the decision to undergo elective cosmetic surgery is not made in a vacuum, and it is easy to overlook the full range of ethical considerations surrounding cosmetic surgery. Many medical ethicists subscribe to an ethical code that centers mainly on the relationship between the doctor and patient, with a focus on respect for autonomy, nonmaleficence, beneficence, and justice. This chapter builds on this framework by extending the scope of actors to include not only the surgeon and the patient but also the media and the overall society. To illustrate this framework, the author uses the example of actress Heidi Montag, who underwent 10 different plastic surgery procedures in one day. The chapter concludes with a discussion of potential correctives for ethical failures in each of these areas.

INTRODUCTION

For most of human existence, biology has been destiny. However, with the advent of cosmetic surgery, this is no longer the case. Jordan (2004) observes that "over the course of the last century, plastic surgery advocates have engaged in a concerted, commercial effort to redefine the human body as a plastic, malleable substance which surgeons can alter and people should want to alter in order to realize their body image ideals" (p. 328). If anything can be corrected, there is now the possibility that one can truly have the perfect body. This shift in technological possibilities raises questions concerning what lines should be drawn concerning body modification; as Clemens (1985) observes, "Technology forces us to deal with complex ethical questions that arise only because the technology creates the situation" (p. 164).

DOI: 10.4018/978-1-5225-5094-5.ch011

Even in cases where the ethics may seem clear, there can be controversy. For example, some portions of the deaf community have fought vehemently against cochlear implants in deaf children (for more on this controversy, see Balkany, Hodges, & Goodman, 1996; Lane & Bahan, 1998). As such, one must proceed with caution when considering the ethics of body modification and enhancement. One thing seems clear: the question of what *can* be accomplished through medical technology may be outpacing our ability as a society to answer what *should* be done. Technoethics provides an entrée into this discussion because, as Luppicini (2009b) explains, "technoethics is techno- and bio-centric (biotechno-centric)" (p. 3). In other words, technoethics allows us to consider the technological aspects of the situation as well as the lived experience of the individuals who would be impacted by the action in question.

Beauchamp and Childress (2001) propose the following biomedical ethical framework that has become widely adopted:

1. *Respect for autonomy* (a norm of respecting the decision-making capacities of autonomous persons)
2. *Nonmaleficence* (a norm of avoiding the causation of harm)
3. *Beneficence* (a group of norms for providing benefits and balancing benefits against risks and costs)
4. *Justice* (a group of norms for distributing benefits, risks, and costs fairly). (p. 12)

However, even these seemingly clear-cut issues can seem at odds sometimes. For example, Beauchamp and Childress (2001) observe that beneficence can sometimes conflict with the principle of autonomy in the case of paternalism (p. 176). Still, Gillon (1994) adds the dimension of scope to this framework and observes that "I have not found anyone who seriously argues that he or she cannot accept any of these prima facie principles or found plausible examples of concerns about health care ethics that require additional moral principles" (p. 188). Nor do I have any issues with these principles, but I do not think that they go far enough in considering the ethics of a given situation because they maintain the focus on the interaction between the patient and physician. In our media saturated world, we must shift the frame to also consider the environment in which we live. In this chapter I will examine the case of cosmetic surgery in particular and propose that we consider: the ethics of the medical professionals who perform and advertise these procedures; the ethics of the media structures that promote a homogenous ideal of beauty; the ethics of those within society who tacitly approve of such procedures; and the ethics of the individual making the decision. I will use the case of actress Heidi Montag to illustrate this framework.

Although many have gone under the knife in the pursuit of beauty, Montag stands out as an exemplar of this trend. Montag underwent ten different plastic surgery procedures in one day, stating, "I had a little bit of Botox, an eyebrow lift, my ears tucked, I had my nose re-aligned, fat injections put into my cheeks, my lips done and I had my chin shaved down" (Berman, 2010, p. C4). Of course, there is more to be done, as she heaps plastic surgery upon plastic surgery: "I would like to get my breasts redone. Because I couldn't get them the size I wanted because they couldn't fit" ("Heidi Says," 2010, p. 31). After her barrage of surgeries, she told *People* magazine: "I see an upgraded version of me. It's a new face and a new energy. It's a new person and I feel like almost all of the things I didn't want to be and who I turned into kind of got chiseled away" (Garcia, 2010, p. 84). The only way that Montag could be herself, it seems, was by removing parts of her flesh. But Montag had no intention of resting on her surgically-enhanced laurels. Says Montag, "Let's just say there's a lot of maintenance. Nobody ages perfectly, so I plan to keep using surgery to make me as perfect as I can be. Because, for me, the surgery is always so rewarding" (Garcia, 2010, p. 88). Because Montag's barrage of surgeries raised significant ethical questions both within and outside of the medical community, she provides an excellent case study with which to examine ethical dimensions of cosmetic surgery.

FOUR ETHICAL DIMENSIONS OF COSMETIC SURGERY

The Surgeon

Bunge (1975) argues that creators and users of technology bear ethical responsibility for making them beneficial (p. 72) and concludes that "the technologist is responsible for his professional work and he is responsible to all those affected by it, not only to his employer" (p. 73). In other words, maintaining a technoethical stance forces the technologist to own his or her actions. One cannot use the technician's defense made famous by Adolf Eichmann that he or she was simply obeying orders (see Arendt, 2006). In the case of the cosmetic surgeon, this means that the customer is not always right and those who perform elective surgery bear a significant ethical burden. In the case of Montag, two facets of the framework proposed by Beauchamp and Childress (2001) stand out: nonmaleficence and beneficence (p. 12).

In the case of plastic surgery, there may be conflicts between nonmaleficence and beneficence when the ill that one corrects is influenced by the very people providing the cure. In her discussion of cosmetic dermatologists, Baumann (2012) notes that they "have the goal of improving their patient's appearance and skin health, but all too often, financial motivation can cloud their judgment" (p. 522). Cantor (2005) likewise notes that the physician's "livelihood depends on performing the very interventions they recommend," but notes that "economic self-interest is less flagrant when a surgeon insists that a sick patient have gallbladder surgery, even if she stands to profit from the procedure, than when a dermatologist sells a patient an expensive cream of dubious value" (p. 155). A similar judgment can be made for cosmetic surgeons. On the freeway near my home, I see billboards for plastic surgeons promoting "beauty for life." Plastic surgeons stand to gain financially by promoting an image of the body as intrinsically flawed and lacking in natural beauty. As Blum (2005) argues, cosmetic surgery "holds out a technological and economic solution (if you have the money, the technology is there) to the very dilemma posed by the way capitalism manages femininity by simultaneously commodifying it, idealizing it, and insisting on its native defects" (p. 110).

Long before the popular press began to read Montag's body, it was read—and written—in great detail by the plastic surgeon that would perform the procedures. Jerslev (2006) describes such a transaction:

The body burdened with the stigmata of the surgeons' marker brutally announces the verdict of bodily incompleteness. It points out that the body does not belong to the one that inhabits it but to another person's objectifying gaze, and it says that the material body is never a finished, singular entity, but a modifiable mass of organic matter. (p. 146)

Jothilakshmi, Salvi, Hayden, and Bose-Haider (2009) argue that "the goals of esthetic surgery are to correct the physical defects that adversely affect a person's body image and ultimately to improve the quality of one's life" (p. 54). But what do we mean when we say "defect"? Western society has coded such naturally occurring variations as pendulous breasts, protruding labia minora, and single eyelids as defects. Nowhere is the desire to correct perceived defects more prominent, however, than in the discourse surrounding aging (see Lin, 2010). Smirnova (2012) suggests that discourses surrounding women and aging

has simultaneously constructed the aging woman as both victim and hero—her body vulnerable and in need of rescue by her will to partake in anti-aging technologies. The technologies themselves are also part of the heroic narrative, masculinized by the rhetoric of neoliberal, rational action backed by scientific and medical authorities. (p. 1236)

In short, a woman who does not fight against the ravages of time is seen as less desirable. As De Roubaix (2011) observes, "Women are obliged to comply with constructs of beauty and normality to remain competitive. Society regards youthfulness as desirable; the mass media both generates and feeds upon these constructs" (p. 15).

Returning to the question of ethics, we are left with the question of "whether women really make free choices in favour of aesthetic surgery under these circumstances" (De Roubaix, 2011, p. 13). Women are placed in the unenviable position of choosing whether to surgically alter their bodies or to matter at all in society. In some ways, this undermines the autonomy of the individual. In advertising the body as defective, one can simultaneously maintain the principle of nonmaleficence from the perspective of the physical body—indeed, may argue that he or she is making the patient better—but may cause psychological harm that will drive the patient to his or her practice to seek relief. As Hardwick-Smith (2011) explains, "Obviously, we should never suggest that a patient's anatomy is 'abnormal.' I DO think that it is important for the patient's self-esteem that she hear that we have seen her type of anatomy many times before, and that she has nothing unusual (even when she does)" (p. 109).

Feminist scholars (e.g., Bordo, 1993; Jeffreys, 2005; Polonijo & Carpiano, 2008; Wolf, 1991) have placed cosmetic surgery within the framework of patriarchal power, but Sanchez Taylor, (2012) entertains the possibility that

with the expansion of the cosmetic surgery industry and the "make over culture" that surrounds it, others choose surgery simply because it is affordable, readily available, fashionable, and so increasingly "normal" to consume surgery in the same way that other beauty and fashion products and services are consumed. (p. 464)

Thus, to claim that those who undergo cosmetic surgery are simply victims of social forces beyond their control is to oversimplify the transaction. Holliday and Sanchez Taylor (2006) argue that "contemporary women who routinely adopt the markers of hypersexualization associated with classed and racialized bodies (such as buttock implants or collagen lips) are not passive but active and desiring (not just desirable)" (p. 191). But the impulse for cosmetic surgery may not be to stand out or to look better than everyone else, but rather to simply fit in. Participants in a study by de Andrade (2010) reported that they sought cosmetic surgery to be "normal," especially after pregnancy. However, one 59-year-old woman stated, "At my age, I have to do it. I have to undergo cosmetic surgery and have a facelift so as to look younger, more beautiful. All my friends are doing it" (de Andrade, 2010, p. 79).

One danger suggested by Gupta (2012) surrounding the commercialization of cosmetic surgery is that "consumers may regard aesthetic surgery as a commodity that is bought rather than a service provided by a trained professional" (p. 548). Despite the desire to respect patient autonomy, the customer is not always right. For some, cosmetic surgery can be seen as a shortcut—a way to get the body one desires in ways that may be otherwise impossible. As Montag notes, "Sure, there are healthier ways to lose weight than stapling your stomach, but you can't exercise your way into bigger boobs or a smaller nose" (Husted, 2009a, p. B03).

The cosmetic surgeon must walk a fine line between respecting the autonomy of the patient and contributing to a culture that pathologizes the body. Consider the example provided by Blum (2003) of the surgeon who advised his patient that in addition to the rhinoplasty that she had planned, he would also "remove her under-eye bags" (p. 276). She notes that "this surgeon has a reputation for doing wonderful eyelid surgery. Unsurprisingly, then, he focuses on the eyes of all prospective patients. This 'flaw' is somehow magnified for him" (p. 277). In this case, it seems that the surgeon transgressed against the principle of autonomy by instilling a sense of doubt concerning the patient's features that was not previously there.

Cosmetic surgeons claim the authority to stand in judgment of the body of the patient and hold the ability to correct flaws in that body. Jordan (2004) notes that "surgical applicants must confront the medical community's ideological perspective on the healthy body and how this influences surgeons' choices about which bodies and desires will receive surgical attention and which will be rejected as inappropriate" (p. 328). The surgeon decides what is wrong with the individual because, as a society, we have outsourced alteration and care of our bodies to medical professionals. We no longer trust ourselves with our own bodies. Although this abdication of autonomy is problematic, this illustrates the need for practitioners to tread carefully when considering the needs of the patient. Harris and Carr (2001) state that "the benefits of [plastic surgery] interventions for the patients concerned are psychological: relief of psychological distress and improvement in social and psychological functioning" (p. 216), but the practitioner must be sure that the flaws corrected are those seen by the patient and not those suggested or created by the surgeon.

The Media

The mass media plays a significant role in individual attitudes toward cosmetic surgery (see Luo, 2013; Solvi et al., 2010; Swami, 2009; Swami et al., 2011; Wen, 2017). Indeed, Swami, Taylor, and Carvalho (2009) found a correlation between celebrity worship and positive attitudes towards cosmetic surgery. It is no great leap to suggest that images of beautiful people may cause some to unfavorably measure themselves against this standard. Most people deal with the fact that they will not look like their favorite celebrity, but for some the pressure is overwhelming; cosmetic surgery offers the potential to come closer to that standard of beauty.

In their discussion of Body Dysmorphic Disorder (BDD), Chan, Jones, and Heywood (2011) explain that "BDD is characterised by time-consuming behaviours such as mirror gazing, comparing particular features to those of others, excessive camouflaging tactics to hide the defect, skin picking and reassurance seeking," explaining that "BDD patients may present to the plastic surgeon requesting multiple cosmetic procedures" (p. 6; for more on BDD diagnosis, see Veale et al., 2012). Kellett, Clarke, and McGill (2008) suggest that those seeking breast augmentation surgery may reflect "a lack of balanced body image or obsessional tendencies" (p. 516). Some have suggested that perceived imperfections are influenced by media images. Berry, Cucchiara, and Davies (2011) provide this explanation of what constitutes the "ideal breast": "there is a common view, perhaps as a consequence of globalization and advertising, of an attractive breast: one full, without ptosis and good symmetry" (p. 1402). In their discussion of labiaplasty, Cartwright and Cardozo (2008) also note that "women requesting surgery report disabling psychological distress associated with a perception that their labia are abnormal in size or shape. . . . The often erroneous perception of abnormality may arise from comparison with women's genitalia as depicted in pornography" (p. 285). Life imitates art.

This assessment works both ways; as people read the bodies in the media, the media also reads the bodies of individuals. Montag's body is no exception here. Supermodel Paulina Porizkova compared Montag to a "cheap, plastic pool float," as she railed against the culture of plastic surgery (Camilli, 2010, p. E5). Babcock (2010), writing for the Spokane *Spokesman Review*, states, "Imagine, 23 years old and already Botoxed, lifted, lipo-ed, and implanted like a blow-up doll. The surgeries were not because of a genetic disfigurement or horrific accident but because, as Montag explained, 'I'm obsessed'" (p. V1). Despite the discomfort this columnist displays with Montag's surgery marathon, it is not actually difficult to imagine; plastic surgery (or rumors thereof) has become cliché among actresses. The surgery was not the shocking thing, but rather the quantity in one day. As Dyens (2001) explains,

We are attracted to Hollywood stars not only because of their biological beauty (i.e., organic effectiveness) but also because of their cultural productivity. What we seek today are bodies sculpted by culture. A Hollywood star, male or female, who has had cosmetic surgery, is a cultural being, and this is what seduces us. (p. 21)

Montag has chosen to fully embrace the socially constructed norms of what ideal femininity should look like and inscribe them on her body. She constructed the ideal of the perfect body not only from her own mind, but from the media and celebrities that infiltrate our minds. Through cosmetic surgery, she has become something more than just Heidi Montag—she becomes an avatar of our cultural norms of beauty.

Scholars have long expressed concern over the media's influence on the body image of both men and women and girls and boys (Aubrey, 2007; Hargreaves & Tiggemann, 2009; Harper & Tiggemann, 2008; Jackson, Jiang, & Chen, 2017; Shields & Heinecken, 2001; Stice, Spangler, & Agras, 2001). Even one of Montag's co-stars expressed misgivings about the potential impact that Montag's actions may have on young girls:

I hope that girls don't read the article, look at the decisions that Heidi made, and think that's normal. She was quoted as saying that every celebrity in Hollywood has these procedures done, every day . . . and that's just not true. I would never want young girls to read that and think it's the standard that they need to be measured by. (Ward, 2010, p. 25)

But there *is* a standard by which everyone is held, which is continually held up in the media. Montag is not the problem, but rather the symptom. A study by Dohnt and Tiggemann (2006) found that girls as young as 5-8 years old had already internalized media messages depicting thinness as the ideal and awareness of dieting as a means of gaining that type of body. Maltby and Day (2011) found a correlation between celebrity worship and those who actually went though with cosmetic surgery. It should come as little surprise that Montag would likewise internalize the media-promoted ideal of perfection and then carve her body into the appropriate shape.

The most pressing ethical consideration for the media, then, is the recognition of the power that the industry holds in shaping culture. As Burgess (1970) explains, "the strategies and motives of any rhetoric

. . . represent an invitation to a life-style, an invitation to adopt a pattern of strategies and motives, verbal and nonverbal, that determine how men and women will function together in culture" (p. 120). As such, language becomes an ethical concern; "We literally speak relations into being, and fashion the world as per the logic of those articulated relations" (Anton & Zhang, 2011, p. 239-240). The media plays a part in the perpetuation of a narrow definition of beauty for both males and females. The Code of Ethics of the Society of Professional Journalists (1996) states that journalists should "minimize harm" and "Show good taste. Avoid pandering to lurid curiosity" (p. 1). This imperative to minimize harm could also be applied to societal harm. Media outlets have the potential to shape the dialogue concerning beauty into something more expansive, but barring this, perhaps the simplest ethical action that the media can take would simply be to leave the individuals who choose to undergo cosmetic surgery alone.

Society

Although there are some evolutionary traits associated with beauty (Barber, 1995), conceptions of beauty are also culturally bound. Cosmetic surgery plays a part in this construction; as Lunceford (2012) puts it, "cosmetic surgery not only reflects but creates our conceptions of what it means to be beautiful" (p. 20). Beauty is socially coded as more desirable and researchers have long observed that a host of positive traits are associated with attractive people (Dion, Berscheid, & Walster, 1972; Nisbett & Wilson, 1977; but see Eagly, Ashmore, Makhijani, & Longo, 1991). This "halo effect" can be leveraged in many ways; attractive people are seen as more intelligent (Kanazawa, 2011; Kanazawa & Kovar, 2004), healthier (Jones et al., 2001), more attractive to employers (Ruetzler, Taylor, Reynolds, Baker, & Killen, 2012; but see Johnson, Podratz, Dipboye, & Gibbons, 2010), more skilled socially (Hope & Mindell, 1994), and make better (and more distinct) first impressions (Lorenzo, Biesanz, & Human, 2010). But the benefits of physical beauty go far beyond romantic potential or career success. Garnham (2013) explains that in contemporary society, the body "becomes the surface of inscription for the choices one makes and can be read in terms of its virtue. Looking 'good' or an attractive appearance thus signifies the ethical subject" (p. 44). This link between morality and beauty is reinforced from an early age (see Baker-Sperry & Grauerholz, 2003; S. Baumann, 2008; Bazzini, Curtin, Joslin, Regan, & Martz, 2010).

Western society has pathologized the body and any perceived defect in the body can be technologically solved through drugs or surgery. Moreover, some have begun to pathologize traits that are simply racial variations (Aquino, 2017; Davis, 2003) or even fetishize these differences, as in the case of the Brazilian butt lift (Lloréns, 2013). The body in its natural state is the problem and cosmetic surgery is the proffered solution. But it is not enough to solve the problem; one must solve it more effectively than others. Montag describes this sense of competition: "Think about the industry I'm trying to go into. My ultimate dream is to be a pop star. I'm competing against the Britney Spearses of the world—and when she was in her prime, it was her sex appeal that sold. Obviously, looks matter; it's a superficial industry" (Garcia, 2010, p. 82). Beauty is a zero-sum game in which failing to measure up physically means losing out to another who has more effectively managed his or her physical appearance. Such sentiments seem consistent with Blum's (2005) assertion that "cosmetic surgery can be seen as a dramatization of the relationship between a woman and an imaginary Other Woman figure . . . who, because of some imaginary set of superior charms, entrances your partner away from you" (p. 110). Plastic surgery allows a woman to become that "other woman," which then places her in competition with the rest of the female population. This is certainly not lost on Montag, who states, "As for other women, if they aren't hating on you, then you're not doing anything right. If women aren't jealous of you, talking about you and cutting you down, then you're a nerd, and I would never want to be that" (Husted, 2009b, p. B03). Jealousy can be a powerful motivator to pursue cosmetic surgery; Arnocky, Perilloux, Cloud, Bird, and Thomas (2016) found that "appearance comparison induced significantly more envy relative to the control condition. Envy in turn significantly predicted cosmetic surgery attitudes, intended facial cosmetic use, and willingness to use diet pills" (p. 79).

The problem, of course, is that there will always be someone who has something that is better. Indeed, research by Calogero, Pina, and Sutton (2014) suggests that "intentions to pursue cosmetic surgery stem (in part) from being in a state of self-objectification—a state where women are focused on how their bodies look in the eyes of others as opposed to what their bodies can do" (p. 202). One dermatologic surgeon described people like Montag as those seeking "physical perfection to satisfy a psychological problem which cannot be helped by multiple surgeries. We as surgeons are not helping our patients by performing surgery on these people'" (Stewart, 2010a, p. K). Once the body begins to be seen as malleable, with parts that are replaceable, there is no limit to what can be done. As Blum (2005) notes, "When you buy a body part for aesthetic reasons, you automatically compare yours to others who have better or worse. Even if you are pleased with a surgical result, you will see the rest of the world as so many possibilities" (p. 105).

How then should bystanders behave in relation to those undergoing cosmetic surgery? Gillon (1994) places societal issues under the category of justice prescribed by Beauchamp and Childress (2001). This makes sense, considering that justice is generally about fairness among a group of people. Rawls (1971) suggests that to determine the justice of a situation, one must approach it with a "veil of ignorance," in which one must decide how to proceed without any knowledge of which side of the transaction he or she would be on. For example, if one would find being a slave unjust, then he or she must find slavery unjust, even if they were to be a slave owner. On the other hand, one might prefer to act as pitcher in a game of baseball, but would find being put in the outfield to be fair as well, despite his or her preferences. In other words, justice does not necessarily mean that everyone would get what they want; only that all parties would find the arrangement to be fair. Gillon (1994) explains, "we should not be surprised that there will always be some people dissatisfied after justice has been done because by definition not everyone's claims can be met," but notes that "societies seek strategies to minimise the destructive effect of such choices, including tendencies to change their strategies over time" (p. 187). This seems reminiscent of Bentham's (1823) utilitarian argument that "It is the greatest happiness of the greatest number that is the measure of right and wrong" (p. vi). Although this is only one of a number of ethical frameworks, it illustrates the stakes surrounding cosmetic surgery. If the goal is to make the potential patient—and society as a whole—happier, how should one achieve that end? One issue noted by Montag is the perceived competition among individuals, especially regarding beauty. Because attraction of and competition for mates serve a biological function, it would likely be too much to ask that people reduce this competition. However, it should not be too much to ask that people are more kind to each other because, as Peterson (2011) writes, we are all vulnerable and these vulnerabilities "help us recognize our need for each other" (p. 46). At the very least, doctors should not abuse their positions of authority as medical experts to exacerbate perceived imperfections in the potential patient.

The Patient

No one exists in a vacuum, and social conceptions of beauty are created not only through exemplars, but also in comparison with others. The body that Montag inhabits has likewise read other bodies in her search for perfection, noting that "When I was shopping for my boobs, I wanted the best, so I sat down and flipped through a bunch of Playboys" (Derakhshani, 2009, p. E02). It seems that Montag chose her breasts much as one searches for a new pair of pants in a catalog. As Blum (2005) observes, "When you don't like a body part, the rest of the world looks like an array of perfect examples of just what you lack. Moreover, once you've bought and paid for an improvement, you want the 'best'" (p. 104).

The catalog in which Montag—and many others like her—chose to browse may not actually provide the goods that she desires. After all, the pages of *Playboy* are filled with surgically and, of course, digitally enhanced breasts. She could not have been innocent of this possibility; speaking of her own experience in posing for *Playboy*, she states, "I didn't fill out one of the bras and they had to Photoshop my boobs bigger, and it was so disheartening. I almost cried" (Garcia, 2010, p. 83). In other words, she is seeking to modify her breasts in ways that may not be possible in the flesh—creating a false set of breasts from a model that is inherently false. Baudrillard (1994) would certainly find such a state amusing with his prediction of the precession of simulacra, but this also speaks to another assertion by Baudrillard (1988): "*Images have become our true sex object*, the object of our desire" (p. 35). It was not simply better breasts that she chose, but rather, *someone's* breasts, which may or may not have been that person's actual breasts. In other words, she chose the *image* of another's breasts. Thus, her statement, "I'm very excited for the world to see the new me, and a real me" (Garcia, 2010, p. 84), seems particularly ironic.

But Montag is not only concerned about the world in abstract, but also seems to crave her husband's approval. Davis and Vernon (2002) suggest a connection between attachment anxiety and cosmetic surgery, stating that "although there are many motives to improve appearance, fear of rejection or loss of a current spouse or lover is clearly among them" (p. 136). This seems particularly evident in Montag's expressed concerns that her husband would not find her sexy. Montag states that after coming home from surgery, "I felt bad that he had to even look at me" (Garcia, 2010, p. 86). When asked if the recovery process tested their relationship, Montag replied, "Asking my husband to take down my pants so that I can go to the bathroom? That's not something I ever wanted to have to do. I mean, you want your husband to look at you and feel sexy, not have him waiting on you hand and foot, feeling like you don't want him to look at you," but concedes that "it took our marriage to another level" (Garcia, 2010, p. 86-88). Montag's story reminded me of when my wife and I came home from the hospital after she gave birth to our son. I recognized that there were some things that she would not be able to do and I did them because our relationship is based on more than just her physical attractiveness. The body can be damaged and must have the opportunity to heal itself; this is a luxury that Montag seems unwilling to give herself. But if one considers the base of the relationship as looking sexy, then he or she must always guard against someone better looking. There is no time for recovery.

The second assumption present in Montag's comments is, perhaps more troubling: that a woman's looks are her most important attribute. In the image-hungry entertainment industry, however, this may be taken as a given. In response to the question, "Does it worry you that people will fixate on your breasts?" Montag responded, "I hope so. They better! That's kind of the point" (Garcia, 2010, p. 83-84). Even so, she pulls back from this slightly, adding, "Sex appeal is really important and it's not saying that you're only sexy if you have big boobs. That's not true at all, and honestly the way I got Spencer, I had no surgery. It was my inner beauty that he loved" (Garcia, 2010, p. 84).

Montag seems to view her body as a set of individual components rather than holistically. Blum (2005) relates a similar impulse in her interviews:

Grabbing a magazine from a nearby table, she pointed to the supermodel on the cover and exclaimed, "Ooh, I love that nose, I want that nose." I ask her why. "It's straight. It's straight and thin. Not the cheekbones. I have the cheekbones. I love the tip—well, I don't know," she said, standing back now, assuming more aesthetic distance, "it's still not thin enough." (p. 104)

When one can deconstruct and reconstruct the body in such a way, it invites a view that the body is no more than the sum of its parts. This can be problematic, if not from an ethical sense, from an aesthetic sense. What works well on one body may not work as well on another. Yet there are deeper underlying concerns that emerge from taking a fragmentary view of the body, specifically the question of when is enough enough? When can one stop altering the body? What parts are acceptable to alter and in what ways? What happens to the sense of the self when one has one person's nose and another person's eyebrows? Most importantly, what happens to our conception of beauty when everybody is able to look the same?

From an ethical standpoint, the potential patient has a moral obligation to him or herself. Recall that one of the ethical principles proposed by Beauchamp and Childress (2001) was respect for the patient's autonomy. Yet Draper and Sorell (2002) explain that "if autonomy in medical ethics is to mean the same as in general ethics—and surely it is supposed to—autonomy must go hand in hand with taking responsibility for what is chosen" (p. 338). The patient is the final arbiter concerning his or her actions. However, the ethical responsibilities do not end with the patient alone. Sider and Clements (1984) argue that "an ethical obligation for health is a fundamental constituent of human morality" and that "we owe our health to ourselves as well as to others" (p. 10). The patient's choices do not affect only him or her, but also family, friends, and others. Surgeries carry risk, and some have become injured (Rajabi et al. 2015; Wimalawansa, Fox, & Johnson, 2014) or even died in the pursuit of beauty (de Casanova & Sutton, 2013; Jiang, Liu, & Chen, 2014). Montag herself notes that there were lasting detrimental effects that she had not anticipated (Furtado, 2010a, p. C4). As such, the patient cannot ethically take a solipsistic view in which his or her own desire for surgical alteration is the measure of all things.

Coda: The Aftermath of Montag's Surgeries

Although Montag was rather positive when she had her surgeries, she later presented a more nuanced view of her quest for physical enhancement. For example, nine months after her barrage of surgeries, she decided that she wanted to have her implants removed and downgraded to a smaller size because of back pain. "I'm desperate to go back to normal," Montag said; "I feel trapped in my own body" (Gillin, 2010, p. 2B). She explains that the implants had also begun to malfunction, necessitating their removal: "My implants were falling through. They were three pounds each so I was really miserable. Obviously, I didn't want to go back into surgery, but it was really necessary" ("Heidi Pratt's Secret Trauma," 2014).

Montag's buyer's remorse went well beyond her enlarged breasts, however. Her biggest regret was not her breasts, but rather her chin. She explains that "I have TMJ now and my jaw hurts. I don't think people do tell you the trauma of what you're going to heal from. I was in so much pain, I actually thought I was going to die" ("Heidi Pratt's Secret Trauma," 2014). She also laments that "Parts of my body definitely look worse than they did pre-surgery," and provides a laundry list of what went wrong, including a

two-inch-long blemish under her chin from her chin reduction, two caterpillar-sized bald spots along her hairline from a brow lift, a horrifying jagged line behind her ears from having her ears pinned back, lumpy legs and four spots left on her lower back and below the buttocks from botched liposuction, a bright red mark inside her right nostril, uneven boobs, a stretched mark on her chest and deep scars around her nipples from a second boob job. (Furtado, 2010a, p. C4)

She also describes the physical toll that surgery exacts on the body: "People have fewer scars from accidents than I have on my body," concluding, "I wish I could jump into a time machine and take it all back. Instead, I'm always going to feel like Edward Scissorhands" (Furtado, 2010b, C16). Montag's husband, Spencer Pratt, echoes this sentiment: "I would definitely say [to] women and men who think there's such a thing as a minor surgical procedure, the second someone is hacking your body it no longer becomes minor surgery" (Ng, 2016). Still, although she's reluctant to say that she regrets the surgeries because "I'm trying not to regret things in my life because that can be a dark path to go down," she concludes, "But I certainly wouldn't do it again and I certainly wouldn't recommend it and I have learned a lot from it and I just want to move forward in a positive way" (Ng, 2016).

Some have suggested that Montag's decision is a symptom of a larger problem. "She has had a lifetime of cosmetic plastic surgery in two years," says plastic surgeon John Di Saia. "It is quite possible that the woman needs some professional help" (Stewart, 2010a, p. Arts K). Montag provides some evidence for this standpoint when she states, "I disliked myself so much. I literally chopped up my own body" ("Heidi Pratt's Secret Trauma," 2014). More recently, she reaffirmed how her mindset influenced her decision to undergo surgery: "It was the hardest time of my life and I feel like I've become a lot stronger from it. And [it] made me look at myself and reflect, 'Why did I do that?' . . . Maybe I needed to have more confidence and be more secure in who I was and not thinking so much about my eyebrows or my this or that" (Ng, 2016). Research has suggested a link between individual conceptions of beauty and willingness to undergo cosmetic surgery. Tylka and Iannantuono (2016) found that a broad conceptualization of beauty for both self and others "was positively related to self-compassion and positive body image quality of life, and inversely related to social comparisons (body, eating, and exercise), anti-fat attitudes, thin-ideal internalization, body surveillance, and contemplation of cosmetic surgery" (p. 78).

In the case of elective cosmetic surgery, it seems prudent to explore with the patient the underlying reasons for surgery. As Zuckerman and Abraham (2008) suggest, "Many girls and women seeking cosmetic surgery might benefit more from therapeutic approaches aimed at improving self-esteem or general body image or those aimed at decreasing depression" (p. 321). This may require a deeper analysis than the surgeon is able to make and in such cases psychiatric evaluation may be warranted (Ericksen & Billick, 2012). This is essential because those who suffer from Body Dysmorphic Disorder (BDD) are unlikely to be satisfied with any surgical intervention. One study found that despite expressing satisfaction concerning the surgery, "only 1 patient no longer had a BDD diagnosis at follow-up: all the other operated patients still had a BDD diagnosis and all but 1 had developed a new site of preoccupation" (Tignol, Biraben-Gotzamanis, Martin-Guehl, Grabot, & Aouizerate, 2007, p. 523). If the aim is beneficence, then cosmetic surgery misses the mark entirely for some patients. Following the principle of beneficence suggests that the least invasive procedure should be attempted first, especially in cases in which the tissue to be altered is healthy and functional. The willingness and desire to undergo ten procedures in one day should be a red flag for any medical practitioner.

But Montag's surgeries were not merely the work of a random woman who wanted to compulsively sculpt her body to her own desires or to please others around her. These surgeries were reported extensively in the media. Some have expressed concern over how such surgeries will influence young people. Diana Zuckerman, president of the National Research Center for Women & Families, put it this way:

Most actresses are already beautiful . . . Then they get surgery to be "more perfect." Then their photos are enhanced to make them look even more beautiful. Then real people—including teens—see these women and these photos and feel terrible because they can't possibly measure up. Then they get plastic surgery, and other "real people" feel badly about their own imperfections in comparison. For this reason, what actresses do really matters. (Cassidy, 2010, p. G1)

As stated above, these images may not even be real when they finally get to the mass media because of the prevalence of photo retouching and alteration. However, some concerns about the effects on adolescents may be somewhat overstated, considering that Theran, Newberg, and Gleason (2010) found only mild attachments in their parasocial interactions with media figures. Still, others (e.g., Brown, Halpern, & L'Engle, 2005) found evidence that adolescent girls take some behavior cues from mass media, especially in relation to sexuality. These parasocial interactions are important because Singh (2015) suggests that there are two impulses leading teenagers to cosmetic surgery: peer group conformity and actual medical problems. If adolescent girls see these women as part of their peer group, this could shift attitudes toward the normalization of cosmetic surgery. Perhaps attitudes have already shifted; Cassidy (2010) reports that "liposuction or breast augmentation have come into vogue as high school graduation presents. But it's not unheard of for 18-year-olds [in rural Pennsylvania] to get new breasts as a graduation gift—or in one [case], as an 18th birthday present" (p. G1).

PROPOSALS FOR ETHICAL COSMETIC SURGERY PRACTICE

The fact that Montag could undergo ten different plastic surgery procedures in one day raises the question of how much is too much. But the ethics of cosmetic surgery transcend any one instance. As I have argued, there is an entire system that must be considered when determining the ethics of cosmetic surgery, especially as the profession has become much more aggressive in its advertising and advocacy through television shows such as *Nip/Tuck*, *Extreme Makeover*, and *The Swan* (see Heyes, 2007; Sender, 2014). This normalization of cosmetic surgery has even seeped into children's picture books (Abate, 2010)! As such, one cannot change this system by simply changing the code of ethics for cosmetic surgeons. This is where a technoethical approach can help elucidate the various pressures that come to bear on the individuals involved in cosmetic surgery. As Luppicini (2009a) explains, technoethical inquiry is "a call for a systems study of the interweaving of technology with human agency within contemporary life and society" (p.19). Montag's surgeries illustrate the different stakeholders in defining beauty: the cosmetic surgeons, the mass media, the individuals who choose to undergo such procedures, and, finally, those around each of us who judge the appearance of others. In order to make ethical judgments, one must consider the entire system. To conclude, I will consider some possible, if quixotic, solutions.

In the case of cosmetic surgery, the aesthetic, ethical, and financial are bound together; Martínez Lirola and Chovanec (2012) explain that

The surgically enhanced body is (1) the key to women's self-esteem, self-confidence and physical perfection, (2) the target of male voyeuristic desire and (3) the medium through which cosmetic surgery providers are able to generate their profit. (p. 503).

This combination creates a significant financial conflict of interest; it's good business to agree with an individual's perceived imperfections. Thus, at the very least, medical practitioners should heed Kant's (1994) demand that one should "Act in such a way that you treat humanity, whether in your own person or in the person of another, always at the same time as an end and never simply as a means" (p. 36). But following the framework proposed by Beauchamp and Childress (2001) of autonomy, nonmaleficence, beneficence, and justice should go beyond the cosmetic surgery practitioners and implications for each individual patient, and also consider the implications for society as a whole. Such an approach on ethics goes well beyond the moment when the patient is placed under anesthesia, and reaches into practices such as advertising, media appearances, informational literature, and counseling. It is not enough to say that surgically modifying an individual into a shape applauded by society counts for beneficence without considering one's role in creating those very ideals.

It seems clear that cosmetic surgery can have positive outcomes in self-perception and behavior, but one must take care to not overstate the positive outcomes, as a meta-analysis of 22 studies by Cook, Rosser, and Salmon (2006) found that with the exception of breast reduction surgery, there was little evidence of increased quality of life after surgery. Moreover, there are the intervening issues of who actually seeks such surgery and the potential long-term effects. Hosseini, Shahgholian, and Abdollahi (2015) found that those who sought cosmetic surgery were less psychologically hardy and more likely to have a negative self-perception. However, Von Soest, Kvalem, Roald, and Skolleborg (2009) found that body image evaluation and self-esteem scores improved after cosmetic surgery and Meningaud et al. (2003) found improvement in anxiety in patients following cosmetic surgery, but notes that those seeking cosmetic surgery were "more anxious" and "more depressed than the general population" (p. 48). On the other hand, von Soest, Kvalem, Skolleborg, and Roald (2009) question whether the increase in extraversion induced by cosmetic surgery "may be due to short-term changes in attitude towards one's own appearance, which in itself serves to legitimate the decision to have undergone cosmetic surgery. Such effects may well diminish over time" (p. 1024-1025).

Perhaps there needs to be some shift in how cosmetic surgeons view their practice; some seem to see themselves more as artists than as doctors. As Baker (2004) put it, "There are those who advocate analysis based on complex measurements to determine what implant shape or size is most desirable. I prefer to use my aesthetic sense when trying to provide balance to the patient's form" (p. 565). However, Henseler et al. (2013) found that "subjective breast assessment, even when it was conducted by experts, lacked accuracy and reproducibility" and advocated the use of digital imaging in breast implant surgery (p. 639). There is a chasm of difference between a cosmetologist and a cosmetic surgeon and taking the aesthetic stance can allow surgeons to overlook ethical considerations of the power that they wield. As Luppicini (2009b) observes, "Technoethics recognizes that there are important ethical considerations when addressing the conduct of an individual with or without a specific technology" (p. 3). When a cosmetic surgeon has the technology to permanently alter one's appearance, he or she should be held to a higher ethical standard than the aesthetician.

Finally, cosmetic surgeons must take care to avoid inflicting harm through their advertising practices. In her discussion of cosmetic labiaplasty, Hardwick-Smith (2011) argues,

Whether communicating verbally or through patient literature or Websites, we should avoid using statements that imply judgment. Should we offer to create a "more beautiful" or "more youthful" appearance by making the labia smaller? Even terms such as "enlarged labia" or "labial hypertrophy" can be viewed as judgmental. Simply calling these procedures "cosmetic vaginal surgery" minimizes misunderstanding and avoids the use of clichés that are more appropriate for over-the-counter make-up sales. The Ob/Gyn doctor is seen by many as the patient's most trusted physician. This gives us an added ethical responsibility. (p. 110)

There is a fine line between promoting one's practice and contributing to the posthumanist idea that the body is intrinsically flawed and in need of surgical intervention. Researchers have noted that there is a correlation between media exposure of depictions of cosmetic surgery and contemplating surgery (Slevec & Tiggemann, 2010). Some have argued that advertisements for cosmetic surgery should be controlled (e.g., Clarke, Drake, Flatt, & Jebb, 2008), but this poses a practical problem of who is to do so. At the very least, advertisements should be ethical, but a content analysis of print advertisements for cosmetic surgeons conducted by Hennink-Kaminski, Reid, and King (2010) found some highly questionable practices, such as ignoring potential risks and side effects and using language that may go against AMA ethical guidelines. Another study by Spilson, Chung, Greenfield, and Walters (2002) also found a significant number of advertisements that were misleading and in violation of the code of ethics of the American Society of Plastic Surgeons, but note that "because such societies are not meant to police all advertisements, discretion is left up to the physician" (p. 1186). Perhaps it is time for more stringent oversight.

In the case of the media, scholars have argued against the unrealistic body types promulgated through the photoshopping of body images (e.g, Reaves, Hitchon, Park, & Yun 2004a, 2004b; Selimbegović & Chatard, 2015). This seems to be a good start, as these norms are internalized even when such bodies are physically impossible. However, there is a more general sense in which the media helps to define norms of beauty. When asked why large breasts were desirable, one woman, who had received breast implants as a high school graduation present, stated,

I would think the media, I mean it's just so, so like stereotypical of what a perfect woman is. You know, big boobs, really skinny, looks like specific celebrities, models and everything. . . . I mean if everybody was fat and had no boobs then I probably wouldn't have wanted them, but if that's the way we grew up, the society you grow up in, you want to look a specific way. Like you would like to have a small waist with a bigger chest. I mean I'm sure that's our American culture in general. (Fowler & Moore, 2012, p. 114)

Perhaps it is too much to ask television, film, and other media to embrace a wider definition of beauty, but as I have explained above, the media plays a large part in defining conceptions of beauty and attitudes toward cosmetic surgery, which is often coded as Caucasian and Western, even in outlets geared toward non-Western, non-Caucasian audiences (see Jung & Lee, 2009).

In the case of the individual who is contemplating cosmetic surgeries, we should change the narrative of how surgery is discussed. For example, in her discussion of the television show *Extreme Makeover*, Heyes (2007) suggests that "electing to have surgery makes one a go-getter, for example, someone who takes charge, not flinching at the prospect of pain, inconvenience, trauma, or risk," while also noting that "resistance to cosmetic surgery is tacitly rendered as a lack of character, and thus can be construed (like resistance to wearing make-up or high heels in an earlier feminist era) only as a failure to make the best of oneself" (p. 28). In short, we must stop considering the possible as equivalent to the inevitable. The desire to compete in the genetic competition of life has resulted in a kind of aesthetic arms race.

As Berman (2010) states, "In previous generations, when women wanted to increase their sex appeal, they turned to Chanel No. 5 and red lipstick. Today, women turn to potentially life-threatening surgeries along with monthly injections of Botox" (p. C4). This impulse to alter the body through surgery is by no means new, of course. Comiskey (2004) states that as cosmetic surgery began to be practiced in the 1920s, medical professionals "defended cosmetic surgery as a noble profession, arguing that it was necessary because of the social importance of beauty in the brutal struggle for existence, particularly for women" (p. 32).

I am not advocating here for a kind of cosmetic surgery shaming, but rather a shift in self-talk concerning beauty. Some procedures seem geared solely to recreate a Western view of beauty, as in the case of blepharoplasty (double eyelid surgery) (Aquino, 2017; Motaparthi, 2010). Activists have long railed against the prevailing Eurocentric model of beauty. Stokely Carmichael (2007), for example, proclaimed that

Beauty in this society is defined by someone with a narrow nose, thin lips, white skin. You ain't got none of that…Can you begin to get the guts to develop a criteria for beauty for black people? Your nose is boss, your lips are thick, you are black, and you are beautiful. Can you begin to do it so that you are not ashamed of your hair and you don't cut it down to the scalp so that naps won't show? Girls are you ready? Obviously it is your responsibility to begin to define the criteria for black people concerning their beauty. ("At Morgan State")

Although Carmichael was arguing for a re-definition of beauty rooted in the realities of African-American bodies, his argument applies to all individuals who do not fit neatly into the media-promulgated norms of beauty.

One should be clear concerning why they seek the desired cosmetic surgery. For example, breast augmentation is relatively common, but why do women choose to undergo this procedure? For some, there is a self-consciousness of the surveillance that we all endure—the fear that we will be assessed and found wanting. As one woman put it, "Well, no one's going to look at me because I'm flat as a board" (Gagné and McGaughey, 2002, p. 823). Another described her self-consciousness around her husband concerning her breasts: "'We'd be in bed and … he'd start to put his arm around me … I'd be thinking, please don't touch my breasts … I couldn't even bear for his hand to be, like, on my waist … I'd just keep moving … [his arm] down to my hips" (Gimlin, 2006, p. 711). But beauty is in the eye of the beholder and many men may prefer small breasts (Furnham & Swami, 2007) or simply be more interested in other body attributes (Dixson, Grimshaw, Linklater, & Dixson, 2011; Wiggins, Wiggins, & Conger, 1968). Frederick, Peplau, and Lever (2008) likewise found that "Although most women in our sample were dissatisfied with their breasts, a majority of men were satisfied with their partner's breasts," a finding that they attribute to overestimating the preferences of the opposite sex (p. 209). In other words, there are many forms of desirability.

But desirability is not the only impulse toward cosmetic surgery. Gimlin (2006) notes that "women who have aesthetic procedures rarely do so with the expectation of becoming beautiful," but rather "have cosmetic surgery in the hope of becoming 'normal'" (p. 711). Some respondents echoed this stance: "I did not want to be too big, that was my biggest thing. I wanted to look natural" (Fowler & Moore, 2012, p. 113). Another said, "I do remember when I had made the decision to have the implants, I didn't want them real big and I wanted them to look like they were mine. Like this is what I grew" (Gagné and McGaughey, 2002, p. 827). But what constitutes normality? There is a broad range of body shapes and types and simply conforming to the average means little from an aesthetic sense. Some have attempted to challenge this homogenization of body types through artistic interventions, such as The Great Wall of Vagina (n.d.), Normal Breast Gallery (2017), and The Shape of a Mother (2016).

Finally, individuals living together in society must change the dialogue surrounding beauty. Humans are judgmental and driven partially by biological imperatives. In seeking a mate, men tend to seek women who embody fertility and health, while women tend to seek men who exhibit status and power, thereby ensuring that they would be able to provide for their offspring (Buss & Schmitt, 1993; Thornhill & Gangestad, 1996), although women are also attuned to male physical attractiveness, especially physical symmetry (Gallup, Frederick, & Pipitone, 2008; Manning, Scutt, & Lewis-Jones, 1998). Moreover, there are beauty standards that transcend culture, such as smooth skin and body symmetry (Fink & Neave, 2005, but see also Grammer, Fink, Møller, & Thornhill, 2003), but within these parameters there is still a range of beauty, some of which is culturally bound (de Casanova, 2004; Sugiyama, 2004). Embracing these differences would be a more ethical stance.

Still, one must allow individuals to make their own choices concerning their bodies. One would think that individuals who had already gone under the knife would have some sympathy for others who chose a similar path, but this does not seem to be the case. For example, one of Gimlin's (2010) participants, who had already had an abdominoplasty, said: "I'm not obsessed about the way I look like some women who have cosmetic surgery. I know that other things matter more . . . my job, my family, my health. These are much more important to me than my appearance". (p. 64). Part of this impulse, Gimlin explains, comes from the mental construction of the "surgical other," who is

motivated by vanity rather than need. In particular, they suggested that whatever she had altered did not really require changing: her breasts were not actually too small; her nose was not really too big; she was not sufficiently overweight to require liposuction. The surgical other is thus presented as being excessively, even obsessively, concerned with minute and inconsequential physical flaws. (Gimlin, 2010, p. 66)

In this way, they are able to maintain some psychological distance while still justifying their own actions. Those who had undergone cosmetic surgery seemed to view those who had breast implants with derision, as if some forms of cosmetic surgery were more acceptable than others. One woman states that she "didn't want a boob job surgeon doing my face." When pressed for clarification on the term "boob job surgeon," she responded, "Um, fast bucks. Flashy. Little concern for the patient. Fast turnaround. They're dealing with clientele that has a different kind of lifestyle, different kind of work ethic than I have" (Gimlin, 2010, p. 68).

Each individual must work within the confines of his or her own circumstances and this includes societal imperatives. Gagné and McGaughey (2002) suggest that "Women electing cosmetic mammoplasty exercise agency, but they do so within the confines of hegemonic gender norms" and that "women are complicitous in disciplining themselves and one another" (p. 835). This brings us full circle to the system of influences surrounding cosmetic surgery. It is impossible to reduce something as complex as the decision to undergo elective surgery to the patient, the surgeon, other individuals, or the media/culture industries. One must look at all of them together.

CONCLUSION

Montag's case provides a cautionary example of how this system plays out and the ethical failures in each dimension. Despite the misgivings of other cosmetic surgeons, there will always be those willing to push the limits of what is possible, performing an extraordinary amount of procedures at one time. This came at a significant financial and personal cost for Montag, whose low self-opinion likely helped to lead her to the operating table. She had fully bought into the idea that her looks were of primary importance and what constituted her value. But she did not come to this conclusion alone. She had internalized a media landscape that celebrates the kind of body that she chose to construct for herself. However, she did so in a way that compartmentalized each individual body part, giving her the breasts of one woman, the nose of another, and eventually resulting in a kind of embodied pastiche of popular culture. This was a consequence of rushing to perform as many surgeries as possible; it was not possible to see how each component would look in relation to the others. As a result, others shamed her for her aesthetic choices while at the same time watching her every move.

Perhaps leaving the spotlight allowed her to reveal her regrets surrounding her surgeries, but these regrets are not hers alone. As Lunceford (2008) explains, "norms are held in place not by a nebulous system, but by each of us" (p. 325). Those who buy into contemporary standards of beauty, those who encourage or engage in cosmetic surgery as a means of self-improvement, those who perform or advertise cosmetic surgery, and those who disparage another's perceived physical imperfections are all part of the system that helped create Heidi Montag.

REFERENCES

Abate, M. A. (2010). "Plastic makes perfect": My beautiful mommy, cosmetic surgery, and the medicalization of motherhood. *Women's Studies*, *39*(7), 715–746. doi:10.1080/00497878.2010.505152

Anton, C., & Zhang, P. (2011). Syntax and ethics: A conversation. *Etc.; a Review of General Semantics*, *68*(3), 238–254.

Aquino, Y. S. J. (2017). "Big eye" surgery: The ethics of medicalizing Asian features. *Theoretical Medicine and Bioethics*, *38*(3), 213–225. doi:10.100711017-017-9395-y PMID:28105531

Arendt, H. (2006). *Eichmann in Jerusalem: A report on the banality of evil*. New York: Penguin Books.

Arnocky, S., Perilloux, C., Cloud, J. M., Bird, B. M., & Thomas, K. (2016). Envy mediates the link between social comparison and appearance enhancement in women. *Evolutionary Psychological Science*, *2*(2), 71–83. doi:10.100740806-015-0037-1

Aubrey, J. S. (2007). The impact of sexually objectifying media exposure on negative body emotions and sexual self-perceptions: Investigating the mediating role of body self-consciousness. *Mass Communication & Society*, *10*(1), 1–23. doi:10.1080/15205430709337002

Babcock, S. (2010, February 20). Plastic front creates poor "perfection." *Spokesman Review*, p. V1.

Baker, J. L. (2004). Choosing breast implant size: A matter of aesthetics. *Aesthetic Surgery Journal*, *24*(6), 565–566. doi:10.1016/j.asj.2004.09.009 PMID:19336211

Baker-Sperry, L., & Grauerholz, L. (2003). The pervasiveness and persistence of the feminine beauty ideal in children's fairy tales. *Gender & Society*, *17*(5), 711–726. doi:10.1177/0891243203255605

Balkany, T., Hodges, A. V., & Goodman, K. W. (1996). Ethics of cochlear implantation in young children. *Otolaryngology - Head and Neck Surgery*, *114*(6), 748–755. doi:10.1016/S0194-5998(96)70097-9 PMID:8643298

Barber, N. (1995). The evolutionary psychology of physical attractiveness: Sexual selection and human morphology. *Ethology and Sociobiology*, *16*(5), 395–424. doi:10.1016/0162-3095(95)00068-2

Baudrillard, J. (1988). The ecstasy of communication (B. Schutze & C. Schutze, Trans.). New York: Semiotext(e).

Baudrillard, J. (1994). *Simulacra and simulation* (S. F. Glaser, Trans.). Ann Arbor, MI: University of Michigan Press.

Baumann, L. (2012). Ethics in cosmetic dermatology. *Clinics in Dermatology*, *30*(5), 522–527. doi:10.1016/j.clindermatol.2011.06.023 PMID:22902224

Baumann, S. (2008). The moral underpinnings of beauty: A meaning-based explanation for light and dark complexions in advertising. *Poetics*, *36*(1), 2–23. doi:10.1016/j.poetic.2007.11.002

Bazzini, D., Curtin, L., Joslin, S., Regan, S., & Martz, D. (2010). Do animated Disney characters portray and promote the beauty-goodness stereotype? *Journal of Applied Social Psychology*, *40*(10), 2687–2709. doi:10.1111/j.1559-1816.2010.00676.x

Beauchamp, T. L., & Childress, J. F. (2001). *Principles of biomedical ethics* (5th ed.). New York, NY: Oxford University Press.

Bentham, J. (1823). A Fragment on Government; Or a Comment on the Commentaries: Being an Examination of What is Delivered on the Subject of Government in General, in the Introduction to Sir William Blackstone's Commentaries: With a Preface. In *Which is Given a Critique on the Work at Large* (2nd ed.). London: E. Wilson and W. Pickering.

Berman, L. (2010, February 3). Heidi Montag throws a curve at young girls; Obsession with "perfection" reinforces women's needless body insecurities. Chicago Sun Times, p. C4.

Berry, M. G., Cucchiara, V., & Davies, D. M. (2011). Breast augmentation: Part III—preoperative considerations and planning. *Journal of Plastic, Reconstructive & Aesthetic Surgery; JPRAS*, *64*(11), 1401–1409.

Blum, V. L. (2003). *Flesh wounds: The culture of cosmetic surgery*. Berkeley, CA: University of California Press.

Blum, V. L. (2005). Becoming the other woman: The psychic drama of cosmetic surgery. *Frontiers: A Journal of Women Studies*, *26*(2), 104-131.

Bordo, S. (1993). *Unbearable weight: Feminism, Western culture, and the body.* Berkeley, CA: University of California Press.

Brown, J. D., Halpern, C. T., & L'Engle, K. L. (2005). Mass media as a sexual super peer for early maturing girls. *The Journal of Adolescent Health, 36*(5), 420–427. doi:10.1016/j.jadohealth.2004.06.003 PMID:15837346

Bunge, M. (1975). Towards a technoethics. *Philosophic Exchange, 6*(1), 69–79.

Burgess, P. G. (1970). The rhetoric of moral conflict: Two critical dimensions. *The Quarterly Journal of Speech, 56*(2), 120–130. doi:10.1080/00335637009382993

Buss, D. M., & Schmitt, D. P. (1993). Sexual strategies theory: An evolutionary perspective on human mating. *Psychological Review, 100*(2), 204–232. doi:10.1037/0033-295X.100.2.204 PMID:8483982

Calogero, R. M., Pina, A., & Sutton, R. M. (2014). Cutting words: Priming self-objectification increases women's intention to pursue cosmetic surgery. *Psychology of Women Quarterly, 38*(2), 197–207. doi:10.1177/0361684313506881

Camilli, D. (2010, April 24). Montag is a "cheap, plastic pool float" after surgery. *The Gazette (Montreal),* p. E5.

Cantor, J. (2005). Cosmetic dermatology and physicians' ethical obligations: More than just hope in a jar. *Seminars in Cutaneous Medicine and Surgery, 24*(3), 155–160. doi:10.1016/j.sder.2005.04.005 PMID:16202953

Carmichael, (Kwame Ture) S. (1971). *Stokely speaks: Black power back to pan-Africanism* [Enki version]. New York: Random House.

Cartwright, R., & Cardozo, L. (2008). Cosmetic vulvovaginal surgery. *Obstetrics, Gynaecology and Reproductive Medicine, 18*(10), 285–286. doi:10.1016/j.ogrm.2008.07.008

Cassidy, S. (2010, January 24). Teens, young adults cut into cosmetic-surgery statistics; Defining beauty breast wishes parental pressure? For the sport of it males do it, too. *Sunday News,* p. G1.

Chan, J. K.-K., Jones, S. M., & Heywood, A. J. (2011). Body dysmorphia, self-mutilation and the reconstructive surgeon. *Journal of Plastic, Reconstructive & Aesthetic Surgery; JPRAS, 64*(1), 4–8. doi:10.1016/j.bjps.2010.03.029 PMID:20392680

Carmichael (Kwame Ture), S. (2007). Stokely speaks: From black power to pan-Africanism. Chicago Review Press.

Clarke, J., Drake, L., Flatt, S., & Jebb, P. (2008). Physical perfection for sale. *Nursing Standard, 23*(8), 26–27. PMID:18655503

Clemens, D. (1985). Technoethics. *Informal Logic, 7*(2&3), 163–165.

Comiskey, C. (2004). Cosmetic surgery in Paris in 1926: The case of the amputated leg. *Journal of Women's History, 16*(3), 30–54. doi:10.1353/jowh.2004.0059

Cook, S. A., Rosser, R., & Salmon, P. (2006). Is cosmetic surgery an effective psychotherapeutic intervention? A systematic review of the evidence. *Journal of Plastic, Reconstructive & Aesthetic Surgery; JPRAS, 59*(11), 1133–1151. doi:10.1016/j.bjps.2006.03.047 PMID:17046622

Davis, D., & Vernon, M. L. (2002). Sculpting the body beautiful: Attachment style, neuroticism, and use of cosmetic surgeries. *Sex Roles, 47*(3/4), 129–138. doi:10.1023/A:1021043021624

Davis, K. (2003). Surgical passing: Or why Michael Jackson's nose makes "us" uneasy. *Feminist Theory, 4*(1), 73–92. doi:10.1177/1464700103004001004

de Andrade, D. D. (2010). On norms and bodies: Findings from field research on cosmetic surgery in Rio de Janeiro, Brazil. *Reproductive Health Matters, 18*(35), 74–83. doi:10.1016/S0968-8080(10)35519-4 PMID:20541086

de Casanova, E. M. (2004). "No ugly women": Concepts of race and beauty among adolescent women in Ecuador. *Gender & Society, 18*(3), 287–308. doi:10.1177/0891243204263351

de Casanova, E. M., & Sutton, B. (2013). Transnational body projects: Media representations of cosmetic surgery tourism in Argentina and the United States. *Journal of World-systems Research, 19*(1), 57–81. doi:10.5195/JWSR.2013.509

De Roubaix, J. A. M. (2011). Beneficence, non-maleficence, distributive justice and respect for patient autonomy—Reconcilable ends in aesthetic surgery? *Journal of Plastic, Reconstructive & Aesthetic Surgery; JPRAS, 64*(1), 11–16. doi:10.1016/j.bjps.2010.03.034 PMID:20457018

Derakhshani, T. (2009, August 13). Sideshow: Low-key farewell to Hughes. *Philadelphia Inquirer,* p. E02.

Dion, K., Berscheid, E., & Walster, E. (1972). What is beautiful is good. *Journal of Personality and Social Psychology, 24*(3), 285–290. doi:10.1037/h0033731 PMID:4655540

Dixson, B., Grimshaw, G., Linklater, W., & Dixson, A. (2011). Eye-tracking of men's preferences for waist-to-hip ratio and breast size of women. *Archives of Sexual Behavior, 40*(1), 43–50. doi:10.100710508-009-9523-5 PMID:19688590

Dohnt, H., & Tiggemann, M. (2006). Body image concerns in young girls: The role of peers and media prior to adolescence. *Journal of Youth and Adolescence, 35*(2), 135–145. doi:10.100710964-005-9020-7

Draper, H., & Sorell, T. (2002). Patients' responsibilities in medical ethics. *Bioethics, 16*(4), 335–352. doi:10.1111/1467-8519.00292 PMID:12956177

Dyens, O. (2001). *Metal and flesh: The evolution of man: Technology takes over.* Cambridge, MA: MIT Press.

Eagly, A. H., Ashmore, R. D., Makhijani, M. G., & Longo, L. C. (1991). What is beautiful is good, but...: A meta-analytic review of research on the physical attractiveness stereotype. *Psychological Bulletin, 110*(1), 109–128. doi:10.1037/0033-2909.110.1.109

Ericksen, W. L., & Billick, S. B. (2012). Psychiatric issues in cosmetic plastic surgery. *The Psychiatric Quarterly, 83*(3), 343–352. doi:10.100711126-012-9204-8 PMID:22252848

Fink, B., & Neave, N. (2005). The biology of facial beauty. *International Journal of Cosmetic Science*, *27*(6), 317–325. doi:10.1111/j.1467-2494.2005.00286.x PMID:18492169

Fowler, L. A., & Moore, A. R. (2012). Breast implants for graduation: A sociological examination of daughter and mother narratives. *Sociology Mind*, *2*(1), 109–115. doi:10.4236m.2012.21014

Frederick, D. A., Peplau, A., & Lever, J. (2008). The Barbie mystique: Satisfaction with breast size and shape across the lifespan. *International Journal of Sexual Health*, *20*(3), 200–211. doi:10.1080/19317610802240170

Furnham, A., & Swami, V. (2007). Perception of female buttocks and breast size in profile. *Social Behavior and Personality*, *35*(1), 1–7. doi:10.2224bp.2007.35.1.1

Furtado, M. (2010a, December 24). Heidi Montag exposes her numerous plastic surgery battle wounds. *The Vancouver Sun (British Columbia)*, p. C4.

Furtado, M. (2010b, December 27). Heidi Montag regrets her cosmetic surgery. *The Daily Gleaner (New Brunswick)*, p. C16.

Gagné, P., & McGaughey, D. (2002). Designing women: Cultural hegemony and the exercise of power among women who have undergone elective mammoplasty. *Gender & Society*, *16*(6), 814–838. doi:10.1177/089124302237890

Gallup, G. G. Jr, Frederick, M. J., & Pipitone, R. N. (2008). Morphology and behavior: Phrenology revisited. *Review of General Psychology*, *12*(3), 297–304. doi:10.1037/1089-2680.12.3.297

Garcia, J. (2010, January 25). Obsessed with being "perfect.". *People*, *73*, 80–88.

Garnham, B. (2013). Designing "older" rather than denying ageing: Problematizing anti-ageing discourse in relation to cosmetic surgery undertaken by older people. *Journal of Aging Studies*, *27*(1), 38–46. doi:10.1016/j.jaging.2012.11.001 PMID:23273555

Gillin, J. (2010, August 26). Montag wants implants out. *St. Petersburg Times*, p. 2B.

Gillon, R. (1994). Medical ethics: Four principles plus attention to scope. *BMJ: British Medical Journal*, *309*(6948), 184–188. doi:10.1136/bmj.309.6948.184 PMID:8044100

Gimlin, D. (2006). The absent body project: Cosmetic surgery as a response to bodily dys-appearance. *Sociology*, *40*(4), 699–716. doi:10.1177/0038038506065156

Gimlin, D. (2010). Imagining the other in cosmetic surgery. *Body & Society*, *16*(4), 57–76. doi:10.1177/1357034X10383881

Grammer, K., Fink, B., Møller, A. P., & Thornhill, R. (2003). Darwinian aesthetics: Sexual selection and the biology of beauty. *Biological Reviews of the Cambridge Philosophical Society*, *78*(3), 385–407. doi:10.1017/S1464793102006085 PMID:14558590

Gupta, S. (2012). Ethical and legal issues in aesthetic surgery. *Indian Journal of Plastic Surgery: Official Publication of the Association of Plastic Surgeons of India*, *45*(3), 547–549. doi:10.4103/0970-0358.105973 PMID:23450235

Hardwick-Smith, S. (2011). Examining the controversy in aesthetic vaginal surgery. *The American Journal of Cosmetic Surgery*, *28*(3), 106–113. doi:10.5992/0748-8068-28.3.106

Hargreaves, D. A., & Tiggemann, M. (2009). Muscular ideal media images and men's body image: Social comparison processing and individual vulnerability. *Psychology of Men & Masculinity*, *10*(2), 109–119. doi:10.1037/a0014691

Harper, B., & Tiggemann, M. (2008). The effect of thin ideal media images on women's self-objectification, mood, and body image. *Sex Roles*, *58*(9), 649–657. doi:10.100711199-007-9379-x

Harris, D. L., & Carr, A. T. (2001). The Derriford appearance scale (DAS59): A new psychometric scale for the evaluation of patients with disfigurements and aesthetic problems of appearance. *British Journal of Plastic Surgery*, *54*(3), 216–222. doi:10.1054/bjps.2001.3559 PMID:11254413

Heidi Pratt's secret trauma and double-d regrets: "I literally chopped up my own body." (2014). *Extra*. Retrieved from http://extratv.com/2014/11/20/heidi-pratts-secret-trauma-and-double-d-regrets-i-literally-chopped-up-my-own-body

Heidi says she'll get more done; Will do some "maintenance." (2010, February 15). *Chicago Sun Times*, p. 31.

Hennink-Kaminski, H., Reid, L. N., & King, K. W. (2010). The content of cosmetic surgery advertisements placed in large city magazines, 1985-2004. *Journal of Current Issues and Research in Advertising*, *32*(2), 41–57. doi:10.1080/10641734.2010.10505284

Henseler, H., Smith, J., Bowman, A., Khambay, B. S., Ju, X., Ayoub, A., & Ray, A. K. (2013). Subjective versus objective assessment of breast reconstruction. *Journal of Plastic, Reconstructive & Aesthetic Surgery; JPRAS*, *66*(5), 634–639. doi:10.1016/j.bjps.2013.01.006 PMID:23402935

Heyes, C. J. (2007). Cosmetic surgery and the televisual makeover. *Feminist Media Studies*, *7*(1), 17–32. doi:10.1080/14680770601103670

Holliday, R., & Sanchez Taylor, J. (2006). Aesthetic surgery as false beauty. *Feminist Theory*, *7*(2), 179–195. doi:10.1177/1464700106064418

Hope, D. A., & Mindell, J. A. (1994). Global social skill ratings: Measures of social behavior or physical attractiveness? *Behaviour Research and Therapy*, *32*(4), 463–469. doi:10.1016/0005-7967(94)90011-6 PMID:8192645

Hosseini, K., Shahgholian, M., & Abdollahi, M.-H. (2015). Hardiness, defense mechanisms, negative self-portrayal scale in applicants and non-applicants of cosmetic surgery. *International Journal of Behavioral Sciences*, *10*(1), 26–31.

Husted, B. (2009a, November 6). A red Letterman day for Crested Butte fan. *Denver Post*, p. B03.

Husted, B. (2009b, August 14). Heidi 'n' seek: Playboy, hubby reveal a bit about her. *Denver Post*, p. B03.

Jackson, T., Jiang, C., & Chen, H. (2017). Associations between Chinese/Asian versus Western mass media influences and body image disturbances of young Chinese women. *Body Image*, *17*, 175–183. doi:10.1016/j.bodyim.2016.03.007 PMID:27110965

Jeffreys, S. (2005). *Beauty and misogyny: Harmful cultural practices in the West*. London: Routledge.

Jerslev, A. (2006). The mediated body. *Nordicom Review*, 27(2), 133–151. doi:10.1515/nor-2017-0235

Jiang, X., Liu, D., & Chen, B. (2014). Middle temporal vein: A fatal hazard in injection cosmetic surgery for temple augmentation. *JAMA Facial Plastic Surgery*, 16(3), 227–229. doi:10.1001/jamafacial.2013.2565 PMID:24577714

Johnson, S. K., Podratz, K. E., Dipboye, R. L., & Gibbons, E. (2010). Physical attractiveness biases in ratings of employment suitability: Tracking down the "beauty is beastly" effect. *The Journal of Social Psychology*, 150(3), 301–318. doi:10.1080/00224540903365414 PMID:20575336

Jones, B. C., Little, A. C., Penton-Voak, I. S., Tiddeman, B. P., Burt, D. M., & Perrett, D. I. (2001). Facial symmetry and judgements of apparent health: Support for a "good genes" explanation of the attractiveness-symmetry relationship. *Evolution and Human Behavior*, 22(6), 417–429. doi:10.1016/S1090-5138(01)00083-6

Jordan, J. (2004). The rhetorical limits of the "plastic body.". *The Quarterly Journal of Speech*, 90(3), 327–358. doi:10.1080/0033563042000255543

Jothilakshmi, P. K., Salvi, N. R., Hayden, B. E., & Bose-Haider, B. (2009). Labial reduction in adolescent population—A case series study. *Journal of Pediatric and Adolescent Gynecology*, 22(1), 53–55. doi:10.1016/j.jpag.2008.03.008 PMID:19241623

Jung, J., & Lee, Y.-J. (2009). Cross-cultural examination of women's fashion and beauty magazine advertisements in the United States and South Korea. *Clothing & Textiles Research Journal*, 27(4), 274–286. doi:10.1177/0887302X08327087

Kanazawa, S. (2011). Intelligence and physical attractiveness. *Intelligence*, 39(1), 7–14. doi:10.1016/j.intell.2010.11.003

Kanazawa, S., & Kovar, J. L. (2004). Why beautiful people are more intelligent. *Intelligence*, 32(3), 227–243. doi:10.1016/j.intell.2004.03.003

Kant, I. (1994). Grounding for the metaphysics of morals (J. W. Ellington, Trans.). In *Ethical philosophy: The complete texts of grounding for the metaphysics of morals and metaphysical principles of virtue (part II of the metaphysics of morals)* (pp. 1–69). Indianapolis, IN: Hackett.

Kellett, S., Clarke, S., & McGill, P. (2008). Outcomes from psychological assessment regarding recommendations for cosmetic surgery. *Journal of Plastic, Reconstructive & Aesthetic Surgery; JPRAS*, 61(5), 512–517. doi:10.1016/j.bjps.2007.08.025 PMID:18316256

Lane, H., & Bahan, B. (1998). Ethics of cochlear implantation in young children: A review and reply from a deaf-world perspective. *Otolaryngology - Head and Neck Surgery*, 119(4), 297–313. doi:10.1016/S0194-5998(98)70070-1 PMID:9781982

Lin, T. J. (2010). Evolution of cosmetics: Increased need for experimental clinical medicine. *Journal of Experimental and Clinical Medicine*, 2(2), 49–52. doi:10.1016/S1878-3317(10)60009-5

Lloréns, H. (2013). Latina bodies in the era of elective aesthetic surgery. *Latino Studies*, *11*(4), 547–569. doi:10.1057/lst.2013.32

Lorenzo, G. L., Biesanz, J. C., & Human, L. J. (2010). What is beautiful is good and more accurately understood: Physical attractiveness and accuracy in first impressions of personality. *Psychological Science*, *21*(12), 1777–1782. doi:10.1177/0956797610388048 PMID:21051521

Lunceford, B. (2008). The walk of shame: A normative description. *Etc.; a Review of General Semantics*, *65*(4), 319–329.

Lunceford, B. (2012). Posthuman visions: Creating the technologized body. *Explorations in Media Ecology*, *11*(1), 7–25. doi:10.1386/eme.11.1.7_1

Luo, W. (2013). Aching for the altered body: Beauty economy and Chinese women's consumption of cosmetic surgery. *Women's Studies International Forum*, *38*, 1–10. doi:10.1016/j.wsif.2013.01.013

Luppicini, R. (2009a). Technoethical inquiry: From technological systems to society. Global Media Journal — Canadian Edition, 2(1), 5-21.

Luppicini, R. (2009b). The emerging field of technoethics. In R. Luppicini & R. Adell (Eds.), *Handbook of research on technoethics* (pp. 1–19). Hershey, PA: Information Science Reference. doi:10.4018/978-1-60566-022-6.ch001

Maltby, J., & Day, L. (2011). Celebrity worship and incidence of elective cosmetic surgery: Evidence of a link among young adults. *The Journal of Adolescent Health*, *49*(5), 483–489. doi:10.1016/j.jadohealth.2010.12.014 PMID:22018562

Manning, J. T., Scutt, D., & Lewis-Jones, D. I. (1998). Developmental stability, ejaculate size, and sperm quality in men. *Evolution and Human Behavior*, *19*(5), 273–282. doi:10.1016/S1090-5138(98)00024-5

Martínez Lirola, M., & Chovanec, J. (2012). The dream of a perfect body come true: Multimodality in cosmetic surgery advertising. *Discourse & Society*, *23*(5), 487–507. doi:10.1177/0957926512452970

Meningaud, J.-P., Benadiba, L., Servant, J.-M., Herve, C., Bertrand, J.-C., & Pelicier, Y. (2003). Depression, anxiety and quality of life: Outcome 9 months after facial cosmetic surgery. *Journal of Cranio-Maxillo-Facial Surgery*, *31*(1), 46–50. doi:10.1016/S1010-5182(02)00159-2 PMID:12553927

Motaparthi, K. (2010). Blepharoplasty in Asian patients: Ethnic and ethical implications. *The Virtual Mentor*, *12*(12), 946–949. doi:10.1001/virtualmentor.2010.12.12.msoc1-1012 PMID:23186822

Nisbett, R. E., & Wilson, T. D. (1977). The halo effect: Evidence for unconscious alteration of judgments. *Journal of Personality and Social Psychology*, *35*(4), 250–256. doi:10.1037/0022-3514.35.4.250

Normal Breast Gallery. (2017). Retrieved from http://www.007b.com/breast_gallery.php

Peterson, V. V. (2011). *Sex, ethics, and communication*. San Diego, CA: Cognella.

Polonijo, A. N., & Carpiano, R. M. (2008). Representations of cosmetic surgery and emotional health in women's magazines in Canada. *Women's Health Issues*, *18*(6), 463–470. doi:10.1016/j.whi.2008.07.004 PMID:19041597

Rajabi, M. T., Makateb, A., Hashemi, H., Holland, E. J., Djalilian, A., & Nerad, J. A. (2015). Disaster in cosmetic surgery: Inadvertent formalin injection during blepharoplasty. *Ophthalmic Plastic and Reconstructive Surgery*, *31*(4), e86–e89. doi:10.1097/IOP.0000000000000110 PMID:26168210

Rawls, J. (1971). *A theory of justice*. Cambridge, MA: Belknap Press of Harvard University Press.

Reaves, S., Hitchon, J. B., Park, S.-Y., & Yun, G. W. (2004a). If looks could kill: Digital manipulation of fashion models. *Journal of Mass Media Ethics*, *19*(1), 56–71. doi:10.120715327728jmme1901_5

Reaves, S., Hitchon, J. B., Park, S.-Y., & Yun, G. W. (2004b). "You can never be too thin"—Or can you? A pilot study on the effects of digital manipulation of fashion models' body size, leg length and skin color. *Race, Gender, & Class*, *11*(2), 140–155.

Ruetzler, T., Taylor, J., Reynolds, D., Baker, W., & Killen, C. (2012). What is professional attire today? A conjoint analysis of personal presentation attributes. *International Journal of Hospitality Management*, *31*(3), 937–943. doi:10.1016/j.ijhm.2011.11.001

Sanchez Taylor, J. (2012). Fake breasts and power: Gender, class and cosmetic surgery. *Women's Studies International Forum*, *35*(6), 458–466. doi:10.1016/j.wsif.2012.09.003

Selimbegović, L., & Chatard, A. (2015). Single exposure to disclaimers on airbrushed thin ideal images increases negative thought accessibility. *Body Image*, *12*, 1–5. doi:10.1016/j.bodyim.2014.08.012 PMID:25260193

Sender, K. (Director). (2014). *Brand new you: Makeover television and the American dream* [DVD]. Northampton, MA: Media Education Foundation.

Shields, V. R., & Heinecken, D. (2001). *Measuring up: How advertising affects self-image*. Philadelphia, PA: University of Pennsylvania Press. doi:10.9783/9780812204025

Sider, R. C., & Clements, C. D. (1984). Patients' ethical obligation for their health. *Journal of Medical Ethics*, *10*(3), 138–142. doi:10.1136/jme.10.3.138 PMID:6502640

Singh, K. (2015). Cosmetic surgery in teenagers: To do or not to do. *Journal of Cutaneous and Aesthetic Surgery*, *8*(1), 57–59. doi:10.4103/0974-2077.155091 PMID:25949026

Slevec, J., & Tiggemann, M. (2010). Attitudes toward cosmetic surgery in middle-aged women: Body image, aging anxiety, and the media. *Psychology of Women Quarterly*, *34*(1), 65–74. doi:10.1111/j.1471-6402.2009.01542.x

Smirnova, M. H. (2012). A will to youth: The woman's anti-aging elixir. *Social Science & Medicine*, *75*(7), 1236–1243. doi:10.1016/j.socscimed.2012.02.061 PMID:22742924

Society of Professional Journalists. (1996). *Code of ethics*. Retrieved from http://www.spj.org/pdf/ethicscode.pdf

Ng, P. (2016). *Exclusive: Heidi Montag reflects on plastic surgery obsession: "I became consumed by this character I was playing."* Retrieved from http://www.etonline.com/tv/189526_heidi_montag_reflects_on_plastic_surgery_obsession/

Solvi, A. S., Foss, K., von Soest, T., Roald, H. E., Skolleborg, K. C., & Holte, A. (2010). Motivational factors and psychological processes in cosmetic breast augmentation surgery. *Journal of Plastic, Reconstructive & Aesthetic Surgery; JPRAS, 63*(4), 673–680. doi:10.1016/j.bjps.2009.01.024 PMID:19268646

Spilson, S. V., Chung, K. C., Greenfield, M. L. V. H., & Walters, M. (2002). Are plastic surgery advertisements conforming to the ethical codes of the American society of plastic surgeons? *Plastic and Reconstructive Surgery, 109*(3), 1181–1186. doi:10.1097/00006534-200203000-00063 PMID:11884856

Stewart, C. (2010a, February 14). Montag took wrong road with plastic surgeries. *Orange County Register,* p. K.

Stewart, C. (2010b, May 9). Heidi Montag plans more surgeries. *Orange County Register*, p. Arts K.

Stice, E., Spangler, D., & Agras, W. S. (2001). Exposure to media-portrayed thin-ideal images adversely affects vulnerable girls: A longitudinal experiment. *Journal of Social and Clinical Psychology, 20*(3), 270–288. doi:10.1521/jscp.20.3.270.22309

Sugiyama, L. S. (2004). Is beauty in the context-sensitive adaptations of the beholder? Shiwiar use of waist-to-hip ratio in assessments of female mate value. *Evolution and Human Behavior, 25*(1), 51–62. doi:10.1016/S1090-5138(03)00083-7

Swami, V. (2009). Body appreciation, media influence, and weight status predict consideration of cosmetic surgery among female undergraduates. *Body Image, 6*(4), 315–317. doi:10.1016/j.bodyim.2009.07.001 PMID:19656747

Swami, V., Campana, A. N. N. B., Ferreira, L., Barrett, S., Harris, A. S., & Tavares, M. C. G. C. F. (2011). The acceptance of cosmetic surgery scale: Initial examination of its factor structure and correlates among Brazilian adults. *Body Image, 8*(2), 179–185. PMID:21354875

Swami, V., Taylor, R., & Carvalho, C. (2009). Acceptance of cosmetic surgery and celebrity worship: Evidence of associations among female undergraduates. *Personality and Individual Differences, 47*(8), 869–872. doi:10.1016/j.paid.2009.07.006

The Great Wall of Vagina. (n.d.). *About the great wall of vagina*. Retrieved from http://www.greatwallof-vagina.co.uk/about

The Shape of a Mother. (2016). Retrieved from http://theshapeofamother.com/

Theran, S. A., Newberg, E. M., & Gleason, T. R. (2010). Adolescent girls' parasocial interactions with media figures. *The Journal of Genetic Psychology, 171*(3), 270–277. doi:10.1080/00221325.2010.483 700 PMID:20836434

Thornhill, R., & Gangestad, S. W. (1996). The evolution of human sexuality. *Trends in Ecology & Evolution, 11*(2), 98–102. doi:10.1016/0169-5347(96)81051-2 PMID:21237770

Tignol, J., Biraben-Gotzamanis, L., Martin-Guehl, C., Grabot, D., & Aouizerate, B. (2007). Body dysmorphic disorder and cosmetic surgery: Evolution of 24 subjects with a minimal defect in appearance 5 years after their request for cosmetic surgery. *European Psychiatry, 22*(8), 520–524. doi:10.1016/j.eurpsy.2007.05.003 PMID:17900876

Tylka, T. L., & Iannantuono, A. C. (2016). Perceiving beauty in all women: Psychometric evaluation of the Broad Conceptualization of Beauty Scale. *Body Image, 17*, 67-81. doi:j.bodyim.2016.02.005

Veale, D., Ellison, N., Werner, T. G., Dodhia, R., Serfaty, M. A., & Clarke, A. (2012). Development of a cosmetic procedure screening questionnaire (COPS) for body dysmorphic disorder. *Journal of Plastic, Reconstructive & Aesthetic Surgery; JPRAS, 65*(4), 530–532. doi:10.1016/j.bjps.2011.09.007 PMID:22000332

von Soest, T., Kvalem, I. L., Roald, H. E., & Skolleborg, K. C. (2009). The effects of cosmetic surgery on body image, self-esteem, and psychological problems. *Journal of Plastic, Reconstructive & Aesthetic Surgery; JPRAS, 62*(10), 1238–1244. doi:10.1016/j.bjps.2007.12.093 PMID:18595791

von Soest, T., Kvalem, I. L., Skolleborg, K. C., & Roald, H. E. (2009). Cosmetic surgery and the relationship between appearance satisfaction and extraversion: Testing a transactional model of personality. *Journal of Research in Personality, 43*(6), 1017–1025. doi:10.1016/j.jrp.2009.07.001

Ward, C. (2010, April 14). From the girl next door to freaky fake. And she's not done with the surgery yet; Exclusive fame-hungry Heidi Montag. *The Mirror (Stafford, Tex.)*, 24–25.

Wen, N. (2017). Celebrity influence and young people's attitudes toward cosmetic surgery in Singapore: The role of parasocial relationships and identification. *International Journal of Communication, 11*, 1234–1252.

Wiggins, J. S., Wiggins, N., & Conger, J. C. (1968). Correlates of heterosexual somatic preference. *Journal of Personality and Social Psychology, 10*(1), 82–90. doi:10.1037/h0026394 PMID:4386664

Wimalawansa, S. M., Fox, J. P., & Johnson, R. M. (2014). The measurable cost of complications for outpatient cosmetic surgery in patients with mental health diagnoses. *Aesthetic Surgery Journal, 34*(2), 306–316. doi:10.1177/1090820X13519100 PMID:24497616

Wolf, N. (1991). *The beauty myth: How images of beauty are used against women*. New York, W.: Morrow.

Zuckerman, D., & Abraham, A. (2008). Teenagers and cosmetic surgery: Focus on breast augmentation and liposuction. *The Journal of Adolescent Health, 43*(4), 318–324. doi:10.1016/j.jadohealth.2008.04.018 PMID:18809128

ADDITIONAL READING

Aquino, Y. S. J., & Steinkamp, N. (2016). Borrowed beauty? Understanding identity in Asian facial cosmetic surgery. *Medicine, Health Care, and Philosophy, 19*(3), 431–441. doi:10.100711019-016-9699-0 PMID:26983846

Atiyeh, B. S., Rubeiz, M. T., & Hayek, S. N. (2008). Aesthetic/cosmetic surgery and ethical challenges. *Aesthetic Plastic Surgery, 32*(6), 829–839. doi:10.100700266-008-9246-3 PMID:18820963

Blum, V. L. (2007). Objects of love: I want a famous face and the illusions of star culture. *Configurations, 15*(1), 33–53. doi:10.1353/con.0.0025

Braun, V. (2005). In search of (better) sexual pleasure: Female genital "cosmetic" surgery. *Sexualities*, *8*(4), 407–424. doi:10.1177/1363460705056625

Davis, K. (1995). *Reshaping the female body: The dilemma of cosmetic surgery*. New York: Routledge.

Davis, K. (2003). *Dubious equalities and embodied differences: Cultural studies on cosmetic surgery*. Lanham, MD: Rowman & Littlefield.

Devereaux, M. (2013). Is medical aesthetics really medical? In P. Z. Brand (Ed.), *Beauty unlimited* (pp. 175–191). Bloomington, IN: Indiana University Press.

Dobson, A. S., McDonald, K., Kirkman, M., Souter, K., & Fisher, J. (2017). Invisible labour? Tensions and ambiguities of modifying the "private" body: The case of female genital cosmetic surgery. In A. S. Elias, R. Gill, & C. Scharff (Eds.), *Aesthetic labour: Rethinking beauty politics in neoliberalism* (pp. 351–368). London: Palgrave. doi:10.1057/978-1-137-47765-1_20

Gilman, S. L. (1999). *Making the body beautiful: A cultural history of aesthetic surgery*. Princeton, NJ: Princeton University Press.

Griffiths, D., & Mullock, A. (2017). Cosmetic surgery: Regulatory challenges in a global beauty market. *Health Care Analysis*, 1–15. doi:10.100710728-017-0339-5 PMID:28247102

Hendrickse, J., Arpan, L. M., Clayton, R. B., & Ridgway, J. L. (2017). Instagram and college women's body image: Investigating the roles of appearance-related comparisons and intrasexual competition. *Computers in Human Behavior*, *74*, 92–100. doi:10.1016/j.chb.2017.04.027

Hyde, M. J. (2010). *Perfection: Coming to terms with being human*. Waco, TX: Baylor University Press.

Lunceford, B. (2014). The ethics of seeking body perfection, with continual reference to Heidi Montag. In S. J. Thompson (Ed.), *Global issues and ethical considerations in human enhancement technologies* (pp. 67–95). Hershey, PA: IGI-Global; doi:10.4018/978-1-4666-6010-6.ch005

Magon, N., & Alinsod, R. (2017). Female cosmetic genital surgery: Delivering what women want. *Journal of Obstetrics and Gynaecology of India*, *67*(1), 15–19. doi:10.100713224-016-0930-y PMID:28242962

Meningaud, J. P., Servant, J. M., Herve, C., & Bertrand, J. C. (2000). Ethics and aims of cosmetic surgery: A contribution from an analysis of claims after minor damage. *Medicine and Law*, *19*(2), 237–252. PMID:10994212

Mousavi, S. R. (2010). The ethics of aesthetic surgery. *Journal of Cutaneous and Aesthetic Surgery*, *3*(1), 38–40. doi:10.4103/0974-2077.63396 PMID:20606994

Oumeish, O. Y. (2001). The cultural and philosophical concepts of cosmetics in beauty and art through the medical history of mankind. *Clinics in Dermatology*, *19*(4), 375–386. doi:10.1016/S0738-081X(01)00194-8 PMID:11535377

Parker, L. S. (1993). Social justice, federal paternalism, and feminism: Breast implants in the cultural context of female beauty. *Kennedy Institute of Ethics Journal*, *3*(1), 57–76. doi:10.1353/ken.0.0158 PMID:11645225

Poster, M. (2007). Swan's way: Care of self in the hyperreal. *Configurations, 15*(2), 151–175. doi:10.1353/con.0.0029

Schermer, M. (2008). On the argument that enhancement is "cheating.". *Journal of Medical Ethics, 34*(2), 85–88. doi:10.1136/jme.2006.019646 PMID:18234944

Sheldon, S., & Wilkinson, S. (1998). Female genital mutilation and cosmetic surgery: Regulating non-therapeutic body modification. *Bioethics, 12*(4), 263–285. doi:10.1111/1467-8519.00117 PMID:11657294

Slevin, K. F. (2010). "If I had lots of money... I'd have a body makeover": Managing the aging body. *Social Forces, 88*(3), 1003–1020. doi:10.1353of.0.0302

Sterodimas, A., Radwanski, H. N., & Pitanguy, I. (2011). Ethical issues in plastic and reconstructive surgery. *Aesthetic Plastic Surgery, 35*(2), 262–267. doi:10.100700266-011-9674-3 PMID:21336881

Testa, G., Carlisle, E., Simmerling, M., & Angelos, P. (2012). Living donation and cosmetic surgery: A double standard in medical ethics? *The Journal of Clinical Ethics, 23*(2), 110–117. PMID:22822698

Wijsbek, H. (2000). The pursuit of beauty: The enforcement of aesthetics or a freely adopted lifestyle? *Journal of Medical Ethics, 26*(6), 454–458. doi:10.1136/jme.26.6.454 PMID:11129847

Yurteri-Kaplan, L. A., Antosh, D. D., Sokol, A. I., Park, A. J., Gutman, R. E., Kingsberg, S. A., & Iglesia, C. B. (2012). Interest in cosmetic vulvar surgery and perception of vulvar appearance. *American Journal of Obstetrics and Gynecology, 207*(5), 428. e421-428. e427. doi:10.1016/j.ajog.2012.06.056

Zylinska, J. (2007). Of swans and ugly ducklings: Bioethics between humans, animals, and machines. *Configurations, 15*(2), 125–150. doi:10.1353/con.0.0028

KEY TERMS AND DEFINITIONS

Autonomy: The right to make decisions and act for oneself, free from coercion.

Beauty: Beauty is culturally bound and differs among groups. The only standards of beauty that seem to transcend culture are features that signal good health, such as symmetry of features.

Beneficence: Working on behalf of the best interests and wellbeing of the patient.

Cosmetic Surgery: Cosmetic surgery is done solely for aesthetic reasons on otherwise healthy, functioning body parts. Common examples include breast implants and rhinoplasty.

Justice: Balancing benefits, risks, and costs fairly.

Medical Ethics: The field of study that examines values and morals in medical practice and prescribes norms of right and wrong conduct. Some questions that medical ethicists grapple with include doctor-assisted suicide, end-of-life care, care for those who are incapacitated or otherwise unable to make decisions for themselves, and medical business and advertising practices.

Nonmaleficence: Avoiding harm whenever possible. This can be best summed up by the common axiom mistakenly ascribed to the Hippocratic Oath: "do no harm."

Chapter 12
Socio–Ethical Impact of the Emerging Smart Technologies

Octavian M. Machidon
Transilvania University of Brasov, Romania

ABSTRACT

Today, technology is being integrated in all social environments, at home, school, or work, shaping a new world in which there is a closer interaction between human and machine than ever before. While every new technology brings along the expected "blessings," there is also the thick end of the stick, namely the potential undesired effects it might cause. Explorative research in smart and enhancing technologies reveals that the current trend is for them to transcend to persuasive technologies, capable of shaping human behavior. In this context, this chapter aims at identifying the social and ethical implications of such technologies, being elaborated after reviewing literature from various research domains. It addresses the implications of today's smart and enhancing technologies on several levels: health repercussions, the social and behavioral changes they generate, and concerns of privacy and security. Also, the chapter emphasizes the need for scientists and researchers to engage not only with the technical considerations, but also with the societal implications mentioned above.

INTRODUCTION

In today's society "smart" things are in the center of attention: smartphones, smart grids, smart meters, smart cars, smart homes, smart cities, and so on, are just a few examples of (until yesterday) ordinary devices and technologies that turned "smart" in the past decade, becoming connected to the Internet, more attractive to customers, and also more pervasive with regard to the user's everyday life. Smart technologies are gaining more and more presence in the user's everyday life; they even enter highly sensitive environments, such as the home. This leads to the emergence of specific ethical issues concerning these new smart socio-technical systems.

Being based on the concept of ambient intelligence (which describes electronic environments that are sensitive and responsive to the presence of people), smart devices are developed by integrating microprocessors and sensors into ordinary objects, making them able to respond to the environment and interact

DOI: 10.4018/978-1-5225-5094-5.ch012

with humans and other smart objects. Today's technology makes it possible for computers to surround and serve humans in every-day life by working non-intrusively in the background. This is referred to as "ubiquitous computing", a concept that has long been foreseen by scientists and researchers (Weiser, 1993). Ubiquitous computing is a method of achieving the most efficient technology that interacts with and surrounds its users while remaining effectively invisible to them. Research in ubiquitous computing has focused on three main topics: natural interfaces (a diversity of communication capabilities between humans and machines), context-aware applications (the application's capability to adapt its behavior based on information from the physical and computational environment), and automated capture and access (for recording and rendering live experiences) (Abowd & Mynatt, 2000). The European Union 1999 IST Programme Advisory Group (ISTAG) vision statement for Framework Programme 5 describes a scenario where "people will be surrounded by intelligent and intuitive interfaces embedded in everyday objects around us and an environment recognizing and responding to the presence of individuals in an invisible way" (Ahola, 2001). This 1999 vision has become today's reality.

A common feature of all smart technologies and devices is the focus on existential experience, the capability of a particular item to provide situation and context-aware services to the users in real time. For example, a smartphone weather application knows how to update the weather forecast based on the user's location (location-awareness). A smart car navigation system can adapt its route based on real-time traffic and weather analysis. A smart grid provides real-time detection and understanding of conditions in order to get a timely response in emergency situations. All these smart products and services are being designed to co-exist in the emerging global Internet-based information architecture named the "Internet of Things" (IoT). The IoT is considered as the ideal backbone for ubiquitous computing by enabling objects to be easily identifiable in smart environments, easing the retrieval of information from the Internet, thus facilitating their adaptive functionality (Fabian, 2008). IoT enables ordinary objects to communicate and interact, therefore becoming smart and providing smart services.

The research presented in this chapter pertains to the field of technoethics. This is an interdisciplinary field that emerged in the 1970's highlighting the moral and social responsibilities that engineers and technologists have for the outcomes of the technological progress and development (Bunge, 1977). Such an approach makes perfect sense given that technology cannot be viewed as a segregated part of society, but a complex, integrated component that influences life on a variety of levels.

Technoethics is defined as an interdisciplinary field concerned with all ethical aspects of technology within a society shaped by technology (Luppicini, 2009). Given the variety and heterogeneity of technologies, and the multitude of fields where they are being used, technoethics brings on the mandatory inter-disciplinary approach needed in order to properly deal with the all the technological processes embedded within all the spheres of life.

This chapter aims, using a technoethical perspective, to identify the specific ethical challenges and concerns that have been raised by the emergence of new smart technologies and to provide specific ideas on how to properly address them in order to benefit safely from the advantages and strongpoints of these technologies, while limiting the potential unintended consequences.

Smart Technology - Smart Users?

The smart devices of today are tending to become extensions of the human brain. Latest generation smartphones offer a variety of features and functions that perform tasks which were normally done by the user's brain. For example, now the user doesn't have to remember important facts, because he can always tap into Google and the search engine offers him within seconds the answer he was looking for. Memory is thus one of the first functions of the brain that can be affected by the usage of smart devices.

The voice of the critics that yearn for a less technical age is getting louder, being amplified by studies that show how the offloading of mental functions to smart electronic devices could cause the brain to become less focused and less reliable. A 2010 study by McGill University researchers reports that depending on GPS to navigate may have a negative effect on the brain function, and especially on the hippocampus (the part involved in memory and navigation process). The study also states that participants who relied on their own to get around had better spatial memory, and a greater hippocampus volume than those using GPS navigation (Konishi & Bohbot, 2010).

One can apply the same judgment to smartphones. By storing phone numbers, appointments, context and location-based information, it gives the user's memory one less important exercise to work on. What was before accomplished using the brain's neurons has now been taken over by technology. So the problem is not with technology itself; the problem comes when a device takes over a function that the human brain was perfectly capable of performing on its own.

An important subject that is of great interest to researchers worldwide is the use of technology in the classroom. It was assumed that technological advances may help students learn better. This includes the use of laptops, tablets and smartphones by students while in class. However, despite this good intent, there seems to be troubling unintended consequences with many of these devices when used in the process of learning. Smart devices are ideally supposed to be used during class for taking notes or accessing useful academic information on the Internet, however students tend to multitask and use the social media, surf the web, chat, or email. Having all these temptations at hand makes it hard to resist. The sad outcome is that by doing two things or more at once, students are not able to fully attend to any of them. In the United States, where technology has been present in the classrooms for several years now, more and more voices of academics are asking for it to be banned.

Recent research has identified serious consequences that the use of technology in class has on the students, the level of laptop use being negatively related to the understanding of course material and overall course performance (Fried, 2008). However, there are also many educational advantages: being used wisely, the laptop can facilitate active learning and problem solving by providing a hands-on approach (Barak et al., 2006). A balanced approach is necessary in order to benefit from the advantages that a laptop or other technological device can provide while reducing the negative impacts generated by inappropriate use that disturb the learning process. Faculty should control and limit the use of technology, allowing it only in classes where it is integrated into the course and needed for specific practical applications.

Technology is not distractive only for students. The effects that the introduction of new communication technologies in workplaces has produced with regard to the workers' concentration level have been the subject of several recent studies (Rennecker & Godwin, 2003; Cameron & Webster, 2005). Productivity is directly influenced by the ability of the worker to stay focused and uninterrupted in a quiet work environment. Research has revealed that with the introduction of new technology the sources of interruption have increased, and also that the main sources today for such interruptions at the workplace are the new communication technologies like e-mail and instant messaging (Röcker, 2010). As they are more attractive and are offering a diverse set of applications and services, smart devices have led to an increase in unwanted interruptions (Cameron & Webster, 2005). Employers might have to carefully control or limit the use of such devices and technologies (like instant messaging, smartphones or tablets) at the workplace in order to maintain an efficient and quiet working environment in cases where productivity or the relationships between coworkers are suffering from technology misuse.

The newly introduced smart technologies are very popular and attractive because they offer high quality sensorial stimulation (high definition video/audio), context and location-aware feedback and the "secure" feeling that everything is under control, anything the user needs to know is only a click away. While these technologies are getting smarter, concerns arise with regard to their effect on the mental capabilities of the user. By offloading cognitive functions that the brain was previously performing to such smart devices, there is the risk of a decrease in the reliability and responsiveness of the brain. Particularly in the case of children, intensive exposure to such devices and technologies might interfere with their development of social skills and intelligence, and with their overall psychological and emotional stability (Healy, 2011).

One of the strongpoints that smart technology is being credited to have is related to helping people perform their activities and improve their lifestyle. For example, Smart Home technology is aimed at enhancing independent living by providing support for aging in place through the facilitation of tasks like cooking, cleaning and health monitoring. However, studies about the acceptance and effects of Smart Home technology on elders have shown that it does not deliver on the promise of sustaining independent living (Peek, 2015), since it is not, so far, tuned to needs, preferences and specific of older people.

Given the concerns stated by various research studies, like the ones mentioned above, a deeper understanding of the effects that smart technology has on its users is needed. It is also clear that such a technology brings a lot of assets and has a great potential if used wisely. Further research should focus on identifying the areas and situations that can benefit from using this type of devices, while underscoring control and limitation measures which can be applied to reduce the negative impacts mentioned above. The users and potential beneficiaries of smart technologies, whether students, employees or parents, should be informed on how to properly make use of such smart devices so that they can maximize the benefits and avoid unwanted consequences.

Health Risks

Another implication of the development of smart devices and technologies is the effect of radiation, since all electrical devices that communicate with each other or the Internet are mainly wireless. As these gadgets are wearable computers, they increase the electromagnetic exposure, the distance between the device and the body influencing intensity. Also, these devices will have a part of their equipment permanently powered on and communicating, in order to maintain their functionality. This will cause a constant exposure to radiation over a long period of time, and on a daily basis – whether at home, in the car, at work or shopping - which affects everyone, both users and non-users of these technologies.

To this date, the way electromagnetic radiation affects physical health is still a subject open to debate for scientists. Several studies were conducted, and many voices point out the potential health hazards that EM (Electromagnetic) radiation could cause in the case of intensive exposure; this environmental effect might have an important impact on the smart object users' lives (Hardell & Sage, 2008; Khurana et al., 2010). There are also concerns about the possibility that RF (Radio frequency) field exposure from cellphones could affect people's health (Blackman, 2009). The World Health Organization (WHO) is conducting an ongoing project named "The International EMF Project" that has been established in order to assess health and environmental effects of exposure to static and time varying electromagnetic fields. In the past decade, the world has known a huge growth in mobile telecommunications, and according to an ITU (International Telecommunication Union) 2013 study there are 6.8 billion mobile-cellular subscriptions worldwide (ITU, 2013). The results of studies of mobile phone risks to human health have been brought to public attention, but many have been criticized due to reported methodological difficulties. However, there are several studies that point out specific hazards that mobile phone radiation causes to different tissues or biological functions (Repacholi, 2001; Khurana et al., 2009; Lönn et al., 2004). While not enough to provide an exhaustive analysis of the subject, these studies should be a strong motivation for deeper research.

A recent and interesting case of a wearable smart device with potential implications on the user's health is the announced Google smart contact lens, which was designed to help people suffering from diabetes monitor their sugar level (Tsukayama, 2014). The device, currently under test, is a soft contact lens integrating a sensor for measuring the glucose level in tears. It also contains a miniature antenna and controller for a wireless transfer of the information gathered by the lens to a device – a computer or monitor – so that the data can be read. Though credited as being of great help to people suffering from diabetes, this device raises important issues regarding the exposure to wireless radiation, since the lens is in permanent contact with the eye and situated in such close proximity to the brain. Extensive medical research is needed for analyzing the implications of the radiation levels for these parts of the body before such a device becomes available, in order to have guarantees that the device can help improve the person's health condition and not worsen it.

There is also research bringing up health issues regarding the Smart City model, where the author argue that adopting such a smart urban model would cause a detachment from places that offer direct access to natural environments, thus diminishing the health benefits of such natural exposure, like: coping with stress, lowering depression, and improving overall mental and physical health (Colding, 2017). Also, this work underlines the existence of a gap, or lack of proper research and debates on dealing with issues about social sustainability in smart cities, including health related aspects with regard to how can digital technologies be integrated so that they can enhance the time spent outdoors.

Due to the potential health hazards identified by the research cited above, extensive further research is needed for a complete and objective evaluation of the health and environmental effects of EM and RF radiation, especially given the current technological trends and the speed of pervasive computing devices in penetrating public and private spaces. Already in many countries "electromagnetic hypersensitivity" has become a social issue, with many people claiming to have medical problems due to exposure to nearby electronic devices. Even though it is still weakly defined and not a recognized medical condition due to its variety of symptoms and health reactions, it is being considered by the WHO as an existing issue that affects many people around the world that are more sensitive to EM fields than others (Leitgeb, 2009). As the public and private spaces become more and more embedded with computing devices and wireless networks, all the parties involved (government agencies, employers, electric companies, electronic device manufacturers and network providers) should provide detailed information on EMF radiation in such spaces in order to properly inform the general population on the exposure to such fields, and should also work on optimizing the environmental factor, taking into consideration the implications of these technologies for human health.

Social Perspective

The smart technology, regardless of its particular implementation, has become a part of the users' social life, being considered as an enhancement of everyday life. This raises a series of questions about the social and behavioral consequences, as well as issues with regard to the privacy and security of the people using such technologies (Nixon et al., 2004).

While it has become one of the most powerful forces in our lives today, one cannot predict how the technology and most of all the innovations regarding it will impact the society and the individual. Many people cannot conceive modern life without computers or technology. More and more every-day objects are turning "smart", being equipped with ambient-intelligence technology, which leads to an increase in the degree of dependency on these devices. Today one can still choose whether or not to rely on a technological device, but given the current trend, the future is seen as predictably a world full of smart objects, where escaping from this technological dependence might not be possible. Such a high dependence on technology could lead to a transfer of control from the individual user to the respective technological device with regard to a specific task or function (Coroama et al., 2004); it also poses the risk that eventual system failures could lead the user to a perceived feeling of helplessness if relying too heavily on smart technology for everyday tasks (Mattern, 2005). A relevant example is the 1987 crash of the stock markets worldwide (also known as "Black Monday") due to malfunctions in the automated program trading – a mechanism that started to be used on Wall Street to make trade easier when computers became highly available, and in which human decision-making is taken out of the equation, buy or sell orders being generated automatically (Bozzo, 2007).

The "computerization" of the world actually re-shapes many of its attributes, changing the social actions and creating new types of interaction between people. The analysis of the unintended consequences of this evolving technology is very relevant for the influence of the Internet and other technological breakthroughs on peoples' lives. Speed and complexity describe the 21st century society, and the technological progress has moved too fast to have been able to cogently consider what impact one innovation or another might have, before they were introduced. However, more recently the evolution has been more incremental (Karlgaard, 2011; Hilbert & Lopez, 2011) and questions have been raised on what technology has brought to peoples' lives.

Smart technology has transcended from small, embedded or wearable devices (e.g. smart watch) to "smart" infrastructures of great complexity and size, like the smart grid and smart cities, which incorporate networks of sensors, actuators, communication devices and so on. Such complex, emergent technologies are being credited not only to have the potential to bring tangible benefits in the way people perform their work or home-related activities, but also to be able to influence people's attitudes and support behavior change, thus becoming persuasive technologies for solving societal challenges (Kulyk, 2016). This concept of persuasive technology however is not without its critics, since it could become an instrument for modelling the society on ideological or behavioral levels in a subliminal manner (Barral, 2014).

In the case of smart cities, the social impact is even more observable and is acknowledged unanimously by researchers in this field, since smart city governance is not mainly a technological issue, but a complex process of institutional change implying appealing visions of socio-technical governance that have a rather political nature, as underlined in a recent review on this topic (Meijer, 2015). The same article argues that smart city governance is about crafting new forms of human collaboration through the use of ICTs to obtain better outcomes and more open governance processes, which basically means that implementing smart city features is not merely a technological process running in the background, but a complex transformation in the people's social life and in the society as a whole.

In a 2012 study, researchers at Tel-Aviv University (TAU) examined how smartphones have impacted the social behavior of their users. They have found that smartphone users changed their behavior with regard to the phone use in public spaces, being 50 percent less likely than regular cell phone users to be bothered by others using their phone and 20 percent less likely to believe that their private phone conversations were irritating to those around them. Also, the study showed that smartphone users were more "attached" to their devices, feeling lost or tense without their phones, while the regular phone users claimed to be feeling free or quiet (Hatuka & Toch, 2012).

Given the fact that enhanced proactivity is one of the capabilities of smart devices (due to their context-awareness) one of the directions of research is using these technologies to assist elderly people and special groups (small children, people with various disabilities). Nevertheless, this target group confronts both developers and policy makers with a series of sensitive issues and challenges because such technologies may also have opposite effects. They could potentially increase isolation and decrease social interaction since family members or caregivers are no longer needed to be in direct contact with the respective person; they also tend to limit the autonomy of the patient, who becomes more tied to his home and potentially deprived of the community and interactions with places such as assisted living facilities (Kaplan & Litewka, 2008).

For example, monitoring blood pressure and heart rate, performing an ECG (electrocardiography) or measuring oxygen saturation can be performed remotely with such technologies, while the elderly patient is in his home, by devices linked to a central system that sends the measurements to a hospital. Despite improving the patient monitoring process, such a scenario deprives the patient of interaction with another person – a nurse for example, who could drop by to see how he is feeling and monitor his health condition.

All these issues, together with others that regard infringement on personal dignity due to invasive surveillance and lack of privacy make the use of enhanced proactive technologies for assisting special groups a sensitive matter still open for debates (Mäyrä & Vadén, 2013). The design process of such enhanced proactive systems should take into consideration social, psychological and physiological aspects, and should have an integrated approach, leading to a strengthening of human relations and interactions while protecting personal dignity and privacy.

Privacy and Security

The privacy issue is specific to all types of smart technologies, since in order to offer context-aware services, they need to collect personal information. From the tasks and functions performed by the smart devices, one can easily determine personal behavior patterns of the user. Also, because of the location-aware feature of most smart gadgets, the user can be tracked and localized in real time. The presence of smart things in the environment creates an invisible surveillance network with serious implications for public and private life, which leads critics to view this "transformation of the surroundings into responsive artifacts and surveillable objects" as "an attempt at a violent penetration of everyday life" (Araya, 1995). Being embedded into the users' surroundings, the activity of smart devices of scanning and storing data can go unnoticed by the persons concerned.

The smartphone, one of the most popular smart devices, stores information about almost everything the user does. Some of it is transmitted to the service provider (incoming/outgoing calls, text messages, how often the user checks his e-mail or browses the Internet, and his location), other is just stored in the device's memory (photos, videos, contacts, passwords, financial information etc...). Also, the smartphone can continuously track the user's location and keep a detailed profile of his current and recent whereabouts. There are also applications and services that while running in the background, collect and transmit data on the Internet. With the smartphone, the distinction between offline and online is no longer possible, as the device is permanently connected. This is a big change compared to the classic systems that people were used to, which collected and exchanged data only during the time the person was using them.

In the same TAU 2012 study, researchers state that smartphone users change their concept of privacy in public spaces; these users are 70 percent more likely than regular cellphone users to believe their phones offer a high degree of privacy, and are more willing to reveal private information while in public spaces. The researchers also show that smartphones create the illusion of a "private bubble" around their users, so that even if they use their smartphone while in public meeting spaces – like parks, city squares, transportation – the users are more caught up in their technology-based communication than their immediate surroundings (Hatuka & Toch, 2012). The smartphone is able to connect its user through the Internet to other people, having a range of features from live video-calls, interactive multiplayer games, and so on. Therefore, the smartphone turn into a "gateway" to another world, either virtual or real, and its user becomes a person that, while physically in a specific location, is simultaneously immersed into other activities – reading a book, chatting, checking the map or the Internet, thus having his attention and psychosomatic functions split between two parallel levels of existence. This explains the "private bubble" effect and also poses high risks for both the smartphone user and the people around him, since it could lead to accidents or other undesirable problems due to diminishing the user's attention and focus on his immediate surroundings.

Another emerging "smart" system that has the potential to intrude into the users' private life is the smart grid. This is a modernized electricity network that uses an intelligent monitoring system to track all electricity flow, integrate alternative sources of electricity (green power), to reduce cost, save energy and increase transparency. Every consumer is monitored by a smart meter that identifies consumption in detail and communicates the information via a network to the central node for monitoring and billing. This new power grid is being promoted and implemented by many governments; its implementation is also a priority in the EU's energy policy plan for the next decade (Giglioli et al., 2010).

Despite of its advantages, the smart grid is being questioned because of its potential to undermine users' privacy, and also because having such a complex architecture and offering remote access to the home power networks of millions of users, any security flaw could be very dangerous (Hadley et al., 2010). By turning "smart", the power grid will increase the amount of personal information available about the users. Infrastructure components together with the consumer devices will acquire data and send it on the network. The new smart meters will provide measurements of the energy use not only at the end of the billing period, but at much shorter intervals, as short as every few minutes.

These periodic readings can offer intimate details about what's going on inside the home: the approximate number of people living there, when they are present, when they are awake or asleep. Also, taking into consideration the fact that the energy fluctuations of many home appliances are somewhat unique, the readings could also reveal what type of appliance was on at a certain moment of the day, and maybe even its make and model (Quinn, 2009). Thus, such a detailed power usage data collection could lead to a potential abusive surveillance. Recent research has proved the ability of extracting even more detailed information from the energy consumption readings, such as the TV channel that is on at a certain moment (Greveler et al., 2012). Since the identifiable information gathered by the smart meters is enough to provide such a detailed perspective of one's intimate life inside his home, special care should be taken by legislators and researchers in charge with implementing the smart grid. A solution needs to be reached that offers household and industrial consumers strong guarantees regarding their privacy. This requires a clear distinction between data needed for billing purposes, which can be collected at a low frequency (once or twice a month) and needs to be linked to a particular individual, and high frequency data (collected every few minutes) that should be anonymized, thus protecting the individual's privacy while maintaining the grid's functionality.

Another concept that has been the subject of many publications and conferences in recent years is the smart Home. This is a house or other living environment that embeds technology for allowing devices and systems to be controlled automatically. Such a home can thus automatically adjust the temperature, level of security and other features by operating a Home Area Network (HAN) than connects the various home devices and communicates with the outside world over the Internet (Networking, 2002). It is considered that this enhancement will allow isolated and passive units like ordinary houses or office buildings to achieve an improved energy-efficiency level, and with this stated goal there is an increasing number of such projects under way, many of them being funded by the European Union's Seventh Framework Programme (EU FP7) (Karnouskos et al., 2011).

An important step in the design and implementation of smart Homes is the development of smart appliances. These are interconnected by means of machine-to-machine (M2M) communications, a concept describing various network protocols that enable connecting and remote-controlling machines with low-cost, scalable and reliable technologies (Niyato et al., 2011); this makes home appliances accessible and controllable through the Internet. They also take advantage of the smart grid's bidirectional communication interface and send detailed individual power usage information to a central data office where it is accessible to the utility provider or the user.

According to a 2013 Research and Markets report (Research and Markets, 2013), the leading vendors of the household appliances market like Whirlpool, Electrolux, Samsung and LG are increasing R&D (research and development) investments in the design and development of smart appliances. The same report states that the mentioned vendors consider this market to have huge potential, with its main driver being the increasing need for power-efficient appliances. However, the cost of smart appliances is still higher than that of their classical counterparts. Even so, according to the same report, analysts have forecasted the smart appliances market to grow at a CAGR (Compounded Annual Growth Rate) of 11.9 percent over the period 2012-2016.

Having in the intimacy of one's home various interconnected sensors and smart devices raises further issues regarding the risks of privacy breaches. Such a scenario changes the way personal data is collected – not by filling a form or taking part in a survey, but while cooking, sleeping or doing ordinary household activities. The information collected in this way can be exposed over a public network and other people can have access to it. Even if the personal data gathered by one smart device might look harmless at a first glance, combined with other information gathered by other devices it might lead to the creation of a digital copy of one's life (Korff, 2013).

Having in the smart Home a network of inter-connected sensors that can record the behavior of the inhabitants, and given the existing smart algorithms for analyzing and interpreting sensor data, the stage is set for influencing the behavior and attitude of people through technology (Strum, 2016). While it is true that such an instrument would be extremely useful for things like encouraging healthy behavior, supporting independent living, or reducing healthcare costs, the issue remains on an ethical level: can one trust the persuasive technology in his home, to which he is exposed every day, to subliminally alter his behavior or attitudes?

With such an increased attention from the major worldwide vendors, R&D in smart appliances should take into consideration security and privacy aspects, since it is much easier to ensure high privacy and security levels for systems in the design and development stages, than to have to deal with these sensitive and important issues afterwards, when resolving them could prove to be a greater engineering challenge.

The available studies analyzing the social reception of the smart home technology have emphasized that despite the highly-marketed afore-mentioned strongpoints of such a smart, integrated transformation of one's home, the strongest feature of public discussion on this topic proved to be related to deep, moral concerns specific to human nature, inequality and trust. At the same time, the solutions to issues like reliability and security, which were also brought up, seemed to have been agreed upon by both public and experts (Balta-Ozkan, 2013). Researchers also found a direct link between the success and performance of a technology as the smart grid, and the acceptance degree of the end users towards such a technology, and solutions for increasing this acceptance rate are more and more being considered to be not of technological nature, but ones that are able to change human values or ideas of morality about the usage of electrical energy (Ponce, 2016).

In trying to protect personal data when dealing with the issues described above, both legal and technological approaches are necessary in order to develop "smarter" privacy and security mechanisms. Lawmakers must enact special laws regarding data protection that should stipulate clearly what types of information can and cannot be collected and sent by electronic devices with regard to user privacy, and what type of data is considered personal. Also, manufacturers and utility/network providers should be required to explicitly mention if the specific device/service collects personal data, what type and in what amount so that the users are informed about potential privacy risks. Last but not least, bioethics must be considered as a crucial partner to smart-home engineering (Birchley, 2016).

Alongside the legal protection, the smart devices and services mentioned above should adapt and implement privacy-enhancing technologies (PET), an approach to protecting personal data conceived by engineers and supported by privacy activists (Korff, 2013) that involves data anonymization and identity management among other privacy protection mechanisms. Such a joint effort uniting lawmakers, researchers and engineers is needed in order to properly deal with the privacy threats raised by these new enhanced proactive technologies.

CONCLUSION

In today's world, technology has entered all the environments, whether public or private, bringing along a series of challenges derived from the close bond that has been established between these new devices and the people using them or being near them.

Being "smart", and thus offering context-aware feedback, and a multitude of functions meant to ease the owner's life, these devices raise concerns due to the risk of over-relying on technology at the expense of using the natural cognitive functions as before.

Smart devices tend to become items of wearable computing, they raise important issues regarding the exposure to electromagnetic and radiofrequency radiation; non-users are also affected, since almost every public or private space is technologized, and devices communicate with one another or the Internet through wireless networks.

Also, the constant information flow (containing personal data regarding location, decisions, contacts, preferences) from such devices towards the operators or the Internet (social networks) makes the privacy and the security of the users more vulnerable than ever before.

As shown in this chapter, such technologies, together with their many assets and potential applications, have ethical and societal implications in various domains and this means that future research in this direction must have a broadened perspective, with various sources of information, an interdisciplinary view and, most of all, a preemptive approach. Future research on any new smart technology should try to find out how and to what degree that particular technology changes and affects the user. Since the technology is getting smarter, the privacy and security mechanisms that protect the users and non-users of these technologies must also adapt and become smart, in order to cope with the newly emerged challenges. Both legal and technical actions should be taken in order to properly regulate the use of the newly enhanced proactive systems and services.

Acceptance studies on smart technologies have shown that these tend to fail in delivering their promises to all age groups, being much more accessible to young people than to the elderly. Lately smart technologies have also become persuasive, which raises an important ethical subject open for debate – how to trust technologies operating in the background around you that can seamlessly influence your behavior and social habits? There is also the question of biosociotechnical sustainability of large, complex technologies, like smart cities, where the impact assessment is not only technical, but implies analyzing how people's social life, and society as a whole, will be shaped by the transition from ordinary to smart urban environments

A major challenge for the future is coping with the dynamic behavior of these technologies; the design and release of new smart devices and services are happening constantly and at a very high rate, thus generating new concerns in many directions. Future research should be proactive, taking into consideration all these implications while showing flexibility and creativity in order to anticipate the challenges and issues of these technologies and prevent potential dangerous consequences before they can occur.

Today, in our society it has become a cliché to state that smart technologies have social implications. This chapter has underlined many of the issues derived from the introduction of such technologies in all social public and private environments. Therefore, it should be expected for this state of things to lead to raising the awareness of social scientists with regard to the social implications of these technologies, in order for the unintended harms to be eliminated and the benefits to be guaranteed.

REFERENCES

Abowd, G. D., & Mynatt, E. D. (2000). Charting past, present, and future research in ubiquitous computing. *ACM Transactions on Computer-Human Interaction*, 7(1), 29–58. doi:10.1145/344949.344988

Ahola, J., (2001). Ambient Intelligence. *ERCIM News*, 47.

Araya, A. A. (1995). Questioning ubiquitous computing. In *Proceedings of the 1995 ACM 23rd annual conference on Computer science* (pp. 230-237). ACM.

Balta-Ozkan, N., Davidson, R., Bicket, M., & Whitmarsh, L. (2013). Social barriers to the adoption of smart homes. *Energy Policy*, 63, 363–374. doi:10.1016/j.enpol.2013.08.043

Barak, M., Lipson, A., & Lerman, S. (2006). Wireless Laptops as Means For Promoting Active Learning In Large Lecture Halls. *Journal of Research on Technology in Education*, 38(3), 245–263. doi:10.1080/15391523.2006.10782459

Barral, O., Aranyi, G., Kouider, S., Lindsay, A., Prins, H., Ahmed, I., ... Cavazza, M. (2014, May). Covert persuasive technologies: bringing subliminal cues to human-computer interaction. In *International Conference on Persuasive Technology* (pp. 1-12). Springer. 10.1007/978-3-319-07127-5_1

Birchley, G., Huxtable, R., Murtagh, M., ter Meulen, R., Flach, P., & Gooberman-Hill, R. (2017). Smart homes, private homes? An empirical study of technology researchers' perceptions of ethical issues in developing smart-home health technologies. *BMC Medical Ethics*, *18*(1), 23. doi:10.118612910-017-0183-z PMID:28376811

Blackman, C. (2009). Cell phone radiation: Evidence from ELF and RF studies supporting more inclusive risk identification and assessment. *Pathophysiology*, *16*(2), 205–216. doi:10.1016/j.pathophys.2009.02.001 PMID:19264460

Bozzo, A. (2007). Players Replay the Crash. *CNBC*. Retrieved February 18, 2014, from http://www.cnbc.com/id/21136884

Bunge, M. (1977). Towards a technoethics. *The Monist*, *60*(1), 96–107. doi:10.5840/monist197760134

Cameron, A. F., & Webster, J. (2005). Unintended consequences of emerging communication technologies: Instant messaging in the workplace. *Computers in Human Behavior*, *21*(1), 85–103. doi:10.1016/j.chb.2003.12.001

Colding, J., & Barthel, S. (2017). An urban ecology critique on the "Smart City" model. *Journal of Cleaner Production*, *164*, 95–101. doi:10.1016/j.jclepro.2017.06.191

Coroama, V., Bohn, J., & Mattern, F. (2004, October). Living in a smart environment - implications for the coming ubiquitous information society. In *Proceedings of the 2004 IEEE International Conference on Systems, Man and Cybernetics* (Vol. 6, pp. 5633-5638). IEEE.

Fabian, B. (2008). *Secure name services for the Internet of Things* (Unpublished doctoral dissertation). Humboldt-Universität zu Berlin, Wirtschaftswissenschaftliche Fakultät.

Fried, C. B. (2008). In-class laptop use and its effects on student learning. *Computers & Education*, *50*(3), 906–914. doi:10.1016/j.compedu.2006.09.006

Giglioli, E., Panzacchi, C., & Senni, L. (2010). *How Europe is approaching the smart grid*. McKinsey on Smart Grid report, McKinsey & Company. Retrieved November 13, 2014, from http://www.mckinsey.com/client_service/electric_power_and_natural_gas/latest_thinking/mckinsey_on_smart_grid

Greveler, U., Justus, B., & Loehr, D. (2012). *Multimedia content identification through smart meter power usage profiles*. Computers, Privacy and Data Protection.

Hadley, M., Lu, N., & Deborah, A. (2010). Smart-grid security issues. *IEEE Security and Privacy*, *8*(1), 81–85. doi:10.1109/MSP.2010.49

Hardell, L., & Sage, C. (2008). Biological effects from electromagnetic field exposure and public exposure standards. *Biomedicine and Pharmacotherapy*, *62*(2), 104–109. doi:10.1016/j.biopha.2007.12.004 PMID:18242044

Hatuka, T., & Toch, E. (2012). *Smart-Spaces: Smartphone's Influence on Perceptions of the Public Space.* Toch Research Group, Tel-Aviv University. Retrieved October 29, 2013, from http://www.aftau.org/site/News2?page=NewsArticle&id=16519

Healy, J. M. (2011). *Endangered Minds: Why Children Dont Think And What We Can Do About I.* New York, NY: Simon and Schuster.

Hilbert, M., & López, P. (2011). The world's technological capacity to store, communicate, and compute information. *Science, 332*(6025), 60–65. doi:10.1126cience.1200970 PMID:21310967

ITU (International Telecommunication Union). (2013). ICT Facts and Figures –. *WORLD (Oakland, Calif.), 2013.* Retrieved from http://www.itu.int/en/ITU-D/Statistics/Documents/facts/ICTFactsFigures2013-e.pdf

Kaplan, B., & Litewka, S. (2008). Ethical challenges of telemedicine and telehealth. *Cambridge Quarterly of Healthcare Ethics, 17*(04), 401–416. doi:10.1017/S0963180108080535 PMID:18724880

Karlgaard, R. (2011). Is Technological Progress Slowing Down? *Forbes Magazine.* Retrieved February 15, 2014, from http://www.forbes.com/sites/richkarlgaard/2011/12/21/is-technological-progress-slowing-down/

Karnouskos, S., Weidlich, A., Kok, K., & Warmer, C. (2011). Field trials towards integrating smart houses with the smart grid. In *Energy-Efficient Computing and Networking* (pp. 114–123). Springer Berlin Heidelberg. doi:10.1007/978-3-642-19322-4_13

Khurana, V. G., Hardell, L., Everaert, J., Bortkiewicz, A., Carlberg, M., & Ahonen, M. (2010). Epidemiological evidence for a health risk from mobile phone base stations. *International Journal of Occupational and Environmental Health, 16*(3), 263–267. doi:10.1179/oeh.2010.16.3.263 PMID:20662418

Khurana, V. G., Teo, C., Kundi, M., Hardell, L., & Carlberg, M. (2009). Cell phones and brain tumors: A review including the long-term epidemiologic data. *Surgical Neurology, 72*(3), 205–214. doi:10.1016/j.surneu.2009.01.019 PMID:19328536

Konishi, K., & Bohbot, V. D. (2010). Grey matter in the hippocampus correlates with spatial memory strategies in human older adults tested on a virtual navigation task. *Proceedings of the 40th Society for Neuroscience annual meeting.*

Korff, S. (2013). PETs in Your Home – How Smart is That? *Symposium on Usable Privacy and Security (SOUPS).*

Kulyk, O. A., Tjin-Kam-Jet-Siemons, L., Oinas-Kukkonen, H., & van Gemert-Pijnen, J. E. W. C. (2016). Fourth International Workshop on Behavior Change Support Systems (BCSS'16): Epic for Change, the Pillars for Persuasive Technology for Smart Societies. In A. Meschtscherjakov, B. de Ruyter, V. Fuchsberger, M. Murer, & M. Tscheligi (Eds.), *Adjunct proceedings of the 11th International Conference on Persuasive Technology, PERSUASIVE 2016* (pp. 92-95). Salzburg, Austria: Center for Human-Computer Interaction, Department of Computer Science, University of Salzburg.

Leitgeb, N. (2009). Electromagnetic hypersensitivity. In *Advances in electromagnetic fields in living systems* (pp. 167–197). Springer New York.

Lönn, S., Ahlbom, A., Hall, P., & Feychting, M. (2004). Mobile phone use and the risk of acoustic neuroma. *Epidemiology (Cambridge, Mass.)*, *15*(6), 653–659. doi:10.1097/01.ede.0000142519.00772. bf PMID:15475713

Luppicini, R. (2008). The emerging field of technoethics. In R. Luppicini & R. Adell (Eds.), *Handbook of Research on Technoethics* (pp. 1–19). Hershey, PA: Information Science Reference. doi:10.4018/978-1-60566-022-6.ch001

Mattern, F. (2005). Leben und Lernen in einer von Informationstechnologie durchdrungenen Welt – Visionen und Erwartungen. In M. Franzen (Ed.), *Lernplattformen (Web-Based Training 2005)* (pp. 39–61). Dübendorf, Switzerland: EMPA-Akademie.

Mäyrä, F., & Vadén, T. (2013). Ethics of Living Technology: Design Principles for Proactive Home Environments. *Human IT. Journal for Information Technology Studies as a Human Science*, *7*(2).

Meijer, A., & Bolívar, M. P. R. (2016). Governing the smart city: A review of the literature on smart urban governance. *International Review of Administrative Sciences*, *82*(2), 392–408. doi:10.1177/0020852314564308

Nixon, P. A., Wagealla, W., English, C., & Terzis, S. (2004). *Security, privacy and trust issues in smart environments. Technical report of the Global and Pervasive Computing Group. Department of Computer and Information Sciences*. Glasgow, UK: University of Strathclyde.

Niyato, D., Xiao, L., & Wang, P. (2011). Machine-to-machine communications for home energy management system in smart grid. *IEEE Communications Magazine*, *49*(4), 53–59. doi:10.1109/MCOM.2011.5741146

Peek, S. T., Aarts, S., & Wouters, E. J. (2017). Can smart home technology deliver on the promise of independent living? A critical reflection based on the perspectives of older adults. Handbook of Smart Homes, Health Care and Well-Being, 203-214.

Ponce, P., Polasko, K., & Molina, A. (2016). End user perceptions toward smart grid technology: Acceptance, adoption, risks, and trust. *Renewable & Sustainable Energy Reviews*, *60*, 587–598. doi:10.1016/j.rser.2016.01.101

Quinn, E. (2009). Privacy and the new energy infrastructure. *SSRN eLibrary*.

Research and Markets. (2013). *Global Smart Appliances Market 2012-2016*. Retrieved February 24, 2014, from http://www.researchandmarkets.com/research/xdchz5/global_smart

Rennecker, J., & Godwin, L. (2003). Theorizing the unintended consequences of instant messaging for worker productivity. *Sprouts: Working Papers on Information Environments. Systems and Organizations*, *3*. Retrieved January 30, 2014, from: http://sprouts.aisnet.org/190/1/030307.pdf

Repacholi, M. H. (2001). Health risks from the use of mobile phones. *Toxicology Letters*, *120*(1), 323–331. doi:10.1016/S0378-4274(01)00285-5 PMID:11323191

Röcker, C. (2010). Social and technological concerns associated with the usage of ubiquitous computing technologies. *Issues in Information Systems*, *11*(1).

Sturm, J. (2017). Persuasive Technology. *Handbook of Smart Homes, Health Care and Well-Being*, 3-12.

Tsukayama, H. (2014). Google's smart contact lens: What it does and how it works. *The Washington Post*. Retrieved February 20, 2014 from http://www.washingtonpost.com/business/technology/googles-smart-contact-lens-what-it-does-and-how-it-works/2014/01/17/96b938ec-7f80-11e3-93c1-0e888170b723_story.html

Valtchev, D., & Frankov, I. (2002). Service gateway architecture for a smart home. *IEEE Communications Magazine, 40*(4), 126–132. doi:10.1109/35.995862

Weiser, M. (1993). Some computer science issues in ubiquitous computing. *Communications of the ACM, 36*(7), 75–84. doi:10.1145/159544.159617

Chapter 13
Energy Consumers' Perspectives on Smart Meter Data:
Privacy and Unjust Algorithmic Discrimination

Jenifer Sunrise Winter
University of Hawaii at Manoa, USA

ABSTRACT

This chapter employs the framework of contextual integrity related to privacy developed by Nissenbaum as a tool to understand consumer response to implementation of residential smart metering technology. To identify and understand specific changes in information practices brought about by the introduction of smart meters, energy consumers were interviewed, read a description of planned smart grid/meter implementation, and were asked to reflect on changes in the key actors involved, information attributes, and principles of transmission. Areas where new practices emerge with the introduction of residential smart meters were then highlighted as potential problems (privacy violations). Issues identified in this study included concern about unauthorized use and sharing of personal data, data leaks or spoofing via hacking, the blurring distinction between the home and public space, and inferences made from new data types aggregated with other personal data that could be used to unjustly discriminate against individuals or groups.

INTRODUCTION

The smart grid is a next-generation electrical power grid intended to upgrade and replace aging infrastructure, enhance energy conservation, and provide real-time information for decision making, allowing energy companies "full visibility and pervasive control over their assets and services" (Farhangi, 2010, p. 19). Whereas the existing power grid is an inefficient, unidirectional pipeline that is unable to access information about residences receiving power in real-time, the smart grid represents the marriage of information and communication technologies (ICTs) and power systems, adding new communication and data management capabilities (Depuru, Wang, Devabhaktuni & Gudi, 2011). The smart grid can

DOI: 10.4018/978-1-5225-5094-5.ch013

be seen as an aspect of broader sociotechnical developments focusing on the sensoring of everyday objects, the Internet of Things. The Internet of Things is described as a "backbone for ubiquitous computing, enabling smart environments to recognize and identify objects, and retrieve information from the Internet to facilitate their adaptive functionality" (Weber & Weber, 2010, p. 1). It is an emerging architecture intended to enable billions or trillions of heterogeneous objects to interact over the Internet. A key component is the development of machine-to-machine communication to automate the exchange of information, goods, and services. These developments represent the integration of the physical world with the virtual world, enabling increased instrumentation and tracking of natural processes. The new types and massive volume of data created in this environment are mined to enhance decision-making in business and government and offer increased convenience and safety (Uckelmann, Harrison, & Michahelles, 2010). One aspect of the Internet of Things is the development of smart cities and homes that, via ICT integration, allow advanced infrastructure monitoring, including smart grid management to govern cost- and resource-efficient use of energy (Khan, Khan, Zaheer, & Khan, 2012; Atzori, Iera & Morabito, 2010). Smart homes can include automatic lighting and power allocation (CERP-IoT, 2010). This use of ICT to lower environmental impact has been referred to as "Green ICT" (Vermesan et al., 2011).

Smart meters, a component of the smart grid, are energy meters installed at residences and used by electric utilities that can capture energy consumption data with more granularity than a traditional electrical meter (see Figure 1).

These data are captured in real-time and transmitted to the utility via a wireless network. In addition to allowing a constant stream of data about a home's energy use, smart meters also allow a utility to send commands to the meter, such as turning off the power due to nonpayment of tariffs or reducing the amount of energy available to a home based on the time of day or type of energy use. In doing so, smart

Figure 1. Residential smart meter

meters "open the door to new and expanded services, such as time-based pricing, load control, budget, billing, high usage alerts, push notifications, and web services for energy management" (Cooper, 2016, p.1). Energy use data is stored and analyzed by the electric company to identify energy usage patterns and related pricing schemes. In the United States, the American Recovery and Reinvestment Act of 2009 funded more than $3.4 billion in grants for smart grid development (Department of Energy, 2011). As of 2015, the United States had installed approximately 65 million smart meters (over 50% of households), rising to 70 million in 2016, and expected to grow to 90 million by 2010 (Cooper, 2016).

THE SMART GRID/SMART METERS IN HAWAII

Hawaii is by far the most petroleum-dependent state in the United States. In 2015, Hawaii used oil for 69.4% of it electricity production, compared to less than 1% nationwide, and electricity prices were more than double the national average (Hawaii State Energy Office, 2017). The existing power grid is limited in regards to incorporation of clean energy sources such as solar or wind power. In 2008, recognizing the long-term economic effects of, and ongoing vulnerabilities imposed by, reliance on oil, the State of Hawaii, in collaboration with the United States Department of Energy, created the Hawaii Clean Energy Initiative (HCEI). The goal of this initiative is to transform Hawaii's economy to one 70% clean-energy-based by 2030 and for the electricity sector to meet 40% of demand by this date. To accomplish this, in addition to alternative fuel sources such as solar and wind power, the HCEI focuses on the deployment of the smart grid. As part of the HCEI agreement between the Hawaiian Electric Company (HECO), the state's largest provider of electrical power, and the State of Hawaii, HECO began testing smart meters in 2006, and in 2008 entered a 15-year definitive agreement to deploy smart meters state-wide (Hawaiian Electric Company, 2008). HECO plans to deploy 448,200 smart meters throughout its service territory by 2018 (Innovation Electricity Efficiency Institute, 2013). This was partially funded by a grant from the ARRA of over 5 million USD (United States Department of Energy, 2011). Smart meter rollout has begun in select neighborhoods in the Honolulu area, with installation at 5,200 households between April and July, 2014 (Shimogawa, 2014).

SECURITY AND PRIVACY CONCERNS ABOUT THE SMART GRID/SMART METERS

The introduction of residential smart meters poses a number of ethical challenges related to security, privacy, and "ensuring social justice both in terms of access and cost of electric power service" (Kostyk & Herkert, 2012, p. 25). First, the granularity of data will greatly increase, enhancing the surveillance capacity of these systems (Bleicher, 2010). Each appliance gives off a signature based on its energy use, making it uniquely identifiable. Even the specific television programs or movies one watches can be deduced via this monitoring (Mills, 2012). Further, manufacturers are increasingly introducing "smart appliances" to the market with features such as remote control from a smartphone or the ability to text an appliance to learn about its state. Smart meters can also interface with these "smart appliances" and control them (e.g., turn them off during peak energy-use periods) (McDaniel & McLaughlin, 2009). Hence, many new types of data can be collected. Further, without secure protection schemes, consumer data may potentially be transferred or sold, willfully or not, and may be aggregated with other data about an individual. Hacking is another issue that has been well documented (e.g., Weber, 2012), and there is potential for spoofed energy usage or surveillance for the purpose of committing crimes. For example, security researchers hacking smart meters were able to determine how many personal computers or televisions were in a home, as well as what media were being consumed (Brinkhaus et al., 2011). These changes threaten to transform the home into a site of surveillance and pose a variety of potential informational injustices. In particular, these new data types and the ways that they can be shared, stored, or mined may reveal patterns about personal behaviors or attributes that could be used to discriminate economically or politically. If the data are not protected due to lapses in security or policies that do not restrict their sale or sharing with other entities, they may be aggregated with other personal data and subject to advanced analytics. In addition, the machine-to-machine communication and processing that is used to collect and analyze these data will greatly increase both the amount of data collected and the analytic capacity used to explore it, introducing an enhanced risk of data error (Winter, 2014). These changes are not just a matter of scope and scale. As Floridi (2005) notes, modern communication technologies are part of an "unprecedented transformation in the very nature (ontology) of the information environment" (p. 186). They do not merely increase the quantity and quality of data collected; they transform humans into informational agents, and each person is essentially constituted by his or her personal information. Informational breaches of this information are thus seen as aggression towards personal identity.

Because smart meter usage in the home represents a dramatic change in the types and amount of data collected about personal energy use, and there is uncertainty about how these data will be shared or stored, it is anticipated that there will be continued public concern, and possible refusal to adopt, smart meters. This type of data collection in the home also challenges the long-standing concept of two privacy spheres: public and private. Because most law in the United States is based on this dichotomy, novel technologies that do not fit well with this split may lead to conflict. While the United States' Fourth Amendment is intended to protect against unreasonable search and seizure, novel technologies have previously highlighted this conflict. For example, in *Kyllo v. United States*, the Supreme Court ruled that law enforcement's use of heat scanners (at the time a novel technology) to detect energy use and identify homeowners cultivating marijuana was unconstitutional because, "In the home... *all* details are intimate details, because the entire area is held safe from prying government eyes" (Christakos & Mehta, 2002, p. 473). In this way, novel technologies such as smart meters can be "disorienting as they reveal the inconstancy of boundaries and fuzziness of definitions" (Nissenbaum, 2010, p. 101).

This chapter examines energy customers' response to implementation of residential smart metering technology. It is motivated towards understanding how we can better foster the development of new systems, practices, and policies that balance the positive potential of smart grid technologies with individuals' rights to privacy and freedom from data-based discrimination. Technologies are not neutral objects, but rather actors in complex, sociotechnical systems. Therefore, new technologies must be examined in the specific contexts of their use (Kling, 2000). To better understand public attitudes about smart meter implantation, this study uses the framework of contextual integrity related to privacy developed by Nissenbaum (2010). Following this framework, the study seeks to identify and understand specific changes in information practices that will be brought about by smart meter implementation and may be perceived as violations of personal privacy and explore the underlying norms that shape these perceptions. Because there have been large roll-outs of smart meter technology over the past several years and numerous concerns have been raised, it is particularly important to understand energy consumers' perspectives in order to design technical systems and related policies that will have moral legitimacy. In the next section, the framework of contextual integrity related to privacy developed by Nissenbaum (2010) is introduced. Then, the method used to explore normative conflicts related to smart meter implementation in residences is described, followed by a results and discussion section that outlines conflicts with novel practices related to smart meters in the home.

THE FRAMEWORK OF CONTEXTUAL INTEGRITY

Although privacy is often cited as a key human right, there are many conflicting beliefs about what it entails (Solove, 2010). Increasingly, there has been acknowledgement that personal conceptions of privacy emerge from rich social contexts. Nissenbaum (2010) argues that privacy is context bound and should be conceived of, not as a right to secrecy or control, but to an "appropriate flow of personal information" in particular contexts (p. 127). This concept is referred to as contextual integrity. The framework of contextual integrity related to privacy is intended to guide assessment of novel practices arising from ICTs. Like Floridi (2005), Nissenbaum argues that previous conceptions of privacy are not able to address the radical changes brought about by systems such as the smart grid and smart meters.

As a descriptive and heuristic tool, the framework of contextual integrity aids insight into individuals' reactions to novel, or changing, ICTs that affect flows of personal information. The framework is also intended to assist in evaluation of moral and political values embedded in systems and practices. Because norms are context-bound, novel systems can create conflict between moral and political values. These might include informational harms, such as unjust discrimination, or threats to personal autonomy and liberty (Nissenbaum, 2010). There is a potential for political or economic discrimination on the part of governments or corporations, who might offer different services, products, or prices, to individuals based on their data profiles (Turow, 2006; Winter, 2014; 2015a). To evaluate a novel technology via the contextual integrity decision heuristic, one uses the following steps: 1) describe the existing practices in context; 2) describe the novel practice in context, along with changes in actors, attributes, and transmission principles; 3) identify the entrenched norms and note how the new technology may come into conflict with existing ones. (If informational norms have been breached, this represents a violation of contextual integrity); 4) evaluate the new informational practices based on moral and political factors, such as implications for justice or democracy; 5) evaluate the moral and political factors in relation to contextual values; and 6) argue for, or against, specific systems or practices based on this analysis (Nissenbaum, 2010).

When assessing a new technology, focus is placed upon whether, in a particular context, it comes into conflict with existing norms. Norms are embedded in systems, and Nissenbaum (2010) highlights their prescriptive nature – that is, they relate to expectations of how one *should* behave in a particular context. The process begins by documenting the existing (prior to the novel technology) practice and identifying the informational norms related to actors who handle the information, attributes of data collected, and how the information is stored or transmitted. Then, to address whether violations have occurred, a comparison must be made between the existing practice and the new practice: "if the new practice generates changes in actors, attributes, or transmission principles, the practice is flagged as violating entrenched informational norms and constitutes a prima facie violation of contextual integrity" (p. 150). While the term has a negative connotation, a "violation" of contextual integrity does not always indicate that development is unjust or lacks moral legitimacy. Instead, it highlights the change so that it can be further assessed in order to determine whether the new practice is morally acceptable, or whether it should be challenged. Nissenbaum (2010) emphasizes that it is possible for the violation, after consideration, to be approved as a morally superior practice. Violations merely pinpoint where there is a conflict between norms: If the new development is more effective in "supporting, achieving, or promoting relevant contextual values," then there is moral justification to replace the entrenched practice (p. 166).

Establishing whether a new informational practice is morally or politically superior requires consideration of general moral and political arguments about privacy. Nissenbaum (2010) notes that these come from a broad array of perspectives addressing the value of privacy (e.g., protecting individuals or groups against informational harms, maintaining personal autonomy, ensuring fairness, justice, and equality, and support of democratic institutions and publics). It is necessary to consider the specific values, ends, purposes, and goals relative to the specific context in order to make this judgment.

This analysis can aid in understanding energy consumers' reaction to ICTs reshaping personal information flows. Where there is resistance or fear in relation to adopting a new technology, it can help to understand the underlying concern (rather than fail to acknowledge it or trivialize it). This makes it useful for predicting when novel technologies are likely to lead to anxiety or rejection, and it highlights these uncertainties for ethical evaluation, opening the process for negotiation between stakeholders.

METHOD

The framework of contextual integrity was employed in this study to identify areas of concern related to emerging practices related to smart meter implementation, highlighting them for ethical evaluation. This study addressed normative conflicts related to smart meter implementation in the home. Smart meters were chosen for analysis because they are a novel technology that alters existing flows of personal information. They are important to evaluate because they are beginning to be widely deployed in other settings, but there has been little public discourse or awareness about them in Hawaii.

To explore energy consumers' perception about context-specific norms of privacy related to smart meters in the home, the researcher conducted in-person, semi-structured interviews. Interviews were chosen because they can elicit more in-depth responses, while permitting the flexibility to follow unexpected directions. Participants were selected based on the following criteria: 1) age of 18 or above; 2) resident of the State of Hawaii, living on Oahu; and 3) living in a dwelling that is serviced by electric power. Maximal variation sampling was employed to select participants reflecting a diversity of perspectives based on age, ethnicity, gender, and socioeconomic status. This study focused on the Island of Oahu, which contains the State's largest urban district, Honolulu. Recruitment was performed online by posting invitations on a local discussion site frequented by a variety of residents and was on a volunteer basis. As demographic categories (gender, age, ethnicity, level of education completed) were saturated, participants in other categories were sought. Interviews were conducted in public locations, at the discretion of the interviewees, and lasted between twenty-five and sixty-five minutes.

The development of interview questions and analysis was guided by the analytic framework of contextual integrity (Nissenbaum, 2010). Interviewees were first asked about their expectations in regards to existing electrical meters so that the prevailing conditions could be documented. Interview questions then sought to gain insight into their perception of *information attributes*, what types of data they thought might be collected about them during such interaction. This included their perception of 1) what types of data may have been collected about them; and how these data might reveal 2) their presence at any given time, and the presence of any other individuals; 3) what appliances they used; and 4) any other information about their activities in their homes. A second set of questions asked participants about the *actors* involved, who they thought had observed these behaviors (human or electronic), and who had handled this information. Other questions addressed *principles of transmission*, whether the participants thought that data was recorded and transmitted. Once the existing practices and expectations were discussed, participants read a short explanation of planned smart grid/meter expansion in their area. The description was not presented as a threat; rather, it described how participants might encounter smart meters in the near future.

After reading about the smart grid/meters, a final set of questions addressed changes to existing practices (and expectations) of privacy. These questions were mirrors of the first set asking about perceptions of information attributes, actors, and principles of transmission in the new environment. Areas where new practices occurred with smart meters were then highlighted by participants as violations of contextual integrity, and these areas were discussed at length to probe for underlying norms.

Interviews were recorded in person with a digital audio recorder and transcribed. In some cases, follow-up clarifying questions were asked of participants to review for accuracy, strengthening objectivity and credibility. Qualitative analysis of the complete transcripts was used to develop themes as they emerged. Transcripts were analyzed and inductively coded using ATLAS.ti Scientific Software. After coding was finalized, data were summarized thematically.

RESULTS AND DISCUSSION

A total of nine participants representing both genders, and a variety of age groups, education levels, and ethnicities participated in the in-depth interview process. Five were male and four female. Three were college graduates, three had completed high school, two had graduate degrees, and one had completed middle school. Three participants were Asian, one African-American, four were mixed ethnicity (Polynesian/Asian or Polynesian/Caucasian), and one was Polynesian. Ages ranged from early twenties to early sixties. All participants resided on the island of Oahu in the State of Hawaii. They represented a variety of professional, service, and technical career paths. To preserve confidentiality, all respondents are represented by a pseudonym in the following discussion.

Existing Practices and Expectations

In order to understand how shifting information practices might be perceived as violations of norms, it was first important to establish informants' perception of the information flows related to their current electric power use at home. A series of questions addressed what data about their energy use they thought were collected, who had access to these data, and how they were stored and transmitted.

Despite announcements on the HECO website and trade news stories, only one of the participants was aware of HECO's smart meter plan (Keala). Two other participants, Pono and Alana lived in neighborhoods where smart meter implementation is scheduled this year. These areas have been targeted by HECO with mailers introducing the smart meter implementation. In these two instances, there was awareness of an "upgrade" to the electrical system, but no special details were recalled. In addition, three of the participants had some awareness of smart meters used on the United States mainland or internationally. Keahi, for example, had lived in South Korea for several years and was familiar with their use there.

In relation to what types of data they expected are presently collected about their home energy use, it was understood by all that their energy utility, in this case HECO, would use this to measure their overall energy use for billing purposes. This was described as a monthly reading that would not offer any specific information other than the total kilowatts-per-hour (kWh) consumed. Keahi also thought that it was possible that some of his smart appliances might measure his energy use and transmit this, and other data, to the manufacturer. However, he acknowledged that this was not currently occurring via the energy utility.

When asked about who would have access to their data, it was agreed that individuals at HECO, who worked in the billing departments, as meter readers, or as policy analysts, would have access to their data. For example, Hauʻoli mentioned that she would not have any concern if the information was "in the right hands… People who specifically need to evaluate, maybe the cost of the electricity or energy that we use." In addition, Keahi, Hauʻoli, and Makana pointed out that they felt it would be appropriate to analyze these data as a way for HECO to offer improved service to consumers. In three cases, an interviewee described a living situation where they paid their electric bill via a proxy – a landlord or tenant association. This is a common situation in Hawaii, where rentals or homeowner/condominium associations may include the cost of electricity in a monthly fee. In these cases, participants agreed that landlords or homeowner associations would also have access to their energy use data. Makana and Keala also noted that aggregate data might be shared with federal or non-profit agencies (e.g., the United States Department of Energy) to study energy use trends for the purpose of developing sustainable energy solutions. Another expectation was that neighbors or passers-by might be aware of energy use (although not having direct access to the data unless they looked at the meter). These were seen as unwelcome, but not particularly intrusive, instances and not likely to be shared in any fashion. These were the only actors that they believed had access to their energy data at present.

Finally, it was understood by all that electronic databases held these data and that they were searchable by the utility. However, it was emphasized by multiple participants that this was acceptable only in relation to the specific actors and purposes mentioned above.

Conflicts with Novel Practices Related to Residential Smart Meters

A number of changes in the types of data collected, actors involved, and transmission techniques led to concerns by the participants. The main themes identified were related to unauthorized use and sharing of personal data, hacking, erosion of the private sphere, inferences about personal behaviors or ideas, and possible discriminatory practices based on analysis of personal data in aggregate form.

First, in all but two cases, there was enthusiasm for some of the promised benefits of smart meters. Energy companies' provision of smart meter displays that provide real-time, personalized feedback to customers so they could monitor and adapt their own energy-related behaviors were cited as appealing by five of the participants. This "green button" data is part of an industry-wide initiative resulting from a 2012 White House call to provide energy use data to energy customers in easy to read formats (Chopra, 2011; Green Button Alliance, 2015). This allows customers to review their own utility-usage data "to gain better insight of waste and inefficiencies; allowing [one] to make adjustments to use fewer resources and even save money" (Green Button Alliance, 2015, para. 2). For participants, this was seen as a way to potentially lower cost via energy use feedback. It was also perceived as an aid to more fairly address energy costs in a shared household. Another cited benefit of smart meters focused on mitigating the broader threat of climate change — how personalized feedback, coupled with behavioral changes, could lead to energy conservation and lessening reliance on imported oil. Pono noted the environmental benefits of smart meters, and said that he had heard about smart meters and smart homes "for a decade now. It's about time we got them." There has been growing public awareness in Hawaii about the threats of climate change, with many prominent news stories forecasting Hawaii and the Pacific region on the forefront of devastating effects such as coastal and inland flooding, ocean acidification, groundwater contamination, and increased risk for megastorms (e.g., Cave, 2014; United States Environmental Protection Agency, 2016; LaFrance, 2017).

Unauthorized Use and Sharing of Personal Data

Participants expressed concern that other, possibly unknown, actors could use their personal data without explicit consent. There was an awareness of increasing amounts of data being collected, sold, and analyzed, as well as uncertainty about who might see it. For example, Keala observed that companies already share personal data and that energy data might be used for targeted marketing:

From what I have seen in the past, companies that collect information tend to share information with other companies. The selling of data, particularly companies that are attempting to market certain things to people. So, if HECO were to sell their demographic information to marketing firms who would do things like send ads based on personal information that would disturb me.

Hau'oli added that "I think when you do have data that's not restricted to paper documents, but things that are online, other people definitely have access to it, unfortunately." Further, participants were concerned that, even if the data were not deliberately shared, they could be accessed without their consent. Keahi noted that there is a great deal of uncertainty about what happens to personal data once they are captured. "Ideally I hope there are constraints on the sharing of this information, that there is this wall of consent that you have to go through, even though it's annoying… but who knows? It's so hard to anticipate how information will move, because there are ways it can be leaked."

In terms of who would possibly want, or have access to the data, there were several ideas. Unethical individuals, corporations, and government agencies were all mentioned multiple times. In regards to the government, there was concern that:

Government agencies could use this data, not for me specifically, but there are people who perhaps are against certain government policies or practices and are in organizations that might want to make changes and perhaps the government might want to keep information on these individuals. It's certainly happened in the past. [Keala]

News coverage revealing the existence of widespread Internet surveillance efforts by the National Security Agency in the United States may be a factor in this concern. In 2013, the Pew Research Center for the People and the Press credited news stories about NSA surveillance with growing public awareness and anxiety about government surveillance (2013). Of particular note is the finding that 70% of respondents believed that NSA surveillance data is used for reasons other than investigating terrorism. Only one participant, Makana, said that he was not concerned about abuse of his energy data: "I can see potential for concern with something like a smart meter or access to your electric usage, but overall I think it is good. I think concerns would be among those who think aliens exist or who think 9-11 is a conspiracy put on by the government."

Moving beyond green buttons, data from the smart grid has also been entering public analysis as companies and smart grid research consortia have begun to make data available to researchers or citizen hackers (St. John, 2014). There are increasing calls from the open data community to provide application programming interfaces (APIs) to anonymized energy data to enable civic hackers to create apps (Tendril, 2012; Raftery, 2013). In these cases, the data sharing has been opt-in and data are anonymized. However, many other anonymized large data sets have been compromised through re-identification. For example, researchers have expressed concern about the re-identification of individuals based on anonymous DNA sequences and public data on the Internet (Gymrek et al., 2013). As noted above, scientists have noted likely climate change impacts to the State of Hawaii, and there is growing public awareness and concern about the effects of sea level rise, ocean acidification, and other damaging trends that threaten the welfare of the Islands. Given the magnitude of the threat and concern about the environment, and the consensus that it would be appropriate for energy companies or non-profits to look for patterns in the data for community improvement, this may emerge as an area where individuals will find sharing these data sets to be acceptable. However, they may not be aware of the risk of anonymized data, so the issue of public awareness and means to better guard against re-identification should be further investigated. This also points to the issue of uncertainty about whether data collected will be used as "expected" and calls for greater transparency throughout the data collection and use cycle.

Whether assurances to not share data are upheld or not, some participants also expressed concern that their information could be intercepted or hacked, either on-site, during transmission, or during storage. Although no participant specifically mentioned knowing of instances of smart meter hacking, four participants mentioned this as a concern. Makana stated that,

With everything I've seen... news stories or articles...about hackers and terrorists taking down our power grid or the Internet in the U.S. I'd assume anyone good with computers could get their hands on that information... The smart meter, if I was a homeowner, would kind of make me want to push towards getting my own solar system just to avoid as much of this as I could.

It should be noted that Makana was the one participant least concerned with his data being intercepted, because he felt that no one would be interested in doing so. He was more concerned about people spoofing energy data, severing his connection to electrical power, or taking control of appliances in his home. This was one instance where concern about negative consequences related to the security of private information led a participant to consider opting out, or resisting, the technology.

This concern about the security of personal data was also addressed. Keala noted that he was "not so sure about the security of the databases that those companies use. People might be able to gather data about me or others that we were unwilling to share." Highlighting the complexity of this problem, the National Institute of Standards and Technology analyzed smart grid technologies and identified over 130 possible logical interfaces that link actors and will require secure standards for protection (National Institute of Standards and Technology, 2010b, 2014). A great deal of technical research related to the smart grid has focused on issues of security, but there are still critical vulnerabilities and no beginning-to-end protection schemes. Even the nation's most heavily secured energy computer systems were reportedly hacked over 150 times between 2010 and 2014 (Bennett, 2015).

Erosion of the Private Sphere

Smart meters are expected to link a variety of everyday behaviors in the home to communication networks, making the home, traditionally the private sphere, a potential site of surveillance. The blurring of the public and private spheres due to ICT increases the probability of sensitive personal information related to political views, religious practices, health, and other intimate practices being shared beyond their original intent or context. Respondents noted that the use of smart meters posed an intrusion into the private sphere, their homes. In fact, this may lead to an erosion of this distinction:

Honestly I don't personally feel that I am doing anything, like, unethical or illegal in my home, but I know there are people that feel that what they do in their own home should not be information that should be available to people outside the home... [Keala]

One participant also noted a related threat from the integration of smart appliances and the smart grid (bridging the discussion into greater concern about the Internet of Things). Keahi noted, "If they collect energy data and then, sort of, glean other data from the devices themselves, I could see that would be a troublesome aspect for me". The erosion of a private sphere is of particular consequence due to the fact that existing laws and regulations in the United States are based on this dichotomy.

Inferences and Data Mining

Participants also raised the question of inferences that could be made about them due to the granularity and volume of data collection. The explosion and availability of real-time data has enabled sophisticated user modeling, and there are many efforts to mine, model, and personalize these data (Jaimes, 2010). In this case, the gathering of novel data types, coupled with the ability to store and share with relative ease dramatically alters personal information flows. All but Makana and Kukane reacted to these changes with anxiety:

I don't like that. Because they can basically tell someone was there, or maybe because of the changes, I bought something. Just the detail of it makes me feel nervous because it's kind of monitoring my daily life in terms of energy consumption. And that could actually reflect.... It's frightening. [What types of things could it reflect?] The fact that it's, like, monitoring... it could be anything. Yea, energy consumption, they have to monitor it, but I don't like the fact that any type of information can be collected. It seems very intervening to my life [Niele].

For Niele, the uncertainty about the scope and granularity of data was a concern, and she criticized the collection of data that was not specific to the purposes she had identified as appropriate (i.e., using it for billing). Keala explicitly linked these inferences to privacy and contrasted the two metering approaches:

I see this as an erosion of privacy, not a complete lack of privacy, but you would be able to infer certain things about a person, I think, by looking at this information. As an overall group, you are seeing trends but you are not necessarily seeing what an individual is doing. But if you have my data you know what I'm doing when I am there. In the past, the amount of power we use in the home, that's a fairly general thing. I don't really see that as that much of an invasion because you can't really determine the sort of thing a person is doing other than using energy. In the smart meter, you can tell [a lot of things], you can infer a lot about this person's personal life based on [this]. I think that's a little too much.

With consumers mesmerized by new appliances, and a lack of transparency about how these new data will be used, Keahi also mentioned energy consumers' general lack of awareness about potential risks:

I was watching the consumer electronics show and that's [smart appliances] just such a huge part now, especially Samsung and LG are really getting into this... so I mean right now for most people they are looking at the consumer side of it. They are very excited about the possibilities of electronics being more responsive and alert, and so I think that part of it is great. But I think in the long term, eventually, we have to think about how is energy data being used? What inferences can people make from it? What companies will be collecting data. That's also equally important, even if it's not as popular.

Typically, regulation is addressed after concrete harms have been documented. However, the time to create legal protections and related system design choices is before system implementation and major problems arise (Weber & Weber, 2010).

Potential for Data Discrimination

While participants in this study were generally enthusiastic about the benefits of smart meters, they also expressed concern that their data could be used for unacceptable purposes. First, invasive, targeted marketing was noted as a possible outcome.

They can tell what types of devices I am using. They could use my personal data to sell stuff... That's a lot of personal data. Maybe they'll find out I use a lot of computers. We have a lot of them. They will know our appliances. They could tell if an appliance is getting old and uses more energy and try to sell us something? Also, that could be used with other kinds of data that they could get. Other people in the household, if you file tax [sic], public records, they would have more data to target me in a compromised way. [Niele]

Haggerty and Ericson (2006) describe the ways in which data surveillance can foster new advertiser-based forms of identity. They argue that an individual's place in this "new constellation of market segments" can be used to discriminate against them, as different groups will receive different commercial offers and communication. Surveillance enables monitoring of these groups, with the embedded system logic subjecting individuals or groups to different levels of scrutiny. This "social sorting" Lyon (2002) enabled by surveillance results in classifications that are "designed to influence and to manage populations and persons thus directly and indirectly affecting the choices and chances of subjects" (p.13). Lyon (2006) further argues that these activities cannot be disengaged from political or ethical tasks.

Hau'oli and Alana were also concerned that corporations would manipulate the data in order make a profit at the expense of consumers. Although both tenants and landlords noted that having personalized records of one's data use could be helpful in assuring individuals were paying their fair share, there was also concern that it could lead to unjust discrimination. For example, a landlord might say, "'Oh there's too many people in that household that are using energy...a particular item or appliance... you really need to cut down.' Or the residential community tells you to cut your appliance [use] or they'll find other tenants" [Hau'oli].

Although none of the participants acknowledged a medical condition that they felt would lead to discrimination, over half of them mentioned a concern about health-related data being inferred from smart meters. Niele said that, "it's kind of horrible, because if I am using some type of medical device, then they'll be able to know as well. That's a lot of personal data!" This was further elaborated by Keahi:

I think something that would be troublesome is the type of devices that companies are collecting data from, the energy use itself would not be troublesome, but perhaps it could give clues to the types of devices that people have in their homes. So, for example, if you have a certain health problem, and a certain device is used in the home to help you, then companies could access or make assumptions or inferences into the types of health problems you have, then I see the trouble there.

Granular smart grid data may infer a variety of health-related data and will link behaviors occurring in the home to the previously protected realm of medical information. Laws related to medical data, such as HIPAA (United States), do not address the data or actors in this case, as the protected health information (PHI) in the Privacy Rule is very limited. Therefore, there is little to prevent the collection or sharing of this information and it will likely be aggregated with other search and purchasing behaviors linked to online profiles. For example, Hill (2012) noted that data aggregators, such as Target, are able to infer things about customers' health by combing through data. In a now-famous example, a teenager buying unscented hand lotion, in conjunction with other seemingly-innocuous items, triggered a pregnancy-related advertisement to be sent to her home during the early stages of her pregnancy. Other data may include de-identified tracking information collected during web browsing that may be re-identifiable when aggregated. The National Institute of Standards and Technology (2010a) noted that insurance companies would be interested in using these data to adjust health care premiums or deny coverage based on private behaviors that might indicate risk of higher health costs.

Consumers' everyday interactions with technologies produce trace data that is aggregated and mined to make inferences about individuals or groups. A few points of information that seem innocuous may reveal sensitive information about health, politics, or may be used to discriminate against individuals seeking housing, immigration eligibility, or employment (Winter, 2014). In the United States' relaxed regulatory environment in regards to personal data protections, data brokers are able to amass and sell "a 'data enrichment' service that provides 'hundreds of attributes' such as age, profession and 'wealth indicators' tied to a particular IP address" (Angwin, 2015, para. 5-6), even for minors. These data can be used to forecast many behaviors and outcomes. For example, health surveillance systems (that are not governed under specific laws for healthcare data) may be able to predict upcoming diagnoses of serious ailments such as pancreatic cancer (McFarland, 2016, para. 3), and these data and assessments can be shared or resold to others. Despite regulatory or legal attempts to prevent abuse of some types of data, in this larger ecosystem, those seeking to monetize these data may simple use non-protected "proxy" fields that are highly correlated to any variables protected by law (Barocas & Selbst, 2016).

Other Sensitive Behaviors

In addition to jeopardizing the privacy of discreet personal data related to health, granular data collection and sharing may also expose sensitive behaviors related to political belief or activity, or any other personal information that could be used to disadvantage certain individuals or groups. The potential issues that arise from this include political and economic discrimination, as well as limiting individuals' freedom of access to information or ability to discuss issues relevant to democratic decision-making in their communities (Winter, 2014). Therefore, this poses a grave risk to constitutional freedoms and civil liberties, and it contributes to a chilling effect on free speech, a society where individuals cannot freely express their opinions due to surveillance concerns. The erosion of the private sphere threatens both privacy and anonymity when engaging in public affairs, and therefore poses a grave risk to participation in democratic discourse. Niele, a foreign national who recently acquired U.S. citizenship via marriage, also imagined a scenario in which immigration officials might use energy data to corroborate her claim to be living with her husband, a U.S. citizen. She emphasized that she and her husband had been living together for over fifteen years before they married, and they themselves would likely not have been affected, but she worried that data errors or incorrect inferences could be used to deny citizenship to others.

CONCLUSION

This study examined energy consumers' perspective about customization and privacy in the context of residential smart meters. Using Nissenbaum's framework of contextual integrity to analyze participants' perceptions about changes in the key actors involved, information attributes, and principles of transmission, a number of points where existing norms about the collection and use of personal information will potentially be violated in everyday interaction with smart meters in the home were identified. A common theme was that participants were in favor of the feedback, potential cost savings, and potential environmental benefit of smart meter implementation, but only where the data collected and shared contributed to those specific goals: "As long as the 'smart' is for the betterment of a community of people versus profit" [Hau'oli].

This study identified several instances where existing norms about the use of one's personal data may be transgressed. In the case of such a conflict, the framework of contextual integrity calls for evidence that new practices are superior, with the onus of proof being placed on advocates of the new practice. Smart meters advocates must demonstrate that individuals' freedom to express political views, engage in information-seeking necessary to take part in communal decisions, and the freedom to go about their legal, daily activities without fear of surveillance will be protected. In this case, the practices flagged in analysis represent an undemocratic shift in power, erosion of personal autonomy, and threat of unjust discrimination.

Individuals should have more awareness and control in managing personal data flows and should be aware of what data are being collected about them and have a say in whether they will be shared with any other entity. The findings of this study highlight the need to identify how much, and what types of, information are required to provide meaningful insights and feedback to power utilities versus what is being sold to data aggregators and has no larger community benefit (or actual community detriment). Principles such as necessary legitimation, purpose specification and limitation, and data minimization as outlined in the European Union's data protection legislation (Pallas, 2012) would mitigate many of the threats identified in this study. In the United States there is, at present, no meaningful legal protection, particularly against corporate intrusions against personal data. In addition to regulatory protections, privacy must be introduced during the earliest stages of system development and be maintained throughout the lifecycle of personal information (Cavoukian & Kursawe, 2012). Privacy by design is a framework adhering to personal privacy protection principles while enabling necessary data collection and analysis. In their case study of smart grid implementation, Cavoukian and Kursawe (2012) concluded that utilities should be required to conduct privacy impact assessments and subsequently collect only data that is necessary for these primary purposes. Further, individuals should not be forced to choose between privacy and energy conservation. A smart grid designed with privacy at its core can serve diverse goals and contexts and provide users with the assurance that their data is well-protected. Uncertainties about smart grid security, the accuracy and reliability of data aggregation, and economic and political motives to gather data indiscriminately for later mining, will only increase the tension between personal privacy and smart meters. Even though HECO will initially allow people to opt-out of smart meter installation, there is potential discrimination due to individuals being denied the more desirable aspects of the developments (which may include economic or other benefits). It is important to understand public concern and to develop systems and policies that accord with social norms and expectations. For example, technical standards, regulations, and laws, should allow more transparency and control. More attention should be focused on how the smart grid is not merely infrastructure but a network that shapes social, political, and economic relations.

REFERENCES

Angwin, J. (2015). Own a Vizio Smart TV? It's watching you. *ProPublica*. Retrieved from https://www.propublica.org/article/own-a-vizio-smart-tv-its-watching-you

Atzori, L., Iera, A., & Morabito, G. (2010). The Internet of Things: A survey. *Computer Networks*, *54*(15), 2787–2805. doi:10.1016/j.comnet.2010.05.010

Barocas, S., & Selbst, A. D. (2016). Big data's disparate impact. *California Law Review*, *104*(3), 671–732.

Bennett, C. (2015, September 9). Energy Dept. hacked 150 times in 4 years. *The Hill*. Retrieved from http://thehill.com/policy/cybersecurity/253130-hackers-cracked-energy-department-150-times-over-four-years

Bleicher, A. (2010). Privacy on the smart grid. *IEEE Spectrum*. Retrieved from: http://spectrum.ieee.org/ energy/the-smarter-grid/privacy-on-the-smart-grid

Brinkhaus, S., Carluccio, D., Greveler, U., Justus, B., Löhr, D., & Wegener, C. (2011). Smart hacking for privacy. *28th Chaos Communication Congress*. Retrieved from: http://events.ccc.de/congress/2011/ Fahrplan/ attachments/1968_28c3-abstract-smart_hacking_for_privacy.pdf

Cave, J. (2014, August 28). Climate change will ruin Hawaii, new study says. *Huffington Post*. Retrieved from http://www.huffingtonpost.com/2014/08/28/climate-change-study-hawaii_n_5731956.html

Cavoukian, A., & Kursawe, K. (2012). Implementing privacy by design: The smart meter case. In *Proceedings of the 2012 IEEE International Conference on Smart Grid Engineering* (pp. 1-8). Piscataway, NJ: IEEE. 10.1109/SGE.2012.6463977

CERP-IoT. European Union, Cluster of European Research Projects on the Internet of Things. (2010). *Vision and challenges for realising the Internet of Things*. Brussels: European Commission – Information Society and Media.

Chopra, A. (2011, September 15). *Modeling a green energy challenge after a blue button*. Retrieved from: http://www.whitehouse.gov/blog/2011/09/15/modeling-green-energy-challenge-after-blue-button

Christakos, H. A., & Mehta, S. N. (2002). Annual review of law and technology. *Berkeley Technology Law Journal*, *2002*, 473.

Cooper, A. (2016, October). *Electric company smart meter deployments: Foundations for a smart grid*. Washington, DC: Innovation Electricity Efficiency Institute.

Depuru, S. S., Wang, L., Devabhaktuni, V., & Gudi, N. (2011). Smart meters for power grid: Issues, advantages, and status. *Renewable & Sustainable Energy Reviews, 15*(6), 2736–2742. doi:10.1016/j.rser.2011.02.039

Farhangi, H. (2010). The path of the smart grid. *IEEE Power & Energy Magazine, 8*(1), 18–28. doi:10.1109/MPE.2009.934876

Floridi, L. (2005). The ontological interpretation of informational privacy. *Ethics and Information Technology, 7*(7), 185–200. doi:10.100710676-006-0001-7

Green Button Alliance. (2015). *Green Button for my home.* Retrieved from http://www.greenbuttondata.org/residential.html

Gymrek, M., McGuire, A. L., Golan, D., Halperin, E., & Erlich, Y. (2013). Identifying personal genomes by surname inference. *Science, 339*(6117), 321–324. doi:10.1126cience.1229566 PMID:23329047

Haggerty, K. D., & Ericson, R. V. (2006). The new politics of surveillance and visibility. In K. D. Haggerty & R. V. Ericson (Eds.), *The new politics of surveillance and visibility* (pp. 3–25). Toronto: University of Toronto Press.

Hawaii State Energy Office. (2017, May). *Hawaii energy facts and figures.* Retrieved from https://energy.hawaii.gov/wp-content/uploads/2011/10/HSEOFactsFigures_May2017_2.pdf

Hawaiian Electric Company. (2008). *Hawaiian Electric selects Sensus FlexNet AMI: Success of pilot projects results in definitive agreement* [Press release]. Retrieved from: http://www.heco.com/vcmcontent/StaticFiles/pdf/Sensus_AMI_HECO_12-23-08_FINAL.pdf

Hill, K. (2012, February 16). How Target figured out a teen girl was pregnant before her father did. *Forbes.* Retrieved from http://www.forbes.com/sites/ kashmirhill/2012/02/16/how-target-figured-out-a-teen-girl-was-pregnant-before-her-father-did/

Innovation Electricity Efficiency Institute. (2013, August). *Utility-scale smart meter deployments: A foundation for expanded grid benefits.* Washington, DC: Innovation Electricity Efficiency Institute. Retrieved from http://www.edisonfoundation.net/iee/Documents/ IEE_SmartMeterUpdate_0813.pdf

Jaimes, A. (2010). Data mining for user modeling and personalization in ubiquitous spaces. In H. Nakashima, H. Aghajan, & J. C. Augusto (Eds.), *Handbook of ambient intelligence and smart environments* (pp. 1015–1038). London: Springer-Verlag. doi:10.1007/978-0-387-93808-0_38

Khan, R., Khan, S. U., Zaheer, R., & Khan, S. (2012). Future Internet: The Internet of Things architecture, possible applications and key challenges. *10th International Conference on Frontiers of Information Technology,* 257-260. 10.1109/FIT.2012.53

Kling, R. (2000). Learning about information technologies and social change: The contribution of social informatics. *The Information Society, 16*(3), 217–232. doi:10.1080/01972240050133661

Kostyk, T., & Herkert, J. (2012). Societal implications of the emerging smart grid. *Communications of the ACM, 55*(11), 34–36. doi:10.1145/2366316.2366328

LaFrance, A. (2017). The ghost of climate-change future. *The Atlantic*. Retrieved from https://www. theatlantic.com/science/archive/2017/05/the-ghost-of-climate-change-future/528471/

Lyon, D. (2002). Surveillance as social sorting: Computer codes and mobile bodies. In D. Lyon (Ed.), *Surveillance as social sorting: Privacy, risk and automated discrimination* (pp. 14–30). London, UK: Routledge.

Lyon, D. (2006). The search for surveillance theories. In D. Lyon (Ed.), *Theorizing surveillance: The panopticon and beyond* (pp. 3–20). Portland, OR: Willand.

McDaniel, P., & McLaughlin, S. (2009). Security and privacy challenges in the smart grid. *IEEE Security and Privacy*, 7(3), 75–77. doi:10.1109/MSP.2009.76

McFarland, M. (2016). What happens when your search engine is first to know you have cancer? *The Washington Post*. Retrieved from https://www.washingtonpost.com/ news/innovations/wp/2016/06/10/ what-happens-when-your-search-engine-is-first-to-know-you-have-cancer/

Mills, E. (2012, Jan 24). *Researcher find smart meters could reveal favorite TV shows*. Retrieved from http://www.cnet.com/news/researchers-find-smart-meters-could-reveal-favorite-tv-shows/

National Institute of Standards and Technology. (2010a). *Introduction to NISTIR 7628: Guidelines for smart grid cyber security*. Gaithersburg, MD: NIST.

National Institute of Standards and Technology. (2010b). Guidelines for smart grid cyber security: Vol. 2. *Privacy and the smart grid*. Gaithersburg, MD: NIST.

National Institute of Standards and Technology. (2014). *Guidelines for smart grid cyber security – Revision 1*. Gaithersburg, MD: NIST.

Nissenbaum, H. (2010). *Privacy in context: Technology, policy, and the integrity of social life*. Stanford, CA: Stanford University Press.

Pallas, F. (2012). Data protection and smart grid communication – the European perspective. In *Proceedings of the 2012 IEEE Innovative Smart Grid Technologies Conference* (pp. 1-8). New York: IEEE. 10.1109/ISGT.2012.6175695

Pew Research Center for the People and the Press. (2013). *Few see adequate limits on NSA surveillance program*. Retrieved October 25, 2013, from http://www.people-press.org/ files/legacy-pdf/7-26-2013%20 NSA%20release.pdf

Raftery, T. (2013, October 10). Utilities should open up API's to their smart meter data [Blog post]. Retrieved from: http://greenmonk.net/2013/10/10/utilities-should-open-up-apis-to-their-smart-meter-data/

Shimogawa, D. (2014, Mar 11). Hawaiian Electric to install smart meters on Oahu. *Pacific Business News*. Retrieved from http://www.bizjournals.com/pacific/news/ 2014/03/11/hawaiian-electric-to-install-smart-meters-on-oahu.html

Solove, D. (2010). *Understanding privacy*. Cambridge, MA: Harvard University Press.

St. John, J. (2014, March 13). Hidden treasure: Two new resources offer up massive amounts of utility data. *Greentechgrid*. Retrieved from: https://www.greentechmedia.com/articles/ read/Energy-Data-Treasure-from-Chattanoogas-Smart-Grid-Incubator-and-Pecan-Str

State of Hawaii, Department of Business, Economic Development and Tourism. (2011). *Renewable energy in Hawaii. Periodic research and data reports on issues of current interest, economic report 2011.* Honolulu, HI: Department of Business, Economic Development & Tourism.

Tendril. (2012, January 20). *NYC Cleanweb Hackathon: Crowdsourcing killer energy apps*. Retrieved from: http://www.tendrilinc.com/blog/nyc-cleanweb-hackathon-crowdsourcing-killer-energy-apps

Turow, J. (2006). Cracking the consumer code: Advertisers, anxiety and surveillance in the digital age. In K. D. Haggerty & R. V. Ericson (Eds.), *The new politics of surveillance and visibility* (pp. 279–307). Toronto: University of Toronto Press.

Uckelmann, D., Harrison, M., & Michahelles, F. (2010). An architectural approach towards the future Internet of Things. In D. Uckelmann & ... (Eds.), *Architecting the Internet of Things*. Berlin: Springer-Verlag Berlin Heidelberg.

United States Department of Energy. (2011, November). *Recovery Act selections for smart grid investment grant award*. Retrieved from http://energy.gov/oe/technology-development/smart-grid/recovery-act-smart-grid-investment-grants

United States Environmental Protection Agency. (2016, August). *What climate change means for Hawaii*. Retrieved from https://19january2017snapshot.epa.gov/sites/production/files/2016-09/documents/climate-change-hi.pdf

Vermesan, O., Friess, P., Guillemin, P., Gusmeroli, S., Sundmaeker, H., Bassi, A., ... Doody, P. (2011). Internet of Things strategic research roadmap. In O. Vermesan & P. Freiss (Eds.), *Global technological and societal trends from smart environments and spaces to green ICT* (pp. 9–52). Aalborg: River Publishers.

Weber, D. C. (2012). *Looking into the eye of the meter*. Presentation at DEFCON 2012. Retrieved from: https://www.youtube.com/watch?v=HeoCOVXRX0w

Weber, R. H., & Weber, R. (2010). *Internet of Things: Legal perspectives*. Berlin: Springer-Verlag Berlin Heidelberg. doi:10.1007/978-3-642-11710-7

Winter, J. S. (2014). Surveillance in ubiquitous network societies: Normative conflicts related to the consumer in-store supermarket experience in the context of the Internet of Things. *Ethics and Information Technology, 16*(1), 27–41. doi:10.100710676-013-9332-3

Winter, J. S. (2015a). Algorithmic discrimination: Big data analytics and the future of the Internet. In J. S. Winter & R. Ono (Eds.), *The future Internet: Alternative visions*. New York: Springer. doi:10.1007/978-3-319-22994-2_8

Winter, J. S. (2015b). Citizen perspectives on the customization/ privacy paradox related to smart meter implementation. *International Journal of Technoethics, 6*(1), 45–59. doi:10.4018/ijt.2015010104

ADDITIONAL READING

boyd, d., Levy, K., & Marwick, A. (2014). The networked nature of algorithmic discrimination. In S. Gangadharan (Ed.) Data and discrimination: Collected essays (pp. 53-57). Washington, DC: Open Technology Institute – New America Foundation.

Cavoukian, A. (2013). Personal Data Ecosystem (PDE)–A Privacy by Design approach to an individual's pursuit of radical control. Digital Enlightenment Yearbook 2013: The Value of Personal Data, 89-101.

Clastres, C. (2011). Smart grids: Another step towards competition, energy security and climate change objectives. *Energy Policy*, *39*(9), 5399–5408. doi:10.1016/j.enpol.2011.05.024

Custers, B. (2013). Data dilemmas in the Information Society: Introduction and overview. In Discrimination and Privacy in the Information Society: Data Mining and Profiling in Large Databases (B. Custers, T. Calders, B. Schermer, & Tal Zarsky, Eds.) (pp. 3–26). New York: Springer.

Davenport, T. H., Barth, P., & Bean, R. (2012). How 'big data' is different. Retrieved from http://sloanreview.mit.edu/article/how-big-data-is-different/

Depuru, S. S. S. R., Wang, L., & Devabhaktuni, V. (2011). Electricity theft: Overview, issues, prevention and a smart meter based approach to control theft. *Energy Policy*, *39*(2), 1007–1015. doi:10.1016/j.enpol.2010.11.037

Efthymiou, C., & Kalogridis, G. (2010, October). Smart grid privacy via anonymization of smart metering data. In *Smart Grid Communications* (SmartGridComm), 2010 First IEEE International Conference (pp. 238-243). IEEE. 10.1109/SMARTGRID.2010.5622050

Fox-Penner, P. (2014). *Smart power anniversary edition: Climate change, the smart grid, and the future of electric utilities*. Washington, D.C.: Island Press.

Grolinger, K., L'Heureux, A., Capretz, M. A., & Seewald, L. (2016). Energy forecasting for event venues: Big data and prediction accuracy. *Energy and Building*, *112*, 222–233. doi:10.1016/j.enbuild.2015.12.010

Kalogridis, G., Efthymiou, C., Denic, S. Z., Lewis, T. A., & Cepeda, R. (2010, October). Privacy for smart meters: Towards undetectable appliance load signatures. In *Smart Grid Communications* (SmartGridComm), 2010 First IEEE International Conference (pp. 232-237). IEEE.

Langheinrich, M. (2001). Privacy by design: Principles of privacy-aware ubiquitous systems. In *Proceedings of the 3rd International Conference on Ubiquitous Computing* (pp. 273-291). London: Springer-Verlag. 10.1007/3-540-45427-6_23

Marmol, F. G., Sorge, C., Ugus, O., & Pérez, G. M. (2012). Do not snoop my habits: Preserving privacy in the smart grid. *IEEE Communications Magazine*, *50*(5), 166–172. doi:10.1109/MCOM.2012.6194398

McKenna, E., Richardson, I., & Thomson, M. (2012). Smart meter data: Balancing consumer privacy concerns with legitimate applications. *Energy Policy*, *41*, 807–814. doi:10.1016/j.enpol.2011.11.049

Sankar, L., Rajagopalan, S. R., Mohajer, S., & Poor, H. V. (2013). Smart meter privacy: A theoretical framework. *IEEE Transactions on Smart Grid*, *4*(2), 837–846. doi:10.1109/TSG.2012.2211046

Tene, O., & Polonetsky, J. (2012). Big data for all: Privacy and user control in the age of analytics. *Nw. J. Tech. & Intell. Prop.*, *11*, xxvii.

Upturn. (2014). Civil rights, big data, and our algorithmic future. Retrieved from https://bigdata.fairness.io/

Wang, W., & Lu, Z. (2013). Cyber security in the Smart Grid: Survey and challenges. *Computer Networks*, *57*(5), 1344–1371. doi:10.1016/j.comnet.2012.12.017

KEY TERMS AND DEFINITIONS

Privacy by Design: Is a framework adhering to personal privacy protection principles while enabling necessary data collection and analysis. It has seven main principles: privacy should be the default setting; privacy should be embedded into design; full functionality; end-to-end security; proactivity not reactivity; visibility and transparency; and respect for user privacy.

Smart Meters: Are energy meters installed at residences and used by electric utilities that can capture energy consumption with more granularity than a traditional electrical meter. Data is captured in real time and transmitted to the utility via a wireless network. In addition to allowing a constant stream of data about a home's energy use, smart meters also allow a utility to send commands to the meter, such as turning off the power due to nonpayment of tariffs or reducing the amount of energy available to a home based on the time of day or type of energy use.

Section 3
Emerging Trends and Future Directions

Chapter 14
Encouraging Digital Civility:
What Companies and Others Can Do

Jacqueline F. Beauchere
Microsoft Corporation, USA

ABSTRACT

The internet, the landmark invention of our lifetime, has brought us great benefit, but along with it, risk and antisocial behavior, including online bullying, hate speech, extremist content, and other ills. Prevention lies in promoting digital citizenship—safe, responsible, and appropriate use of technology and services—and a newer concept, digital civility—online interactions rooted in empathy, respect, and kindness. And, while no one entity can combat these issues alone, internet companies can play their part, as exemplified by the robust tools and resources offered by Microsoft and others. A collective focus, however, is needed to help raise awareness and change behavior, and the responsibility must be shared among the technology industry and government policy makers as well as everyone who uses the internet, including parents and caregivers, educators, and young people. This chapter explores these ideas.

INTRODUCTION

The internet is nothing short of the landmark invention of our lifetime. It has changed forever the way we work, communicate, learn, play, and grow. It has quickened productivity, expanded global commerce, enabled new opportunities for social interaction, and sparked the creation of online communities. Yet, like all public places, the online world is not without its risks and bad actors.

Online bullying and harassment, as well as the digital proliferation of hate speech, extremist content, child sexual abuse imagery, and non-consensual pornography, are just a few of the "parade of horribles" that cross the web on a daily basis. All have garnered significant attention in recent years, highlighted further by the risks associated with live-streaming—the ability of people to broadcast live on the web what they may be doing at any particular moment. While many people, especially active teens, chronicle day-in-the-life updates like selfies, family jokes, or shopping tips for friends, others are broadcasting assaults, rapes, suicides—even murders. Media concentration on the most severe and tragic cases has triggered widespread concern among parents, policy-makers, and civil society.

DOI: 10.4018/978-1-5225-5094-5.ch014

While internet companies cannot be responsible for the online behavior of all individuals, nor be expected to police all corners of the web, the public rightly has an expectation that industry will do its level best to help make the internet safer and more secure for all. If businesses fail or only half-heartedly attempt to meet these expectations, certain groups may shy away from online interactions, abuse and harassment could grow, the promise of a global, connected society will falter—increasing the likelihood that individuals will distrust digital products and services and perhaps even the technology companies themselves.

This public expectation elevates the importance and relevance of the concepts of *digital citizenship*—safe, responsible, and appropriate use of technology and services—and *digital civility*—online interactions rooted in empathy, respect, and kindness. It is essential that internet companies, and indeed all organizations with an online presence, self-assess that they are doing their part to embrace and promote digital citizenship and digital civility among their users. In fact, a collective focus is needed to help raise awareness, educate, and change behavior, involving all internet participants.

Approaches range from philosophical reflections in the emerging field of technoethics (Bertolotti, et. al., 2013 and 2017) to more policy-oriented approaches, such as efforts in the EU, New Zealand, and the United States. In December 2016, the European Commission and Facebook, Microsoft, Twitter, and YouTube announced a Code of Conduct[1] to counter illegal online hate speech. New Zealand enacted the Harmful Digital Communications Act 2015,[2] which includes a range of legal measures to prevent and reduce the impact of "harmful digital communications." And in the United States, 38 states and the District of Columbia have enacted laws criminalizing the distribution of sexually intimate images of individuals without their consent, often referred to as non-consensual pornography or more commonly, "revenge porn."[3]

The aim of this paper is to provide an overview of the steps that Microsoft, a key actor in the technology industry, has taken in its effort to promote online safety, and to offer suggestions for how everyone—the technology industry and policy makers, nongovernmental organizations and academics, as well as internet participants including educators, parents, and young people—can encourage digital civility and citizenship. The paper seeks to demonstrate the business and ethical considerations helping to guide Microsoft's response to some new, topical issues and thereby stimulate additional engagement within the sphere of technoethical studies.

MICROSOFT RESEARCH ON DIGITAL CIVILITY TODAY

As access to the transformational power of technology grew around the world, societies were transfixed by the promise of a truly connected world. Today, however, we find ourselves increasingly aware of the misuse and abuse of online services and their users, as well as physical-world horrors being streamed online for all the world to see. This awareness has led to increased caution, eroding people's confidence in technology as a trustworthy tool and force for good.

In an effort to understand and quantify evolving online social norms, Microsoft conducted research about the state of online interactions and the perceived level of digital civility among users. On Safer Internet Day 2017,[4] we released the results and our first-ever Digital Civility Index—a new measure of people's safety online and their exposure to a defined set of risks.

We surveyed more than 7,000 teens (ages 13 to17) and adults (ages 18 to 74) in 14 countries[5] to gauge their attitudes and perceptions about the state of digital civility today. This sample draws from a population pool that, according to the International Telecommunication Union (ITU) of the United Nations, accounts for about 63 percent of the world's wired population, representing more than two-thirds of the estimated 3.2 billion internet users worldwide and eight of the 11 largest internet markets.[6] We measured the lifetime exposure of those surveyed to 17 forms of online abuse, including harassment, damage to reputation, unwanted contact, and hate speech.[7]

Research results showed that respondents largely find the internet to be a civil place—consumers said they feel that civility online improved over the past year and would continue to improve, so they would expect to continue increasing their online interactions. However, they did express strong concerns about online safety both now and in the future.

The respondents' concerns about safety and security are grounded in their exposure to harm online:

- Almost two in three respondents (65 percent) said they had fallen victim to at least one form of online abuse; that swelled to 78 percent when participants also accounted for the online experiences of their friends and family members.[8] Unwanted contact, trolling, mean treatment, receiving unwanted sext messages, online harassment, and hate speech were the top concerns.
- In addition, half of the respondents reported being extremely or very worried about the risks addressed in the study, and 62 percent said they did not know or were unsure where to get help when they encountered abuse online.
- Meanwhile, 62 percent revealed being extremely or very concerned about future online engagement, with doxing (collecting and broadcasting information about a person without their permission), damage to reputation, and online harassment being their chief fears.

Figure 1. Microsoft Digital Civility Research 2016/2017: Respondents are positive about digital civility, and although they are less optimistic about their security, they plan to keep using the internet.

Trends in Online Safety

PAST YEAR		1 YEAR AHEAD	
74	Consumers felt civility improved in the past year	**94**	Consumers felt civility will get slightly better in the future
112	...but felt their identity and activities were less secure	**104**	...and felt they will continue to be less secure in the future
144	...and they increased the interactions they had online...	**138**	...but will continue to increase their interactions in the future

Figure 2. Microsoft Digital Civility Research 2016/2017: More than half of the respondents and family members or friends experienced unwanted contact.

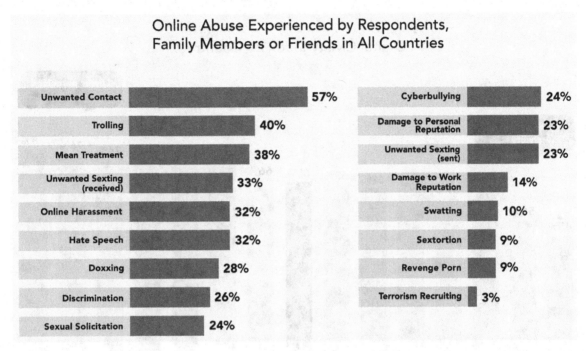

Online Abuse Experienced by Respondents, Family Members or Friends in All Countries

Unwanted Contact	57%		Cyberbullying	24%
Trolling	40%		Damage to Personal Reputation	23%
Mean Treatment	38%		Unwanted Sexting (sent)	23%
Unwanted Sexting (received)	33%		Damage to Work Reputation	14%
Online Harassment	32%		Swatting	10%
Hate Speech	32%		Sextortion	9%
Doxxing	28%		Revenge Porn	9%
Discrimination	26%		Terrorism Recruiting	3%
Sexual Solicitation	24%			

From these results, we created what we're calling Microsoft's Digital Civility Index. We devised the index for each country surveyed, as well as an international reading that includes all 14 countries. The index works like a golf score: the lower the percentage, the lower the respondents' exposure to risk and the higher the perceived level of online civility among people in that country.

Of the countries surveyed, the UK had the highest level of perceived digital civility at 45 percent; South Africa had the lowest at 78 percent. The international Digital Civility Index stands at 65, which means that 65 percent of all people surveyed have been exposed to some harm online. Results also show that, on average, respondents, family members, or friends experienced almost five (4.9) of the 17 types of abuse measured in the study.

The new index builds on the Microsoft Computing Safety Index[9]—a study conducted three times between 2010 and 2013 that gauged the online safety habits and behaviors of consumers—as well as a separate survey about the global pervasiveness of online bullying commissioned by the company in February 2012.[10]

The latter research polled more than 7,600 young people between the ages of 8 and 17 in 25 countries.[11] We asked whether they had encountered a range of negative behaviors online ranging from general meanness, such as teasing or name-calling, to outright cruelty, including the willful intent to harm. More than half of the respondents (54 percent) said they were concerned they would be bullied online; about four in 10 (37 percent) said someone had been mean to them online; and nearly a quarter (24 percent) admitted to having bullied someone else online.

Some of these same issues were revisited four years later in the digital civility research. Across all 14 countries, 9 percent of both teen and adult respondents said they had experienced bullying; 22 percent reported mean treatment online; and 17 percent disclosed that they had been harassed.[12]

Figure 3. Microsoft Digital Civility Research 2016/2017: The index works like a golf score: the lower the percentage, the lower the respondents' exposure to risk and the higher the perceived level of online civility.

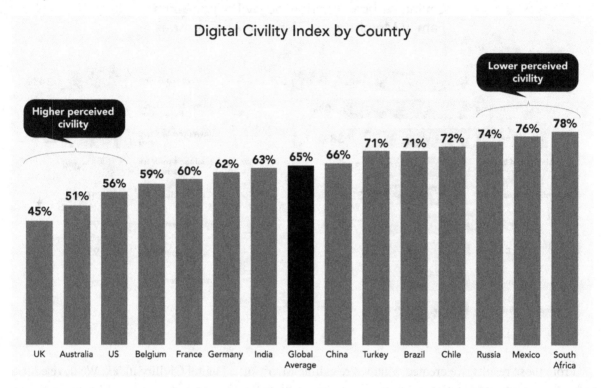

The digital civility research also showed that exposure to online risks has consequences in the physical world, ranging from a loss of trust in others to increased stress, sleep deprivation, and even thoughts of suicide (shown in Figure 4 below). Indeed, 40 percent of respondents said they had become less trusting of people online, and almost a third reported growing less trusting of people offline. More than one in five said they lost sleep, felt stressed, or participated less frequently in blogs and other online forums. Others said they lost a friend, became depressed, endured damage to their personal reputations, or contemplated suicide.

This inaugural round of digital civility research sets the baseline for the initial 14 countries. We are continuing the digital civility research in 2017 and 2018, adding several new countries and establishing a new baseline.

FOSTERING DIGITAL CIVILITY: WHAT MICROSOFT IS DOING

So, what can we learn from the data? Online, people are establishing social norms that include treating each other with respect and dignity, but more can and must be done. Digital civility—which includes the protection of one's identity, needs, and beliefs without harming or degrading another's and is grounded in empathy—must become a universal message and a common-sense behavior so that the internet can be a safe place for everyone.

Figure 4. Microsoft Digital Civility Research 2016/2017: After experiencing harm online, respondents report less trust of others both online and offline.

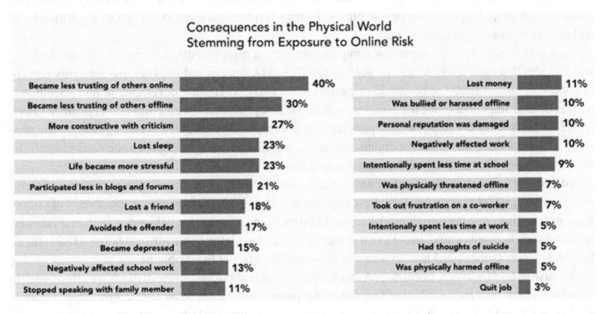

Consequences in the Physical World
Stemming from Exposure to Online Risk

Became less trusting of others online	40%
Became less trusting of others offline	30%
More constructive with criticism	27%
Lost sleep	23%
Life became more stressful	23%
Participated less in blogs and forums	21%
Lost a friend	18%
Avoided the offender	17%
Became depressed	15%
Negatively affected school work	13%
Stopped speaking with family member	11%
Lost money	11%
Was bullied or harassed offline	10%
Personal reputation was damaged	10%
Negatively affected work	10%
Intentionally spent less time at school	9%
Was physically threatened offline	7%
Took out frustration on a co-worker	7%
Intentionally spent less time at work	5%
Had thoughts of suicide	5%
Was physically harmed offline	5%
Quit job	3%

As a starting point for promoting this message, Microsoft launched a Digital Civility Challenge in early 2017,[13] encouraging adults and youth alike to embrace four primary tenets for their interactions online:

- *Treat others as you would like to be treated* by acting with empathy, compassion, and kindness in every interaction, and treating everyone online with dignity and respect.
- *Respect differences* by honoring diverse perspectives, and when disagreements surface, engage thoughtfully and avoid name-calling and personal attacks.
- *Pause before replying* to contrary comments and refrain from posting or sending anything that could hurt someone, damage a reputation, or threaten someone's safety.
- *Stand up for yourself and others* by supporting those who are targets of online abuse or cruelty, reporting activity that threatens anyone's safety (including your own), and preserving evidence of inappropriate or unsafe behavior.

Hundreds took the Digital Civility Challenge, and in the first few weeks following the launch of the campaign, Microsoft's activities around the Digital Civility Index generated more than 5.5 million social media impressions and almost 600 online articles published in 30 countries.

Building on the challenge, in August 2017 Microsoft convened its first Council for Digital Good Summit[14] as part of a one-year pilot program for teens in the United States. Fifteen young people from 12 U.S. states were selected to share their diverse perspectives on the state of online interactions today, as well as their hopes and ideals for what would make online life healthier, safer, and more enjoyable. Each council member drafted an individual manifesto for life online, which the cohort will consolidate into a single catalogue of online norms and publish to the council website as a living work product of this inaugural council.

When discussing Microsoft's focus on an issue such as digital civility or our online safety work in general, people are sometimes surprised to learn that for more than two decades Microsoft has followed a four-part strategy for protecting people online, focusing on technology, self-governance, partnerships, and consumer education and outreach.

First and foremost, as a technology company, we have a responsibility to create software, devices, and services that have safety features—such as family safety settings and mechanisms for easily reporting abuse—built in from the outset. In our effort to self-govern product development and operations, we devise and implement internal policies, standards, and procedures with child and consumer safety top-of-mind, and these extend beyond pure legal requirements. We embrace a vast number of partnerships and collaborate with a host of organizations because no one entity or organization can successfully tackle these significant, novel, and nuanced issues alone.

To educate consumers about online safety and promote the responsible and appropriate use of technology among all internet citizens, we have developed a 360-degree approach: staying abreast of online risks and alerting consumers to those risks; providing tools and resources to help individuals and families better protect themselves; and, in the event someone should fall victim to a scam or scheme, arming them with the resources they need to help address, or preferably, correct the problem.

To raise public awareness of online risks and educate people about how to avoid them, we offer a wealth of online safety materials, including fact sheets for parents and teachers on online grooming,[15] online harassment,[16] and hate speech.[17] On social and digital media, we regularly engage with our friends and followers, offering news, guidance and information about the latest resources, tools, and materials—from Microsoft and others—that can help keep children, teens, and families safer and more secure online.[18]

FOSTERING DIGITAL CIVILITY: A SHARED RESPONSIBILITY

No one entity can successfully promote digital civility on its own. Indeed, creating a safer, more secure internet is a shared responsibility among the technology industry, government policy-makers, non-governmental organizations, academics, and all individual internet participants, including parents and caregivers, educators, and young people. Microsoft suggests a range of activities and behaviors for all participants in this social and technological equation.

What the Technology Industry Can Do

- **Create Purposeful Online Environments:** Services offering users the ability to create and participate in communities must explain the purpose of the online environments they seek to grow. For instance, is the service for gaming and entertainment, buying and selling, communicating, socializing, or dating? Let users know, and recognize that virtual communities cross geographical and cultural boundaries.
- **Institute and Enforce Codes of Conduct:** Service providers must create and make public and conspicuous, in a code of conduct or similar vehicle, what content and activities they both encourage and prohibit, as well as the penalties for failing to respect a company's terms. Companies must take seriously reports about content or conduct that is illegal, incites violence, is discriminatory, or promotes hatred. Balance policies and codes of conduct against fundamental rights, including privacy, free expression, and personal and public safety.

- **Offer Remedies:** Offer easy-to-find, user-friendly online tools to report illegal, inappropriate, or offensive content, and review and address those reports in a timely manner. Be transparent about content takedowns. In turn, provide mechanisms for customers to report and request reinstatement of content they believe was removed in error.

What Law- and Policy-Makers Can Do

- **Deter Online Abuse:** Strengthen laws to deter online exploitation and harassment, and don't inadvertently victimize the people those laws seek to protect. To help ensure this, work closely with child advocacy and victim-support organizations, law enforcement agencies, the technology industry, and youth and their families.
- **Grow Public-Private Partnerships:** Seek input from and collaborate with technology companies, victims' advocates, public health and other experts, and members of civil society. Together, raise awareness of online risks and rewards; educate families, teachers, lawyers, judges, and law enforcement personnel. Devise creative and innovative approaches for encouraging positive, respectful behaviors online and offline. Support, organize, and promote these partnerships through awareness-raising and messaging campaigns, as well as studies and research.
- **Encourage Responsible Industry Practices:** Work with the technology industry and other organizations to agree on foundational principles. Technology providers can then determine the most effective means of implementation. This approach provides industry with the latitude and flexibility required to respond to the ever-changing landscape of online risk.

What the Broader Internet Community Can Do

Individuals can embrace the four primary tenets for online interaction in the Microsoft Digital Civility Challenge described above, while nongovernmental organizations, academics, and others can consider the following:

- **Embrace Pluralism Online:** Work together to encourage and grow a culture of online civility that respects and values different opinions. Embrace free expression, tolerance, and cultural and social diversity. Making room for all perspectives helps to break down echo chambers, spark insights, and improve cooperation.
- **Share Knowledge:** Develop and share educational resources that encourage individuals, families, and communities to proactively engage and prepare—at the earliest ages and stages—for life online.
- **Grow Positive Communities:** Civil societies foster positive, healthy relationships and community. Help build and support safe and trusted online environments where individuals are encouraged and empowered to share, create, learn, and fully participate.

How to Support Digital Civility Among Youth

Calls to action in support of youth—for parents, educators, and young people themselves—all reference a key component: social and emotional learning, which helps to build empathy.

According to the Committee for Children, a nonprofit organization that develops social and emotional learning curriculum, such training emphasizes "communication skills, a focus on achievement, and concern for community. It also promotes positive classroom behavior and academic excellence. Conversely, it helps to reduce in-school conduct problems, aggressive behavior, and emotional stress." [19]

Whatever the online safety issue, Microsoft believes in keeping the lines of communication open among children, teens, and adults. Young people want to know that someone cares, will listen, and will take action, as and when appropriate. Accordingly, parents and caregivers should ask that children report any threats encounter online directly to them.

What Parents and Caregivers Can Do

- **Lead by Example:** Model compassion, kindness, and empathy. Children learn from what adults do. They notice how their elders respond to stress, and they take note if family, friends, neighbors, and even strangers are not being treated with kindness and respect.
- **Encourage Empathy:** Adults can suggest to children that they look at things from others' perspectives, including those who wish to do them harm. Expressing empathy is a key component of social and emotional learning.
- **Watch for Signs:** Is a child upset when online or texting? Does he or she display a reluctance to go to, or stay at, school?

What Educators, Counselors, and School Officials Can Do

- **Teach Digital Citizenship in School:** We live in a digital culture. To thrive, we must teach citizenship skills that encompass a child's complete life both online and in the physical world. Integrate lessons about life online into traditional scholastic curricula, including social studies, health, and language arts classes. Invest in after-school programs so all family members can learn and model healthy online safety skills.
- **Promote Social and Emotional Learning:** Educational approaches that focus on social and emotional learning help develop empathy and prepare youth for success. Core competencies include self-awareness, self-management, and responsible decision-making.
- **Emphasize Civility:** Civility in everyday interactions fosters vibrant, engaged communities. Lead by example and celebrate positive attitudes and behaviors. Acknowledge and appreciate the student voice in the civility dialogue, engage peer leaders to share positive online social norms, and emphasize that most youth are making sound choices online.

What Young People Can Do

Young people can embrace the four primary tenets for online interaction in the Microsoft Digital Civility Challenge described above.

CONCLUSION

If society is to fulfill the promise of the internet, we must encourage digital citizenship and nurture digital civility. We cannot settle for the status quo of hurtful online interactions and must encourage one another to be our best selves online as in real life. We can accomplish this only through a collective focus that harnesses the commitment and resources of technology companies, government policy-makers, businesses with an online presence, and all those who use the internet, including parents, educators, and young people.

ACKNOWLEDGMENT

Microsoft employees around the world contribute to and support the company's work to help protect individuals and families online and to promote digital citizenship and civility. Indeed, this paper is a compilation of the many Microsoft projects and programs that demonstrate the company's role in these efforts. I cannot attempt to name all the individuals at Microsoft, both past and present, who have made and continue to make a daily difference in helping to protect people online. You know who you are, and I thank and applaud you.

That said, I would like to thank the following individuals who helped to shape this research, paper, and work in digital civility from both inside and outside of Microsoft: Dr. Patricia Agatston, Dr. Tommaso Bertolotti, Carol Brown, Donna Corey, Tarleton Gillespie, Marsali Hancock, David Heiner, Michael Karimian, Katie Lowry, John Ruchinskas, and Tom Wong. Your work and dedication are very much appreciated.

REFERENCES

Bertolotti, T., Arfini, S., & Magnani, L. (2017). *Cyber Bullies as Cyborg Bullies*. The Changing Scope of Technoethics in Contemporary Society.

Bertolotti, T., & Magnani, L. (2013). A philosophical and evolutionary approach to cyber-bullying: Social networks and the disruption of sub-moralities. *Ethics and Information Technology*, *15*(4), 285–299. doi:10.100710676-013-9324-3

Lenhart, A. (2016). *Online Harassment, Digital Abuse, and Cyberstalking in America*. Data & Society Research Institute and Center for Innovative Public Health Research. Retrieved August 1, 2017, from https://www.datasociety.net/pubs/oh/Online_Harassment_2016.pdf

KEY TERMS AND DEFINITIONS

Digital Citizenship: The safe, responsible, and appropriate use of technology and services.
Digital Civility: Online interactions rooted in empathy, respect, and kindness.

Digital Literacy: Begins with technological literacy—how to use devices and navigate the internet. It then progresses to learning basic online safety habits, such as the importance of strong and secret passwords to protect accounts and devices, and knowing how to update devices to defend against malware and scams. Digital literacy also means building resilience and self-reliance, which encompasses developing the critical thinking skills needed to assess the accuracy of online information, evaluate situations, make informed decisions, and solve problems encountered online.

Hate Speech: Speech that attacks an individual (or group) based on attributes such as their race, religion, ethnicity, sexual orientation of gender, or a disability.

Online Bullying (or Cyberbullying): The use of electronic technology to tease, demean, or harass someone less powerful.

Online Harassment (or Cyber Harassment): Unwanted contact that is used to intimidate, annoy, or frighten someone using digital means.

Social and Emotional Learning: The process through which people learn to understand and manage cmotions, and feel and show empathy for others to help develop positive relationships, and make effective decisions.

ENDNOTES

[1]   Code of Conduct on Countering Illegal Hate Speech Online. ec.europa.eu/justice/fundamental-rights/files/hate_speech_code_of_conduct_en.pdf

[2]   Harmful Digital Communications Act 2015. www.legislation.govt.nz/act/public/2015/0063/latest/whole.html

[3]   Cyber Civil Rights Initiative. www.cybercivilrights.org

[4]   Safer Internet Day 2017. www.saferinternetday.org/

[5]   Australia, Belgium, Brazil, Chile, China, France, Germany, India, Mexico, Russia, South Africa, Turkey, the United Kingdom, and the United States

[6]   *Global ICT Developments*, United Nations International Telecommunication Union (ITU), 2015. http://www.itu.int/en/ITU-D/Statistics/Pages/stat/default.aspx. (Note: the ITU is continually updating its webpages, so look for reports dated 2015.)

[7]   The survey asked people to note which of the following 17 risks they, a friend, or a family member had been exposed to online: 1) Doxing: The process of collecting and broadcasting information about a person—for example, name, age, email, address, telephone number, photographs—without permission. 2) Swatting: The act of deceiving emergency services (police, fire, medical) into sending an emergency response based on the false report of a critical incident or crime. 3) Hate Speech: Speech that attacks a person or group based on gender, ethnic origin, religion, race, disability, or sexual orientation. 4) Revenge Pornography: A sexually explicit portrayal of one or more people distributed without their consent. 5) Sextortion: When someone threatens to distribute private and sensitive material if the target doesn't provide images of a sexual nature, sexual favors, or money. The perpetrator may also threaten to harm friends or relatives by using information obtained from electronic devices unless there is compliance. 6) Cyberbullying (or Online Bullying): When the internet, cell phones, or other devices are used to send or post text or images intended to hurt,

embarrass, or intimidate another person. 7) Mean Treatment: Words or messages sent to another person online that are unkind, unfair, or malicious. 8) Trolling: A deliberate act to make someone mad or angry using comments in a clever but deceitful manner. 9) Discrimination: When someone is discriminated against or excluded based on gender, ethnic origin, religion, race, disability, or sexual orientation. 10) Receiving Unwanted Sexts: Receiving unwanted sexually explicit messages and imagery. 11) Sending Unwanted Sexts: Sending unwanted sexually explicit messages and imagery. 12) Sexual Solicitation: Asking to engage in sexual activities or talk, or giving personal sexual information that is unwanted. 13) Terrorism Recruiting: An attempt by a terrorist or terrorist organization to recruit someone for the purposes of causing harm. 14) Unwanted Contact: Being personally contacted by phone or in person without an invitation by someone who obtained information online. 15) Damage to Personal Reputation: Damage or destruction to reputation through personal information shared online in blogs, postings, pictures, tweets, videos, etc. 16) Damage to Professional or Work Reputation: Damage or destruction to reputation through work information shared online in blogs, postings, pictures, tweets, videos, etc. 17) Online Harassment: Threats or other offensive behavior (not sexual solicitation) sent online or posted online for others to see.

[8]   When surveying young people, experience has shown us that youth are often more comfortable discussing something that may have happened to a friend or family member than to themselves.

[9]   *Microsoft Computing Safety Index Worldwide Report*, Microsoft, 2013. http://go.microsoft.com/?linkid=9843176

[10]   *Online bullying among youth 8 to 17 years old worldwide,* Youth Online Behavior Study, Microsoft, February 2012. https://aka.ms/YouthOnlineBehaviorStudy

[11]   Youth were surveyed in Argentina, Australia, Brazil, Canada, China, Czech Republic, Egypt, France, Germany, India, Italy, Japan, Malaysia, Morocco, Norway, Pakistan, Poland, Qatar, Russia, Singapore, Spain, Turkey, United Arab Emirates, the United Kingdom, and the United States.

[12]   The findings in our digital civility research showed a remarkable consistency with research on online harassment, digital abuse, and cyberstalking conducted in the United States in 2016 by the Data & Society Research Institute and the Center for Innovative Public Health Research. (https://www.datasociety.net/pubs/oh/Online_Harassment_2016.pdf)

As with our research, these groups found that almost half (47 percent) of internet users surveyed had experienced online harassment or abuse and three-quarters (72 percent) had witnessed at least one harassing behavior online. As in the Microsoft survey, people altered their behaviors to address the risks including censoring their online postings (27 percent), and changing contact information (40 percent) out of fear of online harassment, with some even disconnecting from support networks and information.

[13]   *Promote digital civility.* www.microsoft.com/digitalcivility

[14]   Council for Digital Good, www.microsoft.com/cdg

[15]   *Stay alert to online grooming.* https://aka.ms/OnlineGrooming

[16]   *Dealing with harassment on the internet.* https://aka.ms/OnlineBullyingHarassment

[17]   Teach kids to identify misinformation and hate speech. https://aka.ms/identifymisinformation-hatespeech

[18]   Website: www.microsoft.com/saferonline
Facebook: www.facebook.com/saferonline
Twitter: www.twitter.com/safer_online

[19]   Committee for Children (www.cfchildren.org), Seattle, Washington, United States, is a not-for-profit organization established more than 30 years ago. It has created a social and emotional learning (SEL) curriculum that, as of this writing, is in use in 40 percent of schools in the United States and in 70 other countries. SEL helps to prepare young people for adulthood and success in the 21st century by emphasizing, among other things, communication skills, a focus on achievement, and concern for community. It also promotes positive classroom behavior and academic excellence. Conversely, it helps to reduce in-school conduct problems, aggressive behavior, and emotional stress. Given cultural and societal differences the world over, SEL is by no means a singular response to negative behavior among youth, but it is one approach to consider.

Chapter 15
Algorithms vs. Hive Minds:
Preserving Democracy's
Future in the Age of AI

Rick Searle
IEET, USA

ABSTRACT

From the time of its emergence onto the public scene, the internet has been understood in light of both its dystopian potential for total surveillance and control and its utopian possibilities to enable enhanced forms of freedom. The reality has proven far more complicated with the internet having both helped to weaken institutions and strengthened new forms of authoritarian populism. This chapter argues that these two potentials are deeply interconnected and that the long-term sustainability of democracy requires that we understand and address the connections between our fears and hopes regarding the internet's future.

INTRODUCTION

In 1997 just as the Internet was roaring into public consciousness the inventor of the VRML code, Mark Pesce, attempted to project forward the ultimate destiny of this new "realm" he had helped create. Holding that the telecommunications revolution would likely end in one of two radically different ways, Pesce wrote in his essay *Ignition:*

The power over this realm has been given to you. You are weaving the fabric of perception in information perceptualized. You could – if you choose – turn our world into a final panopticon – a prison where all can be seen and heard and judged by a single jailer. Or you could aim for its inverse, an asylum run by the inmates. The esoteric promise of cyberspace is of a rule where you do as you will; this ontology – already present in the complex system known as the Internet – stands a good chance of being passed along to its organ of perception. (Pesce, 1997)

Certainly Pesce was onto something. As the Internet and its successor mobile technologies unfolded in the two decades following his essay it proved both the ultimate panopticon and a vector for the under-

DOI: 10.4018/978-1-5225-5094-5.ch015

mining of traditional centers of power. It gave us both the NSA and what political theorists characterized variously as "the end of power" (Naím, 2014) or "monitory democracy". (Keane, 2009)

Yet the effect, so far, of this erosion of power has not been to empower democratic citizens and civil discourse but to enable new forms of popular- authoritarian politics and political sectarianism even in some of the most long-lived democracies in the West. (Mounk, 2016)

My task here is to bridge these utopian and dystopian aspects by providing a rough outline of the emergence of Pesce's feared "prison" with a "single jailer" and his hoped for "asylum run by the inmates" in the hope that better understanding our situation will provide a more secure ethical orientation towards the communications technologies which are radically changing the nature of democratic politics.

The following essay is divided into three sections and a brief conclusion. The first section will look at various manifestations of Pesce's panopticon, the economic model that underpins it, along with its manifestation in authoritarian states.

The second section will look at the inverse of this panopticon, the way in which the Internet has enabled lateral, almost leaderless movements to burst onto the scene in the second decade of the 21 century. I characterize these movements and protests as "hive-minds", and in this section, I will explore how these movements both were enabled and suppressed by leveraging features unique to current communications technologies.

The third section will explore how in 2016 the hive-mind was mobilized in the interest of the political right and the way in which this has resulted in calls for greater algorithmic control by Internet platforms. Here I attempt to lay out how, rather than being mutually exclusive predictions regarding the Internet's future, algorithms and hive-minds are instead two manifestations of the same process both of which threaten the future of democracy if not brought under public control.

The final and concluding section will look at some proposals for asserting political control over algorithms and hive-minds and urge us to break free of the founding mythology of the Internet in order to recover our status as democratic citizens.

Mass Surveillance and the Rise of Algorithms

Not all that long ago, people talked of the Internet as if it were a new and distinct domain- *cyberspace*-something separate from the real world with which we had long been acquainted. That is no longer the case, for what has happened over the last generation is that cyberspace has consumed the real world, it has become the overlay through which our reactions with reality are mediated. (Wertheim, 1999)

A peculiar model of how this mediation should work is now found across multiple domains. It is found in the way security services operate, along with much of finance and commerce; it is the basis for new ways of responding to crime, and is deeply influencing the way we organize the cities of our increasingly urbanized planet. It is ultimately a model of *power* that has been made possible by the shrinking size of computer components and the spread of ubiquitous connectivity. It is a model that bears a chilling resemblance to Pesce's feared panopticon.

Only with the 2013 revelations by Edward Snowden was the extent to which US and British security services had leveraged the Internet's architecture for mass surveillance become truly known. (Franceschi-Bicchierai, 2014) Yet a little over a year before Snowden's discoveries were made public, James Bamford laid out how the NSA had built a massive data center in the desert of Utah where:

....the NSA has turned its surveillance apparatus on the US and its citizens. It has established listening posts throughout the nation to collect and sift through billions of email messages and phone calls, whether they originate within the country or overseas. It has created a supercomputer of almost unimaginable speed to look for patterns and unscramble codes. Finally, the agency has begun building a place to store all the trillions of words and thoughts and whispers captured in its electronic net. (Bamford, 2012)

Subsequent revelations, especially those of Snowden, would uncover just how deep the tentacles of this architecture 0f surveillance went, and just what a danger it was to traditional notions of privacy and civil liberties.

The ultimate effect of the outcry engendered by the Snowden revelations, especially among US tech firms that aimed at global markets, was a partial roll back of the surveillance state. In 2015 Congress forced the NSA to end its bulk collection of Americans metadata- the very purpose for which the Utah facility had been built. (Poplin, 2015)

The Snowden revelations, along with a series of infamous hacks like the one against Sonny Corp, also helped spur the increasing popularity of encryption in which even run of the mill Internet users tried to hide their activities from the prying eyes of the state and actors with nefarious intent. (Kuchler, 2014) This led states themselves, which had become dependent upon the new surveillance technologies to go on the offensive against encryption, as the British did with the Investigatory Powers Act of 2016 or "Snooper's Charter". Governments sought to weaken encryption even if this ultimately meant making the Internet more vulnerable to assaults by criminal actors and rival states. (Hern, 2017)

What the Snowden revelations largely failed to do was upend the economic model that had given rise to mass surveillance in the first place. The NSA could only even imagine building such a system because the private sector had been permitted to build an entire communications architecture on the basis of mass surveillance. It had taken the aftermath of dot com bubble and bust for companies to come up with a model of how to monetize the Internet, and almost all of the major tech companies that dominate the Internet, at least in America- and there are only a handful- Google, FaceBook and Amazon, now follow some variant of this model.

That model was to aggregate all the sharing that the Internet seems to naturally produce and offer it, along with other "compliments" for "free" in exchange for one thing: the ability to monitor, measure and manipulate through advertising whoever uses their services. (Economist, 2012) The model went by the name of "personalization" and demanded in the words of Kevin Kelly: "... *total transparency. That is going to be the price. If you want to have total personalization, you have to be totally transparent.*" (Stibel, 2009)

The idea of ubiquitous monitoring only made sense if the flood of information it produced could be effectively organized and searched for valuable pieces of data.

Here was where the revolution in algorithmization and artificial intelligence came into play. In the early 21st century much of individual social interaction came to be mediated by sorting algorithms from recommended movies to selected books, music, and even lovers. (Steiner, 2012)

Monitoring of individuals allowed them to be classed as "types" on the basis of which those individuals became "targets" for, among other things, products, criminal investigation, or scams. Due to the fact that the Internet had become one of the primary ways the individual interacted with the world algorithms defined who an individual was, if not to herself, then for others. (Pariser, 2011) In this era of "Big Data", power flows towards those able to identify and act upon meaningful patterns.

The only major US tech firm pursuing an alternative to this model was Apple, which under the leadership of Tim Cook distinguished itself on the basis of unwavering protection of consumer privacy. (Simonite, 2017) Yet the victory of Apple's model of wouldn't so much represent the realization of Silicon Valley's libertarian, hacker, and counter-culture ethic, as one in which gatekeepers asserted full control over their technology and the user's experience of it. (Wu, 2012)

It was just as likely Apple's model wouldn't survive the era of Big Data enabled AI, for even while the kinds of widespread encryption and ad blocking that might upend the surveillance state and its underlying commercial model became increasingly common, the technology that seemed poised to dominate the early 21st century- artificial intelligence- was dependent upon the open model pursued by Appel's major rivals, a development that might make that company's devotion to privacy ultimately unsustainable.

This is because the companies with the most potent capabilities in AI, which at the moment is based not on any revolution in software so much as in the sheer quantity of data now available for deep learning algorithms to mine, are monopolized by those entities most willing to hoover up and utilize user's every interaction.

Like the competition over land by 19th century imperialist powers, algorithms were used by competing social and economic forces over the territory of *data*. The hunt for faster and better ways to parse data, and deliver it in ways "tailored" to the individual resulted in an artificial intelligence arms race with the major Internet powers, both part of the state, and outside of it, vigorously pursuing and perfecting AI. To quote Andrew Ng of the Chinese search giant Baidu, "whoever wins AI wins the Internet". (Ng, 2014)

This desire to influence targets dovetailed almost perfectly with a revived behaviorism in psychology. As our machines became more rational, human beings, or at least it was being argued, became less so. A key component of tailoring to a targeted individual, which really meant influencing the individual to make preselected consumer and political choices, wasn't monitoring alone but surveillance followed by sophisticated forms of manipulation which were the product of research in the burgeoning field of behavioral economics, so-called "nudging". (Thaler and Sunstein, 2008)

The deliberate crafting of devices and apps to take advantage of the weaknesses identified by psychologist, especially human vulnerability to behavioral addiction, became one of the primary modus operandi of Internet firms. (Alter, 2017) The constant demand for user's attention that was the result of Internet companies' dependence on advertising as their predominant source of revenue resulted in widespread despair over the effect the Internet was having, especially in the age of ubiquitous screens made possible by smart phones, on human productivity and relationships as advertisers became increasingly inescapable. (Wu, 2017)

Yet it was in cities that political manifestation of algorithmization and mass surveillance seemed furthest along. Both developed and developing world cities were being wooed by technology companies and eagerly embracing so-called "smart-cities" where the urban landscape is covered in sensors cameras and related technologies with all this data pumped into "control-centers", which coordinate management responses. Developed world cities, such as New York, have deployed such systems (Singer, 2012), but the adoption of similar technologies in the developing world is more interesting for the simple fact that so much more of humanity lives, and if demographic projections are correct, will live, there where the problems of rapid urbanization are so much more acute. (Kilcullen, 2013)

In addition to general city management systems, technology companies built huge data centers to monitor and respond to one of urban life's perennial problems- crime. Here is how the former CEO of Google, Eric Schmidt described one of the largest and most sophisticated of these crime centers- *Platforma Mexico:*

Housed in an underground bunker in the Secretariat of Public Security compound in Mexico City, this large database integrates intelligence, crime reports and real time data from surveillance cameras and other inputs from across the country. Specialized algorithms can extract patterns, project social graphs and monitor restive areas for violence and crime as well as for natural disasters and other emergencies. (Schmidt, 2013)

Almost unnoticed, such crime centers have proliferated both beyond and within the US, (Priest, 2011) and some were even heralding the arrival of the sorts of "predictive policing" which, until now, was found in the world of science-fiction alone. (Karoliszyn, 2014)

The new authoritarian regimes, especially, found in the tools of mass surveillance powers that would have put the spying capacities of their totalitarian forbearers to shame. (Guriev & Treisman, 2017) The most notorious in this regard was The People's Republic of China where there existed the "Great Firewall" through which the PRC tried to prevent embarrassing information from outside its borders from the eyes of Chinese citizens. (Haas, 2017) In China one also saw what the consequences of surveillance society might be were it to follow its own logic free of the constraints of Western ideas regarding privacy and constraints on the state. There one found state officials forced to wear GPS trackers in an effort to root out corruption, (Walsh, 2017), facial recognition technologies used to monitor the behavior of citizens (Chin & Linn, 2017) along with a much greater proclivity of commercial companies, even if compelled, to share data on users with the state.

Thus, vast areas of the globe have been fleshed out in ways that resemble something like Pesce's panopticon. If that were the whole of the story the future might be very dystopian indeed, but there is another side to it as well.

The Hive- Mind and Digital Utopianism

The fact that we have acquiesced in the construction of an unprecedented system of mass surveillance that is used largely by elites for commercial, financial, political and security purposes should lead to a realization that a great deal of Pesce's panopticon has already been built. It is a system that is too complex for human individuals to control and has been put under the direction of sophisticated algorithms that structure to their owners' purposes an ever increasing amount of human interactions and even our own self-understanding.

However, dark as all of this is, it does not mean that the anarchic and democratic aspects of the Internet Pesce had hoped for are not also present. The media theorists, Clay Shirky was not really wrong when he predicted in 2005 that the 21st century would be an "age of chaos" where loosely coordinated groups would have increasing leverage over society and would out-compete institutions that clung to information monopolies. The flatter and more loosely organized these groups, and the more they abandoned traditional goals such as the profit motive, the more effective, Shirky held, they would ultimately be. (Shirky, 2008)

The revolutions, revolts and protests in the second decade of the 21st century really did seem to embody the flat characteristics of hive minds that had been laid out by the technology writer Kevin Kelly almost twenty years before their eruption. Kelly in his 1994 book *Out of Control* saw in the rise of personal computers and the Internet that connected them the foretaste of a more anarchic, self-organizing, and non-centrally directed order of the hive a "vivi-system" that Kelly thought had four core features:

- The absence of imposed centralized control.
- The autonomous nature of the subunits.
- The high connectivity between subunits.
- The webby nonlinearity of peers influencing peers. (Kelly, 1995).

The Indignado protests in Spain, the Occupy Wall Street Movement in the US, the crowds that toppled governments in Tunisia and Egypt in 2011, and shook Turkey and Brazil in 2013, or the 2014 protests over police brutality in Ferguson Missouri and elsewhere, to name just a few examples, lacked centralized control and were largely leaderless with sub-groups following their own scripts. As Manuel Castells, perhaps the premier theorists of the "networked age" argues these were lateral movements lacking clear revolutionary narratives and driven forward by interactions between individuals that did not belong to an overarching structure. (Castells, 2012)

The tool which made these protests possible was the mobile phone. From an insignificant number of luxury devices wielded by elites, cellular phones became the most rapidly ubiquitized device in human history during the first decade of the 21st century. By 2013 there were 6 billion of them- 4.5 billion of which were in the developing world. More people had access to cell phones than indoor toilets or clean water. (Townsend, 2014)

What sets the Internet era off from those that preceded it is the ease with which it facilitates collaboration between previously unconnected individuals. Steven Johnson calls the kinds of collaborative efforts by small groups enabled by ubiquitous Internet and mobile technologies "peer-to-peer" networks and sees in them a new form of post-representational democracy and a more fluid and citizen centered politics. (Johnson, 2012)

While the constant gadfly of technologists, Evgeny Morozov, not without some degree of justice, complained that the ease of social interaction between distant individuals afforded by the Internet and social media resulted in a kind of lukewarm political involvement he characterized as "slacktivism" (Morozov, 2011), the same platforms he derided did play a significant role in the popular revolts against authoritarian regimes prematurely dubbed the "Arab Spring".

As the sociologist Zeynep Tufekci pointed out in her landmark book on the role of social media in recent political revolts and their aftermath, the very same tools that allowed Westerners to remain connected with hundreds of friends spread all over the world became a means of mobilizing collective grievance. For the first time, citizens in authoritarian societies such as Egypt had access to platforms of information and discussion free of government censors. (Tufekci, 2017)

The increasing presence of these networks in revolt was facilitated by the decline of older institutions that had, as of yet, failed to adapt to the logic of web-like structures. As the vice-chairmen of the consulting firm Kissinger Associates, Joshua Cooper Ramo, points out in his excellent book *The Seventh Sense: Power, Fortune, and Survival in the Age of Networks*- we are entering a tumultuous age in which older forms of power such as political parties, mainline churches and traditional media are being, and will increasingly be, eaten alive by new powers in the form of networks. (Ramo, 2017)

As almost ad hoc groups of like- minded individuals have become empowered traditional institutions appear to have become increasingly weakened. The digital revolution, which has managed to put levels of computational capacity that had once been the possession solely of huge government agencies and large corporations into the hands of literally billions of individuals, really does seem to have had an effect on the ability of traditional power centers to exercise that power, making the control over events more difficult.

Moisés Naím, for one, argues that every large structure in society: armies, corporations, churches and unions are seeing their power decline and are being challenged by small and nimble upstarts empowered by cheap collaborative and coordinating technology. (Naím, 2014)

The communications revolution has significantly lowered the barriers to political organization and speech. Anyone can throw up a website and start organizing for or against some cause. What this has resulted in is a sort of *Cambrian explosion* of political organizations many of which take on the defense of some very specific political interest or cause. Politics as waged by such groups, at least in democratic countries, moves from being representational democracy to what the political theorist John Keane calls "monitory democracy" essentially a society in which media and citizen based groups, largely empowered by the Internet, continually monitor, challenge and check political power. (Keane, 2009)

One form such monitory democracy could take was that of hacktivists groups, most notably, Anonymous. Other than bringing tens of thousands into the streets, nothing seemed to get elite attention so much as the DoS attacks used by Anonymous whose Guy Fawkes masks, borrowed from the dystopian graphic novel and movie "V", became emblematic of the age of protest. (Olson, 2012)

Since 2011, Anonymous and its sister organization Lulz had gone from a group of pranksters and vandals to a movement with both political and moral aspects trying to impose penalties on what they held to be egregious abuses of power. With particular severity authorities went after these types of organizations that challenge elites' very control over the Internet. (Olson, 2012)

The thing that united what I will call digital utopians, whether they were thinkers such as Shriky, Castells, or Johnson or corporate figures such as Google's Schmitt, was that they seemed to believe that the digital revolution by its very nature would lead to an enhanced democratic citizenship. Digital technology seemed tailor made for the victory of democracy and liberalism predicted by Francis Fukuyama in his book *The End of History*. (Fukuyama, 1992) Unfortunately, what has actually occurred has been something very different.

The Hive-Mind Collapses: The End of Digital Utopianism

There are two ways in which I believe Pesce's prediction regarding the future of the Internet went horribly wrong. Pesce saw the future from the standpoint of a kind of techno-Manicheanism. The Internet would end either in an age of anarchic freedom or with a regime of totalitarian surveillance and control. He seems to have not foreseen that a world where the "asylum was run by the inmates" might be something far removed from any idea of an anarchist utopia. At the same time, his techno-Manicheanism blinded him to the possibility that rather than offering us mutually incompatible version of the future, his rival technological panopticon and digital anarchism were caught up in a mutually supporting feedback loop.

While the Internet and its social platforms did indeed power political revolts, such protests were crushed by authoritarian states which leveraged the same capacities of these platforms to surveil users and easily identify and stifle the most influential members of the movement. (Tufekci, 2017) The period in which the Internet has become truly global is also one in which democracy has notably declined. (Freedom House, 2016).

Perhaps much more surprising was how the aforementioned Cambrian explosion of political speech effected established liberal democracies themselves, along with the way such speech itself became automated and algorithmitized whether via the kinds of digital sweatshops that resembled the Amazon platform, Mechanical Turk, or where political speech was taken over by the bots themselves.

The science-fiction writer William Gibson may have predicted something like this when he observed that the era of universal transparency and ubiquitous information wouldn't be one in which conflicts between citizens were settled by reference to shared *facts* but one of increasingly contentious disputes around rival notions of the truth. As Gibson put it in his 2003 essay for the New York Times on the hundredth anniversary of George Orwell's birth, *"The Road to Oceania"*:

I say ''truths,'' however, and not ''truth,'' as the other side of information's new ubiquity can look not so much transparent as outright crazy. Regardless of the number and power of the tools used to extract patterns from information, any sense of meaning depends on context, with interpretation coming along in support of one agenda or another. A world of informational transparency will necessarily be one of deliriously multiple viewpoints, shot through with misinformation, disinformation, conspiracy theories and a quotidian degree of madness. We may be able to see what's going on more quickly, but that doesn't mean we'll agree about it any more readily. (Gibson, 2003)

In the 2016 presidential election the Trump campaign ssemed to embody
Gibson's prediction, and essentially used social media to pull off a sort of coup against the Republican party and the traditional press (Nisenholtz, 2017) Whatever the outcome of current investigations regarding outright collusion between the Trump campaign and the Russian government, many of the ways in which the Russians leveraged digital technologies to influence the election are already known.

During the election, the Russian government utilized upwards of a thousand "trolls" who were paid to spread false stories against both Democratic and Republican candidates whose views were seen as hostile to the Kremlin. (Papenfuss, 2017) The Russian propaganda campaign has an analog in China which likewise employs an army of trolls, though in the latter case they are tasked with spreading positive stories about the government within the PRC itself rather than influence politics abroad. (King, 2017)

Both the Russian and the Chinese troll operations bear some resemblance to Amazon platform – Mechanical Turk- in which digital tasks are divided up among geographically dispersed individuals working on the Internet and directed by a centralized overseer or algorithm. And just as in the case of Mechanical Turk, the work of employees is then used as the data set on which AI that will replace those workers is being trained, the role of trolls is being increasingly turned over to bots. (Reese & Health, 2017)

There is growing evidence of Russian use of bots (short algorithms that perform some predefined tasks) as a tool to influence democratic elections. Bots that were active during the US presidential campaign afterwards went silent only to become active during the French presidential election and which were used to spread negative opinions against Emanuel Macron, a vocal opponent of the Kremlin. (Ferrara, 2017)

The use of such political bots had a clear precursor in the commercial sphere where bots now outnumbered humans on the web. (McMillan, 2017)

A number of pro-Trump bots reportedly used psycho-metric targeting compiled by pulling together data scattered across the Internet to create voter profiles. Voters were then supposedly given targeted messaging with one of the key points of leveraged being an intimate knowledge of what the voter most *feared*. (Doward, 2017)

The role of what was being called "fake-news" in the US presidential election and the British referendum on "Brexit" resulted in increasing calls for Internet platforms to assert editorial control over user generated speech. (Rosenberg, 2017) In addition, the perceived decline of civil political discourse, the shattering of the "Overton Window" (McCutcheon, 2016) led to increasing efforts by these platforms to utilize algorithms to purge themselves of hate speech. (Thompson, 2017) Internet platforms, especially Facebook, began to present themselves as the solution to problems which they themselves bore much of the responsibility for. (LaFrance, 2017)

One plausible outcome to the current period of information wars would be a liberal, benevolent version of the kind of panopticon China was successfully constructing. (Denyer, 2016) Yet just as likely was the possibility that Pesce had missed, that over a long stretch of time, algorithms and the hive-mind would co-exist and remain locked in a mutually reinforcing feedback loop.

The technologist, Jaron Lanier has been among the first to have identified such a feedback loop, a phenomenon that arises from the technology of the Internet itself. Lanier seemed to put his finger on how the technological dynamic seemed to naturally give rise to Pesce's panopticon rather than a flatter more anarchic structure of a hive- mind even when those designing the systems wanted the latter.

Every attempt to create a bottom-up emergent network to coordinate human affairs also facilitates some new hub that inevitably becomes a center of power, even if that was not the intent. These days, if everything is open, anonymous, and copyable, then a search/analysis company with a bigger computer than normal people have access to will come along and measure and model everything that takes place, and then sell the resulting ability to influence events to third parties. The whole supposedly open system will contort itself to that Sovereign Server, creating a new form of centralized power. More openness doesn't work. A Linux always makes a Google. (Lanier, 2014)

Once aware of its existence the feedback loop between algorithms and hive-minds becomes almost ubiquitous. Lanier himself has pointed out how artificial intelligence in its current manifestation is a kind of magic trick. Existing translation software and the like isn't so much intelligent as it is meant to hide and de-monetize for its true creators- the original human translators by which such software has been trained- the end product. Indeed, the "free" Internet is a platform for aggregating the free data its users provide for it. Data which is used to create ever more powerful algorithms to process yet more human generated data. (Lanier, 2014)

Another good place to see where the hive-mind aspirations of Internet users ends up generating a highly concentrated outcome is with the crypto-currency Bitcoin which almost overnight morphed from being the project of cyber-anarchists and libertarians to being dominated by multimillion dollar data centers who were the only ones capable of "mining" the currency and processing its flood of data. (Economist, 2015).

Hive-minds, individuals using personal computational devices in the common pursuit of some goal both train and necessitate centralized, automated platforms (algorithms) to process and manage this data. Rather than being an alternative to the dominance of algorithmic platforms, hive-minds necessitate their existence and increase our need for them. We've seen this process in play in the rise of the mass surveillance, in commerce, machine learning and crypto-currencies.

At the same time, hive-minds weaken those social institutions that have yet to take on the structure of algorithms- institutions such as political parties or the traditional press. The failure of these institutions has so far not resulted in calls to ensure algorithmic platforms serve the larger political and social interests of society, but in calls for them to assert management over the forces they have unleashed.

CONCLUSION

Among those who see the idea of the Internet's destiny in either the rule of algorithms or the freedom of the hive-mind as little more than a piece of Silicon Valley's founding mythology, various solutions to the current impasse have been proposed. Lanier favors revealing the man behind the curtain when it comes to AI combined with ways to monetize data as individual property. (Lanier, 2013) Morozov meanwhile appears to favor the socialization of data as the only way forward (Morozov, 2016) even as some call for the breakup of Internet giants (Dwyer, 2017), and the EU tries to reign them in via regulation. (LA Times, 2017) Perhaps some combination of all of these would be the best way forward, though what such a solution would look like remains unclear.

What is clear is that we are only at the beginning rather the process where digital technologies transform the nature of democratic politics. (Fowler & Goodman, 2017) It is a process where public discourse seems likely to be transformed more than any era since Guttenberg (Eisenstein, 2012) If democracy is to survive this era, the solutions to its problems cannot be brought to us by technologists alone, and the powers which they have unleashed have to, in some sense or other, be brought under public control.

The first step in preserving democracy's future in these conditions is to break ourselves out of Pesce's myth. There is no final utopia out there that awaits us so long as we follow the Internet's inherent logic, but this is not a pessimistic thought. For neither does there await us in the future some everlasting dystopia, so long as we remain human.

REFERENCES

Alter, A. (2017). *Irresistible The Rise of Addictive Technology and the Business of Keeping Us Hooked.* Penguin Group USA.

Bamford, J. (2012). *The NSA Is Building the Country's Biggest Spy Center (Watch What You Say).* Wired.com.

Castells, M. (2012). *Networks of Outrage and Hope: Social Movements in the Internet Age.* Cambridge, UK: Polity.

Chin, J., & Lin, L. (2017, June 26). *China's All-Seeing Surveillance State Is Reading Its Citizens' Faces.* Retrieved July 29, 2017, from https://www.wsj.com/articles/the-all-seeing-surveillance-state-feared-in-the-west-is-a-reality-in-china-1498493020?mod=e2tw

Denyer, S. (2016, May 23). *China's scary lesson to the world: Censoring the Internet works.* Retrieved July 29, 2017, from https://www.washingtonpost.com/world/asia_pacific/chinas-scary-lesson-to-the-world-censoring-the-internet-works/2016/05/23/413afe78-fff3-11e5-8bb1-f124a43f84dc_story.html?tid=ss_tw-amp&utm_term=.052fcf1fe206

Doward, J. (2017, March 4). *Did Cambridge Analytica influence the Brexit vote and the US election?* Retrieved July 29, 2017, from https://www.theguardian.com/politics/2017/mar/04/nigel-oakes-cambridge-analytica-what-role-brexit-trump

Economist (2013). The Silicon Valley Letter. *Economist.* Retrieved from http://www.economist.com/blogs/babbage/2013/12/tech-firms-and-spies

Economist. (2015, January 8). *The magic of mining*. Retrieved July 29, 2017, from https://www.economist.com/news/business/21638124-minting-digital-currency-has-become-big-ruthlessly-competitive-business-magic

Eisenstein, E. L. (2012). *The printing revolution in early modern Europe*. New York, NY: Cambridge University Press. doi:10.1017/CBO9781139197038

Ferrara, E. (2017, July 1). *Disinformation and Social Bot Operations in the Run Up to the 2017 French Presidential Election*. Retrieved July 29, 2017, from https://papers.ssrn.com/sol3/papers.cfm?abstract_id=2995809

Fowler and Goodman. (2017, June 22). *Opinion | How Tinder Could Take Back the White House*. Retrieved July 29, 2017, from https://www.nytimes.com/2017/06/22/opinion/how-tinder-could-take-back-the-white-house.html?smid=tw-share

Franceschi-Bicchierai, L. (2014, July 5). *The 10 Biggest Revelations From Edward Snowden's Leaks*. Accessed July 29, 2017, from http://mashable.com/2014/06/05/edward-snowden-revelations/#w51EfljJMPqx

Freedom House. (2016). *Freedom in the World 2016*. Retrieved July 29, 2017, from https://freedomhouse.org/report/freedom-world/freedom-world-2016

Fukuyama, F. (1992). *The end of history and the last man*. New York: Free Press.

Galván, J. M. (2012). Insights from Christian anthropology for a water-related technoethics. *Water Policy*, *14*(S1), 48. doi:10.2166/wp.2012.004

Gibson, W. (2003, June 24). *The Road to Oceania*. Retrieved July 29, 2017, from http://www.nytimes.com/2003/06/25/opinion/the-road-to-oceania.html

Haas, B. (2017, July 11). *China moves to block internet VPNs from 2018*. Accessed July 29, 2017, from https://www.theguardian.com/world/2017/jul/11/china-moves-to-block-internet-vpns-from-2018?CMP=share_btn_tw

Hern, A. (2017, March 29). *UK government can force encryption removal, but fears losing, experts say*. Accessed July 29, 2017, from https://www.theguardian.com/technology/2017/mar/29/uk-government-encryption-whatsapp-investigatory-powers-act

Johnson, S. (2012). *Future Perfect: The Case for Progress in a Networked Age*. New York: Riverhead Books.

Karoliszyn, H. (2014). Do We Want Minority Report Policing? *Aeon Magazine*. Accessed December 29, 2014. http://aeon.co/magazine/technology/do-we-want-minority-report-policing/

Keane, J. (2009). *The Life and Death of Democracy*. New York: W.W. Norton.

Kelly, K. (1995). *Out of Control: The New Biology of Machines, Social Systems, and the Economic World*. Reading, MA: Addison-Wesley.

Kilcullen, D. (2013). *Out of the Mountains: The Coming Age of the Urban Guerrilla*. New York: Oxford University Press.

King, G. (2017, June 21). *How the Chinese Government Fabricates Social Media Posts for Strategic Distraction, not Engaged Argument*. Retrieved July 29, 2017, from https://gking.harvard.edu/50c

Kuchler, H. (2014, November 4). *Tech companies step up encryption in wake of Snowden*. Accessed July 29, 2017, from https://www.ft.com/content/3c1553a6-6429-11e4-bac8-00144feabdc0

LaFrance, A. (2017, February 17). *The Mark Zuckerberg Manifesto Is a Blueprint for Destroying Journalism*. Retrieved July 29, 2017, from https://www.theatlantic.com/technology/archive/2017/02/the-mark-zuckerberg-manifesto-is-a-blueprint-for-destroying-journalism/517113/

Lanier, J. (2010). *You Are Not a Gadget: A Manifesto*. New York: Alfred A. Knopf.

Lanier, J. (2013). *Who Owns the Future?* New York: Simon and Schuster.

Lanier, J. (2014, November 14). *The Myth Of AI*. Retrieved July 29, 2017, from https://www.edge.org/conversation/jaron_lanier-the-myth-of-ai

LA Times Editorial Board. (2017, June 28). *The EU fires a warning shot at Google and other Internet giants*. Retrieved July 29, 2017, from http://www.latimes.com/opinion/editorials/la-ed-google-antitrust-20170628-story.html

McMillan, R. (2017, June 2). *Bots Now Outnumber Humans on the Web*. Retrieved July 29, 2017, from https://www.wired.com/2014/12/bots-now-outnumber-humans-web/

Mounk, Y. (2016, August 14). *The Week Democracy Died*. Accessed July 29, 2017, from http://www.slate.com/articles/news_and_politics/cover_story/2016/08/the_week_democracy_died_how_brexit_nice_turkey_and_trump_are_all_connected.html

McCutcheon, C. (2016, March 11). *How Trump and Sanders broke the Overton window*. Retrieved July 29, 2017, from https://www.csmonitor.com/USA/Politics/Politics-Voices/2016/0311/How-Trump-and-Sanders-broke-the-Overton-window

Morozov, E. (2011). *The Net Delusion: The Dark Side of Internet Freedom*. New York, NY: PublicAffairs.

Morozov, E. (2016, December 3). *Data populists must seize our information – for the benefit of us all*. Retrieved July 29, 2017, from https://www.theguardian.com/commentisfree/2016/dec/04/data-populists-must-seize-information-for-benefit-of-all-evgeny-morozov

Naím, M. (2014). *The End of Power From Boardrooms to Battlefields and Churches to States, Why Being In Charge Isn't What It Used to Be*. New York: Basic Books.

Nisenholtz, B. B. (2017, March 1). *What Trump Understands About Using Social Media to Drive Attention*. Retrieved July 29, 2017, from https://hbr.org/2017/03/what-trump-understands-about-using-social-media-to-drive-attention

Olson, P. (2012). *We Are Anonymous: Inside the Hacker World of Lulzsec, Anonymous, and the Global Cyber Insurgency*. New York: Little, Brown and Company.

Papenfuss, M. (2017, March 31). *1,000 Paid Russian Trolls Spread Fake News On Clinton, Senate Intelligence Heads Told*. Retrieved July 29, 2017, from http://www.huffingtonpost.com/entry/russian-trolls-fake-news_us_58dde6bae4b08194e3b8d5c4

Pariser, E. (2011). *The Filter Bubble: What the Internet Is Hiding from You.* New York: Penguin Press.

Pasquale, F. (2015). *The Black Box Society: The Secret Algorithms That Control Money and Information.* Harvard UP.

Pesce, M. (1997). Ignition (A Ritual For the Festival of Brigit). *Hyper-real.* Accessed October 6, 2014. http://hyperreal.org/~mpesce/Ignition.html

Poplin, C. M. (2015, November 30). *NSA Ends Bulk Collection of Telephony Metadata under Section 215.* Accessed July 29, 2017, from https://www.lawfareblog.com/nsa-ends-bulk-collection-telephony-metadata-under-section-215

Priest, D., & Arkin, W. M. (2011). *Top Secret America: The Rise of the New American Security State.* New York: Little, Brown and, Company.

Ramo, J. C. (2017). *Seventh sense: Power, fortune, and survival in the age of networks.* Back Bay Books.

Reese, H., & Heath, N. (2016, December 21). *Inside Amazon's clickworker platform: How half a million people are being paid pennies to train AI.* Retrieved July 29, 2017, from http://www.techrepublic.com/article/inside-amazons-clickworker-platform-how-half-a-million-people-are-training-ai-for-pennies-per-task/

Rosenberg, S. (2017, June 30). *Facebook Learns That the Censor's Job Is Never Done.* Retrieved July 29, 2017, from https://shift.newco.co/facebook-learns-that-the-censors-job-is-never-done-3f57a4de7b1b

Schmidt, E., & Cohen, J. (2013). *The New Digital Age: Reshaping the Future of People, Nations and Business.* New York: Random House.

Shirky, C. (2005). *Institutions vs. Collaboration.* TED.

Simonite, T. (2017, July 14). *Apple's Privacy Pledge Complicates Its AI Push.* Accessed July 29, 2017, from https://www.wired.com/story/apple-ai-privacy/

Singer, N. (2012) Mission Control, Built for Cities. *The New York Times.* Accessed January 11, 2015. http://www.nytimes.com/2012/03/04/business/ibm-takes-smarter-cities-concept-to-rio-de-janeiro.html?pagewanted=all&_r=0

Steiner, C. (2012). *Automate This: How Algorithms Came to Rule Our World.* New York: Portfolio/Penguin.

Stibel, J. M. (2009). *Breakpoint: Why the Web Will Implode, Search Will Be Obsolete, and Everything Else You Need to Know about Technology Is in Your Brain.* New York: Palgrave Macmillan.

Sydell, L. (2014). In A Battle For Web Traffic, Bad Bots Are Going After Grandma. *NPR.* Accessed December 29, 2014. http://www.npr.org/blogs/alltechconsidered/2014/07/03/328196199/in-a-battle-for-web-traffic-bad-bots-are-going-after-grandma

Thaler, R. H., & Sunstein, C. (2008). *Nudge: Improving Decisions about Health, Wealth, and Happiness.* New Haven, CT: Yale University Press.

Thompson, N. (2017, June 29). *Instagram Launches An AI System to Blast Away Nasty Comments*. Retrieved July 29, 2017, from https://www.wired.com/story/instagram-launches-ai-system-to-blast-nasty-comments/

Townsend, A. M. (2014). *Smart Cities: Big Data, Civic Hackers, and the Quest for a New Utopia*. New York: W.W Norton & Company.

Tufekci, Z. (2017). *Twitter and Teargas*. London: Yale University Press.

Turner, F. (2006). *From Counterculture to Cyberculture: Stewart Brand, the Whole Earth Network, and the Rise of Digital Utopianism*. Chicago: U of Chicago. doi:10.7208/chicago/9780226817439.001.0001

Walsh, M. (2017, June 29). *Chinese City Starts Tracking Underperforming Officials With GPS*. Retrieved July 29, 2017, from http://www.sixthtone.com/news/1000427/chinese-city-starts-tracking-underper-forming-officials-with-gps

Wertheim, M. (1999). *The Pearly Gates of Cyberspace: A History of Space from Dante to the Internet*. New York: W.W. Norton.

Wu, T. (2012). *The master switch: The rise and fall of information empires*. London. *Atlantic (Boston, Mass.)*, 271–274.

Wu, T. (2017). *The Attention Merchants The Epic Scramble to Get Inside Our Heads*. Vintage Books.

KEY TERMS AND DEFINITIONS

Algorithm: A set of rules and procedures used to organize information or processes usually reified through a machine or computer. In this chapter, especially internet platforms that automate the flow of information.

Artificial Intelligence (AI): Computer algorithms and systems capable that exhibit cognitive behaviors such as language processing or pattern recognition normally reserved for human intelligence.

Democracy: A system of government where the citizens are empowered to make decisions affecting their political community.

Digital Utopianism: The belief that the proper application of digital technology by itself can solve social and political problems and that technological development naturally occurs in the direction that promotes progressive values.

Hive Mind: A form of non-hierarchical, lateral political and social organization that has been enabled by the internet and mobile technologies in which individuals use personal computational devices in the common pursuit of some goal.

Panopticon: A system that centrally monitors and directs the action of those under it based on the hypothetical prison proposed by Jeremy Bentham in the eighteenth century.

Chapter 16
Viral Art Matters:
Using Web–Based Artwork to Fortify Academic Efforts

Alejandra Emilia Iannone
Sparkle Theatricals, USA

ABSTRACT

Over the last two decades, an impactful phenomenon called virality (i.e., when content circulates via internet among an increasingly broad audience at an exponentially rapid rate) has developed. Not all information achieves virality, so the phenomenon invites reflection. Yet, the academic literature on viral artwork is quite sparse. This chapter helps fill a gap in the literature by demonstrating the academic significance of viral art through comparative analysis of three cases where web-based artworks went viral: Ten Hours of Princess Leia walking in NYC, New Beginnings, and McKayla Is Not Impressed. The author argues that viral art merits rigorous study because doing so could, first, augment existing research on other topics; second, fortify philosophy of art investigations; and third, establish aesthetic principles to guide audience engagement with viral artwork.

INTRODUCTION

In the modern era of Web 2.0, participation streamlines web applications; the more people use applications, the better the applications get (O'Reilly, 2005; Wyrwoll, 2014). Some high-tech entrepreneurs go so far as to say that software is "eating the world" (Andreessen, 2011, p.1; O'Hanihan, 2013, p.1). Now, content can be shared far, wide, and fast; moreover, individuals can play the roles of author and reader at the same time (Wyrwoll, 2014). From this context emerges virality, a phenomenon where information circulates via the Internet among an increasingly broad—often global—audience at an exponentially rapid rate.

The contrast between virality and virulence is sometimes lost in ordinary discussion. Since distinguishing the concepts could help sharpen future analyses, this author will do so outright. Describing something as virulent suggests severe, often harmful, effects; for example, virulent diseases are often

DOI: 10.4018/978-1-5225-5094-5.ch016

infectious. Virulence also attributes bitter hostility, as in the sentence, "It was a virulent attack on feminism." On the other hand, going viral is a matter of speed and spread. Viral content could, but need not, be virulent. In fact, most often the opposite is true.

Not all information achieves virality, so the phenomenon invites reflection. Yet, scholars have failed to address the topic; the literature on viral artwork is quite sparse. This does not indicate that investigating viral artwork would be fruitless. Rather, pursuing the topic could yield expansive results.

The purpose of this chapter is to help fill a gap in the literature by demonstrating the academic significance of viral artwork via comparative analysis of three cases where internet-based artworks went viral. This author will argue that viral artwork merits rigorous study, given at least the following three reasons. First, rigorous study of viral artwork can augment existing research on other topics. Second, studying viral artwork can fortify investigations in philosophy of art through extension to the online artworld. Third, scholars could outline aesthetic principles to guide audience engagement with viral artwork.

In what follows, this author will review existing contributions to the academic literature on topics related to viral artwork, including: virality; Internet communications technology; market research; net-art; and online community development. This writer will also point out examples of non-academic and academic investigations about viral artwork. Then, this author will suggest that the academic approach to viral artwork is insufficient; as this author sees it, academics have neglected a valuable subject of study. To test the hypothesis that viral artwork merits rigorous study, this author will analyze three cases of viral artwork, taking into consideration the implications of their respective fates: Ten Hours of Princess Leia walking in NYC, New Beginnings, and McKayla is Not Impressed. With these examples as guides, this writer concludes, as stated above, that rigorous study of viral artwork could: first, augment existing research on other topics; second, fortify investigations in philosophy of art; and third, guide the public toward engagement with viral artwork.

THE CONTEXT OF THE CONVERSATION

Academic Perspectives on Internet Communications Technology

Some academic research on Internet communications technology relates to issues surrounding virality. John Palfrey (2010) argued that state-sponsored control over the technology is not specific to authoritarian regimes. Liu Yangyue (2014) contributed to the dialogue by analyzing the differences in how authoritarian governments' policies – like those in Malaysia – extend to the Internet. Others have studied Internet communications technology used to promote revolution by residents of non-democratic nations. For example, Jason Abbott (2012) shed light on the Internet's broad socio-political impact among citizens of nations ruled authoritarian governments. Abbott argued that social media outlets are unique means for citizens to establish a public sphere, rather than mere communications tools (Abbott, 2012, p. 334). Further, he asserted that Internet communications technologies make political revolution conceivable (Abbott, 2012, p. 334). Still others have addressed how Internet communications technologies can be used for non-democratic efforts. For example, Ian Bremmer argued that there is nothing inherently democratic about the Internet because it amplifies a variety of perspectives, some at odds with democratic ideals (Bremmer, 2010, p. 92).

Other research focuses on the availability of Internet communications technologies across the globe. Aurore J. Kamssu, Jeffrey S. Siekpe, and James A. Ellzy claimed that since interconnected computers are sparse in certain countries, those countries use the Internet less (Kamssu, Siekpe, & Ellzy, 2004, pp. 161–166).

Academic Perspectives on Virality

While earlier research on virality centered upon viral content's cultural impact, one of the most prevalent questions now addressed in the literature is, "What causes virality?" Most approaches to answering this question focus on fields outside art.

Numerous scholars link virality with emotion. Kristin Purcell (Purcell, 2010, p. 6) concluded that people are most likely to view humorous content. Along these lines, Johan Berger and Katharine Milkman claimed that information evoking high-arousal emotions is more prone to virality (Berger & Milkman, 2012, p. 201). Furthermore, they argued that information that provokes positive emotions is most prone to virality (Berger & Milkman, 2012, p. 201). Berger and Milkman (2012) also claimed that individuals are inclined to share content because it caused high-arousal positivity in them. Nisbett and Wilson (1977) made two claims relevant to Berger's & Milkman's assertions. The first – i.e., people prefer to pass along good news – is compatible with Berger's and Milkman's position. The second – i.e., people prefer to share good news because recipients associate positive information with whoever shared – is not. By contrast, Heath (1996) argued that people prefer passing along bad news. Depending on the kind of response bad news evokes, Heath's position could align with Berger's and Milkman's first claim.

Christine Bacareza Balance (2012) used a YouTube case study to argue that content will go viral if it presents emotional hooks to a niche audience (Balance, 2012, pp. 139, 143, 145–146). Along these same lines, Guadango, Rempala, Murphy, and Okdie (2013) provided grounds for three claims: first, that videos evoking emotions are more likely to be shared (Guadango et al., 2013, p. 2318); second, like Berger and Milkman, that positive videos are most likely to be shared (Guadango et al., 2013, p. 2318); and third, that videos evoking negative emotions are more likely to be shared than those evoking no emotion (Guadango et al., 2013, p. 2318).

Guadango, Rempala, Murphy, and Okdie (2013) also claimed that videos sometimes evoke what they call a diffuse emotion. From their point of view, videos that evoke diffuse emotions are less likely to be shared than positive videos, but more likely than negative or non-emotional videos (Guadango et al., p. 2318). In addition, Guadango, Rempala, Murphy, and Okdie (2013) argued that whether an individual is familiar with the person who forwarded a video has no effect on whether the recipient shares the video (Guadango et al., 2013, pp. 2318).

Michele Knobel and Colin Lankshear (2007) focused on Internet memes, i.e., individual pieces of digital cultural information that are manipulated, then shared among people. The Internet-meme (a term derived from Richard Dawkins 1976 discussion of the spread of culture person-to-person) is a rather loose term that describes the propagation of jokes and web content from individual to individual on the Internet (KnowYourMeme, 2016). Memes are most often spread as *image-macros*, i.e. images captioned with (often) witty messages (KnowYourMeme, 2016). *Image macros* can be used to convey reactions on message boards (KnowYourMeme, 2016). The images are usually based around templates found on dedicated websites; anyone with a computer linked to the Internet connection can share their own versions of a meme.

Content also spreads in Graphics Interchange Format. A GIF is a bitmap image format developed by US-based software writer Steve Wilhite while working at the bulletin board service (BBS) provider CompuServe on June 15, 1987. GIF content has since come into widespread usage on the World Wide Web due to the format's wide support and portability. The format supports up to eight bits per pixel for each image, allowing a single image to reference its own palette of up to 256 different colors chosen from the 24-bit RGB color space.

Though Knobel and Lankshear (2007) provided grounds to establish the claim that most memes are intended to provide humorous or social commentary, Guadango, Rempala, Murphy, and Okdie (2013) also pointed out that "the questions persists as to why people find a manipulated picture…humorous enough to both create their own versions and pass along pictures created by others." (Guadango et al., 2013, pp. 2313).

Karine Nahon and Jeff Hemsley (2013) designated four components as crucial in the emerging of a viral event, as opposed to another sort of informational flow: first, the human and social aspects of sharing information from one to another; second, the speed of viral spread; third, the reach in terms of number of people exposed to the content; and fourth, the reach in terms of the distance the information travels by bridging multiple networks.

Other discussions (Barzilai-Nahon, 2008; Feld and Carter, 1998; Kadushin, 2012; Shirky, 2009; Verbrugge, 1977) address the kinds of connections that can exist between individuals, the nature of those connections, and how information is filtered through. Charles Kadushin (2012) characterized *networks* as "conduits of both wanted and unwanted flow" (Kadushin, 2012, 8). Kadushin's idea helps illuminate the related concept of *homophily*: a tendency for the same kinds of people to end up in the same place and get influenced by the place they ended up (Feld and Carter, 1998; Kadushin, 2012; Verbrugge, 1977). *Homophily* has been distilled into two sorts: *status-homophily*, i.e., when individuals share attributes like age, race, sex, marital status, and education; and *value-homiphily*, i.e., when individuals share through attitudes, stereotypes, etcetera (Feld and Carter, 1998; Kadushin, 2012; Verbrugge, 1977). Karine Barzilai-Nahon (2008) and Clay Shirky (2009) claimed that information flow through networks is filter-forwarded (Shirky, 2009) by network gatekeepers (Barzilai-Nahon, 2008) who select, add, withhold, display, channel, shape, manipulate, repeat, time, localize, integrate, disregard, and delete information. In addition, at least two scholars have published on whether people can engage in worthwhile online communication. Katarina Stanoevska-Slabeva (2002) claimed that the most successful online communities encourage community building via meaningful, online dialogue (Stanoevska-Slabeva, 2002, p. 71). Scott Gibbons (2010) presented related evidence for the claim that the Internet might better enable meaningful dialogue than face-to-face interaction. Gibbons' research shows that his high school writing students had better results working on a wiki—i.e., a website that allows users to edit its content—than when they used traditional methods like in-class peer revision. According to Gibbons, anonymity made genuine collaboration possible. (Gibbons, 2010, pp. 37-39).

Perspectives on Viral Art From Outside Academia

The research on viral artwork outside of academia suggests the topic, though inadequately addressed by academics, is nonetheless significant. Of note are the contributions made by Natalie Kitroeff (2014), Hrag Vartanian (2014), Kyle Chayka (2012), and Mike Kelley (2014). Vartanian (2014), who investigated the commentary accompanying viral web content, theorized that comments made about viral artwork affect artists' future productivity (Vartanian, 2014). Furthermore, Vartanian argued that Internet users would react negatively if commentary functions on a viral post are disabled (Vartanian, 2014).

Chayka (2012) used recent cases of viral Web-based artworks—e.g., Tumblrs, music videos— to argue for the claim that works of art are often being created with the potential for virality in mind. His approach raised questions like "Has art failed if it fails to go viral?" Others have argued that virality is a positive phenomenon that brings about desirable effects. Kelley (2014), a viral photographer, described these benefits, which range from increased financial security to a broadened social network. Though fruitful, these discussions lack precision because they rely on limited, definitions of viral art, like R.J. Rushmore's position (2013) that viral art is the "unmediated (digital) distribution of art from artist to public… a digital equivalent to street art and graffiti." (Rushmore, 2013, 315).

Academic Perspectives on Viral Art

Scholar Lasse Huldt Pedersen (2017) is one of the very few who has addressed viral art, though his discussion is lumped together with an analysis of virality. Pedersen's main four questions are: first, what is viral art?; second, how do we approach viral art in a non-objectical way?; third, how can viral art influence our society?; and fourth, is it possible for viral art to function as an opposing force within Gilles Deleuze's theory of societies of control? (Pedersen, 2017, p. 3). Since he makes many shifts between two related, but nonetheless distinct, concepts—viral art and virality, Pedersen's approach ends up cluttered. Yet, given the limited pool of academic research on viral art, his discussion is useful.

Pedersen rejects an object-oriented approach to genres like viral art. According to him, the object-oriented approach may be why producing a bulletproof formula for creating viral content is challenging. Perhaps, as Pedersen sees it, we fail to understand the intricacy of the process of virality because we get caught up on the visually aesthetic properties of the content, where *visual aesthetics* refers to both what our eyes perceive and how our mind makes sense of it (Pedersen, 2017, p. 29). Pedersen suggests that we associate virality "as an effect… considering that an effect is generally produced by something that is produced by an agency or cause…" (Pedersen, 2017, p. 28). What else is left to consider? Pedersen doesn't tell us much, but does say,

Without networks and network clusters of people, viral art cannot really happen, at least in the way we know of virality as of now. It is dependent on a network in order to move around and saturate it, and with viral art, to mediate something. Without this, it lacks the very base qualities that define virality (Pedersen, 2017, p. 30).

Beyond definitional matters, questions also arise regarding what social effects can be achieved through viral art. As Pedersen point out, "Art in relation to digital technologies has come to challenge our views regarding authentic sources of information and content, making us aware about the potential that anything can be fake." (Pedersen, 2017, p. 53).

As an example, Pedersen calls on recent examples of viral video content allegedly created by a woman going by the name Zardulu to demonstrate his point. Zardulu's videos are based on elaborate hoaxes that require that the artists remain unknown and unaffiliated (Pedersen, 2017; Newman, 2016). How, then, do we know about Zardulu? Some who identify as her hired actors contacted the media about projects on which they worked (Pedersen, 2017; Newman, 2016). The most famous videos Zardulu claims responsibility for are: *Selfie Rat*, in which a rat appears to take a self-portrait with a passed-out man's phone on a subway platform; *Pizza Rat*, in which a rat drags a slice of pizza down New York City subway stairs; and *Three-Eyed Gowanus Canal Catfish Project*, in which videoed people claim they caught three-eyed catfish in Brooklyn, New York's Gowanus Canal, showing viewers with alleged taxidermy catfish that have an extra eye in the middle of their foreheads. Zardulu claims the fish are a prop she made.

These videos are captivating examples of deceptive viral content. Nevertheless, the videos can only help guide the discussion on viral art if they count as viral art. Questions remain unresolved. Did the artist Zardulu create these videos? Are these videos mere hoaxes, elegantly presented? If the videos are no more than archival footage of rat and catfish activity, then this author sees no reason to call them artworks. Even if Zardulu created them, this author's position remains the same. For the purpose of this discussion, this author will assume that Zardulu is responsible for these videos.

Like Zardulu's videos, a theatrical magician's illusions are painstakingly choreographed deceptions. Take, for example, *Three-card Monte*, a confidence game in which the victim is tricked into betting a sum of money on the assumption that they can find the *money card* among three, face-down playing cards. When a magician presents *Three-card Monte*, like other theatrical illusions, it is more than a hoax—it is an artwork that fools the eye. Though illusionists make some aesthetic decisions keeping in mind the success of their intended hoax, they also make aesthetic choices based solely on taste. Zardulu is not open about her creative process, so one cannot be sure what, if any, aesthetic choices she made. However, this author maintains that her videos cannot count as artworks if it turns out her aesthetic decisions only took into consideration the success of her intended deception.

Other scholars have addressed viral art. Adam Kirsch (2008) discussed the issues that arise for authors who publish online, which provides some insight on the experience of artists whose art has gone viral. In addition, Mark Amerika's (2004) discussion of net art—art made to be online and experienced from a computer screen (Bookchin & Shulgin 1999)—contextualized virality. Amerika demonstrated that current Web-based art making has roots in net art. As a result, he indicated that contemporary phenomena associated with current Web-based art making—like virality—are historically grounded, thus established as more than passing fads. Amerika's discussion enriched appreciation of the many, varied examples of net art developed since the late 20th century.[1]

Perspectives that Build a Bridge

Jason Koebler (2014) has argued that each time Internet users share a work of visual art on the Internet, something inherent to that artwork—unspecified by Koebler—is lost. Though Koebler does not acknowledge it, his point aligns with another claim made by scholar Walter Benjamin (1936/1968).

In *The Work of Art in the Age of Mechanical Reproduction*, Benjamin argued that the means of reproducing art in his time was categorically different from the way art had been reproduced before (Benjamin, 1936/1968, p. 217). As Benjamin saw it, there were at least three reasons why the means of reproduction in his era—which included photography and film—were different. First, he claimed that inherent in these media is a process of reproduction that could be used to produce an infinite number of detailed prints, none that are the genuine original (Benjamin, 1936/1968, pp. 217–220). Second, he claimed that these technologies allow the work of art to be seen better, e.g., by a process of slow motion or close-up focus (Benjamin, 1936/1968, p. 218). Third, he claimed that these technologies can transport a work of art to situations the original could not reach itself, e.g., transporting the Sistine Chapel to an art history textbook (Benjamin, 1936/1968, p. 218). These points mattered to Benjamin because, as he saw it, works of art have an aura, which he described as the "unique existence in a particular place," that apprehends the work of art in its time and place of creation, giving the original work of art an irreproducible authenticity (Benjamin, 1936/1968, pp. 218–220). According to Benjamin, in the age of mechanical reproduction the aura of a work of art decayed each time the work of art was mechanically reproduced (Benjamin, 1936/1968, pp. 218–220). Thus, for Benjamin, reproductions—like copies of the Mona Lisa— were deteriorations of an original work of art's aura.

Further analysis of Koebler and Benjamin suggests they would disagree on whether the effects of reproduction—mechanical or digital—are desirable. Still, Koebler's view extends elements of Benjamin's position into the contemporary age of digital reproduction. Now, Internet technology has amplified the effect that Benjamin claimed mechanical reproduction had on an artwork. Digital reproduction happens via social media, where original works of art are filtered, cropped, or zoomed in by Internet users who share them, rather than the artists who created them. These contemporary circumstances bring up new questions about the results of digital reproduction. Are heavily altered reproductions of Web-based artworks just new originals with new auras?[2]

AN INTERDISCIPLINARY APPROACH TO VIRAL ART

The discussion above establishes that research addressing virality ranges across the humanities to the sciences. There has also been extensive scholarship surrounding art and aesthetics. Philosophers have theorized about the purposes and perils of art (Aristotle, 335 B.C.E./1961; Beardsley, 1981; Dewey, 1934/1980; Plato, 380 B.C.E/1992; & Tolstoy, 1897/2011). Others have also investigated the role of the audience. Some have focused in particular on questions about the logic of taste (Hume, 1742/2006; Kant 1790/ 2007). Still others have investigated puzzles about intention and interpretation (Hirsch, Jr., 1980; Sontag, 1966/2011; Wimsatt, Jr., & Beardsley C., 1946/1954/1982). Artworks themselves have also been subjected to philosophical scrutiny; theorists in these areas have researched topics like form and content (Bell, 1914) and the project of establishing a definition of the word "artwork" (Danto, 1964; Dickie, 1969 & 1974). Still others have written on artists' characteristics (Nietzsche, 1872/1967).

Yet, where art and virality meet, there is a poor showing in the literature. Since virality often involves a globalization component (in that viral content reaches large sectors of the world's societies), its study requires an interdisciplinary approach. These challenges, in tandem with the deliberate quality that philosophical reasoning requires, may mean that researching the phenomenon will be a slow process. Nonetheless, the existing academic contributions on viral art, though welcome, are insufficient. As stated at the outset, this chapter aims at filling the still-present gap in the literature about viral art.

This author has claimed that viral artwork merits rigorous study because: first, doing so could augment existing research on other topics; second, studying viral artwork can fortify investigations in philosophy of art by relating them to the online environment; and third, establish aesthetic principles to guide audience engagement with viral artwork. Next, this author will illustrate the grounds for that claim by analyzing three viral artworks.

Case One: Ten Hours of Princess Leia Walking in NYC

The first example is *Ten Hours of Princess Leia walking in NYC*, a YouTube video published on November 11, 2014 by co-authors and co-producers Josh Apter and Gary Mahmoud (Apter & Mahmoud, 2014). Throughout the two minute and thirty-four second film, actor Michele McNally walks the sidewalks of various neighborhoods in New York City dressed as Star Wars character Princess Leia. Night falls while McNally traverses the city streets, all the while followed by other actors who bombard her with comments about her appearance. *Ten Hours of Princess Leia walking in NYC* is a satirical film that responds to an earlier YouTube film called *Ten Hours of Walking in NYC as a Woman*. Upon being published on the YouTube channel *Are We There Yet?* the spoof went viral, reaching 2 million views in 2 days. At the time this chapter was written, *Ten Hours of Princess Leia walking in NYC* had three million seven hundred thirty nine thousand five hundred and thirteen views. The YouTube channel that houses this film is now called *Cringe Factory*.

If this author's hypothesis holds, academic study of *Ten Hours of Princess Leia walking in NYC* could augment existing research on other topics. Can careful consideration of this viral film extend the reach of already existing research about topics other than viral artwork? The best way to demonstrate that it can is by undergoing that very critical analysis. With that aim, this author turns to applying Berger's and Milkman's aforementioned conclusions in the field of market research to this case of viral art (Berger & Milkman, 2012, p. 201). Doing so illuminates strengths and weaknesses of their position from an angle not yet considered.

Of viewers who have watched *Ten Hours of Princess Leia walking in NYC*, but have also expressed their opinions of the film, over twenty-nine thousand clicked the thumbs-up icon while just over two thousand and four hundred clicked the thumbs-down. In the comment box below *Ten Hours of Princess Leia walking in NYC*, much of the commentary drifted to other topics, some relevant—like how the parody relates to the original film—some peripheral—like the aesthetic value of the original *Star Wars*—and some hateful and combative—like discussion about feminazis. Nearly every comment below *Ten Hours of Princess Leia walking in NYC* demonstrated high-arousal emotions like anger and amusement.

Since much of the commentary about *Ten Hours of Princess Leia walking in NYC* suggested that viewers felt negatively-charged emotions while watching, the film can function as support for Berger's and Milkman's position that Internet content is more prone to going viral if it evokes high-arousal emotions (Berger & Milkman, 2012, p. 201). Yet, the negative quality of the *Ten Hours of Princess Leia walking in NYC* commentary makes Berger's and Milkman's subsequent claim—i.e., content will most likely to go viral when the emotions aroused are positive rather than negative—a subject for further discussion (Berger & Milkman, 2012, p. 201). Thus, critical analysis of *Ten Hours of Princess Leia walking in NYC* supports and augments, but also extends the scope of already existing investigations in market research.

In line with this author's hypothesis, *Ten Hours of Princess Leia walking in NYC* can also fortify investigations in philosophy of art by extending fundamental questions—covering topics from audience to space to subject matter—to the online environment. "Can audiences grasp artists' intentions?" develops into "Can Web-based parody be effectively communicated to online audiences?" The scope of "Does art composed of controversial content present special ethical concerns?" expands relatively to Internet's vast reach. "Might certain spaces better suit certain artworks?" invites the variation "Might certain digital spaces better suit certain Web-based artworks?"

Furthermore, *Ten Hours of Princess Leia walking in NYC* introduces a new question for philosophers of art relating to all three of the aforementioned topics: is virality indicative of aesthetic value? Leading actor Michele McNally expressed hope that the viral film will bring her, Apter, and Mahmoud more attention in the Film and TV industry. As she puts it, the fact that *Ten Hours of Princess Leia walking in NYC* went viral helps when speaking to a casting director about potential work opportunities (M. McNally, Personal communication, November 19, 2014). Though McNally's point goes without contest in the entertainment industry, what she says brings up a new intellectual puzzle about Web-based art.

Critical consideration of *Ten Hours of Princess Leia walking in NYC* could also lead to some aesthetic principles that guide audience engagement with viral artworks, as this author's hypothesis suggests. This author has already mentioned that the YouTube comment box below *Ten Hours of Princess Leia walking in NYC* is peppered with high-arousal, often negative commentary. Exchanges between individuals often veer in argumentative directions. Sometimes, a *troll* intentionally disrupts on-topic discussion to elicit emotional responses from site users. Overall, the *Ten Hours of Princess Leia walking in NYC* audience engagement experience needs improvement.

Questions about online audience engagement are reminiscent of other inquiries about online community building. Thus, it seems reasonable to model developing discussions about the former on established discussions about the latter. Harking back to Stanoevska-Slabeva's aforementioned claim that the most successful online communities encourage community building through an Internet platform, the focus shifts toward the channels through which viral artworks are shared (Stanoevska-Slabeva, 2002, p. 71). For example, is YouTube—a leading online sharing community that is home to many viral artworks—equipped to encourage meaningful dialogue about Web-based art?

Recent changes in the structure of YouTube's commenting function suggest that the site may be closer to reaching that point. In the past, users would comment under a self-designated alias. Now, comments post under Google+ profile names. Contemporary YouTube users can filter which Google+ members receive their comments and mention other users in their comments. Since the earlier limit of 500 characters has been removed, users can post more developed comments. Moreover, with the new Google Translate support for users, dialogue can occur between individuals who write in different languages.

With this reduction in anonymity comes a decrease in the offensive commentary that has plagued YouTube. Yet, the issues that plagued YouTube commentary have been tempered, rather than eliminated. Gibbons' point about research on classroom learning, in particular his assertion that anonymity is key to encouraging people to communicate critically yet constructively, is well taken (Gibbons, 2010, pp. 37–39).

Case Two: New Beginnings

The second example is *New Beginnings* a YouTube dance film published September 12, 2013 on the *New York City Ballet* YouTube Channel. Featuring dancers Maria Kowroski and Ask la Cour, this three minute and twenty-two second dance film directed by Davi Russo places Christopher Wheeldon's pas de deux *After the Rain* on the 57th floor of 4 World Trade Center, accompanied by Arvo Part's musical composition *Spiegel Im Spiegel* (Russo, Wheeldon, & Part, 2013). Kowroski and la Cour lean, sway, fall, and reach their ways through Wheeldon's synchronized double duets and intricate partnering sequences. As the dance progresses, the camera angle shifts, allowing the viewer to witness moments that might not be visible in a proscenium theater.

At the time this chapter was written, two million two thousand four hundred and six people had viewed *New Beginnings*. Four hundred and seven had left comments. Twelve thousand four hundred and fifty pressed the thumbs-up button below the film, while one hundred and ninety-seven pressed thumbs-down. Most of the comments—many of them positive—were no more than two sentences long. Quite a few of the positive comments were given a thumbs-up. Often, commentators stated that the dance film made them feel calm. Some users said the film was breathtaking. Others said it left them without words.

Critical analysis of New York City Ballet's *New Beginnings* can also benefit existing research operations by extending the reach of scholarship on topics other than viral artwork. As with *Ten Hours of Princess Leia walking in NYC*, rigorous study of *New Beginnings* could expand on Berger's and Milkman's aforementioned claims: first, content that evokes high-arousal emotions is more prone to going viral; and second, that content most prone to going viral when those emotions are positive (Berger & Milkman, 2012, p. 201). Comparing *New Beginnings* and *Ten Hours of Princess Leia Walking in NYC* illuminates this point.

New Beginnings and *Ten Hours of Princess Leia walking in NYC* are nearly the same length. Both have gone viral, though *New Beginnings* had been viewed just under half as many times as *Ten Hours of Princess Leia walking in NYC* at the time this chapter was written. The former was released by an emerging arts organization three years before this chapter was written; the latter by an established, world-famous institution and five years prior. Both were given a thumbs-up by viewers more times than a thumbs-down. Yet, *Ten Hours of Princess Leia walking in NYC* had more views and comments. The comments below *Ten Hours of Princess Leia walking in NYC* indicated the content provoked viewers while those below *New Beginnings* indicated the content placated them.

Though neither of these artworks was released as an official marketing effort, the circumstances surrounding their respective paths to virality bolster Berger's and Milkman's claim that information evoking high-arousal emotions is most prone to achieving virality (Berger & Milkman, 2012, p. 201). Whether Berger's and Milkman's claim can extend into the online artworld—that is, whether artworks evoking high-arousal, positive emotions are most prone to achieving virality—is nonetheless debatable. Still, like *Ten Hours of Princess Leia walking in NYC*, *New Beginnings* demonstrates that study of viral artworks can extend scholarship on other subjects.

Furthermore, as this author's hypothesis suggests, analyzing this viral film could fortify already existing investigations in philosophy of art through extension to the online artworld. For example, the historical context surrounding *New Beginnings* raises the question, "Do social expectations, like patriotism, ensure certain Web-based artworks will go viral?" Following either line of inquiry would extend already existing research on interested versus disinterested aesthetic judgments (Kant 1790/2007). In addition, investigating whether artworks evoking high-arousal, positive emotions are most likely to go viral could expand inquiry about artistic merit so to consider virality as a possible indicator.

In addition, as asserted in this author's hypothesis, by examining the circumstances surrounding *New Beginnings*, scholars could establish standards that could guide audiences toward expressing genuine evaluations about viral artwork. Whatever the cause, the almost totally positive comment pool about *New Beginnings* suggests that candid criticism may have been difficult. Gibbons' aforementioned claim that anonymity makes genuine collaboration possible is, once again, relevant. (Gibbons, 2010, pp. 37–39). Granted, many factors could have caused the comments' homogeneity, from audience demographics— *New Beginnings* was posted on a page frequented by New York City Ballet enthusiasts—to technological components—the Google+ anonymity limits could discourage off-color comments about art that references tragic subject matter. Still, the hyper-positive comment pool signals a snag in the YouTube community structure that might inhibit meaningful dialogue about viral artwork in future. With scholarly research on the subject, however, audiences could be guided toward better-informed engagement with viral artwork.[3]

Case Three: McKayla is Not Impressed

Viral, Web-based artwork extends beyond YouTube films to other digitally born content like memes and GIFs. One well-known example of viral meme and GIF art is *McKayla is Not Impressed*, Gavin Alaoen's Tumblr website, active from 2012 through 2013, that displays Internet memes and GIFs made using a 2012 Associated Press photo of United States gymnast McKayla Maroney.

In the original photo, which went viral itself, Maroney receives her silver medal at the London Summer Olympics in 2012. With arms crossed and lips pursed to the side, she is the picture of dissatisfaction. After the original photo spread online, Web-users started using it to create memes playing off Maroney's disappointed appearance. Some of the creations incorporate famous works of art. Others refer to important moments in history. Still others mention pop culture. Each incorporates the original photo of McKayla, thoroughly unimpressed with the circumstances upon which she is superimposed. As the Tumblr website shows, the McKayla memes have all gone viral. Hundreds to thousands of Internet-users have pressed the like button under each post.

This case demonstrates how this author's hypothesis extends throughout the world of viral artwork. Just as with Web-based films, rigorous study of Web-based graphic artworks that go viral could extend the reach of already existing research in fields other than viral artwork. The circumstances surrounding the *McKayla is Not Impressed* memes can bolster the claims that content is most likely to go viral if it evokes high-arousal, positive emotions like—as most of the McKayla memes do—amusement. Besides, *McKayla is Not Impressed* Tumblr website also gestures toward a new topic for art scholars to investigate—virality's aftermath.

The final post—a GIF showing the creator of *McKayla is Not Impressed* meeting Maroney—is captioned:

So, after all this time since this meme started, I finally got to meet Mckayla! Def a great and wonderful experience. Shoutouts to everyone who's viewed and submitted to the blog, thanks! (Alaoen, 2013)

No new posts have been added on the *McKayla is Not Impressed* Tumblr site since. Most site elements remain accessible, though the feature that allowed users to make their own McKayla meme is now defunct. *McKayla is Not Impressed* has left the pop culture spotlight.

One might reason that the site's impact faded because its no-longer-topical content fails to resonate with modern Web users. Does that conclusion have adequate grounds? If scholars investigate this particular puzzle, they could advance an already existing, larger inquiry into whether artworks can succeed outside of natural habitats (Davies, 2006). Analyzing viral artworks could fortify already existing investigations in philosophy of art by applying them to the online artworld, as this author has hypothesized.

Studying the *McKayla is Not Impressed* Tumblr site could, as with the aforementioned viral artworks, help scholars establish principles to guide audience engagement with viral artwork. As mentioned earlier in this section, the *McKayla is Not Impressed* Tumblr once invited users to submit site content. One could reasonably infer that creating a post for *McKayla is Not Impressed* enhanced contributors' sense of engagement with that community. Yet, the *McKayla is Not Impressed* community fizzled. The incongruity between these two points invites careful investigation of *McKayla is Not Impressed*. Perhaps learning what could encourage audience engagement with viral, Web-based artwork involves recognizing what could extinguish it. All of these points align with this author's hypothesis.

SOLUTIONS AND RECOMMENDATIONS

This chapter began to fill the gap in the literature by demonstrating the academic significance of viral artwork via comparative analysis of three cases where Web-based artworks went viral. After reviewing the related literature from both inside and out of academia, this author hypothesized that viral artwork and the questions it brings up merit rigorous study because doing so would, first, augment existing research on other topics; second, expand in scope efforts in philosophy of art; and third, guide audiences toward better engagement with viral artworks. To illustrate grounds for this position, this author analyzed three cases of Web-based artwork-gone-viral: *Ten Hours of Princess Leia walking in NYC*, *New Beginnings*, and *McKayla is Not Impressed*.

Still, the work has just begun. Even given the associated wealth of investigatory opportunity, the existing research on virality as pertains to art and aesthetics remains insufficient. Though this chapter succeeds in identifying and beginning to fill the aforementioned gap in the literature, the job remains unfinished. Questions raised in this article remain unanswered. Vast numbers of viral artworks remain unanalyzed. A fraction of the various media-sharing platforms have been considered, let alone those yet to be created. Taking into consideration all of these loose ends, one might wonder, "Has this chapter moved us forward after all?" This author maintains that it has. Each of these loose ends shows that researchers have their work cut out for them.

FUTURE RESEARCH DIRECTIONS

This researcher suggests that scholars first focus on adopting a definition for the term *viral artwork*, and then extend the scope of their work by analyzing the positive and negative implications of Web-based artworks' digital locations, audience reach, form, content, and virality status. Future study will likely continue to develop beyond what has been mentioned here, with increased academic attention to viral artwork. Predicting how that may happen is beyond the scope of this chapter.

CONCLUSION

The artworld has become an increasingly digital environment. These changes ushered in fresh ways of making, displaying, and reacting to art. Virality, which is the tendency of an image, video, or piece of information to circulate via Internet among an increasingly broad audience at an exponentially rapid rate, is one such phenomenon.

Though only certain images, videos, and pieces of information go viral, the phenomenon has altered the modern-day artworld overall. As a result, it has also revealed a wide-range of aesthetic, ethical, and metaphysical puzzles. Some of these questions concern definition of terms, as with "What counts as viral artwork?" and "Must artworks evoke high-arousal, positive emotions to go viral?" Others take into account audience—"Can online audiences interpret Web-based artists' intentions?"—moreover, space—"Might certain digital spaces better suit certain Web-based artworks Still other lines of inquiry consider ethics—"Does Web-based art composed of controversial content present ethical concerns?" —merit— "Does virality indicate aesthetic value?" and standards of taste— "By whom and according to which principles should viral artwork be judged?"

The world—in particular, the artworld—is changing. If we aim for scholarship to be impactful, the object of our efforts must adjust. Viral art matters: it is time the literature reflected it.

ACKNOWLEDGMENT

To my family, friends, and collaborators: thank you for your constant support of my artistic and academic endeavors.

This research received no specific grant from any funding agency in the public, commercial, or not-for-profit sectors.

REFERENCES

Abbott, J. (2012). Democracy@internet.org revisited: Analyzing the socio-political impact of the Internet and new social media in East Asia. *Third World Quarterly*, *33*(2), 333–357. doi:10.1080/01436 597.2012.666015

Alaoen, G. (2012). *McKayla is not impressed*. Retrieved from http://mckaylaisnotimpressed.tumblr.com/

Amerika, M. (2004). Expanding the concept of writing: Notes on net art, digital narrative and viral ethics. *Leonardo*, *37*(1), 9–13. doi:10.1162/002409404772827987

Andreessen, M. (2011, August 20). Why software is eating the world. *The Wall Street Journal*. Retrieved from http://www.wsj.com/articles/SB10001424053111903480904576512250915629460

Apter, J., & Mahmoud, G. (2014, November 11). *Ten hours of Princess Leia walking in NYC*. Retrieved from https://www.youtube.com/watch?v=7DCDYSJwwE4

Aristotle. (1961). Poetics (S.H. Butcher, Trans.). New York, NY: Hill and Wang. (Original work published c. 335 B.C.E.)

Balance, C. B. (2012). How it feels to be viral me: Affective labor and Asian American YouTube performance. *Women's Studies Quarterly*, *40*(1/2), 138–152. doi:10.1353/wsq.2012.0016

Barthes, R. (1978). The death of the author. In R. Barthes (Ed.), *Image-music-text* (HeathS., Trans.). (pp. 142–148). New York, NY: Hill and Wang. (Original work published 1967)

Barzilai-Nahon, K. (2008). Toward a theory of network gatekeeping: A framework for exploring information control. *Journal of the American Society for Information Science and Technology*, *59*(9), 1493–1512. doi:10.1002/asi.20857

Beardsley, M. C. (1981). The arts in the life of man. In M. C. Beardsley (Ed.), *Aesthetics: problems in the philosophy of criticism* (2nd ed.; pp. 557–583). Indianapolis, IN: Hackett Publishing Company.

Bell, C. (1914). The aesthetic hypothesis. In C. Bell (Ed.), *Art* (pp. 3–38). New York, NY: G.P. Putnam & Sons.

Benjamin, W. (1968). The work of art in the age of mechanical reproduction. In H. Arendt (Ed.) & H. Zohn (Trans.), Illuminations (pp. 219–226). New York, NY: Schocken Books. (Original work published 1936)

Berger, J., & Milkman, K. L. (2012). What makes online content go viral? *JMR, Journal of Marketing Research*, *49*(2), 192–205. doi:10.1509/jmr.10.0353

Bookchin, N., & Shulgin, A. (1999). Introduction to net.art (1994–1999). *Introduction to net.art (1994-1999)*. Retrieved from http://www.net-art.org/netart_definition

Bremmer, I. (2010). Democracy in cyberspace: What information technology can and cannot do. *Foreign Affairs, 89*(6), 86–92.

Bunting, H. (1998). *_readme*. Retrieved from http://www.irational.org/readme.html

Chayka, K. (2012, June 14). *How going viral has changed art*. Retrieved from http://thecreatorsproject.vice.com/blog/how-going-viral-has-changed-art

Cosics, V. (1998). *Deep ASCII*. Retrieved from http://ljudmila.org/~vuk/

Danto, A. (1964). The artworld. *The Journal of Philosophy, 61*(19), 571–584. doi:10.2307/2022937

Davies, S. (2006). Evolution and culture. In S. Davies (Ed.), *The philosophy of art* (pp. 1–25). Hoboken, NJ: Wiley-Blackwell.

Dewey, J. (1980). Having an experience. In J. Dewey (Ed.), Art as Experience (pp. 36–59). New York, NY: Perigree Books. (Original work published 1934)

Dickie, G. (1969). Defining art. *American Philosophical Quarterly, 6*, 253–256.

Dickie, G. (1974). *Art and the aesthetic*. Ithaca, NY: Cornell University Press.

Electronic Literature Organization. (1999). *What is E-lit?* Retrieved from https://eliterature.org/what-is-e-lit/

Feld, S., & Carter, W. (1998). Foci of activity as changing concepts for friendship. In R. Adams & A. Graham (Eds.), *Placing Friendship In Context* (pp. 136–152). Cambridge, UK: Cambridge University Press.

Gibbons, S. (2010). Collaborating like never before: Reading and writing through a wiki. *English Journal, 99*(5), 35–39.

Guadagno, R. E., Rempala, D. M., Murphy, S., & Okdie, B. M. (2013). What makes a video go viral? An analysis of emotional contagion and Internet memes. *Computers in Human Behavior, 29*(6), 2312–2319. doi:10.1016/j.chb.2013.04.016

Hamilton, J. (2015). *Indirect flights*. Retrieved from http://indirect.flights/

Hayles, K. (2008). *Electronic literature: new horizons for the literary*. Notre Dame, IN: University of Notre Dame Press.

Heath, D. (1996). Modest interventions. In G. Downey & J. Dumit (Eds.), *Cyborgs and citadels* (pp. 67–82). Santa Fe, NM: School of American Research.

Heemskerk, J., & Paesmans, D. (1995). *jodi.org*. Retrieved from http://geogeo.jodi.org/

Hirsch, E. D. Jr. (1980). In defense of the author. In E. D. Hirsch (Ed.), *Jr., Validity in interpretation* (pp. 1–19). New Haven, CT: Yale University Press.

Hollenback, K. (2015). *Simple business machines*. Retrieved from http://www.katehollenbach.com/simple-business-machines/

Hume, D. (2006). Of the standard of taste. In E. F. Miller (Ed.), Essays: Moral, political, and literary (pp. 231–258). New York, NY: Cosimo, Inc. (Original work published 1742)

Kadushin, C. (2012). *Understanding social networks: theories, concepts, and findings*. Oxford, UK: Oxford University Press.

Kamssu, A. J., Siekpe, J. S., & Ellzy, J. A. (2004). Shortcomings to globalization: Using Internet technology and electronic commerce in developing countries. *Journal of Developing Areas*, *38*(1), 151–169. doi:10.1353/jda.2005.0010

Kanarek, Y. (1995). *World of awe*. Retrieved from http://www.worldofawe.net/thejournal/landing/ on July 30, 2017.

Kant, I. (2007). Analytic of the beautiful. In N. Walker (Ed.) & J. C. Meredith (Trans.), The critique of judgment (pp. 26–52). London, UK: Oxford University Press. (Original work published 1790)

Kelley, M. (2014, April 15). My photo went viral and nothing could have prepared me for what happened after. *Fstoppers*. Retrieved from https://fstoppers.com/composite/my-photo-went-viral-and-nothing-could-have-prepared-me-what-happened-after-9517 on July 30, 2017.

Kirsch, A. (2008). The fight for recognition. *Poetry*, *193*(2), 143–148.

Kitroeff, N. (2014, May 19). Why that video went viral. *The New York Times*. Retrieved from http://www.nytimes.com/2014/05/20/science/why-that-video-went-viral.html?_r=0

Knobel, M., & Lankshear, C. (2007). Online memes, affinities, and cultural production. In C. Lankshear, M. Knobel, C. Bigum, & M. Peters (Eds.), *A new literacies sampler* (pp. 199–227). New York: Peter Lang Publishing.

KnowYourMeme. (2017). Retrieved from http://knowyourmeme.com/

Koebler, J. (2014, October 21). When your photo goes viral, the Internet will kill its image quality. *Motherboard*. Retrieved from http://motherboard.vice.com/read/when-your-photo-goes-viral-the-internet-will-kill-its-image-quality

Little, M. (2015, September 21). New York City rat taking home pizza on the subway (Pizza Rat). *YouTube video*. Retrieved from https://www.youtube.com/watch?v=UPXUG8q4jKU

Mendoza, N. (2015). *The Selfie-Selfie-O-Matic*. Retrieved from http://www.neilmendoza.com/portfolio/selfie-selfie-o-matic/

Nahon, K., & Helmsley, J. (2013). *Going Viral*. Cambridge, UK: Polity Press.

News, C. H. (2015, November 23). 'Selfie Rat' snaps photo of himself with sleeping man's phone on subway platform. *YouTube Video*. Retrieved from https://youtu.be/5CvWXG8gqEU

Nietzsche, F. (1967). *The birth of tragedy* (W. Kaufmann, Trans.). New York, NY: Random House. (Original work published 1872)

Nisbett, R. E., & Wilson, T. D. (1977). Telling more than we can know: Verbal reports on mental processes. *Psychological Review, 84*(3), 231–259. doi:10.1037/0033-295X.84.3.231

O'Hanihan, A. (2013). *Without their permission: How the 21ˢᵗ century will be made, not managed.* New York, NY: Business Plus.

O'Reilly. (2005). *Web 2.0: compact definition? O'Reilly radar.* Retrieved from http://radar.oreilly.com/2005/10/web-20-compact-definition.html

OddDaily Clips. (2016, January 21). Three eyed catfish appeared in New York. *YouTube Video.* Retrieved from https://youtu.be/MC4cJTARung

Palfrey, J. (2010). Four phases of internet regulation. *Social Research, 77*(3), 981–996.

Pedersen, L. H. (2017). *The viral art effect: how virality and viral art as a part of our social networks can affect our society and how we perceive interfaces* (Unpublished master's thesis). The University of Bergen, Bergen, Norway.

Plato. (1992). Republic (C.D.C. Reeve, Ed., & G.M.A. Grube, Trans.). Indianapolis, IN: Hackett Publishing Company. (Original work published c. 380 B.C.E.)

Purcell, K. (2010). *The state of the online video.* Washington, DC: Pew Internet & American Life Project.

RozendaalR. (2014). *Abstract browsing.* Retrieved from http://www.newrafael.com/notes-on-abstract-browsing/

Rushmore, R. J. (2013). *Viral art.* Retrieved from http://viralart.vandalog.com/read/buy

Russo, D., Wheeldon, C., & Part, A. (2013, September 12). *New beginnings.* Retrieved from https://www.youtube.com/watch?v=3zMCxmdkcRY

Schmidt, L., & Pipkin, K. R. (2015). *@mothgenerator.* Retrieved from https://twitter.com/mothgenerator?ref_src=twsrc%5Egoogle%7Ctwcamp%5Eserp%7Ctwgr%5Eauthor on July 30, 2017.

Shifman, L. (2013). *MIT press essential knowledge: memes in digital culture.* Cambridge, UK: MIT Press.

Shirky, C. (2009). *Here comes everybody: the power of organizing without organizations.* New York, NY: Penguin.

Sontag, S. (2011). Against interpretation. In Against Interpretation and Other Essays (pp. 3–15). New York, NY: Picador USA. (Original work published 1966)

Stanoevska-Slabeva, K. (2002). Toward a community-oriented design of Internet platforms. *International Journal of Electronic Commerce, 6*(3), 71–95. doi:10.1080/10864415.2002.11044244

Tolstoy, L. (2011). What is art? (W. G. Jones, Ed., & A. Maude, Trans.). London, UK: Bristol Classical Press. (Original work published 1897)

Vartanian, H. (2014, November 13). The downside of art going viral. *Hyperallergic.* Retrieved from http://hyperallergic.com/162244/the-downside-of-art-going-viral/

Verbrugge, L. M. (1977). The structure of adult friendship choices. *Social Forces*, *56*(2), 576–597. doi:10.1093f/56.2.576

Wimsatt, W. K., Jr., & Beardsley, M. C. (1982). The intentional fallacy. In W. K. Wimsatt (Ed.), The verbal icon: Studies in the meaning of poetry. Lexington, KY: University Press of Kentucky. (Original work published 1946, revised in 1954)

Wyrwoll, C. (2014). *Social media: Fundamentals, models, and ranking of user-generated content*. Dordrecht, The Netherlands: Springer. doi:10.1007/978-3-658-06984-1

Yangyue, L. (2014). Controlling cyberspace in Malaysia: Motivations and constraints. *Asian Survey*, *54*(4), 801–823. doi:10.1525/as.2014.54.4.801

KEY TERMS AND DEFINITIONS

Aesthetics: A branch of philosophy that addresses the nature of art, beauty, and taste.

Ethics: The branch of knowledge that deals with moral principles.

GIF: A lossless format for compressing image files.

Globalization: The international integration of countries arising from the convergence of world views.

Meme: An idea, behavior, or style that spreads from person to person within a culture.

Tumblr: A microblogging and social networking website where users post multimedia and other content to a short-form blog.

Twitter: An online news and social networking service where users post and interact with messages restricted to 140 characters.

YouTube: A video-sharing website.

ENDNOTES

[1]   These include: *_readme* (Bunting, 1998), a piece based on a press clipping about Bunting that was reformatted so that many of the words are hyperlinks to other websites; *jodi.org* (Heemskerk & Paesmans, 1995) and *Deep ASCII* (Cosics, 1998), both of which use coding and markup language to make artwork hidden within a website's page source or made entirely out of binary numbers; *World of Awe* (Kanarek, 1995), an ongoing fictional online diary that mixes love letters to cyborgs with 3-D models and landscapes; *Abstract Browsing* (Rozendaal, 2014), a free browser app or Chrome extension that converts any websites original content into contrasting colored boxes that change colors every few seconds; *Indirect Flights* (Hamilton, 2015), an interactive website that provides different and fragmented aerial of the world collages into a dense panorama; *@mothgenerator* (Schmidt & Pipkin, 2015), a Twitter bot that posts imaginary moths of all shapes, sizes, colors, each with a name generates from English and Latin); *Simple Business Machines* (Hollenback, 2015) a visual reconfiguration of buttons, knobs, and faders from a control board; *The Selfie-Selfie-O-Matic* (Mendoza, 2015) arranges its elements (dolls, flower patterns, and frames) in a different way each time; and many cases of electronic literature, that is, literature created on and meant to be read on a stand-alone or networked computer (Hayles, 2008, Electronic Literature Organization).

[2] One way to address this question would be considering the related area of contemporary music composition. As in the past, modern-day recorded songs can have parts, whether instrumental, vocal, or both. These days, however, component parts of a song can be recorded as separate tracks. Once all of a song's stems are recorded, music producers can mix the tracks using software programs and therefore create a cohesive whole. The resultant, unified track is the song. Since modern-day song recording has become a largely digital process, it is possible to alter recorded musical compositions. One way of altering is *remixing*. A *remix* is an alternate version of an already composed song created by adjusting its existing layout. For example, to remix Michael Jackson's *Thriller* one might decrease the original tempo, eliminate the lead vocal line, or add a house beat. The remix would sound different from the original, but still communicate the original song's message. This author's view is that ornamental changes do not alter the original composition's essence. Altering Web-based artwork is like adjusting remixing a song. These adjustments are changes that may conceal, but nonetheless maintain, the original composition's essence.

[3] As mentioned earlier in this chapter, elements of this dialogue have been addressed, e.g., *status-homophily*, *value-homophily*, *filter-fowarding*, and *network-gatekeepers* (Barzilai-Nahon 2008; Feld and Carter, 1998; Kadushin, 2012; Shirky, 2009; Verbrugge, 1977).

Chapter 17
A Technoethical Study of Ethical Hacking Communication and Management Within a Canadian University

Baha Abu-Shaqra
University of Ottawa, Canada

Rocci Luppicini
Universisty of Ottawa, Canada

ABSTRACT

Ethical hacking is an important information security risk management strategy within higher education applied against the growing threat of hacking attacks. Confusion regarding the meaning and ethics of ethical hacking within broader society and which resonates within organizations undermines information security. Confusion within organizations increases unpredictably (equivocality) in the information environment, which raises risk level. Taking a qualitative exploratory case study approach, this chapter pairs technoethical inquiry theory with Karl Weick's sensemaking model to explore the meanings, ethics, uses and practices, and value of ethical hacking in a Canadian university and applies technoethical inquiry decision-making grid (TEI-DMG) as an ethical decision-making model. Findings point to the need to expand the communicative and sociocultural considerations involved in decision making about ethical hacking organizational practices, and to security awareness training to leverage sensemaking opportunities and reduce equivocality in the information environment.

INTRODUCTION

Universities and other higher education institutions represent a tempting target for hackers and are under an increasing risk of hacking attacks. Educational institutions maintain databases of personal information about faculty, staff, and students. Such databases represent a tempting target for cybercriminals who sell stolen personal information on the black market to other criminals for profit (Burrell, n.d.). Cybercrimi-

DOI: 10.4018/978-1-5225-5094-5.ch017

nals may be looking to steal university research. Ethical hacking is an important information security risk management strategy higher education institutions and businesses use against the growing threat of hacking attacks. Implementation challenges within an organization intersect several perspectives within the broader societal/industry context--social/sociocultural, ethical, and technical/technological perspectives. There is confusion (among other challenges) surrounding ethical hacking meaning and ethics within society and which resonates within societal organizations with costs to society. Confusion within organizations increases unpredictably (equivocality) in the information environment which negatively affects information security—it raises hacking risk. Confusion among the general public can manifest in a stigma that can hurt businesses. Confusion undermines innovation and effective policy development.

A social/sociocultural perspective is concerned with a broad question, what is ethical hacking? A key cause of confusion regarding ethical hacking meaning and ethics within society results from a difference in language use (application of the term ethical hacking) between and among engineers and technologists, and non-technologists. This difference can manifest in two ways. First, hacking as a contronym resulting from a tension between two contradictory stakeholder perspectives--hacking as having a positive connotation among engineers and technologists in contrast to the more popular understanding of hacking as being a malicious activity. Second, the terms white, grey, and black hackers and hacking can refer to a type of information security testing or to sociocultural codes. An ethical perspective focuses on fair and efficient (effective) technology implementation--including, whether it should be used or not, and how to implement it effectively so that organizations are protected and the public is served. A technical/technological perspective includes account for broad industry trends, and addresses aspects of hacking technology proliferation and the changing technological landscape of cybersecurity, as well as broader concerns related to problems within the information security management field, such as the metrics problem, the lack of broad industry information security standards, and software interoperability challenges. Importantly, organizational challenges resonating form broader societal practices—notably, confusion regarding ethical hacking meaning and ethics among various stakeholder groups extends into organizations which undermines organizational information security.

Most information security management books on ethical hacking focused on its technical application in information security risk assessment practices. The broader societal context of ethical hacking implementation was less considered. Non-technical challenges involved in the implementation of ethical hacking within higher education organizations intersect several perspectives. The study focused on effective ethical hacking implementation in an higher education organization understood within the broader societal/industry context—within the ethical, social/sociocultural, and technical/technological context. The study explored the research question, What are the meanings, ethics, uses and practices, and value of ethical hacking in a Canadian university? by applying technoethical inquiry theory (Luppicini, 2008A, 2008B, 2010) and Karl Weick's (1969, 1979, 1995) sensemaking model to a case study. This paper addressed a gap within the information security management literature on ethical hacking. The important contribution to knowledge of this study lies in filling in a gap in the literature on information security management that results from the scarcity of research on the communicative and sociocultural considerations involved in the implementation of ethical hacking within organizations, focusing on non-technical aspects, while the dominant scholarship is application and certification oriented focusing on technical and legal aspects.

Technoethical inquiry theory (TEI) is a pragmatic systems theory that highlights knowledge gathering from multiple perspectives, including ethical, technological, political, legal, historical, communicative, and sociocultural (Luppicini, 2010). The goal of TEI is to uncover information related to the efficiency and fairness of ethical hacking use in an organization. The research applied TEI (the five steps) to present a multi-perspective, multi-stakeholder analysis of ethical hacking use in an organization by exploring key stakeholder perspectives about meanings, ethics, uses and practices, and value aspects of implementation. Perspectives were then drawn together to frame a holistic and grounded understanding of the use of ethical hacking in an organization. The TEI-DMG (Technoethical Inquiry Decision-making Grid) was applied to offer a qualitative assessment of efficiency and fairness considerations of ethical hacking implementation within an organization. Data collection consisted of in-depth semi-structured interviews with expert participants representing key stakeholder groups, as well as organizational documentation. Data was coded against the theoretical propositions (Yin, 1994) of TEI during open coding and analyzed using the illustrative pattern matching method (Neuman, 2010).

BACKGROUND

The threat of cyber-attacks on information assets in the private and public sectors is a growing and evolving threat, warns Public Safety Canada (2013A, 2013B, 2013C). There is "no doubt that the frequency and severity of the cyber threat is accelerating. Protecting Canadians in cyberspace will be a constantly evolving challenge" (2013A). The frequency of hacking attacks increases year after year. Every year "those seeking to infiltrate, exploit or attack our cyber systems are more sophisticated and better resourced than the year before" (Public Safety Canada, 2013A, Introduction, para. 5). Over two-thirds of Canadian adults were subject to cybercrime in 2012 (2013B). Canadians are increasingly reliant on the Internet. The Canadian federal government, for example, offers more than 130 commonly used services online, including tax returns, student loan applications, and employment insurance forms. Identity theft costs Canadians nearly $1.9 billion each year (2013A).

Cyber attacks include the unintentional or unauthorized access, use, manipulation, interruption or destruction (via electronic means) of electronic information and/or the electronic and physical infrastructure used to process, communicate and/or store that information. The severity of the cyber attack determines the appropriate level of response and/or mitigation measures: i.e., cyber security. (Public Safety Canada, 2013A)

Hackers pose a security threat in that they can compromise the confidentiality, integrity, or availability of information. Cybersecurity is a process of applying information security measures to protect information CIA (Dhillon, 2007; Reynolds, 2012; Stamp, 2011).

Ethical hacking is a key cybersecurity strategy within higher education institutions. A review of literature found the majority of published books on ethical hacking were either application oriented or certification oriented, emphasizing the use of ethical hacking as a risk assessment process (Engebretson, 2013; Graves, 2010; Harris, Harper, Eagle, & Ness, 2007; Landoll & Landoll, 2005; Regalado et al., 2015; Simpson, Backman, & Corley, 2010). Application type texts typically serve as manuals or how-to guides, while certification oriented texts prepare IT security professionals for several information security related certifications set at various levels of competencies and skills. The texts typically outline the relevant laws and regulations. However, little attention is given to non-technical and non-legal aspects of ethical hacking implementation within organizations. This paper addressed a gap within the information security management literature on ethical hacking. The important contribution to knowledge of this study lies in filling in a gap in the literature on information security management that results from the scarcity of research on the communicative and sociocultural considerations involved in the implementation of ethical hacking within organizations, focusing on non-technical aspects, while the dominant scholarship is application and certification oriented focusing on technical and legal aspects.

Technoethics "attempts to provide conceptual grounding to clarify the role of technology in relation to those affected by it and to help guide ethical problem-solving and decision making in areas of activity that rely on technology" (Luppicini, 2010, p. 5). TEI takes a pragmatic approach to technology assessment—it evaluates its use by weighing the perceived benefits against the perceived costs and side effects with emphasis on efficient and fair technology implementation. TEI is well suited for addressing the research question because there is ethical hacking philosophy alignment with the pragmatic orientation of TEI regarding the approach to gaining knowledge, the axiology, and ethical goals. For both, 1) the goal is improved performance in information security; 2) axiology or value: a pragmatic cost effective, risk based approach to decision making. TEI aligns with the pragmatic philosophical orientation of ethical hacking as a risk-based, cost-effective information security risk assessment strategy with an emphasis on efficient and economical practices; and 3) approach to gaining knowledge: the synthesis of a multi-perspective understanding of an information security system. The epistemology of both aligns with the qualitative case study methodology regarding the centrality of personal experience and context for attaining knowledge, including triangulation via data derived from multiple stakeholder perspectives.

This study explored the research question, What are the meanings, ethics, uses and practices, and value of ethical hacking in a Canadian university? TEI, a systems multi-perspective approach, is suitable to assess ethical hacking implementation within an organization because it theorizes the broader sociocultural and industry context. TEI views organizational challenges through a holistic interdisciplinary lens. Its multi-perspective approach accounts for the broad societal context. As a systems approach, it can explain the dynamics of interaction among various stakeholder groups. Technology implementation challenges intersect disciplines and stakeholder perspectives and should be understood within the broader societal context. A historical background is necessary to explain current confusion resulting from a split in technological/sociocultural perspectives regarding the meaning and ethics of ethical hacking—also necessary historical background relates to the historical role of the mass media and authorities' use of established incriminating terminology in shaping broader societal perceptions about ethical hacking meaning and ethics. Broad perspectives were incorporated into the analysis to help explain what is shaping contemporary social understandings and social response to hacking activities (e.g., enacting laws).

Weick's (1969, 1979) sensemaking model was applied to examine the communicative aspects of ethical hacking implementation by exploring organizational perceptions among key stakeholder groups about the meanings and ethics of ethical hacking as well as the underlying communicative routines. Weick's model was used to examine the organizing processes of enactment and selection of ethical hacking practices. The primary function of organizing is to make sense of the information environment. During enactment, a participant brackets an event or an act such that the environment becomes constituted in a particular way. Selection involves "the imposition of various structures on enacted equivocal displays in an attempt to reduce their equivocality" (Weick, 1979, p. 131). Much of the sensemaking happens during the selection phase. Equivocality is the unpredictability that is inherent in the information environment. Equivocality is likely to be high in organizations in a highly competitive or quickly changing business environment or during a time of crisis. When equivocality is high, and the complexity of the environment allows for multiple explanations of the same event, communication cycles are suggested--

ongoing interpersonal and cross-functional communication (Miller, 2009). Equivocality can be reduced by providing communication opportunities for participants to interact and create common knowledge.

Unpredictability in the information environment within organizations arising from variances in perceptions about ethical hacking meanings, ethics, and practices among key stakeholder groups can be reduced through the selection of assembly rules (instructions) and communication cycles (ongoing interpersonal and cross-functional communication). The existence of risk requires uncertainty (which can be understood as unpredictability). Cybersecurity actors can reduce the risk of hacking by reducing unpredictability in the information environment about ethical hacking organizational aspects. The application of Weick's model within the empirical pragmatic lens of TEI has a practical, scientifically-justified benefit for the participating organization—improving the communicative performance improves the security performance.

METHODOLOGY

This study explored the research question, What are the meanings, ethics, uses and practices, and value of ethical hacking in a Canadian university? TEI (the five steps) was applied to frame an understanding about perceived ethical dimensions--efficiency and fairness--surrounding ethical hacking organizational implementation among key stakeholder groups. These understandings were then presented within a broader societal and industry context. The steps (Luppicini, 2010, p. 73) can be listed as follows:

- **Step 1:** Evaluate the intended ends and possible side effects to discern overall value;
- **Step 2:** Compare the means and intended ends in terms of technical and nontechnical aspects
- (moral, social);
- **Step 3:** Reject any action where the output (overall value) does not balance the input in terms
- of efficiency and fairness;
- **Step 4:** Explore relevant information connected to the perceived effectiveness and ethical
- dimensions of ethical hacking in a Canadian university for key stakeholder groups; and
- **Step 5:** Consider technological relations at a variety of levels.

This study applied the qualitative exploratory case study approach to study how an organization understands and implements ethical hacking within its unique organizational context. A case study is "an empirical inquiry that investigates a contemporary phenomenon within its real-life context, especially when the boundaries between phenomenon and context are not clearly evident" (Yin, 2003, p. 13). A case study can be thought of as a comprehensive method, covering the logic of design, and data collection and analysis techniques. Case studies allow researchers to explore a program, event, activity, process, or individuals in depth because the case study methodology supports a systems exploration and conceptualization of organizational phenomena and practices (Creswell, 2003). Five further arguments in support of the qualitative case study methodology follows. First, the qualitative case study methodology aligns with TEI in its systemic and theoretical orientation regarding data collection and analysis—including triangulation via data derived from multiple perspectives and stakeholder groups. Second, it is suitable when the study focus is on operational links rather than on frequencies. Third, it is suitable when little control over events is expected. Fourth, it is suitable when the focus of the study is on contemporary phenomena within a real-life context (Yin, 1994). Fifth, the qualitative case study methodology is well-suited for capturing the unique complexities of a single case (Stake, 1995). The exploratory approach is appropriate when there is a scarcity of literature on the subject (Stebbins, 2011).

Data collection consisted of in-depth interviews with five IT and information security experts, as well as a comprehensive document review. In-depth interviews are typically done "to solicit people's descriptions and explanations of events taking place in their own environment" (Eid, 2011, p.10). The study employed four triangulation protocols to ensure the accuracy of the findings: 1) Triangulation of measure (Neuman, 2011) or triangulation of data (Yin, 1994) using different sources of data and different measures (perspectives) of ethical hacking; 2) Triangulation of method (Stake, 1995) using in-depth face-to-face interviews with key stakeholder groups within an organization, as well as organizational documentation as two methods of data collection; 3) Triangulation of observers (Neuman, 2011) or member checking (Stake, 1995) whereby the participants were consulted on the interview transcripts so as to counter selective perception and interpretation of the researcher; and 4) Triangulation of theory using two complementary theoretical lenses, TEI and Weick's theory of information organizing.

A purposeful data sampling strategy and sampling of insiders' expert resources was used in pursuit of an ethical and comprehensive analysis. The interview participants, university professors and information security industry professionals, were sought out for their expert knowledge in 1) scholarly ethical hacking research; 2) broad industry trends and best practices in information security management, including information security compliance management, risk assessment, and typical organizational information security policy objectives; 3) organizational practices in ethical hacking, especially in information security management and risk assessment practices; and 4) organizational communication routines related to ethical hacking aspects. Interview experts had a minimum of one year experience in IT and information security management. The participating university was chosen as the research site because i) the needed expert knowledge in internal and external (industry-wide and academic) ethical hacking aspects was found there, ii) there was important cooperation from the IT department in conducting the interviews, and iii) the research site implemented state-of-the-art IT and information security technologies and practices.

The nature of the organizational data about ethical hacking meanings and practices which the researchers had access to, and any challenges in obtaining access to the data, can be understood within the context of a concern by the IT department about divulging information about information security practices which a malicious hacker can exploit. Expert C remarked in relation to publishing organizational information security policies online, a common practice, "if you have something posted online and the bad guys look at it, they know what they have to do to break into somebody's system" (personal communication, April 24, 2014). To acquire permission to conduct in-depth interviews about ethical hacking practices with IT staff at the participating organization, the researchers first had to address two main concerns raised by the IT executive office: 1) Concerns about creating a security vulnerability at the organization by divulging sensitive information about technical or management ethical hacking practices, or by disclosing the identity of the research site or an interview participant; 2) Concerns about safeguarding employee (participant) confidentiality and about job security. The IT department would kindly cooperate with the researchers after the two main mechanisms adopted to address these two concerns were explained. First, the study employed the validation protocol member checking (Stake, 1995) which gave the interview participants the opportunity to review their contributions and quotes and to correct them if necessary before they are included in the final research manuscript. Second, the name of the research site was dropped from the study documents.

In-depth, focused (Yin, 1994), and semi-structured interviews were conducted with a target set time (1 hour) at various locations. The face-to-face interview sessions were audio recorded and the relevant parts were transcribed for accuracy and attentive analysis. Further, interview hand-written notes were taken. The interviews were first transcribed in five separate documents. In each, a table was created to sort expert responses into categories, as they addressed the elements of inquiry—the meanings, ethics, uses and practices, and value of ethical hacking. The five tables were then merged into one table. The juxtaposition of the findings helped the researchers identify common understandings as well as variations in perceptions about the meanings, ethics, uses and practices, and value of ethical hacking in an organization.

FINDINGS AND DISCUSSION

The study explored the meanings, ethics, uses and practices, and value of ethical hacking in a Canadian university. Data addressing the RQ inquiry elements—the meanings, ethics, uses and practices, and value of ethical hacking—were coded against the theoretical propositions (Yin, 1994) of TEI (the 5 steps) during open coding. First, the transcribed interviews were coded. Eight main topic themes emerged. The participating organization had a computer services website accessible from its main website. The researchers examined the website and identified and analyzed 18 documents containing data addressing the inquiry elements. The documents were categorized into four types (informational, policy, reports, and news) and topic themes under each document type were identified. Themes which addressed the four inquiry elements were then merged with the eight interview themes to frame organizational understandings about each ethical hacking element. The understandings were then contextualized within ethical hacking literature and broad industry practices. The study used the illustrative pattern matching method (Neuman, 2010) as the analytic strategy and applied TEI-KW to interpret the data. The illustrative method anchors or illustrates theoretical concepts with empirical evidence. It applies theory to a concrete social setting and organizes data based on theory. "Preexisting theory can provide conceptual empty boxes that you fill with the empirical evidence" (Neuman, 2011, p. 353). In the pattern matching variation of this analytic strategy, concepts or patterns identified in the findings are matched to those derived from theory. The findings (coded and interpreted elements) were used to answer the RQ (Abu-Shaqra & Luppicini, 2016).

The RQ was divided into two sub-questions. Each sub-question was divided into two questions. TEI was applied to analyze sub-question *a*, and Weick's theory was applied to analyze sub-question *b*. Sub-question a) What is the Value, and What are the Management and Technical Uses and Practices of Ethical Hacking in a Canadian University? (What is the Value of Ethical Hacking? And, What are the Management and Technical Uses and Practices of Ethical Hacking?) Sub-question b) What are the Meanings, Ethics, and Communicative Uses and Practices of Ethical Hacking in a Canadian University? (What are the Meanings and Ethics of Ethical Hacking? And, What are the Communicative Practices of Ethical Hacking?)

What Is the Value of Ethical Hacking?

Intended Ends and Possible Side Effects of Ethical Hacking

Participant perceptions about ethical hacking ends (goals) fell under two broad themes, namely, management aspects and technical aspects. Expert A, Expert D, Expert C, and organizational documentation

P2 presented ethical hacking mainly as a tool used to pursue organizational management goals, that is, they emphasized its management utility for the organization. Expert B and Expert E saw it mainly as a technical tool used in vulnerability assessment.

For Expert A, ethical hacking was used to achieve "continuous improvement of information security, in partnership with the greater community." For Expert D, Expert C, and according to documentation P2, ethical hacking was used to protect the information assets. The end goal of ethical hacking use was "to make sure that the application that you are trying to protect is protected," said Expert C. According to organizational documentation P2, information assets, including software, software applications, and data, should be protected from unauthorized alteration or damage--from potential threats to confidentiality, integrity or availability of information. For Expert B, a main goal of ethical hacking was to discover systemic vulnerability sources. Ethical hacking was used to "run in-house vulnerability testing on servers, assess the vulnerabilities in the used software, and explore new sources of vulnerability" (Expert B). For Expert E, in general, the goal of ethical hacking was to identify vulnerabilities and fix them before a hacker exploits them. Ongoing improvement in information security performance is a strategic information security management goal. A second goal is safeguarding the information assets (Dhillon, 2007; Engebretson, 2013; Graves, 2010; Landoll & Landoll, 2005; Peltier, 2004A, 2004B, 2005; Reynolds, 2012).

Perceptions about possible side effects of ethical hacking use in the participating organization entailed sociocultural, technical, and financial perspectives. The primary concern for Expert B and Expert A was sociocultural, namely, that ethical hacking had a PR stigma attached to it. "People may fear their information will be compromised during ethical hacking," said Expert A. The primary concern for Expert E and Expert C was technical, namely, that ethical hacking can damage the information system or destroy data if not performed properly. Secondarily for Expert C, the system may remain exploited after ethical hacking was performed. A secondary concern for Expert A was technical, namely, accidental damage to the system during ethical hacking procedures. The main concern for Expert D was financial, that documents related to ethical hacking (reports and strategy) can get stolen. A secondary concern for Expert D was financial, that investments were needed to upgrade the system. A secondary concern for Expert E was financial, that ethical hacking may be costly.

Perceived Means of Ethical Hacking

Organizational understandings about ethical hacking means (technologies or practices) used in the university focused on the technical application of ethical hacking as a risk assessment methodology using software programs. Expert B, Expert D, Expert E, Expert A, and Expert C agreed both commercial and open source resources were used in information security risk assessment practices. But while Expert B, Expert D, Expert E, and Expert A emphasized the use of open source technologies, Expert C emphasized the use of commercial software.

For Expert A, the organization can use open source technologies for threat risk assessment. Secondarily, the organization can use well established standardized threat risk assessment methodologies. For Expert B, the university would typically use some commercial ethical hacking software, but "when it comes down to the difficult stuff, I think it is mostly open source." For Expert D, primarily, the "IT professional staff can use open source as long as they consult with their superiors." Secondarily, the organization can use hacking open source software such as "script kiddy and download" for free, or it can buy commercial software costing up to $5,000. Primarily for Expert C, commercial software may be more suitable than open source because some application programs that are more suitable for the organization are commercial rather than open source, and commercial software vendors are more likely to have more readily available updated security patches than are open source. Secondarily, "budgetary constraints may drive an organization to the open source route." For Expert E, in general, the information security testing methodology as well as the used software tools were open source based, though commercial tools were also available.

Perceived Value of Ethical Hacking

The value of ethical hacking for the organization can be located in its utility in risk assessment processes, and can be understood from management and technical perspectives. From a management perspective, the organizational value of ethical hacking can be located in its utility as a value system (as a risk based approach) for decision making about suitable security defenses and countermeasures. From a technical perspective, the value of ethical hacking can be located in its utility as a process to understand and prioritize security risks.

Expert B and Expert C emphasized the use of ethical hacking as a pragmatic value system to help make decisions about suitable countermeasures by weighing the risks of being attacked and associated damage costs against the cost and effectiveness of countermeasures, that is, by weighing the costs against benefits. To determine value, estimate how likely is an attack to happen, what are the consequences of that happening, and what would be the cost of preventing this from happening, said Expert B. Secondarily for Expert B and Expert C, ethical hacking was a process or a methodology to help decision makers understand and prioritize risks. The organization cannot perform ethical hacking against all the applications in the environment, they said. "You have to prioritize," argued Expert C. "The Internet layer should be protected first, and then you can work on other things." Similarly, Expert E and organizational documentation P2 emphasized the use of ethical hacking as a process to help decision makers understand and prioritize risks. Expert E argued the professional hacker "asks the client about the value of the assets, assesses the threats and the potential attacks on the assets, and examines the security mechanisms." The organizational documentation P2 emphasized the utility of ethical hacking as a process of risk assessment--as a process of determining the different threats to the information assets, estimating the probability of their occurrence and potential consequences, and determining the costs of increased protection. Secondarily for Expert E and organizational documentation P2, the value of ethical hacking can be found in its utility as a pragmatic, risk based value system for decision making.

What Are the Management and Technical Uses and Practices of Ethical Hacking?

Management Uses and Practices of Ethical Hacking

The organization used ethical hacking in information security management in at least five ways: compliance management (Expert A, Expert D, and Expert C), threat risk assessment (Expert A, Expert E, and Expert B), network assessment (Expert D), design implementation (Expert C), and vulnerability testing (Expert B).

Primarily for Expert A, ethical hacking is commonly used in compliance management. "Most of the industry focuses on security compliance, or security testing, or security validation, or security certification." Ethical hacking "is used to validate and test whether the system is compliant." Ethical hacking was used in the organization to test whether the system was compliant with information security standards (Expert A). Second, for Expert A, threat risk assessment was used as an information security risk management tool. For Expert C, first, ethical hacking as pen testing was used to verify the implementation of the recommended security design; second, it was used in compliance verification, as part of a security audit which aims to verify procedural as well as technical controls. For Expert D, ethical hacking was used in network and applications assessment to lower the risk of illegal access to computing resources. Secondarily for Expert D, it was used to verify that policies were being observed and standards were being met. Expert B said ethical hacking was used in vulnerability testing and in information security threat risk assessment. Expert E argued that, in general, ethical hacking as threat risk assessment is a systematic approach to understanding a) what are the threats, b) what are the assets, c) what is the value of the assets, and d) what is the possibility people will attack these assets.

Technical Uses and Practices of Ethical Hacking

Expert E, Expert A, Expert D, and Expert C agreed that the two main organizational uses of ethical hacking as a technical tool related to its use in risk assessment and vulnerability assessment practices. Expert B emphasized its application in social engineering.

For Expert A, threat risk assessment is a well-established methodology. The steps include 1) "The first thing is to catalogue what you have"; 2) "Then you have to identify what vulnerabilities you have, and for each vulnerability you have to assess what is the value of the damage that can occur, and that can be monetary or public image"; 3) Next is to assess the likelihood of an attack. For Expert D, ethical password hacking, as part of risk assessment, tests the ability to hack a password by using the default factory password search, the dictionary search, social engineering, man-in-the-middle attack, and the brute force search methods. Expert E said that, in general, uses of ethical hacking as a technical tool included its use in vulnerability testing, and its use in threat risk assessment. For Expert B, organizational uses of ethical hacking as a technical tool or strategy included its use in social engineering. For example, Expert B said, an ethical hacker can gather confidential information from users and report on the results, such as how many users gave their passwords. Expert C offered a nuanced view about the application of ethical hacking in risk assessment practices, by outlining three types of information security testing simulation scenarios, subject to the organizational constraints and needs.

What Are the Meanings and Ethics of Ethical Hacking?

The Meanings of Ethical Hacking

Organizational understandings about ethical hacking meanings leaned toward a technical perspective, as hacking (Expert A, Expert E, Expert B, and Expert C), and as vulnerability assessment (secondarily for Expert A, Expert E, and Expert B). Secondarily for Expert C, ethical hacking was "pen testing." Expert D saw ethical hacking primarily as network assessment.

The definition of ethical hacking as hacking among IT professionals at the participating organization was consistent with the view that the term hacking still carried a positive connotation among IT and computer professionals (Palmer, 2001). Expert B said ethical hacking was "just hacking." The use of the term "ethical" is meant to dispel the bad image of hackers. The term ethical hacking is used in opposition to hacking, "to distance yourself from malicious hackers." Secondarily for Expert B, ethical hacking referred to a technical process of "trying to find vulnerabilities in the system before the bad guys do, using the same means." For Expert E, ethical hacking was a practice in the IT industry which involved using hacking technologies to identify vulnerabilities in a network infrastructure. Ethical hacking was also called vulnerability assessment, pen testing, and hacking (Expert E). Expert C said ethical hacking was hacking or pen testing "in the ethical way, in the legal way." Expert A argued that ethical hacking was a hacking process performed to discover vulnerabilities and to test the effectiveness of the information security controls in place. For Expert D, ethical hacking was primarily network assessment, which includes assessing the vulnerability of the network, systems, applications, and how users sign in. There were four different meanings for ethical hacking among the five stakeholder groups: hacking, vulnerability assessment, pen testing, and network assessment. In the computer security context, representing the more strict technical definition, a hacker is someone who seeks and exploits weaknesses in a computer system or network. Most books in information security management on ethical hacking equated it with risk assessment or penetration testing (e.g., Engebretson, 2013; Graves, 2010; Harris, Harper, Eagle, & Ness, 2007; Landoll & Landoll, 2005; Regalado et al., 2015; Simpson, Backman, & Corley, 2010; Sterling, 1993).

The Ethics of Ethical Hacking

Organizational understandings about the ethics of professional ethical hackers fell under two general themes. It is ethical in that it follows a technical process of risk assessment, and it is ethical in that it is legal. In other words, ethical hacking as a technical process of risk assessment (Expert E, Expert B, and Expert A), and ethical hacking as a legal process of risk assessment (Expert D, Expert E, and Expert C).

Expert E recognized ethical hacking as a technical process of threat risk assessment, arguing it was "a systematic approach to understanding a) what are the threats, b) what are the assets, c) what is the value of the assets, and d) what is the possibility people will attack these assets." Expert B argued there was nothing ethical about ethical hacking, "it is a technical process" of risk assessment. Expert A argued "the ethics is about the process of hacking, not the reason the hacking is being done." The ethical hacking process for Expert A, a) does not harm and there is no intent to do harm; b) stipulates an ethical responsibility to avoid harm; c) reports on the findings; d) "recognizes that there are guidelines about what you can do"; e) "recognizes that there is a moral imperative toward the public good"; and f) "recognizes that it is done at a professional capacity."

Expert D and Expert C emphasized the legal aspects of ethical hacking. For Expert D, ethical hackers a) have legal authorization from top level management to perform hacking. They can "hack the system officially; in the legal sense"; b) follow best practices; c) follow organizational policies; and d) recommend to mitigate information security holes. For Expert C, ethical means following a policy or a legally binding agreement. "Ethical is legal." Ethical hackers follow a legal process. They must have permission to hack. "They must have a contract signed with an organization giving them permission to expose company data before starting to hack." Secondarily for Expert E, ethical hackers are usually invited by the asset owner to perform hacking to find vulnerabilities and fix them. They get access legally to the resource, and communicate the results to the owner of the assets.

A meta-ethical analysis can further help clarify the ethics of ethical hacking. Garner and Rosen (1967) outline three key meta-ethical questions that can be used to conduct a meta-ethical analysis: 1) What is the meaning of moral terms or judgments? 2) What is the nature of moral judgments? And 3)

How may moral judgments be defended? The authors consulted well-cited books on ethical hacking, the EC-Council (the International Council of Electronic Commerce Consultants) website, and incorporated perspectives from the interview participants to frame a descriptive, multi-perspective account of ethical hacking ethics. Descriptive ethics of ethical hacking found in well-cited ethical hacking texts included: 1) Ethical hackers should address both systemic vulnerabilities as well as preventive measures (Harris, 2007; Palmer, 2001); 2) The practices of professional ethical hackers are governed by legal frameworks. Ethical hackers should always obtain permission from the data owner before attempting to access the computer system or network (Graves, 2010; Palmer, 2001); and 3) Ethical hackers should gain the trust of clients (Graves, 2010; Palmer, 2001); they should take "all precautions to do no harm to their systems during a pen test" (Graves, 2010, para. 1). For key stakeholder groups: 1) Ethical hacking was ethical in that it followed a technical-pragmatic process of risk assessment (Expert E, Expert B, and Expert A). Expert B argued that there was nothing ethical about ethical hacking, "it is a technical process." Expert A argued "the ethics is about the process of hacking, not the reason the hacking is being done"; 2) Ethical hacking was ethical for being a legal process (Expert D, Expert E, and Expert C). For Expert C, "ethical is legal." Ethical hackers "must have a contract signed with an organization giving them permission to expose company data before starting to hack." For Expert E, ethical hackers are usually invited by the asset owner to perform hacking to find vulnerabilities and fix them. For EC-Council (www.eccouncil. org), a "Certified Ethical Hacker" is

a skilled professional who understands and knows how to look for weaknesses and vulnerabilities in target systems and uses the same knowledge and tools as a malicious hacker, but in a lawful and legitimate manner to assess the security posture of the target system(s).

And an "Ethical Hacker" is

an individual who is usually employed with the organization and who can be trusted to undertake an attempt to penetrate networks and/or computer systems using the same methods and techniques as a Hacker.

Therefore a descriptive account of ethical hacking ethics can be stated as follows: Ethical hackers are skilled and knowledgeable IT and information security professionals usually employed with an organization and who look for vulnerabilities in target systems and can be trusted to "undertake an attempt to penetrate networks and/or computer systems using the same methods and techniques" as a hacker; and who use the same knowledge and tools as malicious hackers but in a lawful and legitimate manner to assess the security posture of target systems. Ethical hackers should address both systemic vulnerabilities as well as preventive measures.

What Are the Communicative Practices of Ethical Hacking?

The communicative information organizing routines underlying variances in perceptions about ethical hacking aspects among key stakeholder groups in the participating organization included: First, communication among the various IT staff about ethical hacking practices usually took place through email (Expert D and Expert C), telephone, memos, or at meetings (Expert D) but there were no formal procedures to communicate about ethical hacking (Expert E, Expert B, and Expert D). As Expert B put it, "there is no standard method of communicating about ethical hacking issues." Second, there was no standard language or symbols used for ethical hacking (Expert E, Expert B, and Expert D). "The use of language about ethical hacking is not standardized," said Expert D. The IT staff did not necessarily use the term ethical hacking to mean the same thing or to refer to the same concept or process. IT professionals in various units would have different perceptions about ethical hacking. "They would not have common knowledge" (Expert D). Third, the IT department was decentralized, comprised of semi-autonomous units, and decision-making was decentralized (Expert D, Expert B, and Expert C). Fourth, communication among the various IT staff about ethical hacking practices was on a need to know basis (Expert C, Expert D, Expert A, and organizational documentation). Expert C said, when a security architect performs pen testing "to verify if the security recommendations were implemented," usually only those directly involved in the testing process are notified. "You only notify those people who are supposed to know about this. You do not notify the entire organization or the entire IT that you are going to do pen testing" (Expert C). Organizational documentation P2 assigned managers of administrative units among other managerial and executive staff responsibility for restricting information to those who really need it to perform their assigned functions for all sensitive information assets.

SOLUTIONS AND RECOMMENDATIONS

Technological Management

Software and computer engineers need to weigh technical, management, legal, ethical, communicative, as well as sociocultural considerations in organizational decision-making about technology implementation. A qualitative decision-making framework that can integrate the diverse interests and priorities of stakeholders is presented. The researchers applied TEI-DMG to the case study for an assessment of ethical hacking value within an organization, as presented in Table 1. Technoethical inquiry decision-making grid (Abu-Shaqra & Luppicini, 2016).

Table 1. Technoethical inquiry decision-making grid (TEI-DMG)

Disciplinary\Stakeholder perspective	Expert A Professor of Computer Engineering, Faculty of Engineering	Expert B Associate Professor of Computer Science, Faculty of Engineering	Expert D Anonymous	Expert E Information Security Researcher	Expert C A Security Architect in a Canadian University	Documents	Total
Communicative	+2						+2
Management	+1	+1	+2	+1	+2	+2	+9
Technical	+2	+3	+1	+4	+4	+1	+15
Social	+2	+1					+3
Financial			+3	+1	+1		+5
Legal							
Policy							
Stakeholder total	7	5	6	6	7	3	34

*Range: Steps 1 to 3.

Going down each column: Assess the weight/importance of each perspective relative to other perspectives for each stakeholder.

Going across each row: Assess the weight of each perspective for each stakeholder, and the relative weight of each perspective against the organizational total weight (the relative importance of each perspective).

TEI-DMG can be thought of as a priority list of interests (values) used to inform effective (efficient and fair) decision-making. The priority levels for disciplinary perspectives for each stakeholder were weighed and mapped onto the decision making grid. Each incidence of emphasis on a certain disciplinary perspective was given one plus point.

Qualitative assessment from TEI steps 1 to 3 showed that the predominant organizational concern was about technical aspects of ethical hacking, at about 44%, followed by management aspects at about 26%, financial aspects at about 14.5%, and communicative aspects at about 6%. The findings suggest that a more expansive consideration of communicative, social, legal, and policy perspectives in decision making about ethical hacking organizational practices would be needed for efficient and fair implementation of the technology. The Stakeholder Priorities grid showed a similar picture, overall—an organizational emphasis on technical aspects at about 46%, and on management aspects at about 21%. However, an interesting picture emerged—the recession of the financial consideration to about 4%, and the rise of the communicative interest to about 12%. The explanation for this difference in emphasis on the financial aspects may be because steps 1 to 3 specifically inquires about ethical hacking means, which is related to a discussion about the cost of ethical hacking software. The rise in relative importance in the communicative aspects may be explained by the fact that communicative aspects were a focus of step 4. Guided by TEI-DMG, findings pointed to the need for a more inclusive or expansive interdisciplinary decision-making process about ethical hacking organizational use. Specifically, findings pointed to the need to expand the communicative and sociocultural considerations involved in decision making about ethical hacking organizational practices.

Communicative Management

Assessment of communicative practices explored perceptions among key stakeholder groups about the meanings and ethics of ethical hacking and how the organization communicated about these aspects (the underlying communicative routines). Four out of five participants (Expert A, Expert E, Expert B, and Expert C) saw that ethical hacking primarily meant hacking, a technical process. Second (secondarily for Expert A, Expert E, and Expert B), it meant vulnerability assessment. Third (secondarily for Expert C), ethical hacking meant penetration testing. Fourth, it meant network assessment (Expert D). Organizational understandings about the ethics of professional ethical hackers fell under two themes. Ethical hacking was seen as a technical process of risk assessment (Expert E, Expert B, and Expert A), and as a legal process of risk assessment (Expert D, Expert E, and Expert C). Variances in perceptions among key stakeholder groups about the various ethical hacking inquiry elements were commonplace. There were four meanings for ethical hacking among the five stakeholder groups. Hacking was the predominant view, followed by vulnerability assessment. Participants were split in their perceptions about the ethics of ethical hacking, one group seeing it as ethical by virtue of it being a technical process (Expert E, Expert B, and Expert A), while the other group deemed it ethical in that it followed a legal process (Expert D, Expert E, and Expert C).

The interview participants offered two main ways which can help reduce the equivocality in the ethical hacking information environment. Expert B, Expert A, and Expert E focused on efficient and autonomous technology use, while Expert D and Expert C focused on security awareness training. Expert D argued that security awareness training can help organizations improve organizational communication about ethical hacking, password security, and user roles and responsibilities. Awareness training can help the organization establish a baseline about the meanings, ethics, and value of ethical hacking, added Expert D. Expert C argued that security awareness training can help users learn about social engineering schemes and how to prevent them, and about best practices in password management.

The IT department can consider adopting communication cycles in the form of scheduled interpersonal meetings. Interpersonal communication among employees can reduce confusion around organizational meanings and uses of ethical hacking. This would give stakeholders the opportunity to reduce the confusion around ethical hacking meanings and uses while creating common understandings as they interact. In line with Weick's theory, findings pointed to information security awareness training for increasing sensemaking opportunities among stakeholders and reducing equivocality in the information environment both about user roles and responsibilities regarding information security aspects, and about the meanings, ethics, uses and practices, and value of ethical hacking for the participating organization.

FUTURE RESEARCH DIRECTIONS

The following research recommendations build on the present discussion and retain emphasis on the study of technology communication, management, and ethical qualitative assessment within organizations. Future research within the same organization can build on the present work to manage aspects of the design and implementation of an information security awareness training program (including structural, cultural, and technical aspects) by incorporating management information systems and knowledge management frameworks with TEI-KW.

Another research direction would be to augment TEI with specialized organizational communication theoretical lenses (in addition to Weick's model) to help achieve a broader understanding about ethical hacking communicative and cultural practices to guide performance improvement through effective decision making. Anthony Giddens's structuration theory can be used to examine how organizational structures can shape the outcome, and how the outcome in turn can reconstitute the structures. Edgar Schein's model of professional culture can be used to examine culture as a group phenomenon, as a pattern of basic assumptions, and as an emergent process to help understand the alignment of the organizational culture (artifacts, values, assumptions) with the technical goals and practices. Finally, research ideas based on methodology include increasing the sample size of participants, conducting the study on more than one organization (three to five big organizations, to investigate industry trends and best practices), and using additional data collection methods, such as direct observation and questionnaires.

CONCLUSION

The researchers studied the technoethics of implementing ethical hacking in a Canadian university taking a qualitative exploratory case study approach. In-depth interviews with key stakeholder groups and a document review were conducted. The study applied TEI-DMG to make a qualitative assessment of ethical hacking technology use, and for advice on efficient and fair ethical hacking decision-making about ethical hacking practices in an organization. The study found disproportionate emphasis on the technical and legal perspectives among key stakeholder groups. Guided by TEI-DMG, findings pointed to the need to expand the communicative and sociocultural considerations involved in decision making about ethical hacking organizational practices.

Communicative analysis was performed using Weick's sensemaking model. Variances in perceptions among key stakeholder groups about ethical hacking meanings, ethics, uses and practices, and value were commonplace. A key finding of the study was that the term ethical hacking is polysemic, depending on the stakeholder's perspective. The key to understanding the intended meaning is to appreciate the intertextuality and context surrounding the use of the term. Within the participating organization, it was used to refer to distinctly different information security concepts or practices. There were four different meanings for the term ethical hacking among the five stakeholder groups: hacking, vulnerability assessment, penetration testing, and network assessment, beside risk assessment (Expert B and Expert D) and threat risk assessment (Expert A and Expert E). Organizational understandings about the ethics of ethical hackers fell under two broad themes, namely, ethical hacking as a technical process of risk assessment (Expert E, Expert B, and Expert A), and ethical hacking as a legal process of risk assessment (Expert D, Expert E, and Expert C). The communicative routines underlying these variances included: 1) Communication among the IT staff about ethical hacking aspects was on a need to know basis; 2) There was no standard language within the organization to refer to ethical hacking practices; and 3) There was no standard method to communicate about ethical hacking aspects within the organization. Guided by Weick's model, the study recommended implementing security awareness training to help reduce equivocality in the information environment and increase sensemaking opportunities towards reaching common understandings and improving information security.

The important contribution to knowledge of this research lies in filling in a gap in the literature that results from the scarcity of research on the communicative and sociocultural considerations involved in the implementation of ethical hacking within organizations, while the dominant scholarship is application and certification oriented (technical and legal aspects). This paper addressed the paucity of organizational communication research on non-technical and non-legal aspects of ethical hacking. The study explored key stakeholder perceptions about the meanings and ethics, and the communicative practices of ethical hacking within an organization. The study applied Weick's theory of organizing to study the communicative aspects of ethical hacking organizational use. Pairing Weick's sensemaking model with TEI allowed for a holistic and systemic examination of ethical hacking communicative aspects. The broad disciplinary context afforded by TEI helped the researchers capture the complexity surrounding ethical hacking meanings and communicative practices.

REFERENCES

Abu-Shaqra, B., & Luppicini, R. (2016). Exploring ethical hacking within a Canadian university. *International Journal of Technoethics*, *7*(1). doi:10.4018/IJT.2016010105

Burrell, B. (n.d.). *Protection from cyber crime: Top 10 security measures for educational institutions*. Retrieved May 7, 2015, from http://www.eset.com/us/resources/content-browser-detail/protection-from-cyber-crime-top-10-security-measures-for-educational-institutions/

Creswell, J. W. (2003). *Research design: Qualitative, Quantitative, and Mixed Methods Approaches.* Thousand Oaks, CA: Sage Publications.

Dhillon, G. (2007). *Principles of information systems security: Text and cases.* John Wiley & Sons.

Eid, M. (Ed.). (2011). *Research methods in communication.* Boston, MA: Pearson.

Engebretson, P. (2013). *The basics of hacking and penetration testing: ethical hacking and penetration testing made easy.* Elsevier.

Garner, R. T., & Rosen, B. (1967). *Moral philosophy: A systematic introduction to normative ethics and meta-ethics.* New York: Macmillan.

Graves, K. (2010). *CEH certified ethical hacker study guide.* John Wiley & Sons.

Harris, S., Harper, A., Eagle, C., & Ness, J. (2007). *Gray hat hacking.* McGraw-Hill, Inc.

Landoll, D. J., & Landoll, D. (2005). *The security risk assessment handbook: A complete guide for performing security risk assessments.* CRC Press. doi:10.1201/9781420031232

Luppicini, R. (2008a). Introducing technoethics. In R. Luppicini & R. Adell (Eds.), *Handbook of research on technoethics* (pp. 1–18). Hershey, PA: Idea Group Publishing. doi:10.4018/978-1-60566-022-6.ch001

Luppicini, R. (2008b). The emerging field of technoethics. In R. Luppicini & R. Adell (Eds.), *Handbook of research on technoethics* (pp. 1–19). Hershey, PA: Information Science Reference. doi:10.4018/978-1-60566-022-6.ch001

Luppicini, R. (2010). *Technoethics and the evolving knowledge society: ethical issues in technological design, research, development, and innovation.* IGI Publishing. doi:10.4018/978-1-60566-952-6

Miller, K. (2009). *Organizational communication: Approaches and processes.* Wadsworth Publishing Company.

Neuman, W. L. (2010). *Social research methods: Qualitative and quantitative approaches.* Pearson.

Neuman, W. L. (2011). Social research methods: Qualitative and quantitative approaches. In M. Eid (Ed.), Research methods in communication (pp. 341-377). Boston, MA: Pearson.

Palmer, C. C. (2001). Ethical hacking. *IBM Systems Journal, 40*(3), 769–780. doi:10.1147j.403.0769

Peltier, T. R. (2004A). *Information Security Policies, Procedures, and Standards: Guidelines for effective information security management.* Boca Raton, FL: Auerbach publications. doi:10.1201/9780203488737

Peltier, T. R. (2004B). Risk analysis and risk management. *Information Systems Security, 13*(4), 44–56. doi:10.1201/1086/44640.13.4.20040901/83732.7

Public Safety Canada. (2013a). *Canada's Cyber Security Strategy.* Retrieved September 30, 2013, from http://www.publicsafety.gc.ca/cnt/rsrcs/pblctns/cbr-scrt-strtgy/index-eng.aspx

Public Safety Canada. (2013b). *An Open Letter to Canadians on Cyber Security Awareness.* Retrieved September 30, 2013, from http://www.publicsafety.gc.ca/cnt/nws/nws-rlss/2013/20131003-eng.aspx

Public Safety Canada. (2013c). *Harper Government announces action plan for cyber security*. Retrieved September 30, 2013, from http://www.publicsafety.gc.ca/cnt/nws/nws-rlss/2013/20130418-eng.aspx

Regalado, D., Harris, S., Harper, A., Eagle, C., Ness, J., Spasojevic, B., & Sims, S. (2015). *Gray hat hacking the ethical hacker's handbook*. McGraw-Hill Education Group.

Reynolds, G. W. (2012). *Ethics in information technology*. Boston, MA: Cengage Learning.

Simpson, M., Backman, K., & Corley, J. (2010). *Hands-on ethical hacking and network defense*. Cengage Learning.

Stake, R. E. (1995). *The art of case study design*. Sage Publications.

Stamp, M. (2011). *Introduction in information security: Principles and practice* (2nd ed.). Hoboken, NJ: John Wiley & Sons, Inc. doi:10.1002/9781118027974

Stebbins, R. A. (Ed.). (2001). *Exploratory research in the social sciences* (Vol. 48). Sage Publications. doi:10.4135/9781412984249

Weick, K. (1969). *The social psychology of organizing*. Reading, MA: Addison-Wesley.

Weick, K. (1979). *The social psychology of organizing*. Reading, MA: Addison-Wesley.

Weick, K. E. (1995). *Sensemaking in organizations*. SAGE Publications, Inc.

Yin, R. K. (1994). *Case study research: Design and methods*. Thousand Oaks, CA: SAGE Publications.

ADDITIONAL READING

Bunge, M. (1967). *Scientific Research II: The Search for Truth*. New York: Springer. doi:10.1007/978-3-642-48138-3

Bunge, M. (1976). The philosophical richness of technology. Proceedings of the Biennial Meeting of the Philosophy of Science Association. Volume 2: Symposia and Invited Papers (pp. 153–172).

Bunge, M. (1977). Towards a technoethics. *The Monist*, *60*(1), 96–107. doi:10.5840/monist197760134

Bunge, M. (1979). A systems concept of society: Beyond individualism and holism. *Theory and Decision*, *10*(1), 13–30. doi:10.1007/BF00126329

Conklin, Wm. A., White, G., Williams, D., Cothren, C., & Davis, R. L. (2017). CompTIA security+ all-in-one exam guide, fifth edition (exam SY0-501). Pearson Education.

Eid, M. (2010). Cyber-Terrorism and Ethical Journalism: A Need for Rationalism. *International Journal of Technoethics*, *1*(4), 1–19. doi:10.4018/jte.2010100101

Floridi, L., & Sanders, J. (2003). Computer ethics: Mapping the foundationalist debate. *Ethics and Information Technology*, *4*(1), 1–24. doi:10.1023/A:1015209807065

Harris, S., & Maymi, F. (2016). *CISSP all-in-one exam guide*. McGraw-Hill, Inc.

Kim, P. (2015). *The hacker playbook 2: Practical guide to penetration testing.* Secure Planet LLC.

Kuhn, T. (1962). *The structure of scientific revolutions.* Chicago: University of Chicago Press.

Luppicini, R. (2013). *Moral, Ethical, and Social Dilemmas in the Age of Technology: Theories and Practice* (pp. 1–379). Hershey, PA: IGI Global; doi:10.4018/978-1-4666-2931-8

Mitcham, C. (1997). *Thinking ethics in technology: Hennebach lectures and papers, 1995-1996.* Golden, CO: Colorado School of Mines Press.

Oriyano. (2016). CEH v9: Certified ethical hacker version 9 study guide. John Wiley & Sons.

Rosenthal, S. B., & Buchholz, R. A. (2000A). *Rethinking business ethics: A pragmatic approach.* New York: Oxford University Press.

Rosenthal, S. B., & Buchholz, R. A. (2000B). The empirical-normative split in business ethics: A pragmatic alternative. *Business Ethics Quarterly, 10*(2), 399–408. doi:10.2307/3857883

Vries, M. J. (2009). A Multi-Disciplinary Approach to Technoethics. In R. Luppicini & R. Adell (Eds.), *Handbook of Research on Technoethics* (pp. 20–31). Hershey, PA; doi:10.4018/978-1-60566-022-6.ch002

Walker, M. (2017). *CEH Certified ethical hacker all-in-one exam guide.* McGraw-Hill Osborne Media.

Weber, K., & Glynn, M. A. (2006). Making sense with institutions: Context, thought and action in Karl Weick's theory. *Organization Studies, 27*(11), 1639–1660. doi:10.1177/0170840606068343

Weick, K. E. (1988). Enacted sensemaking in crisis situations. *Journal of Management Studies, 25*(4), 305–317. doi:10.1111/j.1467-6486.1988.tb00039.x

Weick, K. E. (1990). The vulnerable system: An analysis of the Tenerife air disaster. *Journal of Management, 16*(3), 571–593. doi:10.1177/014920639001600304

Weick, K. E. (1993). The collapse of sensemaking in organizations: The Mann Gulch disaster. *Administrative Science Quarterly, 38*(4), 628–652. doi:10.2307/2393339

Weick, K. E. (2001). *Making Sense of the Organization.* Malden, MA: Blackwell.

Weick, K. E. (2009). Making Sense of the Organization: Vol. 2. *The Impermanent Organization.* Wiley.

Weick, K. E., Sutcliffe, K. M., & Obstfeld, D. (2005). Organizing and the process of sensemaking. *Organization Science, 16*(4), 409–421. Retrieved from http://search.proquest.com/docview/213832611?accountid=14701. doi:10.1287/orsc.1050.0133

Weidman, G. (2014). *Penetration testing: a hands-on introduction to hacking.* No Starch Press.

KEY TERMS AND DEFINITIONS

Equivocality: Unpredictably in the information environment arising from confusion not from ignorance.
Ethical Hacking: When the "good guys" do the hacking.
Hacking: "Cracking the code"; beating or cheating the system.

Information Security Risk Management: The prudent, economical allocation of organizational information security management resources.

Risk: The probability of damage.

Technoethical Inquiry Theory: A systematic, systems pragmatic approach to analyzing the use of technology.

Technoethics: The relation between technology and it ethical use.

Chapter 18
Communication in the E–Culture and Media:
New Trends and Features

Liudmila Vladimirovna Baeva
Astrakhan State University, Russia

ABSTRACT

Online and media cultures have a dominant influence on modern society. This type of culture is characterized by specific forms of expression and ethical and aesthetic features mediated by technology. Virtual communication is one reflection of the phenomena of culture reflected through technology. The chapter identifies the typology of virtual communication using a systems approach as an example of online and media culture. This is based on the analysis of the development of social networks and forms of communication and shows the trends in the dynamics of virtual communication. The new environment, with its distinctive characteristics, indicators, forms, and images, creates new opportunities and new risks for humans and their cultures.

INTRODUCTION

Global technological development, with its own unique characteristics requires detailed study. Its consequences have already caused significant changes in psychology, world views, values, and society. One of the most striking phenomena of the digital age is the formation of online culture and media-culture. Although, the concept "e-culture" is still developing, already it is evident it cannot be compared with anything that has ever existed, necessitating detailed study of the phenomenon.

E-culture, digital or online culture is a new sphere of human activity, associated with the creation of the electronic versions of spiritual and material objects as well as the creative work of virtual objects of science, communication and art. "Electronic" means the representation in a digital form. According to the European tradition, e-culture was originally understood as a form of cultural heritage preservation (Ronchi, 2009), but also a distinction from e-commerce. Later, the term was used for the idea of different objects having electronic or other digital form. Nowadays, "e-culture" is an interdisciplinary concept

DOI: 10.4018/978-1-5225-5094-5.ch018

having components from Philosophy, Cultural Studies, Sociology, Political Science, Economics and of course in the field of information technology. Its subjects and creators are scientists, programmers, artists, representatives of mass media and average users of information systems, who use technology to create electronic forms representing their self-image in the global network Internet. The most important characteristics of e-culture is transparency, global nature and availability for every user. Everyone can become both an user and a creator of online phenomena, enjoying creative freedom and few limitations.

The information age and electronic culture generated virtual space and virtual time, the electronic status of a person, forms a kind of 'third nature' in the world of virtual phenomena. For the last two decades, many of the key spheres of human existence (education, communication, art, science, and creative activity) have dramatically changed. They have primarily been virtualized, that is, transferred from a real-life form into simulated and digital ones. In this sense, the information age has not only united people into a uniform network, but changed the essence of their communication and relations. The invention of remote access technology and the ability for remote communications t resulted in the virtualization of the interpersonal communication. The consequences of this technological leap have changed the way human relate, generated a special electronic form of the culture, and induced new existential and ethical problems that require solutions.

The new trend in the development of electronic cultures is the unique global openness of the information space that creates new opportunities and risks. Virtual communication is more than a transition to a new form of traditional communication.

The goal is to develop a systematization of electronic cultures and virtual communication under the conditions of the information age. Objectives of the study are to better understand the nature and manifestations of electronic culture, the characteristics of virtual communication as one of its forms, and to identify the forms of virtual communication, its types and new trends.

BACKGROUND

Researchers and theorists of the postindustrial or information society have focused on the study of the influence of information technology on culture, society and human beings (Toffler, 1980; Naisbitt, 1982; McLuhan, 1992; Castells, 1997; Drucker, 1998; Stiglitz, 2015). How the society and human beings develop in the technological age is also of interest to theorists (Habermas,1983; Baudrillard, 1995) in terms of socio-cultural approach. Several centers study the general issues of the development of an information society including different aspects of this area of investigation. Examples of the areas under investigation include the development of e-culture, Internet-communication, and the ethics of the information society. Scientists of the University of Milan headed by A.M. Ronchi (2009) and the Virtual Maastricht McLuhan Institute (Netherlands) study the problems of the electronic culture development. The researchers of the International Center for Information Ethics (Karlsruhe, Germany) (Capurro, 2006), the London School of Economics, Department of Media and Communications (UK) (Haddon, 2004), the Center on Computing and Social Responsibility (De Montfort University, UK) (Rogerson, 1998), and the Center for the Study of Information Society of the University of Haifa (Israel) (Raban, 2009), focus on the problem of techno-ethics (Rocci, 2012) that deals with the study of ethical and anthropological issues of the information space.

One of the major problems in modern investigations is the virtualization of the modern human life style, the shift of people from a real being to virtual being. The term 'virtuality' and the concept 'virtual reality' were introduced by Jaron Lanier in the late 1980s. He used these terms to denote the electronic devices, carrying their user to a new dimension of existence, the information world. The digital and interactive environment of technologically produced simulacra that is novel for most individuals, all the things that traditionally they have experience through the sensory perception of the reality.

Scientists in the humanities have been studying the problems of the development of virtual reality interacting with culture (Baudrillard, 1993; Lyotard, 1984; Virilio, 1984; Heller, 2012; Heim, 1993; Girard, (2003; Rivoltella, 2008; Baeva, 2013, 2014).

Baudrillard (1993) thoroughly explored the essence of the human entry into the virtual culture. He determined the ontological status of simulation in terms of the formation of 'hyper-reality', by absorbing and eliminating reality. Baudrillard (1993) believes that the development of science and the world of things led to the appearance of this quasi-reality. A reality is defined as something that may be equivalently reproduced. This definition was formulated postulates that any process can be reproduced precisely in specified conditions. As a result, a reality represents not just a phenomenon which can be reproduced, but one which has been already reproduced, i.e., hyper-reality (Baudrillard, 1993). Discussing the consequences of the virtual hyper reality development, Baudrillard (1993) gave two assessments. On the one hand, he predicts universe cloning as an unconscious choice of the mankind, refusing the natural state in favor of artificial, more viable, and effective things. On the other hand, he asserts that the impetuous development of the virtual will lead to implosion, i.e., blurring of the borders between the real and alternative worlds. In both cases, the object - subject relations replace subject-object ones when the things, the products created by individuals, start swallowing up their originators, manipulating them, and subordinating them to their functioning.

Over the past 50 years, a significant amount of research, devoted to the study of the media has led to the formation of new branches of knowledge, theories, concepts and categories. Key researchers have been investigating the problems of media culture and identifying socio-cultural, philosophic, humanistic, ethical, esthetic and interdisciplinary aspects of studying the media-sphere (McLuhan, 1992; Castells, 1997; Münker, Brouwer, and Reijnen, 1997; Bignell, 2000; Savchuk, 2013).

Contemporary researchers share the opinion that under the conditions of the electronic culture development, information technology has become a major factor in the development of the social environment and the life-world of a person. Furthermore, the means of communication or media becomes a moderator of thought and world view. According to McLuhan (1992), the media is a background and habitat of individuals where they themselves become media, passing through themselves the flow of messages, data and various information and facts. He considers that media environment covers all artifacts, excluding, perhaps, only natural objects (McLuhan, 1992). In the information age, the media background is becoming more and more obvious in its presence and influence. McLuhan (1992) emphasized the three most important properties of the media environment: emergence, inconspicuousness and permanent variability. The media produces energy of an unprecedented scale, creating meanings, images, structures, patterns, ideas, and values. Under modern technological conditions, the media culture is constantly changing and taking new forms (blogs, networks, chats, forums and other). In the view of Savchuk (2013), as a researcher of media philosophy problems, media becomes not only a background but also us, changing our consciousness and rationality. The media becomes a source of cultural coding and modeling of consciousness and plays a key role in forming a special type of rationality and valuable reference points for and individual.

These studies influenced greatly on the author's research providing the theoretical basis for the further development of the ideas.

MAIN FOCUS OF THE CHAPTER

Information technology has greatly influenced the development of the specific culture – electronic, digital or virtual – within recent decades. It generates qualitatively new phenomena, in more and more spheres, like science, art, social interaction, education, mass media, commerce and political systems. E-culture cannot be defined as either material or spiritual culture as it has features of both. After the creation of "the second nature" – "the world of things" a human being in actual fact created "the third nature" – the world of virtual phenomena, that is a specific synthesis of the conscious world and advanced information technologies. The study of e-culture became rapidly important for science and practice as the development of new possibilities and threats as existing forms and expressions of culture appeared. At the same time e-culture also generated new values that became of higher priority for human beings and influenced human world view objectives.

E-culture includes the following phenomena: all electronic forms of modern communication (Internet, cellular communication and smartphone applications, social networking sites, virtual communities, chats, blogs, web-forums, and web-sites), electronic cultural heritage (on-line museums, galleries and exhibitions), on-line education, electronic reconstruction of cities and objects of cultural heritage in their historical and space perspective, computer games including network games, electronic mass media (on-line magazines and newspapers), digital modern art (animation, photo, cinema, music and advertising, created by means of advanced information technologies), electronic reference systems (archives, encyclopedias, dictionaries and libraries), and information programs (security, forms of data security, etc.).

The characteristic features of the electronic culture are:

- Freedom of access, openness for members of the information society;
- Remoteness, real distance from the subject;
- Activity in gaining access to electronic information, including possible participation in developing information content from any point of information society;
- Commercialization (electronic form is used for a wide access to goods, services and resources, the sale of which is basic to the information society) (Bell, 1986);
- Innovative, existence through the implementation and continuous updating of research;
- Technocratic, increased value of technology and technological tools that not only support the culture, but have independent significance;
- Entertaining, providing recreation;
- Normative pluralism, associated with the heterogeneity of content and the expansion of the rights and freedoms of the individual (Capurro, 2010);
- Virtuality form as the existence in an artificially created reality;
- dominance of visual things over conceptual ones;

There are Two main structural types of expression in e-culture:

1. Electronic form of real, traditional cultural objects (e.g., on-line museums, libraries, exhibitions, etc.)
2. Electronic cultural objects in form and essence (computer games, social networking sites, Internet, digital art pieces, etc.)

Each type has its own characteristics, although there are many similarities and shared characteristics. The electronic form and essence of culture is the continuation of, and development from traditional cultural objects, having become an electronic expression (to maintain its value and competitiveness).

The real culture is changing in part its traditional form to compete successfully with new electronic one. E-culture significantly transformed real artifacts, ideas and human being's personas into virtual forms. The extent to which the products of e-culture became the continuation of, and "shell" for "classical" ("pre-informational") culture is beyond measure. It is not possible to compare the value of this phenomenon and achievements of classical culture. The outstanding features of the form and content of this culture is evident and is driving the extension and development of e-culture. The main space of e-culture development is the Internet, as this is where many forms are concentrated. E-culture comprises such areas as communication, leisure and education, that have a significant impact on the human world view. Under the influence of e-culture over last three decades, a new generation grew up with its own values, needs and ethical principles. These may become an active driver of social dynamics in their turn.

In this information age, media culture is the extension of the electronic culture development in diverse forms of communication and information transfer, primarily e-mass media, the Internet, and social networking web-sites. The public nature and global scale of information technologies means that media culture has become the greatest source of influence on individuals; coding and modeling their world views, valuable reference points, aspirations, ideals and behavioral stereotypes. Media culture has proven to be the sphere of the electronic communication which has a real effect on individuals from the first years of their lives despite its virtual form. Children are so influenced by the information culture that media characters and heroes with their bright visual effects, join their families and real people who surround them as the most important moderators of their images and value systems. The visual media culture in which a modern person develops is the manifestation of electronic culture in a technological form. Its meanings and reference points are mostly linked with the modern post-nonclassical age in which the cults of freedom, personality, pluralism, and consumption, is manifest.

Relying on the methods of Baudrillard (1993) and the approaches he followed, the author defines virtualization as the replacement of real processes and phenomena by virtual forms. On the one hand, it deals with the creation of digital analogs and simulations of real culture objects and on the other hand – with the creativity of the new cyberspace and its phenomena. In this case, the consciousness of the subject is a source of new reality, a kind of "the third nature" where the products of mind creativity are combined with the visual images, completed by the information resources. The infinite multiplication of g copies is becoming the peculiarity of the reality virtualization, i.e., "copies of copies" - the digital infinity which distances the objects from their creators.

The information objects, created by individuals instantly become available to the community and acquire new interpretations. They, being unrecognizable and independent of their authors, and produce a boundless quasi-reality. "the world of E" (e-culture, e-education, e-government, e-business, etc.), has become more real and significant in the terms of values, acquiring the status of a hyper-value. More and more spheres of human activity are virtualized; as the border between reality and online worlds is eroded, it turns out individuals are living by the principles of the physical and information world.

The virtualization of culture and the human real world has generated the phenomenon of the virtual communication, defined as the remote interaction and communication with a partner or a group by means of computer and telecommunication systems (Psychology of communication, 2011). Several authors have discussed the concept of the virtual communication in terms of modern culture, technology and postmodernism ideas (Baudrillard, 1993; Castells, 1997; McLuhan, 1992; Masuda 1983; Turkle, 2006).

Communication is an important sphere of a human life and performs many functions including adaptive, educational, the search for the meaning of life, and ethics. Communication an essential human capability, especially if it is filled with profound meaning and feelings. Modern information networks have linked people by means of numerous threads and chains, having overcome the borders of space, language and social convention. The Internet has become, primarily, an instrument for human communication. For the most users, communications is the main value and opportunity of the internet.

The analysis of the development of social networks shows how quickly an entire community forms after the creation of a new Network for communication, despite of the diversity of interactions (Zhou, Ding & Finin, 2011). Communities in social networks are a new kind of community of people, using mostly a virtual form of communication, looking for social activity and self-presentation in wider audience of society and keeping some information about themselves confidential or replacing it with information that is made up to give a different impression.

According to A. Ronchi, Professor at Milan's Polytechnic University, now we should consider the Internet as a defensive wall in respect of social communication (Ronchi, 2009).

Virtual communication can then be seen as the communication form between people by means of information technologies at remote distances with the following features:

- Global character,
- Self-organizing network form,
- Spontaneously formed diverse content,
- Simultaneous participation of a great number of communication subjects,
- Impersonal nature,
- Possibilities for anonymous interaction,
- Coexistence of real interpersonal communications,
- Simulated subjects, objects and relations.

Information and virtual communication assume new functions:

- Global socialization through the creation of a global communication environment for human communication in an "open world",
- Instant information, the notification of all communication participants on events and phenomena as they occur,
- The creation of conditions for informal communication (without censorship) as forms of recreation, rest, and entertainment,
- Adaptation to the social activity of people having problems with real communication,
- The removal of borders between social status, location, and languages.

Social networks have taken the lead in virtual communication, and international networks prevail over the national ones. The most popular and visited social network remains Facebook with a billion registrations and 1,712 billion active users per month. Increasing the number of users and Instagram, with more than half a billion users continue to increase its user base and continually improve its business opportunities. In 2016, the trend in promotion was live. In 2017, this trend continues to grow. The main emphasis will be on video for Facebook. The website has an average of 8 billion video views daily.

Users of Facebook spend 100 million hours viewing video every day. Sharing video in Instagram grew from 30 to 65%, according to a study by Brand Networks. This shows that the visual form of information transfer is increasingly preferred over verbal.

Over the last years there has been a trend for an increasing role for mobile social media users. According Digital in 2016 report, mobile social media users leapt 17%, adding 283 million new users.

Another trend in the world of virtual communication is the increasing role of messengers. The closest competitor to Facebook in 2016, was WhatsApp, the number of users is increased by 50% (1 billion users). Facebook Messenger continues to grow though not at the same stunning rate as WhatsApp. This shows appeal to a mass audience, but the user desire for privacy, individuality, and communication. In 2010-2012 there were social networks for local groups ("Pair", "Path" and other), now they have replaced by messengers. This is important and disturbing news for marketers, since communication by messengers excludes commercial advertising. Global social networks are more exposed to external control than the messengers.

The increasing role of messengers shows that transition from the virtualization of the communication through mass networks to the more personal communities. This solves not only the problems of information transfer and advertising, but reflects the need for traditional selective interpersonal communication. On the other hand, the modern level of the virtual communication and modern control of the networks does not guarantee that individuals can find here the freedom communication which they seek. This freedom as well as the remote transfer of feelings remains illusory. Despite the variety of forms of social communication and the specifics of various social networks, there are common problems and features of an existential nature. The implementation of openness and popularity is associated with the loss of privacy from the tracking systems and at risk of manipulation by commercial advertising. Under these conditions, the user may prefer to maintain communication in the global network, but with the preservation of privacy of communication.

Considering the nature of the subjects' relationship, the variety of information and virtual relationships can be divided into the following main types:

1. Thanks to the electronic communication and the global spread, many people, close to each other in real life, keep in touch with those living apart. This type of communication can be called *distant-traditional* as its essence relies on the traditional relations between people, using the Internet communication and mobile devices only as a technical tool. This communication type is characterized by the subjects knowledge of each other in real life and having a steady relationship (family relationship, professional relations, friendly relations, loving relationships, etc.), but they have to communicate by means of the information resources because they are far from each other, busy, etc. The essence of the traditional human relations of this communication form remains to be "subject – subject" without essential changes and is not simulated. This form of communication has moved, from social networks to instant messengers.

Interpersonal communication is often replaced with its online simulation, displacing such important relationship areas as love and friendship. Researchers note that the number of network romantic relationships has been increased, and virtual relations (called "the Second Life") can sometimes improve people's mental state and help to solve their real problems (Gilbert, Murphy, & Ávalos, 2011). The concept "friendship" is undergoing changes in e-culture, dealing with the loss of stability, social and financial support, and responsibility (Amichai-Hamburger, 2012). The simulation of feelings in these areas facilitates the loss of human existential support and changes moral and ethical milestones related to the understanding of another's value.

Besides this traditional function at the qualitatively new technological development stage, the Internet and social networks caused new communication types that are virtual and partly or completely artificial by the nature.

2. The second communication type can be called *distant-elite* type; it enables the representatives of various elites, who people know from the mass media, and their "followers", whom the elite members do not know personally, to communicate. The most different types of network interaction can be seen in the following range of relationships: blogs of celebrities and discussions about them; forums with leading scientists; writers; and the leading public figures of various areas of public life (politics, economy, religion, law, etc.). In this communication sphere, real people communicate not with "real persons" but their stylized images, or simulacra, which sufficiently display the essential characteristics and the real properties, personal features not available to the discussion are hidden. This communication type is tied to a subject and an artificial image, a simulacrum; it primary function in the virtual communication is the solution of interpersonal problems, and to increase their importance, status, and self-assessment by using the quasi-communication with an elite representative to raise the followers to the "same level".

3. The third communication type joins together the people who do not have any real relations but have the same status. This type communication can be called *"distant-nominal"*. It is characterized by people who do not know each other in real life, know only what the other posted about themselves on the Net, and have opportunity to terminate this interaction at any time without explaining the reasons. This communication has no interpersonal contact as the subjects communicate not personally but representatively, by their digital analogs, avatars (virtual images), and nicknames (a name in the Net). This has made it possible to join together in the Network a huge number of "friends". These are remote users, whose communication is mostly superficial, without commitment, empathy, and involvement in "the world of Other". Its essence is a type of entertainment or recreation, a virtual "party" that is a non-committal amusement among similar people. The communication is completely artificial: simulacrum to simulacrum. The participants create their own phantom image and a virtual hero with the features they want for living different vital scenarios.

Currently, the main trend is that the role of the traditional (real) and *distant-traditional* communication is diminishing and the significance of the *distant-nominal* relations is growing.

Characteristics of the New Forms of Communication and the Impacts we can Expect

1. *Special attention to the presentation of the self.* Virtual communication has a specificity of subject to subject relations, associated both with the presentation of self and the perception of the other. The integral communication aspect is how one represents the manifestation of oneself for the other, the presentation of image, beliefs, interests, feelings, etc. The most important attribute of the communication in the social networks and on forums is to create a profile, a personal web-page indicating the real and fictional achievements and characteristics of the personality to which much

attention is paid. In the most extreme expressions, the self-presentation takes the form narcissism and domination of the Ego value over all others. The constant concentration of the attention on oneself is also expressed in the "selfie" and regular posting of life photos in Instagram.

2. Continuity of the virtual communication stream, zero speed expectations. After the invention of the Internet, the communication has not slowed, on the contrary it has become even more significant for individuals who have forgotten to commune with themselves. Their need to join in the virtual dialogue with others practically became part of their way of being in the world. People of different ages permanently stay in the social networks, communicating on the game portals during for many hours, blogging, and keeping "LiveJournals" (though the role of the latter gradually decreases).. The considerable percentage of users do not restrict themselves to one message a day, they constantly post and repost different information. As a consequence, reading of the messages from "friends" also becomes expected and increases participation on the network. The notification is seen by all community participants, and like a radio effect that multiplies the feedback, it causes chain reactions, a communicative burst.

3. Attenuation of emotional communication. A number of researchers believe that the growth of virtual communication, driven originally by interest in new technologies, have become social phobias. The growth of virtual relations popularity promotes a special type of real communication fear – nomophobia, the aspiration to avoid the real communication (King et al., 2013). It is worth emphasizing that those people who tend to hyper-communication in real life also tend to do so in virtual communication, wishing to use all possible channels to communicate with others. Thus, Internet communication gradually starts replacing real communication, weakening emotional and empathetic relations, but strengthening the possibilities of the self-presentation, narcissism, information exchange, as well as circulation of various "rumors" in "the global village" (in the Net). The desire to use technologies is motivated by the desire to live the happy and full life. However, the use of the technology factor does not qualitatively change the emotional sphere in the vital human world; only the capabilities of overcoming the limits of space and time, and management of external circumstances, have been enhanced (Spahn, 2015).

4. Development of the need to be permanently in virtual communication can turn occasionally into an addiction. In the information environment, individuals find not only new opportunities and freedoms, but also addictions, the main one among which is virtual communication, which in essence is the desire for continuous presence in the Network, fear of reality and interpersonal communication, and loss of interest in life. The most radical approaches equate the Internet addiction to the self-destroying personal pathologies, like the narcotic drug addiction. The neurologist P. Whybrow compares computer addiction with the drug dependence, specifying that computers amplify the excitement and worsen the users' depressions (Fischer, 2012). Internet addiction shows as a desire to stay permanently on-line and interact with virtual partners, as a result, some individuals disregard their health and real social communications, cognitive and creative activity weakens, and the passive form of the reality perception, not processing information, intensifies. There are serious risks of transferring values to the virtual worlds and social networks, making real communication difficult and reducing the ability to solve the vital problems, aggravating destructive thinking and self-destructive behavior. In China, South Korea and Taiwan, Internet addiction has been acknowledged as a diagnosis by medicine, and Internet abuse is considered as a national crisis. In these countries, tens of millions of people are considered to be addicted to the Internet.

5. Simulation of the real relations and the decline in trust. In the electronic culture, a communication problem of the issue of trust in the other virtual partner has arisen. D. Raban (2009) pointed out that modern web-forums show that people substantially trust in the information, told them by unfamiliar people. In a limited sense, human beings live in two worlds in which they do not quite trust, real communication has remained significant, though the value of the interaction with virtual other has still grown within its own set of rules. The interaction with the virtual other, turns out to be vacuous and absurd because these relations include the simulation of feelings, trust, understanding, and involvement in the other's life.

6. Virtualization of the real life. The virtualization does not exclude the real sphere, but rather completes it. People more often combine real communication with the virtual one, the family with a social network, the friendship with the "addition of strangers on the list of friends", the intellectual conversations with the colleagues with the virtual communities of quasi-professional users. An example of this is the appearance of such social networks as Highlight . The areas of real and virtual always intersect, and the elements of the quasi-communication influence real relations and communication, assimilating them to virtual communication. The virtualization of their life style concentrates the individuals' attention on themselves and their needs, changing the world around them into the sphere of the infinite modeling of new products and services replacing traditional values.

The new communication form also produces new ethical problems. R. Capurro (2010), Director of the International Center for Information Ethics (ICIE), (Karlsruhe, Germany) is of the opinion, "The Internet turned into the main infrastructure of the social communication at the local and global levels. The freedom of access should be considered as the fundamental ethical principle like principles of the freedom speech and press. Some of the rights declared in the Universal Declaration of Human Rights, such as a right to freedom of thought, conscience and religion (Article 18), the right to freedom of opinion and expression (Article 19) and the right to freedom of peaceful assembly and association (Article 20) should be accurately defined and interpreted in view of new and unique opportunities of the online digital mass media". Currently, the experts point out that this ethical crisis impacts in such areas of the modern society life as copyright infringement, plagiarism, censorship, interference in the private life within the cyberspace, a digital inequality, and violation of moral standards in advertising. Duff (2008) characterized the modern situation, coming from the information society development as a normative crisis when the maximum freedom does not develop into a high degree of responsibility but creates moral and ethical challenges in the new world.

At first sight, the key characteristic of communication in the virtual online space involves denial of the traditional ethics and etiquette, elimination of all "conventions", norms, taboos, etc. However, virtual communication is not completely free from rules, otherwise it could not occur. Virtual communication has its unwritten code and the official forms of "unlimited freedom" and independence. Norbert Wiener was the first to identify ethical problems in the information space. After the development of social networks a main factor of virtual communication, various options of regulating interpersonal relations in the Net are possible. Shea (1994) presented her book "Netiquette" ten basic rules of Netiquette, i.e., etiquette for those who live in the Network world Rule 1 - Remember the Human; Rule 2 - Adhere to the same standards of behavior online that you follow in the real life; Rule 3 - Know where you are in cyberspace; and so on. These rules would be a basis for the peaceful and constructive co-existence of free Internet users if the users abided by them. Mostly these have remained only an appeal, responded to by few of the users. Perhaps because some rules are abstract, or the principle of the Network is an ethical pluralism.

"The Code of Ethics for the Information Society" in which it was stated that in the information space, as in the real life, the rights and freedoms of a person should be observed was approved at the 36th session of the general UNESCO conference in 2011 (Ethical code, 2011). These ideas were developed in the succeeding years, for example, within the framework of the conference "Internet and Socio-Cultural Transformations in the Information Society" (Sakhalin, 2013) it was noted that total control over the communication in the cyberspace becomes more and more frivolous. The serious content is an insignificant part of whole. The content is oriented on leisure and entertainment, unpretentious taste, replacement and depreciation of the serious and qualitative content. It causes "clip thinking" and essential changes of the collective consciousness.

Despite the codes and rules proposed by the society, most communication in the Internet does not meet these standards and was created in many ways as a form of "freedoms from morals". Proceeding from an optimistic viewpoint, it is possible to expect that the development of the ethics in the virtual sphere will overcome the contemporary pluralism in spite of the fact that the Internet mostly proved to be a version of the freedom from the obligations and norms of the real world.

To promote the development of the human ethical values in virtual interaction, special training courses and trainings are currently designed to help the human beings with adaptation in the Network and formation of certain behavioural guidelines which can also be valuable in real life, as Chang (2011) describes, speaking about teaching the Information Ethics course in China. The modern system of education needs courses like "Ethics of Information Society", "Etiquette of Virtual Communication", and "E-culture and human rights".

Despite new communication technologies, the transition by society of the ideas of the good and evil to the virtual level, has remained unchanged. In the virtual sphere, people are still "condemned to freedom", and the preservation of the moral behavior in the conditions of ethical pluralism is extremely difficult without the conditions of the strict control. Consequently, people have great opportunities for their self-development and self-improvement now.

FUTURE RESEARCH DIRECTIONS

Prospects for the study of these problems is very diverse. Firstly, relevant research in the field of various new forms of virtual communication is required. Communication through social networks has been studied, while the study of the role of messengers still requires attention. It is important to examine not only trends in the development of new forms of communication, but their impact on the culture, the worldview and human values. Another important research direction is the study of media culture as its role in the information world will only increase.

The current trend of the modern society encompasses the decline of the role of the traditional (real) and distant-traditional communication and the increase of the value of the distant-nominal communication. As characteristic features of the distant-nominal communication, the special attention to Ego demonstration, the continuity of virtual communication, weakening of emotional communication, identifying ways to keep virtual communication from becoming and addiction, and the simulation of real relations and decline in trust.

The ethics and etiquette of the virtual communication have been "devised". The external processes of the regulation of the ethical principles of the information society (In this case, it is necessary to recognize the leading role of UNESCO) and the self-organization projects (i.e., design of ethical standards in virtual communities), have taken place. Virtual communication does not change people's moral values but rather facilitates their attenuation and transformation into "relicts" of the traditional reality under the influence of the simulation and game character of the virtual world and of reduced society control. The strict arrangement of the virtual content and its subjection to the proposed codes inevitably will produce the desire to escape from the regulations therefore development of censorship will not resolve this problem. In this author's view, the educational system and cultural life in the information world, to be effective, need to contribute to the socialization of people and their adaptation to new technological conditions without losing sight of social attributes.

An important research trend is the study of information ethics and law. Safety in the future information society will largely depend on these areas of study. The focus will also be on various forms of electronic culture. Their diversity and rapid development set the stage for the emergence of new scientific directions.

CONCLUSION

Many spheres of human life are connecting with the process of virtualization in the context of electronic culture. Some of them are fundamental to human existence. One of these, communication, in the information age features a global, openness, distance interaction, according to its own laws and principles.

Virtual communication is not only a means of communication and a communication technology for the subjects remote from each other, but also an independent phenomenon gaining its own value for, and influence on, a person. The determining features of virtual communication are that it is by nature a simulation, is associated with recreation and does not bear significant conceptual-vital capacity. It is based on real interpersonal relations with traditional communication functions (sense of one's own life; understanding of the other people's value; need for empathy; cooperation; etc.). Thus, the main current trend seen in modern society includes the decline of the role of traditional (real) and distant-traditional communication and an increase in the value of distant-nominal communication. Characteristic features of the distant-nominal communication are the special attention to Ego demonstration; the continuity of the virtual communication; the "radio effect"; the weakening of emotional communication; the desire keep connected to virtual communication to the point of sometimes developing into an addiction; the simulation of real relations and decline in trust. As the result, the real life has been virtualized. In a sense, human beings live in two worlds, which they do not trust in full; offline communication remains important, although the value of virtual communication is developing, with its own rules for interacting. Logging onto Net to "meet" a virtual other, turns out to be insignificant, senseless, as these relationships involve the simulation of feelings, trusting, understanding, and participation in virtual other's life.

Thus, human beings also face a moral choice in the virtual space. There are more possibilities and conditions to violate common morals and ethics of behavior online and that means there are more temptations to do so. Human beings continue to be "condemned to freedom" online, with its new levels and forms. It is much more difficult to keep on behaving morally under the ethical pluralism than under an environment of strict control. However, today, this provides human beings with great possibilities and opportunities for their self-development and self-improvement.

E-culture is not only the duplication of "live" culture, but also new achievements resulting from the application of creative high technologies that provided radically new facilities and trends for self-expression, cognition, and development. The electronic resources multiply the abilities of human beings and give them new liberties and a new world to live in. In this regard, the transition from the real sphere of interaction into the virtual one reduces the importance of interpersonal communication, moral and ethical norms, and traditional ways of life. This study was supported by the RSF under Grant №16-18-10162, «A new type of rationality in the era of medial rotation», Sant-Petersburg State University.

REFERENCES

Amichai-Hamburger, Y., Kingsbury, M., & Schneider, B. H. (2012). Friendship: An old concept with a new meaning? *Computers in Human Behavior*, *29*(1), 33–39. doi:10.1016/j.chb.2012.05.025

Baeva, L. V. (2013). Electronic culture: Experience of philosophical analysis. *Issues of Philosophy*, *5*, 75–83.

Baeva, L. V. (2014). Existential and Ethical Values in an Information Era. *Journal of Human Values*, *20*(1), 33–43. doi:10.1177/0971685813515593

Baudrillard, J. (1993). *Symbolic exchange and death*. Aldershot, UK: Ashgate.

Bignell, J. (2000). *Postmodern Media Culture*. Edinburgh, UK: Edinburgh University Press.

Capurro, R. (2010). Information ethics. *The Information Society*, *5*, 6–15.

Castells, M. (1997). The End of the Millennium, the Information Age: Economy, Society and Culture: Vol. 3. Oxford, UK: Blackwell.

Chang, C. L. (2011). The effect of an information ethics course on the information ethics values of students – A Chinese guanxi culture perspective. *Computers in Human Behavior*, *27*(5), 2028–2038. doi:10.1016/j.chb.2011.05.010

Digital in 2016 report. (2017). Retrieved May 23, 2017, from https://wearesocial.com/uk/special-reports/digital-in-2016)

Drucker, P. F. (1998). The Age of Social Transformation. In G. R. Hickman (Ed.), *Leading Organizations: Perspectives for a New Era* (pp. 538–556). Thousand Oaks, CA: SAGE Publications.

Duff, A. (2008). The normative crisis of the information society. *Cyberpsychology (Brno)*, *2*(1), 3. Retrieved from http://cyberpsychology.eu/view.php?cisloclanku=2008051201&article=3

Ethical code of information society. 36 general conference of UNESCO. (2011). Retrieved February 05, 2015 http://unesdoc.unesco.org/images/0021/002126/212696e.pdf

Fischer, M. A. (2012). *Manic Nation: Dr. Peter Whybrow says we're addicted to stress*. Retrieved February 03, 2016 from http://www.psmag.com/health/manic-nation-dr-peter-whybrow-says-were-addicted-stress-42695/

Forbes. (n.d.). *5 hot on-line social networks*. Retrieved June 27, 2017 from http://m.forbes.ru/article.php?

Gilbert, R. L., Murphy, N. A., & Ávalos, C. M. (2011). Communication Patterns and Satisfaction Levels in Three-Dimensional Versus Real-Life Intimate Relationships. *Cyberpsychology, Behavior, and Social Networking, 14*(10), 585–589. doi:10.1089/cyber.2010.0468 PMID:21381970

Girard, B., & Siochrú, S. O. (2003). *Communicating in the information society*. Geneva: United Nations Research Institute for Social Development.

Habermas, J. (1985). *Theorie der Kommunikativen Handelns*. Frankfurt am Main, Germany: Suhrkamp Verlag.

Heim, M. (1993). *The Metaphysics of Virtual Reality*. New York: Oxford University Press.

Heller, P. B. (2012). Technoethics: The Dilemma of Doing the Right Moral Thing in Technology Applications. *International Journal of Technoethics, 3*(1), 14–27. doi:10.4018/jte.2012010102

King, A. L. S., Valença, A. M., Silva, A. C. O., Baczynski, T., Carvalho, M. R., & Nardi, A. E. (2013). Nomophobia: Dependency on virtual environments or social phobia? *Computers in Human Behavior, 29*(1), 140–144. doi:10.1016/j.chb.2012.07.025

Lyotard, J.-F. (1984). *The Postmodern Condition: A Report on Knowledge*. Minneapolis, MN: Minnesota Press and Manchester University Press.

Masuda, Y. (1983). The Information Society as Post-Industrial Society. Washinton: D. C. McLean, A. (2011), Ethical frontiers of ICT and older users: cultural, pragmatic and ethical issues. *Ethics and Information Technology, 13*(4), 313–326.

McLuhan, H. M., & McLuhan, E. (1992). Laws of Media: The New Science. Toronto: Academic Press.

Münker, S., Brouwer, J., & Reijnen, L. (1997). *Interfacing realities*. Rotterdam: V2

Naisbitt, J. (1982). *Megatrends: Ten New Directions Transforming Our Lives*. New York: A Warner Communications Company.

Pair: a social networking app just for couples. (n.d.). Retrieved February 12, 2017 from website: http://www.fastcodesign.com/1669435/pair-a-social-networking-app-just-for-couples

Path. (n.d.). *Who we are*. Retrieved February 12, 2017 from https://path.com/about

Raban, D. R. (2009). Self-presentation and the value of information in Q&A websites. *Journal of the American Society for Information Science and Technology, 60*(12), 2465–2473. doi:10.1002/asi.21188

Rivoltella, P. C. (2008). *Knowledge, Culture and Society in the Information Age. In Digital Literacy: Tools and Methodologies for Information Society*. IRM Press.

Rocci, L. (2012). *International Journal of Technoethics*. An Official Publication of the Information Resources Management Association.

Ronchi, A. M. (2009). *E-Culture*. New York: Springer-Verlag, LLC.

Savchuk, V. V. (2013). *Media Philosophy. Attack reality*. Saint-Petersburg, Russia: Academic Press.

Shea, V. (1994). *The Core rules of Netiquette*. Retrieved December 20, 2016 from http://www.albion.com/netiquette/corerules.html

Spahn, A. (2015). Can Technology make us happy? Ethics, Spectator's happiness and the value of achievement. Well-being in contemporary society. Springer International Publishing.

Stiglitz, J. E., & Greenwald, B. C. (2015). *Creating a learning society: A new approach to growth, development, and social progress*. New York: Columbia University Press. doi:10.7312tig17549

Toffler, A. (1980). *The Third Wave*. New York: Bantam Books.

Toffler, A. (1991). *Powershift: knowledge, wealth and violence in the 21st century*. New York: Bantan.

Turkle, Sh. (2006). A Nascent Robotics Culture: New Complicities for Companionship. *AAAI Technical Report Series (World Health Organization)*.

Veltman, K. H. (2004). Towards a Semantic Web for Culture. *Journal of Digital Information*, *4*(4). Retrieved September 12, 2016 from http://jodi.ecs.soton.ac.uk/Articles/v04/i04/Veltman/

Virilio, P. (1991b). *The Lost Dimension*. New York: Semiotext. (Original work published 1984)

Whybrow, P. (2012). *Manic Nation*. Retrieved from http://www.psmag.com/health/manic-nation-dr-peter-whybrow-says-were-addicted-stress-42695

World map of social networks. (n.d.). Retrieved May 10, 2017 from http://vincos.it/world-map-of-social-networks/

Zhou, L., Ding, L., &Finin, T. (2011). How is the Semantic Web evolving? A Dynamic Social Network Perspective. *Computers in Human Behavior, 27*, 1294-1302.

KEY TERMS AND DEFINITIONS

Digital Information and Virtual Communication: Is the communication form between people by means of information technologies at remote distances with the following features: global character, the self-organizing network form, the spontaneously formed diverse content, simultaneous participation of a great number of communication subjects, impersonal nature, possibilities of anonymous interaction, coexistence of real interpersonal communications, and artificial simulacrum (nominal) relations.

E-Culture, Online Culture, or Digital Culture: Is a new sphere of the human activity, associated with the creation of the electronic copies of spiritual and material objects as well as the creative work of the virtual objects of science, communication, and art.

Ethics of Information Society: Ethical principles, norms, rules of behavior of people in the conditions of a virtual form of communication (the internet, games, mobile communication, etc.), directed on formation of valid, humane, legal space for communication.

Nomophobia: The view of mental disorders developing under the influence of virtualization of communication, which manifests itself as a fear of and a desire to avoid real socializing and meeting people.

Types of E-Culture Expression: 1) Electronic form of former (traditional, classical – here not electronic) cultural objects (e.g., on-line museums, libraries, exhibitions, etc.). 2) Electronic cultural objects in form and essence (computer games, social networking sites, internet, digital art pieces, etc.).

Virtual Objectivization: Blurring the boundaries between personal and social phenomena in a virtual interaction that converts human values and outlook.

Virtualization: Is the process when the real processes and phenomena are replaced by the virtual forms. On the one hand, it deals with the creation of digital analogs and simulations of the real culture objects, and on the other hand, it deals with the creativity of the new cyberspace and its phenomena.

Compilation of References

Abate, M. A. (2010). "Plastic makes perfect": My beautiful mommy, cosmetic surgery, and the medicalization of motherhood. *Women's Studies*, *39*(7), 715–746. doi:10.1080/00497878.2010.505152

Abbott, T. K. (1898). *Kant's Critique Of Practical Reason And Other Works On The Theory Of Ethics*. London: Longmans, Green.

Abbott, J. (2012). Democracy@internet.org revisited: Analyzing the socio-political impact of the Internet and new social media in East Asia. *Third World Quarterly*, *33*(2), 333–357. doi:10.1080/01436597.2012.666015

Abney, K. (2014). Robotics, ethical theory, and metaethics: A guide for the perplexed. In Robot Ethics. The ethical and social implications of robotics. MIT Press.

Abowd, G. D., & Mynatt, E. D. (2000). Charting past, present, and future research in ubiquitous computing. *ACM Transactions on Computer-Human Interaction*, *7*(1), 29–58. doi:10.1145/344949.344988

Abu-Shaqra, B., & Luppicini, R. (2016). Exploring ethical hacking within a Canadian university. *International Journal of Technoethics*, *7*(1). doi:10.4018/IJT.2016010105

Achterhuis, H. (1998). *De erfenis van de utopie*. Amsterdam: Ambo.

Adler J. (2012, August 3). Raging Bulls: How Wallstreet got addicted to light-speed trading. *Wired*.

Ahlstedt, J., & Villyson, J. (2012). High Frequency Trading. *Research Paper*, 1-8.

Ahola, J., (2001). Ambient Intelligence. *ERCIM News*, 47.

Akbulut, Y., Sahin, Y. L., & Eristi, B. (2010). Development of a scale to investigate cybervictimization among online social utility members. *Contemporary Educational Technology*, *1*, 46–59.

Alaoen, G. (2012). *McKayla is not impressed*. Retrieved from http://mckaylaisnotimpressed.tumblr.com/

Allen, C., Wallach, W., & Smit, I. (2006). Why machines ethics. *IEEE Intelligent Systems*, *21*(4), 12–17. doi:10.1109/MIS.2006.83

Alley, R. (2013). *The drone debate. Sudden bullet or slow boomerang?* New Zealand: Victoria University of Wellington.

Alpert, S. (2008). Neuroethics and nanoethics: Do we risk ethical myopia? *Neuroethics*, *1*(1), 55–68. doi:10.100712152-007-9001-5

Alter, A. (2017). *Irresistible The Rise of Addictive Technology and the Business of Keeping Us Hooked*. Penguin Group USA.

Altmann, J., Asaro, P., Sharkey, N., & Sparrow, R. (2013). Armed military robots. *Ethics and Information Technology*, *15*(2), 73–76. doi:10.100710676-013-9318-1

Amerika, M. (2004). Expanding the concept of writing: Notes on net art, digital narrative and viral ethics. *Leonardo*, *37*(1), 9–13. doi:10.1162/002409404772827987

Amichai-Hamburger, Y., Kingsbury, M., & Schneider, B. H. (2012). Friendship: An old concept with a new meaning? *Computers in Human Behavior*, *29*(1), 33–39. doi:10.1016/j.chb.2012.05.025

Andersen, S. (2005). Stimulants and the developing brain. *Trends in Pharmacological Sciences*, *26*(5), 237–243. doi:10.1016/j.tips.2005.03.009 PMID:15860370

Anderson, M., & Anderson, S. L. (2007). Machine ethics: Creating an ethical intelligent agent. *AI Magazine*, *28*(4), 15–26.

Anderson, M., & Anderson, S. L. (2007). Machine Ethics: Creating an Ethical Intelligent Agent. *AI Magazine*, *28*(4), 15–26.

Andreessen, M. (2011, August 20). Why software is eating the world. *The Wall Street Journal*. Retrieved from http://www.wsj.com/articles/SB10001424053111903480904576512250915629460

Angwin, J. (2015). Own a Vizio Smart TV? It's watching you. *ProPublica*. Retrieved from https://www.propublica.org/article/own-a-vizio-smart-tv-its-watching-you

Annas, G. J. (2007). Imagining a New Era of Neuroimaging, Neuroethics, and Neurolaw. *American Journal of Law & Medicine*, *33*(2-3), 163–170. doi:10.1177/009885880703300201 PMID:17910155

Antal, A., Alekseichuk, I., Bikson, M., Brockmöller, J., Brunoni, A. R., Chen, R., ... Paulus, W. (2017). Low intensity transcranial electric stimulation: Safety, ethical, legal regulatory and application guidelines. *Clinical Neurophysiology*, *34*(0), 4022–4026. PMID:28709880

Antal, A., & Herrmann, C. S. (2016). Transcranial Alternating Current and Random Noise Stimulation: Possible Mechanisms. *Neural Plasticity*. PMID:27242932

Anton, C., & Zhang, P. (2011). Syntax and ethics: A conversation. *Etc.; a Review of General Semantics*, *68*(3), 238–254.

Apter, J., & Mahmoud, G. (2014, November 11). *Ten hours of Princess Leia walking in NYC*. Retrieved from https://www.youtube.com/watch?v=7DCDYSJwwE4

Aquino, Y. S. J. (2017). "Big eye" surgery: The ethics of medicalizing Asian features. *Theoretical Medicine and Bioethics*, *38*(3), 213–225. doi:10.100711017-017-9395-y PMID:28105531

Araya, A. A. (1995). Questioning ubiquitous computing. In *Proceedings of the 1995 ACM 23rd annual conference on Computer science* (pp. 230-237). ACM.

Arendt, H. (2006). *Eichmann in Jerusalem: A report on the banality of evil*. New York: Penguin Books.

Arigo, J. (2000). The Ethics of Weapons Research: A Framework for Discourse between Insiders and Outsiders. *Journal of Power and Ethics*, *1*, 303–327.

Aristotle. (1961). Poetics (S.H. Butcher, Trans.). New York, NY: Hill and Wang. (Original work published c. 335 B.C.E.)

Arkin, R. C. (2007). *Governing lethal behavior: Embedding ethics in a hybrid deliberative/reactive robot architecture* (Technical report GIT-GVU-07-11). Atlanta, GA: Georgia Institute of Technology.

Arkin, R. (2009). *Governing lethal behavior in autonomous robots*. Boca Raton, FL: CRC Press. doi:10.1201/9781420085952

Arkin, R. C. (2009). Ethical robots in warfare. *IEEE Technology and Society Magazine, 28*(1), 30–33. doi:10.1109/MTS.2009.931858

Arnocky, S., Perilloux, C., Cloud, J. M., Bird, B. M., & Thomas, K. (2016). Envy mediates the link between social comparison and appearance enhancement in women. *Evolutionary Psychological Science, 2*(2), 71–83. doi:10.100740806-015-0037-1

Arnsten, A., & Li, B. (2005). Neurobiology of executive functions: Catecholamine influences on prefrontal cortical functions. *Biological Psychiatry, 57*(11), 1377–1384. doi:10.1016/j.biopsych.2004.08.019 PMID:15950011

Arun, P., & Sahni, S. (2014). Methylphenidate and suicidal ideation: Report of two cases. *Indian Journal of Psychiatry, 56*(1), 79–81. doi:10.4103/0019-5545.124721 PMID:24574564

Asaro, P. (2007). Robots and responsibility from a legal perspective. In *Proceedings of the 8th IEEE 2007 International Conference on Robotics and Automation.* IEEE.

Asaro, P. M. (2008). How just could a robot war be? In A. Briggle, K. Waelbers, & Ph. Brey (Eds.), *Current issues in computing and philosophy* (pp. 50–64). Amsterdam: IOS Press.

Asaro, P. M. (2009). Modeling the moral user. *IEEE Technology and Society, 28*(1), 20–24. doi:10.1109/MTS.2009.931863

Ashby, W. R. (1962) Principles of the self-organizing system. In *Principles of self-organization: Transactions of the University of Illinois Symposium.* London: Pergamon Press.

Atzori, L., Iera, A., & Morabito, G. (2010). The Internet of Things: A survey. *Computer Networks, 54*(15), 2787–2805. doi:10.1016/j.comnet.2010.05.010

Aubrey, J. S. (2007). The impact of sexually objectifying media exposure on negative body emotions and sexual self-perceptions: Investigating the mediating role of body self-consciousness. *Mass Communication & Society, 10*(1), 1–23. doi:10.1080/15205430709337002

Auriel, E., Hausdorff, J., & Giladi, N. (2009). Methylphenidate for the treatment of Parkinson disease and other neurological disorders. *Clinical Neuropharmacology, 2*(32), 75–81. doi:10.1097/WNF.0b013e318170576c PMID:18978488

Babcock, S. (2010, February 20). Plastic front creates poor "perfection." *Spokesman Review,* p. V1.

Baeva, L. V. (2013). Electronic culture: Experience of philosophical analysis. *Issues of Philosophy, 5,* 75–83.

Baeva, L. V. (2014). Existential and Ethical Values in an Information Era. *Journal of Human Values, 20*(1), 33–43. doi:10.1177/0971685813515593

Bainbridge, W. (2007). Governing Nanotechnology: Social, Ethical and Human Issues. In Springer Handbook of Nanotechnology (pp. 1823-1840). Springer Berlin Heidelberg.

Bainbridge, W., & Rocco, M. (Eds.). (2005). Managing Nano-, Bio-, Info- Cogno Innovations: Converging Technologies in Society. National Science Foundation.

Bainbridge, W. S. (Ed.). (2013). *Converging technologies for improving human performance: Nanotechnology, biotechnology, information technology and cognitive science.* Springer Science & Business Media.

Bainbridge, W. S., & Roco, M. C. (2006). *Managing Nano-Bio-Info-Cogno Innovations.* Springer. doi:10.1007/1-4020-4107-1

Baker, J. L. (2004). Choosing breast implant size: A matter of aesthetics. *Aesthetic Surgery Journal, 24*(6), 565–566. doi:10.1016/j.asj.2004.09.009 PMID:19336211

Baker-Sperry, L., & Grauerholz, L. (2003). The pervasiveness and persistence of the feminine beauty ideal in children's fairy tales. *Gender & Society*, *17*(5), 711–726. doi:10.1177/0891243203255605

Balance, C. B. (2012). How it feels to be viral me: Affective labor and Asian American YouTube performance. *Women's Studies Quarterly*, *40*(1/2), 138–152. doi:10.1353/wsq.2012.0016

Balkany, T., Hodges, A. V., & Goodman, K. W. (1996). Ethics of cochlear implantation in young children. *Otolaryngology - Head and Neck Surgery*, *114*(6), 748–755. doi:10.1016/S0194-5998(96)70097-9 PMID:8643298

Balta-Ozkan, N., Davidson, R., Bicket, M., & Whitmarsh, L. (2013). Social barriers to the adoption of smart homes. *Energy Policy*, *63*, 363–374. doi:10.1016/j.enpol.2013.08.043

Bamford, J. (2012). *The NSA Is Building the Country's Biggest Spy Center (Watch What You Say)*. Wired.com.

Bandura, A. (1999). Moral disengagement in the perpetration of inhumanities. *Personality and Social Psychology Review*, *3*(3), 193–209. doi:10.120715327957pspr0303_3 PMID:15661671

Bankman, I. N., & Janselewitz, S. J. (1995, September). Neural waveform detector for prosthesis control. In *Engineering in Medicine and Biology Society, 1995., IEEE 17th Annual Conference* (Vol. 2, pp. 963-964). IEEE. 10.1109/IEMBS.1995.579382

Banks, D. (1998). Neurotechnology. *Engineering Science and Education Journal*, *7*(3), 135–144. doi:10.1049/esej:19980306

Barak, M., Lipson, A., & Lerman, S. (2006). Wireless Laptops as Means For Promoting Active Learning In Large Lecture Halls. *Journal of Research on Technology in Education*, *38*(3), 245–263. doi:10.1080/15391523.2006.10782459

Barber, N. (1995). The evolutionary psychology of physical attractiveness: Sexual selection and human morphology. *Ethology and Sociobiology*, *16*(5), 395–424. doi:10.1016/0162-3095(95)00068-2

Barke, R. (1986). Science Technology and Public Policy. Washington, DC: Congressional Quarterly Press.

Barocas, S., & Selbst, A. D. (2016). Big data's disparate impact. *California Law Review*, *104*(3), 671–732.

Barral, O., Aranyi, G., Kouider, S., Lindsay, A., Prins, H., Ahmed, I., ... Cavazza, M. (2014, May). Covert persuasive technologies: bringing subliminal cues to human-computer interaction. In *International Conference on Persuasive Technology* (pp. 1-12). Springer. 10.1007/978-3-319-07127-5_1

Barthes, R. (1978). The death of the author. In R. Barthes (Ed.), *Image-music-text* (HeathS., Trans.). (pp. 142–148). New York, NY: Hill and Wang. (Original work published 1967)

Barzilai-Nahon, K. (2008). Toward a theory of network gatekeeping: A framework for exploring information control. *Journal of the American Society for Information Science and Technology*, *59*(9), 1493–1512. doi:10.1002/asi.20857

Baudrillard, J. (1988). The ecstasy of communication (B. Schutze & C. Schutze, Trans.). New York: Semiotext(e).

Baudrillard, J. (1993). *Symbolic exchange and death*. Aldershot, UK: Ashgate.

Baudrillard, J. (1994). *Simulacra and simulation* (S. F. Glaser, Trans.). Ann Arbor, MI: University of Michigan Press.

Baumann, L. (2012). Ethics in cosmetic dermatology. *Clinics in Dermatology*, *30*(5), 522–527. doi:10.1016/j.clindermatol.2011.06.023 PMID:22902224

Baumann, S. (2008). The moral underpinnings of beauty: A meaning-based explanation for light and dark complexions in advertising. *Poetics*, *36*(1), 2–23. doi:10.1016/j.poetic.2007.11.002

Bazzini, D., Curtin, L., Joslin, S., Regan, S., & Martz, D. (2010). Do animated Disney characters portray and promote the beauty-goodness stereotype? *Journal of Applied Social Psychology*, *40*(10), 2687–2709. doi:10.1111/j.1559-1816.2010.00676.x

Beardsley, M. C. (1981). The arts in the life of man. In M. C. Beardsley (Ed.), *Aesthetics: problems in the philosophy of criticism* (2nd ed.; pp. 557–583). Indianapolis, IN: Hackett Publishing Company.

Beauchamp, T. L., & Childress, J. F. (2001). *Principles of biomedical ethics* (5th ed.). New York, NY: Oxford University Press.

Beauchere, J. (2013). Online 'safety' as a state of being. *Microsoft on the Issues*. Retrieved from http://bit.ly/1eiOJCE

Beauchere, J. (2017). *Encouraging Digital Civility: What Companies and Others Can Do*. Academic Press.

Beavers, A. F. (2012). Moral machines and the threat of ethical nihilism. In P. Lin, K. Abney, & G. A. Bekey (Eds.), *Robot ethics. The ethical and social implications of robotics* (pp. 333–344). Cambridge, MA: The MIT Press.

Bell, C. (1914). The aesthetic hypothesis. In C. Bell (Ed.), *Art* (pp. 3–38). New York, NY: G.P. Putnam & Sons.

Benanti, P. (2010). From Neuroskepticism to Neuroethics: Role of Morality in Neuroscience That Becomes Neurotechnology. *AJOB Neuroscience*, *1*(2), 39–40. doi:10.1080/21507741003699264

Benjamin, W. (1968). The work of art in the age of mechanical reproduction. In H. Arendt (Ed.) & H. Zohn (Trans.), Illuminations (pp. 219–226). New York, NY: Schocken Books. (Original work published 1936)

Benjamin, M. (2012). *Drone warfare: Killing by remote control*. New York: OR Books.

Bennett, C. (2015, September 9). Energy Dept. hacked 150 times in 4 years. *The Hill*. Retrieved from http://thehill.com/policy/cybersecurity/253130-hackers-cracked-energy-department-150-times-over-four-years

Bennett, T., & Holloway, K. (2017). Motives for illicit prescription drug use among university students: A systematic review and meta-analysis. *The International Journal on Drug Policy*, *44*, 12–22. doi:10.1016/j.drugpo.2017.02.012 PMID:28343063

Bentham, J. (1823). A Fragment on Government; Or a Comment on the Commentaries: Being an Examination of What is Delivered on the Subject of Government in General, in the Introduction to Sir William Blackstone's Commentaries: With a Preface. In *Which is Given a Critique on the Work at Large* (2nd ed.). London: E. Wilson and W. Pickering.

Berger, J., & Milkman, K. L. (2012). What makes online content go viral? *JMR, Journal of Marketing Research*, *49*(2), 192–205. doi:10.1509/jmr.10.0353

Berger, T. W., & Glanzman, D. L. (Eds.). (2005). *Toward replacement parts for the brain: implantable biomimetic electronics as neural prostheses*. MIT Press.

Berger, T. W., Hampson, R. E., Song, D., Goonawardena, A., Marmarelis, V. Z., & Deadwyler, S. A. (2011). A cortical neural prosthesis for restoring and enhancing memory. *Journal of Neural Engineering*, *8*(4), 046017. doi:10.1088/1741-2560/8/4/046017 PMID:21677369

Berman, L. (2010, February 3). Heidi Montag throws a curve at young girls; Obsession with "perfection" reinforces women's needless body insecurities. Chicago Sun Times, p. C4.

Berman, S., O'Neill, J., Fears, S., Bartzokis, G., & London, E. (2008). Abuse of amphetamines and structural abnormalities in the brain. *Annals of the New York Academy of Sciences*, *1141*(1), 195–220. doi:10.1196/annals.1441.031 PMID:18991959

Bernal, J. D. (1939). *The Social Function of Science*. London: Routledge and Kegan Paul.

Bernardinelli, Y., Nikonenko, I., & Muller, D. (2014). Structural plasticity: Mechanisms and contribution to developmental psychiatric disorders. *Frontiers in Neuroanatomy, 8*. PMID:25404897

Berry, M. G., Cucchiara, V., & Davies, D. M. (2011). Breast augmentation: Part III—preoperative considerations and planning. *Journal of Plastic, Reconstructive & Aesthetic Surgery; JPRAS, 64*(11), 1401–1409.

Bertolotti, T. (2011). Facebook has it: The irresistible violence of social cognition in the age of social networking. *International Journal of Technoethics, 2*(4), 71–83. doi:10.4018/jte.2011100105

Bertolotti, T., Arfini, S., & Magnani, L. (2017). *Cyber Bullies as Cyborg Bullies*. The Changing Scope of Technoethics in Contemporary Society.

Bertolotti, T., & Magnani, L. (2013). A philosophical and evolutionary approach to cyber-bullying: Social networks and the disruption of submoralities. *Ethics and Information Technology, 15*(4), 285–299. doi:10.100710676-013-9324-3

Berube, D. M. (2012). Decision ethics and emergent technologies: The case of nanotechnology. *European Journal of Law and Technology, 1*(3), 1–8. Retrieved from http://ejlt.org/article/view/78

Betts, L. R. (2016). *Cyberbullying: Approaches*. Springeralden, MA: Consequences, and Interventions. doi:10.1057/978-1-137-50009-0

Bhat, C. S. (2008). Cyber bullying: Overview and strategies for school counsellors, guidance of officers, and all school personnel. *Australian Journal of Guidance & Counselling, 18*(01), 53–66. doi:10.1375/ajgc.18.1.53

Bignell, J. (2000). *Postmodern Media Culture*. Edinburgh, UK: Edinburgh University Press.

Bilder, R., Volavka, J., Lachman, H., & Grace, A. (2004). The catechol-O-methyltransferase polymorphism: Relations to the tonic-phasic dopamine hypothesis and neuropsychiatric phenotypes. *Neuropsychopharmacology, 29*(11), 1943–1961. doi:10.1038j.npp.1300542 PMID:15305167

Bingham, P. M. (1999). Human uniqueness: A general theory. *The Quarterly Review of Biology, 74*(2), 133–169. doi:10.1086/393069

Birchley, G., Huxtable, R., Murtagh, M., ter Meulen, R., Flach, P., & Gooberman-Hill, R. (2017). Smart homes, private homes? An empirical study of technology researchers' perceptions of ethical issues in developing smart-home health technologies. *BMC Medical Ethics, 18*(1), 23. doi:10.118612910-017-0183-z PMID:28376811

Bird, K., & Sherwin, M. J. (2005). *American Prometheus The Triumph and Tragedy of J. Robert Oppenheimer*. New York: Alfred A Knopf.

Blackman, C. (2009). Cell phone radiation: Evidence from ELF and RF studies supporting more inclusive risk identification and assessment. *Pathophysiology, 16*(2), 205–216. doi:10.1016/j.pathophys.2009.02.001 PMID:19264460

Bleicher, A. (2010). Privacy on the smart grid. *IEEE Spectrum*. Retrieved from: http://spectrum.ieee.org/ energy/the-smarter-grid/privacy-on-the-smart-grid

Blum, V. L. (2005). Becoming the other woman: The psychic drama of cosmetic surgery. *Frontiers: A Journal of Women Studies, 26*(2), 104-131.

Blum, V. L. (2003). *Flesh wounds: The culture of cosmetic surgery*. Berkeley, CA: University of California Press.

Boggio, P. S., Rigonatti, S. P., Ribeiro, R. B., Myczkowski, M. L., Nitsche, M. A., Pascual-leone, A., & Fregni, F. (2008). A randomized, double-blind clinical trial on the efficacy of cortical direct current stimulation for the treatment of major depression. *The International Journal of Neuropsychopharmacology, 11*(2), 249–254. doi:10.1017/S1461145707007833 PMID:17559710

Bookchin, N., & Shulgin, A. (1999). Introduction to net.art (1994–1999). *Introduction to net.art (1994-1999).* Retrieved from http://www.net-art.org/netart_definition

Bordo, S. (1993). *Unbearable weight: Feminism, Western culture, and the body.* Berkeley, CA: University of California Press.

Borducchi, D., Gomes, J. S., Akiba, H., Cordeiro, Q., Borducchi, J. M., Valentin, L., ... Dias, Á. M. (2016). Transcranial direct current stimulation effects on athletes' cognitive performance: An exploratory proof of concept trial. *Frontiers in Psychiatry, 7*, 183. doi:10.3389/fpsyt.2016.00183 PMID:27965597

Bostrom, N. (2002). Existential risks: Analyzing Human Extinction Scenarios and Related Hazards. *Journal of Evolution and Technology / WTA, 9*.

Bostrom, N. (2003). Human Genetic Enhancements: A transhumanist Perspective. *The Journal of Value Inquiry, 37*(4), 493–506. doi:10.1023/B:INQU.0000019037.67783.d5 PMID:17340768

Bostrom, N., & Sandberg, A. (2009). Cognitive Enhancement: Methods, Ethics, Regulatory Challenges. *Science and Engineering Ethics, 15*(3), 311–341. doi:10.100711948-009-9142-5 PMID:19543814

Boyden, E. S., Zhang, F., Bamberg, E., Nagel, G., & Deisseroth, K. (2005). Millisecond-timescale, genetically targeted optical control of neural activity. *Nature Neuroscience, 8*(9), 1263–1268. doi:10.1038/nn1525 PMID:16116447

Bozzo, A. (2007). Players Replay the Crash. *CNBC.* Retrieved February 18, 2014, from http://www.cnbc.com/id/21136884

Braidotti, R. (2013). *The posthuman.* Cambridge, UK: Polity Press.

Breit, S., Schulz, J. B., & Benabid, A. L. (2004). Deep brain stimulation. *Cell and Tissue Research, 318*(1), 275–288. doi:10.100700441-004-0936-0 PMID:15322914

Bremmer, I. (2010). Democracy in cyberspace: What information technology can and cannot do. *Foreign Affairs, 89*(6), 86–92.

Brey, P. (2000). Technology as extension of human faculties. *Metaphysics, Epistemology, and Technology. Research in Philosophy and Technology, 19*.

Brinkhaus, S., Carluccio, D., Greveler, U., Justus, B., Löhr, D., & Wegener, C. (2011). Smart hacking for privacy. *28th Chaos Communication Congress.* Retrieved from: http://events.ccc.de/congress/2011/Fahrplan/ attachments/1968_28c3-abstract-smart_hacking_for_privacy.pdf

Britannica Online Encyclopedia. (2012). *Cybercrime.* Retrieved, October 15, 2012, from: www.britannica.com/EB-checked/topic/130595/cybercrime

Brogaard, J.A. (2011). High Frequency Trading, information, and profits. Government of Science. *The future of computer trading in Financial markets – Foresight Driver Review – DR 10.*

Brown, J. D., Halpern, C. T., & L'Engle, K. L. (2005). Mass media as a sexual super peer for early maturing girls. *The Journal of Adolescent Health, 36*(5), 420–427. doi:10.1016/j.jadohealth.2004.06.003 PMID:15837346

Brunstetter, D., & Braun, M. (2011). The implications of drones on the just war tradition. *Ethics & International Affairs, 25*(3), 337–358. doi:10.1017/S0892679411000281

Budanov, V. G. (2015) Conceptual model of socio-anthropological projections of converging NBICS-technologies In Socio-anthropological resources transdisciplinary research in the context of innovative civilization: Collected papers of international scientific webinar. Kursk.

Buglass, S. L., Binder, J. F., Betts, L. R., & Underwood, D. M. (2017). Motivators of online vulnerability: The impact of social network site use and FOMO. *Computers in Human Behavior, 66*, 248–255. doi:10.1016/j.chb.2016.09.055

Bunge, M. (1977). Towards a technoethics. *Monist, 60*(1), 96–107. doi: 013410.5840/monist19776

Bunge, M. (1975). Towards a technoethics. *Philosophic Exchange, 6*(1), 69–79.

Bunge, M. (1977). Towards a Technoethics. *The Monist, 60*(1), 96–107. doi:10.5840/monist197760134

Buniak, L., Darragh, M., & Giordano, J. (2014). A four-part working bibliography of neuroethics: part 1: overview and reviews – defining and describing the field and its practices. *Philosophy, Ethics, and Humanities in Medicine; PEHM, 9*(9), 1–14. doi:10.1186/ 1747-5341-9-9 PMID:24885037

Bunting, H. (1998). *_readme*. Retrieved from http://www.irational.org/readme.html

Burgess, P. G. (1970). The rhetoric of moral conflict: Two critical dimensions. *The Quarterly Journal of Speech, 56*(2), 120–130. doi:10.1080/00335637009382993

Burns, A., Ow, H., & Wiesner, U. (2006). Fluorescent core–shell silica nanoparticles: Towards "Lab on a Particle" architectures for nanobiotechnology. *Chemical Society Reviews, 35*(11), 1028–1042. doi:10.1039/B600562B PMID:17057833

Burrell, B. (n.d.). *Protection from cyber crime: Top 10 security measures for educational institutions*. Retrieved May 7, 2015, from http://www.eset.com/us/resources/content-browser-detail/protection-from-cyber-crime-top-10-security-measures-for-educational-institutions/

Buss, D. M., & Schmitt, D. P. (1993). Sexual strategies theory: An evolutionary perspective on human mating. *Psychological Review, 100*(2), 204–232. doi:10.1037/0033-295X.100.2.204 PMID:8483982

Calipari, E., & Jones, S. (2014). Sensitized nucleus accumbens dopamine terminal responses to methylphenidate and dopamine transporter releasers after intermittent-access self-administration. *Neuropharmacology, 82*, 1–10. doi:10.1016/j.neuropharm.2014.02.021 PMID:24632529

Callahan, D. (2012). *The roots of bioethics: Health, progress, technology, death*. Oxford University Press. doi:10.1093/acprof:oso/9780199931378.001.0001

Calogero, R. M., Pina, A., & Sutton, R. M. (2014). Cutting words: Priming self-objectification increases women's intention to pursue cosmetic surgery. *Psychology of Women Quarterly, 38*(2), 197–207. doi:10.1177/0361684313506881

Cameron, A. F., & Webster, J. (2005). Unintended consequences of emerging communication technologies: Instant messaging in the workplace. *Computers in Human Behavior, 21*(1), 85–103. doi:10.1016/j.chb.2003.12.001

Camilli, D. (2010, April 24). Montag is a "cheap, plastic pool float" after surgery. *The Gazette (Montreal)*, p. E5.

Cantor, J. (2005). Cosmetic dermatology and physicians' ethical obligations: More than just hope in a jar. *Seminars in Cutaneous Medicine and Surgery, 24*(3), 155–160. doi:10.1016/j.sder.2005.04.005 PMID:16202953

Capurro, R. (2010). Information ethics. *The Information Society, 5*, 6–15.

Carmichael (Kwame Ture), S. (2007). Stokely speaks: From black power to pan-Africanism. Chicago Review Press.

Carmichael, (Kwame Ture) S. (1971). *Stokely speaks: Black power back to pan-Africanism* [Enki version]. New York: Random House.

Cartwright, R., & Cardozo, L. (2008). Cosmetic vulvovaginal surgery. *Obstetrics, Gynaecology and Reproductive Medicine, 18*(10), 285–286. doi:10.1016/j.ogrm.2008.07.008

Cassidy, S. (2010, January 24). Teens, young adults cut into cosmetic-surgery statistics; Defining beauty breast wishes parental pressure? For the sport of it males do it, too. *Sunday News*, p. G1.

Castells, M. (1997). The End of the Millennium, the Information Age: Economy, Society and Culture: Vol. 3. Oxford, UK: Blackwell.

Castells, M. (2012). *Networks of Outrage and Hope: Social Movements in the Internet Age*. Cambridge, UK: Polity.

Cavalcanti, A., & Freitas, R. A. Jr. (2005). Nanorobotics control design: A collective behavior approach for medicine. *NanoBioscience. IEEE Transactions on, 4*(2), 133–140. PMID:16117021

Cave, J. (2014, August 28). Climate change will ruin Hawaii, new study says. *Huffington Post*. Retrieved from http://www.huffingtonpost.com/2014/08/28/climate-change-study-hawaii_n_5731956.html

Cavoukian, A., & Kursawe, K. (2012). Implementing privacy by design: The smart meter case. In *Proceedings of the 2012 IEEE International Conference on Smart Grid Engineering* (pp. 1-8). Piscataway, NJ: IEEE. 10.1109/SGE.2012.6463977

CERP-IoT. European Union, Cluster of European Research Projects on the Internet of Things. (2010). *Vision and challenges for realising the Internet of Things*. Brussels: European Commission – Information Society and Media.

Chalmers, D., & Clark, A. (1998). The extended mind. *Analysis, 58*(1), 7–19. doi:10.1093/analys/58.1.7

Champagne, M., & Tonkens, R. (2015). Bridging the responsibility gap in automated warfare. *Philosophy & Technology, 28*(1), 125–137. doi:10.100713347-013-0138-3

Chang, C. L. (2011). The effect of an information ethics course on the information ethics values of students – A Chinese guanxi culture perspective. *Computers in Human Behavior, 27*(5), 2028–2038. doi:10.1016/j.chb.2011.05.010

Chan, H. Y., Aslam, D. M., Wiler, J. A., & Casey, B. (2009). A novel diamond microprobe for neuro-chemical and-electrical recording in neural prosthesis. *Microelectromechanical Systems. Journalism, 18*(3), 511–521.

Chan, J. K.-K., Jones, S. M., & Heywood, A. J. (2011). Body dysmorphia, self-mutilation and the reconstructive surgeon. *Journal of Plastic, Reconstructive & Aesthetic Surgery; JPRAS, 64*(1), 4–8. doi:10.1016/j.bjps.2010.03.029 PMID:20392680

Chapin, J. K. (2004). Using multi-neuron population recordings for neural prosthetics. *Nature Neuroscience, 7*(5), 452–455. doi:10.1038/nn1234 PMID:15114357

Chappelle, W., McDonald, K., & McMillan, K. (2011). *Important and critical psychological attributes of USAF MQ-1 predator and MQ-9 reaper pilots according to subject matter experts*. School of Aerospace Medicine. doi:10.21236/ADA545552

Chayka, K. (2012, June 14). *How going viral has changed art*. Retrieved from http://thecreatorsproject.vice.com/blog/how-going-viral-has-changed-art

Cheon, J., & Lee, J. H. (2008). Synergistically integrated nanoparticles as multimodal probes for nanobiotechnology. *Accounts of Chemical Research, 41*(12), 1630–1640. doi:10.1021/ar800045c PMID:18698851

Chin, J., & Lin, L. (2017, June 26). *China's All-Seeing Surveillance State Is Reading Its Citizens' Faces*. Retrieved July 29, 2017, from https://www.wsj.com/articles/the-all-seeing-surveillance-state-feared-in-the-west-is-a-reality-in-china-1498493020?mod=e2tw

Chopra, A. (2011, September 15). *Modeling a green energy challenge after a blue button*. Retrieved from: http://www. whitehouse.gov/blog/2011/09/15/modeling-green-energy-challenge-after-blue-button

Christakos, H. A., & Mehta, S. N. (2002). Annual review of law and technology. *Berkeley Technology Law Journal, 2002*, 473.

Clark, A. (1998a). *Being there: Putting brain, body, and world together again*. MIT Press.

Clark, A. (1998b). Embodiment and the Philosophy of Mind. *Royal Institute of Philosophy, 43*(Supplement 43), 35–51. doi:10.1017/S135824610000429X

Clark, A. (1999). An embodied cognitive science? *Trends in Cognitive Sciences, 3*(9), 345–351. doi:10.1016/S1364-6613(99)01361-3 PMID:10461197

Clark, A. (2003). *Natural-Born Cyborgs. Minds, Technologies, and the Future of Human Intelligence*. Oxford, UK: Oxford University Press.

Clark, A. (2008). *Supersizing the mind. embodiment, action, and cognitive extension*. Oxford, UK: Oxford University Press. doi:10.1093/acprof:oso/9780195333213.001.0001

Clarke, J., Drake, L., Flatt, S., & Jebb, P. (2008). Physical perfection for sale. *Nursing Standard, 23*(8), 26–27. PMID:18655503

Clatworthy, P., Lewis, S., Brichard, L., Hong, Y., Izquierdo, D., Clark, L., ... Robbins, T. (2009). Dopamine release in dissociable striatal subregions predicts the different effects of oral methylphenidate on reversal learning and spatial working memory. *The Journal of Neuroscience, 29*(15), 4690–4696. doi:10.1523/JNEUROSCI.3266-08.2009 PMID:19369539

Clemens, D. (1985). Technoethics. *Informal Logic, 7*(2&3), 163–165.

Cliff, D., Brown, D., & Treleaven, Ph. (2010a). Technology trends in the financial markets: A 2020 vision. In UK Governments Foresight Project, The Future of Computer Trading in Financial Markets. Government Office for Science London.

Cliff, D., & Northrop, L. (2010b). The global financial markets: an Ultra-Large-Scale Systems Perspective. In *The future of Computer Trading in Financial Markets Driver review - DR 4* (p. 47). Government Office for Science London.

Clynes, M., & Kline, N. (1960, September). Cyborgs and space. *Astronautics, 26–27*, 74–76.

Coeckelbergh, M. (2013). Drones, information technology, and distance: Mapping the moral epistemology of remote fighting. *Ethics and Information Technology, 15*(2), 87–98. doi:10.100710676-013-9313-6

Coeckelbergh, M. (2014). The moral standing of machines: Towards a relational and non-cartesian moral hermeneutics. *Philosophy & Technology, 27*(1), 61–77. doi:10.100713347-013-0133-8

Coghill, D., Seth, S., Pedroso, S., Usala, T., Currie, J., & Gagliano, A. (2014). Effects of methylphenidate on cognitive functions in children and adolescents with attention-deficit/hyperactivity disorder: Evidence from a systematic review and a meta-analysis. *Biological Psychiatry, 76*. PMID:24231201

Colding, J., & Barthel, S. (2017). An urban ecology critique on the "Smart City" model. *Journal of Cleaner Production, 164*, 95–101. doi:10.1016/j.jclepro.2017.06.191

Collste, G., Duquenoy, P., George, C., Hedström, K., Kimppa, K., & Mordini, E. (2006). ICT in medicine and health care: Assessing social, ethical and legal issues. Social Informatics: An Information Society for all? In *Remembrance of Rob Kling. Proceedings of the Seventh International Conference on Human Choice and Computers* (pp. 297-308). Retrieved August 1, 2017, from https://eprints.mdx.ac.uk/2040/1/Duquenoy-ICT_in_Medicine_and_Health_Care_social_ethical_issues_preprint.pdf

Comiskey, C. (2004). Cosmetic surgery in Paris in 1926: The case of the amputated leg. *Journal of Women's History*, *16*(3), 30–54. doi:10.1353/jowh.2004.0059

Cook, S. A., Rosser, R., & Salmon, P. (2006). Is cosmetic surgery an effective psychotherapeutic intervention? A systematic review of the evidence. *Journal of Plastic, Reconstructive & Aesthetic Surgery; JPRAS*, *59*(11), 1133–1151. doi:10.1016/j.bjps.2006.03.047 PMID:17046622

Cooney, B. (2004). *Posthumanity: thinking philosophically about the future*. Rowman & Littlefield.

Cooper, A. (2016, October). *Electric company smart meter deployments: Foundations for a smart grid*. Washington, DC: Innovation Electricity Efficiency Institute.

Coroama, V., Bohn, J., & Mattern, F. (2004, October). Living in a smart environment - implications for the coming ubiquitous information society. In *Proceedings of the 2004 IEEE International Conference on Systems, Man and Cybernetics* (Vol. 6, pp. 5633-5638). IEEE.

Cortese, F. (2013a). *Transhumanism, Technology & Science: To Say It's Impossible Is To Mock History Itself*. Institute for Ethics & Emerging Technologies. Retrieved November 17, 2015, from http://ieet.org/index.php/IEET/more/cortese20130612

Cortese, F. (2013b). The Hubris of Neoluddism. *H+ Magazine*. Retrieved November 17, 2015, from http://hplusmagazine.com/2013/06/07/the-hubris-of-neo-luddism/

Cortese, F. (2013c). Three Spectres of Immortality: A Talk From the Radical Life Extension Conference in Washington D.C. *H+ Magazine*. Retrieved November 17, 2015, from http://hplusmagazine.com/2013/10/16/three-spectres-of-immortality-a-talk-from-the-radical-life-extension-conference-in-washington-d-c/

Cortese, F. (2014). Heidegger On The Existential Utility Of Death. In C. Tandy (Ed.), Death And Anti-Death, Volume 12: One Hundred Years After Charles S. Peirce (1839-1914) (pp. 131-136). Ann Arbor, MI: Ria University Press.

Cosics, V. (1998). *Deep ASCII*. Retrieved from http://ljudmila.org/~vuk/

Creswell, J. W. (2003). *Research design: Qualitative, Quantitative, and Mixed Methods Approaches*. Thousand Oaks, CA: Sage Publications.

Crnkovic, G. D., & Curuklu, B. (2012). Robots: Ethical by design. *Ethics and Information Technology*, *14*(1), 61–71. doi:10.100710676-011-9278-2

Crootof, R. (2015). War, responsibility, and killer robots. *North Carolina Journal of International Law and Commercial Regulation*, *40*(4), 909–932.

Crootof, R. (2016). A meaningful floor for 'meaningful human control'. *Temple International and Comparative Law Journal*, *30*, 53–62.

Culbertson, L. (2007). "Human-ness", "dehumanisation" and performance enhancement. *Sport. Ethics and Philosophy*, *1*(2), 195–217. doi:10.1080/17511320701439877

Cummings, M. L. (2006). Automation and accountability in decision support system interface design. *Journal of Technology Studies*, *32*(1), 23–31. doi:10.21061/jots.v32i1.a.4

Danto, A. (1964). The artworld. *The Journal of Philosophy*, *61*(19), 571–584. doi:10.2307/2022937

Davidson, J., & Martellozzo, E. (2013). Exploring young people's use of social networking sites and digital media in the internet safety context: A comparison of the UK and Bahrain. *Information Communication and Society*, *16*(9), 1456–1476. doi:10.1080/1369118X.2012.701655

Davies, A. T. (1988). *Infected Christianity*. Montreal: McGill-Queen's University Press.

Davies, S. (2006). Evolution and culture. In S. Davies (Ed.), *The philosophy of art* (pp. 1–25). Hoboken, NJ: Wiley-Blackwell.

Davis, D., & Vernon, M. L. (2002). Sculpting the body beautiful: Attachment style, neuroticism, and use of cosmetic surgeries. *Sex Roles*, *47*(3/4), 129–138. doi:10.1023/A:1021043021624

Davis, K. (2003). Surgical passing: Or why Michael Jackson's nose makes "us" uneasy. *Feminist Theory*, *4*(1), 73–92. doi:10.1177/1464700103004001004

Davis, N. J. (2013). Neurodoping: Brain Stimulation as a Performance-Enhancing Measure. *Sports Medicine (Auckland, N.Z.)*, *43*(8), 649–653. doi:10.100740279-013-0027-z PMID:23504390

Davis, N. J. (2014). Transcranial stimulation of the developing brain: A plea for extreme caution. *Frontiers in Human Neuroscience*, *8*(August), 8–11. PMID:25140146

de Andrade, D. D. (2010). On norms and bodies: Findings from field research on cosmetic surgery in Rio de Janeiro, Brazil. *Reproductive Health Matters*, *18*(35), 74–83. doi:10.1016/S0968-8080(10)35519-4 PMID:20541086

de Casanova, E. M. (2004). "No ugly women": Concepts of race and beauty among adolescent women in Ecuador. *Gender & Society*, *18*(3), 287–308. doi:10.1177/0891243204263351

de Casanova, E. M., & Sutton, B. (2013). Transnational body projects: Media representations of cosmetic surgery tourism in Argentina and the United States. *Journal of World-systems Research*, *19*(1), 57–81. doi:10.5195/JWSR.2013.509

De Jong, K., Olds, J., & Giordano, J. (2011). *National Neuroscience: Ethics, Legal and Social Issues Conference* (No. 202069). George Mason University.

De Roubaix, J. A. M. (2011). Beneficence, non-maleficence, distributive justice and respect for patient autonomy—Reconcilable ends in aesthetic surgery? *Journal of Plastic, Reconstructive & Aesthetic Surgery; JPRAS*, *64*(1), 11–16. doi:10.1016/j.bjps.2010.03.034 PMID:20457018

Debatin, B., Lovejoy, J. P., Horn, A. K., & Hughes, B. N. (2009). Facebook and online privacy: Attitudes, behaviors, and unintended consequences. *Journal of Computer-Mediated Communication*, *15*(1), 83–108. doi:10.1111/j.1083-6101.2009.01494.x

Dedoncker, J., Brunoni, A. R., Baeken, C., & Vanderhasselt, M.-A. (2016). The effect of the interval-between-sessions on prefrontal transcranial direct current stimulation (tDCS) on cognitive outcomes: A systematic review and meta-analysis. *Journal of Neural Transmission (Vienna, Austria)*, *123*(10), 1159–1172. doi:10.100700702-016-1558-x PMID:27145765

Deng, B. (2015, July). The robot's dilemma. Working out how to build ethical robots is one of the horniest challenges in artificial intelligence. *Nature*, *523*, 25–26.

Dennett, D. (2003). *Freedom Evolves*. New York: Viking.

Denning, T., Matsuoka, Y., & Kohno, T. (2009). Neurosecurity: Security and privacy for neural devices. *Neurosurgical Focus*, *27*(1), E7. doi:10.3171/2009.4.FOCUS0985 PMID:19569895

Denyer, S. (2016, May 23). *China's scary lesson to the world: Censoring the Internet works*. Retrieved July 29, 2017, from https://www.washingtonpost.com/world/asia_pacific/chinas-scary-lesson-to-the-world-censoring-the-internet-works/2016/05/23/413afe78-fff3-11e5-8bb1-f124a43f84dc_story.html?tid=ss_tw-amp&utm_term=.052fcf1fe206

Depuru, S. S., Wang, L., Devabhaktuni, V., & Gudi, N. (2011). Smart meters for power grid: Issues, advantages, and status. *Renewable & Sustainable Energy Reviews*, *15*(6), 2736–2742. doi:10.1016/j.rser.2011.02.039

Derakhshani, T. (2009, August 13). Sideshow: Low-key farewell to Hughes. *Philadelphia Inquirer*, p. E02.

Detert, J. R., Treviño, L. K., & Sweitzer, V. L. (2008). Moral disengagement in ethical decision making: A study of antecedents and outcomes. *The Journal of Applied Psychology*, 93(2), 374–391. doi:10.1037/0021-9010.93.2.374 PMID:18361639

Dewey, J. (1980). Having an experience. In J. Dewey (Ed.), Art as Experience (pp. 36–59). New York, NY: Perigree Books. (Original work published 1934)

Dhillon, G. (2007). *Principles of information systems security: Text and cases*. John Wiley & Sons.

Dickie, G. (1969). Defining art. *American Philosophical Quarterly*, 6, 253–256.

Dickie, G. (1974). *Art and the aesthetic*. Ithaca, NY: Cornell University Press.

Dickson, D. (1988). *The New Politics of Science*. Chicago: The University of Chicago Press.

Digital in 2016 report. (2017). Retrieved May 23, 2017, from https://wearesocial.com/uk/special-reports/digital-in-2016)

Dion, K., Berscheid, E., & Walster, E. (1972). What is beautiful is good. *Journal of Personality and Social Psychology*, 24(3), 285–290. doi:10.1037/h0033731 PMID:4655540

Dixson, B., Grimshaw, G., Linklater, W., & Dixson, A. (2011). Eye-tracking of men's preferences for waist-to-hip ratio and breast size of women. *Archives of Sexual Behavior*, 40(1), 43–50. doi:10.100710508-009-9523-5 PMID:19688590

Dohnt, H., & Tiggemann, M. (2006). Body image concerns in young girls: The role of peers and media prior to adolescence. *Journal of Youth and Adolescence*, 35(2), 135–145. doi:10.100710964-005-9020-7

Donnelly, S. B. (2005, December 4). Long-distance warriors. *Time Magazine*.

Doward, J. (2017, March 4). *Did Cambridge Analytica influence the Brexit vote and the US election?* Retrieved July 29, 2017, from https://www.theguardian.com/politics/2017/mar/04/nigel-oakes-cambridge-analytica-what-role-brexit-trump

Dowling, J. P. (2013). *Schrodinger's killer app. Race to build the world's first quantum computer*. Boca Raton, FL: Taylor & Francis. doi:10.1201/b13866

Draper, H., & Sorell, T. (2002). Patients' responsibilities in medical ethics. *Bioethics*, 16(4), 335–352. doi:10.1111/1467-8519.00292 PMID:12956177

Dredge, R., Gleeson, J., & de la Piedad Garcia, X. (2014). Presentation on Facebook and risk of cyberbullying victimization. *Computers in Human Behavior*, 40, 16–22. doi:10.1016/j.chb.2014.07.035

Dresler, M., Sandberg, A., Ohla, K., Bublitz, C., Trenado, C., Mroczko-Wąsowicz, A., ... Repantis, D. (2013). Non-pharmacological cognitive enhancement. *Neuropharmacology*, 64, 529–543. doi:10.1016/j.neuropharm.2012.07.002 PMID:22828638

Drucker, P. F. (1998). The Age of Social Transformation. In G. R. Hickman (Ed.), *Leading Organizations: Perspectives for a New Era* (pp. 538–556). Thousand Oaks, CA: SAGE Publications.

Dubljević, V. (2015). Principles of Justice as the Basis for Public Policy on Psychopharmacological Cognitive Enhancement. *Law, Innovation and Technology*, 4, 1.

Dubljević, V., & Ryan, C. J. (2015). Cognitive enhancement with methylphenidate and modafinil: Conceptual advances and societal implications. *Neuroscience and Neuroeconomics*, 4.

Duff, A. (2008). The normative crisis of the information society. *Cyberpsychology (Brno)*, 2(1), 3. Retrieved from http://cyberpsychology.eu/view.php?cisloclanku=2008051201&article=3

Dunlap, Ch. J. Jr. (n.d.). Accountability and autonomous weapons: Much ado about nothing. *Temple International and Comparative Law Journal*. (forthcoming)

Dunne, J. (1993). *Back to the Rough Ground: "Phronesis" and "Techne"*. Modern Philosophy and in Aristotle.

Dyens, O. (2001). *Metal and flesh: The evolution of man: Technology takes over*. Cambridge, MA: MIT Press.

Dyer, G. (2010). *War: The new edition*. New York: Random House.

Eagly, A. H., Ashmore, R. D., Makhijani, M. G., & Longo, L. C. (1991). What is beautiful is good, but...: A meta-analytic review of research on the physical attractiveness stereotype. *Psychological Bulletin*, *110*(1), 109–128. doi:10.1037/0033-2909.110.1.109

Eaton, M. L., & Illes, J. (2007). Commercializing cognitive neurotechnology—the ethical terrain. *Nature Biotechnology*, *25*(4), 393–397. doi:10.1038/nbt0407-393 PMID:17420741

Economist (2013). The Silicon Valley Letter. *Economist*. Retrieved from http://www.economist.com/blogs/babbage/2013/12/tech-firms-and-spies

Economist. (2015, January 8). *The magic of mining*. Retrieved July 29, 2017, from https://www.economist.com/news/business/21638124-minting-digital-currency-has-become-big-ruthlessly-competitive-business-magic

Edwards, Cortes, Wortman-Jutt, Putrino, Bikson, Thickbroom, & Pascual-Leone. (2017). Transcranial Direct Current Stimulation and Sports Performance. *Frontiers in Human Neuroscience*. 10.3389/fnhum.2017.00243

Eid, M. (Ed.). (2011). *Research methods in communication*. Boston, MA: Pearson.

Einstein, A. (n.d.). *Correspondence with Franklin Delano Roosevelt from August 2, 1939*. Retrieved from http://hyper-textbook.com/eworld/einstein.shtml#first

Eisenhower, D. (n.d.). *D. Farewell address to the nation on January 17, 1961*. Retrieved from http://www.ourdocuments.gov/doc.php?flash=true&doc=90

Eisenstein, E. L. (2012). *The printing revolution in early modern Europe*. New York, NY: Cambridge University Press. doi:10.1017/CBO9781139197038

Ekelhof, M. A. C. (n.d.). Complications of a common language: Why it is so hard to talk about autonomous weapons. *Journal of Conflict and Security Law*. (forthcoming)

Electronic Literature Organization. (1999). *What is E-lit?* Retrieved from https://eliterature.org/what-is-e-lit/

Engebretson, P. (2013). *The basics of hacking and penetration testing: ethical hacking and penetration testing made easy*. Elsevier.

Ericksen, W. L., & Billick, S. B. (2012). Psychiatric issues in cosmetic plastic surgery. *The Psychiatric Quarterly*, *83*(3), 343–352. doi:10.100711126-012-9204-8 PMID:22252848

Eronia, O. (2012). Doping mentale and concetto di salute: A possibile regolamentazione legislative? *Archivio penale*, 3.

Ethical code of information society. 36 general conference of UNESCO. (2011). Retrieved February 05, 2015 http://unesdoc.unesco.org/images/0021/002126/212696e.pdf

ETICA Project. (2011). Retrieved August 1, 2017, from http://www.etica-project.eu/

ETICA Report Summary. (2011). Retrieved August 1, 2017, from http://cordis.europa.eu/result/rcn/56066_en.html

Fabian, B. (2008). *Secure name services for the Internet of Things* (Unpublished doctoral dissertation). Humboldt-Universität zu Berlin, Wirtschaftswissenschaftliche Fakultät.

Faiola, A., & Matei, S. A. (2005). Cultural cognitive style and web design: Beyond a behavioral inquiry into computer-mediated communication. *Journal of Computer-Mediated Communication*, *11*(1), 375–394. doi:10.1111/j.1083-6101.2006.tb00318.x

Farah, M. J. (2005). Neuroethics: The practical and the philosophical. *Trends in Cognitive Sciences*, *9*(1), 34–40. doi:10.1016/j.tics.2004.12.001 PMID:15639439

Farah, M. J., Illes, J., Cook-Deegan, R., Gardner, H., Kandel, E., King, P., ... Wolpe, P. R. (2004). Neurocognitive enhancement: What can we do and what should we do? *Nature Reviews. Neuroscience*, *5*(5), 421–425. doi:10.1038/nrn1390 PMID:15100724

Faraone, S., Spencer, T., Madras, B., Zhang-James, Y., & Biederman, J. (2014). Functional effects of dopamine transporter gene genotypes on in vivo dopamine transporter functioning: A meta-analysis. *Molecular Psychiatry*, *19*(8), 880–889. doi:10.1038/mp.2013.126 PMID:24061496

Farhangi, H. (2010). The path of the smart grid. *IEEE Power & Energy Magazine*, *8*(1), 18–28. doi:10.1109/MPE.2009.934876

Farmer, J. D., & Skouras, Sp. (2010). *An ecological perspective on the future of computer trading*. Government Office for Science London.

Feld, S., & Carter, W. (1998). Foci of activity as changing concepts for friendship. In R. Adams & A. Graham (Eds.), *Placing Friendship In Context* (pp. 136–152). Cambridge, UK: Cambridge University Press.

Ferrara, E. (2017, July 1). *Disinformation and Social Bot Operations in the Run Up to the 2017 French Presidential Election*. Retrieved July 29, 2017, from https://papers.ssrn.com/sol3/papers.cfm?abstract_id=2995809

Fettahoglu, E., Satilmis, A., Gokcen, C., & Ozatalay, E. (2009). Oral megadose methylphenidate ingestion for suicide attempt. *Pediatrics International*, *51*(6), 844–845. doi:10.1111/j.1442-200X.2009.02929.x PMID:20158630

Fetz, E. E. (2007). Volitional control of neural activity: Implications for brain–computer interfaces. *The Journal of Physiology*, *579*(3), 571–579. doi:10.1113/jphysiol.2006.127142 PMID:17234689

Fielding, M. (2006). Robotics in future land warfare. *Australian Army Journal*, *3*(2), 99–108.

Fieser, J., & Dowden, B. (2007). Just war theory. *The Internet Encyclopedia of Philosophy*. Retrieved June 26, 2017, from http//www.iep.utm.edu/j/justwar.htm

Finance Watch. (2012). Investing not Betting. Making Financial markets serve society. *Finance Watch*.

Fink, B., & Neave, N. (2005). The biology of facial beauty. *International Journal of Cosmetic Science*, *27*(6), 317–325. doi:10.1111/j.1467-2494.2005.00286.x PMID:18492169

Fins, J. J. (2007). Mind wars: Brain research and national defense. *Journal of the American Medical Association*, *297*(12), 1382–1383. doi:10.1001/jama.297.12.1382

Fischer, M. A. (2012). *Manic Nation: Dr. Peter Whybrow says we're addicted to stress*. Retrieved February 03, 2016 from http://www.psmag.com/health/manic-nation-dr-peter-whybrow-says-were-addicted-stress-42695/

Fischer, J. M., & Ravizza, M. (1998). *Responsibility and control: A theory of moral responsibility*. Cambridge, UK: Cambridge University Press. doi:10.1017/CBO9780511814594

Fitzsimonds, J. R., & Mahnken, T. G. (2007). Military officer attitudes toward UAV adoption: Exploring institutional expediments to innovation. *Joint Forces Quarterly*, *46*(3), 96–103.

Floridi. (2013). *The ethics of information*. Oxford, UK: Oxford University Press.

Floridi, L. (2005). The ontological interpretation of informational privacy. *Ethics and Information Technology*, *7*(7), 185–200. doi:10.100710676-006-0001-7

Foddy, B. (2011). Enhancing Skill. In Enhancing Human Capacities. Oxford, UK: Blackwell. doi:10.1002/9781444393552. ch23

Foddy, B. (2008). Risks and asterisks: neurological enhancements in baseball. In *Your Brain on Cubs: Inside the Heads of Players and Fans*. Washington, DC: Dana Press.

Forbes. (n.d.). *5 hot on-line social networks*. Retrieved June 27, 2017 from http://m.forbes.ru/article.php?

Forge J. (2007b). No Consolation for Kalashnikov. *Philosophy Now*, 6-8.

Forge, J. (2004). The Morality of Weapons Research. *Science and Engineering Ethics*, *10*(3), 531–542. doi:10.100711948-004-0010-z PMID:15362709

Forge, J. (2007a). What are the Moral Limits of Weapons Research? *Philosophy in the Contemporary World*, *14*(1), 79–88. doi:10.5840/pcw200714120

Forge, J. (2008). *The Responsible Scientist: A Philosophical Analysis*. Pittsburgh, PA: Pittsburgh University Press.

Forge, J. (2009). Proportionality, Just War Theory and Weapons Innovation. *Science and Engineering Ethics*, *15*(1), 25–38. doi:10.100711948-008-9088-z PMID:18802788

Forge, J. (2010). A Note on the Definition of Dual-Use. *Science and Engineering Ethics*, *16*(1), 111–117. doi:10.100711948-009-9159-9 PMID:19685170

Forge, J. (2011). *The Morality of Weapons Research*. Wiley-Blackwell International Encyclopaedia of Ethics.

Forge, J. (2012). *Designed to Kill: The Case Against Weapons Research*. Dordrecht: Springer.

Forge, J. (2017a). *Science, Ethics and Weapons Research in Encyclopedia of Information Science and Technology* (4th ed.). Hershey, PA: IGI Global.

Forge, J. (2017b). *The Morality of Weapons Design and Development: Emerging Research and Opportunities*. Hershey, PA: IGI global.

Fowler and Goodman. (2017, June 22). *Opinion | How Tinder Could Take Back the White House*. Retrieved July 29, 2017, from https://www.nytimes.com/2017/06/22/opinion/how-tinder-could-take-back-the-white-house.html?smid=tw-share

Fowler, L. A., & Moore, A. R. (2012). Breast implants for graduation: A sociological examination of daughter and mother narratives. *Sociology Mind*, *2*(1), 109–115. doi:10.4236m.2012.21014

Fox, M. D., Snyder, A. Z., Vincent, J. L., Corbetta, M., Van Essen, D. C., & Raichle, M. E. (2005). The human brain is intrinsically organized into dynamic, anticorrelated functional networks. *Proceedings of the National Academy of Sciences of the United States of America*, *102*(27), 9673–9678. doi:10.1073/pnas.0504136102 PMID:15976020

Franceschi-Bicchierai, L. (2014, July 5). *The 10 Biggest Revelations From Edward Snowden's Leaks.* Accessed July 29, 2017, from http://mashable.com/2014/06/05/edward-snowden-revelations/#w51EfljJMPqx

Frederick, D. A., Peplau, A., & Lever, J. (2008). The Barbie mystique: Satisfaction with breast size and shape across the lifespan. *International Journal of Sexual Health, 20*(3), 200–211. doi:10.1080/19317610802240170

Freedom House. (2016). *Freedom in the World 2016.* Retrieved July 29, 2017, from https://freedomhouse.org/report/freedom-world/freedom-world-2016

Freitas, R. A. (1999). *Basic capabilities.* Georgetown, TX: Landes Bioscience.

Freitas, R. A. (2002). The future of nanofabrication and molecular scale devices in nanomedicine. *Studies in Health Technology and Informatics,* 45–60. PMID:12026137

Freitas, R. A., & Havukkala, I. (2005). Current status of nanomedicine and medical nanorobotics. *Journal of Computational and Theoretical Nanoscience, 2*(1), 1–25.

Freitas, R. A. Jr. (2005). Nanotechnology, nanomedicine and nanosurgery. *International Journal of Surgery, 3*(4), 243–246. doi:10.1016/j.ijsu.2005.10.007 PMID:17462292

Freitas, R. A., & Nanomedicine, V. I. (2003). *Biocompatibility.* Georgetown, TX: Landes Bioscience.

Fried, C. B. (2008). In-class laptop use and its effects on student learning. *Computers & Education, 50*(3), 906–914. doi:10.1016/j.compedu.2006.09.006

Frodl, T. (2010). Comorbidity of ADHD and Substance Use Disorder (SUD): A neuroimaging perspective. *Journal of Attention Disorders, 14*(2), 109–120. doi:10.1177/1087054710365054 PMID:20495160

Frodl, T., & Skokauskas, N. (2012). Meta-analysis of structural MRI studies in children and adults with attention deficit hyperactivity disorder indicates treatment effects. *Acta Psychiatrica Scandinavica, 125*(2), 114–126. doi:10.1111/j.1600-0447.2011.01786.x PMID:22118249

Fukuyama, F. (1992). *The end of history and the last man.* New York: Free Press.

Fukuyama, F. (2002). *Our Posthuman Future: Consequences of the Biotechnology Revolution.* London: Profile Books.

Furnham, A., & Swami, V. (2007). Perception of female buttocks and breast size in profile. *Social Behavior and Personality, 35*(1), 1–7. doi:10.2224bp.2007.35.1.1

Furtado, M. (2010a, December 24). Heidi Montag exposes her numerous plastic surgery battle wounds. *The Vancouver Sun (British Columbia),* p. C4.

Furtado, M. (2010b, December 27). Heidi Montag regrets her cosmetic surgery. *The Daily Gleaner (New Brunswick),* p. C16.

Gagné, P., & McGaughey, D. (2002). Designing women: Cultural hegemony and the exercise of power among women who have undergone elective mammoplasty. *Gender & Society, 16*(6), 814–838. doi:10.1177/089124302237890

Galbraith, J. K. (1967). The New Industrial State. Boston: Houghton Mifflin.

Galliott, J. C. (n.d.). *Military robots: Mapping the moral landscape.* Farnham: Ashgate. (forthcoming)

Gallup, G. G. Jr, Frederick, M. J., & Pipitone, R. N. (2008). Morphology and behavior: Phrenology revisited. *Review of General Psychology, 12*(3), 297–304. doi:10.1037/1089-2680.12.3.297

Galván, J. M. (2012). Insights from Christian anthropology for a water-related technoethics. *Water Policy*, *14*(S1), 48. doi:10.2166/wp.2012.004

Garcia, J. (2010, January 25). Obsessed with being "perfect.". *People*, *73*, 80–88.

Garner, R. T., & Rosen, B. (1967). *Moral philosophy: A systematic introduction to normative ethics and meta-ethics.* New York: Macmillan.

Garnham, B. (2013). Designing "older" rather than denying ageing: Problematizing anti-ageing discourse in relation to cosmetic surgery undertaken by older people. *Journal of Aging Studies*, *27*(1), 38–46. doi:10.1016/j.jaging.2012.11.001 PMID:23273555

Garraway, C. (2009). The doctrine of command responsibility. In J. Doria, H.-P. Gasser, & M. C. Bassiouni (Eds.), *The legal regime of the international criminal court* (pp. 703–725). Leiden: Nijhoff. doi:10.1163/ej.9789004163089.i-1122.194

Gasson, M., Hutt, B., Goodhew, I., Kyberd, P., & Warwick, K. (2005). Invasive neural prosthesis for neural signal detection and nerve stimulation. *International Journal of Adaptive Control and Signal Processing*, *19*(5), 365–375.

Gazzaley, A., Cooney, J. W., McEvoy, K., Knight, R. T., & D'esposito, M. (2005). Top-down enhancement and suppression of the magnitude and speed of neural activity. *Journal of Cognitive Neuroscience*, *17*(3), 507–517. doi:10.1162/0898929053279522 PMID:15814009

Geelen, J. (2012). *The Emerging Neurotechnologies: Recent Developments and Policy Implications.* Policy Horizons Canada.

Gert, B. (2004). *Common Morality.* Oxford, UK: Oxford University Press. doi:10.1093/0195173716.001.0001

Gert, B. (2005). *Morality: Its Nature and Justification* (Revised Edition). Oxford, UK: Oxford University Press. doi:10.1093/0195176898.001.0001

Gertz, N. (2011). *Technology and suffering in war.* Paper presented at Technology and Security, University of North Texas.

Gibbons, S. (2010). Collaborating like never before: Reading and writing through a wiki. *English Journal*, *99*(5), 35–39.

Gibson, W. (2003, June 24). *The Road to Oceania.* Retrieved July 29, 2017, from http://www.nytimes.com/2003/06/25/opinion/the-road-to-oceania.html

Giglioli, E., Panzacchi, C., & Senni, L. (2010). *How Europe is approaching the smart grid.* McKinsey on Smart Grid report, McKinsey & Company. Retrieved November 13, 2014, from http://www.mckinsey.com/client_service/electric_power_and_natural_gas/latest_thinking/mckinsey_on_smart_grid

Gilbert, R. L., Murphy, N. A., & Ávalos, C. M. (2011). Communication Patterns and Satisfaction Levels in Three-Dimensional Versus Real-Life Intimate Relationships. *Cyberpsychology, Behavior, and Social Networking*, *14*(10), 585–589. doi:10.1089/cyber.2010.0468 PMID:21381970

Gillepsie. (2014). *The relevance of algorithms.* Retrieved from http://www.tarletongillespie.org/essays/Gillespie%20-%20The%20Relevance%20of%20Algorithms.pdf

Gillin, J. (2010, August 26). Montag wants implants out. *St. Petersburg Times,* p. 2B.

Gillon, R. (1994). Medical ethics: Four principles plus attention to scope. *BMJ: British Medical Journal*, *309*(6948), 184–188. doi:10.1136/bmj.309.6948.184 PMID:8044100

Gimlin, D. (2006). The absent body project: Cosmetic surgery as a response to bodily dys-appearance. *Sociology*, *40*(4), 699–716. doi:10.1177/0038038506065156

Gimlin, D. (2010). Imagining the other in cosmetic surgery. *Body & Society, 16*(4), 57–76. doi:10.1177/1357034X10383881

Giordano, J. (Ed.). (2012). *Neurotechnology: Premises, potential, and problems.* CRC Press. doi:10.1201/b11861

Giordano, J., Akhouri, R., & McBride, D. K. (2009). Implantable Nano-Neurotechnological Devices: Consideration of Ethical, Legal, and Social Issues and Implications. *Journal of Long-Term Effects of Medical Implants, 19*(1), 83–93. doi:10.1615/JLongTermEffMedImplants.v19.i1.80 PMID:20402632

Girard, B., & Siochrú, S. O. (2003). *Communicating in the information society.* Geneva: United Nations Research Institute for Social Development.

Goethe, J. W. v. (1988). *Faust, Part I* (German-English ed.). New York: Bantam Classics.

Goodall, S., Howatson, G., Romer, L., & Ross, E. (2012). Transcranial magnetic stimulation in sport science: A commentary. *European Journal of Sport Science.* doi:10.1080/17461391.2012.704079 PMID:24444227

Gordijn, B. (2006). Converging NBIC technologies for improving human performance: A critical assessment of the novelty and the prospects of the project. *The Journal of Law, Medicine & Ethics, 4*(34), 726–732. doi:10.1111/j.1748-720X.2006.00092.x PMID:17199814

Gore, A. (n.d.). *BrainyQuote.com.* Retrieved August 31, 2017, from BrainyQuote.com Web site: https://www.brainyquote.com/quotes/quotes/a/algore457743.html

Grammer, K., Fink, B., Møller, A. P., & Thornhill, R. (2003). Darwinian aesthetics: Sexual selection and the biology of beauty. *Biological Reviews of the Cambridge Philosophical Society, 78*(3), 385–407. doi:10.1017/S1464793102006085 PMID:14558590

Graves, K. (2010). *CEH certified ethical hacker study guide.* John Wiley & Sons.

Gray, G. J. (1959). *The warriors: Reflections on men in battle.* New York: Harper & Row.

Green Button Alliance. (2015). *Green Button for my home.* Retrieved from http://www.greenbuttondata.org/residential.html

Greene, J. (2004). Article. *Philosophical Transactions of the Royal Society of London. Series B, Biological Sciences, 359*, 1776.

Greenhill, L., Pliszka, S., & Dulcan, M. (2002). Practice Parameter for the Use of Stimulant Medications in the Treatment of Children, Adolescents, and Adults. *Journal of the American Academy of Child and Adolescent Psychiatry, 41*(2), 26S–49S. doi:10.1097/00004583-200202001-00003 PMID:11833633

Greveler, U., Justus, B., & Loehr, D. (2012). *Multimedia content identification through smart meter power usage profiles.* Computers, Privacy and Data Protection.

Grossman, D. (1995). *On killing: The psychological cost of learning to kill in war and society.* Boston: Little, Brown and Company.

Guadagno, R. E., Rempala, D. M., Murphy, S., & Okdie, B. M. (2013). What makes a video go viral? An analysis of emotional contagion and Internet memes. *Computers in Human Behavior, 29*(6), 2312–2319. doi:10.1016/j.chb.2013.04.016

Gunkel, D. J. (2012). The machine question. Critical perspectives on AI, robots, and ethics. Cambridge, MA: The MIT Press.

Gupta, S. (2012). Ethical and legal issues in aesthetic surgery. *Indian Journal of Plastic Surgery: Official Publication of the Association of Plastic Surgeons of India, 45*(3), 547–549. doi:10.4103/0970-0358.105973 PMID:23450235

Guston, D. H. & Keniston, Kenneth. Editors. (1994). The Fragile Contract, University Science and the Government, Cambridge, MA: The MIT Press.

Gymrek, M., McGuire, A. L., Golan, D., Halperin, E., & Erlich, Y. (2013). Identifying personal genomes by surname inference. *Science*, *339*(6117), 321–324. doi:10.1126cience.1229566 PMID:23329047

Haas, B. (2017, July 11). *China moves to block internet VPNs from 2018*. Accessed July 29, 2017, from https://www.theguardian.com/world/2017/jul/11/china-moves-to-block-internet-vpns-from-2018?CMP=share_btn_tw

Haberer, J. (1969). *Politics and the Community of Science*. New York: Van Nostrand Reinhold.

Habermas, J. (1985). *Theorie der Kommunikativen Handelns*. Frankfurt am Main, Germany: Suhrkamp Verlag.

Hadley, M., Lu, N., & Deborah, A. (2010). Smart-grid security issues. *IEEE Security and Privacy*, *8*(1), 81–85. doi:10.1109/MSP.2010.49

Haggerty, K. D., & Ericson, R. V. (2006). The new politics of surveillance and visibility. In K. D. Haggerty & R. V. Ericson (Eds.), *The new politics of surveillance and visibility* (pp. 3–25). Toronto: University of Toronto Press.

Hamidi, M., Johson, J. S., Feredoes, E., & Postle, B. R. (2011). Does high-frequency repetitive transcranial magnetic stimulation produce residual and/or cumulative effects within an experimental session? *Brain Topography*, *23*(4), 355–367. doi:10.100710548-010-0153-y PMID:20623171

Hamilton, J. (2015). *Indirect flights*. Retrieved from http://indirect.flights/

Hammond, D. (2005). Philosophical and Ethical Foundations for systems thinking. *TripleC (Cognition, Communication, Co-operation), 3*(2), 20-27.

Han, X., Qian, X., Bernstein, J. G., Zhou, H. H., Franzesi, G. T., Stern, P., ... Boyden, E. S. (2009). Millisecond-timescale optical control of neural dynamics in the nonhuman primate brain. *Neuron*, *62*(2), 191–198. doi:10.1016/j.neuron.2009.03.011 PMID:19409264

Haraway, D. (1991). A cyborg manifesto: Science, technology, and socialist feminism in the late twentieth century. In D. Haraway (Ed.), *Simians, Cyborgs and Women: The Reinvention of Nature* (pp. 149–182). New York, NY: Routledge.

Hardell, L., & Sage, C. (2008). Biological effects from electromagnetic field exposure and public exposure standards. *Biomedicine and Pharmacotherapy*, *62*(2), 104–109. doi:10.1016/j.biopha.2007.12.004 PMID:18242044

Hardwick-Smith, S. (2011). Examining the controversy in aesthetic vaginal surgery. *The American Journal of Cosmetic Surgery*, *28*(3), 106–113. doi:10.5992/0748-8068-28.3.106

Hargreaves, D. A., & Tiggemann, M. (2009). Muscular ideal media images and men's body image: Social comparison processing and individual vulnerability. *Psychology of Men & Masculinity*, *10*(2), 109–119. doi:10.1037/a0014691

Harper, B., & Tiggemann, M. (2008). The effect of thin ideal media images on women's self-objectification, mood, and body image. *Sex Roles*, *58*(9), 649–657. doi:10.100711199-007-9379-x

Harris, D. L., & Carr, A. T. (2001). The Derriford appearance scale (DAS59): A new psychometric scale for the evaluation of patients with disfigurements and aesthetic problems of appearance. *British Journal of Plastic Surgery*, *54*(3), 216–222. doi:10.1054/bjps.2001.3559 PMID:11254413

Harris, J. (2012). Chemical cognitive enhancement: is it unfair, unjust, discriminatory, or cheating for healthy adults to use smart drugs?—-2. In J. Illes & B. Sahakian (Eds.), *Oxford Handbook of Neuroethics*. Oxford, UK: Oxford University.

Harris, S., Harper, A., Eagle, C., & Ness, J. (2007). *Gray hat hacking*. McGraw-Hill, Inc.

Hatuka, T., & Toch, E. (2012). *Smart-Spaces: Smartphone's Influence on Perceptions of the Public Space.* Toch Research Group, Tel-Aviv University. Retrieved October 29, 2013, from http://www.aftau.org/site/ News2?page=NewsArticle&id=16519

Hawaii State Energy Office. (2017, May). *Hawaii energy facts and figures.* Retrieved from https://energy.hawaii.gov/ wp-content/uploads/2011/10/HSEOFactsFigures_May2017_2.pdf

Hawaiian Electric Company. (2008). *Hawaiian Electric selects Sensus FlexNet AMI: Success of pilot projects results in definitive agreement* [Press release]. Retrieved from: http://www.heco.com/vcmcontent/StaticFiles/pdf/Sensus_AMI_ HECO_12-23-08_FINAL.pdf

Hayles, K. (2008). *Electronic literature: new horizons for the literary.* Notre Dame, IN: University of Notre Dame Press.

Healy, D. (2008). Birth, Ritalin, Prozac, Viagra, Death. In T. C. Bennett & I. Karpin (Eds.), *Brave New World of Health* (pp. 112–128). Sydney: The Federation Press.

Healy, J. M. (2011). *Endangered Minds: Why Children Dont Think And What We Can Do About I.* New York, NY: Simon and Schuster.

Heath, D. (1996). Modest interventions. In G. Downey & J. Dumit (Eds.), *Cyborgs and citadels* (pp. 67–82). Santa Fe, NM: School of American Research.

Heemskerk, J., & Paesmans, D. (1995). *jodi.org.* Retrieved from http://geogeo.jodi.org/

Heetderks, W. J. (1988). RF powering of millimeter-and submillimeter-sized neural prosthetic implants. *Biomedical Engineering. IEEE Transactions on, 35*(5), 323–327. PMID:3397079

Heidegger, M. (1927). *Being and time (Dutch edition).* Nijmegen: SUN.

Heidegger, M. (1977). *The question concerning technology and other essays.* New York: Harper & Row Publishers Inc.

Heidi Pratt's secret trauma and double-d regrets: "I literally chopped up my own body." (2014). *Extra.* Retrieved from http://extratv.com/2014/11/20/heidi-pratts-secret-trauma-and-double-d-regrets-i-literally-chopped-up-my-own-body

Heidi says she'll get more done; Will do some "maintenance." (2010, February 15). *Chicago Sun Times,* p. 31.

Heim, M. (1993). *The Metaphysics of Virtual Reality.* New York: Oxford University Press.

Heller, P. B. (2012). Technoethics: The Dilemma of Doing the Right Moral Thing in Technology Applications. *International Journal of Technoethics, 3*(1), 14–27. doi:10.4018/jte.2012010102

Hellström, T. (2013). On the moral responsibility of military robots. *Ethics and Information Technology, 15*(2), 99–107. doi:10.100710676-012-9301-2

Helmchen, H., & Sartorius, N. (Eds.). (2010). *Ethics in Psychiatry European Contributions.* Springer. doi:10.1007/978-90-481-8721-8

Helmer, S. M., Pischke, C. R., Van Hal, G., Vriesacker, B., Dempsey, R. C., Akvardar, Y., ... Zeeb, H. (2016). Personal and perceived peer use and attitudes towards the use of nonmedical prescription stimulants to improve academic performance among university students in seven European countries. *Drug and Alcohol Dependence, 168,* 128–134. doi:10.1016/j. drugalcdep.2016.08.639 PMID:27639131

Henckaerts, J.-M., & Doswald-Beck, L. (2009). Customary international humanitarian law: Vol. I. *Rules.* Cambridge, UK: ICRC and Cambridge University Press.

Hendershott & Riordan, R. (2009). *Algorithmic Trading and Information.* Econ papers No. 09-08. Working Papers NET Institute.

Hendershott, T., & Moulton, P. C. (2011). Automation, speed, and stock market quality: The NYSE's hybrid. *Journal of Financial Markets, 14*(4), 568–604. doi:10.1016/j.finmar.2011.02.003

Hennink-Kaminski, H., Reid, L. N., & King, K. W. (2010). The content of cosmetic surgery advertisements placed in large city magazines, 1985-2004. *Journal of Current Issues and Research in Advertising, 32*(2), 41–57. doi:10.1080/1 0641734.2010.10505284

Henseler, H., Smith, J., Bowman, A., Khambay, B. S., Ju, X., Ayoub, A., & Ray, A. K. (2013). Subjective versus objective assessment of breast reconstruction. *Journal of Plastic, Reconstructive & Aesthetic Surgery; JPRAS, 66*(5), 634–639. doi:10.1016/j.bjps.2013.01.006 PMID:23402935

Hern, A. (2017, March 29). *UK government can force encryption removal, but fears losing, experts say.* Accessed July 29, 2017, from https://www.theguardian.com/technology/2017/mar/29/uk-government-encryption-whatsapp-investigatory-powers-act

Hesapcioglu, S., Goker, Z., Bilginer, C., & Kandil, S. (2012). Methylphenidate Induced Psychotic Symptoms: Two Cases Report. *Journal of Medical Cases.*

Hester, D. M. (2001). *Community as healing: pragmatist ethics in medical encounters.* Rowman & Littlefield.

Hetke, J. F., & Anderson, D. J. (2002). Silicon microelectrodes for extracellular recording. Handbook of Neuroprosthetic Methods, 163-91.

Heyes, C. J. (2007). Cosmetic surgery and the televisual makeover. *Feminist Media Studies, 7*(1), 17–32. doi:10.1080/14680770601103670

Heylighen, F., Heath, M., & Van Overwalle, F. (2004). The emergence of distributed cognition: a conceptual framework. *Proceedings of Collective Intentionality IV.*

Hilbert, M., & López, P. (2011). The world's technological capacity to store, communicate, and compute information. *Science, 332*(6025), 60–65. doi:10.1126cience.1200970 PMID:21310967

Hill, K. (2012, February 16). How Target figured out a teen girl was pregnant before her father did. *Forbes.* Retrieved from http://www.forbes.com/sites/kashmirhill/2012/02/16/how-target-figured-out-a-teen-girl-was-pregnant-before-her-father-did/

Hill, A. T., Fitzgerald, P. B., & Hoy, K. E. (2016). Effects of Anodal Transcranial Direct Current Stimulation on Working Memory: A Systematic Review and Meta-Analysis of Findings from Healthy and Neuropsychiatric Populations. *Brain Stimulation, 9*(2), 197–208. doi:10.1016/j.brs.2015.10.006 PMID:26597929

Hirsch, E. D. Jr. (1980). In defense of the author. In E. D. Hirsch (Ed.), *Jr., Validity in interpretation* (pp. 1–19). New Haven, CT: Yale University Press.

Hissam, S., Klein, M., & Moreno, G. A. (2013). *Socio-Adaptive systems challenge problem Workshop report.* Carnegie Mellon Software Engineering Institute Chicago. CMU/SEI-2013-SR-010.

Hoberman, J. (1992). *Mortal Engines. The Science of Performance and the Dehumanization of Sport.* New York: The Free Press.

Hofstadter, R. (1964). *The Paranoid Style in American Politics and Other Essays.* Cambridge, MA: Harvard University Press.

Holland, J. H. (1992). Genetic Algorithms. *Scientific American, 267*(July), 66–72. doi:10.1038cientificamerican0792-66

Hollenback, K. (2015). *Simple business machines.* Retrieved from http://www.katehollenbach.com/simple-business-machines/

Holliday, R., & Sanchez Taylor, J. (2006). Aesthetic surgery as false beauty. *Feminist Theory, 7*(2), 179–195. doi:10.1177/1464700106064418

Holme, S., & McNamee, M. (2011). Physical Enhancement: What Baseline, Whose Judgment? In Enhancing Human Capacities. Oxford, UK: Blackwell.

Hölzel, B., Carmody, J., Vangel, M., Congleton, C., Yerramsetti, S., Gard, T., & Lazar, S. (2011). Mindfulness practice leads to increases in regional brain gray matter density. *Psychiatry Research, 191*(1), 36–43. doi:10.1016/j.pscychresns.2010.08.006 PMID:21071182

Hope, D. A., & Mindell, J. A. (1994). Global social skill ratings: Measures of social behavior or physical attractiveness? *Behaviour Research and Therapy, 32*(4), 463–469. doi:10.1016/0005-7967(94)90011-6 PMID:8192645

Horvath, J. C., Forte, J. D., & Carter, O. (2015). Quantitative review finds no evidence of cognitive effects in healthy populations from single-session transcranial direct current stimulation (tDCS). *Brain Stimulation, 8*(3), 535–550. doi:10.1016/j.brs.2015.01.400 PMID:25701175

Hosseini, K., Shahgholian, M., & Abdollahi, M.-H. (2015). Hardiness, defense mechanisms, negative self-portrayal scale in applicants and non-applicants of cosmetic surgery. *International Journal of Behavioral Sciences, 10*(1), 26–31.

Housden, C. R., Morein-Zamir, S., & Sahakian, B. J. (2011). Cognitive Enhancing Drugs: Neuroscience and Society. In Enhancing Human Capacities. Oxford, UK: Blackwell.

Human Right Council. (2013). *Report of the special rapporteur on extrajudicial,summary or arbitrary executions, Christof Heyns (A/HRC/23/47).* United Nations.

Hume, D. (2006). Of the standard of taste. In E. F. Miller (Ed.), Essays: Moral, political, and literary (pp. 231–258). New York, NY: Cosimo, Inc. (Original work published 1742)

Husain, M., & Mehta, M. (2011). Cognitive enhancement by drugs in health and disease. *Trends in Cognitive Sciences, 15*(1), 28–36. doi:10.1016/j.tics.2010.11.002 PMID:21146447

Husted, B. (2009a, November 6). A red Letterman day for Crested Butte fan. *Denver Post,* p. B03.

Husted, B. (2009b, August 14). Heidi 'n' seek: Playboy, hubby reveal a bit about her. *Denver Post,* p. B03.

Ihde, D. (2009). The Designer Fallacy and Technological Imagination. In P. Vermass & … (Eds.), *Philosophy and Design* (pp. 51–60). Berlin: Springer.

Illes, J., Kirschen, M. P., & Gabrieli, J. D. (2003). From neuroimaging to neuroethics. *Nature Neuroscience, 6*(3), 205–205. doi:10.1038/nn0303-205 PMID:12601375

Innovation Electricity Efficiency Institute. (2013, August). *Utility-scale smart meter deployments: A foundation for expanded grid benefits.* Washington, DC: Innovation Electricity Efficiency Institute. Retrieved from http://www.edisonfoundation.net/iee/Documents/ IEE_SmartMeterUpdate_0813.pdf

International Organization for Standardization. (2011). *Robots for industrial environments - Safety requirements.* Retrieved June 26, 2017, from http://www.iso.org/iso/iso_catalogue/catalogue_tc/catalogue_detail.htm?csnumber=36322

Inukai, Y., Saito, K., Sasaki, R., Tsuiki, S., Miyaguchi, S., Kojima, S., ... Onishi, H. (2016). Comparison of Three Non-Invasive Transcranial Electrical Stimulation Methods for Increasing Cortical Excitability. *Frontiers in Human Neuroscience, 10*(December), 1–7. PMID:28082887

Isaacs, R. E., Weber, D. J., & Schwartz, A. B. (2000). Work toward real-time control of a cortical neural prothesis. *Rehabilitation Engineering. IEEE Transactions on, 8*(2), 196–198. PMID:10896185

Isa, T., Fetz, E. E., & Müller, K. R. (2009). Recent advances in brain–machine interfaces. *Neural Networks, 22*(9), 1201–1202. doi:10.1016/j.neunet.2009.10.003 PMID:19840893

Isenberg, D. (2007). Robots replace trigger fingers in Iraq. *Asia Times Online*. Retrieved June 26, 2017, from http://www.atimes.com/atimes/Middle_East/IH29Ak01.html

ITU (International Telecommunication Union). (2013). ICT Facts and Figures –. *WORLD (Oakland, Calif.), 2013*. Retrieved from http://www.itu.int/en/ITU-D/Statistics/Documents/facts/ICTFactsFigures2013-e.pdf

Jackson, A., Moritz, C. T., Mavoori, J., Lucas, T. H., & Fetz, E. E. (2006). The Neurochip BCI: Towards a neural prosthesis for upper limb function. *Neural Systems and Rehabilitation Engineering. IEEE Transactions on, 14*(2), 187–190.

Jackson, T., Jiang, C., & Chen, H. (2017). Associations between Chinese/Asian versus Western mass media influences and body image disturbances of young Chinese women. *Body Image, 17*, 175–183. doi:10.1016/j.bodyim.2016.03.007 PMID:27110965

Jacob, M. C. (Ed.). (2000). *The Politics of Western Science*. Amherst, MA: Humanity Books.

Jaimes, A. (2010). Data mining for user modeling and personalization in ubiquitous spaces. In H. Nakashima, H. Aghajan, & J. C. Augusto (Eds.), *Handbook of ambient intelligence and smart environments* (pp. 1015–1038). London: Springer-Verlag. doi:10.1007/978-0-387-93808-0_38

Jausovec, N., & Jausovec, K. (2014). Increasing working memory capacity with theta transcranial alternating current stimulation (tACS). *Biological Psychology, 96*(1), 42–47. doi:10.1016/j.biopsycho.2013.11.006 PMID:24291565

Jausovec, N., Jausovec, K., & Pahor, A. (2014). The influence of theta transcranial alternating current stimulation (tACS) on working memory storage and processing functions. *Acta Psychologica, 146*(1), 1–6. doi:10.1016/j.actpsy.2013.11.011 PMID:24361739

Jeffreys, S. (2005). *Beauty and misogyny: Harmful cultural practices in the West*. London: Routledge.

Jerslev, A. (2006). The mediated body. *Nordicom Review, 27*(2), 133–151. doi:10.1515/nor-2017-0235

Jiang, X., Liu, D., & Chen, B. (2014). Middle temporal vein: A fatal hazard in injection cosmetic surgery for temple augmentation. *JAMA Facial Plastic Surgery, 16*(3), 227–229. doi:10.1001/jamafacial.2013.2565 PMID:24577714

Johnson, A. M., & Axinn, S. (2013). The morality of autonomous robots. *Journal of Military Ethics, 12*(2), 129–141. doi:10.1080/15027570.2013.818399

Johnson, N., Zao, G., Hunsader, E., Qi, H., Johnosn, N., Meng, J., & Tivnan, B. (2013). Abrupt rise of new machine ecology beyond human response time. *Scientific Reports, 3*(1), 2627. doi:10.1038rep02627 PMID:24022120

Johnson, S. (2012). *Future Perfect: The Case for Progress in a Networked Age*. New York: Riverhead Books.

Johnson, S. K., Podratz, K. E., Dipboye, R. L., & Gibbons, E. (2010). Physical attractiveness biases in ratings of employment suitability: Tracking down the "beauty is beastly" effect. *The Journal of Social Psychology, 150*(3), 301–318. doi:10.1080/00224540903365414 PMID:20575336

Jonas, H. (1984). The Imperative of Responsibility. In *Search of Ethics for the Technological Age*. University of Chicago Press.

Jones, B. C., Little, A. C., Penton-Voak, I. S., Tiddeman, B. P., Burt, D. M., & Perrett, D. I. (2001). Facial symmetry and judgements of apparent health: Support for a "good genes" explanation of the attractiveness-symmetry relationship. *Evolution and Human Behavior*, *22*(6), 417–429. doi:10.1016/S1090-5138(01)00083-6

Jonsen, A. R. (1998). *The Birth of Bioethics*. Oxford University Press.

Jordan, B. (2007). Half of predators fielded have been lost. *Air Force Times*. Retrieved June 26, 2017, from http://www.airforcetimes.com/news/2007/02/AFpredatorlosses070223

Jordan, J. (2004). The rhetorical limits of the "plastic body.". *The Quarterly Journal of Speech*, *90*(3), 327–358. doi:10.1080/0033563042000255543

Jothilakshmi, P. K., Salvi, N. R., Hayden, B. E., & Bose-Haider, B. (2009). Labial reduction in adolescent population—A case series study. *Journal of Pediatric and Adolescent Gynecology*, *22*(1), 53–55. doi:10.1016/j.jpag.2008.03.008 PMID:19241623

Joy, B. (2000). Why the future doesn't need us. *Nanoethics–The Ethical and Social Implications of Nanotechnology*, 17-39.

Juergensmeyer, M. (2000). *Terror in the Mind of God: The Global Rise of Religious Violence*. Oakland, CA: University of California Press.

Jung, J., & Lee, Y.-J. (2009). Cross-cultural examination of women's fashion and beauty magazine advertisements in the United States and South Korea. *Clothing & Textiles Research Journal*, *27*(4), 274–286. doi:10.1177/0887302X08327087

Kaag, J., & Kaufman, W. (2009). Military frameworks: Technological know-how and the legitimization of warfare. *Cambridge Review of International Affairs*, *22*(4), 585–606. doi:10.1080/09557570903325496

Kaczynski, T. J. (2008). *Industrial Society and Its Future*. Wingspan Press.

Kadushin, C. (2012). *Understanding social networks: theories, concepts, and findings*. Oxford, UK: Oxford University Press.

Kahane, G. (2011). Reasson to Feel, Reasons to Take Pills. In R. Ter Muelen, J. Savulescu, & G. Kahane (Eds.), *Enhancing human capacities*. Malden, MA: Blackwel.

Kalivas, P., & Volkow, N. (2011). New medications for drug addiction hiding in glutamatergic neuroplasticity. *Molecular Psychiatry*, *16*(10), 974–986. doi:10.1038/mp.2011.46 PMID:21519339

Kamssu, A. J., Siekpe, J. S., & Ellzy, J. A. (2004). Shortcomings to globalization: Using Internet technology and electronic commerce in developing countries. *Journal of Developing Areas*, *38*(1), 151–169. doi:10.1353/jda.2005.0010

Kanai, R., Chaieb, L., Antal, A., Walsh, V., & Paulus, W. (2008). Frequency-dependent electrical stimulation of the visual cortex. *Current Biology*, *18*(23), 1839–1843. doi:10.1016/j.cub.2008.10.027 PMID:19026538

Kanarek, Y. (1995). *World of awe*. Retrieved from http://www.worldofawe.net/thejournal/landing/ on July 30, 2017.

Kanazawa, S. (2011). Intelligence and physical attractiveness. *Intelligence*, *39*(1), 7–14. doi:10.1016/j.intell.2010.11.003

Kanazawa, S., & Kovar, J. L. (2004). Why beautiful people are more intelligent. *Intelligence*, *32*(3), 227–243. doi:10.1016/j.intell.2004.03.003

Kant, I. (2007). Analytic of the beautiful. In N. Walker (Ed.) & J. C. Meredith (Trans.), The critique of judgment (pp. 26–52). London, UK: Oxford University Press. (Original work published 1790)

Kant, I. (1994). Grounding for the metaphysics of morals (J. W. Ellington, Trans.). In *Ethical philosophy: The complete texts of grounding for the metaphysics of morals and metaphysical principles of virtue (part II of the metaphysics of morals)* (pp. 1–69). Indianapolis, IN: Hackett.

Kaplan, B., & Litewka, S. (2008). Ethical challenges of telemedicine and telehealth. *Cambridge Quarterly of Healthcare Ethics, 17*(04), 401–416. doi:10.1017/S0963180108080535 PMID:18724880

Kaplan, R. D. (2006, September). Hunting the Taliban in Las Vegas. *Atlantic Monthly*, 81–84.

Karlgaard, R. (2011). Is Technological Progress Slowing Down? *Forbes Magazine.* Retrieved February 15, 2014, from http://www.forbes.com/sites/richkarlgaard/2011/12/21/is-technological-progress-slowing-down/

Karnouskos, S., Weidlich, A., Kok, K., & Warmer, C. (2011). Field trials towards integrating smart houses with the smart grid. In *Energy-Efficient Computing and Networking* (pp. 114–123). Springer Berlin Heidelberg. doi:10.1007/978-3-642-19322-4_13

Karoliszyn, H. (2014). Do We Want Minority Report Policing? *Aeon Magazine.* Accessed December 29, 2014. http://aeon.co/magazine/technology/do-we-want-minority-report-policing/

Kasparbauer, A., Rujescu, D., Riedel, M., Pogarell, O., Costa, A., Meindl, T., ... Ettinger, U. (2014). Methylphenidate Effects on Brain Activity as a Function of SLC6A3 Genotype and Striatal Dopamine Transporter Availability. *Neuropsychopharmacology.* PMID:25220215

Kass, L. (2001). Preventing a brave new world. *Technology and Values: Essential Readings*, 311-322.

Kasten, F. H., Dowsett, J., & Herrmann, C. S. (2016). Sustained aftereffect of α-tACS lasts up to 70 minutes after stimulation. *Frontiers in Human Neuroscience, 10*, 245. doi:10.3389/fnhum.2016.00245 PMID:27252642

Kaurin, P. (2013). Courage behind a screen. In B. J. Strawser (Ed.), *Killing by remote control: The Ethics of an unmanned military*. New York: Oxford University Press.

Keane, J. (2009). *The Life and Death of Democracy*. New York: W.W. Norton.

Keegan, J., & Holmes, R. (1986). *Soldiers: A history of men in battle*. New York: Viking.

Kellett, S., Clarke, S., & McGill, P. (2008). Outcomes from psychological assessment regarding recommendations for cosmetic surgery. *Journal of Plastic, Reconstructive & Aesthetic Surgery; JPRAS, 61*(5), 512–517. doi:10.1016/j.bjps.2007.08.025 PMID:18316256

Kelley, M. (2014, April 15). My photo went viral and nothing could have prepared me for what happened after. *Fstoppers.* Retrieved from https://fstoppers.com/composite/my-photo-went-viral-and-nothing-could-have-prepared-me-what-happened-after-9517 on July 30, 2017.

Kelly, K. (1995). *Out of Control: The New Biology of Machines, Social Systems, and the Economic World*. Reading, MA: Addison-Wesley.

Kershnar, S. (2013). No moral problem. In B. J. Strawser (Ed.), *Killing by remote control: The ethics of an unnmanned military*. Oxford, UK: Oxford University Press. doi:10.1093/acprof:oso/9780199926121.003.0011

Khan, R., Khan, S. U., Zaheer, R., & Khan, S. (2012). Future Internet: The Internet of Things architecture, possible applications and key challenges. *10th International Conference on Frontiers of Information Technology*, 257-260. 10.1109/FIT.2012.53

Khurana, V. G., Hardell, L., Everaert, J., Bortkiewicz, A., Carlberg, M., & Ahonen, M. (2010). Epidemiological evidence for a health risk from mobile phone base stations. *International Journal of Occupational and Environmental Health*, *16*(3), 263–267. doi:10.1179/oeh.2010.16.3.263 PMID:20662418

Khurana, V. G., Teo, C., Kundi, M., Hardell, L., & Carlberg, M. (2009). Cell phones and brain tumors: A review including the long-term epidemiologic data. *Surgical Neurology*, *72*(3), 205–214. doi:10.1016/j.surneu.2009.01.019 PMID:19328536

Khushf, G. (2005). The use of emergent technologies for enhancing human performance: Are we prepared to address the ethical and policy issues? *Public Policy and Practice*, *4*(2), 1-17. Retrieved August 1, 2017, from http://www.ipspr. sc.edu/ejournal/ej511/ George%20Khushf%20Revised%20Human%20Enhancements1.htm

Kilcullen, D. (2013). *Out of the Mountains: The Coming Age of the Urban Guerrilla*. New York: Oxford University Press.

Kim, Y., Teylan, M., Baron, M., Sands, A., Nairn, A., & Greengard, P. (2009). Methylphenidate-induced dendritic spine formation and FosB expression in nucleus accumbens. *Proceedings of the National Academy of Sciences of the United States of America*, *106*(8), 2915–2920. doi:10.1073/pnas.0813179106 PMID:19202072

King, G. (2017, June 21). *How the Chinese Government Fabricates Social Media Posts for Strategic Distraction, not Engaged Argument*. Retrieved July 29, 2017, from https://gking.harvard.edu/50c

King, A. L. S., Valença, A. M., Silva, A. C. O., Baczynski, T., Carvalho, M. R., & Nardi, A. E. (2013). Nomophobia: Dependency on virtual environments or social phobia? *Computers in Human Behavior*, *29*(1), 140–144. doi:10.1016/j. chb.2012.07.025

King, P. (1995). Abelard's Intentionalist Ethics. *The Modern Schoolman*, *72*(2), 213–231. doi:10.5840choolman1995722/316

Kirilenko, A., Kyle, A.S., Samadi, M., & Tuzun, T. (2011). *The Flash Crash: The impact of High Frequency Trading on an Electronic Market*. DOI: 10.2139/ssrn.1686004

Kirsch, A. (2008). The fight for recognition. *Poetry*, *193*(2), 143–148.

Kitroeff, N. (2014, May 19). Why that video went viral. *The New York Times*. Retrieved from http://www.nytimes. com/2014/05/20/science/why-that-video-went-viral.html?_r=0

Kjaer, T., Bertelsen, C., Piccini, P., Brooks, D., Alving, J., & Lou, H. (2002). Increased dopamine tone during meditation-induced change of consciousness. *Brain Research. Cognitive Brain Research*, *13*(2), 255–259. doi:10.1016/S0926-6410(01)00106-9 PMID:11958969

Kling, R. (2000). Learning about information technologies and social change: The contribution of social informatics. *The Information Society*, *16*(3), 217–232. doi:10.1080/01972240050133661

Knobel, M., & Lankshear, C. (2007). Online memes, affinities, and cultural production. In C. Lankshear, M. Knobel, C. Bigum, & M. Peters (Eds.), *A new literacies sampler* (pp. 199–227). New York: Peter Lang Publishing.

KnowYourMeme. (2017). Retrieved from http://knowyourmeme.com/

Koebler, J. (2014, October 21). When your photo goes viral, the Internet will kill its image quality. *Motherboard*. Retrieved from http://motherboard.vice.com/read/when-your-photo-goes-viral-the-internet-will-kill-its-image-quality

Konishi, K., & Bohbot, V. D. (2010). Grey matter in the hippocampus correlates with spatial memory strategies in human older adults tested on a virtual navigation task. *Proceedings of the 40th Society for Neuroscience annual meeting*.

Korff, S. (2013). PETs in Your Home – How Smart is That? *Symposium on Usable Privacy and Security (SOUPS)*.

Kostarelos, K. (2006). The emergence of nanomedicine: A field in the making. *Nanomedicine (London)*, *1*(1), 9–12. doi:10.2217/17435889.1.1.1 PMID:17716200

Kostyk, T., & Herkert, J. (2012). Societal implications of the emerging smart grid. *Communications of the ACM*, *55*(11), 34–36. doi:10.1145/2366316.2366328

Kowalski, R. M., Limber, S. P., & Agatston, P. W. (2012). Cyberbullying: Bullying in the Digital Age (2nd ed.). Malden, MA: Academic Press.

Kozasa, E., Sato, J., Lacerda, S., Barreiros, M., Radvany, J., Russell, T., ... Amaro, E. Jr. (2012). Meditation training increases brain efficiency in an attention task. *NeuroImage*, *59*(1), 745–749. doi:10.1016/j.neuroimage.2011.06.088 PMID:21763432

Kraemer, F., van Overveld, K., & Peterson, M. (2011). Is there an ethics of algorithms. *Ethics and Information Technology*, *13*(3), 251–260. doi:10.100710676-010-9233-7

Kringelbach, M. L., & Aziz, T. Z. (2009). Deep brain stimulation. *Journal of the American Medical Association*, *301*(16), 1705–1707. doi:10.1001/jama.2009.551 PMID:19383961

Krishnan, A. (2009). *Killer robots. Legality and ethicality of autonomous weapons*. Farnham, MA: Ashgate Publishing Limited.

Krishnan, A. (2009). *Killer robots: Legality and ethicality of autonomous weapons*. Burlington, VT: Ashgate.

Kuchler, H. (2014, November 4). *Tech companies step up encryption in wake of Snowden*. Accessed July 29, 2017, from https://www.ft.com/content/3c1553a6-6429-11e4-bac8-00144feabdc0

Kudlow, P., Treurnicht Naylor, K., Xie, B., & McIntyre, R. (2013). Cognitive enhancement in Canadian medical students. *Journal of Psychoactive Drugs*, *45*(4), 360–365. doi:10.1080/02791072.2013.825033 PMID:24377176

Kulyk, O. A., Tjin-Kam-Jet-Siemons, L., Oinas-Kukkonen, H., & van Gemert-Pijnen, J. E. W. C. (2016). Fourth International Workshop on Behavior Change Support Systems (BCSS'16): Epic for Change, the Pillars for Persuasive Technology for Smart Societies. In A. Meschtscherjakov, B. de Ruyter, V. Fuchsberger, M. Murer, & M. Tscheligi (Eds.), *Adjunct proceedings of the 11th International Conference on Persuasive Technology, PERSUASIVE 2016* (pp. 92-95). Salzburg, Austria: Center for Human-Computer Interaction, Department of Computer Science, University of Salzburg.

Kurzweil, R. (2005). *The singularity is near: When humans transcend biology*. New York: Viking Penguin.

LA Times Editorial Board. (2017, June 28). *The EU fires a warning shot at Google and other Internet giants*. Retrieved July 29, 2017, from http://www.latimes.com/opinion/editorials/la-ed-google-antitrust-20170628-story.html

LaFrance, A. (2017). The ghost of climate-change future. *The Atlantic*. Retrieved from https://www.theatlantic.com/science/archive/2017/05/the-ghost-of-climate-change-future/528471/

LaFrance, A. (2017, February 17). *The Mark Zuckerberg Manifesto Is a Blueprint for Destroying Journalism*. Retrieved July 29, 2017, from https://www.theatlantic.com/technology/archive/2017/02/the-mark-zuckerberg-manifesto-is-a-blueprint-for-destroying-journalism/517113/

Lambert, N., & Hartsough, C. (1998). Prospective Study of Tobacco Smoking and Substance Dependencies Among Samples of ADHD and Non-ADHD Participants. *Journal of Learning Disabilities*, *31*(6), 533–544. doi:10.1177/002221949803100603 PMID:9813951

Landoll, D. J., & Landoll, D. (2005). *The security risk assessment handbook: A complete guide for performing security risk assessments*. CRC Press. doi:10.1201/9781420031232

Lane, H., & Bahan, B. (1998). Ethics of cochlear implantation in young children: A review and reply from a deaf-world perspective. *Otolaryngology - Head and Neck Surgery, 119*(4), 297–313. doi:10.1016/S0194-5998(98)70070-1 PMID:9781982

Lanier, J. (2014, November 14). *The Myth Of AI*. Retrieved July 29, 2017, from https://www.edge.org/conversation/jaron_lanier-the-myth-of-ai

Lanier, J. (2010). *You Are Not a Gadget: A Manifesto*. New York: Alfred A. Knopf.

Lanier, J. (2013). *Who Owns the Future?* New York: Simon and Schuster.

Lawson, C. (2010). Technology and the extension of human capabilities. *Journal for the Theory of Social Behaviour, 40*(2), 207–223. doi:10.1111/j.1468-5914.2009.00428.x

Lee, P. (2012). Remoteness, risk and aircrew Ethos. *Air Power Review, 15*(1), 1–19.

Leitgeb, N. (2009). Electromagnetic hypersensitivity. In *Advances in electromagnetic fields in living systems* (pp. 167–197). Springer New York.

Lenhart, A. (2016). *Online Harassment, Digital Abuse, and Cyberstalking in America*. Data & Society Research Institute and Center for Innovative Public Health Research. Retrieved August 1, 2017, from https://www.datasociety.net/pubs/oh/Online_Harassment_2016.pdf

LeUnes, A. (2011). *Sport Psychology*. London: Icon Books.

Leveringhaus, A. (2016). Drones, automated targeting and moral responsibility. In E. D. Nucci & F. Santoni de Sio (Eds.), *Drones and responsibility. Legal, philosophical and socio-technical perspectives on remotely controlled weapons* (pp. 169–181). London: Routledge.

Leveringhaus, A. (2016). *Ethics and Autonomous Weapons*. London: Palgrave. doi:10.1057/978-1-137-52361-7

Levy, N. (2007). *Neuroethics: Challenges for the 21st century*. Cambridge University Press. doi:10.1017/CBO9780511811890

Lewis, M. (2014). Flash boys. Cracking the money code. New York, Penguin Group.

Libet, B., Gleason, C. A., Wright, E. W., & Pearl, D. K. (1983). Time of conscious intention to act in relation to onset of cerebral activity (readinesspotential): The unconscious initiation of a freely voluntary act. *Brain, 106*, 623–642. doi:10.1093/brain/106.3.623 PMID:6640273

Lichocki, P., Kahn, P. Jr, & Billard, A. (2011). The Ethical Landscape of Robotics. *IEEE Robotics & Automation Magazine, 18*(1), 39–50. doi:10.1109/MRA.2011.940275

Lier van B. (2013). Can machines communicate? The Internet of Things and Interoperability of Information. *Engineering Management Research, 2*(1), 55–66.

Lier van B. (2013). Luhmann meets Weick: Information Interoperability and Situational Awareness. *Emergence, 15*(1), 71–95.

Lier, B. (2015). Advanced Manufacturing and Complexity Science Ultra-Large-Scale Systems, Emergence and Self-Organisation. ICSTCC 2015.

Lier, B., & Hardjono, T. W. (2010). Luhmann meets the Matrix. Exchanging and sharing information in network-centric environments. *Journal of Systemics, Cybernetics and Informatics, 3*, 68–72.

Lin, P., Bekey, G., & Abney, K. (2008). *Autonomous military robotics: Risk, ethics, and design*. San Luis Obispo: California Polytechnic State University. doi:10.21236/ADA534697

Lin, T. J. (2010). Evolution of cosmetics: Increased need for experimental clinical medicine. *Journal of Experimental and Clinical Medicine, 2*(2), 49–52. doi:10.1016/S1878-3317(10)60009-5

Lippman, A. (1991). Prenatal genetic testing and screening: Constructing needs and reinforcing inequities. *American Journal of Law & Medicine, 1-2*(17), 15–50. PMID:1877608

Little, M. (2015, September 21). New York City rat taking home pizza on the subway (Pizza Rat). *YouTube video*. Retrieved from https://www.youtube.com/watch?v=UPXUG8q4jKU

Lloréns, H. (2013). Latina bodies in the era of elective aesthetic surgery. *Latino Studies, 11*(4), 547–569. doi:10.1057/lst.2013.32

Loeb, G. E., McHardy, J., Kelliher, E. M., & Brummer, S. B. (1982). Neural prosthesis. *Biocompatibility in Clinical Practice, 2*, 123-149.

Loland, S. (2009). The ethics of performance-enhancing technology in sport. *Journal of the Philosophy of Sport, 36*(2), 152–161. doi:10.1080/00948705.2009.9714754

Lönn, S., Ahlbom, A., Hall, P., & Feychting, M. (2004). Mobile phone use and the risk of acoustic neuroma. *Epidemiology (Cambridge, Mass.), 15*(6), 653–659. doi:10.1097/01.ede.0000142519.00772.bf PMID:15475713

Looby, A., & Earleywine, M. (2011). Expectation to receive methylphenidate enhances subjective arousal but not cognitive performance. *Experimental and Clinical Psychopharmacology, 19*(6), 433–444. doi:10.1037/a0025252 PMID:21875224

López-Frías, J. (2014). *Mejora humana y dopaje en la actual filosofía del deporte* (Unpublished doctoral dissertation). Facultad de Filosofía, Universidad de Valencia.

Lorenzo, G. L., Biesanz, J. C., & Human, L. J. (2010). What is beautiful is good and more accurately understood: Physical attractiveness and accuracy in first impressions of personality. *Psychological Science, 21*(12), 1777–1782. doi:10.1177/0956797610388048 PMID:21051521

Lowe, C. R. (2000). Nanobiotechnology: The fabrication and applications of chemical and biological nanostructures. *Current Opinion in Structural Biology, 10*(4), 428–434. doi:10.1016/S0959-440X(00)00110-X PMID:10981630

Luber, B., & Lisanby, S. H. (2014). Enhancement of human cognitive performance using transcranial magnetic stimulation (TMS). *NeuroImage, 85*, 961–970. doi:10.1016/j.neuroimage.2013.06.007 PMID:23770409

Luber, B., Stanford, A., Bulow, P., Nguyen, T., Rakitin, B., Habeck, C., ... Lisanby, S. (2008). Remediation of sleep-deprivation-induced working memory impairment with fMRI-guided transcranial magnetic stimulation. *Cerebral Cortex, 18*(9), 2077–2085. doi:10.1093/cercor/bhm231 PMID:18203694

Luber, B., Steffener, J., Tucker, A., Habeck, C., Peterchev, A. V., Deng, Z.-D., ... Lisanby, S. H. (2013). Extended remediation of sleep deprived-induced working memory deficits using fMRI-guided transcranial magnetic stimulation. *Sleep, 36*(6), 857–871. doi:10.5665leep.2712 PMID:23729929

Lucas, G. (2011). *Industrial challenges of military robotics*. Paper presented at the conference The Ethics of Emerging Military Technologies of International Society for Military Ethics (ISME), San Diego, CA. Retrieved from http://isme.tamu.edu/ISME11/isme11.html

Lucas, G. Jr. (2011). Industrial challenges of military robotics. *Journal of Military Ethics, 10*(4), 274–295. doi:10.1080/15027570.2011.639164

Luders, E., Toga, A., Lepore, N., & Gaser, C. (2009). The underlying anatomical correlates of long-term meditation: Larger hippocampal and frontal volumes of gray matter. *NeuroImage*, *45*(3), 672–678. doi:10.1016/j.neuroimage.2008.12.061 PMID:19280691

Luhmann, N. (1995). *Social systems*. Stanford, CA: Stanford University Press.

Lunceford, B. (2008). The walk of shame: A normative description. *Etc.; a Review of General Semantics*, *65*(4), 319–329.

Lunceford, B. (2012). Posthuman visions: Creating the technologized body. *Explorations in Media Ecology*, *11*(1), 7–25. doi:10.1386/eme.11.1.7_1

Luo, W. (2013). Aching for the altered body: Beauty economy and Chinese women's consumption of cosmetic surgery. *Women's Studies International Forum*, *38*, 1–10. doi:10.1016/j.wsif.2013.01.013

Luppicini, R. (2008). The Emerging Field of Technoethics. In R. Luppicini & R. Adell (Eds.), *Handbook of Research on Technoethics*. Academic Press. Retrieved from www.igi-global.com/emerging-field-technoethics

Luppicini, R. (2009). Technoethical inquiry: From technological systems to society. Global Media Journal – Canadian Edition, 2(1), 5-21.

Luppicini, R. (2009a). Technoethical inquiry: From technological systems to society. Global Media Journal — Canadian Edition, 2(1), 5-21.

Luppicini, R. (2008). The emerging field of technoethics. In R. Luppicini & R. Adell (Eds.), *Handbook of Research on Technoethics* (pp. 1–19). Hershey, PA: Idea Group Publishing. doi:10.4018/978-1-60566-022-6.ch001

Luppicini, R. (2009). Technoethical Inquiry: From Technological Systems to Society. *Global Media Journal*, *2*(1), 5–21.

Luppicini, R. (2010). *Technoethics and the Evolving Knowledge Society: Ethical Issues in Technological Design, Research, Development, and Innovation*. Hershey, PA: IGI Global; doi:10.4018/978-1-60566-952-6

Luppicini, R. (2010b). The technological r/evolution. *International Journal of Technoethics*, *1*(1), i–ii.

Luppicini, R. (2012). *Ethical Impact of Technological Advancements and Applications in Society*. Hershey, PA: IGI Global. doi:10.4018/978-1-4666-1773-5

Luppicini, R. (Ed.). (2012a). *Handbook of Research on Technoself: Identity in a Technological Society* (Vols. 1-2). Hershey, PA: Idea Group Publishing.

Luppicini, R., & Adell, R. (2009). *Handbook of Research on Technoethics* (Vols. 1–2). Hershey, PA: IGI Global; doi:10.4018/978-1-60566-022-6

Lustenberger, C., Boyle, M. R., Foulser, A. A., Mellin, J. M., & Fröhlich, F. (2015). Role of Frontal Alpha Oscillations in Creativity HHS Public Access. *Cortex*, *67*, 74–82. doi:10.1016/j.cortex.2015.03.012 PMID:25913062

Lynch, Z. (2004). Neurotechnology and society (2010–2060). *Annals of the New York Academy of Sciences*, *1013*(1), 229–233. doi:10.1196/annals.1305.016 PMID:15194618

Lyon, D. (2002). Surveillance as social sorting: Computer codes and mobile bodies. In D. Lyon (Ed.), *Surveillance as social sorting: Privacy, risk and automated discrimination* (pp. 14–30). London, UK: Routledge.

Lyon, D. (2006). The search for surveillance theories. In D. Lyon (Ed.), *Theorizing surveillance: The panopticon and beyond* (pp. 3–20). Portland, OR: Willand.

Lyotard, J.-F. (1984). *The Postmodern Condition: A Report on Knowledge*. Minneapolis, MN: Minnesota Press and Manchester University Press.

MacIntyre, A. (1981). *After Virtue*. Notre Dame, IN: University of Notre Dame Press.

MacIntyre, A. (1989). The Virtues, the Unity of a Human Life and the Concept of a Tradition. In S. Hauerwas & L. Gregory Jones (Eds.), *Why Narrative?* (pp. 89–110). Grand Rapids, MI: W.B. Eerdmans.

Magnani, L. (2007). *Morality in a Technological World. Knowledge as Duty*. Cambridge, UK: Cambridge University Press. doi:10.1017/CBO9780511498657

Magnani, L. (2009). *Abductive Cognition: The Epistemological and Eco-Cognitive Dimensions of Hypothetical Reasoning*. Berlin: Springer. doi:10.1007/978-3-642-03631-6

Magnani, L. (2011). *Understanding Violence. Morality, Religion, and Violence Intertwined: a Philosophical Stance*. Berlin: Springer.

Magnuson, S. (2008, May). Armed robots sidelined in Iraq. *National Defense Magazine*.

Maher, B. (2008). Poll results: Look who's doping. *Nature, 452*(7188), 674–675. doi:10.1038/452674a PMID:18401370

Maier, L., Liechti, M., Herzig, F., & Schaub, M. (2013). To Dope or Not to Dope: Neuroenhancement with Prescription Drugs and Drugs of Abuse among Swiss University Students. *PLoS One, 8*(11), e77967. doi:10.1371/journal.pone.0077967 PMID:24236008

Makris, N., Biederman, J., Valera, E., Bush, G., Kaiser, J., Kennedy, D. N., ... Seidman, L. (2007). Cortical thinning of the attention and executive function networks in adults with attention-deficit/hyperactivity disorder. *Cereb cortex, 17*(6), 1364–1375. doi:10.1093/cercor/bhl047 PMID:16920883

Malsch, I., & Hvidtfelt-Nielsen, K. (2010). *Nanobioethics: ObservatoryNano 2nd Annual Report on Ethical and Societal Aspects of Nanotechnology*. ObservatoryNano.

Maltby, J., & Day, L. (2011). Celebrity worship and incidence of elective cosmetic surgery: Evidence of a link among young adults. *The Journal of Adolescent Health, 49*(5), 483–489. doi:10.1016/j.jadohealth.2010.12.014 PMID:22018562

Manchester, W. (1979). *Goodbye darkness: A memoir of the pacific war*. New York: Dell Publishing Company.

Manning, J. T., Scutt, D., & Lewis-Jones, D. I. (1998). Developmental stability, ejaculate size, and sperm quality in men. *Evolution and Human Behavior, 19*(5), 273–282. doi:10.1016/S1090-5138(98)00024-5

Markowitz, J., Devane, C., Pestreich, L., Patrick, K., & Muniz, R. (2006). A Comprehensive In Vitro Screening of d-, l-, and dl- threo-Methylphenidate: An Exploratory Study. *Journal of Child and Adolescent Psychopharmacology, 16*(6), 687–698. doi:10.1089/cap.2006.16.687 PMID:17201613

Marquand, A., O'Daly, O., De Simoni, S., Alsop, D., Maguire, R., Williams, S., ... Mehta, M. (2012). Dissociable effects of methylphenidate, atomoxetine and placebo on regional cerebral blood flow in healthy volunteers at rest: A multi-class pattern recognition approach. *NeuroImage, 60*(2), 1015–1024. doi:10.1016/j.neuroimage.2012.01.058 PMID:22266414

Marsden, E. (1969). *Greek and Roman Artillery: Historical Development*. Oxford, UK: Oxford University Press.

Marshall, S. L. A. (2000). *Men against fire: The problem of battle command*. Norman, OK: University of Oklahoma Press.

Martínez Lirola, M., & Chovanec, J. (2012). The dream of a perfect body come true: Multimodality in cosmetic surgery advertising. *Discourse & Society, 23*(5), 487–507. doi:10.1177/0957926512452970

Martin, M. J., & Sasser, C. W. (2010). *Predator: The remote-control air war over Iraq and Afghanistan: A pilot's story*. Minneapolis, MN: Zenith Press.

Mastroianni, G. R. (2011). The person–situation debate: Implications for military leadership and civilian–military relations. *Journal of Military Ethics*, *10*(1), 2–16. doi:10.1080/15027570.2011.561636

Masuda, Y. (1983). The Information Society as Post-Industrial Society. Washinton: D. C. McLean, A. (2011), Ethical frontiers of ICT and older users: cultural, pragmatic and ethical issues. *Ethics and Information Technology*, *13*(4), 313–326.

Mattern, F. (2005). Leben und Lernen in einer von Informationstechnologie durchdrungenen Welt – Visionen und Erwartungen. In M. Franzen (Ed.), *Lernplattformen (Web-Based Training 2005)* (pp. 39–61). Dübendorf, Switzerland: EMPA-Akademie.

Matthias, A. (2011). *Is the concept of an ethical governor philosophically sound?* Paper presented at the Tilting Perspectives: Technologies on the Stand: Legal and Ethical Questions in Neuroscience and Robotics, The Netherlands.

Matthias, A. (2004). The responsibility gap: Ascribing responsibility for the actions of learning automata. *Ethics and Information Technology*, *6*(3), 175–183. doi:10.100710676-004-3422-1

Mäyrä, F., & Vadén, T. (2013). Ethics of Living Technology: Design Principles for Proactive Home Environments. *Human IT. Journal for Information Technology Studies as a Human Science*, *7*(2).

McCarthy, H., Skokauskas, N., & Frodl, T. (2014). Identifying a consistent pattern of neural function in attention deficit hyperactivity disorder: A meta-analysis. *Psychological Medicine*, *44*(04), 869880. doi:10.1017/S0033291713001037 PMID:23663382

McCutcheon, C. (2016, March 11). *How Trump and Sanders broke the Overton window*. Retrieved July 29, 2017, from https://www.csmonitor.com/USA/Politics/Politics-Voices/2016/0311/How-Trump-and-Sanders-broke-the-Overton-window

McDaniel, P., & McLaughlin, S. (2009). Security and privacy challenges in the smart grid. *IEEE Security and Privacy*, *7*(3), 75–77. doi:10.1109/MSP.2009.76

McFarland, M. (2016). What happens when your search engine is first to know you have cancer? *The Washington Post*. Retrieved from https://www.washingtonpost.com/ news/innovations/wp/2016/06/10/what-happens-when-your-search-engine-is-first-to-know-you-have-cancer/

McLuhan, H. M., & McLuhan, E. (1992). Laws of Media: The New Science. Toronto: Academic Press.

McLuhan, M. (1964). *The Gutenberg galaxy: The making of typographic man*. Toronto: University of Toronto Press.

McLuhan, M. (1966). *Understanding media: The extensions of man*. Toronto: University of Toronto Press.

McLuhan, M., & Fiore, Q. (1967). *The medium is the massage*. New York: Random House.

McLuhan, M., Fiore, Q., & Agel, J. (1968). *War and peace in the global village* (Vol. 127). New York: Bantam books.

McLuhan, M., & McLuhan, E. (1988). *Laws of media: The new science* (Vol. 1). Toronto: University of Toronto Press.

McMillan, R. (2017, June 2). *Bots Now Outnumber Humans on the Web*. Retrieved July 29, 2017, from https://www.wired.com/2014/12/bots-now-outnumber-humans-web/

Meadors, T. (2011). *Virtual jus in bello: Teaching just war with video games*. Paper presented at the The Ethics of Emerging Military Technologies, University of San Diego.

Meagher, R. (1988). Techne. *Perspecta*, *24*, 159–164. doi:10.2307/1567132

Meagher, R. E. (2006). *Herakles gone mad: Rethinking heroism in an age of endless war*. Northampton, UK: Olive Branch Press.

Meijer, A., & Bolívar, M. P. R. (2016). Governing the smart city: A review of the literature on smart urban governance. *International Review of Administrative Sciences*, *82*(2), 392–408. doi:10.1177/0020852314564308

Mendoza, N. (2015). *The Selfie-Selfie-O-Matic*. Retrieved from http://www.neilmendoza.com/portfolio/selfie-selfie-o-matic/

Meningaud, J.-P., Benadiba, L., Servant, J.-M., Herve, C., Bertrand, J.-C., & Pelicier, Y. (2003). Depression, anxiety and quality of life: Outcome 9 months after facial cosmetic surgery. *Journal of Cranio-Maxillo-Facial Surgery*, *31*(1), 46–50. doi:10.1016/S1010-5182(02)00159-2 PMID:12553927

Menkveld, A. J. (2014). High-Frequency Traders and Market Structure. *Financial Review*, *49*(2), 333–344. doi:10.1111/fire.12038

Menkveld, A. J., & Zoican, M. A. (2014). Need for Speed? Exchange Latency and Market Quality. *Journal of Financial Economics*, *14*, 71–100.

Merkel, R., Boer, G., Fegert, J., Galert, T., Hartmann, D., Nuttin, B., & Rosahl, S. (2007). *Intervening in the brain. Changing psyche and society*. Berlin: Springer.

Meyers, C. (2014). Neuroenhancement in Reflective Equilibrium: A Qualified Kantian Defense of Enhancing in Scholarship and Science. *Neuroethics*, *7*(3), 287–298. doi:10.100712152-014-9212-5

Miah, A. (2004). Genetically Modified Athletes. London: E&FN Spon (Routledge).

Miah, A. (2011). Physical Enhancement: The State of Art. In Enhancing Human Capacities. Oxford, UK: Blackwell.

Milgram, S. (1974). *Obedience to authority: An experimental view*. London: Tavistock.

Miller, A. S., & Price, D. K. (1966). Review of The Scientific Estate. *Duke Law Journal*, *2*(Spring), 622–629. doi:10.2307/1371547

Miller, K. (2009). *Organizational communication: Approaches and processes*. Wadsworth Publishing Company.

Mills, E. (2012, Jan 24). *Researcher find smart meters could reveal favorite TV shows*. Retrieved from http://www.cnet.com/news/researchers-find-smart-meters-could-reveal-favorite-tv-shows/

Moller, A. C., & Deci, E. L. (2010). Interpersonal control, dehumanization, and violence: A self-determination theory perspective. *Group Processes & Intergroup Relations*, *13*(1), 41–53. doi:10.1177/1368430209350318

Mooney, C. (2005). *The Republican War on Science*. New York: Basic Books.

Moore, A., & Malinowski, P. (2009). Meditation, mindfulness and cognitive flexibility. *Consciousness and Cognition*, *18*(1), 176–186. doi:10.1016/j.concog.2008.12.008 PMID:19181542

Moore, G. E. (1965). Cramming more components onto integrated circuits. *Electronics (Basel)*, *38*(8), 114–117.

Moor, J. H. (2006, July). The nature, Importance and Difficulty of Machine Ethics. *IEEE Intelligent Systems*, *21*, 18–21. doi:10.1109/MIS.2006.80

Moreno, J. D. (2011). *The Body Politic, The Battle Over Science in America*. New York: Bellevue Literary Press.

Morozov, E. (2016, December 3). *Data populists must seize our information – for the benefit of us all*. Retrieved July 29, 2017, from https://www.theguardian.com/commentisfree/2016/dec/04/data-populists-must-seize-information-for-benefit-of-all-evgeny-morozov

Morozov, E. (2011). *The Net Delusion: The Dark Side of Internet Freedom*. New York, NY: PublicAffairs.

Morrison, M., & Cornips, L. (2012). Exploring the role of dedicated online biotechnology news providers in the innovation economy. *Science, Technology & Human Values, 3*(37), 262–285. doi:10.1177/0162243911420581

Morton, W., & Stockton, G. (2000). Methylphenidate Abuse and Psychiatric Side Effects. *The Journal of Clinical Psychiatry, 2*, 159–164. PMID:15014637

Motaparthi, K. (2010). Blepharoplasty in Asian patients: Ethnic and ethical implications. *The Virtual Mentor, 12*(12), 946–949. doi:10.1001/virtualmentor.2010.12.12.msoc1-1012 PMID:23186822

Mounk, Y. (2016, August 14). *The Week Democracy Died.* Accessed July 29, 2017, from http://www.slate.com/articles/news_and_politics/cover_story/2016/08/the_week_democracy_died_how_brexit_nice_turkey_and_trump_are_all_connected.html

Mueller, S., Costa, A., Keeser, D., Pogarell, O., Berman, A., Coates, U., ... Meindl, T. (2014). The effects of methylphenidate on whole brain intrinsic functional connectivity. *Human Brain Mapping, 35*(11), 5379–5388. doi:10.1002/hbm.22557 PMID:24862742

Mukerji, N. (2016). Autonomous killer drones. In E. D. Nucci & F. Santoni de Sio (Eds.), *Drones and responsibility. Legal, philosophical and socio-technical perspectives on remotely controlled weapons* (pp. 197–214). London: Routledge.

Müller, D. J., & Dufrene, Y. F. (2008). Atomic force microscopy as a multifunctional molecular toolbox in nanobiotechnology. *Nature Nanotechnology, 3*(5), 261–269. doi:10.1038/nnano.2008.100 PMID:18654521

Müller, V. C. (2016). Autonomous killer robots are probably good news. In E. D. Nucci & F. Santoni de Sio (Eds.), *Drones and responsibility. Legal, philosophical and socio-technical perspectives on remotely controlled weapons* (pp. 67–81). London: Routledge.

Mulquiney, P. G., Hoy, K. E., Daskalakis, Z. J., & Fitzgerald, P. B. (2011). Improving working memory: Exploring the effect of transcranial random noise stimulation and transcranial direct current stimulation on the dorsolateral prefrontal cortex. *Clinical Neurophysiology, 122*(12), 2384–2389. doi:10.1016/j.clinph.2011.05.009 PMID:21665534

Münker, S., Brouwer, J., & Reijnen, L. (1997). *Interfacing realities.* Rotterdam: V2

Nahon, K., & Helmsley, J. (2013). *Going Viral.* Cambridge, UK: Polity Press.

Naím, M. (2014). *The End of Power From Boardrooms to Battlefields and Churches to States, Why Being In Charge Isn't What It Used to Be.* New York: Basic Books.

Naisbitt, J. (1982). *Megatrends: Ten New Directions Transforming Our Lives.* New York: A Warner Communications Company.

Nakao, T., Radua, J., Rubia, K., & Mataix-Cols, D. (2011). Gray Matter Volume Abnormalities in ADHD: Voxel-Based Meta-Analysis Exploring the Effects of Age and Stimulant Medication. *The American Journal of Psychiatry, 168*(11), 1154–1164. doi:10.1176/appi.ajp.2011.11020281 PMID:21865529

Nash, R. F. (Eds.). (1990). American Environmentalism, Readings in Conservation History. New York: McGraw Hill.

National Institute of Standards and Technology. (2010a). *Introduction to NISTIR 7628: Guidelines for smart grid cyber security.* Gaithersburg, MD: NIST.

National Institute of Standards and Technology. (2010b). Guidelines for smart grid cyber security: Vol. 2. *Privacy and the smart grid.* Gaithersburg, MD: NIST.

National Institute of Standards and Technology. (2014). *Guidelines for smart grid cyber security – Revision 1.* Gaithersburg, MD: NIST.

National Research Council. (2005). *Autonomous vehicles in support of naval operations*. Washington, DC: The National Academies Press.

National Research Council. (2014). *Convergence: facilitating transdisciplinary integration of life sciences, physical sciences, engineering, and beyond*. National Academies Press; doi:10.17226/18722

Neuman, W. L. (2011). Social research methods: Qualitative and quantitative approaches. In M. Eid (Ed.), Research methods in communication (pp. 341-377). Boston, MA: Pearson.

Neuman, W. L. (2010). *Social research methods: Qualitative and quantitative approaches*. Pearson.

News, C. H. (2015, November 23). 'Selfie Rat' snaps photo of himself with sleeping man's phone on subway platform. *YouTube Video*. Retrieved from https://youtu.be/5CvWXG8gqEU

Ng, P. (2016). *Exclusive: Heidi Montag reflects on plastic surgery obsession: "I became consumed by this character I was playing."* Retrieved from http://www.etonline.com/tv/189526_heidi_montag_reflects_on_plastic_surgery_obsession/

Niemeyer, C. M. (2004). *Nanobiotechnology*. Nanobiotechnology. Encyclopedia of Molecular Cell Biology and Molecular Medicine. doi:10.1002/3527602453

Nietzsche, F. (1967). *The birth of tragedy* (W. Kaufmann, Trans.). New York, NY: Random House. (Original work published 1872)

Nisbett, R. E., & Wilson, T. D. (1977). Telling more than we can know: Verbal reports on mental processes. *Psychological Review*, *84*(3), 231–259. doi:10.1037/0033-295X.84.3.231

Nisbett, R. E., & Wilson, T. D. (1977). The halo effect: Evidence for unconscious alteration of judgments. *Journal of Personality and Social Psychology*, *35*(4), 250–256. doi:10.1037/0022-3514.35.4.250

Nisenholtz, B. B. (2017, March 1). *What Trump Understands About Using Social Media to Drive Attention*. Retrieved July 29, 2017, from https://hbr.org/2017/03/what-trump-understands-about-using-social-media-to-drive-attention

Nissenbaum, H. (2010). *Privacy in context: Technology, policy, and the integrity of social life*. Stanford, CA: Stanford University Press.

Nitsche, M. A., Fricke, K., Henschke, U., Schlitterlau, A., Liebetanz, D., Lang, N., ... Paulus, W. (2003). Pharmacological modulation of cortical excitability shifts induced by transcranial direct current stimulation in humans. *The Journal of Physiology*, *553*(1), 293–301. doi:10.1113/jphysiol.2003.049916 PMID:12949224

Nixon, P. A., Wagealla, W., English, C., & Terzis, S. (2004). *Security, privacy and trust issues in smart environments. Technical report of the Global and Pervasive Computing Group. Department of Computer and Information Sciences*. Glasgow, UK: University of Strathclyde.

Niyato, D., Xiao, L., & Wang, P. (2011). Machine-to-machine communications for home energy management system in smart grid. *IEEE Communications Magazine*, *49*(4), 53–59. doi:10.1109/MCOM.2011.5741146

Noorman, M. (2014). Responsibility practices and unmanned military technologies. *Science and Engineering Ethics*, *20*(3), 809–826. doi:10.100711948-013-9484-x PMID:24142234

Noorman, M., & Johnson, D. G. (2014). Negotiating autonomy and responsibility in military robots. *Ethics and Information Technology*, *16*(1), 51–62. doi:10.100710676-013-9335-0

Normal Breast Gallery. (2017). Retrieved from http://www.007b.com/breast_gallery.php

O'Hanihan, A. (2013). *Without their permission: How the 21ˢᵗ century will be made, not managed*. New York, NY: Business Plus.

O'Reilly. (2005). *Web 2.0: compact definition? O'Reilly radar*. Retrieved from http://radar.oreilly.com/2005/10/web-20-compact-definition.html

OddDaily Clips. (2016, January 21). Three eyed catfish appeared in New York. *YouTube Video*. Retrieved from https://youtu.be/MC4cJTARung

Office of the Surgeon General. (2006). Mental health advisory team (MHAT) IV Operation Iraqi Freedom 05-07, Final Report. Washington, DC: United States Department of the Army.

Okano, A., Fontes, E., Montenegro, R., Farinatti, P., Cyrino, E., Li, L., ... Noakes, T. D. (2013). Brain stimulation modulates the autonomic nervous system, rating of perceived exertion and performance during maximal exercise. *British Journal of Sports Medicine*, 49(18), 1213–1218. doi:10.1136/bjsports-2012-091658 PMID:23446641

Olson, P. (2012). *We Are Anonymous: Inside the Hacker World of Lulzsec, Anonymous, and the Global Cyber Insurgency*. New York: Little, Brown and Company.

Olsthoorn, P., & Royakkers, L. M. M. (2011). *Risks and robots – Some ethical issues*. Paper presented at the conference The Ethics of Emerging Military Technologies of International Society for Military Ethics (ISME), San Diego, CA. Retrieved from http://isme.tamu.edu/ISME11/isme11.html

Oppenheimer, R. (1953, July). Atomic Weapons and American Policy. *Foreign Affairs*, 31, 523–535.

Oppenheimer, R. (1955). *The Open Mind*. New York: Simon and Schuster.

Orend, B. (2006). *The morality of war*. Orchard Park, NY: Broadview Press.

Oreskes, N., & Conway, E. M. (2010). The Merchants of Doubt. New York: Bloomsbury Press.

Oreskes, N. (2004, June). Science and Public Policy: What's proof got to do with it? *Environmental Science & Policy*, 7(5), 369–383. doi:10.1016/j.envsci.2004.06.002

Osofsky, M. J., Bandura, A., & Zimbardo, P. G. (2005). The role of moral disengagement in the execution process. *Law and Human Behavior*, 29(4), 371–393. doi:10.100710979-005-4930-1 PMID:16133946

Pair: a social networking app just for couples. (n.d.). Retrieved February 12, 2017 from website: http://www.fastcodesign.com/1669435/pair-a-social-networking-app-just-for-couples

Palfrey, J. (2010). Four phases of internet regulation. *Social Research*, 77(3), 981–996.

Pallas, F. (2012). Data protection and smart grid communication – the European perspective. In *Proceedings of the 2012 IEEE Innovative Smart Grid Technologies Conference* (pp. 1-8). New York: IEEE. 10.1109/ISGT.2012.6175695

Palmer, C. C. (2001). Ethical hacking. *IBM Systems Journal*, 40(3), 769–780. doi:10.1147j.403.0769

Papenfuss, M. (2017, March 31). *1,000 Paid Russian Trolls Spread Fake News On Clinton, Senate Intelligence Heads Told*. Retrieved July 29, 2017, from http://www.huffingtonpost.com/entry/russian-trolls-fake-news_us_58dde6bae4b08194e3b8d5c4

Pariser, E. (2011). *The Filter Bubble: What the Internet Is Hiding from You*. New York: Penguin Press.

Parkin, B. L., Ekhtiari, H., & Walsh, V. F. (2015). Non-invasive Human Brain Stimulation in Cognitive Neuroscience: A Primer. *Neuron*, 87(5), 932–945. doi:10.1016/j.neuron.2015.07.032 PMID:26335641

Pasquale, F. (2015). *The Black Box Society: The Secret Algorithms That Control Money and Information*. Harvard UP.

Path. (n.d.). *Who we are.* Retrieved February 12, 2017 from https://path.com/about

Patrick, K., Mueller, R., & Gualtieri, C. (1987). *Psychopharmacology: The Third Generation of Progress* (H. Y. Meltzer, Ed.; 3rd ed.). New York: Raven press.

Pedersen, L. H. (2017). *The viral art effect: how virality and viral art as a part of our social networks can affect our society and how we perceive interfaces* (Unpublished master's thesis). The University of Bergen, Bergen, Norway.

Peek, S. T., Aarts, S., & Wouters, E. J. (2017). Can smart home technology deliver on the promise of independent living? A critical reflection based on the perspectives of older adults. Handbook of Smart Homes, Health Care and Well-Being, 203-214.

Peltier, T. R. (2004A). *Information Security Policies, Procedures, and Standards: Guidelines for effective information security management.* Boca Raton, FL: Auerbach publications. doi:10.1201/9780203488737

Peltier, T. R. (2004B). Risk analysis and risk management. *Information Systems Security, 13*(4), 44–56. doi:10.1201/1 086/44640.13.4.20040901/83732.7

Pérez-Triviño, J.L. (2011). Gene Doping and the Ethics of Sport: Between Enhancement and Posthumanism. *International Journal of Sports Science, 1*(1).

Pérez-Triviño, J.L. (2015). Equality of Access to Enhancement Technology in a Posthumanist Society. *Dilemata, 19.*

Pérez-Triviño, J. L. (2013). Cyborgsportpersons: Between Disability and Enhancement. *Physical Culture and Sport Studies and Research, 57*(1). doi:10.2478/pcssr-2013-0003

Perlmutter, J. S., & Mink, J. W. (2006). Deep brain stimulation. *Annual Review of Neuroscience, 29*(1), 229–257. doi:10.1146/annurev.neuro.29.051605.112824 PMID:16776585

Pesce, M. (1997). Ignition (A Ritual For the Festival of Brigit). *Hyper-real.* Accessed October 6, 2014. http://hyperreal. org/~mpesce/Ignition.html

Peterson, V. V. (2011). *Sex, ethics, and communication.* San Diego, CA: Cognella.

Pew Research Center for the People and the Press. (2013). *Few see adequate limits on NSA surveillance program.* Retrieved October 25, 2013, from http://www.people-press.org/ files/legacy-pdf/7-26-2013%20NSA%20release.pdf

Pino, B. (2010). Re-assessing ecology of tool transparency in epistemic practices. *Mind & Society, 9*(1), 85–110. doi:10.100711299-010-0071-4

Pitzer, K. S. (n.d.). *Letter dated April 2, 1952.* Retrieved January 16, 2015 from http://vault.fbi.gov/rosenberg-case/ robert-j.-oppenheimer

Plato. (1992). Republic (C.D.C. Reeve, Ed., & G.M.A. Grube, Trans.). Indianapolis, IN: Hackett Publishing Company. (Original work published c. 380 B.C.E.)

Poel, I., & Royakkers, L. (2011). Ethics, technology and engineering. Chichester, UK: John Wiley and Sons Ltd.

Polonijo, A. N., & Carpiano, R. M. (2008). Representations of cosmetic surgery and emotional health in women's magazines in Canada. *Women's Health Issues, 18*(6), 463–470. doi:10.1016/j.whi.2008.07.004 PMID:19041597

Ponce, P., Polasko, K., & Molina, A. (2016). End user perceptions toward smart grid technology: Acceptance, adoption, risks, and trust. *Renewable & Sustainable Energy Reviews, 60,* 587–598. doi:10.1016/j.rser.2016.01.101

Pontius, A. A. (1973). Neuro-ethics of 'walking' in the newborn. *Perceptual and Motor Skills, 37*(1), 235–245. doi:10.2466/ pms.1973.37.1.235 PMID:4728008

Poplin, C. M. (2015, November 30). *NSA Ends Bulk Collection of Telephony Metadata under Section 215*. Accessed July 29, 2017, from https://www.lawfareblog.com/nsa-ends-bulk-collection-telephony-metadata-under-section-215

Popper, K. (1947). *The Open Society and its Enemies* (Vol. 1). London: Routledge.

Porsdam,, M. S., & Sahakian, B. J. (2015). The increasing lifestyle use of modafinil by healthy people: Safety and ethical issues. *Current Opinion in Behavioral Sciences*, 4.

Price, D. (1965). *The Scientific Estate*. Cambridge, MA: The Bellknap Press of Harvard University.

Priest, D., & Arkin, W. M. (2011). *Top Secret America: The Rise of the New American Security State*. New York: Little, Brown and, Company.

Public Safety Canada. (2013a). *Canada's Cyber Security Strategy*. Retrieved September 30, 2013, from http://www.publicsafety.gc.ca/cnt/rsrcs/pblctns/cbr-scrt-strtgy/index-eng.aspx

Public Safety Canada. (2013b). *An Open Letter to Canadians on Cyber Security Awareness*. Retrieved September 30, 2013, from http://www.publicsafety.gc.ca/cnt/nws/nws-rlss/2013/20131003-eng.aspx

Public Safety Canada. (2013c). *Harper Government announces action plan for cyber security*. Retrieved September 30, 2013, from http://www.publicsafety.gc.ca/cnt/nws/nws-rlss/2013/20130418-eng.aspx

Purcell, K. (2010). *The state of the online video*. Washington, DC: Pew Internet & American Life Project.

Quinn, E. (2009). Privacy and the new energy infrastructure. *SSRN eLibrary*.

Raban, D. R. (2009). Self-presentation and the value of information in Q&A websites. *Journal of the American Society for Information Science and Technology*, *60*(12), 2465–2473. doi:10.1002/asi.21188

Raffensperger, C., & Tickner, J. (Eds.). (1999). *Protecting public health and the environment: Implementing the precautionary principle*. Washington, DC: Island Press.

Rafferty, R., & Vander Ven, T. (2014). "I hate everything about you": A qualitative examination of cyberbullying and on-line aggression in a college sample. *Deviant Behavior*, *35*(5), 364–377. doi:10.1080/01639625.2013.849171

Raftery, T. (2013, October 10). Utilities should open up API's to their smart meter data [Blog post]. Retrieved from: http://greenmonk.net/2013/10/10/utilities-should-open-up-apis-to-their-smart-meter-data/

Rajabi, M. T., Makateb, A., Hashemi, H., Holland, E. J., Djalilian, A., & Nerad, J. A. (2015). Disaster in cosmetic surgery: Inadvertent formalin injection during blepharoplasty. *Ophthalmic Plastic and Reconstructive Surgery*, *31*(4), e86–e89. doi:10.1097/IOP.0000000000000110 PMID:26168210

Ramirez. (2011). *High Frequency Trading*. Retrieved from http://www.google.nl/url?sa=t&rct=j&q=&esrc=s&source=web&cd=2&ved=0CCkQFjAB&url=http%3A%2F%2Fre.vu%2Fdoc-download%2Fluzorlandoramirez%2F129619%2Fwork_example-luz.orlando.ramirez-highfrequencytrading.149252.1340385848.pdf&ei=4O8uVIm8CYSjPKO3gdgE&usg=AFQjCNF8239BS1WMAB865KebjUqmDDklig&bvm=bv.76802529,d.ZWU

Ramo, J. C. (2017). *Seventh sense: Power, fortune, and survival in the age of networks*. Back Bay Books.

Rawlins, F. I. G. (1950). Episteme and Techne. *Philosophy and Phenomenological Research*, *10*(3), 389–397. doi:10.2307/2103272

Rawls, J. (1971). *A theory of justice*. Cambridge, MA: Belknap Press of Harvard University Press.

Reaves, S., Hitchon, J. B., Park, S.-Y., & Yun, G. W. (2004a). If looks could kill: Digital manipulation of fashion models. *Journal of Mass Media Ethics*, *19*(1), 56–71. doi:10.120715327728jmme1901_5

Reaves, S., Hitchon, J. B., Park, S.-Y., & Yun, G. W. (2004b). "You can never be too thin"—Or can you? A pilot study on the effects of digital manipulation of fashion models' body size, leg length and skin color. *Race, Gender, & Class*, *11*(2), 140–155.

Reese, H., & Heath, N. (2016, December 21). *Inside Amazon's clickworker platform: How half a million people are being paid pennies to train AI*. Retrieved July 29, 2017, from http://www.techrepublic.com/article/inside-amazons-clickworker-platform-how-half-a-million-people-are-training-ai-for-pennies-per-task/

Regalado, D., Harris, S., Harper, A., Eagle, C., Ness, J., Spasojevic, B., & Sims, S. (2015). *Gray hat hacking the ethical hacker's handbook*. McGraw-Hill Education Group.

Rennecker, J., & Godwin, L. (2003). Theorizing the unintended consequences of instant messaging for worker productivity. *Sprouts: Working Papers on Information Environments. Systems and Organizations*, 3. Retrieved January 30, 2014, from: http://sprouts.aisnet.org/190/1/030307.pdf

Repacholi, M. H. (2001). Health risks from the use of mobile phones. *Toxicology Letters*, *120*(1), 323–331. doi:10.1016/S0378-4274(01)00285-5 PMID:11323191

Repantis, D., Schlattmann, P., Laisney, O., & Heuser, I. (2010). Modafinil and methylphenidate for neuroenhancement in healthy individuals: A systematic review. *Pharmacological Research*, *62*(3), 187–206. doi:10.1016/j.phrs.2010.04.002 PMID:20416377

Report of the Staffs of the CFTC and SEC to the Joint Advisory Committee on Emerging Regulatory Issues. (2010). *Findings regarding the market events of May 6, 2010*. Author.

Research and Markets. (2013). *Global Smart Appliances Market 2012-2016*. Retrieved February 24, 2014, from http://www.researchandmarkets.com/research/xdchz5/global_smart

Resek, C. (Ed.). (1964). *War and the Intellectuals*. Indianapolis, IN: Hackett Publishing Co.

Resnick, D. (2013). Is Weapons Research Immoral? *Metascience*, *23*(1), 105–107. doi:10.100711016-013-9834-y

Reynolds, G. W. (2012). *Ethics in information technology*. Boston, MA: Cengage Learning.

Rhodes, R. (1986). *The Making of the Atomic Bomb. Harmonsworth, UK*. Penguin.

Rigby, K., & Smith, P. K. (2011). Is school bullying really on the rise? *Social Psychology of Education*, *14*(4), 441–455. doi:10.100711218-011-9158-y

Rihill, T. (2007). *The Catapult*. Yardley, PA: Westholme.

Rippen, H., & Risk, A. (2000). e-Health code of ethics (May 24). *Journal of Medical Internet Research*, *2*(2), e9. doi:10.2196/jmir.2.2.e9 PMID:11720928

Rivoltella, P. C. (2008). *Knowledge, Culture and Society in the Information Age. In Digital Literacy: Tools and Methodologies for Information Society*. IRM Press.

Rizza, C., & Pereira, A. G. (Eds.). (2013). *Social networks and Cyber-bullying among teenagers: EU Scientific and Policy report*. Publications Office of the European Union.

Robbins, T., & Arnsten, A. (2009). The Neuropsychopharmacology of Fronto-Executive Function: Monoaminergic Modulation. *Annual Review of Neuroscience*, *32*(1), 267–287. doi:10.1146/annurev.neuro.051508.135535 PMID:19555290

Robinson, J. J. D., Wagner, N.-F., & Northoff, G. (2015). Is the Sense of Agency in Schizophrenia Influenced by Resting-State Variation in Self-Referential Regions of the Brain? *Schizophrenia Bulletin*, *42*(2), 270–276. doi:10.1093chbulbv102 PMID:26221048

Rocci, L. (2012). *International Journal of Technoethics*. An Official Publication of the Information Resources Management Association.

Röcker, C. (2010). Social and technological concerns associated with the usage of ubiquitous computing technologies. *Issues in Information Systems*, *11*(1).

Roco, M. C., & Bainbridge, W. S. (Eds.). (2002). Converging technologies for improving human performance: nanotechnology, biotechnology, information technology and cognitive science. NSF-DOC Report, June 2002, Arlington, VA.

Roco, M. C. (2004). Science and technology integration for increased human potential and societal outcomes. *Annals of the New York Academy of Sciences*, *1013*(1), 1–16. doi:10.1196/annals.1305.001 PMID:15194603

Ron, B., Meulen, R., Malizia, A., & Vos, R. (2011). Scientific, ethical, and social issues in mood enhancement. In Enhancing Human Capacities. Oxford, UK: Blackwell.

Ronchi, A. M. (2009). *E-Culture*. New York: Springer-Verlag, LLC.

Rosenberg, S. (2017, June 30). *Facebook Learns That the Censor's Job Is Never Done*. Retrieved July 29, 2017, from https://shift.newco.co/facebook-learns-that-the-censors-job-is-never-done-3f57a4de7b1b

Roskies, A. (2002). Neuroethics for the new millenium. *Neuron*, *35*(1), 21–23. doi:10.1016/S0896-6273(02)00763-8 PMID:12123605

Rossi, S., Hallett, M., Rossini, P. M., & Pascual-Leone, A. (2009). Safety, ethical considerations, and application guidelines for the use of transcranial magnetic stimulation in clinical practice and research. *Clinical Neurophysiology*, *120*(12), 2008–2039. doi:10.1016/j.clinph.2009.08.016 PMID:19833552

Rothblatt, M. (2011). Won't mindclones only be for the rich and famous? *Institute for Ethics & Emerging Technologies*. Retrieved November 17, 2015, from http://ieet.org/index.php/IEET/more/rothblatt20110321

Royakkers, L. M. M., & Topolski, A. R. (2014). Military robotics & relationality: criteria for ethical decision-making. In J. van den Hoven, N. Doorn, T. Swierstra, B.-J. Koops, & H. Romijn (Eds.), *Responsible innovation 1. Innovative solutions for global issues* (pp. 351–367). Dordrecht: Springer. doi:10.1007/978-94-017-8956-1_20

Royakkers, L. M. M., & Van Est, Q. (2010). The cubicle warrior: The marionette of digitalized warfare. *Ethics and Information Technology*, *12*(3), 289–296. doi:10.100710676-010-9240-8

RozendaalR. (2014). *Abstract browsing*. Retrieved from http://www.newrafael.com/notes-on-abstract-browsing/

Rubia, K., Alegria, A., Cubillo, A., Smith, A., Brammer, M., & Radua, J. (2013). Effects of Stimulants on Brain Function in Attention-Deficit/Hyperactivity Disorder: A Systematic Review and Meta-Analysis. *Biological Psychiatry*, *76*(8), 616–628. doi:10.1016/j.biopsych.2013.10.016 PMID:24314347

Ruetzler, T., Taylor, J., Reynolds, D., Baker, W., & Killen, C. (2012). What is professional attire today? A conjoint analysis of personal presentation attributes. *International Journal of Hospitality Management*, *31*(3), 937–943. doi:10.1016/j.ijhm.2011.11.001

Rushmore, R. J. (2013). *Viral art*. Retrieved from http://viralart.vandalog.com/read/buy

Russo, D., Wheeldon, C., & Part, A. (2013, September 12). *New beginnings*. Retrieved from https://www.youtube.com/watch?v=3zMCxmdkcRY

Russo, S., Dietz, D., Dumitriu, D., Morrison, J., Malenka, R., & Nestler, E. (2010). The addicted synapse: Mechanisms of synaptic and structural plasticity in nucleus accumbens. *Trends in Neurosciences*, *33*(6), 267–276. doi:10.1016/j.tins.2010.02.002 PMID:20207024

Sahakian, B., & Morein-Zamir, S. (2007). Professor's little helper. *Nature*, *450*(7173), 1157–1159. doi:10.1038/4501157a PMID:18097378

Salomon, J.-J. (1973). *Science and Politics* (N. Lindsay, Trans.). Cambridge, MA: MIT Press.

Sanchez Taylor, J. (2012). Fake breasts and power: Gender, class and cosmetic surgery. *Women's Studies International Forum*, *35*(6), 458–466. doi:10.1016/j.wsif.2012.09.003

Sánchez, X., & Lejeune, M. (1999). Práctica Mental y deporte. ¿Qué sabemos después de casi un siglo de investigación? *Revista de Psicología del Deporte*, *8*(1).

Sandberg, A. (2011). Cognition Enhancement: Upgrading the Brain. In Enhancing Human Capacities. Oxford, UK: Blackwell.

Sandel, M. (2007). *The case against Perfection*. Cambridge, MA: Harvard University Press.

Sandel, M. (2007). *The Case against Perfection: Ethics in the Age of Genetic Engineering*. Belknap Press of Harvard University Press.

Sandel, M. (2012). The Case against Perfection. In S. Holland (Ed.), *Arguing About Bioethics* (pp. 93–105). New York: Routledge.

Sanguineti, V., Giugliano, M., Grattoarola, M., & Morasso, P. (2001). 14 Neuro-Engineering: From neural interfaces to biological computers. *Communications Through Virtual Technologies: Identity, Community, and Technology in the Communication Age*, *1*, 233.

Sattler, S., Sauer, C., Mehlkop, G., & Graeff, P. (2013). The rationale for consuming cognitive enhancement drugs in university students and teachers. *PLoS One*, *8*(7), e68821. doi:10.1371/journal.pone.0068821 PMID:23874778

Sauseng, P., Klimesch, W., Heise, K. F., Gruber, W. R., Holz, E., Karim, A. A., ... Hummel, F. C. (2009). Brain Oscillatory Substrates of Visual Short-Term Memory Capacity. *Current Biology*, *19*(21), 1846–1852. doi:10.1016/j.cub.2009.08.062 PMID:19913428

Savchuk, V. V. (2013). *Media Philosophy. Attack reality*. Saint-Petersburg, Russia: Academic Press.

Savulescu, J. (2007). Gene therapy, transgenesis and chimeras: is the radical genetic alteration of human beings a threat to our humanity? In J. Savulescu (Ed.), *Quest of Ethical Wisdom: How the Practical Ethics of East and West Contribute to Wisdom*. Oxford, UK: Oxford Uehiro Centre for Practical Ethics.

Scharre, P. D. (2015). The opportunity and challenge of autonomous systems. In Autonomous systems. Issues for Defence Policymakers. NATO Headquarters Supreme Allied Command. Allied Command Transformation.

Schechtman, M. (2014). *Staying Alive—Personal Identity, Practical Concerns, and the Unity of a Life*. New York: Oxford University Press. doi:10.1093/acprof:oso/9780199684878.001.0001

Schleim, S. (2012). Brains in context in the neurolaw debate: The examples of free will and "dangerous" brains. *International Journal of Law and Psychiatry*, *35*(2), 104–111. doi:10.1016/j.ijlp.2012.01.001 PMID:22289293

Schmidt, L., & Pipkin, K. R. (2015). *@mothgenerator*. Retrieved from https://twitter.com/mothgenerator?ref_src=twsrc%5Egoogle%7Ctwcamp%5Eserp%7Ctwgr%5Eauthor on July 30, 2017.

Schmidt, E., & Cohen, J. (2013). *The New Digital Age: Reshaping the Future of People, Nations and Business*. New York: Random House.

Schulzke, M. (2013). Autonomous weapons and distributed responsibility. *Philosophy & Technology, 26*(2), 203–219. doi:10.100713347-012-0089-0

Schwartz, A. B. (2004). Cortical neural prosthetics. *Annual Review of Neuroscience, 27*(1), 487–507. doi:10.1146/annurev.neuro.27.070203.144233 PMID:15217341

Schwarz, E. (2017). *Death machines: The ethics of violent technologies*. Manchester, UK: Manchester University Press.

Schweren, L., Hartman, C., Zwiers, M., Heslenfeld, D., van der Meer, D., Franke, B., ... Hoekstra, P. (2014). Combined stimulant and antipsychotic treatment in adolescents with attention-deficit/hyperactivity disorder: A cross-sectional observational structural MRI study. *European Child & Adolescent Psychiatry*. PMID:25395383

Searle, J. (1980). Minds, brains, and programs. *Behavioral and Brain Sciences, 3*(3), 417–457. doi:10.1017/S0140525X00005756

Seidman, L., Valera, E., & Makris, N. (2005). Structural brain imaging of attention-deficit/hyperactivity disorder. *Biological Psychiatry, 57*(11), 1263–1272. doi:10.1016/j.biopsych.2004.11.019 PMID:15949998

Sela, T., Kilim, A., & Lavidor, M. (2012). Transcranial alternating current stimulation increases risk-taking behavior in the Balloon Analog Risk Task. *Frontiers in Neuroscience, 6*, 1–11. doi:10.3389/fnins.2012.00022 PMID:22347844

Selimbegović, L., & Chatard, A. (2015). Single exposure to disclaimers on airbrushed thin ideal images increases negative thought accessibility. *Body Image, 12*, 1–5. doi:10.1016/j.bodyim.2014.08.012 PMID:25260193

Sender, K. (Director). (2014). *Brand new you: Makeover television and the American dream* [DVD]. Northampton, MA: Media Education Foundation.

Serruya, M. D., Hatsopoulos, N. G., Paninski, L., Fellows, M. R., & Donoghue, J. P. (2002). Brain-machine interface: Instant neural control of a movement signal. *Nature, 416*(6877), 141–142. doi:10.1038/416141a PMID:11894084

Shachtman, N. (2007, October 18). *Robot cannon kills 9, wounds 14*. Wired.com.

Shain, W., Spataro, L., Dilgen, J., Haverstick, K., Retterer, S., Isaacson, M., & Turner, J. N. (2003). Controlling cellular reactive responses around neural prosthetic devices using peripheral and local intervention strategies. *Neural Systems and Rehabilitation Engineering. IEEE Transactions on, 11*(2), 186–188. PMID:12899270

Shang, Y., Wang, X., Shang, X., Zhang, H., Liu, Z., Yin, T., & Zhang, T. (2016). Repetitive transcranial magnetic stimulation effectively facilitates spatial cognition and synaptic plasticity associated with increasing the levels of BDNF and synaptic proteins in Wistar rats. *Neurobiology of Learning and Memory, 134*, 369–378. doi:10.1016/j.nlm.2016.08.016 PMID:27555233

Shanks, R., Ross, J., Doyle, H., Helton, A., Picou, B., Schulz, J., ... Lloyd, S. (2015). Adolescent exposure to cocaine, amphetamine, and methylphenidate cross-sensitizes adults to methamphetamine with drug- and sex-specific effects. *Behavioural Brain Research, 281*, 116–124. doi:10.1016/j.bbr.2014.12.002 PMID:25496784

Shannon, C. E. (1948). A mathematical theory of communication. *The Bell System Technical Journal, 27*(3), 379–423. doi:10.1002/j.1538-7305.1948.tb01338.x

Sharkey, N. (2008). Cassandra or false prophet of doom: AI robots and war. *IEEE Intelligent Systems, 23*(4), 14–17. doi:10.1109/MIS.2008.60

Sharkey, N. (2010). Saying 'no!' to lethal autonomous targeting. *Journal of Military Ethics*, *9*(4), 369–383. doi:10.108 0/15027570.2010.537903

Shaw, S., Shah, L., Jolly, A., & Wylie, J. (2008). Identifying heterogeneity among injection drug users: A cluster analysis approach. *American Journal of Public Health*, *98*(8), 1430–1437. doi:10.2105/AJPH.2007.120741 PMID:18556614

Shea, V. (1994). *The Core rules of Netiquette*. Retrieved December 20, 2016 from http://www.albion.com/netiquette/corerules.html

Shields, V. R., & Heinecken, D. (2001). *Measuring up: How advertising affects self-image*. Philadelphia, PA: University of Pennsylvania Press. doi:10.9783/9780812204025

Shifman, L. (2013). *MIT press essential knowledge: memes in digital culture*. Cambridge, UK: MIT Press.

Shimogawa, D. (2014, Mar 11). Hawaiian Electric to install smart meters on Oahu. *Pacific Business News*. Retrieved from http://www.bizjournals.com/pacific/news/ 2014/03/11/hawaiian-electric-to-install-smart-meters-on-oahu.html

Shirky, C. (2005). *Institutions vs. Collaboration*. TED.

Shirky, C. (2009). *Here comes everybody: the power of organizing without organizations*. New York, NY: Penguin.

Shulman, S. (2008). *Undermining Science, Suppression and Distortion in the Bush Administration*. Oakland, CA: University of California Press.

Shumay, E., Chen, J., Fowler, J., & Volkow, N. (2011). Genotype and Ancestry Modulate Brain's DAT Availability in Healthy Humans. *PLoS One*, *6*. PMID:21826203

Sider, R. C., & Clements, C. D. (1984). Patients' ethical obligation for their health. *Journal of Medical Ethics*, *10*(3), 138–142. doi:10.1136/jme.10.3.138 PMID:6502640

Simonite, T. (2017, July 14). *Apple's Privacy Pledge Complicates Its AI Push*. Accessed July 29, 2017, from https://www.wired.com/story/apple-ai-privacy/

Simon, R. (1993). *Fair Play. Sports, values and society*. Boulder, CO: Westview Press.

Simpson, M., Backman, K., & Corley, J. (2010). *Hands-on ethical hacking and network defense*. Cengage Learning.

Simpson, T. W., & Müller, V. C. (2016). Just war and robots' killings. *The Philosophical Quarterly*, *66*(263), 302–322. doi:10.1093/pq/pqv075

Singer, N. (2012) Mission Control, Built for Cities. *The New York Times*. Accessed January 11, 2015. http://www.nytimes.com/2012/03/04/business/ibm-takes-smarter-cities-concept-to-rio-de-janeiro.html?pagewanted=all&_r=0

Singer, P. W. (2009). *Wired for war: The robotics revolution and conflict in the 21st century*. New York: The Penguin Press.

Singer, P. W. (2009). *Wired for war: The robotics revolution and conflict in the twenty-first century*. New York: Penguin Books.

Singer, P. W. (2010). The future of war. In G. Dabringer (Ed.), *Ethical and legal aspects of unmanned systems: Interviews* (pp. 71–84). Vienna: Institute for Religion and Peace.

Singh, K. (2015). Cosmetic surgery in teenagers: To do or not to do. *Journal of Cutaneous and Aesthetic Surgery*, *8*(1), 57–59. doi:10.4103/0974-2077.155091 PMID:25949026

Sinnott-Armstrong, W. (2002). Gert Contra Consequentialism. In W. Sinnott-Armstrong & R. Audi (Eds.), Rationality, Rules and Ideals. Lanham, MD: Roman and Littlefield.

Slevec, J., & Tiggemann, M. (2010). Attitudes toward cosmetic surgery in middle-aged women: Body image, aging anxiety, and the media. *Psychology of Women Quarterly, 34*(1), 65–74. doi:10.1111/j.1471-6402.2009.01542.x

Slim, H. (2007). *Killing civilians: Method, madness and morality in war.* Hurst Company.

Smart, J. J. C., & Haldane, J. J. (2003). *Atheism and theism.* Blackwell Publishing. doi:10.1002/9780470756225

Smirnova, M. H. (2012). A will to youth: The woman's anti-aging elixir. *Social Science & Medicine, 75*(7), 1236–1243. doi:10.1016/j.socscimed.2012.02.061 PMID:22742924

Smith, G. B. (1991). Heidegger, Technology and Postmodernity. *The Social Science Journal, 28*(3), 369c–389. doi:10.1016/0362-3319(91)90019-Z

Snowball, A., Tachtsidis, I., Popescu, T., Thompson, J., Delazer, M., Zamarian, L., ... Cohen Kadosh, R. (2013). Long-term enhancement of brain function and cognition using cognitive training and brain stimulation. *Current Biology, 23*(11), 987–992. doi:10.1016/j.cub.2013.04.045 PMID:23684971

Society of Professional Journalists. (1996). *Code of ethics.* Retrieved from http://www.spj.org/pdf/ethicscode.pdf

Solove, D. (2010). *Understanding privacy.* Cambridge, MA: Harvard University Press.

Solvi, A. S., Foss, K., von Soest, T., Roald, H. E., Skolleborg, K. C., & Holte, A. (2010). Motivational factors and psychological processes in cosmetic breast augmentation surgery. *Journal of Plastic, Reconstructive & Aesthetic Surgery; JPRAS, 63*(4), 673–680. doi:10.1016/j.bjps.2009.01.024 PMID:19268646

Sontag, S. (2011). Against interpretation. In Against Interpretation and Other Essays (pp. 3–15). New York, NY: Picador USA. (Original work published 1966)

Sontag, L. M., Clemans, K. H., Graber, J. A., & Lyndon, S. T. (2011). Traditional and cyber aggressors and victims: A comparison of psychosocial characteristics. *Journal of Youth and Adolescence, 40*(4), 392–404. doi:10.100710964-010-9575-9 PMID:20680425

Spahn, A. (2015). Can Technology make us happy? Ethics, Spectator's happiness and the value of achievement. Well-being in contemporary society. Springer International Publishing.

Sparrow, R. (2007). Killer robots. *Journal of Applied Philosophy, 24*(1), 62–77. doi:10.1111/j.1468-5930.2007.00346.x

Sparrow, R. (2009). Building a better warbot: Ethical issues in the design of unmanned systems for military applications. *Science and Engineering Ethics, 15*(2), 169–187. doi:10.100711948-008-9107-0 PMID:19048395

Sparrow, R. (2011). Robotic weapons and the future of war. In P. Tripodi & J. Wolfendale (Eds.), *New wars and new soldiers: Military ethics in the contemporary world* (pp. 117–133). Farnham, UK: Ashgate.

Sparrow, R. (2011). Robotic weapons and the future of war. In J. Wolfendale & P. Tripodi (Eds.), *New wars and new soldiers* (pp. 117–133). Burlington: Ashgate.

Spencer, T., Brown, A., Seidman, L., Valera, M., Makris, N., Lomedico, A., ... Biederman, J. (2013). Effect of Psychostimulants on Brain Structure and Function in ADHD: A Qualitative Literature Review of MRI-Based Neuroimaging Studies. *The Journal of Clinical Psychiatry, 74*(09), 902–917. doi:10.4088/JCP.12r08287 PMID:24107764

Spilson, S. V., Chung, K. C., Greenfield, M. L. V. H., & Walters, M. (2002). Are plastic surgery advertisements conforming to the ethical codes of the American society of plastic surgeons? *Plastic and Reconstructive Surgery, 109*(3), 1181–1186. doi:10.1097/00006534-200203000-00063 PMID:11884856

Spranger, T. M. (Ed.). (2012). *International neurolaw: A comparative analysis.* Springer. doi:10.1007/978-3-642-21541-4

Sridharan, D., Levitin, D. J., & Menon, V. (2008). A critical role for the right fronto-insular cortex in switching between central-executive and default-mode networks. *Proceedings of the National Academy of Sciences of the United States of America*, *105*(34), 12569–12574. doi:10.1073/pnas.0800005105 PMID:18723676

St. John, J. (2014, March 13). Hidden treasure: Two new resources offer up massive amounts of utility data. *Greentech-grid*. Retrieved from: https://www.greentechmedia.com/articles/ read/Energy-Data-Treasure-from-Chattanoogas-Smart-Grid-Incubator-and-Pecan-Str

Stahl, B. C., & Rogerson, S. (2009). Landscapes of ethical issues of emerging ict applications in europe. In *Proceedings of the Eighth International Conference of Computer Ethics: Philosophical Enquiry* (pp. 719 – 738). Nomiki bibliothiki.

Stake, R. E. (1995). *The art of case study design*. Sage Publications.

Stamp, M. (2011). *Introduction in information security: Principles and practice* (2nd ed.). Hoboken, NJ: John Wiley & Sons, Inc. doi:10.1002/9781118027974

Stanoevska-Slabeva, K. (2002). Toward a community-oriented design of Internet platforms. *International Journal of Electronic Commerce*, *6*(3), 71–95. doi:10.1080/10864415.2002.11044244

State of Hawaii, Department of Business, Economic Development and Tourism. (2011). *Renewable energy in Hawaii. Periodic research and data reports on issues of current interest, economic report 2011*. Honolulu, HI: Department of Business, Economic Development & Tourism.

Stebbins, R. A. (Ed.). (2001). *Exploratory research in the social sciences* (Vol. 48). Sage Publications. doi:10.4135/9781412984249

Steiner Chr. (2013). *Automate this: How algorithms took over our markets, our jobs, and the world*. New York: Penguin Group.

Steiner, C. (2012). *Automate This: How Algorithms Came to Rule Our World*. New York: Portfolio/Penguin.

Stewart, C. (2010a, February 14). Montag took wrong road with plastic surgeries. *Orange County Register*, p. K.

Stewart, C. (2010b, May 9). Heidi Montag plans more surgeries. *Orange County Register*, p. Arts K.

Stibel, J. M. (2009). *Breakpoint: Why the Web Will Implode, Search Will Be Obsolete, and Everything Else You Need to Know about Technology Is in Your Brain*. New York: Palgrave Macmillan.

Stice, E., Spangler, D., & Agras, W. S. (2001). Exposure to media-portrayed thin-ideal images adversely affects vulnerable girls: A longitudinal experiment. *Journal of Social and Clinical Psychology*, *20*(3), 270–288. doi:10.1521/jscp.20.3.270.22309

Stieglitz, T., Schuetter, M., & Koch, K. P. (2005). Implantable biomedical microsystems for neural prostheses. *Engineering in Medicine and Biology Magazine, IEEE*, *24*(5), 58–65. doi:10.1109/MEMB.2005.1511501 PMID:16248118

Stieglitz, T., Schuettler, M., & Meyer, J. U. (2000). Micromachined, polyimide-based devices for flexible neural interfaces. *Biomedical Microdevices*, *2*(4), 283–294. doi:10.1023/A:1009955222114

Stiglitz, J. E., & Greenwald, B. C. (2015). *Creating a learning society: A new approach to growth, development, and social progress*. New York: Columbia University Press. doi:10.7312tig17549

Strawser, B. J. (2011). *Two bad arguments for the justification of autonomous weapons*. Paper presented at Technology and Security, University of North Texas.

Sturm, J. (2017). Persuasive Technology. Handbook of Smart Homes, Health Care and Well-Being, 3-12.

Sugiyama, L. S. (2004). Is beauty in the context-sensitive adaptations of the beholder? Shiwiar use of waist-to-hip ratio in assessments of female mate value. *Evolution and Human Behavior, 25*(1), 51–62. doi:10.1016/S1090-5138(03)00083-7

Suhler, C. L., & Churchland, P. S. (2011). The Neurobiological Basis of Morality. In J. Illes & B. J. Sahakian (Eds.), *The Oxford Handbook of Neuroethics* (pp. 33–58). Oxford, UK: Oxford University Press.

Sullins, J. (2010). RoboWarfare: Can robots be more ethical than humans on the battlefield? *Ethics and Information Technology, 12*(3), 263–275. doi:10.100710676-010-9241-7

Suthana, N., Haneef, Z., Stern, J., Mukamel, R., Behnke, E., Knowlton, B., & Fried, I. (2012). Memory Enhancement and Deep-Brain Stimulation of the Entorhinal Area. *The New England Journal of Medicine, 366*(6), 502–510. doi:10.1056/NEJMoa1107212 PMID:22316444

Swami, V. (2009). Body appreciation, media influence, and weight status predict consideration of cosmetic surgery among female undergraduates. *Body Image, 6*(4), 315–317. doi:10.1016/j.bodyim.2009.07.001 PMID:19656747

Swami, V., Campana, A. N. N. B., Ferreira, L., Barrett, S., Harris, A. S., & Tavares, M. C. G. C. F. (2011). The acceptance of cosmetic surgery scale: Initial examination of its factor structure and correlates among Brazilian adults. *Body Image, 8*(2), 179–185. PMID:21354875

Swami, V., Taylor, R., & Carvalho, C. (2009). Acceptance of cosmetic surgery and celebrity worship: Evidence of associations among female undergraduates. *Personality and Individual Differences, 47*(8), 869–872. doi:10.1016/j.paid.2009.07.006

Swierstra, T., & Rip, A. (2007). Nano-ethics as NEST-ethics: Patterns of moral argumentation about new and emerging science and technology. *NanoEthics, 1*(1), 3–20. doi:10.100711569-007-0005-8

Sydell, L. (2014). In A Battle For Web Traffic, Bad Bots Are Going After Grandma. *NPR.* Accessed December 29, 2014. http://www.npr.org/blogs/alltechconsidered/2014/07/03/328196199/in-a-battle-for-web-traffic-bad-bots-are-going-after-grandma

Szostek. (2011). Studies of Interactions between human traders and Algorithmic trading systems. Government Office for Science London.

Takagi, M. (2012). Safety and Neuroethical Consideration of Deep Brain Stimulation as Psychiatric or Dementia Treatment. *Asian Bioethics Review, 4*(1), 48–64.

Tamorri, S. (2004). *Neurociencias y deporte. Psicología deportiva y procesos mentales del atleta.* Barcelona: Ed. Paidotribo.

Tansley, A. G. (1935, July). The use and abuse of vegetational concepts and terms. *Ecology, 16*(3), 284–307. doi:10.2307/1930070

Taylor, J. S. (1995). Neurolaw: Towards a new medical jurisprudence. *Brain Injury: [BI], 9*(7), 745–751. doi:10.3109/02699059509008230 PMID:8680401

Tendril. (2012, January 20). *NYC Cleanweb Hackathon: Crowdsourcing killer energy apps.* Retrieved from: http://www.tendrilinc.com/blog/nyc-cleanweb-hackathon-crowdsourcing-killer-energy-apps

Thaler, R. H., & Sunstein, C. (2008). *Nudge: Improving Decisions about Health, Wealth, and Happiness.* New Haven, CT: Yale University Press.

The Great Wall of Vagina. (n.d.). *About the great wall of vagina.* Retrieved from http://www.greatwallofvagina.co.uk/about

The Shape of a Mother. (2016). Retrieved from http://theshapeofamother.com/

The White House. (1965). *Restoring the Quality of our Environment, Report of the Environmental Pollution Panel.* President's Science Advisory Committee.

Theran, S. A., Newberg, E. M., & Gleason, T. R. (2010). Adolescent girls' parasocial interactions with media figures. *The Journal of Genetic Psychology, 171*(3), 270–277. doi:10.1080/00221325.2010.483700 PMID:20836434

Thompson, M. (2007). V-22 Osprey: A flying shame. *Time.* Retrieved June 26, 2017, from http://www.time.com/time/politics/article/0,8599,1665835,00.html

Thompson, N. (2017, June 29). *Instagram Launches An AI System to Blast Away Nasty Comments.* Retrieved July 29, 2017, from https://www.wired.com/story/instagram-launches-ai-system-to-blast-nasty-comments/

Thornhill, R., & Gangestad, S. W. (1996). The evolution of human sexuality. *Trends in Ecology & Evolution, 11*(2), 98–102. doi:10.1016/0169-5347(96)81051-2 PMID:21237770

Tignol, J., Biraben-Gotzamanis, L., Martin-Guehl, C., Grabot, D., & Aouizerate, B. (2007). Body dysmorphic disorder and cosmetic surgery: Evolution of 24 subjects with a minimal defect in appearance 5 years after their request for cosmetic surgery. *European Psychiatry, 22*(8), 520–524. doi:10.1016/j.eurpsy.2007.05.003 PMID:17900876

Tobaiqy, M., Stewart, D., Helms, P., Williams, J., Crum, J., Steer, C., & McLay, J. (2011). Parental reporting of adverse drug reactions associated with attention-deficit hyperactivity disorder (ADHD) medications in children attending specialist paediatric clinics in the UK. *Drug Safety, 34*(3), 211–219. doi:10.2165/11586050-000000000-00000 PMID:21332245

Toffler, A. (1980). *The Third Wave.* New York: Bantam Books.

Toffler, A. (1991). *Powershift: knowledge, wealth and violence in the 21st century.* New York: Bantan.

Tolstoy, L. (2011). What is art? (W. G. Jones, Ed., & A. Maude, Trans.). London, UK: Bristol Classical Press. (Original work published 1897)

Tonkens, R. (2009). A challenge for Machine Ethics. *Minds and Machines, 19*(3), 421–438. doi:10.100711023-009-9159-1

Tonn, B. (2006). Co-volution of Social Science and Emerging Technologies. *Managing nano-bio-info-cogno innovations*, 309-335.

Townsend, A. M. (2014). *Smart Cities: Big Data, Civic Hackers, and the Quest for a New Utopia.* New York: W.W Norton & Company.

Tsukayama, H. (2014). Google's smart contact lens: What it does and how it works. *The Washington Post.* Retrieved February 20, 2014 from http://www.washingtonpost.com/business/technology/googles-smart-contact-lens-what-it-does-and-how-it-works/2014/01/17/96b938ec-7f80-11e3-93c1-0e888170b723_story.html

Tufekci, Z. (2017). *Twitter and Teargas.* London: Yale University Press.

Turkle, Sh. (2006). A Nascent Robotics Culture: New Complicities for Companionship. *AAAI Technical Report Series (World Health Organization).*

Turner, D., Robbins, T., Clark, L., Aron, A., Dowson, J., & Sahakian, B. (2003). Relative lack of cognitive effects of methylphenidate in elderly male volunteers. *Psychopharmacology, 168*(4), 455–464. doi:10.100700213-003-1457-3 PMID:12734634

Turner, F. (2006). *From Counterculture to Cyberculture: Stewart Brand, the Whole Earth Network, and the Rise of Digital Utopianism.* Chicago: U of Chicago. doi:10.7208/chicago/9780226817439.001.0001

Turow, J. (2006). Cracking the consumer code: Advertisers, anxiety and surveillance in the digital age. In K. D. Haggerty & R. V. Ericson (Eds.), *The new politics of surveillance and visibility* (pp. 279–307). Toronto: University of Toronto Press.

Tylka, T. L., & Iannantuono, A. C. (2016). Perceiving beauty in all women: Psychometric evaluation of the Broad Conceptualization of Beauty Scale. *Body Image, 17,* 67-81. doi:j.bodyim.2016.02.005

Uckelmann, D., Harrison, M., & Michahelles, F. (2010). An architectural approach towards the future Internet of Things. In D. Uckelmann & ... (Eds.), *Architecting the Internet of Things.* Berlin: Springer-Verlag Berlin Heidelberg.

United States Department of Energy. (2011, November). *Recovery Act selections for smart grid investment grant award.* Retrieved from http://energy.gov/oe/technology-development/smart-grid/recovery-act-smart-grid-investment-grants

United States Environmental Protection Agency. (2016, August). *What climate change means for Hawaii.* Retrieved from https://19january2017snapshot.epa.gov/sites/production/files/2016-09/documents/climate-change-hi.pdf

Urban, K., & Gao, W. (2012). Evolution of the Study of Methylphenidate and Its Actions on the Adult Versus Juvenile Brain. *Journal of Attention Disorders.* PMID:22923783

Urban, K., & Gao, W. (2014). Performance enhancement at the cost of potential brain plasticity: Neural ramifications of nootropic drugs in the healthy developing brain. *Frontiers in Systems Neuroscience, 8,* 38. doi:10.3389/fnsys.2014.00038 PMID:24860437

US Department of Defense. (2013). *Unmanned systems integrated roadmap 2013-2038.* Washington, DC: Government Printing Office.

Valtchev, D., & Frankov, I. (2002). Service gateway architecture for a smart home. *IEEE Communications Magazine, 40*(4), 126–132. doi:10.1109/35.995862

Van de Poel, I. R., & Royakkers, L. M. M. (2011). *Ethics, engineering and technology.* Oxford, UK: Blackwell.

Van de Poel, I. R., Royakkers, L. M. M., & Zwart, S. D. (2015). *Moral responsibility and the problem of many hands.* New York: Routledge.

Van de Voort, M., Pieters, W., & Consoli, L. (2015, March). Refining the ethics of computer-made decisions: A classification of moral mediation by ubiquitous machines. *Ethics and Information Technology, 17*(1), 41–56. doi:10.100710676-015-9360-2

Van der Marel, K., Klomp, A., Meerhoff, G., Schipper, P., Lucassen, P., Homberg, J., ... Reneman, L. (2014). Long-term oral methylphenidate treatment in adolescent and adult rats: Differential effects on brain morphology and function. *Neuropsychopharmacology, 39*(2), 263–273. doi:10.1038/npp.2013.169 PMID:23851400

Van der Meer, L., Costafreda, S., Aleman, A., & David, A. S. (2010). Self-reflection and the brain: A theoretical review and meta-analysis of neuroimaging studies with implications for schizophrenia. *Neuroscience and Biobehavioral Reviews, 34*(6), 935–946. doi:10.1016/j.neubiorev.2009.12.004 PMID:20015455

Van Inwagen, P. (1975). The incompatibility of free will and determinism. *Philosophical Studies, 27*(3), 185–199. doi:10.1007/BF01624156

van Lier, B. (2015). The enigma of context within network-centric environments. *Cyber-Physical Systems, 1*(1), 46–64. doi:10.1080/23335777.2015.1036776

Vanhaudenhuyse, A., Demertzi, A., Schabus, M., Noirhomme, Q., Bredart, S., Boly, M., ... Laureys, S. (2011). Two distinct neuronal networks mediate the awareness of environment and of self. *Journal of Cognitive Neuroscience, 23*(3), 570–578. doi:10.1162/jocn.2010.21488 PMID:20515407

Vartanian, H. (2014, November 13). The downside of art going viral. *Hyperallergic*. Retrieved from http://hyperallergic.com/162244/the-downside-of-art-going-viral/

Veale, D., Ellison, N., Werner, T. G., Dodhia, R., Serfaty, M. A., & Clarke, A. (2012). Development of a cosmetic procedure screening questionnaire (COPS) for body dysmorphic disorder. *Journal of Plastic, Reconstructive & Aesthetic Surgery; JPRAS, 65*(4), 530–532. doi:10.1016/j.bjps.2011.09.007 PMID:22000332

Veltman, K. H. (2004). Towards a Semantic Web for Culture. *Journal of Digital Information, 4*(4). Retrieved September 12, 2016 from http://jodi.ecs.soton.ac.uk/Articles/v04/i04/Veltman/

Verbeek, P. P. (2005). *What things do: Philosophical reflections on technology, agency, and design*. University Park, PA: Pennsylvania State University Press.

Verbeek, P. P. (2009). Moralizing technology: On the morality of technological artifacts and their design. In D. M. Kaplan (Ed.), *Readings in the philosophy of technology* (pp. 226–242). Plymouth: Rowman & Littlefield Publishers.

Verbeek, P.-P. (2008). Cyborg intentionality: Rethinking the phenomenology of human–technology relations. *Phenomenology and the Cognitive Sciences, 7*(3), 387–395. doi:10.100711097-008-9099-x

Verbrugge, L. M. (1977). The structure of adult friendship choices. *Social Forces, 56*(2), 576–597. doi:10.1093f/56.2.576

Vermesan, O., Friess, P., Guillemin, P., Gusmeroli, S., Sundmaeker, H., Bassi, A., ... Doody, P. (2011). Internet of Things strategic research roadmap. In O. Vermesan & P. Freiss (Eds.), *Global technological and societal trends from smart environments and spaces to green ICT* (pp. 9–52). Aalborg: River Publishers.

Verroker, M. (2005). Drug use and abuse in sport. In D. R. Mottram (Ed.), *Drugs in Sport*. London: Routledge.

Vesali, C. E. (2002). History of Drugs in Sport. *International Sports Studies, 24*(1).

Vicente, J. P. (2013). The American way of remote air warfare. *Journal of Military Studies, 4*(1). doi:10.1515/jms-2016-0185

Virilio, P. (1991b). *The Lost Dimension*. New York: Semiotext. (Original work published 1984)

Volkow, N. (2012). Long-term safety of stimulant use for ADHD: Findings from nonhuman primates. *Neuropsychopharmacology, 37*(12), 2551–2552. doi:10.1038/npp.2012.127 PMID:23070200

Volkow, N., & Swanson, J. (2008). Does Childhood Treatment of ADHD With Stimulant Medication Affect Substance Abuse in Adulthood? *The American Journal of Psychiatry, 165*(5), 553–555. doi:10.1176/appi.ajp.2008.08020237 PMID:18450933

Volkow, N., Wang, G., Fowler, J., Fischman, M., Foltin, R., Abumrad, N., ... Pappas, N. (1999). Methylphenidate and cocaine have a similar in vivo potency to block dopamine transporters in the human brain. *Life Sciences, 65*(1), 7–12. doi:10.1016/S0024-3205(99)00225-8 PMID:10403500

Volkow, N., Wang, G.-J., Fowler, J., & Tomasi, D. (2012). Addiction Circuitry in the Human Brain. *Annual Review of Pharmacology and Toxicology, 10*(1), 321–336. doi:10.1146/annurev-pharmtox-010611-134625 PMID:21961707

von Soest, T., Kvalem, I. L., Roald, H. E., & Skolleborg, K. C. (2009). The effects of cosmetic surgery on body image, self-esteem, and psychological problems. *Journal of Plastic, Reconstructive & Aesthetic Surgery; JPRAS, 62*(10), 1238–1244. doi:10.1016/j.bjps.2007.12.093 PMID:18595791

von Soest, T., Kvalem, I. L., Skolleborg, K. C., & Roald, H. E. (2009). Cosmetic surgery and the relationship between appearance satisfaction and extraversion: Testing a transactional model of personality. *Journal of Research in Personality, 43*(6), 1017–1025. doi:10.1016/j.jrp.2009.07.001

Wadia, P. (2010). The Notion of 'Techne' in Plato. *Philosophical Studies, 31*, 148–158.

Wagner, N.-F., Robinson, J., & Wiebking, C. (2015). The ethics of neuroenhancement: Smart drugs, competition and society. *International Journal of Technoethics, 6*(1), 1–20. doi:10.4018/ijt.2015010101

Waite, C., & Bourke, L. (2013). Using the cyborg to re-think young people's uses of Facebook. *Journal of Sociology*. DOI: 10.1177/1440783313505007

Wallach, W., & Allen, C. (2009). *Moral machines. Teaching robots right from wrong.* New York: Oxford University Press. doi:10.1093/acprof:oso/9780195374049.001.0001

Wall, Croarkin, McClintock, Murphy, Bandel, & Sim, & Sampson. (2013). Neurocognitive effects of repetitive transcranial magnetic stimulation in adolescents with major depressive disorder. *Frontiers in Psychiatry, 4*(1).

Walsh, D. (2012). *Changing Technology in Capital Markets: A Buy side evaluation of HFT and Dark Trading.* Commissioned research for the Financial Services Council.

Walsh, M. (2017, June 29). *Chinese City Starts Tracking Underperforming Officials With GPS.* Retrieved July 29, 2017, from http://www.sixthtone.com/news/1000427/chinese-city-starts-tracking-underperforming-officials-with-gps

Walther, J. B., Loh, T., & Granka, L. (2005). Let me count the ways: The interchange of verbal and nonverbal cues in computer-mediated and face-to-face affinity. *Journal of Language and Social Psychology, 24*(1), 36–65. doi:10.1177/0261927X04273036

Ward, C. (2010, April 14). From the girl next door to freaky fake. And she's not done with the surgery yet; Exclusive fame-hungry Heidi Montag. *The Mirror (Stafford, Tex.)*, 24–25.

Watkins, P. (n.d.). Filmography and an account of the controversy over the film *The War Game*. Retrieved January 10, 2015 from http://pwatkins.mnsi.net/warGame.htm

Watson, P. (1978). *War on the mind: The military uses and abuses of psychology.* New York: Basic Books.

Weaver, W. (1948). Science and Complexity. *American Scientist, 36*, 536–544. PMID:18882675

Weber, D. C. (2012). *Looking into the eye of the meter.* Presentation at DEFCON 2012. Retrieved from: https://www.youtube.com/watch?v=HeoCOVXRX0w

Weber, R. H., & Weber, R. (2010). *Internet of Things: Legal perspectives.* Berlin: Springer-Verlag Berlin Heidelberg. doi:10.1007/978-3-642-11710-7

Weick, K. (1969). *The social psychology of organizing.* Reading, MA: Addison-Wesley.

Weick, K. E. (1995). *Sensemaking in organizations.* SAGE Publications, Inc.

Weiser, M. (1993). Some computer science issues in ubiquitous computing. *Communications of the ACM, 36*(7), 75–84. doi:10.1145/159544.159617

Weizenbaum, J. (1977). *Computer power and human reason: From judgement to calculation.* New York: W. H. Freeman & Company.

Welsh, A. (2008). *What is Honor? A Question of Moral Imperatives.* New Haven, CT: Yale University Press.

Wen, N. (2017). Celebrity influence and young people's attitudes toward cosmetic surgery in Singapore: The role of parasocial relationships and identification. *International Journal of Communication, 11*, 1234–1252.

Wertheim, M. (1999). *The Pearly Gates of Cyberspace: A History of Space from Dante to the Internet*. New York: W.W. Norton.

Wexler, A. (2016). The practices of do-it-yourself brain stimulation: Implications for ethical considerations and regulatory proposals. *Journal of Medical Ethics*, *42*(4), 211–215. doi:10.1136/medethics-2015-102704 PMID:26324456

Whetham, D. (2012). Remote killing and drive-by wars. In D. W. Lovell & I. Primoratz (Eds.), *Protecting civilians during violent conflict: Theoretical and practical issues for the 21st century* (pp. 199–214). Aldershot, UK: Ashgate.

Whybrow, P. (2012). *Manic Nation*. Retrieved from http://www.psmag.com/health/manic-nation-dr-peter-whybrow-says-were-addicted-stress-42695

Wiener, N. (1948). *Cybernetics or control and communication in the animal and the machine*. New York: John Wiley & Sons.

Wiggins, J. S., Wiggins, N., & Conger, J. C. (1968). Correlates of heterosexual somatic preference. *Journal of Personality and Social Psychology*, *10*(1), 82–90. doi:10.1037/h0026394 PMID:4386664

Wilens, T., Faraone, S., Biederman, J., & Gunawardene, S. (2003). Does Stimulant Therapy of Attention-Deficit/Hyperactivity Disorder Beget Later Substance Abuse? A Meta-analytic Review of the Literature. *Pediatrics*, *111*. PMID:12509574

Wimalawansa, S. M., Fox, J. P., & Johnson, R. M. (2014). The measurable cost of complications for outpatient cosmetic surgery in patients with mental health diagnoses. *Aesthetic Surgery Journal*, *34*(2), 306–316. doi:10.1177/1090820X13519100 PMID:24497616

Wimsatt, W. K., Jr., & Beardsley, M. C. (1982). The intentional fallacy. In W. K. Wimsatt (Ed.), The verbal icon: Studies in the meaning of poetry. Lexington, KY: University Press of Kentucky. (Original work published 1946, revised in 1954)

Winter, J. S. (2014). Surveillance in ubiquitous network societies: Normative conflicts related to the consumer in-store supermarket experience in the context of the Internet of Things. *Ethics and Information Technology*, *16*(1), 27–41. doi:10.100710676-013-9332-3

Winter, J. S. (2015a). Algorithmic discrimination: Big data analytics and the future of the Internet. In J. S. Winter & R. Ono (Eds.), *The future Internet: Alternative visions*. New York: Springer. doi:10.1007/978-3-319-22994-2_8

Winter, J. S. (2015b). Citizen perspectives on the customization/ privacy paradox related to smart meter implementation. *International Journal of Technoethics*, *6*(1), 45–59. doi:10.4018/ijt.2015010104

Wolf, N. (1991). *The beauty myth: How images of beauty are used against women*. New York, W.: Morrow.

Wolf, S. M. (2008). Neurolaw: The big question. *The American Journal of Bioethics*, *8*(1), 21–22. doi:10.1080/15265160701828485 PMID:18236328

Woods, A. J., Antal, A., Bikson, M., Boggio, P. S., Brunoni, A. R., Celnik, P., ... Nitsche, M. A. (2016). A technical guide to tDCS, and related non-invasive brain stimulation tools. *Clinical Neurophysiology*, *127*(2), 1031–1048. doi:10.1016/j.clinph.2015.11.012 PMID:26652115

World map of social networks. (n.d.). Retrieved May 10, 2017 from http://vincos.it/world-map-of-social-networks/

Wu, T. (2012). *The master switch: The rise and fall of information empires*. London. *Atlantic (Boston, Mass.)*, 271–274.

Wu, T. (2017). *The Attention Merchants The Epic Scramble to Get Inside Our Heads*. Vintage Books.

Wyrwoll, C. (2014). *Social media: Fundamentals, models, and ranking of user-generated content*. Dordrecht, The Netherlands: Springer. doi:10.1007/978-3-658-06984-1

Xuyang, W., & Yuzhuo, Z. (2011). Law philosophy analysis: Application of medical instruments for direct reading and influence of the activities of cranial nerve. In *Computer Science & Education (ICCSE), 2011 6th International Conference on* (pp. 293-296). IEEE.

Yangyue, L. (2014). Controlling cyberspace in Malaysia: Motivations and constraints. *Asian Survey, 54*(4), 801–823. doi:10.1525/as.2014.54.4.801

Yildiz, O., Sismanlar, S., Memik, N., Karakaya, I., & Agaoglu, B. (2011). Atomoxetine and methylphenidate treatment in children with ADHD: The efficacy, tolerability and effects on executive functions. *Child Psychiatry and Human Development, 42*(3), 257–269. doi:10.100710578-010-0212-3 PMID:21165694

Yin, R. K. (1994). *Case study research: Design and methods*. Thousand Oaks, CA: SAGE Publications.

Young, D. C. (1984). *The Olympic Myth of Greek Amateur Athletics*. Chicago: Ares Publishers.

Zeidan, F., Johnson, S., Diamond, B., David, Z., & Goolkasian, P. (2010). Mindfulness meditation improves cognition: Evidence of brief mental training. *Consciousness and Cognition, 19*(2), 597–605. doi:10.1016/j.concog.2010.03.014 PMID:20363650

Zeman, A. (2003). *Consciousness: A user's guide*. London: Yale University Press.

Zhao, H., Qiao, L., Fan, D., Zhang, S., Turel, O., Li, Y., ... He, Q. (2017). Modulation of Brain Activity with Noninvasive Transcranial Direct Current Stimulation (tDCS): Clinical Applications and Safety Concerns. *Frontiers in Psychology*, 8. PMID:28539894

Zhou, L., Ding, L., &Finin, T. (2011). How is the Semantic Web evolving? A Dynamic Social Network Perspective. *Computers in Human Behavior, 27*, 1294-1302.

Zuckerman, D., & Abraham, A. (2008). Teenagers and cosmetic surgery: Focus on breast augmentation and liposuction. *The Journal of Adolescent Health, 43*(4), 318–324. doi:10.1016/j.jadohealth.2008.04.018 PMID:18809128

About the Contributors

Rocci Luppicini is an Associate Professor in the Department of Communication and Director of E-Business Technologies within the Faculty of Arts at the University of Ottawa (Canada). He also acts as the editor-in-chief for the International Journal of Technoethics and is a leading expert in technology studies (TS), media studies, and technoethics. He has published over 25 peer reviewed articles and has authored and edited several books including, Online Learning Communities in Education (IAP, 2007), the Handbook of Conversation Design for Instructional Applications (IGI, 2008), Trends in Canadian Educational Technology and Distance Education (VSM, 2008), the Handbook of Research on Techno-ethics: Volume I &II (with R. Adell) (IGI, 2009), Technoethics and the Evolving Knowledge Society: Ethical Issues in Technological Design, Research, Development, and Innovation (2010), Cases on Digital Technologies in Higher Education: Issues and Challenges (with A. Haghi) (IGI, 2010), and the Handbook of Research on Technoself: Identity in a Technological Society:Vol I &II (IGI, 2013).

* * *

Baha Abu-Shaqra is a doctoral student in the PhD in Electronic Business program, Faculty of Engineering, University of Ottawa, Canada. He holds an MA in Communication from the University of Ottawa, and a BJ (Bachelor of Journalism) from the University of King's College, Halifax, Nova Scotia, Canada. His doctoral thesis explores ethical hacking education and management within higher education institutions. His research interests include the problem of rising student hacking crime and ethical hacking education in higher education, dual-use open source technologies, cybersecurity management, technoethical inquiry theory applications in technology assessment and ethical decision making, the application of Weick's organizational information theory and Beer's viable system model to improve information security within organizations, and the application of Beer's VSM to model new business units within organizations and to design autonomous organizational systems.

Selene Arfini is a PhD candidate in Philosophy at the University of Chieti and Pescara and member of Computational Philosophy Laboratory at the Dept. of Humanities, Philosophy Section at the University of Pavia. Her research interests fall in the domains of epistemology, philosophy of science, epistemic cognition, and philosophy of cognitive science. Her current work involves the foundation of an epistemology of ignorance (including the analysis of ignorance distribution in certain cognitive niches), the study of the methodology of thought experiments, and it is framed in the dialog between extended cognition, cognitive niches construction, and the project of the "Naturalization of Logic" recently initiated by Dov Gabbay and John Woods.

Liudmila Vladimirovna Baeva is a Full Professor, PhD of Philosophy, Dean of Department of Social Communication, Professor of Chair of Philosophy of Astrakhan State University. The Expert of Analytical Centre under the Government of the Russian Federation, Expert of Russian Academia of Science. Author of over 200 scientific articles and 6 monographs. Research interests focus on the field of axiology, philosophical anthropology, philosophy of media, e-culture and the study of the information society issues. Member of the Russian Philosophical Society and the Russian Political Science Association, member of editorial board of the international journal "Socioloska luca: Journal of Social Anthropology, Social Demography & Social Psychology" (Montenegro), the international journal "The Caspian Region: Economics, Politics and Culture" (Russian), Journal "Philosophical Problems of Information Technologies and Cyberspace" (Russia). Member of World Congress of Philosophy in Istanbul, Seoul, Athens. This study was supported by the Russian Scientific Foundation under Grant Project No. 16-18-10162, Saint-Petersburg State University.

Jacqueline Beauchere is the Chief Online Safety Officer at Microsoft Corporation. In this role, Ms. Beauchere is responsible for all aspects of Microsoft's online safety strategy, including cross-company policy creation and implementation, influence over consumer safety features and functionality, and communications to and engagement with a variety of external audiences. She currently serves as an advisory board member to the U.K. government-sponsored WePROTECT Global Alliance to End Child Sexual Exploitation Online Advisory Board. She has previously served as Microsoft's representative to the boards of directors of the National Cyber Security Alliance, the Technology Coalition, and the Family Online Safety Institute. Ms. Beauchere has spent more than 17 years at Microsoft leading various groups and efforts that evangelize the company's commitment to help create safer, more trusted online experiences for people of all ages and abilities. Before joining Microsoft, Ms. Beauchere was an attorney in private practice in New Jersey, New York, and Washington, D.C. A second-career lawyer, she spent 12 years as a real-time financial news correspondent and editor-in-charge, most recently with Reuters America, Inc., in New York.

Tommaso Bertolotti is Adjunct Professor of Cognitive Philosophy at the University of Pavia, Italy, and teaching & research assistant at Télécom ParisTech, France. His main research areas include philosophy of technology, applied and social epistemology, philosophy and cognitive science of religion. On top of several articles on peer reviewed journals, he authored "Patterns of Rationality: Recurring Inferences in Science, Social Cognition and Religious Thinking" (Springer, 2015) and co-edited with Lorenzo Magnani the "Springer Hanbdook of Model-Based Science" (2017).

John Forge is a philosopher who spent his whole academic career in departments of History and Philosophy of Science and Science and Technology Studies, and which explains, in part, why his work now focuses on science in its social and political context. The present essay reflects those interests. Forge is the author of The Responsible Scientist, which won a number of prizes. He was originally from England where he was mostly educated, but attended Cornell in the sixties, and has lived and worked in Australia since 1974.

Jai Galliott is a defence analyst and expert on the socio-ethical and strategic issues associated with the employment of emerging technologies, including cyber systems, autonomous vehicles and soldier augmentation technologies as they affect Australia and the world abroad. Galliott has received competitive research funding from the Commonwealth Goverment, Defence Science and Technology Organisation, and the Australian Army. He served briefly as an officer of the Royal Australian Navy prior to commencing his academic career and is an associate of the Consortium on Emerging Technologies, Military Operations, and National Security (CETMONS), the Consortium for Robotics and Unmanned Systems Education and Research (CRUSER) and is a member of the Institute for Ethics and Emerging Technologies (IEET). He has spoken on defence and strategic studies at prestigious venues including Oxford University and the United Nations in Geneva, as well as for ABC Television and the BBC World Service.

Elena Georgievna Grebenshchikova (Dr. Habil) is Head of the Center of Scientific Information and Research on Science, Education and Technologies, Institute for Scientific Information on Social Sciences of the Russian Academy of Science, Moscow, Russia and associate professor of the Department of bioethics, Pirogov Russian National Research Medical University, Moscow, Russia. Her main research interest is the ethical problems of technoscience, especially biotechnological innovations. She is author of over 60 papers and book "Transdisciplinary Paradigm: Science-Innovation-Society" (2012).

Alejandra Emilia Iannone is an interdisciplinary artist now living in the Twin Cities after calling New York City home for ten years. She is the Founder and Creative Co-Director of Sparkle Theatricals, a Minneapolis-based performance group whose mission is to immerse artists and audiences of all ages in experiences that celebrate curiosity and inspire laughter. Alejandra has had the privilege of performing at venues like the Josie Robertson Plaza at Lincoln Center, Carnegie Hall, Jacob's Pillow, the Ailey Citigroup Theater, and the Versace Mansion. Her writing has been published by DIYdancer, Dancer's Turn, and the International Journal of Technoethics. She is a citizen of Argentina and the U.S.A.

Brett Lunceford (Ph.D., Pennsylvania State University) focuses on the intersections between the body, sexuality, and technology. He is the author of the book Naked Politics: Nudity, Political Action, and the Rhetoric of the Body and more than three dozen journal articles and book chapters. His work has appeared in such journals as ETC: A Review of General Semantics, Explorations in Media Ecology, International Journal of Technoethics, Journal of Contemporary Rhetoric, Rhetoric & Public Affairs, and Theology & Sexuality. He currently serves as President of the Media Ecology Association.

Octavian M. Machidon graduated as B. Eng. in Applied Electronics from the Electrical Engineering & Computer Science Faculty at Transylvania University in 2009 and as M. Eng. in Integrated Electronic & Communication Systems – specialized in Embedded Systems – from the same Faculty in 2011. He obtained the Ph.D. degree in Electronics Engineering and Telecommunications at the same university. Since 2015 he is an Assistant Lecturer at the university's Electronics and Computers Department. Before his academic career, he worked in the semiconductor industry at eASIC Corporation, as an engineer responsible with the design and implementation of integrated circuits in the eASIC technology. His current research interests cover VLSI microelectronics, embedded systems, remote engineering, reconfigurable and distributed computing, and the ethics of information and communication technology.

Lorenzo Magnani, philosopher and cognitive scientist, is professor of Philosophy of Science at the University of Pavia, Italy, and directs its Computational Philosophy Laboratory. His recent books include Morality in a Technological World (2007), and Abductive Cognition. The Epistemological and Eco-Cognitive Dimensions of Hypothetical Reasoning (2009) and Understanding Violence. Intertwining of Morality, Religion, and Violence: A Philosophical Stance (2011). In 1998 he started the series of International Conferences on Model-Based Reasoning (MBR). Since 2011 he is the editor of the Book Series Studies in Applied Philosophy, Epistemology and Rational Ethics (SAPERE), Springer, Heidelberg/Berlin. He also co-edited with Tommaso Bertolotti the "Springer Hanbdook of Model-Based Science" (2017).

Peter Olsthoorn is associate professor in Military Leaderschip and Ethics at the Netherlands Defence Academy. Besides leadership and ethics, het teaches on armed forces and society, war and media, and on ethics and fundamental rights in the European Joint Master's in Strategic Border Management. His research is mainly on topics such as military virtues, military medical ethics, drones and the ethics of border guarding. Among his publications are Honor in Political and Moral Philosophy (State University of New York Press 2015) and Military Ethics and Virtues: An Interdisciplinairy Approach for the 21st century (Routledge 2010).

Jose-Luis Perez-Trivino is senior lecturer in Philosophy of Law at Universitat Pompeu Fabra and associate professor. He is Bachelor in Laws and Bachelor in Philosophy. Dr. Pérez-Triviño conducted some research stays at Uehiro Center for Practical Ethics of the University of Oxford, and in Heidelberg (Germany), Genova (Italy) and Córdoba (Argentina) universities. He performed several speeches and communications in different universities and international conferences. Dr. Pérez-Triviño holded an associate director position in the Department of Law and has been manager of the UPF PhD Programme in Laws (2007-2010). Currently, he is director of the teaching innovation division (UQUID) of the Faculty of Laws. Also, he is President of the Spanish Association of Philosophy of Sport (Asociación Española de Filosofía del Deporte), director of Fair Play Journal (Fair Play, Revista de Filosofía, Ética y Derecho del Deporte), and co-founder of the board of directors of the Latin Association of Philosophy of Sport (Associación Latina de Filosofía del Deporte).

Gabriel R. Ricci is Professor of Humanities at Elizabethtown College where he teaches ethics and political philosophy. His research interests are in time consciousness and phenomenology and he is the editor of the book series Religion and Public Life and Culture and Civilization published by Routledge, Taylor and Francis.

Jeffrey Robinson (M Psych) began his career working as a senior Psychometrist at the St. Lawrence Valley Correctional Treatment Centre - Secure Treatment Unit (SLVCTC) for approximately 9 years after graduating with a Master in Psychology (Forensic) from Bond University, Australia. The SLVCTC is a provincial jail and treatment center for mentally disorder offenders. While there he developed several treatment programs for both high and low functioning mentally disordered offenders. He also conducted various types of psychological assessments, including risk, cognitive, ADHD, and other types of assessments. He took a research sabbatical working at the Mind, Brain and Neuroethics lab at the Royal Ottawa Health Care Group. After this he worked at the Forensic Treatment Unit, a secure forensic hospital treating individuals who were found to be not criminal responsible of a variety of offenses; and has since resumed his post at the SLVCTC.

Lambèr Royakkers is associate professor in Ethics and Technology at the Department School of Innovation Sciences of the Eindhoven University of Technology. He has studied mathematics, philosophy, and law. His research has an interdisciplinary character and is on the interface between ethics, law and technology, especially artificial intelligence and robotics. He has (co-)authored more than 10 books, including Ethics, Engineering and Technology (Wiley-Blackwell 2011), Moral Responsibility and the Problem of Many hands (Routledge 2015), and Just Ordinary Robots: Automation from Love to War (CRC Press 2017). Royakkers is co-editor of the Robotics & Automation Engineering Journal.

Rick Searle is a writer and educator living in central Pennsylvania. He is an affiliate scholar for the Institute for Ethics and Emerging Technology where his essays occur regularly and a member of The Fundamental Questions Institute. He is the author and editor of the book Rethinking Machine Ethics in the Age of Ubiquitous and an essayist in the books: "How can humanity steer the future?", along with "Wandering towards a goal: how can mindless mathematical laws give rise to aims and intentions." He blogs at Utopia or Dystopia: where past meets future.

Ben van Lier (1957) is director Strategy & Innovation at Centric, a Dutch IT company. In this capacity, he focuses on research and analysis of developments in the interface between organisations and technology. Alongside his work at Centric, he obtained his PhD from the Rotterdam School of Management in 2009 (Erasmus University Rotterdam). In 2013, he was appointed Professor at Steinbeis University Berlin. In this role he is focused on qualitative research into topics as systems and complexity theory, interoperability of information and the network-centric approach. In 2015 he was also appointed Professor at the University of Applied Science Rotterdam focused on the development of the (industrial) internet of things. Both roles he fulfils alongside his work at Centric.

Nils-Frederic Wagner is Assistant Professor of Philosophy at the University of Duisburg-Essen in Germany. Previously, he was appointed as postdoctoral fellow at the University of Ottawa's Mind, Brain Imaging and Neuroethics Research Unit, and contract instructor in the Department of Philosophy at Carleton University, both in Canada. Wagner holds a PhD in Philosophy from the University of Göttingen in Germany. During his MA studies in Philosophy and Sociology at the University of Göttingen, he spent one year as an EAP scholar at the University of California, Santa Barbara. His work focuses on empirically-informed Ethics; particularly on issues in Neuroethics and Bioethics. As well as on Philosophy of Mind and Action, and Philosophy of Neuroscience.

Jenifer Sunrise Winter is Associate Professor at the University of Hawaii at Manoa and the Co-Director of the Pacific Information and Communication Technology for Development Collaborative. Her research deals broadly with ethics of emerging information and communication technologies. In particular, she investigates privacy and surveillance, digital inequalities, and algorithmic discrimination in the context of Big Data and the Internet of Things. A related area of research explores data governance and stewardship, including use of Big Data for the public good. She is refining a set of models derived from text mining and expert interviews in the domain of personal health data and expanding this to other Big Data domains. A third area of inquiry relates to the future of Internet of Things/artificial intelligence governance. She co-edited The Future Internet: Alternative Visions and has authored dozens of works addressing emerging information policy issues.

Index

Stay Current on the Latest Emerging Research Developments

Become an IGI Global Reviewer for Authored Book Projects

Premier Reference Source

Emerging GIS Applications for Emergency and Disaster Management

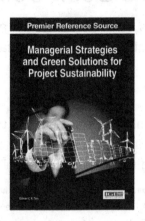

Premier Reference Source

Managerial Strategies and Green Solutions for Project Sustainability

Premier Reference Source

Comparative Approaches to Using R and Python for Statistical Data Analysis

Premier Reference Source

Solutions for High-Touch Communications in a High-Tech World

The overall success of an authored book project is dependent on quality and timely reviews.

In this competitive age of scholarly publishing, constructive and timely feedback significantly decreases the turnaround time of manuscripts from submission to acceptance, allowing the publication and discovery of progressive research at a much more expeditious rate. Several IGI Global authored book projects are currently seeking highly qualified experts in the field to fill vacancies on their respective editorial review boards:

Applications may be sent to:
development@igi-global.com

Applicants must have a doctorate (or an equivalent degree) as well as publishing and reviewing experience. Reviewers are asked to write reviews in a timely, collegial, and constructive manner. All reviewers will begin their role on an ad-hoc basis for a period of one year, and upon successful completion of this term can be considered for full editorial review board status, with the potential for a subsequent promotion to Associate Editor.

If you have a colleague that may be interested in this opportunity,
we encourage you to share this information with them.

Printed in the United States
By Bookmasters